Pharmacologic Aspects of Aging

GARNEAU HALL   TOTE, '80

Pharmacologic Aspects of Aging

EDITORS

LOUIS A. PAGLIARO, M.S., Pharm.D., Ph.D.

Associate Professor,
Faculty of Pharmacy and Pharmaceutical Sciences,
University of Alberta,
Edmonton, Alberta

ANN M. PAGLIARO, R.N., B.S.N., M.S.N.

Associate Professor,
Faculty of Nursing,
University of Alberta,
Edmonton, Alberta

WITH 45 ILLUSTRATIONS

THE C. V. MOSBY COMPANY

ST. LOUIS • TORONTO • LONDON   1983

MOSBY

A TRADITION OF PUBLISHING EXCELLENCE

Editor: **Chester L. Dow**
Assistant editor: **Sally Gaines**
Manuscript editor: **Linda L. Duncan**
Designer: **Nancy Steinmeyer**
Production: **Jeanne A. Gulledge**

The C.V. Mosby Company
11830 Westline Industrial Drive, St. Louis, Missouri 63141

Library of Congress Cataloging in Publication Data

Main entry under title:

Pharmacologic aspects of aging.

    Includes index.
    1. Geriatric pharmacology. I. Pagliaro,
Louis A. II. Pagliaro, Ann M. [DNLM: 1. Drug
therapy—In old age. WT 100 P536]
RC953.7.P44 1983   615'.1   82-14096
ISBN 0-8016-3748-2

GW/VH/VH 9 8 7 6 5 4 3 2 1   01/D/093

Contributors

LAWRENCE H. BLOCK, Ph.D.

Professor of Pharmaceutics, School of Pharmacy, Duquesne University, Pittsburgh, Pennsylvania

JAMES W. COOPER, Ph.D., F.C.P.

Associate Professor, Head, Department of Pharmacy Practice, School of Pharmacy, University of Georgia, Athens, Georgia

RONALD T. COUTTS, Ph.D., D.Sc., F.C.I.C., F.R.I.C., F.P.S., F.R.S.C.

Assistant Dean and Professor, Faculty of Pharmacy and Pharmaceutical Sciences, University of Alberta, Edmonton, Alberta

ABRAM J.D. FRIESEN, B.S., M.A., Ph.D.

Associate Professor, Faculty of Pharmacy and Pharmaceutical Sciences, University of Alberta, Edmonton, Alberta

BRUCE H. KRUG, Pharm.D.

Consultant and Director, Clinical Services, Howard & Morris Institutional Services, Baltimore, Maryland

PETER P. LAMY, Ph.D., F.A.G.S.

Professor and Director, Institutional Pharmacy Programs, Chairman, Department of Pharmacy Practice and Administrative Science, School of Pharmacy, University of Maryland, Baltimore, Maryland

JOHN W. LEVCHUK, B.S., M.S., M.Ed., Ph.D.

Associate Professor, College of Pharmacy, Center for the Health Sciences, University of Tennessee, Memphis, Tennessee

DOROTHY V. LUNDIN, R.N., M.S.

Formerly Assistant Professor, School of Nursing, University of Minnesota, Minneapolis, Minnesota

ANN M. PAGLIARO, R.N., B.S.N., M.S.N.

Associate Professor, Faculty of Nursing, University of Alberta, Edmonton, Alberta

LOUIS A. PAGLIARO, M.S., Pharm.D., Ph.D.

Associate Professor, Faculty of Pharmacy and Pharmaceutical Sciences, University of Alberta, Edmonton, Alberta

JOHN J. PETO, B.Sc., M.D., Dipl. (A.C.P.), F.R.C.P.(C.)

Assistant Professor, Division of Geriatric Medicine, Faculty of Medicine, University of Alberta, Edmonton, Alberta

W.A. RITSCHEL, Dr. Phil., Dr. Univ., Mr. Pharm., F.A.S.A., F.C.P.

Professor of Pharmacokinetics and Biopharmaceutics, College of Pharmacy; Professor of Pharmacology and Cell Biophysics, College of Medicine; Co-Director of Clinical Pharmacokinetics Service, University Hospital, University of Cincinnati, Cincinnati, Ohio

DUNCAN ROBERTSON, M.B., B.S., F.R.C.P.(C.), F.A.C.P., M.R.C.P.(U.K.)

Professor and Head of Geriatric Medicine, College of Medicine, University of Saskatchewan, Saskatoon, Saskatchewan

DAVID SKELTON, M.B., B.S., M.R.C.S., M.R.C.P., M.R.C.G.P.

Professor of Geriatric Medicine, Chairman of the Division of Geriatric Medicine, University of Alberta; Chief of Staff, Youville Memorial Hospital, Edmonton, Alberta

JEFFREY R. SOLOMON, Ph.D.

Executive Vice-President, Altro Health-Rehabilitative Services, New York, New York

KEITH WALKER, M.B., Ch.B., F.R.C.Path., F.R.C.P.(C.)

Clinical Professor in Pathology, Department of Laboratory Medicine, University of Alberta; Director, Division of Medical Biochemistry, University of Alberta Hospital, Edmonton, Alberta

AUDREY S. WEINER, M.P.H.

Assistant Administrator, Medical and Ancillary Services, Hebrew Home for the Aged at Riverdale, Bronx, New York

To our grandmother, Caterina Scalise, an active octogenarian, whose love, support, and encouragement have been invaluable.

Do not regret growing old—it is a privilege denied to many.

Preface

The administration of medications and the monitoring of their effects in the elderly comprise one of the most important and complex aspects of health care. This area of drug therapy is becoming a major concern to growing numbers of health care practitioners because of the constantly increasing elderly population and the resultant shift of health care attention and emphasis from the treatment of acute to chronic conditions that require drug therapy.

There is, therefore, a definite need for an authoritative text and reference book that presents a unique and comprehensive coverage of the areas associated with geriatric drug therapy. The purpose of this book is to present a comprehensive, referenced, and easily accessible compilation of pharmacologic, clinical, and psychosocial data concerning the use and effect of drugs in the elderly. This book is written accordingly for all practitioners currently involved in geriatric care and for students who are assimilating knowledge of geriatric drug therapy.

Each chapter covers a major area related to geriatric drug therapy. The contributing authors, recognized authorities in their respective fields of expertise, have been chosen on the basis of their clinical experience and interest in specific areas relating to drug therapy in the elderly. These authors bring from their varied backgrounds and experiences a depth and scope of knowledge in re-

lation to geriatric drug therapy that has been sorely missing from other geriatric drug therapy texts. They also represent and demonstrate the optimization of drug therapy for the elderly, which can be achieved only by an interdisciplinary team approach to the problems of geriatric drug therapy. Evaluations, comments, and recommendations based on each author's personal experience and interpretation of the literature are included in each chapter; such statements reflect solely the opinion of the author and may not represent the opinions of the editors or publisher.

The drugs discussed in this text and listed in the general index are referred to by their nonproprietary (generic) names; however, practitioners who use trade (brand) names of medications may gain access to the information they seek by consulting Appendix C. This appendix lists drug trade names alphabetically and gives the nonproprietary name(s) of the active ingredient(s) for prescription and nonprescription products that are marketed in either Canada or the United States.

All doses discussed in this text are approximate. In all cases variability in drug response because of genetic or physiologic differences may necessitate alterations in dose or dosage regimen. Drug information centers, package inserts, and other authoritative references should be consulted whenever there is further question about a particular use or dose of a drug.

By using the information presented in this text, practitioners and students should better understand the unique and complex aspects of drug therapy in the elderly. We hope that, with this knowledge and understanding, the older person will be provided with the maximum benefits of drug therapy together with a minimum of adverse effects.

Louis A. Pagliaro
Ann M. Pagliaro

Contents

Pharmacologic Aspects of Aging

Introduction

Louis A. Pagliaro

Ann M. Pagliaro

The older adult suffers two to five times the frequency of adverse effects from drug therapy as the younger adult, and from 5% to 30% of elderly hospital admissions may be associated with inappropriate drug therapy. (See Chapter 11 for a comprehensive overview of this problem.) Drug therapy must be tailored to meet the individual needs of each older person and must take into consideration such factors as health and disease state, socioeconomic and psychologic status, genetic predisposition, known allergies, and prescription and nonprescription medication use. These areas must be carefully assessed to devise drug regimens that provide optimum therapeutic benefit with a minimum of adverse effects.

SPECIAL DRUG CONSIDERATIONS IN THE ELDERLY

Those involved with the health care of the elderly are often not adequately aware of the effects of aging on the selection and management of drug therapy. This is often a result of many factors, including a low level of suspicion, more than one prescriber providing drug therapy, lack of inquiry into self-medication with nonprescription drugs, atypical presentation of symptoms in the elderly (e.g., higher pain threshold, more referred pain), ascription of symptoms to "old age," not considering changes in hearing and vision when communicating with older persons about health matters, and lack of the time necessary to adequately assess the older person. This text is concerned with the special drug considerations of the elderly.

Physiologic changes

Physiologic changes that occur as a natural result of aging profoundly influence drug therapy in the elderly. The physiologic changes in body systems that are involved with the absorption, distribution, metabolism, and elimination of drugs that occur with aging need special consideration including changes in the composition of body mass and hepatic and renal function. Chapters 6, 7, and 8 discuss both the physiologic changes that occur as a natural consequence of aging and the resultant clinical implications.

Before proceeding, so as not to inadvertently contribute to the stereotype defined by Butler (1975) as "agism," it should be noted that the physiologic changes noted here and throughout the text are "average" changes that occur in the elderly. That is to say, aging is a unique and individual process that occurs at different rates in different individuals. Chronologic age is not always the best parameter for estimating physiologic condition.

Composition of body mass. Several changes occur in the composition of body mass as a nat-

1

ural consequence of aging. There is increased fat body tissue, as opposed to lean body tissue, that can cause delayed onset of action of some medications followed by accumulation on repeated dosing with fat-soluble drugs (e.g., barbiturates, diazepam, lidocaine). There is also reduction of heart, kidney, and muscle mass, which can result in toxic blood or tissue levels of a drug when a "normal" adult dose is administered. Total body fluid also decreases as a percentage of total body weight from 55% in the younger adult to 45% in the elderly adult.

Hepatic function. Although most drugs are normally metabolized in the elderly, the rates of some forms of hepatic metabolism, such as hydroxylation and conjugation reactions, have been demonstrated to be significantly decreased on the average for several drugs (e.g., acetaminophen, antipyrine). This decrease is associated with longer half-lives of elimination for these drugs; however, these findings cannot be generalized to all other drugs. It should also be noted that the elderly may be more susceptible to drug-induced liver toxicity (e.g., hepatitis caused by isoniazid) than are younger adults.

Renal function. Renal blood flow and the dependent mechanisms of glomerular filtration and tubular secretion are decreased in the elderly. There is also a reduction in the number of functioning nephrons. Consequently, drugs that are eliminated predominantly in unchanged form through the kidneys (e.g., digoxin, gentamicin, kanamycin, lithium, penicillin) remain in the body longer than usual and have longer half-lives of elimination. If dosages are not reduced, overdosing will increasingly result as will the severity and the frequency of adverse and side effects.

Thus decreased functional reserve in a variety of body systems (e.g., cardiovascular, hepatic, renal) and the resultant lack of a "safety margin" with which to cope with drug effects may cause the elderly to experience more seemingly paradoxic drug responses and side effects than other age groups. These effects may also be caused by age-related changes in the volume of distribution

and the structure, number, or sensitivity of drug receptors.

Volume of distribution

The volume of distribution of many drugs is reduced in the elderly. A factor affecting volume of distribution in the elderly is a significantly reduced albumin concentration. The concentration of free (active) drug can be significantly higher than expected when a normal adult dose of a highly protein-bound drug (e.g., meperidine, phenytoin, phenylbutazone, warfarin) is administered to an elderly person. Greater "competition" of drugs for protein binding sites also exists, and the potential for drug interactions mediated through a protein binding mechanism is significantly increased.

Disease states can also influence the volume of distribution. For example, the presence of congestive heart failure can reduce the volume of distribution of many drugs (e.g., digoxin, furosemide, lidocaine) so that a "normal" adult dose may result in toxic blood levels.

Drug receptors

It has been observed for some time that the elderly appear to be particularly susceptible or resistant to the effects of certain drugs (e.g., barbiturates). Most of these effects can be explained by the physiologic changes previously discussed; however, it has been postulated that these effects may be caused, at least in part, by decreased numbers of drug receptors and/or by the decreased responsiveness of some drug receptors in the elderly.

Multiple disease states and polypharmacy

Multiple disease states and polypharmacy involving prescription and nonprescription medications are very common in the elderly. Therefore drug-drug and drug-disease state interactions are more frequently observed in this age group. For example, interactions involving psychotherapeutic agents that additively or synergistically depress the sensorium are especially troublesome. They contribute to poor self-esteem and to the significant number of elderly who are inappropriately classified as suffering from senile dementia.

A comprehensive analysis of drug interactions in the elderly is found in Chapter 8.

Geriatric dosing

The factors previously discussed emphasize the need for special consideration of dosing and monitoring the effects of medications in the elderly. Because these factors are relatively newly discovered and have not previously been given wide attention, dosing in the elderly is not as exact as in the young. In the young, specific dosages and general formulas are available. However, it is only for very few drugs that an exact dosage has been identified for the elderly, and the only equations that have been devised are as yet necessarily complex and laborious to use. Guidelines that have been devised for dosing in the elderly are found in Chapters 10 and 12.

PRINCIPLES OF GERIATRIC DRUG THERAPY

Those involved in the health care of the elderly should be aware of the following questions in relation to the pharmacologic aspects of aging and should answer them carefully when working with the older individual:

1. Is drug therapy necessary?
2. What is the therapeutic end point of therapy?
3. Is the drug correct?
4. Is the dosage correct?
5. Is the dosage form correct?
6. What adverse or side effects may occur?
7. What drug interactions may occur?
8. Is the drug correctly labeled and packaged?

9. Who is responsible for drug administration?
10. Is the older person compliant?
11. Can any medications be discontinued?

Specific drug therapy regimens have not been widely developed for the elderly; thus each of the previously noted principles will be briefly commented on.

Is drug therapy necessary?

Often, drug therapy is *not* the therapy of first choice in the elderly, who, because of the natural consequences of aging, are more likely to have multiple medical conditions, each of which necessitates some form of therapy.

In considering a drug regimen, it must be determined if alternate "therapy" may be used to treat the client's problem. For example, can a sedative or hypnotic be avoided if the client receives increased physical activity, avoids caffeinated beverages in the evening, avoids large volumes of fluids near bedtime, or drinks a warm glass of milk before going to bed? It should be noted that milk does contain the amino acid tryptophan, which may have a sedating effect on the central nervous system. Another example might be that an antidepressant can be avoided if voluntary visiting is arranged to decrease the older person's loneliness or if the medication(s) causing the depression (e.g., reserpine) is stopped.

What is the therapeutic end point of therapy?

Rational drug therapy should always be associated with a general goal (e.g., cure of a condition, relief of symptoms, prolongation of life) and a predefined end point that can indicate whether or not the goal has been (or is being) achieved. Quantitative measures (e.g., blood pressure of 130/90) should be established to serve as indicators of success or failure of drug therapy. Other measures may also serve as indicators that the drug therapy should be reevaluated, or a time frame (e.g., every 6 months) may be associated with this variable. Drug therapy should never be "p.r.n." for an indefinite period without a definite time frame for reevaluation.

Is the drug correct?

Misdiagnosis is particularly common in the elderly. It is hoped, as more educational programs are designed and more specially prepared professionals in elderly health promotion and care become available, this problem will decrease. Commonly misdiagnosed and misprescribed conditions in the elderly involve the use of cardiac glycosides to treat dependent peripheral edema without congestive heart failure; the use of cardiac glycosides in the elderly who have temporary congestive heart failure, perhaps caused by anemia or a severe respiratory tract infection, but which resolved itself when the primary condition was treated; and the use of antipsychotics in the elderly when their confusion was caused by other medications that they were taking.

Similar types of problems commonly seen in the elderly also include the prescription of a drug that is the drug of choice for the particular disease state in a younger adult but which is contraindicated in the elderly because of the physiologic factors noted earlier. Another consideration is the treatment of the condition whenever possible with a different drug that has fewer or less severe side effects even if it is not "the textbook drug of choice."

Is the dosage correct?

As previously noted, specific dosages have not yet been generally determined for the elderly. However, we know that loading doses are often not needed and that smaller than normal adult doses are usually required to prevent toxicity resulting from the physiologic changes (e.g., decreased renal function, decreased volume of distribution) that occur as a natural consequence of aging. Some medications, such as antibiotics and diuretics, may need to be administered in higher

than "normal" doses if the desired therapeutic response is not obtained. In general, therefore, the elderly often require more follow-up than younger adults to adequately adjust and properly titrate drug dosage to their individual needs.

Is the dosage form correct?

Some elderly persons find liquids easier to swallow than capsules or tablets. A change in dosage form may significantly increase compliance. Sometimes suppositories may be preferred. The bioavailability of a drug can be significantly changed, however, by changing the dosage form, and the dose must be adjusted accordingly.

What adverse or side effects may occur?

Those involved with geriatric care must not only be aware of and monitor adverse or side effects, but they should also be sure that the client is aware of any adverse or side effects that might occur. The older person should know what side effects to expect, which side effects indicate that the medication should be discontinued, or when the clinician should be consulted. Involvement in the regimen will not only increase compliance but will also help minimize unwanted and unnecessary sequelae that might otherwise arise.

Orthostatic hypotension is a particularly troublesome side effect for the elderly. Falls may result that often lead to fractures and hospitalization. Any antihypertensive drug, including the thiazide diuretics, may cause this effect. The elderly should be cautioned about the problem of orthostatic hypotension and receive instruction in measures that may minimize its occurrence. For example, older persons should be instructed to lie in bed for a few minutes on awakening until completely awake. They should then sit up in bed for a few minutes and then sit on the edge of the bed with their feet and legs dangling over the edge for several minutes before getting up. This will allow the body's baroreceptors to readjust from the horizontal to the standing position, thus helping to minimize orthostatic hypotension on arising.

More specific details on adverse drug reactions can be found in Chapter 11.

What drug interactions may occur?

Because of a variety of factors, including polypharmacy and decreased albumin concentration, the elderly are at a particular risk of experiencing a drug interaction. In addition, because of their decreased functional reserve (as previously noted), the probability of the interaction having an adverse effect is significantly increased.

It is always necessary to be aware of drug interactions that may occur and of their potential severity. For example, does the interaction necessitate a change in therapy, and, if so, which drug can be safely substituted? The client must also be carefully informed about which drugs and foods may interact and should thus be avoided.

Specific details on drug interactions that are commonly encountered in the elderly can be found in Chapter 8.

Is the drug correctly labeled and packaged?

In addition to the information usually required (e.g., name of medication, strength, quantity, dosage, name of client, name of prescriber) and auxilliary information (e.g., major potential side effects; activities, foods, and drugs to avoid), the elderly client often has other special drug labeling and packaging needs. Is the print on the labels large enough for the client to read? Does the client read English? If not, are directions available in the foreign language, or is a responsible family member available who reads English and can assist? Can the elderly client open "childproof" containers?

Who is responsible for drug administration?

Can the older person administer the medication? For example, is vision or psychomotor skill adequate for the older person to administer insulin? Can complicated multidrug regimens be followed, or is confusion or forgetfulness a problem? Possible solutions include having a family member administer the medications, using special injection equipment, or developing memory aids (e.g., dosing cards, calendars, or containers) to assist in "remembering" when the medications should be taken. It may be helpful to use dosing regimens or longer acting dosage forms that need to be administered only once daily (e.g., phenothiazines), once weekly (e.g., large doses of vitamin D for osteomalacia), or once monthly (e.g., fluphenazine decanoate). Professional assistance with administration of medications may be required for the elderly person who lives at home.

Currently, 5% to 10% of elderly persons reside in geriatric long-term care facilities, and as more live to older age these numbers will increase. There is an increasing need for specialized drug-related knowledge and delivery systems to meet the needs of this segment of the elderly population. A detailed discussion and analysis of drug therapy in relation to geriatric long-term care facilities can be found in Chapters 3, 4, and 5.

Is the older person compliant?

Estimates of noncompliance in the elderly range from 20% to 80%. If the previous questions are carefully answered, the major reasons for noncompliance will have been effectively dealt with. In addition, the clinician should ensure that the older person has been provided with both verbal and written instructions in relation to drug therapy, ask the older person to repeat the instructions to assess comprehension of the directions (i.e., the appropriate directions may have been correctly given, but this does not ensure that the older person understood them), and finally, explain to the older adult the importance of compliance.

The concept of self-care should also be fostered as much as possible in the elderly in relation to their individual capabilities and limitations. Provided with proper education, guidance, and support, the older person can be assisted in maintaining and assuming as much of the responsibility as possible for self-care in relation to drug therapy.

A detailed analysis of compliance is found in Chapter 1. In addition, problems related to inadequate education and guidance, including drug misuse in the elderly and geriatric poisoning, are discussed in Chapters 2 and 9, respectively.

Can any medications be discontinued?

When new medication regimens are being considered, the previous regimens should be thoroughly reevaluated, and those medications, both prescription and nonprescription, that are no longer needed should be discontinued. Not only will this save time, money, and the trouble of taking unnecessary medication, but it may also improve the individual's quality of life by eliminating unnecessary side effects (e.g., mental confusion) by decreasing the presence or potential of adverse drug interactions.

When a medication is removed from a drug regimen, it should be ascertained if a change in dosage of the remaining drugs is necessary. For example, if a medication that enhances drug metabolism (e.g., phenobarbital) is discontinued, then the dosage of another drug that the older person is taking (e.g., warfarin) may need to be decreased to prevent toxicity, since it will not continue to be metabolized at the same rate. This same procedure should be followed when any medication is added to a drug regimen. For example, if a medication that enhances drug metabolism (e.g., phenobarbital) is started, then the dosage of another drug that the individual is taking (e.g., warfarin) may need to be increased to obtain the same pharmacologic effect.

SUMMARY

This introduction has focused on clinician-directed drug therapy and the inherent problems associated with prescribing, dispensing, and administering medications and the monitoring of their effects in the elderly. Although drug ther-

apy for the older person must be carefully selected and individually tailored to avoid unwarranted effects, those involved with the health care of the elderly must *not* let old age be used as a criterion to withhold rationally formulated drug therapy that may improve the quality and dignity of life for the elderly.

BIBLIOGRAPHY

Butler, R.N.: Why survive? Being old in America, New York, 1975, Harper & Row, Publishers, Inc.

Coleman, J.H., and Dorevitch, A.P.: Rational use of psychoactive drugs in the geriatric patient, Drug Intell. Clin. Pharm. **15:**940, 1981.

Dietsche, L.M., and Pollmann, J.N.: Alzheimer's disease: advances in clinical nursing, J. Gerontol. Nurs. **8:**97, 1982.

Foxall, M.J.: Elderly patients at risk of potential drug interactions in long-term care facilities, West. J. Nurs. Res. **4:**133, 1982.

Garcia, C.A., Reding, M.J., and Blass, J.P.: Overdiagnosis of dementia, J. Am. Geriatr. Soc. **29:**407, 1981.

Greenblatt, D.J., Sellers, E.M., and Shader, R.I.: Drug disposition in old age, N. Engl. J. Med. **306:**1081, 1982.

Hayes, M.H., Langman, M.J., and Short, A.H.: Changes in drug metabolism with increasing age: warfarin binding and plasma proteins, Br. J. Clin. Pharm. **2:**69, 1975.

Hayter, J.: Why response to medication changes with age, Geriatr. Nurs. **2:**411, 1981.

Lamy, P.P.: Special features of geriatric prescribing, Geriatrics **36:**42, 1981.

Lenhart, D.G.: The use of medications in the elderly population, Nurs. Clin. North Am. **11:**135, 1976.

Lerner, R.: Sleep loss in the aged: implications for nursing practice, J. Gerontol. Nurs. **8:**323, 1982.

Mullen, E.M., and Granholm, M.: Drugs and the elderly patient, J. Gerontol. Nurs. **7:**108, 1981.

Playfer, J.R., et al.: Age related differences in the disposition of acetanilide, Br. J. Clin. Pharmacol. **6:**529, 1978.

Ritschel, W.A.: Pharmacokinetics approach to drug dosing in the aged, J. Am. Geriatr. Soc. **24:**344, 1976.

Sloan, R.W.: How to minimize side effects of psychoactive drugs, Geriatrics **37:**51, 1982.

Steinberg, S.: Drug therapy in the elderly—problems and recommendations, On Continuing Pract. **8:**15, 1981.

CHAPTER 1

Medication-taking behavior and compliance in the elderly

Dorothy V. Lundin

Now keep this straight
You take 1 red pill
Every 2 hours and
2 blue pills every hour
And ½ a yellow pill before
Every meal and
2 speckled orange pills between lunch and dinner
Followed by 3 green pills
Before bedtime unless you haven't
Had a bowel movement, in which case. . . .
Good luck!

A plaque bearing these curious words occupied a prominent spot above a desk at a large hospital station where physicians wrote and nurses transcribed orders.

I never learned the intent of the person responsible for hanging it. Could it have been done in frustration, after someone overheard "going-home instructions" that were ludicrous in their ambiguity? Or was it meant to be a subtle reminder to physicians and nurses preparing to instruct and educate clients about a collection of potent drugs the latter would have full responsibility for taking?

Whatever the intent, it is illustrative of a num-ber of drug problems related to compliance and behavior.

The issues of medication-taking behavior and compliance are important for all clients. In the elderly client particularly a number of variables increase the significance of behavior patterns and compliance with medical regimens.

Of tremendous importance for society is the impact that the increasing proportion of elderly will have in the years ahead.

More people are living to older age than ever before. Whereas in 1900 there were only 3 million Americans aged 65 years and over, comprising 4% of the population, in 1979 there were 24 million, comprising 11% of the population. By the year 2030, people 65 years and over will number 50 million and comprise 17% of the U.S. population (U.S. Department of Health, Education, and Welfare, 1979b). A similar pattern has also been observed and predicted for other industrialized countries. For example, in 1950 there were little over 1 million Canadians aged 65 years and over, comprising less than 8% of the population; in 1979 there were 2 million, comprising 9% of the population. By the year 2025, people 65 years and over will number almost 6 million and comprise 17% of the Canadian population (Stone and Fletcher, 1981).

It is obvious that prevention of problems related to medication taking must assume a high priority. Because 80% of the elderly have one or more chronic conditions and their medical treatment accounts for about 30% of the nation's health care expenditures, potential economic disaster for both the individual elderly person and for society in general exists. Parallel forecasts can also be made for other industrial countries. In addition, there is the potential for an escalating number of health hazards if the medical regimen for treating an increasing number of chronic diseases in the elderly person fails to keep pace with that person's diminished capacity to handle that regimen.

In the late 1930s mystical medical treatment for whatever ailed the client was prevalent. One example that impressed me as a young student nurse in my first community health experience was the vivid array of aspirin tablets in five colors that was used to treat clients in the emergency hospital of a large, well-known industry. In the 1950s and 1960s some physicians labeled prescription medications that they dispensed. More often the admonition was, "If I want my clients to know what they're getting, I'll tell them!"

Throughout the 1970s the trend to accord medication consumers the right to participate in their own health care decisions was noted in some teaching materials (Bruya, 1979). Information was posted in health care agencies and was made available in brochures to clients. I have observed, however, that including the consumer-client as a full participant was more often given lip service only and was, in fact, a rare exception in actual practice.

Paralleling the period of concealing the identity of medication from the consumer was a period of according absolute and unquestioned authority to the prescriber. Even in the 1980s the elderly, whose physician-client contacts began much earlier, are still reluctant to question that

perceived authority. Rather than complying with a regimen that is unacceptable, the elderly simply discontinue drug therapy rather than seek revision.

Podell (1975) noted that most clients try to hide compliance problems probably because of their respect for, affection for, or fear of the physician. In addition, many elderly still live by the old attitude "The doctor will tell me what I need to know."

If one were to apply the figures that 5% of the elderly reside in long-term care facilities at any one time (Butler, 1975) and then look ahead to the year 2030 when there are projected to be 50 million elderly in the United States, one quickly sees the dilemma. Suppose the same percent of elderly required institutionalization and inherently related services in the year 2030. The simple mathematics of the situation shows that although the percent of elderly is increasing, there may well be a proportionate concomitant reduction in professionals and facilities available to provide services to those elderly.

High quality nursing homes often have waiting lists of up to 3 years, and classified advertisements contain weekly pleas for nurses and geriatric assistants, for hospitals and nursing homes.

Lublin (1980), describing the dilemma of the nurse shortage, cited the increasing number of elderly and the sophisticated care they receive as being important contributing factors to the increasing shortage of nurses in the years ahead.

The American Hospital Association predicts 120,000 nursing position vacancies by the mid-1980s for U.S. hospitals alone, calling the situation an acute nationwide nursing shortage ("Where Jobs Go Begging," 1980).

If the only reason for keeping elderly persons functional in their own homes were to keep them out of institutions, it would seem an imperative goal viewed in terms of alternatives.

All these factors only point up the need for all elderly health care consumers and all of those who will be elderly in the future to become informed health care consumers.

COMPLIANCE AND NONCOMPLIANCE

A mass of literature, starting with a trickle in the 1960s and increasing to a deluge by 1980, has accumulated on the subject of the compliant or noncompliant consumer. In 1975 "Patient Compliance" became a separate listing in *Cumulated Index Medicus* (U.S. Government Printing Office, 1975).

No attempt will be made to use one definition of noncompliance as a term here. Beginning with the Curtis study (1961), in which criteria for drug errors included drugs taken but not ordered, drugs ordered but not taken, and drugs ordered but taken in incorrect doses, and the Schwartz et al. study (1962), in which additional criteria of incorrect timing and lack of understanding of purpose were included, various clusters of criteria have been referred to as noncompliance. It is important that the reader realize that, for the purposes of looking at compliance with medication regimen, investigators, almost without exception, have individually defined compliance with variations of criteria, differing one from another. Various measures of compliance follow:

1. Biochemical assays of the medication or a metabolite in the blood
2. Measure of blood level of specific drug against arbitrary predetermined blood level reading below which the client was noncompliant
3. Pill count and liquid medication measure
4. Client report
5. Presence of drug in the urine
6. Combination pill count and urine test
7. Combination pill count and client report
8. Client interview measured against clinician interview
9. Assessing deviation from total regimen in terms of comprehension and compliance
10. Composite index of client's perception, physician's perception, and an independent review of records
11. Literal adherence to prescription label doses and directions by client report, as ascertained by interview
12. Mechanical monitor measuring the number of times the medication container was opened against the number of doses that should have been taken

Compliance, or adherence, and noncompliance, deviation, or default have been referred to, discussed, and measured in numerous studies.

Data were compiled from 246 papers on compliance in one study, and the factors that most commonly interfered with compliance were assessed (Blackwell, 1979).

The specificity or objectivity employed has varied widely in studies. For example, in the Brand and Smith study (1974) of compliance with physicians' recommendations, elderly client interviews were measured against physician interviews.

Clinite and Kabat (1976) defined error and measured medication errors against opportunity for errors by tablet count and interview.

Hecht (1974) measured compliance with medication regimens by a combination of tablet counts and urine tests. Error greater than one tablet or one negative urine test constituted noncompliance.

Hemminki and Heikkilä (1975), in studying compliance with prescription instruction, included drugs taken for 1 week, but did not include prescribed drugs that were omitted.

In one study of compliance involving a short-term antimicrobial therapy regimen, pills were counted and liquid medication was measured. Absence at the end of 10 days of 70% or more of the amount dispensed constituted compliance (Lima et al., 1976).

Macdonald, Macdonald, and Phoenix (1977) included misuse of old drugs and taking borrowed drugs, in addition to underutilization and overutilization of the medication, to determine compliance.

Norell (1979) employed a medication monitor in a study to improve compliance. Each time the bottle was opened constituted use of the drug and was counted and compared with the number of drug doses that should have been used.

Parkin et al. (1976) measured medication in home visits to elderly persons who were discharged from hospitals and looked at deviation from the total drug regimen in terms of both comprehension and compliance.

Spreit et al. (1980), measuring adherence by the elderly to medication regimens, counted leftover drugs returned after 1 month of treatment.

Davis (1968) used a composite index of compliance: clients' perceptions, physicians' perceptions, and an independent review of client records.

Spector et al. (1978) arrived at a relative medication compliance measure for clients who were taking the same drug by arbitrarily setting a drug-blood level reading below which the client was considered noncompliant.

In defining criteria for compliance, to measure the effect of education on compliance in the elderly, Lundin et al. (1980) looked at the literal adherence to prescription label instructions and assessed compliance by interview.

Although these studies were not all conducted with elderly subjects, they comprise examples of the variations used in obtaining compliance measures and at the same time identify one big problem in geriatric therapy: the inability to obtain from the literature a consistent or standard index for, or even a definition of, compliance.

Smith (1976) sees noncompliance with medication regimens as one of the major unsolved therapeutic problems confronting pharmacy and medicine.

I would also include noncompliance as a problem confronting nursing. Because nurses comprise the largest body of health professionals (Ryden, 1978), nurses are in the strategic position of having the most access to patients. Nursing holds a tremendous potential for facilitating compliance and appropriate medication-taking behavior.

A number of researchers have examined the overall results of compliance.

Marston (1970) reviewed literature dealing with compliance with medical regimens. However, she was not able to identify from her study a "clear picture" of determinants of compliance.

Morris and Halperin (1979) reviewed the literature reporting effects of written drug information on client knowledge and compliance. They too found that the diversity of definitions, measuring devices, and other factors prevented interpretation from a single unifying perspective.

Looking at drug regimens and treatment compliance as part of a larger issue, Blackwell (1979) observed, "The lack of a clear consensus in the compliance literature, coupled with increasing complexity of the issues, contributes some skepticism and even cynicism about the significance of the compliance problem."

Discussing the compliance issue with respect to medication regimens, Smith (1976) listed three areas being studied by researchers: (1) How many persons do not take their medications properly? (2) Why do they not follow instructions? (3) What can be done to improve compliance? The first issue has been answered by many. A conservative estimate and a working figure appears to be that about one third of all clients are noncompliant with medication orders in some way. Regardless of the figure given, or the criteria for determining "properly," the number is of such significance that it cannot be ignored.

The impact of having one third of medication therapy omitted or misused in terms of health professionals' wasted effort, wasted time, and wasted money is great. The cost in terms of health hazards to clients steadily increases as complex medical regimens continue to include more and more potent prescription drugs.

Despite the effort and expense of drug studies to determine the effects of drugs, little attention has been devoted to compliance with drug regimens (Blackwell, 1973).

Today in the prevention and treatment of disease many potent and costly medications are used. Largely, these drugs have specific indications, dosage levels, and other criteria that, to be effective, must be closely followed. Obviously, then, optimum effectiveness of a medication is closely allied with proper use (Hammel and Johnson, 1974).

Mazzullo, Lasagna, and Griner (1974) observed, "It is paradoxical for physicians to expend a great deal of effort giving procainamide to hospitalized patients in 'tailor-made' regimens if, upon discharge, many patients do not take the drug as they did in the hospital."

Boyd et al. (1974) concluded that the progress in developing new drugs for successful treatment of disease is of little consequence if clients do not obtain and consume the medication as prescribed.

Nazarian (1976) said it well in his summary when he noted that the physician's careful examination, performance of indicated tests, and prescription, along with the pharmacist's careful preparation of medication and adherence to the physician's instructions, may all be "costly exercises in futility if the medication does not find its way into the patient."

Although compliance has frequently been directly referred to or indirectly treated as specifically a client problem, Lamy (1978) observed that prescription problems of elderly persons have ranged from inappropriate drug use by clients to inappropriate prescribing.

MEDICATION-TAKING BEHAVIORS

As a basis for proposing strategies for improving client compliance with medication regimens, it is necessary that the most prevalent behaviors be identified. These behaviors, related to medication taking, have been documented in available literature and apply to many elderly clients.

The elderly may not be able to open child-proof caps (Jenkins, 1979). Because of vision impairment, clients often cannot read prescription labels (Plant, 1977; Lofholm, 1978; Jenkins, 1979). Clients may also take medications according to size or color of tablets (Lundin, 1978).

Each reader may have a hair-raising story of hazardous medication-taking practices involving taking medication according to size (e.g., taking "a big pill for stronger action" or "a little pill for mighty results"). But the inadvertent interchange of look-alike tablets is a very real hazard for clients whose regimen includes tablets that are similar in appearance (Feder, 1978).

Clients may take borrowed drugs. They obtain medications from more than one physician and have prescriptions filled at more than one pharmacy (Lundin, 1978; Lundin et al., 1980). Consequently, it is inevitable that they take duplications of drugs inadvertently, sometimes because of different names or different appearances of identical products.

The elderly may omit medications, or they may take the wrong dose. They may take medications at the wrong times. They often take drugs without knowledge of, or with incorrect knowledge of, the purpose for them. They may self-medicate with over-the-counter drugs or with prescription medications left from a previous illness. They often take medication that has a more impressive appearance or that is prescribed for what is perceived to be the more vital concern, such as for a heart condition (Schwartz et al., 1962).

In addition to many of the previously mentioned behaviors, Latiolais and Berry (1969) also found clients who:

1. Take more medication than prescribed per dose
2. Take more doses per day than prescribed
3. Discontinue the drug before the prescribed time
4. Take less per dose or fewer doses per day than prescribed
5. Take outdated medication
6. Take two or more therapeutically contraindicated medications
7. Do not get prescriptions filled
8. Do not understand directions
9. Forget to take medications

Clients often do not understand what to expect

from the prescribed medication or what to do when they forget to take a tablet (Ley, Jain, and Skilbeck, 1976). If the medication has not worked in the expected manner by the expected day, it may very well be discontinued without the older person realizing that some drugs take a longer period of time to exert their effects than others.

Clients may prematurely discontinue medications (Boyd et al., 1974). Some clients may discontinue medications because they feel well or no longer have symptoms for which they began the drug. Stimson (1974) attributes this practice to the attitude that people take medications when they are ill and not when they are feeling better.

Clients may not have their prescriptions filled or refilled because they lack either the money to pay for the drugs or the transportation to obtain them (Hammel and Johnson, 1974).

They may take some drugs with foods that inhibit absorption, or they may fail to take medications with sufficient amounts and kinds of liquids (Lundin, 1978).

Clients often chew medications that should be swallowed whole and conversely swallow whole those that should be chewed (Plant, 1977). In addition, they may take their medications with meals even though 30% to 50% of medications have decreased absorption when taken with food (Lofholm, 1978).

Clients sometimes conceal noncompliance. Their self-report conflicts with objective measures (Cole and Emmanuel, 1971).

Clients sometimes order prescriptions by mail or telephone or have others pick them up, thus eliminating any opportunity for face-to-face consultation or reinforcement of the physician's instructions by the pharmacist.

Clients may take more than one medication and often take a complex regimen of drugs for a number of chronic and acute diseases. The complexity of regimens has correlated with increased noncompliance in some studies. Increased numbers of medication have been predictive of decreased compliance (Latiolais and Berry, 1969; Hulka et al., 1975; Parkin et al., 1976).

Clients often lack knowledge about the safety of over-the-counter medications. For example, in one study all persons responding to a question to identify contraindications for aspirin use saw aspirin as safe and knew of no contraindications for its use (Matte and McLean, 1978). In Matte and McLean's study clients decided when to take laxatives for constipation, and their definition of constipation varied from lack of a bowel movement in 4 days to just an "uncomfortable feeling." Most of the respondents in the study did not consider vitamins to be drugs.

I also documented a similar finding in which several over-the-counter drugs were regularly consumed but were denied as being medication (1978).

Some clients "figure out for themselves" what they should be doing with a prescription medication rather than consult their pharmacist (Moore, 1978), and others often take medications for the wrong purpose and at improper dosage intervals (Boyd et al., 1974).

Sometimes clients distinguish "medications," which are seen as safe and familiar, from "drugs," which are considered dangerous (Stimson, 1974). Stimson has suggested that "drugs" are possibly seen as what "drug addicts" use.

Clients often take medications prescribed by more than one physician and have prescriptions filled at more than one pharmacy (Lundin et al., 1980). As a result, the client may be taking duplicated medications without the client, the physician, or the pharmacist being aware of the duplication.

Some clients do not perceive noncompliance as a threat to their medical situation for various reasons (Becker, Drachman, and Kirscht, 1974; Rosenstock, 1975). They sometimes avoid prescribed medication simply because they do not like it. Clients also sometimes register dissatisfaction with their physician by failure to comply (Francis, Korsch, and Morris, 1969).

Behaviors that adversely affect compliance

In order that compliance be seen in its proper perspective it is necessary that each elderly person's medication-taking behavior be evaluated individually. It is clear from the lengthy, nonexhaustive list of identified behaviors that a solution to the problem of noncompliance will rarely involve a single factor. The following compilation of behaviors that adversely affect compliance should serve as a stimulus:

1. Inability to open childproof caps on medication container
2. Inability to read prescription and/or auxiliary labels
3. Taking medications according to size of the tablet or capsule
4. Taking medications according to color of tablet
5. Taking borrowed medications
6. Obtaining prescriptions from more than one prescriber
7. Obtaining medications from more than one pharmacy
8. Failing to take prescribed medications
9. Taking medications at the wrong time
10. Doubling doses to make up for missed doses
11. Taking medication with incorrect knowledge or no knowledge of it
12. Self-medicating with over-the-counter drugs
13. Self-medicating with leftover prescription medications
14. Taking the medication with the more impressive appearance or the one that is prescribed for what is perceived to be the more vital concern
15. Taking more than the prescribed dose
16. Taking less medication per dose than ordered
17. Taking more doses per day than prescribed
18. Taking fewer doses per day than prescribed
19. Discontinuing medication prematurely because of feeling well
20. Discontinuing medication prematurely because of feeling no better
21. Taking outdated medication
22. Taking medication by the wrong route
23. Taking two or more therapeutically contraindicated medications
24. Failing to have prescription filled
25. Failing to comprehend directions
26. Forgetting to take medications
27. Misunderstanding of what outcome to expect from the medication
28. Not understanding what to do when a dose is missed
29. Failing to fill prescription because of lack of money or transportation
30. Taking medication with food that inhibits absorption
31. Taking medication without sufficient kinds and amounts of fluids
32. Chewing medications that should be swallowed whole
33. Swallowing whole medications that should be chewed or dissolved
34. Concealing noncompliance from health professionals
35. Ordering medications by mail or telephone, thereby missing verbal directions, information, and reinforcement
36. Taking complex regimens of medications
37. Taking over-the-counter drugs without knowledge of safety precautions
38. Taking prescription and over-the-counter drugs without knowledge of hazardous interactions
39. Denying that certain over-the-counter preparations such as vitamins and antacids are drugs
40. Interpreting ambiguous directions each in their own way
41. Taking medications for the wrong purpose
42. Taking medications at incorrect dosage intervals

43. Not perceiving noncompliance as being a threat to the medical situation
44. Avoiding medication because of the disliked taste
45. Failing to follow the drug regimen because of dissatisfaction with the clinician
46. Consuming alcoholic beverages and foods that may interact with prescribed medications
47. Radically changing smoking habits without informing the clinician (either significant increase or decrease)
48. Storing medications in inappropriate areas

Health professionals engaged in assessing the elderly will do well to identify comparable behaviors as well as search for additional behaviors that inhibit optimum adherence to the medical regimen.

REASONS FOR CLIENTS' NONCOMPLIANCE WITH MEDICAL REGIMENS

Having seen examples of the many ways people misuse medications, it is necessary to look at some of the reasons these behaviors occur, although reasons for misuse and associated behaviors are sometimes the same:

1. Complex interplay of sociocultural factors
2. Ideas and attitudes
   a. that medications should not be taken when one is well
   b. that the body needs to be given a rest from medications
   c. that the body may become dependent on drugs
3. Family's and friends' influence
4. Previous experience with unwanted drug actions
5. Previous experience with ineffectiveness of medication
6. Dissatisfaction with clinician's action, which is contrary to expected action
7. Misunderstanding of rationale for prescription

8. Dissatisfaction with prescriber
9. Tension in clinician-client relationship
10. Clinician request for information without reciprocal giving of feedback
11. Complexity of regimen
12. Increasing number of drugs involved correlates positively with increasing noncompliance
13. Age-old misbeliefs
14. Incomplete or inadequate label instructions
15. Need to interpret instructions without adequate knowledge to do so
16. Forgetting of verbal instructions
17. Lack of knowledge of content of over-the-counter drugs and prescription medications leading to additive action or duplication
18. Denial that the product is a drug
19. Taking of medication prescribed by more than one clinician without the knowledge of all clinicians involved
20. Failure to hear verbal instructions (impaired hearing)
21. Failure to see label or auxiliary instructions (impaired vision)
22. Misinterpretation of prescription instructions
23. Misunderstanding of formulation of pharmaceuticals
24. Absence of responsibility for own medication taking in hospitals
25. Clinician's lack of time to give instructions
26. Clinician's failure to give directions
27. Lack of money to buy medications
28. Lack of transportation to secure medications
29. Inadequately written prescriptions
30. Failure of pharmacist to reinforce physician's intended therapeutic regimen
31. Failure of clinician to give comprehensible directions
32. Failure of dispensing clinician to give storage directions and directions in relation to food, fluid, frequency, doses per episode,

maximum doses per week, and disposal directions

33. Self-diagnosis that they are cured
34. Dislike of the taste of medication
35. Belief that medications "make them sick"
36. Belief that they need more medication than was ordered
37. Loss of medication
38. Incongruence between what clients think they are to do and what the clinician thinks they are doing
39. Perception of over-the-counter drugs as "safe" because they do not require a prescription
40. Lack of respect for medication
41. Powerful advertising on television, radio, billboards, and in magazines
42. Low level of concern for health
43. Belief in own invulnerability
44. Disbelief that medical therapy will reduce a present threat
45. Adverse side effects from medication

Becker and Maiman (1975), after an extensive survey of the available literature, noted that "patient noncompliance has become the best documented, but least understood, health-related behavior."

Before dealing with methods for improving compliance, I intend to list from the literature and from personal experience what appear to be major reasons why elderly persons are noncompliant with their medication regimens.

Amarasingham (1980) identified in noncompliance a complex interplay of sociocultural factors and suggested looking at these factors when assessing both negative and positive responses to pharmacologic therapy.

Stimson (1974) pointed to some attitudes and ideas clients have: (1) that they should not take medications when they are well and thus they discontinue drugs when symptoms subside, (2) that the body needs to be given a rest from medications, and (3) that the body may become dependent on drugs. He also found that family's and friends' influence is a factor in whether there is compliance or noncompliance and that clients discontinue medications because of experiences with unwanted drug actions, such as drowsiness.

Clients comply or do not comply based on the expectation of what the physician's action will be. For example, dissatisfied with the action, many clients will not take the offered prescription medication (Stimson, 1974).

Clients often fail to comply because they do not understand the rationale for treatment or because the physician prescribes what has been ineffective previously. In a study by Francis, Korsch, and Morris (1969) noncompliance was higher in clients who were dissatisfied with the prescriber than in those who were not.

Davis (1968) identified client noncompliance in terms of an authoritative client-passively accepting physician combination. Noncompliance resulted if there was evidence of tension in the physician-client relationship. Also, if the physician asked for information without giving feedback, noncompliance was more likely.

The complexity of the regimen and the number of drugs involved correlate with a higher probability of medication error ("Non-compliance," 1979).

Lundin et al. (1980) also learned that long-standing attitudes, perhaps passed on from previous generations, contributed to noncompliance (e.g., "You always take medicine with food or milk"). Other reasons for noncompliance that clients identified were incomplete or inadequate label instructions and the need for the client to interpret label instructions without technical knowledge to do so; forgetting verbal instructions; lack of knowledge about the contents of over-the-counter and prescription medications, which lead to duplication of medication; lack of knowledge about the hazards of taking medications simultaneously prescribed by more than one physician without full knowledge of both prescribers; failure to hear instructions verbally given; impaired vision, which prevented some from reading auxiliary labels; and denying that the product was a medication.

Misinterpretation of prescription instructions plays a role in noncompliance. Mazzullo, Lasagna, and Griner (1974), for example, discovered that a wide range of interpretations for the same direction held potential for "therapeutic failure or iatrogenic illness as a consequence of mistaken interpretation."

One misinterpretation that occurred in a survey I conducted (1978) involved one person's interpreting a physician's directive to "hold on to the old medications" as meaning "Take them! Don't discard them." This noncompliance in turn revealed an even more hazardous noncompliant practice of judging how the client would take the different sizes of white tablets to "come out even," depending on the size and color of the tablet. This misunderstanding of the formulation of pharmaceuticals may be unbelievable to the reader of this text, but I believe after hearing many persons refer to their tablets as "exactly like the doctor gave me before," when referring to treatment for a different illness, that it is easy to underestimate the prevalence and the seriousness of the belief that "if it looks the same, it is the same."

Latiolais and Berry (1969) suggested that the prevalent practice of giving each medication dose to the client for the duration of the hospital stay may be a factor in the unreliability of clients when control is returned to them at discharge.

Perhaps some elderly persons are noncompliant because they are at a particular chronologic age. Schwartz et al. (1962) found increased noncompliance in persons above 75 years of age. Lofholm (1978) identified the highest rate of noncompliance in persons between the ages of 75 and 79 years. Boyd et al. (1974) found that persons 65 years and over had the lowest comprehension level of any age group.

One would be more inclined, however, to correlate advanced years with correspondingly complex regimens that accompany chronic diseases associated with the "older" elderly.

Many clients state that they do not ask physicians questions because physicians are too busy, have too many people in the waiting room, or do not seem interested, and these have to be considered as reasons for noncompliance. When asked what the physicians' directions were, many clients reply, "The doctor didn't tell me." The physician's failure to give instructions adds to the list of reasons for noncompliance. Whether the patient forgot those instructions, did not hear them, or none were given, the directions were not received for implementation by the client.

Some clients do not take prescribed medications because they lack the money to buy them (Malahy, 1966).

Inadequately written prescriptions must assume a high rank in the order of explanations for noncompliance. A number of authors cite examples of inadequately written prescriptions (Malahy, 1966; Hermann, 1973; Powell, Cali, and Linkewich, 1973; Mazullo et al., 1974; Rosenstock, 1975; Gorrell, 1977; Lundin, 1978). Inadequately written prescriptions, in turn, preclude the pharmacist from determining the client's understanding as well as keep the pharmacist from reinforcing directions (Powell, Cali, and Linkewich).

The failure of pharmacists to give comprehensible directions (Boyd et al., 1974), or in fact to give any directions, contributes further to reasons for noncompliance. Often medications are dispensed without the pharmacist's directions, which should include directions for storing, directions for taking medications in relation to fluids and meals, and directions pertaining to frequency, disposal of remaining medication, maximum dose per episode, and maximum dose per week.

In addition to the reasons for noncompliance already listed are a number from Madden's study (1973). Clients (1) stopped the medication because they thought they were cured, (2) disliked taking medication, (3) lost the medication, (4) felt the medication made them sick, and (5) added doses because they felt they needed additional medication.

Hulka et al. (1976) explained noncompliance in terms of absence of concordance, that is, the lack of congruence between what clients think they are to do and what the physician thinks they are doing.

Matte and McLean (1978) identified those clients who took over-the-counter drugs thinking they must be safe because they could be purchased without a prescription.

One other explanation that appears to be the basis for some failure to comply is simply a lack of respect for medications of any kind.

Matte and McLean (1978) demonstrated by a survey how misinformed and ignorant the public is with respect to self-medication regarding contraindications of over-the-counter drugs, the amount of product to take, the use or purpose of it, and other misconceptions.

Lofholm (1978) also noted the evidence of over-the-counter drug use to be correlated positively with Sunday afternoon television commercials viewed by elderly residents.

It appears, from the literature reviewed, that noncompliance can be classified as either intentional or unintentional. It can be a deliberate choice not to comply based on what appears to be sound judgment to the elderly person. For example, a person for whom an antibiotic was ordered for 10 days may decide on the fifth day to discontinue the medication because "my pain and fever are gone, so I don't need this any longer." An example of inadvertent failure to comply, might occur when a person whose diuretic prescription label directions state "take daily" chooses to take it once a day at bedtime. Whether noncompliance is deliberate or unintentional, the therapeutic effect is the same. Having become aware of the numerous identified reasons why the elderly fail to comply with medical regimens, the astute health professional, in seeking optimum adherence, will be alert to the many reasons for noncompliance and to the relevance for each specific situation.

STRATEGIES FOR IMPROVING COMPLIANCE

It would seem most practical here to focus on strategies that have been useful and effective in improving compliance. Following is a list of techniques to improve compliance:

Techniques useful primarily to nurses

1. In-hospital observing of the client's ability to open childproof medication containers and substituting when appropriate
2. In-hospital testing of the client's ability to take the medication (adequate motor skills) and substituting a different medication form when possible and necessary
3. Assessing the client's ability to read label and auxiliary instructions and providing legible directions
4. Supervising self-administration during hospitalization, accompanied by client teaching

Technique useful to nurses or physicians

5. Contracting between the client and health professional

Techniques useful to nurses, pharmacists, and physicians

6. Assessing the accuracy of comprehension of instructions and reinforcing intended directions
7. Including a verbal review of medication instructions
8. Having the medication present and visible when reviewing directions with the client
9. Client teaching:
   a. one-to-one teaching with demonstration and feedback
   b. group instruction
   c. group discussion
   d. audiovisuals
   e. programmed learning
   f. participation of significant others
10. Encouraging the client to bring all medications for review when visiting the health professional
11. Emphasizing to the client the health professional's readiness to be of service

12. Making the client an active participant in treatment
13. Individualizing regimens to the client's routine and life-style
14. Providing printed supplementary instructions boldly printed in black, at the appropriate reading level, in language the client can read; including a literate significant other in instruction if the client is illiterate

Techniques useful primarily to physicians

15. Allowing client-physician negotiation
16. Keeping a client "report card"
17. Providing other involved health professionals with copies of the specific, unambiguous directions given to the client
18. Avoiding routine multiple prescribing (to reduce the complexity of the regimen)
19. Reducing doses per day (to decrease the complexity of the regimen) whenever appropriate
20. In multiple prescribing, prescribing brands that are dissimilar in appearance to avoid client confusion with look-alike tablets
21. Providing prescriptions that are legible, specific, detailed, and unambiguous

Techniques useful primarily to pharmacists

22. Assuring completeness of prescription label instructions
23. Assuring legibility of printed label instructions
24. Counseling and reinforcing physician's directions in a private setting
25. Providing the client with information pamphlets that answer commonly asked questions about certain medications
26. Issuing medication cards listing all drugs, including over-the-counter drugs that the patient is taking, to carry at all times
27. Coordinating and dispensing of hospital and home medications so the size, color, and shape are identical, as well as coding the patient record in order that refills continue to be identical
28. Influencing physicians by requesting explicit directions for prescription labeling if not provided by the prescriber
29. Giving additional verbal and written information when relevant
30. Expanding role to include team involvement with nurses and physicians
31. Translating inexact times into exact hours if frequency and times of administration are essential to medication's usefulness

Techniques useful to nurses and pharmacists

32. Providing memory aids individualized for the client:
    a. Cueing
    b. Color coding
    c. Circling hour on a clock face affixed to the container
    d. Placing brightly colored instructions and dose timing in a conspicuous spot
    e. Setting alarm clocks to remind the patient to take the medication
    f. Providing a written list to cross off medication when taken
    g. Using a daily sheet on which every dose and medication taken is written sequentially
    h. Using a weekly calendar with pockets containing the medication stapled to the day, date, and time

Technique useful to physicians and pharmacists

33. Ascertaining what medications (inclusive list) the client is taking

Can the client open the container and take the medication prescribed? Even though some areas mandate their use, some elderly clients cannot open childproof caps. For these clients regular screw tops or other more easily opened caps are available and can usually be substituted on request. If elderly persons do not discover that they cannot manage a childproof cap until they have it in their own homes, the only alternatives may be to either not take the medication, leave the cover off, or transfer medication to another container. These practices are not only hazardous to children but also to the elderly themselves because of the potential for mislabeled containers, deterioration, and spillage.

Actions to avert the childproof cap problem and other potential problems include physical assessment by nurses in hospitals before giving instructions to accompany medications that clients are taking home (Schwartz, 1975; Atkinson, Gibson, and Andrews, 1978). Can clients open the cap? Can they put the pills in their mouths; that is, are their motor skills adequate for self-administration? The person should be allowed to demonstrate this ability, and if the childproof cap is a handicap, substitutions should be made. The drug form may even be inappropriate.

Similarly, when clients go directly from physician to a pharmacy, the pharmacist must bear the professional burden of determining the appropriateness of childproof caps and substitute when appropriate.

Can the client read the prescription label, auxiliary labels, and supplementary directions? There are two alternatives that are available to the elderly who are alone and whose labels are illegible to them. They can either rely on memory of instructions, if given, or interpret them in the context of their knowledge of previous medications.

Some elderly persons suffer from visual impairment (Lofholm, 1978) and often cannot read fine print (Plant, 1977). Several authors have stressed the need for bold, black lettering of instructions (Sharpe and Mikeal, 1974; Schwartz, 1975; Jessup, 1978; Brock, 1980; Lundin et al., 1980). Others have pointed out the imperative need for the older person to be able to read printed instructions and have emphasized that instructions be typewritten (Lamy and Kitler, 1971). Certainly, if written directions are to be followed, they must be read, and this implies an obligation for health professionals, especially pharmacists, as well as manufacturers of medications, to meet this need.

Forgetfulness has been cited as another cause for noncompliance (Lofholm, 1978). Researchers

and authors have tested and suggested various devices or memory aids for helping the elderly remember to take their medications. Often the memory aid involves a simple process, such as putting the medication where it is visible; having special locations for specific medications where the location serves as the memory aid, for example, placing the morning medication container by the box of cereal that is opened every morning; turning the bottle upside down when the drug dose is taken; and so forth.

Some memory aids that have been determined to improve compliance have included the use of a clock face on the prescription label, with the times of administration circled, and brightly colored instruction labels with dosage times posted in a prominant spot (Lima et al., 1976).

Alarm clocks set to remind clients of hard-to-remember dosage regimens have been suggested in situations when taking medications with meals is inappropriate (Jessup, 1978).

One memory aid that is effective in increasing medication compliance is the use of a calendar (Boyd et al., 1974; Podell, 1975; Clinite and Kabat, 1976; Macdonald, Macdonald, and Phoenix, 1977; Wardless and Davie, 1977; Jessup, 1978; Lofholm, 1978). Variations on the use of the calendar include writing down the medication each time it is taken, providing monthly calendars with matching color coding to the medication and time to take, stapling medications in small pockets directly to the calendar, and providing tear-off calendars with verbal instructions.

I have found that an effective method for improving compliance in some clients is simply to have them write the date on a small pad of paper each morning and record each medication as taken throughout the day, discarding the page after the last medication is taken at the end of the day.

One strategy for improving compliance, which has been discussed by Benarde and Mayerson (1978), is "patient-physician negotiation." They have based their teachings on a few elementary principles: (1) securing and maintaining compliance are essential parts of client management; (2) to reduce conflict of purposes, each party must understand the other's viewpoint; (3) the onus is on the physician to provide a setting in which the client can feel at ease; and (4) basic helping relationships or communication skills are necessary tools of the physician.

One can further apply Benarde and Mayerson's teachings in a process sequence. For example, if physicians who respect the client as a person communicate on the same level with the client (e.g., sitting and facing the client rather than standing and looking down on him, maintaining eye contact, talking at the level of client comprehension, acknowledging feelings, picking up nonverbal cues and responding to them, and employing open-ended questions), then the physician's assessment of client concerns will have an optimum basis for being accurate.

The plan will be a mutual sharing of goals with each participant, client and physician, concretely describing his own goals and objectives for achieving them.

The intervention would be the actual carrying out of therapy with both participants having identified what responsibility they bear for success based on their negotiation.

In the evaluation of therapy both participants again will look at whether therapy is successful, whether modes for achieving it are acceptable, and whether some responsibilities may need to be renegotiated.

It behooves all health professionals to think in terms of Bednarde and Mayerson's (1978) maxim: "Put the ill at ease." They conclude that the physician has no chance for improving compliance unless clients are active participants in the process and are convinced of the physician's readiness to treat them as equals.

Gillum and Barsky (1974) also suggest using the negotiation process as one way to achieve a given therapeutic goal. The client and physician choose from alternatives the one or ones most likely to meet with compliance, starting with a simple regimen. The physician reinforces compliant behavior by positive reinforcement before renegotiating a more complex regimen in order to achieve greater likelihood of compliance.

A similar strategy for improving compliance, "contracting," has also been studied and described (Steckel and Swain, 1977). The principles are closely allied with negotiation but usually rely on the specific written identification of what each party will do to fulfill the terms of the contract. The outcomes desired must be so clearly delineated that anyone can observe or measure them. Steckel and Swain use written contracts and stress the need to set the client up for success. That is, by using small steps or increments that can be achieved, the client can produce the ultimate desired behavior.

In an earlier report one physician described the agreement he extracted from clients, which in effect said, "You take your medication as I order and record every dose you take, and I will grade your 'report card' when you bring that record in" (Reichert, 1976). This is a verbal form of contracting. Clients had to demonstrate compliant behavior to derive the satisfaction of reinforcement (i.e., acceptance by the physician) when they produced the report or grade. Although this may be seen as demeaning or juvenile by some, it worked to achieve the objective of taking the medication correctly. Whether the goal was stabilization of blood pressure at an acceptable level or some other equally desirable goal, it worked for this physician and a number of clients.

The card provided by Reichert (1976) on which he expected his clients to record medications as they took them could have served effectively as a memory aid as well as a completion of a contract.

Supplemental written information has been used by a number of researchers, including Brands (1967), who suggested identifying information with the client's name, drug name, and prescription number as it appears on prescription medication. He suggested putting all possible information on the label but providing typewritten supplements in addition to the label. Clinite and Kabat (1976) provided specially prepared printed data sheets with information about the specific medication as did Fox (1969), Madden (1973), Sharpe and Mikeal (1974), Podell (1975), McKenney (1977), and Lundin et al. (1980).

Ideally, every printed supplementary medication information sheet should be individualized. Because this will rarely occur, there are prepared printed medication sheets for about 500 of the most frequently used medications available to all health professionals seeking optimal response from a medication regimen (Smith, 1977; Griffith, 1978). The health educator will still have to determine the appropriateness of the reading level for each client before using this sheet and perhaps supplement it with additional necessary information.

The Raygor Readability Estimate (Raygor, 1976), which is quick and easy to use for the purpose of determining the client's reading level and for preparing written material at the desired level of the elderly population involved, would be an appropriate and accessible tool (Fig. 1-1).

Written supplementary information is not only useful to the client who did not hear instructions, who forgot them, or who felt anxiety and confusion about the results of instructions but also provides for families, friends, or other health professionals information that they may use to reinforce the physician's intended advice consistently.

Fox (1969) and Hildebrand (1972) prepared printed instructions for categories of drugs and checked the appropriate drug name before giving information sheets to clients.

Although a number of persons have suggested giving information verbally, most would agree that verbal information alone is not effective in reducing noncompliance. Among those for whom verbal information would be only part of the package is Brands (1967). He advocates using a guideline list of what every client should know about the medication and also a list of what every

pharmacist's obligation is. He stresses providing verbal counseling in privacy and a typewritten label and written reinforcement of verbal information. Boyd et al. (1974) also stress that pharmacists provide verbal counseling in confidence and assure completeness of label instructions. Clinite and Kabat (1976) advocate providing verbal review with their printed data sheets. Fox (1969) values verbal information but finds it inadequate without repetition.

Hulka et al. (1976) suggest reinforcing client learning beginning with the physician and pharmacist and continuing with follow-up visits. They suggest that for reinforcement to be most effective, medications should be present at the conference so that both the physician and client can identify the medication with the instruction. Schwartz (1975), in effect, makes the same suggestion: instructions should be given after prescriptions are filled rather than being given on pieces of paper that may have no meaning to the client.

Ley, Jain, and Skilbeck (1976) prepared information pamphlets that explained to clients various aspects of their medication. The clients were anxious or depressed, but it was determined that information that explained why they did not derive instant response from drugs and what to do if they missed a medication dose decreased noncompliance. These authors suggest that an appreciable amount of noncompliance is based on simple failure to understand.

Other researchers who emphasize the necessity for assessing client understanding are Lamy and Kitler (1971). Mazzullo, Lasagna, and Griner (1974) discovered a wide range of misinterpretation, even of unambiguous instructions, and see the need for physicians to review instructions with clients in advance to reduce misinterpretation of directions when the medication is received.

Cole and Emmanuel (1971) documented a high rate of self-medication accuracy in clients who had a pharmacist consultation at hospital discharge. They saw the high client-to-physician

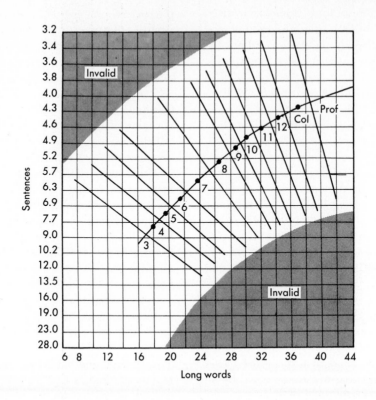

LONG WORDS

Directions

Count out three 100-word passages near the beginning, middle, and end of a selection or book. Count proper nouns but not numerals.

1. Count sentences in each passage, estimating to nearest tenth.
2. Count words with six or more letters.
3. Average the sentence length and word length over the three samples, and plot the average on the graph.

Example

	Sentences	6+ Words
A	6.0	15
B	6.8	19
C	6.4	17
Total	19.2	51
Average	6.4	17

Note mark on graph. Grade level is about 5.

FIG. 1-1

The Raygor Readability Estimate. (Courtesy Alton L. Raygor, University of Minnesota.)

ratio along with the rapid development of new drugs as making pharmacist consultation imperative.

The increasing complexity of medication regimens has correlated positively with increasing noncompliance (Marston, 1970; Matthews and Hingson, 1977). Several researchers have looked at reducing dosage schedules to the least number per day. Fischer (1980) suggests that multiple doses be eliminated wherever possible, which would cut costs in most cases as well. Although recognizing that single doses may not be possible for or tolerated by some clients, he suggests simplification whenever possible, stressing close monitoring when clients are following new or unapproved scheduling.

Matthews and Hingson (1977) also suggest avoiding a divided dose regimen, particularly in multiple drug regimens, wherever this can be achieved. They note that the routine prescribing of laxatives, tranquilizers, vitamins, and other such drugs makes the regimen complex. One other possibility suggested by this team for simplifying dosage schedules is a combination medication, but only when the correct ratio of drugs has been previously arrived at for the individual.

Education has long been recognized as a method useful in changing behavior and therefore in improving compliance. It is a strategy that can be effectively used by any well-informed and educated member of the health professional team—nurse, pharmacist, or physician. When content is approved by professionals, teaching can also be done by paraprofessionals or health educators.

According to Rosenberg (1971), neglecting client education is as serious as neglecting medical treatment. He defines information as "the imparting of facts from an object to a subject" and says that "education takes place when the individual interprets and integrates the information in such a manner as to bring about attitudinal and/or behavioral change." Rosenberg suggests that teaching methods found useful are group instruction, group discussion, audiovisuals, and family participation.

Gillum and Barsky (1974), Johns (1976), Plant (1977), and Haynes, Sackett, and Taylor (1980) stress the importance of clients having an opportunity to be active participants in their own care. Gillum and Barsky include individualized education, repetition, reduction of anxiety level, and accommodation among their strategies for improving compliance. Matthews and Hingson (1977) observed in one study that when clients were involved in decision making and were taught how to observe the impact of their illness, they seemed to be motivated to comply.

Several writers have said in various ways that client education is too important to be left to chance (Schwartz, 1975; Matte and McLean, 1978; Lundin et al., 1980).

Neely and Patrick (1968), Rosenberg (1971), Parkin et al. (1976) all stress beginning client medication education in the hospital for the hospitalized client. Neely and Patrick and Parkin et al. suggest supervising self-administration of medications during hospitalization to prepare the client for safe independent functioning at the time of discharge.

Many listings have been published about what clients should know about their medications. Most lists include the following:

1. Who it is for
2. Name of the drug
3. Dosage
4. Route of administration
5. Frequency of administration
6. When to take
7. How to take
8. Purpose of the drug
9. Maximum doses per day (per week, if relevant)
10. How long to continue
11. How to store
12. Refill information
13. What food, drink, other drugs, or activities to avoid
14. Side effects to expect
15. What to expect if the prescribed medication is not taken

There are other aspects of drug education that

need to be considered here. One issue is the relevance of drug education to the future elderly. Greater consumer education about safety and about the danger of drugs is needed (Piao Chien, Townsend, and Townsend, 1978). Matte and McLean (1978) suggest that although regulation of advertising is one technique for attacking the problem of ignorance and misinformation, teaching tomorrow's consumers, beginning at the primary level, is the place to start. They suggest using pharmacists as educators and providing education for all generations. The elderly could be taught by the use of television, pamphlets, and so forth. I agree with starting with primary students and including all ages but suggest that nurses be included in the teaching team so that it is a collaborative and planned approach. Although the special expertise of the pharmacist is essential, nurses, by virtue of their numbers and the diversity of their roles, are an integrating force in a particularly pivotal position (Ryden, 1978). Johns (1976), recognizing society's change from passive to active participation, sees nurses in positions to involve clients actively and to prepare them to participate as contributing team members. She sees nurses as surveillants who can obtain clues, recognize signs of desirable or undesirable drug effects, and act as confidants because they are the most consistently available health professionals.

Evaluation is an integral part of any teaching effort, whether it is in the form of feedback in the client's own words to determine understanding (as Clinite and Kabat suggest) or whether it is in the form of a posttest, following a more formal teaching approach. Without evaluation, teachers may be able to say they taught, but they will not know what learners learned.

Client education and information benefit both the client and physician, thus enabling an effective working relationship to take place and allowing individual clients to coordinate their own health care (Gaeta and Gaetano, 1977; Parish, 1977). To permit clients to be effective coordinators, there are other aspects of client education

that are important: (1) teaching clients to ask questions, (2) teaching clients what to ask, and (3) teaching clients what to tell their physician, pharmacist, or nurse.

Before prescribing and dispensing, physicians and pharmacists need to know all the drugs that clients are taking. I suggest (1978) that clients bring all drugs that they are taking when visiting the physician and ask that the drugs be reviewed. Others, including Piao Chien, Townsend, and Townsend (1978), have suggested that pharmacists issue medication cards listing all drugs, including over-the-counter drugs, that clients are taking, which they would then carry at all times to present to their physician or pharmacist, or in any emergencies. Whether the client presents the medications or the list of medications, it is important that all physicians and pharmacists be aware of all medications, prescription and nonprescription, being taken regardless of their source.

After taking a drug clients need to inform prescribers when unusual or unexpected side effects occur. Clients need to be taught to inform prescribers and pharmacists about all known drug allergies or previous drug reactions.

It is important that clients who are on a medication regimen inform their health care providers that they smoke or drink alcohol and inform them when their smoking or drinking habits change radically (e.g., when a heavy smoker quits smoking).

Questions clients need to learn to ask if regimens are to be simplified and compliance improved include the following: (1) Do I still need this drug? (2) What can I expect it to do? (3) Are there any side effects that I can expect?

When a new or different medication is prescribed, clients need to ask, "Will I now be able to stop other medications?"

If clients have difficulty swallowing tablets or capsules whole, they need to ask the pharmacist before crushing tablets or opening capsules or ask if another drug form is available.

Clients need to learn to ask for information

about every aspect of a medication's use and handling if the answers are not readily apparent in verbal instructions, on prescription labels, or in supplemental written information (see list on p. 23).

Clients need to be taught some simple safety measures with respect to medication in order to comply with medication regimens:

1. Never take another person's medications.
2. Never give medications to another person.
3. Never keep expired or discontinued drugs but dispose of them safely.
4. Never mix more than one medication in a container.
5. Always keep medications in their original containers.
6. Never take medication from an unlabeled container.
7. Never keep medications at the bedside (except specified medications for breathing or for the heart) because double doses might be taken accidentally.
8. Follow medication regimens according to prescriber directions for the dose, frequency, method of taking, and so forth.
9. Always consult physician, nurse, or pharmacist about any directions not clearly understood rather than guess.
10. Always store medications according to pharmacists' directions.

The physician plays a key role in medication education. Physicians know why they are prescribing a particular medication and what results to expect. It is the physician who will initiate client education by means of adequate prescription label instructions (Powell, Cali, and Linkewich, 1973). Although other health professionals may teach effectively, client education is ultimately the physician's responsibility (Marsh and Perlman, 1972; Rosenstock, 1975). For physicians whose major areas of expertise have become diagnosing and treating, it is necessary that they depend on others to teach (Rosenberg, 1971) and to delegate their teaching duties.

Nurses have a dual advocacy role (Brock, 1980). They most frequently are in positions of supervising or observing medication taking and of teaching ways to avoid errors in a wide variety of settings where they can be alert to those circumstances where errors occur. At the same time, nurses are able to interpret and reinforce physicians' orders when those orders are unambiguous and specific.

Pharmacists have a dual role as well. Having received the physician's communication, the prescription, they in turn are responsible for communicating directions to the client intended by the physician and necessary because of the medication. They are responsible for verifying with physicians any question about the clarity of an order and for making suggestions to physicians when pharmacists' knowledge would benefit the client. Jessup (1978) suggests that it is the pharmacist's responsibility to question the advisability of a medication, to suggest medications, and to consult with physicians when there is duplication or conflict. Lofholm (1978) sees the selection of drugs as pharmacists' responsibility. For example, if hearing impairment already exists or if one medication in the regimen already has the potential for producing auditory nerve damage, pharmacists can select a drug without potential for producing hearing loss.

For improved compliance and optimum medication-taking behavior in the elderly client, it seems clear that only nurse-pharmacist-physician collaboration will achieve that end. Powell, Cali, and Linkewich (1973) have said, "The prescription is a means of communication from a physician to a pharmacist to a patient." A model for client medication education should also include the informed registered nurse in a communication network involving all four members of this important team for teaching, for reinforcing teaching, and for consistency of education (Fig. 1-2).

Strategies for reducing noncompliance, which are uniquely pharmacist strategies, include the following:

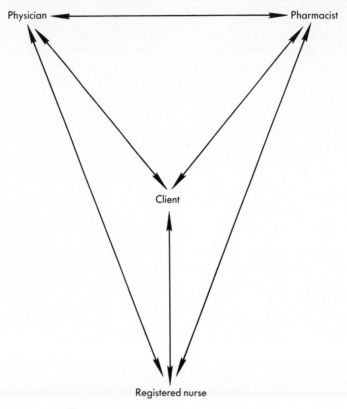

FIG. 1-2

Client medication education model.

1. Hospital and home medication supplies should be coordinated so that the size, color, and shape of the medication taken in the hospital is the same as the going-home supply (Atkinson, Gibson, and Andrews, 1978). I believe that these should be coded on client profiles or prescription records so that refills are also identical.

2. Complete, explicit, legible labeling of medications should be included.

3. Additional instruction relevant to the specific medication should be given.

4. Translation of inexact times into exact hours, if frequency and time are important to the medication's usefulness, should be provided.

5. The pharmacist's readiness to be of service should be emphasized to the client (Madden, 1973).

6. The expansion of roles to include involvement with clients and other health professions because of the expertise they possess must take place (Madden, 1973).

7. The guidelines of the American Pharmaceutical Association and the American Society of Internal Medicine must be literally adhered to (Griffenhagen, 1974).

Physician liability for failure to advise clients about their medications has already been determined in the past. Pharmacists also may very well be held liable if they fail to assume this professional responsibility (Fox, 1969).

PHYSICIANS: THE KEY

Clinicians must defy Voltaire, who said, "A physician is a person who pours drugs of which he knows little into a body of which he knows less" (Helps, 1967). They should demonstrate understanding of every medication prescribed and of the elderly individual for whom it is prescribed before undertaking medication therapy.

One must look at whether the dominant behavior really constitutes noncompliance or whether it results from misprescribing. Smith and Stead (1974), from their experience with an elderly man's suicide attempt, said that attendants had retrieved 46 bottles containing 10,685 still untaken prescribed tablets when bringing him to a hospital. The authors questioned the wisdom of prescribing for the elderly in such a manner (i.e., many tablets per day; a number of prescriptions, each with different directions) that compliance is unlikely (see Chapter 9, "Geriatric Poisoning").

This is probably an extreme case, but surely many practitioners can testify to the prevalence of this practice with many examples of client after client bringing bags full of prescription bottles when coming to hospitals, clinics, and other health care settings.

This has been called the "Cop-Out Age" (Twerski, 1973), and because of physicians' tendencies to help, they often become accessories to society's copouts.

Although there are many good reasons for prescribing drugs for clients of all ages who have an assortment of disorders, the aged adult is more susceptible to both side effects and therapeutic effects for a number of physiologic reasons (see Chapters 6, "Physiologic Changes and Clinical Manifestations of Aging," and 10, "Pharmacokinetics in the Aged"). Extreme caution, therefore, is needed in selecting both the appropriate medications and dosage regimens for the elderly. Some geriatric principles of pharmacotherapeutics include the following: (1) discontinuing a drug is often more beneficial than starting one, (2) use the lowest possible dose, (3) use the fewest number of drugs possible, (4) do not use a drug if the side effects are worse than the symptoms for which it is taken, (5) assess the response to drugs frequently and stop useless drugs (Besdine, 1979) (see "Introduction").

I am by no means suggesting that every person who goes to a physician expecting to come away with a prescription is one of the cop-outs Twerski spoke of, or that the physician who writes that expected prescription is one of society's cop-outs, but the client and the prescriber both need to reevaluate their behaviors in terms of Twerski's "cop-outs." I am reminded of my aged mother's pain and disability after an improperly attended fracture. When the pain was most troublesome at the time she was seeing her physician, she asked, "Can you do something for my arm?" or "Can't you help my arm so I can sleep at night?" He succumbed to this plea by prescribing a medication that, within a few days, caused confusion and disorientation and had to be discontinued. Yet she knew, as did the physician, that there was scarcely any medication that she could take without unfavorable results.

Society has endured the massive media advertising effort to sell drugs and has supported it by buying the advertised drugs. When the message seems to be that there is a harmless medication for everything, can it not be assumed that consumers will ask for and expect physician compliance with their every request?

Twerski (1973) sees the problem of "chemophilia" as grave and the widespread chemophilia in society as a manifestation of mass maladjustment. He argues that the role of the physician, with respect to chemicals, is to intervene only when there is pathology. I maintain that inherent in this description is an advocacy role, not only for the physician but also for the nurse and the pharmacist. It seems that education about medications and respect for medications is the most important intervention for use against empty requests for another medication. Yet in no way must one discourage the client's legitimate description of symptoms and events on which the clinician bases accurate diagnosis and therapy. It is a fine line to tread. Education of the consumer now and in the future has a preventive function that is essential. It is imperative that health professionals who have not yet assumed this educator role do so at once.

Svarstad (1976), after reviewing studies to determine why clients do not follow medical advice, discovered that noncompliance was higher when physicians failed to give feedback after asking for information. She had assumed that physicians' expectations regarding medication use would be simple and unambiguous and would be communicated in such a way that clients would know what those expectations were after verbal and prescription label instructions. She found these assumptions to be unwarranted.

She learned instead that physicians often failed to express expectations explicitly and failed to provide written reinforcement of verbal expectations. There was inconsistency between the physicians' prescriptions and the labels attached by pharmacists, and in 29% of the cases no information was given about the purpose and/or names of the medications. Furthermore, she validated the wall plaque message on the opening page of this chapter by finding that some physicians typically referred to the medications by their shape, size, or color!

When a composite index was used to measure physician's written and verbal instructions, she found a positive correlation between the amount of physician instruction, the accuracy of client perceptions, and client conformity. She worked with the hypotheses that (1) clients cannot comply without having an accurate perception of the physician's expectations and (2) clients' perceptions of those expectations will be more accurate if physicians communicate explicitly, provide written copies of expectations, and inform clients of the names and purposes of drugs.

When physicians were given a score based on the quality of physician-client interactions with respect to seven areas of content, there was positive correlation between the physicians' high ef-

fort to motivate the client and the high behavioral conformity of the client. When the amount of physician instruction was taken into account, the client conformity rate was above the rate for low physician instruction.

It is essential that the physician adhere to the following:

1. Remember the association between compliance and a considerate, courteous, and friendly approach.
2. Explain in complete, comprehensible, and unambiguous terms the what, why, when, and how of the medication.
3. Remember that the current timing of doses has become demanding and that there can be no room for misinterpretation (Hermann, 1973).
4. Advise clients regarding information pertinent to over-the-counter drugs (Matte and McLean, 1978).
5. Advise with respect to forbidden foods in explicit terms, not "vague admonitions." Monitor compliance to the medication regimen (Lamy and Kitler, 1971).
6. Remember that teaching the elderly will necessarily involve using large, bold, black print, accommodating for hearing impairment, and slowing the pace of the "teacher" to the slowed pace of the "learner."
7. Accompany oral instructions with a resource that elderly clients can take with them, such as the supplementary information sheet. Remembering that a large portion of the population is functionally illiterate when confronted with printed materials and that many older elderly persons as a group have had less than an eighth grade education (Lundin et al., 1980), prepare supplementary education below this reading level. A technique that is both quick and easy to compute without machines is the Raygor Readability Estimate (Raygor, 1976), illustrated earlier in this chapter (Fig. 1-1).

Although there seem to be few researchers in

agreement regarding the amount of alcohol consumption by the elderly, it does seem important to comment on medication-alcohol interaction. Of the 100 most frequently prescribed drugs, more than half contain at least one ingredient known to interact adversely with alcohol (see Chapter 8, "Drug Interactions in the Geriatric Client").

A communication to physicians and other health professionals by the Surgeon General (Richmond, 1979) included the following cautions:

1. Routinely document the history and scrutinize the pattern of alcohol consumption for individual patients to determine the possible relationship between presenting complaints and mixing drugs with alcohol.
2. Be alert to the possible interaction of prescribed, over-the-counter, or illicit drugs—singly or in combination—with alcohol.
3. Pay careful attention to the section in the package insert that deals with drug-alcohol interactions and consult the current medical literature and references for specific problems.
4. Limit as much as is practical the quantity of drugs dispensed with any one prescription and monitor the patient with regular follow-ups for unexpected reactions to the medication.
5. Consider, both in the choice of therapy and in the evaluation of the patient, the likelihood of the patient's adherence to your admonition (and that of the warning label on the prescription) against using alcohol while taking medication.

The suggestion that health professionals teach elderly persons to inform their physicians that they smoke and also when they radically change their smoking habits is empty education if physicians do not make a point of discovering what changes this will imply for prescribing medication. Smoking of tobacco should be considered as one of the primary sources of drug interactions in humans.

An example of one complication is that smokers used to higher doses of theophylline may be in danger of getting too much of the drug if they quit smoking and their drug dose is not adjusted

as the smoking effect wears off over a period of up to 3 months. Studies have also shown that smokers may need larger and more frequent doses of some drugs to get the same effect as nonsmokers (U.S. Government Printing Office, 1979a).

THE CLIENT'S RIGHT TO CHOOSE

This chapter would not be complete without some reference to questions that are increasingly arising. Is total compliance necessary? How important is compliance? What part do clients' rights play in this scenario?

Despite the flavor of disobedience there is about a noncompliant patient, a behavior unacceptable to a traditionally authoritarian profession, it seems that many clinicians are now demonstrating behavior changes. Sometimes helped by peer review, their self-awareness has persuaded these same physicians, who are concerned about the noncompliant client, that they can be wrong and that the client, on occasion, would do well to ignore their instructions ("Noncompliance," 1979).

Sackett (1978), in a discussion of standards for compliance trials, points out the necessity for scrutinizing compliance-improving strategies for their potential to produce harm. He further admonishes that the scheme for getting clients to swallow a new drug should be approached with the same skepticism as the drug itself.

In every clinician-client interaction there is an implicit expectation of compliance that accompanies the clinician's prescription or proscription, along with the right of the client to choose not to comply. Amarasingham (1980), in her study of social and cultural perspectives on medication refusal, has identified this refusal as indicating a discrepancy between the client's understanding of medication and what the prescriber intended. Although she studied psychiatric patients and drug therapy, her reference to "medication as message" seems applicable to all clients and their medications. She observed, "We need to be aware of the meaning of the drug in the patient's social world and of the possibility that a refusal to take medication is an attempt to manipulate ambiguous or unacceptable social definitions."

It is clear that total compliance is imperative if some clients are to function at all, for example, the client requiring permanent replacement thyroid hormone after total thyroidectomy or the insulin-dependent diabetic for whom omission of only a few doses of prescribed medication could be disastrous. On the other hand, the clinical significance of deviation from the optimal medication schedule has not been established for most drugs (Hermann, 1973).

In a social system where television viewers are bombarded with messages extolling the virtues of drugs, where some of the most strikingly illustrated pages of popular magazines assure readers that a particular drug will cure what ails them, where information about disease treatment is detailed in newspapers and magazines, where medication self-help literature is readily available in most libraries and many bookstores, the clinician is only one source of information. Without discounting Amarasingham's concepts (1980), it is still the responsibility of clinicians to make a better case for what they propose than for what competing sources of information offer, if they are to expect compliance.

Stimson (1974) said, "In investigating the use of prescribed medicines we therefore have to take account of the patient as a decision making individual living in a culture from which he is receiving information about health and illness."

Slack (1977), in discussing the "patient's right to decide," has suggested that physicians might do well to inquire of clients whether they intend to adhere to a prescribed regimen and to abandon the notion that they are responsible for controlling clients. He suggests that clients who elect not to adhere to a physician's directives are no more noncompliant than the person who, after seeking a friend's advice about a job, elects not to

take it—they are simply exercising the same freedom of choice.

Slack (1977) suggests that physicians should "stop thinking in terms of compliance, recognize the right of patients to make their own medical decisions, and help them to do so." Here I see the key phrase to be "help them to do so." Having clearly spelled out what may occur as the result of taking medication, including benefits, risks, side effects, and so forth, and having clearly explained what clients may expect realistically if they follow another course, clinicians have fulfilled the responsibility for which they were sought.

REFERENCES

Amarasingham, L.R.: Social and cultural perspectives on medication refusal, Am. J. Psychiatry **137**:353, 1980.

Atkinson, L., Gibson, I., and Andrews, J.: An investigation into the ability of elderly patients continuing to take prescribed drugs after discharge from hospital and recommendations concerning improving the situation, Gerontology **24**:225, 1978.

Becker, M.H., Drachman, R.H., and Kirscht, J.P.: A new approach to explaining sick-role behavior in low-income populations, Am. J. Public Health **64**:205, 1974.

Becker, M.H., and Maiman, L.A.: Sociobehavioral determinants of compliance with health and medical care recommendations, Med. Care **13**:10, 1975.

Benarde, M.A., and Mayerson, E.W.: Patient-physician negotiation, J.A.M.A. **239**:1413, 1978.

Besdine, R.W.: Observations on Geriatric Medicine, U.S. Department of Health, Education, and Welfare, Public Health Service, Pub. No. 79-162, Washington, D.C., 1979, U.S. Government Printing Office.

Blackwell, B.: Drug therapy: patient compliance, N. Engl. J. Med. **289**:249, 1973.

Blackwell, B.: The drug regimen and treatment compliance. In Haynes, R.B., Taylor, D.W., and Sackett, D.L., editors: Compliance in health care, Baltimore, 1979, The Johns Hopkins University Press.

Boyd, J.R., et al.: Drug defaulting. II. Analysis of noncompliance patterns, Am. J. Hosp. Pharm. **31**:485, 1974.

Brand, F.N., and Smith, R.T.: Medical care and compliance among the elderly after hospitalization, Int. J. Aging Hum. Dev. **5**:331, 1974.

Brands, A.J.: Complete directions for prescription medication, J. Am. Pharm. Assoc. **7**:634, 1967.

Brock, A.: Self-administration of drugs in the elderly: nursing responsibilities, J. Gerontol. Nurs. **6**:398, 1980.

Bruya, M.A.: Medication principles and oral administration. In Sorensen, K.C., and Luckmann, J., editors: Basic nursing, Philadelphia, 1979, W.B. Saunders Co.

Butler, R.N.: Why survive? Being old in America, New York, 1975, Harper & Row, Publishers, Inc.

Clinite, J.D., and Kabat, H.F.: Improving patient compliance, J. Am. Pharm. Assoc. **16**:74, 1976.

Cole, P., and Sr. Emmanuel: Drug consultation: its significance to the discharged hospital patient and its relevance as a role for the pharmacist, Am. J. Hosp. Pharm. **28**:954, 1971.

Curtis, E.B.: Medication errors made by patients, Nurs. Outlook **9**:290, 1961.

Davis, M.S.: Variations in patients' compliance with doctors' advice: an empirical analysis of patterns of communication, Am. J. Public Health **58**:274, 1968.

Feder, R.: Small white pills, N. Engl. J. Med. **298**:463, 1978.

Fischer, R.G.: Compliance oriented prescribing: simplifying drug regimens, J. Fam. Pract. **3**:427, 1980.

Fox, L.A.: Written reinforcement of auxiliary directions for prescription medications, Am. J. Hosp. Pharm. **26**:334, 1969.

Francis, V., Korsch, B.M., and Morris, J.J.: Gaps in doctor-patient communication, N. Engl. J. Med. **280**:535, 1969.

Gaeta, J.J., and Gaetano, R.J.: The elderly: their health and the drugs in their lives, Dubuque, Iowa, 1977, Kendall/Hunt Publishing Co.

Gillum, R.F., and Barsky, A.J.: Diagnosis and management of patient noncompliance, J.A.M.A. **228**:1563, 1974.

Gorrell, R.L.: And now—a word of warning, Prof. Pharm. **4**:1, 1977.

Griffenhagen, G.B.: Prescription writing and prescription labeling: for a better informed patient, J. Am. Pharm. Assoc. **14**:654, 1974.

Griffith, H.W.: Drug information for patients, Philadelphia, 1978, W.B. Saunders Co.

Hammel, J., and Johnson, K.: Patient education with the elderly, Minn. Pharm. **28**:8, 1974.

Haynes, R.B., Sackett, D.L., and Taylor, D.W.: How to detect and manage low patient compliance in chronic illness, Geriatrics **35**:91, 1980.

Hecht, A.B.: Improving medication compliance by teaching outpatients, Nurs. Forum **13**:112, 1974.

Helps, Sir A.: Friends in counsel. In Stevenson, B., editor: The home book of quotations, ed. 10, New York, 1967, Dodd, Mead, & Co.

Hemminki, E., and Heikkilä, J.: Elderly people's compliance with prescription and quality of medication, Scand. J. Soc. Med. **3**:87, 1975.

Hermann, F.: The outpatient prescription label as a source of medication errors, Am. J. Hosp. Pharm. **30**:155, 1973.

Hildebrand, R.: Drug information for Rx patient, Illinois Pharm., p. 208, July 1972.

Hulka, B.S., et al.: Medication use and misuse: physician-patient discrepancies, J. Chronic Dis. **28**:7, 1975.

Hulka, B.S., et al.: Communication, compliance, and concordance between physicians and patients with prescribed medications, Am. J. Public Health **66**:847, 1976.

Jenkins, G.H.C.: Drug compliance and the elderly patient, Br. Med. J. **13**:124, 1979.

Jessup, L.E.: Nursing responsibilities in drug administration. In Kayne, R.C., editor: Drugs and the elderly, rev. ed., Los Angeles, 1978, University of Southern California Press.

Johns, M.P.: The nurse and drug surveillance, Drug Info. J. **10**:75, 1976.

Lamy, P.P.: Drug prescribing for the elderly: an overview of the problem. In Beber, C.R., and Lamy, P.P., editors: Medication management and education of the elderly, symposium, Washington, D.C., May 1, 1978.

Lamy, P.P., and Kitler, M.E.: Drugs and the geriatric patient, J. Am. Geriatr. Soc. **19**:23, 1971.

Latiolais, D.J., and Berry, C.C.: Misuse of prescription medications by outpatients, Drug Intell. Clin. Pharm. **3**:271, 1969.

Ley, P., Jain, V.K., and Skilbeck, C.E.: A method for decreasing patients' medication errors, Psychol. Med. **6**:599, 1976.

Lima, J., et al.: Compliance with short-term antimicrobial therapy: some techniques that help, Pediatrics **57**:383, 1976.

Lofholm, P.: Self-medication by the elderly. In Kayne, R.C., editor: Drugs and the elderly, rev. ed., Los Angeles, 1978, University of Southern California Press.

Lublin, J.S.: Critical condition: severe nurse shortage forces some hospitals to close beds or units, Wall Street J., p. 18, August 18, 1980.

Lundin, D.V.: Medication taking behavior of the elderly: a pilot study, Drug Intell. Clin. Pharm. **12**:518, 1978.

Lundin, D.V., et al.: Education of independent elderly in the responsible use of prescription medications, Drug Intell. Clin. Pharm. **14**:335, 1980.

Macdonald, E.T., Macdonald, J.B., and Phoenix, M.: Improving drug compliance after hospital discharge, Br. Med. J. **2**:618, 1977.

Madden, E.E., Jr.: Evaluation of outpatient pharmacy patient counseling, J. Am. Pharm. Assoc. **13**:437, 1973.

Malahy, B.: The effect of instruction and labeling on the number of medication errors made by patients at home, Am. J. Hosp. Pharm. **23**:283, 1966.

Marsh, W.W., and Perlman, L.V.: Understanding congestive heart failure and self-administration of digoxin, Geriatrics **27**:65, 1972.

Marston, M.V.: Compliance with medical regimens: a review of the literature, Nurs. Res. **19**:312, 1970.

Matte, D.A., and McLean, W.M.: Self-medication abuse or misuse? Drug Intell. Clin. Pharm. **12**:603, 1978.

Matthews, D., and Hingson, R.: Improving patient compliance: a guide for physicians, Med. Clin. North Am. **61**:879, 1977.

Mazzullo, J.J., III, Lasagna, L., and Griner, P.F.: Variations in interpretation of prescription instructions, J.A.M.A. **227**:929, 1974.

McKenney, J.M.: Compliance and pharmacists, Prof. Pharm. **4**:1, 1977.

Moore, S.R.: Medication taking behavior of the elderly, Drug Intell. Clin. Pharm. **12**:739, 1978.

Morris, L.A., and Halperin, J.A.: Effects of written drug information on patient knowledge and compliance: a literature review, Am. J. Public Health **69**:47, 1979.

Nazarian, L.F.: Pharmacist's role in patient compliance, Prof. Pharm. **3**:1, 1976.

Neely, E., and Patrick, M.L.: Problems of aged persons taking medications at home, Nurs. Res. **17**:52, 1968.

Non-compliance: does it matter? Br. Med. J. **2**:1168, 1979.

Norell, S.E.: Improving medication compliance: a randomised clinical trial, Br. Med. J. **2**:1031, 1979.

Parish, P.: The doctors and patients handbook of medicines and drugs, New York, 1977, Alfred A. Knopf, Inc.

Parkin, D.M., et al.: Deviation from prescribed drug treatment after discharge from hospital, Br. Med. J. **2**:686, 1976.

Piao Chien, C., Townsend, E.J., and Townsend, A.R.: Substance use and abuse among the community elderly: the medical aspect, Addict. Dis. **3**:357, 1978.

Plant, J.: Educating the elderly in safe medication use, Hospitals **51**:97, 1977.

Podell, R.N.: Noncompliance and strategies for improvement, Nutley, N.J., 1975, Roche Laboratories.

Powell, R., Cali, T.J., and Linkewich, J.A.: Inadequately written prescriptions, J.A.M.A. **226**:999, 1973.

Raygor, A.L.: The Raygor readability estimate: a quick and easy way to determine difficulty, paper presented at the National Reading Conference, Atlanta, December 2, 1976.

Reichert, P.: Patients who won't take their medicine, Consultant **16**:116, 1976.

Richmond, J.B.: Surgeon General's advisory, Washington, D.C., 1979, U.S. Department of Health, Education, and Welfare, Public Health Service.

Rosenberg, S.G.: A case for patient education, Hosp. Formulary Manage. **6**:14, 1971.

Rosenstock, I.M.: Patients' compliance with health regimens, J.A.M.A. **234**:402, 1975.

Ryden, M.: Nursing's response (by profession) on the impact of public safety and demographics, paper presented at the Human Aging III Conference, Minneapolis, April 7, 1978.

Sackett, D.L.: Compliance trials and the clinician, Arch. Intern. Med. **138**:23, 1978.

Schwartz, D.: Safe self-medication for elderly outpatients, Am. J. Nurs. **75**:1808, 1975.

Schwartz, D., et al.: Medication errors made by elderly chronically ill patients, Am. J. Public Health **52**:2018, 1962.

Sharpe, T.R., and Mikeal, R.L.: Patient compliance with antibiotic regimens, Am. J. Hosp. Pharm. **31**:479, 1974.

Slack, W.V.: The patient's right to decide, Lancet **2:** 240, 1977.

Smith, D.J.: Patient compliance with medication regimens, Drug Intell. Clin. Pharm. **10:**386, 1976.

Smith, D.L.: Medication guide for patient counseling, Philadelphia, 1977, Lea & Febiger.

Smith, S.E., and Stead, K.C.: Non-compliance or misprescribing? Lancet **1:**937, 1974.

Spector, R., et al.: Does intervention by a nurse improve medication compliance? Arch. Intern. Med. **138:**36, 1978.

Spriet, A., et al.: Adherence of elderly patients to treatment with pentoxifylline, Clin. Pharmacol. Ther. **27:**1, 1980.

Steckel, S.B., and Swain, M.A.: Contracting with patients to improve compliance, Hospitals **51:**81, 1977.

Stimson, G.V.: Obeying doctor's orders: a view from the other side, Soc. Sci. Med. **8:**97, 1974.

Stone, L.O., and Fletcher, S.: Aspects of population aging in Canada, a chartbook, Ottawa, 1981, Statistics Canada and National Advisory Council on Aging.

Svarstad, B.L.: Physician-patient communication and patient conformity with medical advice. In Mechanics, D., editor: The growth of bureaucratic medicine: an inquiry into the dynamics of patient behavior and the organization of medical care, New York, 1976, John Wiley & Sons, Inc.

Twerski, A.J.: The colossal copout, Penn. Med., **76:**22, 1973.

U.S. Government Printing Office: Cumulated index medicus, 16, Washington, D.C., 1975.

U.S. Government Printing Office: Drug effects can go up in smoke, U.S. Department of Health, Education, and Welfare, PHS, FDA, No. 79-3086, 1979a.

U.S. Government Printing Office: Healthy people, U.S. Department of Health, Education, and Welfare PHS, No. 79-55071, 1979b.

Where jobs go begging even in recession, U.S. News & World Report, p. 60, August 11, 1980.

Wandless, I., and Davie, J.W.: Can drug compliance in the elderly be improved? Br. Med. J. **1:**359, 1977.

CHAPTER 2

Drug misuse in the elderly

Jeffrey R. Solomon

Audrey S. Weiner

A text on geriatric drug therapy would be incomplete if it did not focus attention on the nature and scope of drug misuse in the elderly. Although having no formal place in either the therapeutic or efficacious use of medicines, inappropriate drug-taking patterns among the elderly increasingly influence their health. Medication misuse by the elderly can be defined as noncompliance with a therapeutic regimen, including the use of nonprescription as well as prescription medication. Intrinsic to this definition is an understanding that misuse includes both overutilization and underutilization of drugs as well as dysfunctional interactions (see Chapter 8, "Drug Interactions in the Geriatric Client").

Misuse patterns among the elderly have a variety of causes. In some cases poverty, which affects a disproportionate number of older persons, results in prescribed medications not being taken because of their cost. Furthermore, older persons often stop a medication unilaterally without discussion with health care providers because of dissatisfaction with its lack of results. Sometimes this occurs as a result of inadequate client education. For example, a clinician who prescribes an antidepressant but who does not inform the client that the desired results will not be seen for several weeks runs the risk of the client deciding to discontinue the medication. Sometimes the patient who expects that a drug

prescribed for one chronic condition will affect symptoms of other conditions will choose to stop using the medication. This is often seen with prescribing patterns for medications affecting congestive heart failure, high blood pressure, diabetes, and other chronic illnesses that may themselves be symptom free during their early stages.

GERONTOLOGIC CONSIDERATIONS

A theme that is consistent throughout the problem of drug misuse relates to the expectations of clients as they interact with the reality of drugs' therapeutic benefits. The fountain of youth, the object of Ponce de León's quest, is found neither in prescription nor in over-the-counter medications. Consequently, many ravages of normal or pathologic aging may not be reversed by reliance on drugs. In 1930 Freud addressed this reality (Strachey, 1961):

Life, as we find it, is too hard for us; it brings us too many pains, disappointments and impossible tasks. In order to bear it, we cannot dispense with palliative measures . . . there are perhaps three such measures: powerful deflection, which causes to make light of our misery; substantive satisfactions, which diminish it; and intoxication, which make us insensitive to it.

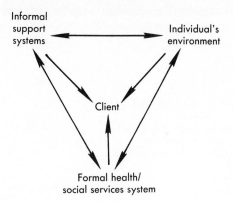

Informal support systems

Individual's environment

Client

Formal health/ social services system

FIG. 2-1

Systems affecting patterns of medication misuse in the elderly.

The synergism of unfulfilled expectations of life, the nearness of death, and the physical, psychologic, and social impact of what old age brings blend together to assist the older person in seeking solutions. The solutions may become part of a silent conspiracy between the older person and any number of caring family members, friends, and professional health care providers. These human systems, which are part of the ecology of the older client, share in the conspiracy because they too find the vicissitudes of life, as played out in old age, too difficult. Although well intentioned, many clinicians continue to rely on medications to replace time-consuming patient education as a means of alleviating anxiety, depression, and a variety of chronic somatic complaints. As Western society moves increasingly from the extended to the nuclear family structure, family members encourage the use of the medical system and the potential misuse of drugs (Fig. 2-1).

RESEARCH FINDINGS

Despite the tremendous growth in gerontologic research, there has only been minimal attention given to the area of legally available prescription and over-the-counter drug use by the elderly.

Research on geriatric drug use has addressed, for the most part, the 5% of the elderly population who live in institutions, but 95% maintain themselves in the community and have the responsibility for their own health and drug management. Furthermore, the overwhelming emphasis on drug-taking behavior research has focused on the problems associated with the use of illicit drugs, especially by younger persons.

No universally accepted theory on drug misuse by the elderly exists. Most theories deal with the pathology assumed to exist in any form of use or reliance on drugs (Guttman, 1977). There is, however, a consistent theme that speaks to drug use serving as a reaction to normal physical, psychosocial, and economic losses that occur throughout the aging process. In his Pulitzer Prize winning book *Why Survive? Being Old in America* Butler (1975) suggests one approach:

> Ultimately, interests must focus on clarifying the complex, interwoven elements necessary to produce and support physical and mental health up to the very end of life rather than our present preoccupation with "curing" ills after they develop.

At the most fundamental level health status is the basic barometer of personal aging for many older persons (Larsen, 1978; Hickey, 1980). The perception of advancing age, one's own and others, is clearly related to health status and concomitant issues relating to independence. Hickey suggests that concern about the status of one's health in the later years is a result of at least three distinct subconcerns. First, there is a fear of the loss of personal independence and autonomy; that is, aging may change one's life-style and limit the pursuit of one's preferences, thereby causing the older person to be dependent on others for physical survival. Second, the economic cost of prolonged health care presents a very realistic fear of reliance on others. This must be taken in the context of the reality that a major change occurs in the economic structure of the older person as the result of retirement. This, together with the impact of inflation on retirement income planning, magnifies these realistic fears. Finally, anxiety about the aging process itself is often expressed through concerns about illness. Thought patterns focusing on sickness, most especially chronic conditions, elicit concerns about aging, the irreversibility of disease, and ultimately, death.

These losses must be seen within the context of other losses that are part of senescence. It is important to note that for purposes of this discussion, normal aging and pathologic aging with disease do not present significantly different clinical pictures. In addition to the factors just listed, the theme of loss is predominant within the psychosocial framework of the older person. The elderly person, in addition to losing income from a job, loses the status that society attributes to the work place. Elderly persons also lose friends, relatives, and contemporaries to death and debilitating illness. Furthermore, they lose functional capacity in each of the five senses and major body systems (musculoskeletal, cardiovascular, respiratory, nervous and special senses, gastrointestinal, urinary, integumentary, reproductive, and endocrine) as a result of the normal aging process (see Chapter 6). Whether manifested by loss of taste, eyesight, or muscle power or whether postural changes occur, the older person is continuously reminded of the ravages of old age.

Although we have spoken of normal aging as not synonymous with illness, it is important to note that approximately 80% to 86% of the elderly suffer from one or more chronic diseases or conditions, compared with only 40% of persons under 65 years of age. Guttman (1977) presents the ten most chronic conditions and the proportion of elderly afflicted by each*:

---

*From Guttman, E.: A survey of drug taking behavior of the elderly, Washington, D.C., 1977, National Institute on Drug Abuse, U.S. Department of Health, Education, and Welfare.

CHRONIC DISEASE OR CONDITION	ELDERLY AFFLICTED (%)
Arthritis and rheumatism	33%
Hearing impairments	22%
Heart disease	17%
High blood pressure	16%
Visual impairments	15%
Digestive system disorders	12%
Chronic sinusitis	10.6%
Mental and emotional disorders	10.5%
Genitourinary disorders	8%
Other cardiovascular disorders	7.5%

Lenhardt (1976) includes the following ten geriatric conditions as those for which drugs are most frequently prescribed: heart disease; hypertension; arthritis; mental and emotional disorders; gastrointestinal disorders; urinary tract infections; diabetes; respiratory tract disorders, such as coughs, sore throats, and influenza; circulatory-related disorders; and chronic skin disorders.

Each person represents a self-contained ecologic system in which there is a careful balance between every range of physical and psychologic factors. Consequently, it is impossible to present these realities of the physiologic aspects of aging without observing and identifying a range of psychologic reactions that are observed in the older person. By no means should one assume that psychopathology automatically follows with the onset of old age. However, one should note that psychopathology is more prevalent in old age than in any other life period and, as with physical disorders, many psychopathologic illnesses are subject to treatment through the efficacious use of medications.

Specifically, the most common forms of psychopathology that are seen in the elderly are depression, organic brain syndrome, paranoid states, anxiety, and hypochondriasis. Although psychopathology may be defined as the point at which any of these (or other) defined states affects one's perception and adaptation to environment, it is understandable that even in normal aging, resultant feelings relating to the previously mentioned changes may trigger bouts of depression or anxiety. Once again, given these bodily changes, hypochondriasis as the result of an excessive concern with one's body has a logical basis. Often, physical changes, in conjunction with minor memory loss or disorientation associated with early organic mental syndrome, manifest themselves in paranoid reactions. Ultimately, each of these five forms of psychopathology may be the result of reactions to normal aging processes as defined by changes noted in the elderly.

While these physical and psychologic changes are occurring, the older person's social networks are also undergoing change. In Western society women tend to marry men older than themselves. In conjunction with a woman's longer life span, a disproportionate number of elderly women, compared to elderly men, results. In the year 2000 there will be 154 older women for each 100 older men. For those over the age of 85 the proportion increases to 202 older women for each 100 older men. Most older men are married; most older women are single (often as a result of widowhood).

The social role change of moving from worker to retiree has been previously noted. As society has become more industrialized, the grandparent role has changed significantly. The nuclear family is becoming more widespread as a result of increasing mobility, vocational patterns, and economic realities. Therefore the elder's role in the extended family in which a given individual may have been raised is no longer the norm (National Council on Aging, 1975). Economic concerns and fear of crime are also cited as other major social consequences that influence aging.

Therefore one can identify a theoretical framework within which drug misuse in the elderly operates. The biopsychosocial forces involved in the conditions previously enumerated predispose the older person to needing help. The nature of this help takes a variety of forms, most often ego syntonic and socially acceptable. However, for large numbers of older persons reliance on chemical alternatives to assist in the natural drive to homeostasis becomes a norm.

USE OF LEGAL DRUGS

Drug misuse and abuse literature is broadly divided into two categories: that relating to legal drugs and that concerned with illicit drug patterns. The overwhelming pattern of drug misuse in the elderly population concerns itself with the inappropriate use of legal drugs and is the focus of this text. However, a brief review of illicit drug use is of interest to provide a complete perspective of this problem. Whittington and Petersen (1979) suggest that the lack of data regarding the use of all illegal chemical substances necessitates the limitation of discussion to opiate use. Incidence data for all patients admitted to the U.S. Public Health Service Hospital in Lexington, Kentucky (1963), indicated that less than 4% of the population were over 60 years of age. Similarly, data from the methadone maintenance program at Roosevelt Hospital, New York, showed that only 0.5% of the 34,000 methadone clients in New York City were over 60 years of age. Whittington and Petersen further suggest that although patterns of illicit use are low, these and other figures are an underrepresentation of incidence. In this context it is hypothesized that older addicts camouflage their habits through a variety of sources to avoid legal harassment and scrutiny. This includes relying on the neighborhood pusher, switching from a more expensive and scarce drug such as heroin to the more accessible hydromorphone (Dilaudid), and modifying patterns of use as necessary.

It is important to understand overall drug use patterns among the elderly. The elderly comprise less than 11% of the current North American population, yet they receive approximately 25% of all prescriptions (Petersen and Whittington, 1977). Furthermore data suggest that the elderly also consume a disproportionately large amount of over-the-counter drugs (Petersen and Thomas, 1975). Source data on elderly persons treated in a hospital emergency room for nonfatal but acute drug reactions were collected for all 1128 persons treated at Jackson Memorial Hospital in Miami, Florida, during 1972. Among all admissions, 5.4% were aged 50 years and over. The most striking feature within this population was that each admission involved the use of a legal, as opposed to an illicit, drug. Of these, 80.9% misused psychotropic drugs. More than 10% had taken an overdose of a nonanalgesic. Those drugs most frequently misused were diazepam, secobarbital, amobarbital, phenobarbital, and propoxyphene.

A 1978 study that assessed drug use patterns of well elderly in Michigan found that not one individual was identified as "drug free." Of those studied, 71% used prescription medications; 54% used over-the-counter drugs; and 20% used home remedies. Nearly one out of four persons interviewed was taking four or more prescription medications concurrently. Approximately one half of the sample reported the use of over-the-counter analgesics, laxatives, and/or antacids from four to five times a week. Finally, one third of those interviewed indicated that they saved their unused medicines, believing that they might need to use them again (Seniors and Substance Abuse Task Force, 1978). These data are similar to those found in other studies such as those conducted by the Cathedral Foundation and the Miami Jewish Home and Hospital for the Aged (Solomon, 1977; Ad Hoc Subcommittee on Aging, 1979).

CONSIDERATIONS IN MEDICATION MISUSE

It is important to review the characteristics of drug misuse as well as its origin. One must first appreciate the limited therapeutic "window" in which many medications operate. For clients to obtain the efficacious effect of medication, the dosage must be adequate to affect the physiologic system. At the same time, especially in light of the physical changes in the older person (e.g., body weight, metabolic function, and endocrine function) (see Chapter 6, "Physiologic Changes and Clinical Manifestations of Aging"), prescribing patterns need to focus on reaching that plateau without encountering the difficulties inherent in overmedication and going beyond that window, which narrows with age. Careful titration by the prescribing clinician is an essential prerequisite to successful drug therapy.

A number of potential reasons for drug misuse exist (Conference Proceedings, 1975):

1. Elderly persons may reject drugs because of a perceived threat to their sense of autonomy and dignity.
2. The very changes that occur in the aging process may affect drug use. For example, sensory losses make reading small labels and hearing verbal instructions difficult. Arthritic changes often make bottles, especially those with childproof safety caps, difficult for older persons to maneuver.
3. The economics of aging often affect drug misuse. Many older persons do not buy drugs because they cannot afford them. They may be limited by lack of transportation to publicly funded clinics and other eleemosynary sources of medications. Consequently, they may substitute less expensive over-the-counter preparations or home remedies for prescribed regimens.
4. The sheer number of medications required increase the possibility of error and increase the potential for dangerous drug interactions.
5. Because of the relative paucity of client education by clinicians, clients often do not know how much medication to take, how often it needs to be taken, or how long to take a specific drug. Thus clients are often not aware of the potential side effects of the drugs, and they do not understand whether the drug is better taken before or after eating. They may also be unaware of

when the therapeutic benefit might begin, what feelings they should have while taking the drugs, and whether there are any potentially hazardous interactions with certain foods, other drugs, or activities.

Patterns of misuse

The patterns of misuse can be further characterized as follows:

1. Overdose—Clients take too much of the drug that a clinician overprescribes for them.
2. Medication omission—Clients decide on their own initiative to omit taking a prescribed medication.
3. Self-selection—Clients make judgments regarding medications to be taken at any specific point.
4. Duplication—Clients use a number of clinicians (e.g., physician, podiatrist, dentist, pharmacist, nurse) without sharing previous drug regimen with each. This results in the simultaneous use of medicines prescribed by different clinicians at different times, often for the same symptoms.
5. Clinician instruction—Clients may be told to take a drug as needed, not knowing the parameters of the symptomatology that should result in drug taking.
6. Pill swapping—Clients share drugs with one another as they would share home remedies, recipes, and other products relating to activities of daily living.
7. Expired medications—As indicated by the Michigan study, clients may retain unused prescription drugs and take them on a subsequent occasion.
8. Automatic refills—Clients may continually have prescriptions refilled without consulting a physician.
9. Iatrogenesis—Clinicians may prescribe inappropriate medications and dosages.
10. Telephone prescriptions—Clients request

and receive prescriptions from the physician over the telephone without a thorough evaluation.
11. Organic mental changes—Clients' mental conditions may be deteriorating, causing forgetfulness and confusion with resultant errors in medication-taking patterns.

In 1975 the United States National Institute on Drug Abuse conducted a conference on the perspectives of drug abuse in the elderly. The conference concluded that clients' noncompliance was an issue of serious concern, indicating that 25% to 60% of clients make errors in self-administration of prescribed medications. The 1978 Michigan Study on Drug Abuse Patterns is consistent in its findings through self-reporting: 30% of the elderly interviewed had stopped taking medication earlier than directed; 20% had not filled a prescription at all; and 14% had varied the prescribed dosage (see Chapter 1, "Medication-taking Behavior and Compliance in the Elderly").

It is significant that our health care systems are predicated on self-care with the exception of institutionally based acute and long-term care (reflecting only a small minority of interactions with the impaired older person). Ambulatory care requires client self-management. One has to decide when to see a physician, when to take medicines, how to take medicines, and when to stop taking medicines. Unfortunately, little attention is paid to one's education in relation to the management of one's own health. Whether one looks at either the preventive or the restorative aspects of clinical health care management, most individuals rely on professionals when, in fact, the client role often predominates. In a 1977 study by the Cathedral Foundation the following was revealed: 100% of the persons indicated that they wanted to know more about the medications they take, including the medication's name, directions relating to administration, how the medication works, and the disorder it treats; 53% expressed the need to understand the information displayed on medication labels; 73% wanted to learn about the medication's side effects; and 47% wanted to know what to do with outdated and unused prescriptions.

PROGRAM APPROACHES

A number of program approaches have been identified to deal with the problem of drug misuse among the elderly. Gollub (1978) categorized three types of programs:

1. Intervention programs: Initiated by health providers who regularly deal with diagnosis, prescriptions, and drug administration, these programs are aimed at direct one-to-one counseling.
2. Intervention and treatment programs: Identifying persons whose problems of drug misuse include chemical dependency, these programs seek to reach out; refer; provide treatment, including individual and group behavioral therapeutic modalities; and offer drug education.
3. Indirect programs: In light of the nature of the cause of drug misuse among the elderly these programs provide health and social service supports necessary to encourage older persons to live more independent and active lives, thereby minimizing the intrapsychic needs that may lead to the abuse of medications.

In conjunction with previously mentioned data regarding the need and desire for the elderly to know more about medications, several educational processes have been developed. Gaetano and Epstein (1977) maintain that through an educational process the drug use behavior of the elderly can be changed to make it a more positive factor in an individual's life, thereby limiting it to appropriate use. This process involves a need for the elderly to accept change in knowledge, attitudes, or behavior. The authors argue that to the degree that these values and attitudes might be changed, there is a direct benefit in the well-being of the elderly as well as an indirect benefit in significant cost savings for unneeded or in-

appropriate medications. They suggest that primary efforts should be made in consumer programs. This is supported in other reports (Plant, 1977) in which arguments are made for the overwhelming cost benefits related to consumer education as opposed to health provider education.

Several formats for the provision of consumer education have been identified. First, the provision of formal education, offered in community colleges, adult education programs, or other institutions where learning is a primary function, is one direct approach. A second involves a community service approach in which human service agencies are the providers of education. Prevention programs have been offered in such places as senior centers, nutrition sites, and community mental health centers. Often a peer counseling approach is taken. For example, the United States Administration on Aging has provided support for this concept through the development of a peer counseling training program at the University of Miami Institute for the Study of Aging. The National Institute on Drug Abuse has prepared resource material for drug education as identified in its Elder Ed Program. Examples of successful community-based approaches include the Med Ed Program of the Miami Jewish Home and Hospital for the Aged, which operates the Douglas Gardens Community Mental Health Center, Senior Adult Day Centers, and the Service Workers Action Team (SWAT) project.

Essentially, this agency has identified medication education as a priority and delivers a packaged Med Ed program through its full range of community-based health and social services for the elderly. This includes a clinician's review of all prescribed and over-the-counter medications used by service clients, including dosage, expiration date, related symptomatology, and duplication. In this context it is not unusual for the clinician to be presented with a shoebox filled with medications that are currently being taken. This medication review is followed by individual and/or group medication education sessions and client-specific case management to remedy any system-produced misuse patterns. Examples of group education programs include "Use of Generic Medications"; "Hypertension and Its Control"; and "Your Role in the Health Care System." Information brochures that are part of an outreach mechanism are sensitive to cultural aspects within the community. Specifically, in the case of Miami, they are trilingual, using English, Spanish, and Yiddish reflecting the primarily elderly populations in Miami, of which more than 60% are foreign born (Fig. 2-2).

Another approach is The Door of Osceola County, Florida, a drug counseling agency that has made the transition from the provision of drug abuse counseling exclusively for adolescents and young adults who abuse illicit drugs to drug misuse education as a comprehensive program aimed at the elderly consumer and health care professionals within its target area. The Door recently initiated an outpatient counseling center that focuses on prescription medication misuse by the elderly. Outreach services, conducted at community centers in residential areas, are de-

---

Medication & the Elderly
Do's

Tell your doctor about all the medications you are taking.

Carefully follow directions on all medications.

Be sure you know when and how to take your drugs.

Throw away out-of-date medications.

Ask your pharmacist to keep a record of all your prescriptions.

Medication & the Elderly
Don'ts

Don't take someone else's medications or offer them yours.

Don't mix medications without your doctor's approval.

Don't put drugs into different or unlabeled bottles.

Don't assume all over-the-counter medicines are safe for you. Check with your doctor first.

Don't mix alcohol and drugs.

Warning: Drugs may be hazardous to your health.

Miami Jewish Home & Hospital for the Aged at Douglas Gardens.

Medicinas y Personas de Edad Avanzada
Los "Haga"

Repórtele a su Doctor todas las medicinas que está tomando.

Sea cuidadoso en seguir las instrucciones de sus medicinas.

Este seguro de cuando y como tomar sus drogas.

Bote las medicinas con fecha vencida.

Pídale a su farmacéutico que le mantenga record de sus prescripciones.

Medicinas y Personas de Edad Avanzada
Los "No Haga"

Ni tome de otros, ni ofrezca a otros medicinas.

No mezcle medicinas sin la aprobación de su médico.

No ponga sus medicinas en pomos o envases sin letreros.

No crea que todas las medicinas sin recetas son inofensivas. Chequee primero con su doctor.

No tome bebidas alcohólicas con sus medicinas.

Advertencia: Los drogas pueden dañar su salud.

Miami Jewish Home & Hospital for the Aged at Douglas Gardens.

Miami Jewish Home & Hospital for the Aged at Douglas Gardens.

FIG. 2-2

Multilingual brochure providing drug information to the elderly.

signed to maximize accessibility to services. The approach identified at The Door is comprehensive because it attempts to educate the elderly services provider while, at the same time, assists in the development of a more knowledgeable consumer. Complementing these services, a task force of elderly persons has been developed to advise local social service agencies and increase the effectiveness of referrals.

The third approach is that of identifying and providing education to the health care provider. At a conference sponsored by the National Institute on Drug Abuse in 1975 the conferees identified a number of aspects in the provision of these educational services. The first is that a prerequisite to any health education program is stimulating interest among individuals involved in care of the aged. Second, there must be recognition of the limited training in gerontology and geriatrics in schools of medicine, pharmacy, nursing, social work, and psychology. Consequently, even the well-trained provider may not have the tools to work effectively in the area of drugs and the elderly. Furthermore, as part of the general negative attitude toward the elderly that exists in Western society, which has been labeled "ageism" (Butler, 1975), professionals tend to have stereotypic views about and significant gaps in the knowledge required for the provision of good health care for the aged. "Ageism" in this regard is similar to other attitudinal belief systems such as racism and sexism. Finally, there needs to be a recognition of the iatrogenic components of drug misuse among the elderly, with concomitant programmatic thrusts in this arena.

INTERVENTION PROGRAMS: HEALTH CARE PROVIDERS

Several methods for intervention in the area of drug misuse have been developed. The first method calls for monitoring programs used predominantly in institutional settings. Generally, monitoring has been related to issues of drug inventory control rather than quality assurance in terms of therapeutic use. Nevertheless, the

potential for monitoring within a number of settings exists. Computer technology permits storage of client drug profile data. With appropriate programming, potentially hazardous drug interactions can be identified, alerting the clinician to possible iatrogenic drug misuse. The limitations of such a monitoring system is that iatrogenesis is only one part of drug misuse: that relating to the health care professional. In no way will this monitoring address the problems caused by the self-management of medications by the client. Prospective monitoring systems are presently being placed in numerous settings. Among the more sophisticated programs that have been developed are those at the University of Southern California; the Medical University of South Carolina, Family Practice Clinic; and the Drug Intake and Management System (DIMES) in Massachusetts. Retrospective monitoring programs exist in a number of clinics and health settings serving the elderly (Gollub, 1979).

One advantage of these retrospective approaches is that they are more readily able to monitor in both institutional and community settings. A sophisticated process used by the Mediphor Program of Stanford, California, allows the client to enter the pharmacy with one or more prescriptions. Corresponding to data entered in a remote computer terminal by the pharmacist, the central computer formats a prescription label and sends the information back to the remote pharmacy. At the same time, an interaction search is performed by the central computer, matching the newly prescribed drug(s) against previously stored data in the client profile. If a potential drug interaction is found, a short message ("mini-alert") is relayed to the label printer at the pharmacy, indicating the client's name, interacting drugs, and a short description of the anticipated interactions. Mini-alerts are divided into two groups: (1) those interactions for which telephone notification and consultation with the prescribing physician is desirable before dispensing the medication and (2) those interactions that, because of lesser immediacy and severity, do not require such notification. For both groups, a full interaction report is printed by the computer and sent to the prescriber the following day.

Several approaches have been developed to provide intervention through monitoring training programs for pharmacists in the community and institutions. Others are pharmacy oriented but are designed for nurses and other health care professionals. Generally, they require the health care professional to view all clients as potential drug misusers. They stress the need to provide the client with adequate knowledge concerning drugs in order to avoid potential problem areas. They suggest that certain characteristics may contribute to drug misuse: client characteristics, such as physical and mental health; client perspectives and expectations, such as failure to comprehend the nature and seriousness of an illness; and failure to appreciate the value of the medication in dealing with the illness, such as the consequences of noncompliance. Finally, they urge the maintenance of comprehensive client records and profiles so that drug misuse prevention may become part of the ordinary protocol involving drug dispensing.

RESEARCH ISSUES

Guttman (1977), in a survey of drug-taking behavior in the elderly, identified a consistent pattern of self-perception by prescription drug users: lowered self-esteem and lowered self-estimation of individual capabilities. This further documents the need for additional information on the role that legal drugs play in a person's ability to cope with life. Further research is needed on social measures that may be taken to improve the self-image and the self-attitudes of the elderly drug misuser. The present state of research on drug misuse and the elderly is limited and has not yet focused on some of the root causes of misuse. The relationship between the causes of inappropriate drug dependence and the effects of inappropriate drug dependence on self-esteem requires further investigation.

Significant research on drug use is also necessary. Retrospective peer review has identified patterns of excessive prescribing by certain clinicians, and replicative approaches might do the same with regard to misuse of drugs by the individual. Furthermore, questions of individual economics and drug use might lead to a better understanding in terms of the overall pharmacologic issue. Needless to say, clinical studies with specific focus on the elderly would greatly expand the base of knowledge, thus resulting in a decrease of iatrogenic drug misuse.

ADVOCACY ISSUES

Finally, increased governmental involvement in the problems of drug misuse, both as health care and consumer issues, may well be observed in the future. Presently, advocates for the aged are calling for legislative changes that would require prescriptions to be labeled with the name of the condition for which the medication is prescribed in lay terms. Mandates for labeling prescriptions with an expiration date for the specific medication are also being advocated. Just as combined economic, consumer, and health care efforts resulted in numerous changes in laws regarding generic formulas, issues of drug misuse in the elderly may well be addressed in public policy arenas.

SUMMARY

Although the clinician cannot mitigate the process of normal and abnormal aging, it is the responsibility of any aging-services practitioner to approach care from a holistic client perspective. This includes the following:

1. Comprehensive physical, psychosocial, and environmental assessment to determine presenting problems, personal supports, use of service delivery systems, and present medication patterns
2. Treatment patterns that address the whole person rather than a disease entity
3. Appropriate titration/prescription of drugs recognizing the physiology of the older client

4. Education regarding dosage, potential side effects, interactions with foods, and anticipated results of the medication regimen; inclusion of the dosage recommendation on drug labels
5. Follow-up through office or telephone contact to assure appropriate patterns of use

These recommendations advocate a nontraditional approach to health care reflective of the realities and needs of the older person. It is important to consider the potential options for formal and informal assessment and system follow-up through families, friends, caregivers, and other social and health care providers.

REFERENCES

Ad Hoc Subcommittee on Aging of the Committee on Health and Rehabilitative Services of the Florida House of Representatives: Aging: a realistic commitment, Tallahassee, Fla., 1979.

Butler, R.: Why survive? Being old in America, New York, 1975, Harper & Row, Publishers, Inc.

Cathedral Foundation: Medication use and misuse study among older persons, unpublished paper, 1977.

Gaetano, R.J., and Epstein, B.T.: Drugs and the elderly: strategies and techniques for consumer education, unpublished paper, 1977.

Gollub, J.: Psychoactive drug misuse among the elderly: a review of prevention and treatment programs. In Kayne, R.C., editor: Drugs and the elderly, Los Angeles, 1978, The Ethel Andros Gerontology Center.

Gollub, J.: Psychoactive drug misuse among the elderly: a review of prevention and treatment programs. In National Institute on Drug Abuse: The aging process and psychoactive drug use, Washington, D.C., 1979, U.S. Department of Health, Education, and Welfare.

Guttman, E.: A survey of drug taking behavior of the elderly, Washington, D.C., 1977, National Institute on Drug Abuse, U.S. Department of Health, Education, and Welfare.

Hickey, T.: Health and aging, Monterey, Calif., 1980, Brooks/Cole Publishing Co.

Institute for the Study of Aging: Drug management and the older adult: a peer counseling approach—manual for training delivery, Coral Gables, Fla., 1977, University of Miami.

Larsen, R.: Thirty years of research on the subjective well being of older Americans, J. Gerontol. **33**:109, 1978.

Lenhardt, D.G.: The use of medications in the elderly population, Nurs. Clin. North Am. **11**(1):135, 1976.

National Council on Aging: The myth and reality of aging in America, Washington, D.C., 1975.

National Institute on Drug Abuse: Drug use and the elderly: perspectives and issues, Conference proceedings, Washington, D.C., 1975, U.S. Department of Health, Education, and Welfare.

National Institute on Drug Abuse: Elder-Ed: An education program for older Americans—using medicines wisely, Washington, D.C., 1979, U.S. Department of Health, Education, and Welfare.

Petersen, D.M., and Thomas, C.: Acute drug reactions among the elderly, J. Gerontol. **30**:552, 1975.

Petersen, D.M., and Whittington, F.J.: Drug use among the elderly: a review, J. Psychedelic Drugs **9**:25, 1977.

Plant, J.: Educating the elderly in safe medication use, Hospitals **51**:97, 1977.

Seniors and Substance Abuse Task Force: Substance abuse among Michigan senior citizens: current issues and future decisions, Lansing, Mich., 1978, Michigan Office of Services to the Aging.

Solomon, J.: The chemical timebomb: drug misuse by the elderly, Contemp. Drug Probl. **6**:231, 1977.

Strachey, J., editor: The standard edition of the complete psychological works of Sigmund Freud, vol. 21, London, 1961, Hogarth Press.

Whittington, F.J., and Petersen, D.M.: Drugs and the elderly. In Petersen, D.M., Whittington, F.J., and Payne, B.P., editors: Drugs and the elderly—social and pharmacological issues, Springfield, Ill., 1979, Charles C Thomas, Publisher.

CHAPTER 3

Monitoring drug therapy for the long-term care client

James W. Cooper

This chapter will present an approach to drug therapy assessment for the long-term care client. There are four purposes for drug therapy assessment in the long-term care client:

1. To establish a verified problem list
2. To verify drug therapy administration and effect
3. To anticipate, detect, and prevent drug-related problems
4. To encourage the most appropriate use of drugs

In long-term care the first basic drug therapy responsibility is to understand how drugs are being used by establishing a verified problem and therapy list (Fig. 3-1). This is a team responsibility of all health care practitioners concerned with the care of the client. The problem list and the record of accomplishments by the client should be combined to provide a concise therapy history.

The second purpose is to verify drug therapy administration and effect. Beyond accounting for controlled substances, one should compare the doses dispensed with those administered. Also, there should be an attainable therapeutic goal that can be identified through objective and subjective parameters for each active problem.

Third, one should anticipate, detect, and prevent drug-related problems. Drug-related prob-

lems include drug misuse, such as medication errors and client noncompliance (Chapters 1 and 2), adverse drug reactions (Chapter 11), and drug interactions (Chapter 8).

The fourth purpose is to encourage the most appropriate use of drugs. This last purpose is actually composed of the first three purposes, if the overall goal is to encourage the most appropriate use of drugs in the facility.

The problem-oriented medical record (POMR) is ideally suited for documentation of care of the elderly long-term care client.

By keeping a complete list of all problems from the data base, recognizing possible subjective (S) and objective (O) findings regarding each problem, assessing (A) the problem, and determining the therapeutic plan (P), one has a concise, convenient, centralized approach to record keeping (i.e., SOAP). In contrast, the traditional source-oriented or "scatter" charting commonly found in acute or episodic care is a less preferable approach to client care documentation.

The five-step problem-oriented approach follows (see also p. 46):

1. Obtain data base
2. Write problem list
3. Match problem list with therapy
4. Evaluate therapeutic goal attainment
5. Complete review and document pertinent findings

STEP 1 — ESTABLISH DATA BASE

A logical beginning for obtaining or creating a data base is the discharge summary (if applicable), which is available when a client has been transferred from a hospital to a long-term care facility. In addition, physician history and physical, nurse assessment and history, subsequent nurses' notes, and progress notes on subsequent periodic evaluations should also be obtained. Assessments and periodic evaluations from the social worker and dietician (or nutritionist) are also valuable. Finally, an area often neglected is the client's history of drug use before admission. Problems can be listed in a format such as that found in Fig. 3-1.

Fig. 3-2 is a medication survey that can be included with facility admitting forms. This form should be completed by the client or the client's family before or at the time of admission.

The survey process, preferably combined with a client or family interview, can help to determine the client's pharmacy(ies) and physician(s) and all medications currently being taken or that have been taken during the past 6 months. Drugs should be brought in to be identified and verified in order to correlate therapy with the verified active problem list. In addition, the client or family is asked to bring in *all* drugs, medications, "cures," and nonprescription drugs.

In the second phase the client should be asked if any drugs are being taken for symptoms, conditions, or disease states as a cross-check (e.g., if the older person does not take any drugs or medications, then what is taken for irregularity or constipation?). (See Fig. 3-2.) Often, health care practitioners will find that the older person is not taking any "drugs" but is taking a "water pill," Ex-Lax, or Kaopectate because these are not thought of as drugs or medicine; they are simply things "taken for something." Many lay people, particularly elderly clients and to some extent their families, do not regard drugs in the same fashion that health professionals do. A review of symptoms (e.g., headache, constipation) with

some drug examples will frequently refresh the memories of most elderly persons and their families. The form presented in Fig. 3-2 can easily be modified to include drugs most commonly used in different geographic areas.

The final portion of the drug history seeks to determine, by five different methods, whether the client has had any problems with drugs. First, does the client have any allergies? If allergies are found, an attempt should be made to verify "allergenicity." It has been demonstrated that about 40% of what clients think are "allergies" are actually side effects, intolerances to drugs, or unrelated events (Adler and DeChristofaro, 1977).

Text continued on p. 51.

Step 1. *Obtain or create data base.* *

(Initially and monthly)
  From:
  Discharge summary (when applicable)
  Physician history and physical (and progress notes)
  Nurses' assessment and history (and nurses' notes)
  Social worker assessment (annual evaluation)
  Dietary/nutritional assessment (monthly evaluation)
  Drug history/survey

Step 2. *Write a problem list in these terms:*

  1. Chronology
  2. Sequence
  3. Activity (active or past status post [S/P])

Step 3. *Match problem list with therapy.*

(Initially and monthly)
  Recognize that some drugs may not *relate to an active problem.*
  Discontinue *unnecessary and duplicative therapy.*

Step 4. *Evaluate attainment of therapeutic goal for each active pharmacotherapeutically treatable problem. Recognize that data may be insufficient for evaluation.*

Step 5. *Complete review and document pertinent findings.*

Recognize that inadequacy of data base may be a problem.

```
                            CLIENT PROBLEM LIST

Clinical Pharmacy Service                          School of Pharmacy

                              Physician's name_____

Client's name_____ Age/ht-wt/race/sex_____

Adm-rev. date(s)_____ Facility_____ CC_____

Adm-PE-ROS-VS _____ Adm-AbNLab tests_____
```

Date	No.	Active problems	Tx/Rx Plans/ results	Date Onset	Resolved	Inactive problems

Problems include established diagnosis, physiologic abnormality, signs and symptoms, laboratory test or physical abnormality, psychologic problem, socioeconomic problems, past operations and procedures, adverse drug reactions and interactions, and compliance with therapy (past or present).

FIG. 3-1

Client problem list.

```
                                               Client's name _____
Health care
facility      _____ Physician's name _____

TO:  The client or your family

                            MEDICATION SURVEY

1.  The purpose of this survey is to gather as much data as we possibly can con-
    cerning the medications that you have taken over the past several months.
    This information will be tabulated and communicated to your physician so that
    he will have available to him a complete picture of your medication history.

    All data furnished are solely hospital or nursing home property and will be
    treated with strict confidentiality.  Please provide as much information as
    you can.

2.  Please list the names and addresses of pharmacies or drugstores where you
    have had prescriptions filled in the last 6 months:

         NAME                                        ADDRESS

    _____      _____

    _____      _____

    _____      _____

    _____      _____

3.  Please list the names of all physicians, dentists, podiatrists, or other
    persons whom you have seen for health needs in the past 6 months.

    _____

    _____

    _____

    _____

4.  Please list the medications, both prescription and nonprescription, that you
    have been taking over the last year.  If you do not know the name of the med-
    ications, please list the prescription number and pharmacy where obtained and
    give the best physical description of the drug (e.g., color, size, shape).
    If possible, please bring in all your current medications for identification.
    They will be returned to you after they have been identified.

    The following list may help you to remember some of the medications, drugs,
    patent medicines, or "cures" you have taken.  Please give as much information
    as possible.  Thank you.
```

FIG. 3-2

Medication survey.

Have you, in the last 6 months, taken or been advised to take any of the following for:

SYMPTOMS	DRUGS	HOW LONG (days, weeks, months)

4.1   Irregularity   _____ Milk of Magnesia   _____
       Constipation   _____ Ex-Lax, Dulcolax   _____
                            _____ Mineral oil, Haley's M-O _____
                            _____ Other_____   _____

4.2   Diarrhea   _____ Kaopectate, Pepto-Bismol _____
       Runny stools   _____ Donnagel, Lactinex, Lomotil _____
                            Paregoric

4.3   Upset stomach   _____ Alka-Seltzer, Bromo-Seltzer _____
       Ulcer medication   _____ Baking soda   _____
                            _____ Tums, Rolaids   _____
                            _____ Gelusil, Maalox, Mylanta _____
                            _____ Other _____ _____

4.4   Aches and pains   _____ Aspirin, Anacin   _____
       Headaches   _____ Bufferin, BC powders   _____
       Arthritic and   _____ Codeine, Darvon, Demerol _____
         rheumatic pain   _____ Decadron, cortisone   _____
                            _____ Prednisone   _____
                            _____ Other_____   _____

4.5   Eye preparations   _____ Phospholine Iodide   _____
       Glaucoma   _____ Humersol, Isopto Carpine _____
       Red, irritated eyes _____ Visine, Pilocarpine   _____
                            _____ Other _____ _____

4.6   Ear preparations   _____ Auralgan   _____
                            _____ Other _____ _____

4.7   Colds   _____ Antihistamines   _____
       Hayfever   _____ Aspirin, Tylenol   _____
       Stuffy nose   _____ Neo-Synephrine   _____
                            _____ Cold tablets, Contac   _____
                            _____ Cough syrup, Nyquil   _____
                            _____ Other _____ _____

4.8   Birth control hormones _____ Oral contraceptives   _____
       "The Pill"   _____ Other _____ _____

4.9   Heart medications   _____ Digitalis   _____
                            _____ Nitroglycerin   _____
                            _____ Quinidine, Pronestyl   _____
                            _____ Other _____ _____

FIG. 3-2 — cont'd.

Medication survey—cont'd.

	SYMPTOMS	DRUGS	HOW LONG (days, weeks, months)
4.10	High blood pressure Water pills Potassium	_____ Diuril (water pill) _____ Reserpine, Ser-Ap-Es _____ Aldomet _____ Esimil _____ Catapres, Inderal _____ Kaochlor _____ Klorvess _____ Slow-K	_____ _____ _____ _____ _____ _____ _____ _____
4.11	Asthma, bronchitis Emphysema	_____ Tedral, Amesec, Bronkotabs _____ Prednisone _____ Isuprel aerosol _____ Epinephrine aerosol _____ Decadron, cortisone _____ Other _____	_____ _____ _____ _____ _____ _____
4.12	Nerve pills Tranquilizers	_____ Librium, Thorazine _____ Valium, Mellaril _____ Meprobamate (Miltown, _____ Equanil) _____ Other _____	_____ _____ _____ _____ _____
4.13	Insomnia	_____ Sominex, Nytol, Dalmane _____ Seconal, Doriden, Quaalude _____ Nembutal, Noludar, Noctec _____ Chloral hydrate _____ Other _____	_____ _____ _____ _____ _____
4.14	Antibiotics Infections	_____ Penicillin _____ Tetracycline _____ Erythromycin _____ Sulfa _____ Other	_____ _____ _____ _____ _____
4.15	Blood clotting Blood thinners Anticoagulants	_____ Coumadin _____ Heparin _____ Other _____	_____ _____ _____
4.16	Blood builders Anemia drugs	_____ Iron tablets, Geritol _____ Fem-Iron _____ Folic acid _____ B_{12} shots _____ Vitamins _____ Other _____	_____ _____ _____ _____ _____ _____
4.17	Diabetes	_____ Insulin _____ Orinase _____ Diabinese _____ Other _____	_____ _____ _____ _____

FIG. 3-2, cont'd.
Medication survey—cont'd.

```
         SYMPTOMS                    DRUGS                       HOW LONG
                                                            (days, weeks, months)

  4.18   Hemorrhoids          _____ Anusol                  _____
                              _____ Preparation H           _____
                              _____ Medicone, Tucks         _____
                              _____ Other_____        _____

  4.19   Skin conditions—dry  _____ Neosporin               _____
         eczema, psoriasis,   _____ Tegrin, Mazon           _____
         athlete's foot, corns, _____ Keri, Vioform         _____
         dandruff, infections _____ Other_____        _____

  4.20   Other conditions     _____         _____
                              _____         _____
                              _____         _____
                              _____         _____
                              _____         _____
```

5.   Do you or have you ever had:

  5.1   Any problems with drugs? ____Yes ____No (Please list)
        _____
        _____
        _____

  5.2   Any allergies to foods, drugs, pets, or environment? ____Yes ____No

  5.3   A family history of allergy? ____Yes ____No

  5.4   A drug discontinued because of rash, itching, nausea, or vomiting?
        ____Yes ____No

  5.5   Difficulty in swallowing tablets or capsules? ____Yes ____No

  5.6   Or been told that you have had a reaction to a drug, shot, or
        medicine? ____Yes ____No

  5.7   Have you been in a hospital in the last year? ____Yes ____No
        If yes, which hospital?

6. Please return this form to your pharmacist as soon as possible.

FIG. 3-2, cont'd.

Medication survey—cont'd.

If a client is asked if a drug has ever been discontinued because it produced rash, itching, nausea or vomiting, difficulty in breathing, or difficulty in swallowing tablets or capsules, one has a cross-check of symptoms with reactions.

Some people confuse difficulty in taking drugs with allergy. For example, some elderly persons have stated that they were allergic to digoxin because they developed anorexia, nausea, and emesis and that they were thus sure that they had an allergy and could not take digoxin. Another example concerns an older person who had digoxin prescribed for a high output type of cardiac failure secondary to chronic lung disease. When the drug did not help her cardiac failure, the prescriber discontinued the drug. The client assumed that she was therefore allergic to digoxin. Allergies should be verified, not only from the standpoint of the older person's understanding of the drug but also perhaps, in some cases, to see that the client is not denied a potentially lifesaving drug, such as penicillin. Clients who have developed nausea, stomach upset, or diarrhea after taking penicillins or other antibiotics may often confuse these side effects with "allergy." Some clients associate difficulty in swallowing tablets and capsules with allergy.

Finally, one should ask if the client has ever been told that he has had a reaction to a drug. Many clients will state, "No, I'm not allergic to anything, but the doctor said I can't take penicillin." The question of whether the client has been in the hospital in the last year is particularly pertinent in determining problems related to drugs. The survey process is less preferable to interviewing each client or the family, but in many cases this personal contact is not possible. If the allergy data base is incomplete, every effort should be made to complete the drug history. The completed drug history should be

---

_____ Date

HEALTH CARE FACILITY

_____

Notice of medication history

Physician's name _____

Client's name _____ Room number _____

Members of the Pharmacy Department staff have compiled a medication history through an interview with your client.

1. Medications that your client was taking at the time of admission to the hospital are listed for your information below:

Medication	Compliance			Presc. No.	Pharmacy
	Yes	Irreg.	No		

2. Verified sensitivities, allergies, or adverse reactions:

   a. Drugs

   b. Food

   c. Environment

3. Pharmacist's remarks: _____
   _____
   _____
   _____

                                        _____
                                                (Pharmacist's name)

FIG. 3-3

Notice of medication history.

placed in the history and physical section of the chart (Fig. 3-3).

The final concept in obtaining and creating a data base is to recognize that inadequacy in data can be a problem. Sometimes, simply not enough is known for the caregiver to make a judgment. This should always be kept in mind when one uses professional judgment.

At this point a drug regimen review (DRR) sheet procedure should be considered (Fig. 3-4). The initial drug regimen review and subsequent assessment can also serve as a record of the client's review and problems. In Fig. 3-4 the facility and the client's name, age, race, and sex are listed along with the height and weight to calculate an ideal body weight. The attending physician before and during the hospital stay, the admission date, dates of review, the chief complaint, past medical history in abbreviated form, drugs used before admission (from the survey process and/or discussions with the family), any admission physical examination findings, the review of body systems, and laboratory test findings that are considered abnormal and might need further consideration should be noted. It should be reemphasized that some of this latter information can be gained from a recent hospital discharge summary and other sources of information from the hospital (e.g., nurses' notes, drug orders). Expensive admission laboratory costs can be saved by some long-term care clients if the health practitioner asks for a copy of the last hospital laboratory results that were performed before the client was transferred to the long-term care facility. The top portion of the DRR sheet is a summary of the data base information.

STEP 2 — WRITING A PROBLEM LIST

At this point a problem list should be written. Problems included are listed on the bottom of the DRR sheet. Problems, both past and present, refer not only to what are commonly thought of as problems, such as established diagnosis, but also to any physiologic abnormality (e.g., dehydration), signs or symptoms, abnormal laboratory tests, physical abnormality or functional loss (e.g., hearing or sight impairment, loss of limb), psychologic problems, socioeconomic problems, past operations and procedures, adverse drug reactions or interactions, and past and present compliance with therapy. Special attention should be given to the terms *past* and *present*. This is not only an initial problem list; it is to be used to update the problem list on a monthly basis (Fig. 3-1). As part of their basic drug regimen review responsibility, health care professionals should document reasons why any therapy was initiated or discontinued.

Chronology, sequence, and activity are considered in terms of the most recent problems or most significant problems listed first, followed by what is usually a natural sequence (e.g., hypertension with subsequent congestive heart failure followed by any problems in treating congestive heart failure, (such as hypokalemia or dehydration). It is essential to consider whether the problem is active or whether it is something that happened and that was resolved in the past (S/P).

STEP 3 — MATCHING THE PROBLEM LIST WITH THERAPY

The third step in the initial and subsequent assessments is to match the problem list with admission and subsequent therapy. This is when the first real check of the older person's admission medications occurs. For each active problem the client should be receiving some type of therapy. It is essential to be cognizant of all possible modalities of therapy besides drugs that can be used (e.g., physical, psychologic, nutritional, radiologic, and surgical). It is important, however, to recognize that some drugs, especially psychotropic drugs, may not relate to any active problem. On the other hand, some problems may have been overlooked at the time of admission (e.g., glaucoma) or inappropriately treated. Fig.

DRUG REGIMEN REVIEW SHEET

Facility_____ Physician's name_____

Client's name/age/sex/race/ht/wt_____

Adm. date_____ Date(s) of review_____ CC_____

PMH_____ Drugs PTA_____

(Adm) PE-ROS_____ AbNlab tests (adm.)_____

Problems*/ procedure	Therapy	Results/question	Date Noted	Resolved
1.				
2.				
3.				
4.				
5.				
6.				
7.				
8.				

(Use back for others)

(Other drugs/treatments)_____

(No problem/p.r.n.)_____

DRR

1. Orders: given (V/O, T/O, R/O)_____ Transcribed_____ Filled_____ Stop?_____

   Charted_____ Nurses' notes_____ Kardex_____ Administered_____ Dose/timing_____

2. Drug interaction with: Disease (DOC)_____ Other drugs_____

   Lab tests_____

   Other_____

3. ADR (classify): a. mild/moderate/severe; b. toxic/allergic/idiosyncratic/side; c. unknown/

   doubtful/possible/documented=definite. List each a, b, and c and dates in problem list.

   _____

4. Compliance-evidence from: Physician_____ RPh_____ N-client_____

   Family/friends_____

5. Client/family education indicated (?)_____

6. Tx indicated (?)_____ Prophylactic_____ Cost-related_____

7. Parameters: Efficacy_____ Toxicity_____

8. Data: Sufficient_____ Insufficient_____

9. Kidney function_____ Hepatic function/albumin_____

10. RPh actions (and dates)_____

    _____

11. MD actions (and dates)_____

    _____

12. RN/other actions (and dates)_____

    _____

*Problems include established diagnosis, physiologic abnormality, signs and symptoms, laboratory test or physical abnormality, psychologic problem, socioeconomic problems, past operations and procedures, adverse drug reactions and interactions, and compliance with therapy (past or present).

FIG. 3-4

Drug regimen review sheet.

Drug Use Review Sheet

Client _____

Month/year	Problems noted/communicated	Results

FIG. 3-4, cont'd.
Drug regimen review sheet—cont'd.

3-5 is a completed drug regimen review of a client who had multiple problems of congestive heart failure, treated with furosemide and digoxin; a history of digitalis toxicity; moderate renal impairment; and a probable personal overuse of a potassium chloride (KC1) salt substitute that, combined with KCl solid dosage form, inadvertently led to hyperkalemia. A further complication was malnutrition for which the client received multiple vitamins and minerals and presumably three appetizing meals a day. The client had a stroke with complete recovery, a peptic ulcer with hemorrhage, a lumbar spine fracture, and medications as needed (p.r.n.), including flurazepam for sleep. Once the problem list is established and an attempt is made to match drugs with therapy, a drug may be found for which there is no problem, especially with p.r.n. drugs for sedation, agitation, or restlessness. This raises a question about why a client is taking some neuroactive drugs. It is important to note this on the problem sheet because in some cases inappropriate use of the drug itself can be a problem (see Chapter 11, "Adverse Drug Reactions in the Geriatric Client"). At the time of admission unnecessary drugs and duplicate therapy can be reduced if a team conference is held, involving the physician, nurse, and pharmacist.

Periodic regimen review

Once the problem list is established and updated on a periodic basis, subsequent review of the drug regimen should be considered. The first step is to bring together the essential data elements for this review: (1) the pharmacy dispensing and drug records, (2) the medication administration record (MAR), and (3) the client's chart. With the chart, pharmacy records, and MAR sheet, the drug regimen review nine-part checklist (listed under DRR of Fig. 3-5) can be completed. The first step is to look for medication errors. This includes making sure that orders were given by correct protocol; that all verbal, telephone, and routine orders were verified

and transcribed correctly (frequent source of errors); that orders were filled and labeled correctly; that stop order policy was instituted and put into effect; and that drugs were not given beyond the stop date. On the other hand, it is necessary to be sure that medication was not discontinued that should have been continued. Were the drugs charted on the MAR? The most frequent long-term care medication error is simply failure to chart or give the dose (Cheung and Kayne, 1975). Nurses' notes should reflect all stat and p.r.n. doses given as well as results of the doses. They should reflect all client drug-related problems of drug use (appropriate and inappropriate) and any adverse reaction or interaction noted. If there is a nurses' Kardex, which in some areas can be incorporated with the MAR into a combined form, does it agree with the chart, MAR, and pharmacy records for orders?

Were the doses actually administered? If a comparison of doses dispensed (or replaced in a unit dose system) with those signed off is made, a good estimate of whether the drug was actually given or not can be obtained, particularly because dose omission is the most common medication error in the long-term care facility (Cheung and Kayne, 1975). It is essential to know if a drug was given before a determination of therapeutic benefit can be made.

Were the dose and timing appropriate? Some drugs should be scheduled before, with, or after meals or antacids. The most frequent scheduling problem is rescheduling of antacids, one or two every hour or 2 hours before the administration of digoxin, iron salts, and tetracyclines to prevent decreased total absorption (Hansten, 1979).

In summary, the first step is really a search for medication errors.

Drug interaction

Was there any drug interaction with the disease (appropriate or inappropriate)? Was, in fact, the therapy of choice used? At this point the at-

DRUG REGIMEN REVIEW SHEET

Facility _Sunnyside N.H_____ Physician's name _Roberts_____

Client's name/age/sex/race/ht/wt _Hanna Allen/ 88/ F/ W/ 5'4"/ 92 lb_

Adm. date _8-26-79_____ Date(s) of review _1-25-80_____ CC _No c/o___

PMH _CHF_____ Drugs PTA _see "Notice of Medication History"_

(Adm) PE-ROS _slight pedal edema_____ AbN lab tests (adm.) _none performed___

Problems*/ procedure	Therapy	Results/question	Date Noted	Resolved
1. CHF	Na restriction Lasix 20 mg q.d.	No edema, SOB	1-25-80	
2.	Slow K t.i.d.	Possible hyperkalemia	"	1-27-80
3.	Lanoxin 0.125 mg daily	NoS3; pulse 38 to 44	"	
4. Malnutrition	Multivitamin daily	Weight increase 92 to 98 lb	"	
5. S/P CVA	Haldol 1 mg p.r.n. (?)	Complete recovery		1968
6. S/P Peptic ulcer		GI hemorrhage		1978
7. S/P Fx Lumbar spine	Darvocet-N-100 q 4 to 6 hr p.r.n.		1-25-78	
8. S/P Dig tox		Mod. renal impairment? K?		1978

(Use back for others)

(Other drugs/treatments) _Dalmane 15 mg h.s. p.r.n._____

(No problem/p.r.n.)_____

DRR

1. Orders: given (V/O, T/O, R/O)___✓___ Transcribed___✓___ Filled___✓___ Stop?___✓___

   Charted___✓___ Nurses' notes___✓___ Kardex___✓___ Administered___✓___ Dose/timing___✓___

2. Drug interaction with: Disease (DOC)_____ Other drugs_____

   Lab tests_____

   Other _K+ supplement with Co-Salt, Stat K = 8.0 mEq/l, 1/25/80 Digoxin 1.1 ng/ml_

3. ADR (classify): a. mild/moderate/severe; b. toxic/allergic/idiosyncratic/side; c. unknown/

   doubtful/possible/documented=definite. List each a, b, and c and dates in problem list.

   _hx dig. toxicity, possible hyperkalemia_____

4. Compliance-evidence from: Physician___✓___ RPh___✓___ N-client _Client___

   Family/friends _source of Co-Salt_____

5. Client/family education indicated (?) _regarding Co-Salt by RN and RPh_____

6. Tx indicated (?)___✓___ Prophylactic _Haldol ?_____ Cost-related_____

7. Parameters: Efficacy___✓___ Toxicity___✓___

8. Data: Sufficient_____ Insufficient _Need stat K+ and digoxin level_

9. Kidney function _med. failure_____ Hepatic function/albumin_____

10. RPh actions (and dates) _Called physician stat 1/25/80_____

11. MD actions (and dates) _Ordered stat K+, digoxin level, hold Slow K and Co-Salt 1/25/80_

12. RN/other actions (and dates) _Instructed client's family to take salt substitute home and_
    not bring in any other drugs or food/supplements

*Problems include established diagnosis, physiologic abnormality, signs and symptoms, laboratory test or physical abnormality, psychologic problem, socioeconomic problems, past operations and procedures, adverse drug reactions and interactions, and compliance with therapy (past or present).

FIG. 3-5

Completed drug regimen review sheet.

tainment of therapeutic effect should be determined. Were there any interactions with other drugs, laboratory tests, or other modalities, such as in the drug-dietary example given in Fig. 3-5? In this example the client was on a sodium-restricted diet. The client's family, concerned over her poor appetite and weight loss, decided, "Since she can't take salt we'll bring in a salt substitute." It was not known at the time that she had moderate renal impairment with a serum creatinine level of 2.2 mg/100 ml to 2.5 mg/100 ml (normal = 0.7 mg/100 ml to 1.5 mg/100 ml) with a calculated clearance of about 20 ml/min to 25 ml/min (normal = 100 ml/min to 125 ml/min). As a consequence of her renal impairment, her ingestion of solid KCl (24 mEq/day), and the salt substitute containing potassium, which was sprinkled in liberal quantities on her food, the patient became very drowsy, showing a pulse rate of 38 to 44 and alternating second- and third-degree block on the ECG. The stat serum potassium level was 8.0 mEq/l (normal = 3.5 mEq/l to 5.0 mEq/l), digoxin was 1.1 ng/ml (normal = 0.8 ng/ml to 2.5 ng/ml), and the client was being evaluated for pacemaker insertion. The solid dosage form of KCl and the salt substitute were stopped, and furosemide was increased to 60 mg/day. Subsequent monthly reviews found the client to have a serum potassium level of 4.1 mEq/l to 4.8 mEq/l, a pulse rate ranging from 68 to 84, a good appetite, and a 10-pound weight gain.

Compliance

For purposes of review, "physician compliance" simply means that the prescriber acknowledges and responds to any communication. If poor communication is a problem, it should be resolved by the medical director and administrator. The same communication should not be rewritten every month; it can be simply noted as "refer to prior month's note on clients of Dr. X." Persistent communication difficulties should be noted in the progress notes, especially if detrimental care or results are observed.

"Pharmacist compliance" refers to requested labeling, supply, or system changes. This is particularly important when there are multiple providers of drugs and a separate consultant pharmacist.

"Nurse compliance" deals with requested improvement in documentation of drug administration, accountability, and other medication-related problems.

In Fig. 3-5 the client, family, and friends obviously were not compliant with the request not to bring in any drugs, dietary items, or foodstuffs. These problems must be documented in the progress notes. Two clients in my 12-facility practice experience who were stabilized with insulin, titrated to an American Diabetic Association diet *and* to what food the family would bring in, developed hypoglycemic coma and died when their families went on vacation. When clients consistently refuse medications, this should be noted in progress notes and brought to the prescriber's attention for resolution.

Education of the elderly and family

When problems such as those previously discussed are noted, some education of those involved should take place. These problems may also illustrate the need for in-service training.

Treatment indicated

This is a significant area that relies on knowledge of therapeutics. It is sometimes difficult to arrive at a judgment even in team conferences, but pertinent questions should be asked*:

1. *Arthritic pain.* Is the client using p.r.n. pain medication more than twice a day? If so, could regularly scheduled acetaminophen or aspirin be of benefit? If pain with inflammation is present with aspirin at full doses, could newer nonsteroidal anti-inflammatories, such as ibuprofen, be tried?

---

*For a more complete consideration of therapeutics see Chapter 12, "Drug Therapy in Clinical Geriatric Medicine."

Have placebos been used if a psychosomatic component is present? Are any signs of anemia, gastrointestinal (GI) upset, or blood loss present?

2. *Other pain.* If pain is severe, are analgesics given prophylactically after evaluation?

3. *High blood pressure.* Have blood pressure readings been in the range of 120/70 to 140/90? Should isolated systolic pressures greater than 160 to 180 with diastolic pressure less than 90 be treated? Is there any baseline and periodic serum chemistry? Are there any complaints of cramping, dizziness, unsteadiness, sedation, or depression? Have sodium restriction, weight loss, and exercise been attempted? Is dehydration a problem?

4. *Congestive heart failure.* Was failure secondary to respiratory tract infection or chronic lung disease? Could digoxin be cautiously withdrawn and furosemide used instead? Are S_3 gallop, paroxysmal nocturnal dyspnea, shortness of breath, peripheral edema, and pulse rates outside 60 to 100 present or absent? Have baseline and periodic serum electrolytes, creatinine, and (if indicated) digoxin levels been determined, especially if the client weighs less than 100 pounds, is taking 0.25 mg digoxin daily, has a loss of appetite, and has lost weight?

5. *Angina pectoris.* Has the client used sublingual nitroglycerin on a regular basis? If so, would oral or topical forms on a regular basis help? If regular vasodilator or β-blocker therapy is used, are blood pressure and pulse rate acceptable?

6. *Dysrhythmia.* Are the pulse rate and rhythm taken daily? Are preferred agents being used? Could blood levels be obtained to determine therapeutic range attainment? Is the client symptomatic?

7. *Altered coagulation.* Are prothrombin times being performed for oral anticoagulants? If so, are they therapeutic? Are

any platelet-affecting or interacting drugs being used? How long should anticoagulants be used after cardiac or cerebral infarct or pulmonary embolism?

8. *Diabetes.* Have diet, weight reduction, and exercise been attempted? Are the client and family compliant with dietary restrictions? Is fasting blood sugar significantly elevated when adjusted for age? Are there any signs or symptoms of hypoglycemia? Is a β-blocker being used?

9. *Thyroid.* Was thyroid therapy started before 1970 or for weight reduction? Has a thyroid profile been done 6 weeks after thyroid therapy was stopped? Are signs of hypothyroidism or hyperthyroidism present?

10. *Osteoporosis.* Is there radiologic evidence? Have benefit and risk ratios of estrogens, calcium and vitamin D, and/or fluoride been weighed?

11. *Corticosteroid use.* Has tapering been attempted? Have locally acting dosage forms been tried? Is adrenal axis suppression present? Have nonsteroidal anti-inflammatories or allergy preventatives such as cromolyn been tried?

12. *Bronchodilator therapy.* Are wheezing, bronchospasm, or objective spirometry measurements present? Has theophylline to therapeutic blood levels been tried? Were sympathomimetics then added? Are GI upset, heart irregularities, or tremors present? Are hydration and physical therapy being used? Have corticosteroids been used in the past?

13. *Allergy and rhinitis.* Is excessive sedation present? Is the client helped for more than 2 weeks at a time? Has alternating antihistamines been tried?

14. *Eyes.* Are eyes continually red and irritated? Have artificial tears been used? Has intraocular pressure been measured and fundus been assessed? Can the client read comfortably?

15. *Ears.* Is excessive cerumen, pain, or swell-

ing present? Have ototoxic drugs been used?

16. *GI system.* Is heartburn present, or is gut pain relieved by antacids, cimetidine, and/or anticholinergics? Are drugs with anticholinergic side effects being used? Is constipation or diarrhea present? Is there any change in bowel habits? Is there any upper or lower quadrant pain? Have bulk-forming agents been tried for chronic diarrhea (after stool culture)?

17. *Genitourinary system.* Has the client had recurrent UTIs? Should a catheter be left in place in absence of urethral obstruction? Should asymptomatic bacteriuria be treated? Has the prostate been evaluated in males with a history of UTIs? If nephrotoxic drugs are used, are the doses determined on the basis of lean body weight and creatinine clearance?

18. *Neurologic therapy.* Are multiple neuroactive substances being used for sedation, sleep, anxiety, restlessness, agitation, confusion, cough and pain? If so, can any be eliminated or used intermittently? Has dose reduction been attempted? Were target symptoms of senile dementia or organic brain syndrome helped? Is the client oversedated? Have decubitis ulcer or pneumonia developed since sedation was started? If anticonvulsants are used, are ataxia, nystagmus, or seizures still present? If so, are drug blood levels available? Are all sedating drugs given from late afternoon to early evening?

19. *Psychotherapy.* Is depression present? If endogenous depression is being treated, have adequate doses been given and all classes of antidepressants been tried? Is the lowest possible dose of an antipsychotic drug being used?

20. *Cerebral and peripheral vasodilators.* Have cerebral or peripheral vascular problems been helped within a 1- to 3-month period?

21. *Topical therapy.* Are all treatments being given and signed off? Has adequate nutritional supplementation been given to the client?

22. *Vitamin, mineral, and nutritional supplements.* Were baseline blood studies and nutritional assessments made? Has ideal body weight been attained? Is there any evidence of hematologic or nutritional deficits? Is appetite poor? After thorough assessment of poor appetite and anemia, have liquid "tonics" and/or vitamin and mineral preparations been tried? If infection, chronic collagen vascular disease, or other chronic disease is present, is adequate nutritional supplementation being given?

23. *Antiinfectives.* Were they given as ordered for the full stop-order period? Was the dose adequate or excessive for weight and renal and hepatic function? Did the condition improve? Have secondary infections been noted?

24. *Hypnotics.* Are hypnotics used every night? Is carry-over sedation present? Has every second or third night been tried? Have fewer doses been tried? Are there any drugs, such as antidepressants, anticonvulsants, sympatholytic antihypertensives, with sedative effects that could be given before bedtime to reduce the need for hypnotics?

Prophylactic therapy

Positive and negative sides should both be considered. Would prophylactic aspirin therapy be of benefit in the "completed" stroke client? Would one-half to one tablet of trimethoprim-sulfamethoxazole daily benefit the client who has had more than two acute UTIs in the past 6 months? Do methenamine salts work in catheterized clients? The benefit of long-term anticoagulants for those experiencing transient ischemic attacks and for those who risk hemorrhagic strokes may be difficult to justify.

Cost-related questions

Is a less expensive drug available? Is the drug in the formulary (facility or third-party drug list)? If not, is a covered alternative available? Was a cephalosporin prescribed for a UTI when the organism was sensitive to a sulfonamide?

Parameters of efficacy or toxicity

Are there sufficient parameters to judge drug effect? Without blood pressures to evaluate antihypertensives or hemoglobin/hematocrit to evaluate hematologic therapy, the question of whether data are sufficient or insufficient becomes obvious.

Sufficient or insufficient data

In many cases it is hard to say unequivocally that sufficient data regarding a client are present, in particular, depending on whether physical and laboratory data are sufficient or insufficient. It is difficult to make a statement that sufficient data are present until one looks at what results or questions one has for each type of therapy. For example, with the client taking potassium-depleting diuretics or potassium supplements, knowledge of the serum potassium level is needed.

Kidney and hepatic function

Are there sufficient kidney or hepatic function data when drugs are excreted primarily through these routes? Have serum creatinine and albumin levels been determined, especially when drugs such as digoxin, injectable aminoglycosides, central nervous system depressants, anticonvulsants, salicylates, anti-inflammatories, or anticoagulants are being used? Increased drug toxicity is seen particularly in the elderly client, most often when there is a functional decrease in renal and hepatic function as well as in albumin level (American Pharmaceutical Association, 1979).

Communication

This section documents what communications and actions occurred with a particular client. The reverse side (Fig. 3-4) documents further problems and their disposition. From a review of progress notes, nurses' notes, team discussions, or a communication log (any questions anyone has about drugs, drug effects and need, or any wastage), as well as problems noted in Figs. 3-6 and 3-7, it is obvious that there are a number of convenient ways to communicate and document problems.

STEP 4—EVALUATION OF GOAL ATTAINMENT

Has the therapeutic goal for each actively treated problem been met? This is a straight-forward approach. For example, in a client who has a history of high blood pressure, what are the blood pressure readings of the past month? If three consecutive readings are below 120/70 or over 140/90 to 160/95, or isolated systolic pressures are over 160 to 180, antihypertensive therapy should be reevaluated (O'Malley and O'Brien, 1980). (See list on pp. 58-60 for other examples.) The same process would apply to solving drug-related problems (e.g., Why is the client not responding to regular acetaminophen for chronic pain? Is the medication being refused?).

STEP 5—COMPLETING THE REGIMEN REVIEW

This step involves bringing together all particular drug regimen review findings for a particular client and documenting problems that need to be solved. Beyond this is a responsibility to see that communications are directed to those who can formulate solutions to individual problems. Figs. 3-6 and 3-7 illustrate documentation and resolution.

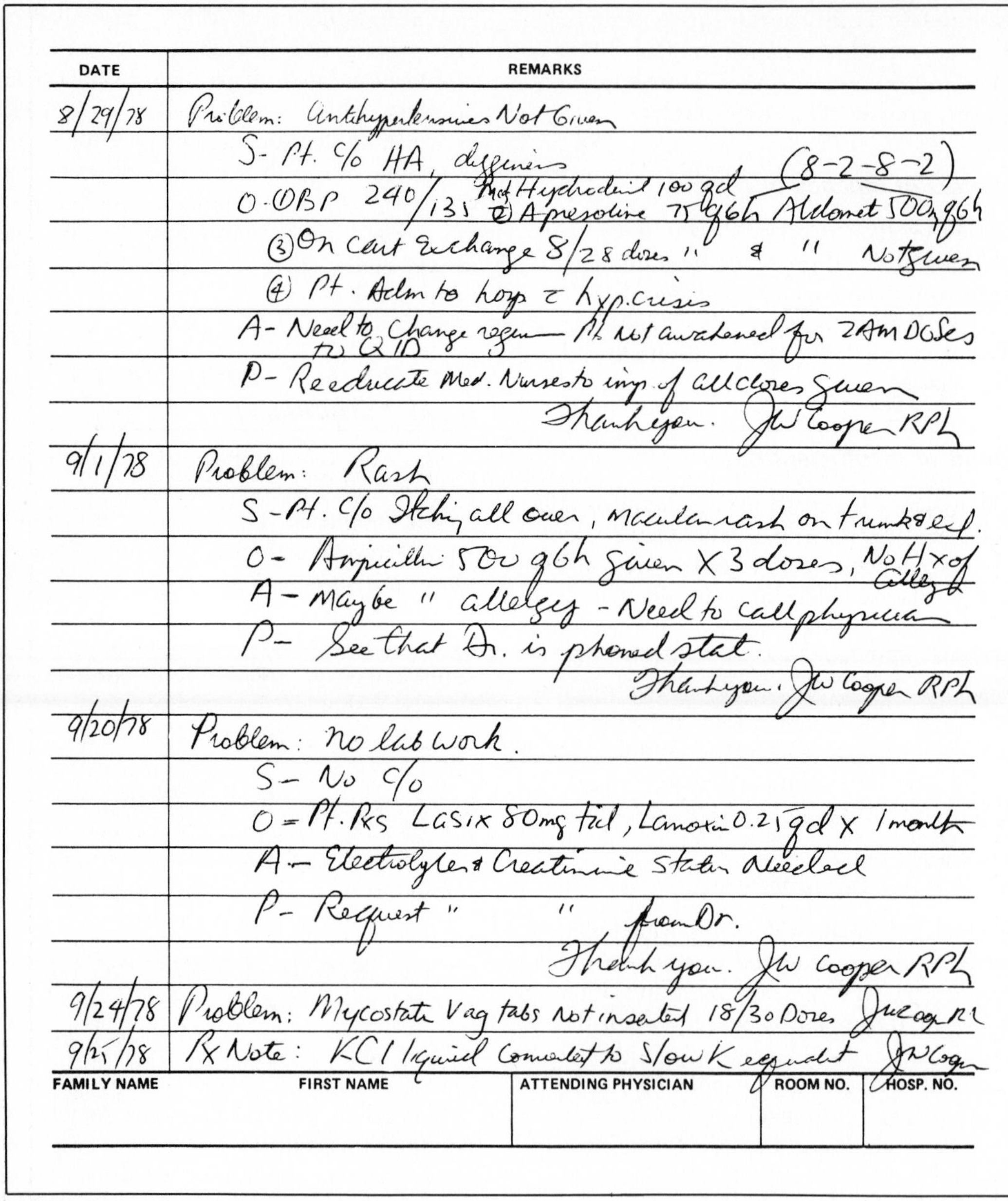

DATE	REMARKS
8/29/78	Problem: Antihypertensives Not Given
	S- Pt. c/o HA, dizziness
	O- OBP 240/135 ① Hydrodiuril 100 qd (8-2-8-2) ② Apresoline 75 q6h Aldomet 500 q6h
	③ On cart Exchange 8/28 doses " & " Not given
	④ Pt. Adm to hosp c hyp. crisis
	A- Need to change regm — Pt. not awakened for 2AM Doses to QID
	P- Reeducate Med. Nurses to imp. of all doses given
	Thank you. JW Cooper RPh
9/1/78	Problem: Rash
	S- Pt. c/o Itching all over, macular rash on trunk & ext.
	O- Ampicillin 500 q6h given X 3 doses, No Hx of allergy
	A- Maybe " allergy - Need to call physician
	P- See that Dr. is phoned stat.
	Thank you. JW Cooper RPh
9/20/78	Problem: No lab work.
	S- No c/o
	O = Pt. Rxs Lasix 80mg tid, Lanoxin 0.25 qd X 1 month
	A- Electrolytes & Creatinine Status Needed
	P- Request " " from Dr.
	Thank you. JW Cooper RPh
9/24/78	Problem: Mycostatin Vag tabs Not inserted 18/30 Doses JW Cooper RPh
9/25/78	Rx Note: KCl liquid Converted to Slow K equivalent JW Cooper
FAMILY NAME	FIRST NAME	ATTENDING PHYSICIAN	ROOM NO.	HOSP. NO.

FIG. 3-6

Physicians' progress notes.

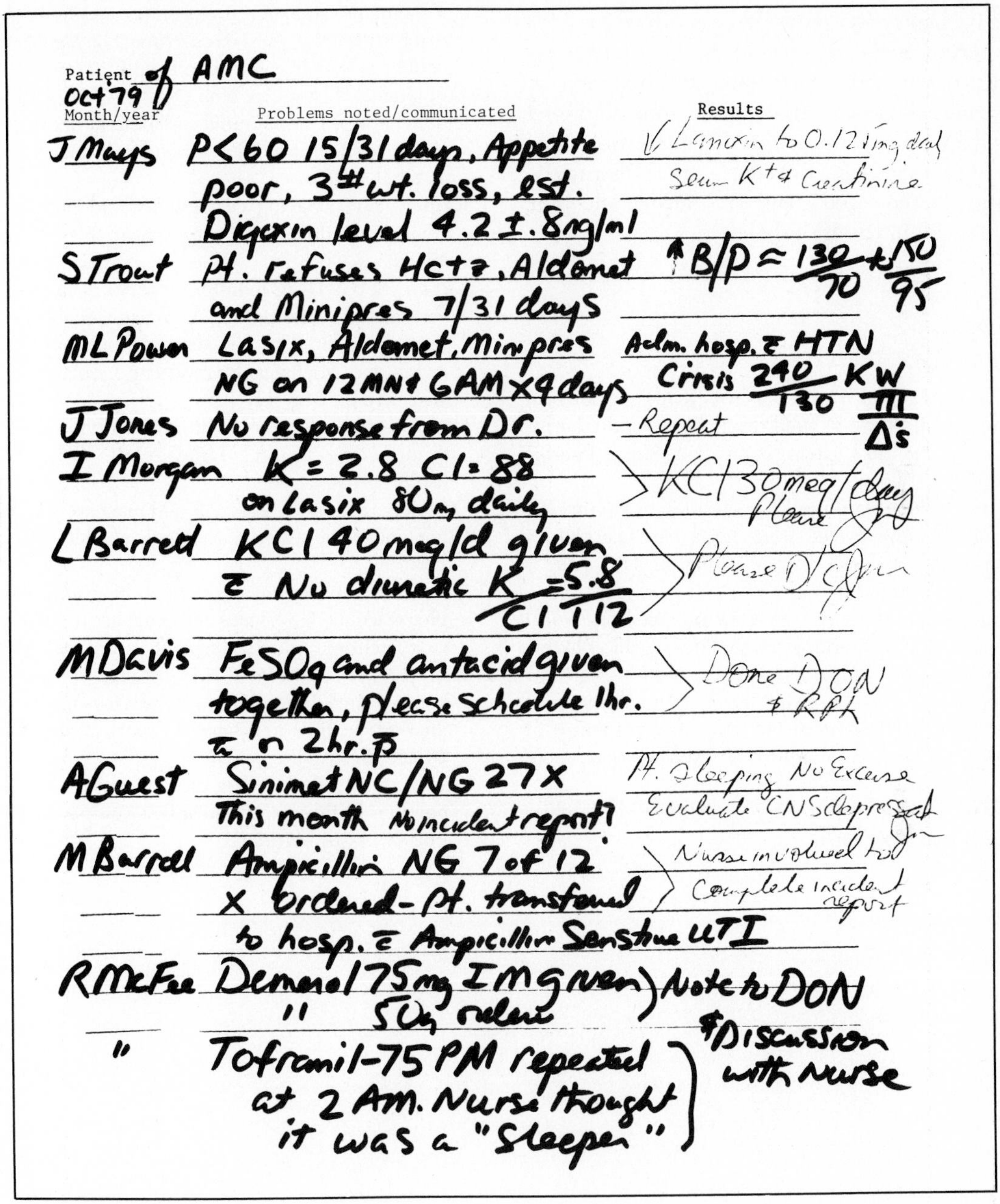

Patient of AMC
Oct 79
Month/year
Problems noted/communicated | Results

J Mays — P<60 15/31 days, Appetite poor, 3# wt. loss, est. Digoxin level 4.2 ±.8 ng/ml — ✓ Lanoxin to 0.125 mg deal Serum K+ & Creatinine

S Trout — Pt. refuses Hct⁷, Aldomet and Minipres 7/31 days — ↑B/P ≈ 130 → 150 / 70 / 95

ML Powen — Lasix, Aldomet, Minipres NG on 12MN & 6AM x 9 days — Adm. hosp. ē HTN Crisis 240 KW / 130 / III Δ's

J Jones — No response from Dr. — —Repeat

I Morgan — K = 2.8 Cl = 88 on Lasix 80mg daily — > KCl 30 meq/day Please

L Barrett — KCl 40 meq/d given ē No diuretic K = 5.8 Cl = 112 — > Please D/C

M Davis — FeSO₄ and antacid given together, please schedule 1hr. ā or 2hr. p̄ — > Done to DON & RPh

A Guest — Sinimet NC/NG 27X This month. No incident report? — Pt. sleeping No Excuse Evaluate CNS depressed

M Barrell — Ampicillin NG 7 of 12 X ordered — pt. transferred to hosp. ē Ampicillin Sensitive UTI — > Nurse involved to Complete incident report

R McFee — Demerol 75 mg IM given " 50 mg reliev — > Note to DON

" — Tofranil—75 PM repeated at 2 AM. Nurse thought it was a "Sleeper" — > §Discussion with Nurse

FIG. 3-7

Drug use review sheet.

SUMMARY

This chapter has presented a methodology for monitoring medication use in the long-term care facility client. For more detailed discussion of pathophysiologic and therapeutic considerations see Chapters 6, "Physiologic Changes and Clinical Manifestations of Aging"; 10, "Pharmacokinetics in the Aged"; and 12, "Drug Selection and Dosage in the Elderly."

REFERENCES

Adler, D.M., and DeChristofaro, R.A.: A study to distinguish between valid drug allergy and adverse drug reaction in a patient population, Hosp. Pharm. **12**:556, 1977.

American Pharmaceutical Association: Monitoring drug therapy in the long term care patient: a workbook for pharmacists, Washington, D.C., 1979, The Association.

Cheung, A., and Kayne, R.: An application of clinical pharmacy in extended care facilities, Calif. Pharm. **23**:22, 1975.

Cooper, J.W., and Bagwell, C.G.: Contributions of the consultant pharmacist to rational drug therapy in the long term care facility, J. Am. Geriatr. Soc. **27**:513, 1978.

Hansten, P.D.: Drug interactions, ed. 4, Philadelphia, 1979, Lea & Febiger.

Kabat, H.F., et al.: Drug utilization review in SNFS—a manual system for preforming sample studies of drug utilization, U.S. Department of Health, Education, and Welfare, Public Health Service, Bureau of Quality Assurance, Pub. No. 76-3002, 1975.

Kidder, S.W.: The potential cost-benefit of drug monitoring services in skilled nursing facilities, N.A.R.D. J. **23**:21, 1978a.

Kidder, S.W.: Saving cost quality and people: drug reviews in long-term care, Am. Pharm. **18**:18, 1978b.

Kidder, S.W.: Drug monitoring services in long-term care facility—the potential cost and quality impact, paper presented to the State of Michigan Office of Aging and Michigan Pharmacists Association, Lansing, Mich., May 11, 1980.

Letourneau, K.N.: Drug utilization review in an extended care facility. Drug Intell. Clin. Pharm. **8**:108, 1974.

O'Malley, K., and O'Brien, E.: Management of hypertension in the elderly, N. Engl. J. Med. **307**:1397, 1980.

Strandberg, L.R., et al.: Effect of comprehensive pharmaceutical services on drug use in long term care facilities, Am. J. Hosp. Pharm. **37**:92, 1980.

Thompson, J., and Floyd, R.: Cost-analysis of comprehensive consultant pharmacist services in the skilled nursing facility: a progress report, Calif. Pharm. **26**:22, 1978.

Vlasses, P.H., et al.: Drug therapy review in a skilled nursing facility: an innovative approach, J. Am. Pharm. Assoc. **17**:92, 1977.

CHAPTER 4

Quality assurance of drug therapy in the geriatric long-term care facility

John W. Levchuk

When focus is placed on the quality assurance of drug therapy, the frame of reference shifts from the monitoring of drugs that are prescribed for an individual client to the monitoring of collective drug use in a client population. The assurance of the quality of drug therapy is a recognized responsibility for all inpatient institutions. Because of the interdisciplinary nature of the institutional provision of drug therapy, a variety of health workers have an interest in it.

The way in which pharmaceutical services are provided varies from institution to institution. In larger institutions and in institutions with a greater intensity of care pharmaceutical services are usually provided by an organized pharmacy department staffed by full-time pharmacists. The director of the pharmacy is expected to assume responsibility for establishing and conducting a quality assurance program. In institutions that are smaller or that provide a lower intensity of care, pharmaceutical services are usually provided by contracted pharmacists who periodically visit the facility. When contract pharmacists are not responsible for the quality assurance of drug therapy, then a member of the institution's full-time staff, such as the director of nursing or the medical supervisor, needs to assume that responsibility. Because a variety of health workers are responsible for the process of quality assurance in the geriatric long-term care facility, the terms *evaluator* or *health care evaluator* are used throughout this chapter.

The concept of quality assurance is derived from or related to several broad theories, models, and principles. Selected ones are briefly reviewed in this chapter as a conceptual framework of quality assurance: the systems model, performance objectives and standards, program planning, and management by exceptions. By understanding these underlying theories, models, and principles, an evaluator can creatively design a quality assurance program to effectively meet local needs.

Two aspects of the quality assessment of drug therapy deserve special attention: (1) the selection and use of criteria for measurement and (2) the use of the client's medication chart as the dominant source document for data. Two sections are devoted to each of these topics. Finally, some recommendations are offered for the implementation of a quality assurance program to improve drug therapy in the geriatric long-term care facility.

This chapter reinforces the general philosophy that quality assurance is a positive force to actuate desired change and thus provides a logical, systematic, and effective way for a team of concerned health providers to actively strive for the continuous improvement of the quality of care.

CONCEPTUAL FRAMEWORK OF QUALITY ASSURANCE

Quality assurance is a structured, formal procedure for applying the concepts of quality control to program activities as well as to products (Stolar, 1975). It has the purpose of assuring that a program measures up to standards and expectations. As a process, it is a continuous, dynamic, cyclic effort of (1) definition, evaluation, redefinition, and reevaluation of services; and (2) implementation of educational or correctional activities. A model for the quality assurance of

drug therapy in the geriatric long-term care facility is shown in Fig. 4-1.

The development of a system for the quality assurance of drug therapy should occur within a framework of five related sets of underlying principles: (1) a therapeutic assessment cycle, (2) the systems model, (3) performance objectives and standards, (4) program planning, and (5) management by exceptions. Each of these will now be discussed in relation to the development of a quality assurance model for drug therapy.

Therapeutic assessment cycle

Within any institution, a health care evaluator is concerned with all aspects of drug therapy, such as which drugs are available, how they are prescribed, how they are used, and how clients respond to them. The following goals can serve as an evaluator's broad frame of reference for a quality assurance program for drug therapy. To achieve quality of drug therapy in the broadest sense, all of the following must be achieved:

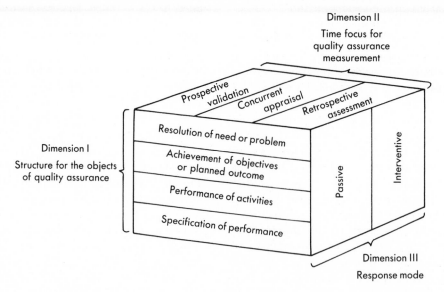

FIG. 4-1

A model for the quality assurance of drug therapy in the geriatric long-term care facility.

1. Pharmaceutical services will be consistent with client care needs and the goals and objectives of the parent institution.
2. Only the best quality of pharmaceuticals will be available for client care in the institution at the lowest possible cost.
3. The most appropriate drug therapy will be prescribed for every client.
4. The right drug will be given to the right client at the right time, in the right strength and dosage form, and by the right route of administration.
5. Services will be consistently of high quality and will meet all legal, professional, and national standards for pharmaceutical services.
6. Services will be provided efficiently and at the most appropriate level of cost-effectiveness.

Two levels of decision making are involved in the institutional use of drugs: direct and indirect (Fig. 4-2). The focus of direct decision making is on the medical problem of a client at a specific point in time. Based on the needs of that client, and in keeping with accepted prescribing and drug use practices, decisions are made about the diagnosis, treatment, and care of that client. A decision is made to follow a specific plan for a specific client in anticipation of a desired outcome; the plan itself is a judgment that represents the best course of action based on the knowledge and information at hand. As action is taken, the client changes from one state to a new state. Any change in the state of the client creates new information as input to decision making. Decision making continues but is based on new information. This interactive process between decision making, planned intervention, and change in client status results directly in the final outcome of the client's health. Qualitatively, the client's condition either improves or does not improve as a result of intervention. Similarly, the client either does or does not suffer from an iatrogenic problem. These two dichotomies depict the two most elemental dimensions that can be used to measure final outcome from planned therapeutic

intervention: effectiveness of intervention and complication(s) from intervention.

The focus of indirect decision making is on the overall quality of drug therapy in an institution. With information derived from the collective experience of therapeutic effectiveness of prescribing practices, or from the rate of iatrogenic problems arising from drug use, decisions are made about the quality of care received by the elderly and about how that quality might be improved. These kinds of decisions are retrospec-

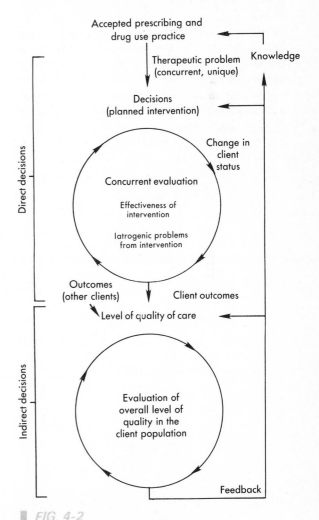

FIG. 4-2

Therapeutic assessment cycle.

tive and noninteractive with respect to a current course of therapy for a particular older person.

Three predominant types of decisions are made about the overall use of drugs in an institution. First, judgments are made about the extent to which a standard of care is being achieved throughout the institution. Second, if standards are not being achieved, decisions are made for the development and implementation of a specific plan of action to change actual practices so that they will be more in line with accepted practices of prescribing and drug use. Third, if standards are being met or exceeded consistently, decisions can be made pertaining to the reevaluation and upgrading of the standards themselves. As action is taken, the *institution* (rather than an individual client) changes from one state to a new state. To evaluate the effectiveness of the institution in providing quality drug therapy, the health care evaluator may conduct adverse drug reaction surveillance programs to identify the incidence of untoward reactions,

drug use reviews to define drug response or use rates, and comparative reviews for the pharmacy and therapeutics committee (in larger institutions).

The systems model

The systems model helps to describe the object of quality assurance. By definition it is an array of interrelated and interdependent components designed to accomplish a particular objective according to plan (Cleland and King, 1972). This definition can be represented by a well-known systems model:

Input → Process → Output

This simple model is quite powerful in its ability to aid an evaluator in defining and analyzing an organization. Because the quality of drug therapy is heavily dependent on effective dissemination and application of a rapidly changing knowledge base (Millis, 1975), the form of the systems model

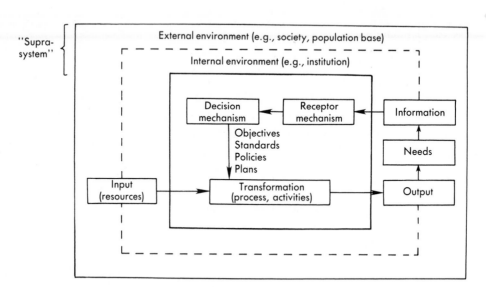

FIG. 4-3

The systems model. (From Management: a systems approach, by D.I. Cleland and W.R. King. Copyright © 1972, McGraw-Hill Book Company. Used with the permission of McGraw-Hill Book Company.)

depicted in Fig. 4-3 emphasizes a flow of information and includes a decision-making component (Cleland and King, 1972). The model also differentiates between an external and an internal environment.

"Output" is defined by performance objectives for the system and results from its operation. "Process" depicts what the system does, how it operates, and what procedures are followed to transform input into output. In the delivery of pharmaceutical services the tendency has been to focus on the activities of providing services as if they were the ends themselves; to apply the systems model the planner of services needs to reorient thinking by starting with the whys of doing something rather than with the whats and hows of doing it.

When one is using the systems model to define the points of reference for the quality assurance of drug therapy, drug therapy can be defined as a process factor or an output factor, depending on the needs of the evaluator (Table 4-1).

Drug therapy is difficult to measure. As a process it must be measured indirectly because no satisfactory, direct measures exist. As an outcome there is no single direct measure to define the concept of "drug therapy." Thus, in the assessment of the quality of drug therapy, the ability to assign appropriate measures of client outcome has not been well developed. Two noteworthy exceptions are the indirect measurements of the incidences of adverse drug reactions and other drug-induced problems. Generally, it is easier to design a quality assurance program around a reduction of inappropriate drug use than around an improvement of appropriate use.

The systems model can be used to aid in the selection of meaningful factors to measure. One way to do this is to consider possible reasons why outcomes may be less than effective, efficient, or desirable. Following are some questions that might be asked:

1. Are resources appropriate for the process?
2. Are assumptions that link resources and process valid?
3. Are processes appropriate for achieving the desired outcome?
4. Are assumptions that link processes and outcomes valid?
5. Are resources being used and processes carried out according to plan?

If factors to measure outcomes cannot be identified, then selection of several relevant process measures (there certainly is no dearth of easily measured process factors in prescribing and using drugs) would bolster inferences about outcomes.

In summary, a systems model is a tool to help define the focus for a quality assurance program.

Performance objectives and standards

Criteria are essential elements in the accountability of any program or service. The term *criteria* has been defined as "predetermined elements against which aspects of the quality of a medical service may be compared" (Visconti, 1979). Objectives and standards are criteria that may be used to determine the quality of prescribing and the use of pharmaceuticals in an institution. Both objectives and standards may be

TABLE 4-1   **Two systems views of drug therapy**

System component	As process	As output
Suprasystem	Population of clients in an institution	Client care provided by an institution
Output	Restoration or maintenance of client's health or ability to function	*Patterns of drug therapy*
Process	*Prescribing practices*	Therapeutic decision making

specified for any level of the systems model, that is, for inputs, processes, and outcomes.

A major difference between objectives and standards is their dynamism. Objectives connote a dynamic state of a program or one of its components by indicating a change from an existing state to a new state. Conversely, standards maintain a static state by describing a desired but existing level of performance.

The development of criteria is perhaps among the most time-consuming and difficult intellectual exercises of quality assurance. Visconti (1979) has recommended that criteria for the evaluation of quality of drug use should be based on the steps of the drug use process as defined by Knapp et al. (1974). The steps identified by Knapp et al. have been modified to fit the institutional setting:

1. Determination of a need for a drug by the prescriber. This involves diagnosis and a choice, in general terms, between drug and non–drug therapy.
2. Selection of a specific therapeutic entity. This involves a decision about therapeutic category and active ingredient.
3. Selection of regimen. This involves determination of the route of administration, dosage form, strength, dosage quantity, and length of therapy.
4. Obtaining the drug product. The most appropriate drug product must be selected and procured for the client.
5. Administration and consumption of the drug product. Unless the client is using a self-medication program, institutional personnel are responsible for correct administration of prescribed drugs.
6. Feedback about the effects of a client's drug therapy provided to all concerned. Therapeutic efforts are perceived and interpreted by the client, the prescriber, and relevant others.

Given these steps, with the evaluation of quality in mind, several questions become apparent:

1. Was the prescribed therapy the one of choice for the client at the time of prescribing?
2. Was the prescribed drug the agent of choice?
3. Did the prescribed drug fit the diagnosis and other aspects of the client's medical needs?
4. Did the prescribed drug regimen include redundancies or superfluities?
5. Were objective tests used when necessary to determine which drug or dosage regimen would be best (e.g., selection of an antibiotic based on sensitivity testing, selection of a dosage schedule for an aminoglycoside based on blood level evaluation)?
6. Was dosage adjusted when indicated (e.g., for impaired metabolism, debilitation, impaired excretion, or old age)?
7. Was therapy administered for an appropriate period of time (e.g., penicillin for 10 days)?

These questions, as well as others, can provide the framework for identifying criteria for the evaluation of the quality of prescribed drug use in an institution. Health care evaluators must have, of course, complete and up-to-date knowledge about the therapeutic selection and use of pharmaceutical products before they can write objectives and standards that are specific to the agents, disease state, or client. Furthermore, there is greater chance to select criteria that would have considerable meaning in evaluating the medical care process if they are selected on the basis of complete knowledge.

Thus far the measurability of observable criteria has been stressed. However, a *subjective* may be used if an objective or measurable standard cannot be stated. Subjectives are written in areas where it is difficult to measure or confirm the actual attainment of an objective. Subjectives are expressed in terms of a number of specific verifiable activities or events that, when accomplished, should logically lead to the desired or future state or condition (Raia, 1974). In a similar frame of reference different types of recordings on the client's chart may need to be sorted into objective and subjective findings. Sorting is appropriate if there is concern about the relative worth between objective and subjective findings.

Pulliam (1974) has categorized several examples of differentiation between objective and subjective findings:

1. Criteria to evaluate drug effects
   a. *Direct effects measured objectively.* Few such criteria are available, but an assay of plasma concentrations of the drug being evaluated is one example.
   b. *Associated effects measured objectively.* Periodic assay of serum potassium permits an assessment of the hypokalemic response to diuretic therapy.
   c. *Associated effects measured subjectively.* The degree of orthostatic symptoms reported by a client taking an antihypertensive agent is one example.
2. Criteria to evaluate disease alterations or prevention
   a. *Objective changes in basic abnormalities.* The changes in blood pressure when treating the hypertensive client is an example.
   b. *Objective changes in associated abnormalities.* Abnormalities of the fundus, which are associated with accelerated hypertension, may be followed as measures of improvement.
   c. *Subjective changes in associated abnormalities.* A decrease in frequency and severity of headaches that are associated with hypertension is an indicator of a change in the disease.
3. Criteria to evaluate the client's status
   a. *Objective changes in the signs of client status.* A decrease in body temperature or other objective signs of client well-being are grouped under this heading.
   b. *Subjective changes in the symptoms of disease.* Alterations in the pattern, frequency, or severity of pain reflect this type of subjective criteria.

In summary, criteria are essential for quality assurance. The more precise and measurable the criteria, the greater the degree of objectivity of judgments derived from measurement. However, measurement should not be abandoned in the absence of measurable criteria; subjectives may be used instead. The specific elements to be measured are defined by the nature of the program and the purposes of quality assurance.

Program planning

Planning is an intellectual process that involves seeking appropriate goals, setting specific objectives, determining how they are to be achieved, and selecting ways to determine how it will be known that they are being achieved. The latter activity indicates that the design of a quality assurance effort is intertwined with the planning of the program to be evaluated or, in the case of an existing program, the specification of performance standards, policies, and procedures.

A planning model (Fig. 4-4) depicts the steps in the process of planning. Evaluation is often depicted as the last step. Essentially, this refers to the act of evaluation in which the operating program is the object of evaluation. The act of evaluation includes collecting data, making judgments based on that data, and modifying the program accordingly. The design of an evaluation plan should be performed parallel with and in reference to program planning.

The objects of performance evaluation are created as a result of planning. Through planning, performance objectives and standards are identified and specified. When objectives, standards, operational configuration, and program activities and procedures are known, the quality assurance plan may be developed. The quality assurance plan identifies what is to be measured and how, when, and under what conditions measurement is to take place.

When one plans a quality assurance program,

The process for program planning.

an attempt should be made to achieve optimum use of personnel time. The application of four general principles helps to assure this: (1) build a quality assurance program around a fixed ratio of available time/available personnel to total time/total personnel to conduct the program, (2) identify critical factors for evaluation, (3) periodically reassess those criteria that should be evaluated, and (4) maintain a continuous activity.

Management by exceptions

Management by exceptions (MBE) is a planned strategy of managerial control by which

an evaluator's attention is turned, as a result of planned dissemination of information, only to those situations that require review or for which corrective action is necessary. With MBE the evaluator, in the absence of any alerting information, still remains assured that a program is operating in conformance with plans and standards. An effective MBE strategy operates when an evaluator is notified only when significant instances, patterns, or levels of nonconformity with objectives or standards have arisen.

A plan for MBE begins with the specification of the exceptions. The MBE plan for the evaluation of a program specifies what information (resulting from the measurement of input, processes, and outcomes) gets to what people, at what times, and under what conditions. Informed decisions are then made about appropriate managerial response. An MBE program allows quality assurance to interact with program activities through informed decisions about planned change.

Exceptional instances. Defined levels of performance establish the expectation against which actual measured performance can be evaluated. An instance of performance is exceptional when it deviates from the standard. Knowledge of these exceptions to the standards is of primary interest to the evaluator. If a single instance of serious deviation from performance standards occurs, prompt evaluation and intervention may be necessary to avert further serious effects on patients, costs, or other factors. The alerting mechanism that is designed to inform the necessary people of exceptional instances should be sensitive enough to pick up serious deviations and should be responsive enough to transmit them quickly. However, for those critical factors where no single serious deviation has occurred, planned periodic review of trend data is necessary. For drug therapy it is expected that the direct medical care decision-making process be responsive to serious deviations from standards. Those deviations of drug therapy that would be detectable primarily from the evaluation of trend data then constitute the dominant theme of a quality assurance program. Also of interest in the evaluation of quality is the rate and nature of those serious deviations that are taken care of at the direct decision-making level. Two notable examples of the latter are changes in antibiotic therapy because of overgrowth of nonsusceptible organisms or the initiation of antibiotic therapy because of infusion-associated nosocomial infection.

Exceptions from a standard can be positive as well as negative. A positive exception would prompt a different response than would a negative exception. If performance is below standard, the intervention can be corrective. If above standard, the standard itself may be upgraded. The evaluation of trends should be used to determine if higher than expected levels of performance are significant enough to warrant upgrading a standard.

Trend data for positive exceptions take two dominant forms, each leading to a different managerial response. First, a consistently occurring positive exception creates a new norm that can be used to define the standard at a higher level. For example, the standards for dose omissions in a unit dose system might be 0.5% of the total medication error rate and 30% of all medication errors. If an institution demonstrates consistent rates of 0.4%/25% over several months, then the institution should accept the new norm as its standard.

An episodically and irregularly occurring positive exception may be detected from a review of data. In this instance, having detected desirable deviation from a standard, reasons for the deviation should be sought. Once these reasons are identified, the program can be modified to be more effective, and the standard can be upgraded accordingly. For example, perhaps a nursing unit occasionally shows an omission error rate of 0.3%/24%, whereas all other units consistently show 0.5%/30%. Probing may reveal that an extra procedure not in the policy or procedure manual is being followed by a particular shift.

This procedure should be identified, isolated, tested, and, if indeed effective, incorporated into the institution's set of routine procedures for everyone to follow. The standard, of course, can be upgraded as well. Incidents such as these may seem insignificant in themselves but, when evaluated as an array, can be rather powerful tools for accountability.

Charting exceptional performance. The managerial chart is a useful tool for the evaluation of exceptional performance. On a separate graph for every critical factor the measurement of performance (y-axis) versus the point in time that the measurement was taken (x-axis) is plotted. Trends become quite obvious at a glance (Fig. 4-5). For example, a monthly sensitivity chart was maintained in an antibiotic monitoring program (Greenlaw, 1977).

Three reference lines preprinted on the chart can be useful. The central line indicates the level of criterion performance used as the standard. The two other lines on the chart in Fig. 4-5 represent two levels of significant deviations from the standard. Any deviation that is greater than these "significant deviation" lines would represent an exceptional case. In essence, then, tolerance limits are established to accommodate naturally occurring deviation resulting from chance alone.

Cost is also a factor to consider in establishing tolerance limits. In particular, the cost of nonintervention should be weighed against the cost of intervention. Tolerance limits can be appropriately set for something at a level at which it would be more costly (in the broadest sense of the word) to ignore than to intervene.

In summary, MBE is a philosophy of preventive management. With good management everything should run smoothly and according to plan. Everything is theoretically routine and accounted for. With the MBE concept even the unexpected would be handled in a planned manner.

Of course, unexpected activities and events may surface from time to time. Through the quality assurance program the evaluator is alerted to significant exceptions. Evaluation of trends of

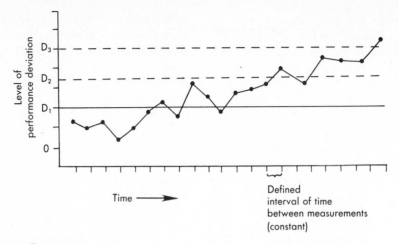

FIG. 4-5

The managerial chart, D_1, "Baseline" (no significant level of deviation); D_2, "Alert" level (a significant level of deviation has occurred); D_3, "Failure" or "Shutdown" level (serious or major deviation has occurred).

both positive and negative exceptions can lead to program improvement. The managerial chart can be used easily and effectively to identify trends in the level of quality of drug therapy.

THE MEASUREMENT OF PROCESSES

Outcomes constitute the ideal measurement criteria for the evaluation of the quality of health care. Several disadvantages exist for the measurement of outcomes in health care (Greenfield et al., 1975). Some are relevant to the evaluation of drug therapy:

1. Ultimate outcomes, such as death or restoration to normal functioning, may occur late in therapy and would therefore be untimely to use.
2. Outcomes themselves are subject to the influence of many intervening variables (some known, some not known; some controllable, some not).
3. Information for many outcomes is not available without resorting to costly and time-consuming research.
4. The practicality of measuring the full breadth of all relevant outcomes is problematic (e.g., psychosocial aspects of drug therapy).

For the geriatric client, measured outcomes may be the culmination of a succession of episodes of care that has been provided in a variety of settings, with the long-term care facility being perhaps only the latest setting. Given this situation, episodic review of the quality of the management (with drug therapy as well as any other form of intervention) of chronic illness can be associated with few if any readily measurable positive outcomes (Donabedian, 1968). On the other hand, the incidence of iatrogenic effects from medical management is a readily measurable negative outcome. However, the usefulness of measuring adverse reactions as outcomes of drug therapy is limited, especially if the incidence is low. If the rates of adverse reactions are low, which could be expected in episodic review of care in the geriatric facility, the rate of administration is possibly a useful process to measure as a proxy for an outcome measure (Greenfield et al., 1978). Thus, although outcome measures are to be encouraged, the state of the art in the quality assurance of drug therapy is to measure process. This is particularly true for the long-term care facility. Although quality assurance is familiar in the hospital setting, it is only beginning to develop in the long-term care facility (Krikorian, 1979). It should again be noted that drug use per se is not an outcome of medical care; it is a process. In many instances, however, the measurement of aspects of the process of drug use can serve as a good approximation for the outcomes of medical care (Greenfield et al., 1978).

Several purposes can be fulfilled through drug use review: regulatory, punitive, educative, preventive, interventive, and the decision about who pays how much for which drugs. The list of references at the end of this chapter includes some examples of drug use review programs that have been undertaken to determine which one of these approaches might be useful in an institution to improve rational drug therapy. Some aspects of those programs will be discussed.

Perhaps among the first attempts to measure the process of drug use in the institutional setting was the regular review of the nursing unit. This has long been a basic responsibility of the consultant pharmacist (Hassan, 1974). The pharmacist, using a checklist of safe storage and labeling criteria (pp. 76 and 77), observes actual practices on the unit. Although nonconformance would be corrected on the spot, records of patterns of nonconformance with standards are useful to determine, for example, the content of in-service education programs. The literature abounds with examples of the evaluation of aspects of the drug distribution system to promote client safety through proper handling, storage, and administration of medications. The outcomes of these processes in connection with the quality assurance of drug therapy are, however, input

factors. Because these outcomes are primarily functions of the drug distribution system, the evaluation of medication errors should also be considered as an evaluation of the quality of input factors. In addition, the American Society of Hospital Pharmacists (1978) stated five criteria for assuring rational drug use through adequate pharmaceutical services:

1. A pharmacy medication profile is maintained for all inpatients and for those outpatients routinely receiving care at the institution.
2. The pharmacy receives a direct copy of the physician's order form, not a transcription.
3. There is a written procedure for the reporting and review of adverse drug reactions.
4. There is a formalized drug use review program integrated with overall hospital client care review activities.
5. Drug products included in the formulary are selected through formal consideration of their merits by the Pharmacy and Therapeutics Committee.

To measure the process of drug therapy, emphasis should be placed on the decisions and actions of the providers (Donabedian, 1968). Many criteria that have been used to evaluate drug therapy have focused on prescribing decisions. At the University of Maryland model criteria for drug orders were established in which conservative prescribing limits were specified for an acceptable dose and quantity of a drug (Knapp et al., 1974). In some cases additional criteria were mentioned; for example, for erythromycin they noted, "Any prescription calling for a regimen other than a dose every 4 to 6 hours for at least ten days falls outside these criteria." These Maryland criteria were developed to provide a start for a local drug use review committee that would expand or modify the criteria as needed by the local program.

A small community hospital based its criteria to evaluate effective prescribing practices on those indications and manner of use approved by the U.S. Food and Drug Administration. Using

Model program for the nursing unit medication review

Policy

The pharmacy department (or consultant pharmacist) is responsible for the control of all pharmaceuticals in the institution. Drugs stored at the nursing unit must be maintained in such a way as to ensure patient safety, proper environmental conditions of storage according to each drug's requirements, and adequate security. The pharmacy department (or consultant pharmacist) establishes standards for safe, proper, and secure storage. Nursing unit personnel are responsible for day-to-day compliance with those standards.

Procedure

1. The pharmacy department (or consultant pharmacist) will publish, revise, and distribute standards for safe, proper, and secure storage of drugs in all areas of the hospital.
2. A pharmacist will assist nursing unit personnel to comply with these standards by means of regularly scheduled nursing station medication reviews and in-service education.
3. Nursing station medication reviews will be conducted monthly at each nursing unit. Using a checklist, the pharmacist will check prevailing storage conditions against the standards that follow. A pharmacist will contact the nursing unit supervisor at least 48 hours in advance of the review. The review will take place at a scheduled time mutually agreeable to the pharmacist and the supervisor. The supervisor will accompany the pharmacist during the review. Irregularities will be corrected during the review whenever practical. If deemed appropriate, a follow-up review will be conducted within 24 hours to ascertain if irregularities not corrected during the initial review have been corrected.
4. Serious, numerous, or consistent discrepancies may result in unannounced spot-checks by pharmacy personnel between monthly reviews.
5. Copies of the review report will be kept by the pharmacy department (or consultant pharmacist) and the nursing unit. A copy of each review report will be forwarded to the supervisory authority of nursing services.
6. The nursing unit supervisor is responsible for discussing outcomes of the medication review with unit personnel and for assuring

day-to-day compliance with drug storage regulations.
7. The pharmacy department (or consultant pharmacist) will periodically conduct in-service training on these policies, procedures, and standards for new nursing personnel. All new nursing personnel are required to attend this orientation session. In-service training activities will be conducted whenever deemed appropriate to minimize irregularities and to maintain compliance with standards.

Standards

(These are written in question form to aid in self-evaluation. Activities to aid in compliance are suggested.)

1. Do all drug containers bear the label of the pharmacy department of this hospital or a pharmacy (if the institution uses contracted pharmaceutical services)?
   a. Return to the pharmacy for proper labeling.
2. Are all drugs readily identifiable according to name, unit strength, dosage form, and route of administration?
   a. Return to the pharmacy for proper labeling.
   b. Contact the pharmacist to suggest revision of labeling for difficult products.
3. Do any containers have illegible, mutilated, or soiled labels?
   a. Return to the pharmacy for relabeling or reissue.
4. Are there any drugs found that have been discontinued because the client has died, has been discharged, or the order has been canceled?
   a. Return to the pharmacy for credit or discarding.
5. Are drug samples in the medication cabinet?
   a. If the physician has supplied for a client, contact the pharmacist.
   b. If they are nursing unit personnel's "private stock," remove them from client care area and keep them with other personal belongings.
6. Is there an excess quantity of certain floor stock items?
   a. Remove excess; call the pharmacist to pick them up and to review the auto-

---

Model program for the nursing unit medication review—cont'd

matic replenishment quantity/mechanism.

7. Are non–drug items found in the cabinets?
   a. Remove all non–drugs from all drug storage areas.
8. Are internal preparations separated from external preparations?
   a. Separate.
   b. Rearrange cabinet area if necessary.
9. Are there any medications at the nursing station or at the client's bedside that the client brought from home?
   a. Send to the pharmacy or hold for the consultant pharmacist. If the client has been taking these medications on order of the physician, notify the pharmacist. If the client has been taking or intends to take these medications without the order of the physician, contact the physician and pharmacist.
10. Are ophthalmic solutions dated according to time of initial use?
    a. Remove and discard if time of initial use cannot be readily determined.
11. Do reconstituted injectables and oral liquid medications have a reconstitution date and/or an expiration date on the label, and is the unit strength of medications readily identifiable?
    a. Remove and discard if improperly labeled.
12. Are outdated drugs anywhere on the unit?
    a. Remove and discard.
13. Do any drugs show evidence of deterioration?
    a. Remove and contact pharmacist.
14. Have any investigational drugs been placed on the unit by a physician?
    a. Contact the pharmacist.
15. Are drugs and biologics requiring refrigera-

tion found in the drug cabinet (i.e., not refrigerated)?
    a. Remove and discard.
16. Are those drugs that do not require refrigeration found in the refrigerator?
    a. Remove and consult pharmacist.
17. Is the refrigerator temperature set low enough (no more than 4° C)? Is there a working thermometer present? Is the refrigerator working properly?
18. Are cabinets clean and neat?
19. Are all cabinets locked whenever there is no registered nurse in the immediate area? Is the narcotic cabinet always locked except when in actual use? Are keys to medication cabinets left lying around on tabletops?
    a. Instill in unit personnel the importance of security measures for all drug products.
    b. If any unit personnel notices regular noncompliance or break in security pertaining to any drugs, drug orders, or client medication records, contact the pharmacy department.
20. Are delivered drugs quickly consigned to proper storage areas?
    a. Analyze delegation of responsibility of unit personnel.
21. Are drug orders kept in such a way that they will not get lost, mixed up, or misplaced before being forwarded to the pharmacy? Are drug orders, considered privileged information, handled and placed on the unit in such a way to maintain their security?
    a. Review what unit personnel do with orders and formulate definite handling procedures.
22. Are medication preparation areas neat, free from clutter and distraction, and conducive to orderly, undistracted medication setup?

---

those criteria, the hospital's review committee compared actual prescribing practices against them, classifying drug orders into one of three categories: (1) drug was used as approved; (2) drug was not used in an approved manner, but there was substantial documentation in the literature to justify its use; and (3) drug was not used in an approved manner, and no documented evi-

dence would be found in the literature to support its use (Kelly, White, and Miller, 1975).

Well-designed lists of criteria can be used for rapid initial screening of the appropriateness of drug orders. Charts can be rapidly reviewed for selected drugs. Selected aspects of the use of those drugs can be quickly compared with the standards for use. In connection with the three

Specific standards for appropriate injectables

1. *Vitamin B12*
   a. *One injection per month for vitamin B12 deficiency states (i.e., pernicious anemia or malabsorption syndromes, including the autonomic neuropathy sometimes associated with diabetes).*
   b. *Two injections within one 2-week period for severe debilitation (following trauma, severe infections, operations, acute alcoholism). This will occur rarely in the doctor's office.*
2. *B-complex*
   For severe nutritional problems where the patient is not able to take medication by mouth or where there are malabsorption syndromes, this will be approved. This will occur rarely in the doctor's office.
3. *Imferon—for iron deficiencies where*
   a. *Patient has demonstrated intolerance of or unresponsiveness to oral iron.*
   b. *Patient needs immediate initiation of therapy for severe iron deficiency anemia (1 injection).*
4. *Gamma globulin*
   a. *For prevention or modification of rubeola or infectious hepatitis where direct contact has been proved.*
   b. *Bruton-type agammaglobulinemia.*
   c. *In certain cases using special immune*

   globulin derived from sera of individuals hyperimmunized to a specific disease.
5. *Antibiotics*
   a. *Long-acting, all-purpose or combination repository, containing benzathine penicillin in the appropriate doses, is an approved method of treatment in patients with suspected or proven Group A betahemolytic streptococcal conditions such as strep throat, acute tonsillitis, acute otitis media, acute sinusitis, or acute pharyngitis (1 injection per illness episode).*
   b. *Erythromycin, cephalosporin, or lincomycin when patient is allergic to penicillin in streptococcal condition.*
   c. *In gonococcal disease, penicillin (or ampicillin) is indicated (spectinomycin and tetracycline, in that order, if allergic to penicillin).*
   d. *In syphilis, penicillin is also indicated (erythromycin and tetracycline, in that order, if allergic to penicillin). Multiple injections in syphilis are indicated. In areas where there are public health clinics, however, appropriate injections will be covered (allowed for payment) only on those dates of service prior to*

From Lohr, K.N., Brook, R.H., and Kaufman, M.A.: Quality of care in the New Mexico Medicaid Program (1971-1975): the effect of the New Mexico Experimental Medical Care Review Organization on the use of antibiotics for common infectious diseases, Med. Care 18(1 Suppl.): 1, 1980.

categories of appropriateness that were previously listed drugs passing the screen would fall into the first category; that is, the drug was used as approved. Drugs not passing the screen would be drugs that had not been used as approved. These selected instances would then be subjected to peer review, or some other intense evaluation, to determine whether or not substantial documentation existed to justify a drug's nonapproved use in a particular instance. As an example of a screening process for a specific class of drugs, a list of criteria was developed by the New Mexico Medicaid program as a way to screen prescribing

practices (Lohr, Brook, and Kaufman, 1980). A trained clerical person screened prescribed medications by comparing them with a list of standards for the appropriate use of injectables (above and on p. 79) to determine which orders were appropriate and which would be subjected to peer review. Criteria for rapid screening of large groups of prescription orders for several drugs have also been developed and their application described (Brandon et al., 1977).

A potentially inappropriate set of criteria may result if their selection is derived from reference to a fixed-sequence algorithm or protocol. A

Specific standards for appropriate injectables — cont'd

the first day that clinic services are available.

6. *Injectable expectorants or cough medicines. Never! Example: Gomenol*

7. *Estrogens*
   Estrogens for menopausal syndromes will be covered (allowed for payment) only when the patient cannot take the drug orally, and the claim documents this situation.

8. *Influenza vaccine*
   a. *For patients over 65 years.*
   b. *For patients under 65 years who are severely medically debilitated (e.g., severe respiratory or cardiac problems).*

9. *The use of ACTH is limited to diagnosis (in the plasma cortisol test to assess adrenal cortical function) or in the treatment of the following conditions:*
   a. *Certain cases of multiple sclerosis.*
   b. *Certain cases of myasthenia gravis.*
   c. *Certain cases of inflammatory bowel syndrome.*

10. *Tetanus Toxoid and DPT boosters are medically appropriate and may be paid whenever there is evidence of a trauma such as a laceration, burn, abrasion, animal bite, puncture wound, etc.*

11. *Lidocaine (Xylocaine) and procaine (Novocain) are medically appropriate if a necessity for local anesthesia.*

12. *Antiasthmatics*
    The following injections are medically ap-

propriate for claims with a diagnosis of asthma:
   a. *epinephrine*
   b. *aminophylline*
   c. *Sus-phrine [epinephrine]*
   d. *adrenaline [in] oil*

13. *Antiemetics*
    When nausea and vomiting is indicated on the claim and an injection is given, all claims must be reviewed by a physician. The drugs listed below are examples of injections which must be reviewed:
   a. *Compazine [prochlorperazine]*
   b. *Dramamine [dimenhydrinate]*
   c. *Phenergan [promethazine]*
   d. *Sparine [promazine]*
   e. *Tigan [trimethobenzamide]*
   f. *Vistaril [hydroxyzine]*
   g. *Atarax [hydroxyzine]*

14. *Myochrysine and Solganal (Gold)*
    Injections of Myochrysine and Solganal for juvenile and adult rheumatoid arthritis are medically appropriate. These injections are given once a week for a period of 3 to 4 months. After this initial 3- to 4-month period, these injections will be given once a month. Any injections falling outside these guidelines must be sent to professional review.

15. *Dilantin [phenytoin] and phenobarbital*
    Injections of Dilantin or phenobarbital are medically appropriate if the diagnosis is epilepsy or seizures.

---

fixed-sequence algorithm assumes that there is only one correct medical decision at each decision point in the care of a client. With this assumption a fixed linear chain of activities or events results, and criteria are defined accordingly. In many instances a variety of "correct" decisions may be available at any decision point, depending on the prevailing conditions and findings of the client. A branched chain of activities and events is consistent with medical logic. For example, if the client has problem set A, the appropriate action is B. If, on the other hand, the client with problem set A has variation X, the

appropriate action would be $B(X)$. Both would be two separate actions and hence pathways from the decision points. Criteria pertaining to the measurement of process along pathway X may be irrelevant to pathway $B(X)$. Or worse, the expected value for a given criterion may differ as a function of the pathway. These differences must be taken into consideration in the selection of criteria.

The concept of mapping branched decision pathways has been used to develop criteria for the quality assessment of the medical management of diabetes mellitus (Greenfield et al.,

1975). Criteria (p. 82) were developed to reflect sequential medical decision making that would be required on the basis of specific findings for an individual client at a particular time. A map was created for the selected criteria in such a way that each criterion would lead to a subsequent deci-

sion or action based on a finding or value (Fig. 4-6)*:

*Modified from Greenfield, S., et al.: Peer review by criteria mapping: criteria for diabetes mellitus, Ann. Intern. Med. **83:**761, 1975.

DIAGNOSIS

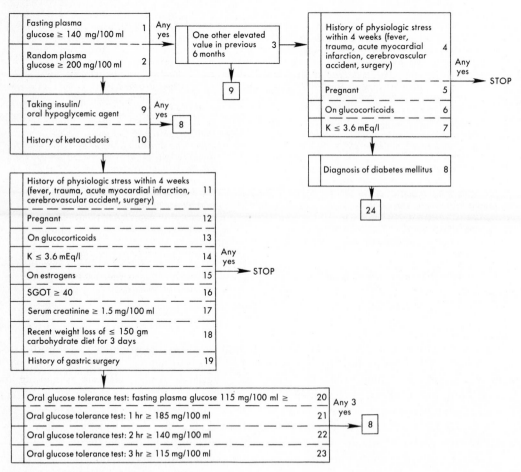

Add 10 mg/100 ml for each decade over age 50.

FIG. 4-6

Abstractor maps for diagnosis and management. (Modified from Greenfield, S., et al.: Ann. Intern. Med. **83:**761, 1975.)

MANAGEMENT

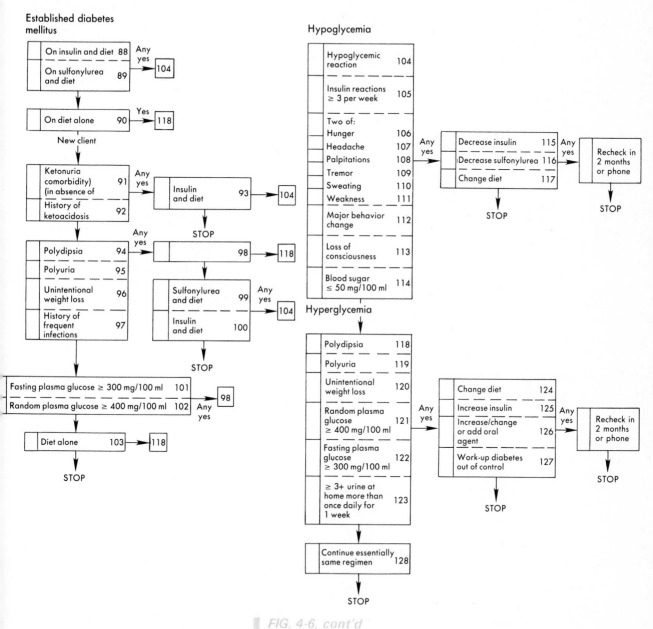

FIG. 4-6, cont'd

Abstractor maps

A. Established diabetes mellitus
  1. If client is on any of the following regimens, check for hypoglycemia (see below); if hypoglycemia is absent, check for hyperglycemia (see below); if both hypo- and hyperglycemia are absent, continue essentially the same regimen:
    a. On insulin and diet
    b. On sulfonylurea and diet
  2. If client is on the following regimen, check only for hyperglycemia (see below); if hyperglycemia is absent, continue essentially same regimen:
    a. On diet alone
  3. Checking for hypoglycemia: if client has any one of the symptoms or signs or test results listed below, change regimen (decreased insulin and/or decreased sulfonylurea and/or change diet) and follow-up (recheck in <2 months or phone):
    a. Hypoglycemic reaction
    b. Insulin reactions >3 per week
    c. Two or more of:
      (1) Hunger
      (2) Headache
      (3) Palpitations
      (4) Tremor
      (5) Sweating
      (6) Weakness
    d. Major change in behavior
    e. Loss of consciousness
    f. Blood sugar <50 mg/100 ml (i.e., 50 mg%)
  4. Checking for hyperglycemia: if client has any one of the signs or test results listed below, change regimen (add/increase insulin and/or increase/change type/add oral agent and/or change diet and/or work-up "diabetes out of control") and follow-up (recheck in <2 months or phone):
    a. Polydipsia
    b. Polyuria
    c. Unintentional weight loss

    d. Random plasma glucose >400 mg/100 ml (i.e., 400 mg%)
    e. Fasting plasma glucose >300 mg/100 ml (i.e., 300 mg%)
    f. >3 + urine at home more than once daily for a week (in absence of Somogyi phenomenon: post-hypoglycemic hyperglycemia)
B. New client with diabetes mellitus (or client with diabetes mellitus not previously on a regimen)
  1. Choose insulin and diet if any of the following:
    a. History of ketoacidosis
    b. Ketonuria
  2. Choose diet plus insulin or sulfonylurea if 1a and 1b are absent, but any one of the following is/was present:
    a. Polydipsia
    b. Polyuria
    c. Unintentional weight loss
    d. Fasting plasma glucose >300 mg/100 ml (i.e., 300 mg%)
    e. Random plasma glucose >400 mg/100 ml (i.e., 400 mg%)
    f. History of frequent infections
    Thereafter, follow criteria for an established client on same regimen.
  3. Choose diet alone if 1a and 1b and 2a through 2f are all absent (that is, fasting plasma glucose <300 mg/100 ml or random plasma glucose <400 mg/100 ml). Thereafter, follow criteria for an established client on same regimen.

The following model is presented as a way to plan the analysis of drug therapy problems (Witte et al., 1980)*:
  1. Inappropriate indication for medication
    a. No clinical indication for a prescribed drug is documented.

---

b. No drug is ordered where there is a documented indication.
2. Inappropriate selection of drug
   When the prescribed medication:
   a. Is used in combination with another drug, a particular disease state, or diet potentially causing an unintended or undesired effect in the prophylaxis, diagnosis, or therapy of the patient.
   Included are cases of inappropriate drug-drug combination, drug-disease combination, drug-laboratory combination, or physical-drug incompatibility.
   b. Warrants an adjuvant drug that was not used in the therapy (e.g., the use of pyridoxine with isoniazid therapy).
   c. Is more expensive than an equivalent alternative drug (e.g., amoxicillin for ampicillin).
3. Inappropriate choice of regimen
   a. When use of the drug is in excess of the generally accepted dose or duration of therapy.
   b. When the prescribed dosage form or route of administration makes it difficult for the patient to comply or is pharmacologically ineffective.
   c. When the drug is not used in sufficient quantities or at appropriate intervals consistent with generally accepted therapeutic regimens to achieve the desired pharmacologic effect (e.g., underdosing).
4. Inappropriate monitoring for effectiveness of drug therapy
   a. There is lack of clinical data or validation of data to show improvement in the patient's clinical condition after an appropriate time period of being on the drug.
   b. There is a worsening of the patient's clinical condition after an appropriate time on the drug, and no action is taken to evaluate therapy.
   c. A suspected adverse drug reaction is occurring, and no action is taken to validate or manage the unintended or undesired response.

This model focuses on classes of decision points in the selection and evaluation of a course of drug therapy for a particular client. It appears to be a useful framework for the mapping of branched decision pathways for a disease-specific regimen of drug therapy for clients in a geriatric long-term care facility.

Before leaving the subject of the measurement of process, it is important to note one study that offers an interesting example of how the measurement of drug use (process) can indeed serve as a meaningful approximation of the outcome of treatment. Greenfield et al. (1978) investigated the use of short-term outcome criteria to assess the quality of care for clients with osteoarthritis. The researchers selected osteoarthritis as the model because of its high incidence in society, its high frequency among users of medical care services, its vague indeterminate nature as a disease entity, and the fact that many geriatric clients in a long-term care facility might be undergoing treatment for osteoarthritis. A lengthy list of disease-specific outcome measures were selected: functional capacity, level of pain, rate of orthopedic surgery, social participation, outlook on life, and drug use.

To measure drug use as an outcome factor a panel of multidisciplinary physicians agreed on an optional, state of the art, customary level of drug use that would be expected in a population of clients with osteoarthritis within 1 year of medical intervention*:

   Of clients, 0% should be taking the following:
   steroids
   oxycodone
   meperidine
   any narcotic
   Of clients, 22% to 75% are expected to be taking one of the following:

---

*Modified from Greenfield, S., et al.: Development of outcome criteria and standards to assess the quality of care for patients with osteoarthritis, J. Chronic Dis. 1:375, 1978.

phenylbutazone
ibuprofen
naproxen
aspirin
acetaminophen
tolmetin
indomethacin
fenoprofen

Less than 2% are expected to be taking one of the following:
codeine
propoxyphene
pentazocine

Less than 10% are expected to be taking one of the following:
probenecid
allopurinol

Less than 50% are expected to be taking a new nonsteroid anti-inflammatory drug:
ibuprofen
tolmetin
indomethacin
naproxen
ketoprofen
fenoprofen

Of clients, 0% are taking 2 or more drugs simultaneously that are toxic to the gastrointestinal tract:
aspirin
indomethacin
tolmetin
phenylbutazone
ibuprofen
naproxen
fenoprofen
aspirin-acetaminophen-codeine
prednisone
other oral steroid

Less than 10% are expected to receive 4 or more injections in one joint per year

After a year of medical intervention the current drug therapy for each client in the sample was recorded. To assess the level of quality of care with respect to drug therapy, physicians measured rates of drug use from the pooled data and compared these figures with the established criteria. Incidentally, all of the data for this eval-uation were available in the client record, with the exception of the determination of the number of injections per joint. That information was obtained easily from client interview by questionnaire.

In summary, although the measurement of process is the state of the art with respect to the assessment of the quality of drug therapy, there are numerous opportunities for drug use reviews to provide important information that would approximate outcomes of care. The selection of criteria is among the most important aspects of the measurement problem. To aid in the development of criteria, the following guide, an adaptation of the steps used by Greenfield et al. (1978), may be useful:

1. Organize a panel of clinicians who can provide an appropriate interdisciplinary perspective to the development of criteria.
2. Establish an operational definition of the client population to be studied. Create an algorithm to be used to test clients to determine if they would be members of the population of interest.
3. Identify factors outside the influence of medical care that would adversely affect the quality of care.
4. Identify criteria that would be disease specific, explicit, sensitive to the dynamics of sequential medical decision making, and reflective of the state of the art. Criteria should be sensitive enough to discriminate between differences (e.g., changes in status of a client or group, differences between clients or groups) in the short term, with respect to when medical intervention occurred.
5. Select an array of criteria that correlates well with and is representative of the major relevant outcomes from therapy, including physical, physiologic, and psychosocial outcomes.
6. Establish an effective and reliable measurement plan.

THE CLIENT'S MEDICATION CHART

The client's chart is the dominant, and often the only, source used to obtain data for drug use reviews. Individuals who perform drug use reviews must be thoroughly acquainted with the proper use and limitations of the chart for these purposes. It is not my intent to discuss proper use of the chart for conducting drug use reviews in the long-term care facility. To learn the proper use of the client record for drug use review, the reader is encouraged to consult the self-study program published by the American Pharmaceutical Association (1978).

The reliability of the results from chart review can be compromised considerably if the procedure for chart review is unreliable or poorly planned; if the desired data are not typical chart inclusions; if chart entries are omitted, inaccurate, or incomplete; or if the reviewer must interpret chart data to conform to recording requirements. The combined information from the three chart reviews that are described will help illustrate these factors.

Segal, Thompson, and Floyd (1979) studied prescribing patterns in a skilled nursing facility. The charts of 50 randomly selected clients (of 250 occupants) were subjected to a detailed analysis. The assumptions that the authors made are applicable to the typical study protocol involving chart review. When reviewing a chart, they assumed that the diagnoses were correct, charting was accurate, all problems were noted, laboratory data were correct, history of allergies was accurate, and drugs had been administered as ordered. (Note that if these or any other activities are questionable, the health care evaluator has a basis to design and conduct an evaluation of those performance factors. Some published studies have reported such evaluations, as will be noted.)

Several types of criteria were reviewed for each drug prescribed, including diagnostic indication for use, route of administration, and dosage interval. For each of these the chart reviewer determined if the ordered medication was appropriate or inappropriate. The reviewer also assessed the amount of dosage, determining if it was potentially toxic, therapeutic, or subtherapeutic. In addition, the number of detected drug interactions (drug-drug, drug-disease, drug-diet) were recorded for each chart. For adverse drug reactions data were recorded as "none," "doubtful," "possibly clinically significant," and "probably clinically significant." The actual standards used by the reviewer to make these decisions were determined on the basis of personal knowledge because standards were not specified in the publication. Hence personal judgment may have been a key factor in determining the value assigned to each measure. Some purists in the field of measurement may question the reliability of a study that deviates from the absolute guarantee of unbiased, totally objective measures. However, from a practical perspective, others might argue that the degree of guarantee should be based on the reasons for conducting the study and the proposed use of the results.

After Segal, Thompson, and Floyd (1979) obtained their data, they summarized the results by tabulating drugs versus factors in a variety of configurations. From the analysis of their results, the authors were able to conclude that certain prescribers were associated with underdosing while others showed a pattern of therapeutically nonjustifiable high doses and that the orders for some drugs were associated with potentially toxic doses, adverse drug reactions, or potential interactions.

A chart review technique was used to screen anticoagulant doses (Meinhold, Reale, and Miller, 1979). Data for several dosing factors in a chart were compared with an anticoagulant dosing protocol. The method for the development of the protocol of that study is noteworthy. A step-by-step, clinically sequenced protocol was established from the results of a literature review. A questionnaire was prepared by creating an item for each step in the protocol. A panel of 30 physicians, pharmacists, and nurses was selected on the basis of authorship of articles or active practice relating to the use of anticoagulants. Each panelist was asked to respond "agree/disagree/modify" for each term in the questionnaire. The final protocol represented a modification of the majority view of the panelists. From the results of this chart review, printed in-service educational material was distributed to correct the nonconformity that was detected between data in the chart and specifications in the protocol.

Krikorian (1979) studied the extent of errors pertaining to recording data about medication on the client's chart. The extent of recording errors found in his study is cause for considerable concern about the reliability of the client chart as a source document for drug use studies. From 709 charts that were scrutinized during a 4-month period, Krikorian found that the reasons for nonadministration of a medication were not documented (164 errors); medications were not all charted or the reasons for not charting were not noted (152 errors); discrepancies existed between physicians' orders and the nurses' medication Kardex (37 errors); and other less frequent problems were also noted. Krikorian's guidelines for conducting the chart review may be useful to others for their own chart review, regardless of purpose. A team of people were involved, each person having a defined set of tasks to perform. A fixed time (1 hour per day) was specified for chart review. This differs from the tendency to specify a fixed number of charts. During the fixed time interval a variable number of charts were reviewed. Ten to twelve were often actually reviewed, although the team had a goal of fifteen. The reviews were performed at a designated time, with the actual time rotating from day to day on a continuous cycle. The time was selected to avoid disruption. Each day a different floor was selected for chart review.

The previous synopses should illustrate some of the pitfalls that can be avoided in designing a chart review. Even with its inherent limitations the client's chart still remains among the best source documents for the studies of drug therapy in an institution. Following is a summary of a study that illustrates the very meaningful results that can be obtained from a relatively easy and straightforward chart review.

An intense, short-term survey was performed on p.r.n. orders in a nursing home (Howard, Strong, and Strong, 1977). All drug orders were scrutinized. From the data on the p.r.n. orders, evaluators were able to determine the average number of drugs with a p.r.n. order per client (3.2, representing 58% of the average number of current drug orders in effect per client). The evaluators recorded any specific directions that may have accompanied a p.r.n. order and questioned the nurse regarding her understanding of the p.r.n. order. From their findings the authors claimed that overuse of the p.r.n. order and a lack of the nurse's clear understanding of the meaning of that order placed the elderly at unnecessary risk. The authors felt that the problem could be remedied by increased nursing awareness and strengthened requirements for physician review of medication orders for clients.

IMPLEMENTATION

From the many studies and methodologic approaches that have been described in the literature, many tasks for the implementation of a program of the quality assurance of drug therapy have been described and used. From careful study of the well-planned experiences of others, a general pattern emerges for an effective approach to quality assurance. Accordingly, the following considerations are recommended.

Administrative authority

Individual physicians, nurse practitioners, and, in some cases, other clinicians are ultimately responsible for the quality of care afforded to their clients. The institution is responsible for assuring the total well-being of its clients. At a minimum, then, the institution must see that each client not be subjected to care that is of a lower quality than the recognized standard. Beyond this, however, many institutions strive to offer the best quality of care within the constraints of available resources. In this regard it is well established (e.g., in legal decisions, in accreditation and regulatory standards, and in common practice) that the institution has the right and the obligation to protect its interests with respect to the quality of care afforded to its clients (Holder, 1978). In this regard physicians, for example, are expected to yield certain individual prerogatives to the common good of the institution as a whole (Hirsch, Morris, and Moritz, 1979). The professional practice standards of other groups of health professionals, such as nurses and pharmacists, stress activities that promote the quality of care. Furthermore, the ultimate quality of care received by institutionalized elderly persons is the result of a team effort. For these as well as other reasons it is important that the process of quality review receives full administrative sanction.

In many institutions the authority to conduct a quality assurance program may already exist in one or more places through the organized medical staff or through the institution's administrative structure. If such authority is not formalized, accreditation standards or the federal conditions of participation in the Medicare or Medicaid program provide minimum standards for establishing administrative authority.

Organizational structure

One principle of good management is that if something is worth doing, then plan it, organize it, do it with established policies and procedures, operate it as a controlled operation, and hold it accountable. In other words, formalize it in the organization. If quality assurance is worth doing, this principle of good management should apply to it as well. As mentioned, diverse groups of clinicians in an institution have interests in the

quality of care. Because of the nature of their responsibilities, many committees and staffs, such as an infections committee, a pharmacy and therapeutics committee, a medical audit committee, and an in-service education staff, would be grateful recipients of results from a quality assurance program. These committees and staffs themselves often perform activities that constitute, functionally speaking, quality assurance. In addition, some departments have established quality assurance efforts, and groups of individuals have from time to time undertaken quality assurance studies (several published studies on antibiotic use attest to this). Perhaps the most significant contribution that could be made from an organizational perspective would be to apply that one good principle of management to assure that quality assurance is being conducted as a planned, organized, systematic, accountable, and institution-wide effort.

Because of the existing diversity of interest and activity in quality assurance and the overall structure of the institution, perhaps the most important initial administrative decision about organization would be related to the appropriate degree of centralization-decentralization of authority and responsibility that should exist. A second important decision would be to establish linkages between, for example, the in-service education program, the medical staff, nursing services, the pharmacy department or the consultant pharmacist, the pharmacy and therapeutics committee, the infections committee, and the medical audit committee, or their equivalents.

Team effort

All those interested in quality assurance should participate. Reports of experiences with interdisciplinary committees, task forces, study groups, and reference panels have received favorable comments. A team effort is appropriate for at least four important activities of quality assurance: (1) selecting goals and objectives for the quality assurance program, (2) establishing priorities of problems to be assessed, (3) creating criteria, and (4) interpreting the results for purposes of selecting the most appropriate corrective action. Depending on the nature of a particular study, a team effort may also be appropriate for selecting the methodology for data collection.

Goals and objectives

Periodic selection and reassessment of goals and objectives help to direct limited resources (quality assurance is a personnel-intense process) to meaningful enterprises. Two types of goals are appropriate for the quality assurance of drug therapy in an institution: those for the continuous evaluation of selected aspects of drug therapy (e.g., antibiotic usage rates) and those for short-term, "as needed" projects (e.g., the previously discussed study of p.r.n. medications).

Selected review

In selecting topics for study or review when time and human resources are limited, clinicians should look for problems where they are most likely to occur, such as those drugs most frequently prescribed (Brandon, 1977); those with the greatest potential for adverse drug reactions, misuse, or overuse (Hoffmann, 1980); or those that are the most costly. Another approach to the selection of the topic could be based on the significance of the health problem. For example, the selection of a health problem to be studied could depend on its severity, its impact on the overall quality of medical care, the potential for improving client care by studying the problem, or the potential use of the problem as a tracer. For a geriatric long-term care facility it has been suggested that at least one study should be in progress at any given time (Stewart, Kabat, and Wertheimer, 1976).

Criteria and data collection methods

The best criteria and methods must be selected. Inappropriate or meaningless criteria and poor data collection methods are perhaps the weakest links in studies of quality assurance. The most relevant criteria are those that have been selected as a way to measure variables that have been selected because of their relevance to the objectives of a particular study. In selecting criteria, good principles for identifying and testing their validity and reliability should be employed. Through the design of the study a close relationship between activities and measurements must be assured. Results from measurements must permit generalizations to be made about, for example, conformance to standards, achievement of objectives, or changes according to plan. Unlike "traditional" research, the intention behind drug use studies is not to establish a global cause-effect relationship (i.e., to test hypotheses and contribute to theory) but rather to narrowly focus on relatively local objectives to contribute to policy-making ability. The principles of design employed should follow those of traditional research.

Periodic review

Quality assurance is a cycle. Results from the review process and components of the program should be periodically reviewed and revised for the next cycle.

Implementation of decisions and dissemination of information

Quality assurance, as will be recalled, is, above all, a vehicle for improvement. Health regulatory agencies have their own agenda for medical audit that relate to accountability and the financing of medical care more than anything else; their purposes should not be confused with the managerial reasons for quality assurance. As a managerial function, quality assurance provides benchmarks of progress, conformance, and achievement. The reason for conducting quality assurance studies is to identify if intervention is necessary to improve performance. Thus the bottom line of a quality assurance program is to assure that decisions are implemented and that the necessary changes take place. A major fault that exists in many organizations is that good decisions are never implemented. A quality assurance program should have the necessary administrative encouragement and support to follow through on findings. Some follow-through activities are to provide educational programs; to refer matters to committee; to introduce or redesign a form, policy, or procedure; to establish a regulation; or to require a consultation from a specialist to approve certain drug orders. To instill meaning into the quality assurance process and to close the loop of the quality assurance cycle, the necessary authority to include the correctional phase in the program must be provided.

In addition to the recommendations just mentioned for the quality assurance program, the following three points may be worthwhile to consider with respect to individual studies.

Pilot study. A trial run on a limited scale may help identify and correct unanticipated problems in implementing the study design. Some common examples have been flaws in data collection forms; erroneous assumptions about availability, identifiability, or extractability of data from charts; awkward data collection procedures; or unfeasible client monitoring activities. Other purposes of a pilot study might include the validation of measurement criteria and the establishment of interrater reliability.

Three-phased review. For efficiency and effectiveness a chart review process can include an initial rapid screen, a secondary screen of questionable charts, and a full committee review of charts most likely to have a significant problem (Kelly et al., 1975).

Cost-effectiveness. Any study has an associated cost. That cost should be considered with respect to the effectiveness of the study in meeting its objectives or in effecting a change in drug therapy. Williamson (1978) claims that a structured procedure is more effective than a nonstructured one for identifying the cost-effectiveness of topics for quality assurance. Williamson's procedure includes the selection and use of a priority-setting

team, a training session, an incubation period, a priority-setting meeting, and the final selection of topics.

Quality assurance, as a managerial device to improve the quality of drug therapy, has many promises and limitations. Even with its limitations, a well-designed program can detect significant deficiencies and lead to substantial improvements in care. For a program to be successful, the effort needs knowledgeable and conscientious people backed by a supportive administration and health care staff.

REFERENCES

American Pharmaceutical Association: Monitoring drug therapy in the long-term care facility: an APhA self-study program for pharmacists, Washington, D.C., 1978, The Association.

American Society of Hospital Pharmacists: Model quality assurance program for hospital pharmacies, Washington, D.C., 1978, The Society.

Brandon, B.M., et al.: Drug usage screening criteria, Am. J. Hosp. Pharm. **34:**146, 1977.

Cleland, D.I., and King, W.R.: Management: a systems approach, New York, 1972, McGraw-Hill, Inc.

Donabedian, A.: Promoting quality through evaluating the process of care, Med. Care **6:**181, 1968.

Feinstein, A.R., and Kramer, M.S.: Clinical biostatistics. LIII. The architecture of observer/method variability and other types of process research, Clin. Pharmacol. Ther. **28:**551, 1980.

Greenfield, S., et al.: Peer review by criteria mapping: criteria for diabetes mellitus, Ann. Intern. Med. **83:**761, 1975.

Greenfield, S., et al.: Development of outcome criteria and standards to assess the quality of care for patients with osteoarthritis, J. Chronic Dis. **31:**375, 1978.

Greenlaw, C.W.: Antimicrobial drug use monitoring by a hospital pharmacy, Am. J. Hosp. Pharm. **34:**835, 1977.

Hassan, W.E., Jr.: Hospital pharmacy, ed. 3, Philadelphia, 1974, Lea & Febiger.

Hirsch, C.S., Morris, R.C., and Moritz, A.R.: Handbook of legal medicine, ed. 5, St. Louis, 1979, The C.V. Mosby Co.

Hoffmann, R.P.: General suggestions for auditing antibiotic usage, Hosp. Pharm. **15**:143, 1980.

Holder, A.R.: Medical malpractice law, ed. 2, New York, 1978, John Wiley & Sons, Inc.

Howard, J.B., Strong, K.E., Sr., and Strong, K.E., Jr.: Medication procedures in a nursing home: abuse of p.r.n. orders, J. Am. Geriatr. Soc. **25**:83, 1977.

Kelly, W.N., White, J.A., and Miller, D.E.: Drug use review in a community hospital, Am. J. Hosp. Pharm. **32**:1014, 1975.

Knapp, D.A., et al.: Development and application of criteria in drug use review programs, Am. J. Hosp. Pharm. **31**:648, 1974.

Krikorian, J.: Quality control enhanced by chart review, Hospitals **53**(21):97, 1979.

Lohr, K.N., Brook, R.H., and Kaufman, M.A.: Quality of care in the New Mexico Medicaid program (1971-1975): the effect of the New Mexico Experimental Medical Care Review Organization on the use of antibiotics for common infectious diseases, Med. Care **18**:1, 1980.

Meinhold, J.M., Reale, E.O., and Miller, W.A.: Audit of anticoagulant therapy of pulmonary embolus, deep vein thrombosis, and thrombophlebitis, Am. J. Hosp. Pharm. **36**:214, 1979.

Millis, J.S.: Pharmacists for the future: the report of the study commission on pharmacy, Ann Arbor, Mich., 1975, University of Michigan Health Administration Press.

National Coordinating Committee on Large Volume Parenterals: Recommended guidelines for quality assurance in hospital centralized intravenous admixture services, Am. J. Hosp. Pharm. **37**:645, 1980.

Pulliam, C.C.: Evaluating therapeutic accomplishments, Am. J. Hosp. Pharm. **31**:880, 1974.

Raia, A.P.: Managing by objectives, Glenview, Ill., 1974, Scott, Foresman, & Co.

Richardson, W.C., Shortell, S.M., and Campbell, W.W.: The conduct and usefulness of evaluation research in health-care delivery, Am. J. Pharm. Educ. **42**:447, 1978.

Segal, J.L., Thompson, J.F., and Floyd, R.A.: Drug utilization and prescribing patterns in a skilled nursing facility: the need for a rational approach to therapeutics, J. Am. Geriatr. Soc. **27**:117, 1979.

Stewart, J.E., Kabat, H.R., and Wertheimer, A.I.: Drug usage review sample studies in long-term care facilities, Am. J. Hosp. Pharm. **33**:138, 1976.

Stolar, M.H.: Quality assurance for hospital pharmacy. I. Basic concepts, Am. J. Hosp. Pharm. **32**:276, 1975.

Visconti, J.A.: Drug use review. In Smith, M.C., and Brown, T.R., editors: Handbook of institutional pharmacy practice, Baltimore, 1979, The Williams & Wilkins Co.

Williamson, J.W.: Formulating priorities for quality assurance activity: description of a method and its application, J.A.M.A. **239**:631, 1978.

Witte, K.W., et al.: Drug regimen review in skilled nursing facilities by consulting clinical pharmacists, Am. J. Hosp. Pharm. **37**:820, 1980.

CHAPTER 5

Drug therapy review guidelines for geriatric long-term care facilities

Peter P. Lamy

Bruce H. Krug

The nursing home industry's average annual growth from 1965 to 1979 was 16.9%. During that time expenditure rose from $2.1 billion to $17.8 billion. In 1980 nursing home care demanded 8.8% of the nation's total health care expenditures, and this figure is expected to rise to 10% by 1990.

The U.S. Commerce Department reported that expenditures for nursing home care in 1981 were $24.5 billion. The department also attempted to forcast expenditures for this decade. According to these projections, annual nursing home costs will rise by 17.1% by the end of 1982, more than any other segment of the nation's health care expenses, reaching $28.7 billion. Furthermore, the rise will not be arrested but will continue, leading to expenditures of $48 billion in 1986 and $76 billion in 1990 (Hickox, 1982; "Congress to Cope," 1982).

Recognizing this trend, both the U.S. Senate and House of Representatives have scheduled

Modified from Lamy, P.P., and Krug, B.H.: Drug therapy review in nursing homes: proposed standards and guidelines, Contemp. Pharm. Pract. 4:125, 1981. Permission granted by the American Pharmaceutical Association.

hearings on the financing and organization of long-term care systems focusing on alternatives to institutionalization as part of the continuum of care and exploring more competitive reimbursement programs. Thus the exact dynamics of the nursing home field cannot be predicted, but it is clear that it will grow and continue to grow rapidly. The reason that it will continue to grow rests with population statistics.

INCREASE IN THE NUMBER OF ELDERLY

There has been a decline in the mortality rate for the extreme aged population (those 85 years and older) of 26% between 1966 and 1977 (Rosenwaike, Yaffe, and Sagi, 1980). This rate is accelerating as documented by statistics that show that between 1933 and 1966 the rate declined by only 10%. These data explain, in part, the most astonishing demographic characteristics of the twentieth century: those 85 years and older constitute the fastest growing segment in the U.S. population, increasing annually by 40%. Their number will double in the next 20 years.

The real and projected increase in the number of extreme aged should be of particular concern to health care professionals practicing in nursing homes. Little is known about this population. Almost nothing is known about their nutritional status, which can influence health and drug action, because the Health and Nutrition Examination Survey only examined persons who were not confined to institutions and who were between 1 and 74 years of age.

It has been suggested, however, that nutritional deficiencies are seldom if ever identified but that a significant number of the extreme aged in nursing homes are probably chronically malnourished despite the fact that they are able to eat. It would, then, be important to improve the nutritional value and caloric density of their diets, which is probably done most successfully by means of geriatric enteral hyperalimentation (Ross, 1981; Tomaiolo, Enman, and Kraus, 1981).

CHRONIC DISEASE IN THE ELDERLY

Although it has been predicted that chronic disease will occupy a smaller proportion of the typical life span, there is no question that many of the extreme aged have high systolic blood pressure levels, and there is still no agreement as to whether or not they should be treated. Furthermore, among the very old, women outnumber men by a ratio of at least 2 to 1, and that ratio rises to 3 to 1 among nursing home residents.

Many surveys have shown that women receive more drugs than men, and many drugs, such as penicillin and heparin, have a different effect on women. Even the normal adult dose is generally an overdose for a female patient, and the elderly person is simply smaller than the "normal" adult. It is, therefore, not surprising that gender is a determinant of the frequency and characteristics of adverse drug reactions. Therefore the very old female nursing home resident is particularly at risk to the hazards of drug action (Lamy, 1981a and 1981b).

Almost 80% of the elderly, compared with those younger than 65 years of age, have one or more chronic diseases, and multipathology increases with increasing age. The extreme aged are more susceptible to disease (Lamy, 1980e), particularly chronic disease. The therapeutic goal, then, becomes one of managing rather than curing the disease, and long-term treatment with suppressive or maintenance therapy is necessary.

It is important to keep the therapeutic goal in mind. A change in the therapeutic goal should not simply be based on new information. For example, it is now recognized that strict diabetic control can probably impede the development of small vessel disease, such as nephropathy and retinopathy. Strict control can only be obtained by the use of insulin, but considerations other than "strict" control should enter into a decision to switch an elderly person from an oral hypoglycemic to insulin. This would involve patient comfort, anticipated life span, intercurrent diseases, and other factors. Therapy must be individualized. Tight therapeutic goals and aggressive treatment may be appropriate for some elderly persons in nursing homes. On the other hand, lack of aggressive treatment may be appropriate for others.

Pneumonia may, on occasion, be "the old man's friend," but pressure sores, conjunctivitis, and urinary tract infections are not. In the former condition, aggressive treatment for infectious disease may not be indicated, but nontreatment of the latter conditions would definitely not be in the patient's best interest (Avorn, 1981).

New information should be incorporated in the development of a patient's treatment regimen if it promises to prevent other diseases or to maintain a patient's quality of life. Serious consideration, therefore, should be given to recent literature reports that there is increasing evidence that serious complications, such as ventricular ectopic activity, may develop in asymptomatic hypokalemic patients, possibly leading to sudden death (Holland, Nixon, and Kuhnert, 1980), and that any established and routine monitoring functions should be changed (Multicenter Diuretic Cooperative Study Group, 1981) to include serum potassium levels.

DRUGS AND THE ELDERLY

The declining health status of the elderly population is mirrored by the increasing drug use among this population. In nursing homes nearly one third of the elderly patients receive more than 8 drugs daily, some as many as 12 and 16 drugs (Office of Long Term Care, 1976). This picture is complicated by the fact that the elderly exhibit a modified drug response resulting mainly from altered pharmacokinetics (see Chapter 10). This occurs because of altered distribution, metabolism, and excretion of drugs. Underlying these alterations are physiologic and pathologic changes that are responsible for diminished hepatic and renal function, alteration in body composition, alteration in blood flow, and a decrease and qualitative change in protein binding of drugs (Triggs and Nation, 1975; Triggs, Nation, and Long, 1975; Crooks, O'Malley, and Stevenson, 1976; Lamy and Vestal, 1976; Hollister, 1977; Richey and Bender, 1977; Vestal, 1978). (See Chapters 6 and 10.)

This reduced capability to handle drugs often leads to altered, unexpected, and even bizarre drug responses in older adults, particularly when they use multiple drugs. Adverse drug reactions (ADRs) increase with age, and in one study 24% of patients over 81 years of age experienced adverse drug effects, compared with 11% of those who were 31 to 40 years old (Seidl et al., 1966). In another study the incidence of adverse drug effects rose from 3% in patients 20 to 29 years old to 21% in those 70 to 79 years (Hurwitz, 1969).

Many studies have looked at adverse drug reactions in the acute care setting (Seidl et al., 1966; Hoddinot, 1967; Ogilvie and Ruedy, 1967; Borda, Slone, and Jick, 1968; Hurwitz and Wade, 1969). Approximately 15% to 30% of patients in acute care settings will experience one or more adverse drug reactions during their stay. About 3% to 5% of hospital admissions to medical services are a result of adverse drug reactions. The average hospital stay is doubled for persons experiencing ADRs. The majority of ADRs are preventable (Cheung and Kayne, 1975). A recent study found that of 325 patients admitted to an intensive care unit in the course of 1 year, 41 (12.6%) were hospitalized because of iatrogenic disease. Many of these patients had concomitant serious illness. Nevertheless, 19 patients (46.3%) were admitted with iatrogenic disease resulting from therapeutic or technical errors that were potentially avoidable. Twenty-three patients were admitted suffering iatrogenic disease caused by drug administration; roughly one third of these were caused by adverse drug reactions and two thirds were caused by therapeutic errors (Trunet et al., 1980). (See Chapter 11 for a more complete discussion of adverse drug reactions in the elderly.)

Similar data for long-term care facilities are scarce. However, one must anticipate that they would be much more serious because of increased age; generally less advantageous physical, mental, functional, and nutritional status; and the larger number of drugs generally administered to nursing home residents.

Laventurier et al. (1976) found that 22% of nursing home residents were exposed to potentially interacting drugs, compared to 6.2% of an ambulatory population studied. Cheung and Kayne (1975) reviewed 100 consecutive admissions from nursing homes to acute care institutions and found that 15% to 17% were probably caused by drug-related illness. Perhaps, then, one way to address this problem is to keep in mind those drugs that are most likely to interact and those that have been shown to put the elderly most at risk to hazardous drug action (see Chapter 8).

It seems that diuretics are most often responsible for adverse effects, but drugs such as antihypertensives, antiparkinsonian agents, psychotropics, and digitalis glycosides, in that order, pose the most serious risk to the elderly (Williamson and Chopin, 1980). Drug-drug interactions are often expected although they are difficult to evaluate in complex clinical cases. However, the interactions of drugs with nutritional status or with intercurrent diseases have been given little attention and probably occur at a much higher rate than expected (Lamy, 1980a and 1980b). Based on these and similar considerations, it has often been suggested that these problems could be averted if the elderly received fewer drugs. This seems to be a somewhat naive and simplistic approach to the problem because several drugs, even as many as six or seven, may be needed to manage multiple chronic diseases in the elderly (Lamy, 1980c); however, many problems and conditions may be adversely affected by drugs (Table 5-1).

To address these problems, there should be a team of health professionals, consisting of a physician, nurse, and pharmacist, who have access to dietary and nutritional advice. The team would study each older person's problems, proposed therapeutic goal(s), the possibility of non–drug treatment, the advisability of exercise and other activities, and other related factors. Particular attention should be paid to the need and use of "p.r.n." drugs and the possibility of standing orders that may address problems in the absence of the prescriber.

AN APPROACH TO OPTIMUM DRUG THERAPY IN THE ELDERLY

Something more is needed to bring about optimum drug therapy for the elderly, particularly for those elderly residing in long-term care facilities. This was recognized in 1974 when the Department of Health, Education, and Welfare mandated that pharmacists provide monthly drug therapy reviews for each resident receiving medicaid-reimbursed drug treatment in a skilled nursing facility ("Standards for Certification," 1974). Pharmacists have found that the monthly drug regimen review is effective in the disease management of elderly residents in skilled nursing

TABLE 5-1 **Possible relationships between patient factors and drugs**

Patient Condition/problem/status	Drugs
Medically defined conditions (diagnoses)	Conditions may be helped by drugs Conditions may be caused by drugs Drug use may be unjustified or inappropriate
Medical status	Status may be positively or adversely affected by drugs Intercurrent diseases may be adversely affected
Functional status (e.g., mobility, bowel and bladder function)	Status may be positively or adversely affected by drugs
Nutritional status	Status may be supported or depleted by drugs
Psychosocial status	Status may be supported or aggravated by drugs
Special treatments and procedures	Drugs may be used in preference to non–drug measures Certain procedures may not be indicated with drug treatment

facilities (McGhan, Wertheimer, and Martilla, 1980; Miller et al., 1980).

Dr. Janice Caldwell, former director, Division of Long Term Care of the Health Care Financing Administration, seems to agree. In a letter to Tim Webster, Executive Director of the American Society of Consultant Pharmacists, she noted that "current evidence indicates that the 1974 skilled nursing facility regulation which requires a monthly drug regimen review by a pharmacist has considerable potential for improving quality [of care] and reducing costs. . . . this benefit [should] be extended to intermediate care facility patients."

Numerous health care professionals, including many pharmacists, have described the need for and effectiveness of the cautious approach to geriatric medicine in the long-term care facility. Intervention has ranged from improving prescribing patterns, monitoring drug therapy, unit dose packaging, and devising methods to decrease drug waste and p.r.n. drugs, to establishing prepaid or capitation methods of payment.* Still the Comptroller General of the United States (1980) has reported that two major problems have not yet been dealt with adequately:

1. There is no readily accessible, single source of information on drug use and monitoring.
2. The Department of Health and Human Services (HHS) has not defined the scope of "medication review."

Furthermore, data are not readily available to determine quality of care in terms of appropriateness of care (Liu and Mossey, 1980).

"Appropriateness" of care is difficult to establish in a long-term care facility. Because of the advanced age, the multiple disease conditions often present, and the physical disabilities of residents in these facilities, multiple confounding diagnoses and problems are often encountered and possibly often overlooked. This almost mandates a quality review that is based on characteristics other than standard diagnostic categories and standard drug treatment.

▌ ▒▒▒▒ INDICATORS

Subsequently, proposed regulations have been published to extend drug-regimen review to intermediate care facilities (Department of Health and Human Services, 1980). These have severe shortcomings as do the indicators that are

---

*Lang and Kabat, 1970; Letourneau, 1974; Hood, Lemberger, and Stewart, 1975; Rawlings and Frisk, 1975; Rawlings and Mathieson, 1976; Vlasses et al., 1976; Brodie, Lofholm, and Benson, 1977; Ciullo and Shepherd, 1977; Cooper and Bagwell, 1978; Patry and Kroeger, 1978; Howard, Strong, and Strong, 1978; Stewart et al., 1978; Martilla and Green, 1979; Naccarto, Bell, and Lamy, 1979; Segal, Thompson, and Floyd, 1979; Shepherd, 1979; Zimmer, 1979; Brown and DeSimone, 1980; Levine, 1980; Strandberg et al., 1980a and 1980b; Brown, 1981; Carter, Small, and Garnett, 1981; Vancura and Martilla, 1981; Young et al., 1981.

Certification procedures for use of antidepressants*

1. *More than two changes of an antidepressant within a 7-day period. Commonly used antidepressants follow:*

Generic names	Brand names	Usual daily dose
amitriptyline	Elavil	100 to 300 mg/day
desipramine	Norpramin, Pertofrane	100 to 300 mg/day
doxepin	Adapin, Sinequan	100 to 300 mg/day
imipramine	Tofranil, SK-pramine	100 to 300 mg/day
nortriptyline	Aventyl, Pamelor	50 to 150 mg/day
protriptyline	Vivactil	20 to 60 mg/day

2. *The use of antidepressants listed in number 1 in excess of one half the listed dosage ranges for patients over 65.*
3. *The use of the antidepressants listed in number 1 in excess of the listed dosage ranges.*

Proposed indicators of poor medication review.

---

intended for surveyors of nursing facilities (Lamy, 1980d).

One problem is the rigid application of indicators. Admittedly, they are simply designed to let a surveyor determine "good" or "bad" practices. An example is given in Table 5-2. These indicators, which will help surveyors determine the effectiveness of the pharmacy consultant, went into effect in April 1982 and were incorporated into the State Operations Manual for Provider Certification.

Six common antidepressants are listed above. The problem is that "changes" are looked at but not the use of the drug in a multiple drug regimen, in which many drugs may well have anticholinergic side effects. Furthermore, dosage ranges are predicated on adjustment as suggested by the American Psychiatric Society. Often, however, it has been shown that this may lead to underdosing in certain individuals. A higher dose, however, would automatically seem to indicate poor prescribing and consulting procedures. Since the inception of the list, however, the tetracyclics and the tricyclic dibenzoxazepines have been marketed, and the bicyclics are not far behind. This emphatically shows that any type of monitoring must also be capable of changing with changing availability of drugs and changing concepts of geriatric care.

PHARMACY STANDARDS AND GUIDELINES FOR SKILLED NURSING FACILITIES

Some time ago, the Baltimore City Professional Standards Review Organization Long-Term Care Committee, Quality Assurance Subcommittee, requested us to develop meaningful pharmacy standards and guidelines by which the quality of pharmacy services could be evaluated. These standards were subsequently accepted and are now being tested in several large skilled nursing facilities.

Because a meaningful drug regimen review has not yet been defined or described, it is suggested that these guidelines serve both as a framework for surveyor assessment of drug regimen reviews and as minimum practice standards for pharmacists performing reviews. For the surveyor, they serve only as indicators of good regimen review or its lack because in any given clinical situation good reasons may cause deviation from them. In most cases use of the indicators cannot lead to a definitive finding of compliance or noncompliance. Their application and findings, when taken as a whole, may indicate, however, that there is noncompliance or poor practice, which should be further investigated.

Quite obviously, direct communication with the person performing the drug regimen review may be necessary, and, therefore, inclusion of the consulting pharmacist in the actual survey may be advantageous.

The consultant pharmacist can use these guidelines as a framework to develop methods needed to perform drug regimen reviews. They point out the types of issues that need to be assessed but are not intended to be a step-by-step guide. This would be impossible because in any given practice different issues need to be considered and incorporated into the process. The size of the institution, the resident mix, the nature of the medical staff and nursing staff, the availability of laboratory facilities, drug use, and similar considerations all would influence the type of review to be undertaken. Some problems discovered repeatedly during individual drug regimen reviews may suggest a general pattern. Should this occur, an audit (Appendix 5-1) rather than individual reviews would address and assess the issue more effectively (Michocki, Wiser, and Lamy, 1981). Furthermore, it is likely that suggestions for changes in prescribing are more readily accepted when given in general, impersonal terms rather than in specific comments written on the chart. Also, an audit may reveal problems that chart reviews on a patient-by-patient basis would not reveal.

Krug (1981) gained an impression from numerous regimen reviews that digoxin level determinations in one institution might be misused. Although these levels can unquestionably be beneficial in certain clinical situations, they may be misused, and the cost (at $25 to $40) may not be justified. The proper use and interpretation of serum digoxin concentrations are hampered by a number of important facts:

1. The "normal" values have been determined from clinically toxic and nontoxic groups. There is considerable overlap, and "normal" values are often found in toxic patients, whereas "toxic" levels are found in clinically nontoxic patients (Braunwald and Klucke, 1965; Beller et al., 1971). Thus a serum digoxin determination can rarely be used as a diagnosis of toxicity or nontoxicity. It is, however, the most useful measure in light of the patient's clinical status.

2. Factors other than high serum levels can

contribute to digoxin toxicity. Among them are serum potassium levels; the ratio of intracellular-to-extracellular potassium; calcium and magnesium concentrations; pH; hypoxia; and the patient's thyroid status (Ingelfinger and Goldman, 1976).

3. Effective control of the ventricular rate in the elderly with atrial fibrillation or flutter, by blockade of the AV node, may require digoxin levels considered in the "toxic" range.

4. Levels that have not yet reached steady state (i.e., those taken before steady state is reached or taken less than 6 hours after an oral dose) are misleading and often meaningless.

An audit, according to the criteria presented in Appendix 5-2, was performed at a large extended care facility. It yielded the following results:

1. Of all blood levels determined, 82% were requested by two physicians who cared for fewer than 50% of patients.

2. Of the blood levels ordered, 60% did not meet the criteria. Many were ordered monthly as a matter of routine.

3. Of the levels, 25% were performed (blood was drawn) when a steady state had not yet been reached or too soon after an oral dose.

4. Appropriate use of digoxin levels could save the facility over $4000 annually.

These results were used in subsequent monthly drug regimen reviews as well as in a letter from the medical director to the attending physicians. A reaudit would assess the effectiveness of the audit and the intervention.

The use of iron preparations presents another area in which an audit would be appropriate and helpful. Iron use is prevalent in long-term care facilities (Lamy and Krug, 1978), mainly to treat iron deficiency anemia and nonspecific complaints, and it is commonly viewed as a harmless substance (U.S. National Center for Health Statistics, 1974). Yet iron therapy is not without risk (Wintrobe, 1974; Souajian, 1975; AMA Drug Evaluations, 1977; Lamy and Krug, 1978). In one facility the use of iron was thought to be less than optimum, and the Pharmacy and Therapeutics Committee suggested an audit (Appendix 5-3). The audit revealed the following (Krug, 1979):

1. Anemia was a nearly universal finding in the elderly receiving iron. However, iron therapy in 60% of patients receiving it did not meet the criteria. Thus, although iron was used to treat anemia, rather than used prophylactically, many patients did not have further workup indicative of iron deficiency.

2. Nearly 88% of patients received an appropriate dose. Suboptimum therapy, in terms of dosing, was not a universal problem.

3. Fewer than one third of the elderly received expensive and/or irrational (combination) products.

4. Approximately 35% of patients were receiving iron for more than 1 year, despite a lack of documented response.

5. About 50% of patients received, in addition to iron, other hematinics, indicating a "shotgun" approach.

6. Nearly 80% of patients were inadequately monitored for response to iron therapy.

The results were disseminated to the prescribing staff through in-service programs. A reaudit revealed no improvement in the prescribing of iron. The intervention had failed. Other means are being developed to improve this problem area.

This finding pointed to the need that an audit must be designed to identify problems and to correct them. Only a reaudit will be able to confirm or deny the effectiveness of the specific intervention.

With these comments in mind, the following proposed pharmacy standards are presented, which consist of suggestions for medication review and proposed surveyor's guidelines.*

Text continued on p. 104.

---

*Based in part on the surveyor's indicators published concurrently with the newly proposed federal regulations.

Medication review

A. *Purpose*
   The purpose is to evaluate each patient's individual drug regimen (including dietary orders and non–drug measures, such as physical therapy) and to identify current drug problems and potential drug problems that affect the quality of care and appropriate use of pharmacy patient care services in long-term care facilities (LTCF)

B. *Pharmacy medication review*
   The medication review must be based on the patient's physical and psychologic status. A complete drug regimen review includes a review of all patient records by a pharmacist, followed by recommendations and notes where appropriate.
   1. *Review is performed monthly. Frequency may be increased when indicated by patient status and in case of major therapy changes. Follow-up between regular reviews should occur.*
   2. *There should be documentation of findings in the patient's medical record.*
   3. *Review is considered complete only with written response by the physician to the pharmacist's comments and recommendations in the patient's medical record.*

C. *Medication administration*
   1. *Medication shall be administered as ordered by the physician.*
   2. *The following are considered drug administration or transcription errors and should be so noted by the pharmacist:*
      a. *Wrong drug*
      b. *Outdated drug*
      c. *Unordered drug*
      d. *Incorrect strength*
      e. *Wrong dosage form*
      f. *Missed or omitted dose without documentation (e.g., refused, patient on leave of absence from facility)*
      g. *Wrong route of administration*
      h. *Wrong time of administration (more than 60 minutes from ordered time or before meals rather than after)*
      i. *Incorrect duration (administered for shorter or longer period of time than ordered)*
      j. *Lack of appropriate documentation on patient's record of administration of p.r.n. drug or patient response to p.r.n. or stat medications*

D. *Stop orders*
   Stop orders for appropriate drugs are to be established by the Pharmacy Services Committee.

E. *Availability of drugs*
   1. *Drugs not needed stat shall be available to the patient within a period of time acceptable to the Pharmacy Services Committee as appropriate for the facility's patients, unless otherwise ordered by the physician.*
   2. *If a drug is not available within the established time, the physician shall be notified immediately by the nurse with documentation of notification in the medical record.*
   3. *Procedures shall be developed by the Pharmacy Services Committee for obtaining drugs needed in the facility when an emergency arises.*

F. *Documentation of rationale for drug use*
   1. *Rationale for drug use cannot be reviewed by the pharmacist unless the following patient and therapy variables are noted:*
      a. *Intercurrent diseases that could affect the choice and effect of a drug*
      b. *Patient's pathophysiologic status: renal function, hepatic function, and total body weight. (Note: If data are absent, pharmacist shall request these values so that a rational review may take place.)*
      c. *Patient's nutritional status and dietary orders*
      d. *Results of all laboratory tests ordered*
   2. *The physician shall include in the progress notes the rationale for the initiation of or significant changes in drug therapy.*
   3. *The note should be written in such a manner that any reviewer or member of the health care team can understand the goal(s) of therapy and contribute where appropriate.*

Surveyor's guidelines*

Purpose: TO IDENTIFY POTENTIAL DRUG THERAPY PROBLEMS

NOTE: *An important measure of good patient care is physician response to recommendations by the consultant pharmacist following medication review.*
The physician's response serves several purposes: (1) it documents the receipt of the comment, (2) it serves to notify the pharmacist that comments have been received, and (3) it serves to enhance the educational and patient care functions of the process. The consultant pharmacist has an obligation to see that comments reach the intended recipient, and the physician's response serves to complete this process.

GUIDELINES *The surveyor's guidelines are presented in the left-hand column. Pertinent comments and rationale are documented in the right-hand column.*

Guidelines	Comments
DOSE REDUCTION	
1. In general, a reduction in the dose of most drugs from that recommended for the "average" adult is expected, based primarily on diminished renal function in the elderly	Reduction in renal function with aging is well recognized (Bender, 1964; Rowe et al., 1976). Thus the need for reduced doses of drugs eliminated by the kidneys must be anticipated (Triggs and Nation, 1975; Crooks, O'Malley, and Stevenson, 1976; Richey and Bender, 1977; Lamy, 1979). The effects of aging on liver function are less well characterized. However, reduced doses of drugs that are metabolized by the liver may also be necessary (Crooks, O'Malley, and Stevenson, 1976; Richey and Bender, 1977). There are also alterations in protein binding, fat/lean body ratio, and volumes of distribution (Triggs and Nation, 1975; Crooks, O'Malley, and Stevenson, 1976; Richey and Bender, 1977; Vestal, 1978; Lamy, 1979). Finally, the elderly may have altered drug sensitivity regardless of these changes (Vestal, 1978).
2. Antipsychotic drugs ordered in excess of one half of the listed dose for the "average" adult; for older adults with organic brain syndrome, the dose should be reduced by one half again (i.e., one fourth of the "average" adult dose)	The elderly are more sensitive to the effects of these drugs. The most troublesome side effects include orthostatic hypotension, sedation, anticholinergic effects, extrapyramidal effects, and tardive dyskinesia (Prein, Haber, and Caffey, 1975; "Dementia and Problems of Aging," 1979; Comptroller General, 1980; Hier and Caplan, 1980). *Continued.*

Pharmacy standards (side margin)

*Based in part on the surveyor's indicators published concurrently with the newly proposed federal regulations.

Surveyor's guidelines—cont'd

Pharmacy standards

Guidelines	Comments
INAPPROPRIATE DURATION OF THERAPY	
1. Drugs administered beyond established stop-order policies	
2. Drugs administered p.r.n. as directed every day for 30 days or more NOTE: *Some consultants suggest a much shorter maximum p.r.n. time than 30 days (i.e., 7 to 10 days). Others feel that a drug may be needed for a short time, but if a regular prescription is written, the drug is likely to be continued for a longer period.*	*P.R.N. drug use is a well documented area of neglect in the LTCF (Ingman et al., 1975); Howard, Strong, and Strong, 1977). This is an attempt to identify inappropriate use of p.r.n. medications. If drugs are needed on a regular basis, in general they should be ordered so that meaningful assessment of therapy can take place.*
3. Antidepressants used for less than 3 days	*The tricyclics, in general, will take several days and often up to 2 to 4 weeks to exert their full effects (Jarvick, 1970). Thus short-term use of these agents is inappropriate. For these reasons, frequent dose changes would be inappropriate.*
4. Antipsychotics used, in general, for less than 3 days (some deviations may be expected for some injections.)	*Antipsychotics, as is the case for antidepressants, take several days of continuous therapy to exert their optimum effect, and thus p.r.n. or short-term use would seem inappropriate.*
5. Hypnotic drugs used for more than 7 consecutive days NOTE: *This obviously would not apply to a patient transferred from another institution who may have received a hypnotic for a prolonged period of time. Sudden withdrawal may then be hazardous.*	*Hypnotics should not be used as long-term routine therapy. This is particularly true in the elderly (Exton-Smith, 1967). In addition to producing hangover, these drugs interfere with normal sleep patterns and lose their effectiveness with prolonged use (Greenblatt and Miller, 1974). Nightmares and delirium can occur with termination of long-term use. There is evidence that flurazepam possesses some advantages over the barbiturates (Kales et al., 1977).*
6. Antibiotic ophthalmic drugs used for more than 10 days	*Continued need for any antibiotic, in this case for the eye, should be reassessed frequently to document continued need and patient response.*

Pharmacy standards

Guidelines	*Comments*
INAPPROPRIATE MULTIPLE THERAPY	
1. Multiple orders of the same drug or class of drug for the same patient	*Polypharmacy is common in the LTCF (Office of Long Term Care, 1976). One reasonable attempt to limit this would be to eliminate duplication of medications. This would be expected to reduce costs as well as improve care (Ingman et al., 1975).*
2. The use of more than one type of multi-vitamin per day	*Specific deficiencies should be treated individually. The "shotgun" approach is to be discouraged. As a general supplement, there is no evidence that the use of multiple combination products has any advantage over the use of one appropriate multivitamin supplement.*
3. The use of two or more laxatives concurrently, including p.r.n. medications	*Laxative use is high in the LTCF (Lamy and Krug, 1978). Multiple laxative therapy may be a clue to inappropriate laxative use. It is desirable that the effects of one preparation are assessed before additional ones are added to the regimen.*
4. The concomitant use of hypnotic drugs	*Hypnotic use is a problem. There is no evidence that therapy with combined agents possesses any advantage over the judicious use of a single agent (Greenblatt and Miller, 1974).*
5. The concomitant use of any of the antipsychotics, unless need is documented by a psychiatrist	*There is no evidence that therapy with combined antipsychotics has any advantage over the proper use of one single agent (Casey et al., 1961; Freeman, 1967; Jarvick, 1970). Attempts to mix these drugs to minimize side effects have been largely disappointing (Freeman, 1967).*
6. Antibiotic-steroid mixtures for ophthalmic use, unless ordered by an ophthalmologist	*Long-term use of topical steroids can increase intraocular pressure. Topical steroids also exhibit cataractogenic properties (Kitazawa, 1970; Theodore, 1975).*

Continued.

Surveyor's guidelines—cont'd

Guidelines	*Comments*
INAPPROPRIATE CHANGE IN THERAPEUTIC REGIMEN	
1. More than two changes of antidepressants within a 7-day period	*This was discussed under "Inappropriate Duration of Therapy," number 3.*
2. Change from one dosage form to another without follow-up	*The dosage form may have an important influence on drug absorption and, thus, action. Important examples include digoxin, phenytoin, and theophylline.*

INAPPROPRIATE SIGNS, SYMPTOMS, AND LABORATORY TESTS

APICAL PULSE

1. Elderly persons receiving digitalis therapy who have not had apical pulse rate and rhythm recorded daily	*Pulse rate and rhythm are important parameters to monitor both digitalis efficacy and toxicity. Both apical and peripheral pulses should be taken. If the apical pulse rate is greater than the peripheral pulse rate, then a pulse deficit, as occurs in atrial fibrillation, is present. The apical pulse is always more accurate than the peripheral pulse.*
2. Elderly persons using β-blocker therapy who do not have a daily pulse rate recorded or who have a pulse consistently below 50	*Bradycardia is a significant side effect of β-blockers.*
3. Elderly persons using antidysrhythmic therapy who have not had an apical pulse recorded daily	*The apical pulse is an important therapeutic and toxicity parameter for monitoring antidysrhythmic therapy.*

HEMATOLOGY

1. Elderly persons receiving anticoagulant therapy (except minidose heparin) who have not had some assessment of clotting function at least every month and a hematocrit at least every 3 months	*A monthly prothrombin time is the minimal acceptable frequency for monitoring warfarin. Full dose heparin would need more frequent blood work assessment but is unlikely to be encountered in a LTCF. A hematocrit is an important means of identifying occult bleeding in the patient receiving anticoagulants.*
2. Elderly persons receiving iron preparations, folic acid, or vitamin B$_{12}$ who have not had a red blood cell assessment (i.e., hemoglobin/hematocrit and peripheral blood smears) before therapy, during the first month of therapy, and at least every 6 months thereafter	*These tests are necessary to properly identify anemia and are needed to avoid a "shotgun" approach to therapy. Repeat tests (hemoglobin/hematocrit) are needed to document response to therapy, thus reaffirming the diagnosis.*

Pharmacy standards

Guidelines	**Comments**
SERUM ELECTROLYTES	
1. Elderly persons receiving diuretics who have not had serum electrolyte (Na^+, K^+, Cl^-, HCO_3^-) determinations and a blood urea nitrogen test (BUN) within 30 days after initiation of therapy or significant change in dose; tests should be routinely repeated every 6 months	Diuretics may profoundly alter the electrolyte balance and cause dehydration; this is particularly true in the elderly (Vestal, 1978). These tests should be performed soon after initiation of or change in therapy to identify potential problems.
2. Elderly persons receiving digitalis therapy who have not had a renal function test (BUN, creatinine) before initiation of therapy, a baseline serum electrolyte determination within 30 days of therapy, and routine determinations every 6 months thereafter NOTE: For patients with labile renal function, *creatinine clearance,* not *serum creatinine,* should be used as an indicator of renal function.	Digoxin is highly dependent on renal function for elimination, and the elderly often have decreased renal function (Bender, 1964; Rowe et al., 1976). A baseline renal function test is needed in choosing a dose. Because alterations in electrolytes (particularly K^+ and Ca^{++}) may affect digoxin sensitivity, a baseline should be obtained and followed during therapy. This is particularly important in elderly persons taking concurrent diuretic therapy.
URINARY TESTS	
1. Elderly persons receiving methenamine therapy whose urinary bacterial count has not been determined at least once within 30 days of initiation of therapy	Methenamine salts are effective only for suppression of bacteriuria and are ineffective as initial treatment. Acute infections must be eliminated before therapy is begun (Lamy, 1980e).
2. Elderly persons receiving methenamine therapy who have not had a determination of urine pH before initiation of therapy and frequently enough thereafter to assure maintenance of an acidic urine	An acidic pH is necessary for effective methenamine therapy. Optimal pH is 5.5, and there is essentially no effect when the urinary pH is above 6.2 (Musher and Griffith, 1974; Naccarto, Bell, and Lamy, 1979).
3. Elderly persons receiving nitrofurantoin therapy	
a. Whose BUN or creatinine has not been determined before initiation of therapy	Nitrofurantoin is not concentrated sufficiently in the urine if renal function is diminished (Product Information, Norwick-Eaton Pharmaceuticals); thus adequate renal function should be assured.
b. Whose urine bacterial count has not been determined at least once every 30 days after therapy has begun	This is a routine assessment parameter in monitoring chronic suppressive therapy.

Continued.

Surveyor's guidelines—cont'd

Guidelines	Comments
MISCELLANEOUS	
1. Elderly persons who repeatedly lose seizure control while receiving anticonvulsant therapy	*Loss of seizure control may indicate inadequate therapy or inappropriate therapy.*
2. Elderly persons receiving thyroid drugs who have not had a reassessment of thyroid function with a change in maintenance dose or when the clinical condition dictates	*In general adequacy of thyroid replacement should be documented by thyroid function tests as a confirmation of clinical response (Ingbar and Woeber, 1978).*
3. Elderly persons receiving antihypertensive therapy who have not had a blood pressure determination at least weekly, unless stable	*Elderly persons may exhibit changing needs for these medications, and blood pressure should be monitored to assure efficacy and to detect side effects (e.g., orthostatic hypotension).*
NOTE: *Blood pressure should be assessed and recorded with the patient in the supine, sitting, and standing positions.*	
4. Elderly persons receiving insulin who have not had a urinary glucose and ketone test at least weekly	*This is self-explanatory.*
NOTE: *These, or more accurate blood tests, need to be performed daily for labile diabetics.*	
5. Elderly persons receiving insulin or an oral hypoglycemic who have not had a fasting blood sugar or a 2-hour postprandial test at least every 90 days	*Fasting blood sugar determination is needed because the results of the urine test may be somewhat undependable: they are interfered with by many drugs and diseases, and the renal threshold for glucose increases with age (Koda-Kimble, 1979).*

Pharmacy standards

OTHER AREAS OF CONSIDERATION

As previously pointed out, the suggested guidelines can form only a framework; they do not cover all areas of importance or all areas where consultant pharmacists can importantly contribute to the care of the elderly by applying their knowledge of pharmacokinetics, toxicology, and drug costs. One important area is the use of antibiotics in long-term care facilities. Although in many (but not all) instances antibiotics are prescribed based on sensitivity testing, the fact that

this information alone does not assure appropriate therapy is often overlooked. Simply put, the drug must reach the desired site of action. Thus it may not be at all unusual to see antibiotics used in the management of urinary tract and respiratory tract infections and pressure sores, which may well be indicated based on sensitivity testing but which would not be effective. Examples would include the use of oral carbenicillin to treat wound infections, the use of cephalosporins to treat meningitis, nitrofurantoin to treat infections in patients with poor renal function, and the use of oral aminoglycosides to treat patients with systemic (nonintestinal) infections. In short, the laboratory reports only the sensitivity of an organism to a particular drug in vitro but does not indicate that the drug would be effective in vivo.

Sensitivity reports also imply that all drugs in a certain class would be effective (e.g., first-generation cephalosporins, penicillinase-resistant penicillins, tetracyclines). Although this is not always true, this information can be valuable for other reasons as well. For example, a laboratory might report sensitivity to cephalosporins, established by using a cephaloridine disk. Yet cephaloridine should not be selected because it is the most toxic of all cephalosporins. The pharmacist, having studied the laboratory report, can then suggest a drug that is least toxic to a specific patient and also, importantly, the least expensive of the clinically effective drugs.

Pharmacokinetic knowledge will permit the consultant pharmacist to advise on the proper dose (both loading and maintenance) to be selected, based on the patient's renal status, age, weight, and other factors.

It is also important to consider other patient characteristics. Many elderly patients experience problems with swallowing solid oral dosage forms. Obviously, some means of easing problems with drug administration must then be suggested. It is common to note the crushing of solid oral dosage forms in long-term care facilities as well as the increased use of liquid dosage forms. The pharmacist is qualified to advise both the nursing and medical staff on the stability of crushed medications, the cost of alternative liquid dosage forms, availability and effectiveness of liquid dosage forms as compared with solid dosage forms, the characteristics of particular solid dosage forms such as enteric-coated or sustained-release tablets, and the potential for gastrointestinal irritation of specific dosage forms and changes in dosage forms (e.g., crushing of tablets). All these considerations can then lead to an informed suggestion about the best dosage form to use for a particular patient.

SUMMARY

Pharmacist-performed drug regimen review was originally mandated in 1974. Several studies have demonstrated the cost benefit of these reviews. It has also been suggested that these reviews may promote rational prescribing and decrease medication errors.

APPENDIX 5-1

CONSIDERATIONS REGARDING AN AUDIT

1. Time spent in developing objective, specific, reliable, and well-focused criteria will pay rich dividends in producing useful data.
2. Audit objectives should be simple.
3. Assessment of large or complex problems will be more difficult than initially realized and will most likely not result in better data than a simple audit.
4. Constructive, multidisciplinary, corrective actions should be planned. Different methodologies may have to be used in different facilities.
5. A reaudit is absolutely necessary to assess the effectiveness of intervention(s).

APPENDIX 5-2

CRITERIA FOR DIGOXIN LEVEL AUDIT*

Indication

1. Subtherapeutic response
   a. No improvement or worsening of congestive heart failure or atrial fibrillation
   b. Unstable on admission with suspected noncompliance
2. Suspected toxicity
   a. New dysrhythmia
   b. Non–cardiac signs of toxicity
3. Suspected alteration of pharmacokinetics
   a. Elevated BUN or serum creatinine
   b. Anyone 55 years or older receiving greater than 0.125 mg/day of digoxin
   c. Any change in BUN or serum creatinine
4. Follow-up of abnormal level

---

*Presented to and accepted by the facility's Pharmacy and Therapeutics Committee.

Performance

1. Sampling time
   a. At least 6 hours after last oral dose
2. Steady state should be achieved before observing level
   a. Without loading dose: after 7 days of maintenance therapy
   b. With full loading dose: 6 hours after first maintenance dose

Evaluation/action

1. Serum level
   a. Less than 0.5 ng/ml—increase dose or discontinue drug
   b. 0.5 to 2.1 ng/ml—no change unless less than 1.4 ng/ml and symptomatic of disease under treatment
   c. Greater than 2.1 ng/ml
      (1) Symptomatic: hold and decrease dose
      (2) Asymptomatic: hold (optional) and decrease dose, unless patient is in atrial fibrillation and not clinically toxic

APPENDIX 5-3

CRITERIA FOR IRON UTILIZATION AUDIT

1. Use criteria
   a. Determination of presence of iron deficiency anemia
      (1) Hematocrit and/or hemoglobin below normal for sex (Wintrobe, 1974)
      (2) Peripheral blood smear and/or red cell indices compatible with microcytic/hypochromic anemia; mean corpuscular volume (MCV) below normal for sex; mean corpuscular hemoglobin concentration (MCHC) may or may not be reduced but should not be elevated (Wintrobe, 1974)
      (3) Anemia indicated by decreased serum iron, increased iron binding capacity, and decreased transferrin saturation. These tests are costly. If the first two criteria are met, a therapeutic trial may be initiated (Wintrobe, 1974; Wintrobe and Bunn, 1977).
      (4) The response to iron (see 3a) will serve to document the cause of the anemia as iron deficiency if the therapeutic trial has been performed.

   b. Determination of cause of anemia
      (1) Stool for occult blood and, when indicated, other diagnostic tests are needed to determine the cause of the anemia (Wintrobe, 1974; Wintrobe and Bunn, 1977).
2. Process criteria
   a. Dose: in general, a dose of 100 mg/day elemental iron should be provided. This will produce a response equal to that of the traditional 200 mg dose (McGanity and Cannon, 1959; Wintrobe, 1974; AMA Drug Evaluations, 1977). If iron is to be administered with meals, 200 mg daily should be administered (McGanity and Cannon, 1959).
   b. Preparation: ferrous sulfate tablets are low in cost and are generally well accepted by patients. They should be used. Other single entity iron preparations are acceptable if better patient acceptance is documented at an equivalent dose of iron. Preparations containing ascorbic acid, other hematinics or vitamins, or sustained-release preparations are usually no more effective than ferrous sulfate and should not be used.
   c. Duration of treatment: iron administration should be continued for 6 months after the anemic state has been normalized. This will replenish the iron stores. Further use of iron is only based on specific indications, such as inability to provide sufficient iron in the diet or continued blood loss (Wintrobe, 1974; AMA Drug Evaluations, 1977).
   d. Time of administration: iron preparations should not be coadministered (within 2 hours) with tetracycline or antacid products containing divalent or trivalent cations (e.g., Al^{+++}, Ca^{++}, Mg^{++}) (Hall and Davis, 1969; Hansten, 1979).
   e. Monitoring of therapy: effectiveness of iron therapy must be monitored through
      (1) Reticulocyte count between days 4 and 9 (Wintrobe, 1974; Wintrobe and Bunn, 1977).
      (2) Hemoglobin determination, monthly, until normal (Wintrobe, 1974).
   f. Documentation
      (1) Presence of anemia should be documented in the problem list.
      (2) Patient intolerance (constipation, dyspepsia) should be documented in the progress notes.
3. Outcome criteria
   a. Reticulocyte count should show a definite in-

crease (over 2% corrected) on initial determination. This indicates patient response (Wintrobe, 1974; Wintrobe and Bunn, 1977). If no increase is noted, anemia is unresponsive to iron.

  b. Hemoglobin should be within normal limits within 6 to 8 weeks (Wintrobe, 1974; Wintrobe and Bunn, 1977).

  c. Cause of anemia should have been identified.

REFERENCES

American Medical Association: Drug evaluations: ed. 3, Littleton, Mass., 1977, Publishers Science Group.

Avorn, J.: Nursing-home infections: the context, N. Engl. J. Med. **305:**759, 1981.

Beller, G.A., et al.: Digitalis intoxication—a prospective clinical study with serum level correlations, N. Engl. J. Med. **284:**989, 1971.

Bender, A.D., The effect of increasing age on the distribution of peripheral blood flow in man, J. Am. Geriatr. Soc. **13:**192, 1964.

Borda, I.T., Slone, D., and Jick, H.: Assessment of adverse drug reactions within a drug surveillance program, J.A.M.A. **205:**645, 1968.

Braunwald, E., and Klucke, F.J.: Digitalis, Annu. Rev. Med. **16:**371, 1965.

Brodie, D.C., Lofholm, P., and Benson, R.A.: A model for drug use review in a skilled nursing facility, J. Am. Pharm. Assoc. **17:**617, 1977.

Brown, C.H.: Automatic stop-order policy for p.r.n. medications in skilled nursing facilities, Contemp. Pharm. Pract. **4:**59, 1981.

Brown, C.H., and DeSimone, E.M.: Use of p.r.n. medications in skilled nursing facilities, Contemp. Pharm. Pract. **3:**209, 1980.

Carter, B.L., Small, R.E., and Garnett, W.R.: Monitoring digoxin therapy in two long-term care facilities, J. Am. Geriatr. Soc. **29:**263, 1981.

Casey, J.F., et al.: Combined drug therapy of chronic schizophrenics, Am. J. Psychiatry **117:**997, 1961.

Cheung, A., and Kayne, R.: An application of clinical pharmacy services in extended care facilities, Calif. Pharm. **23:**22, 1975.

Ciullo, J., and Shepherd, M.: Drug discard patterns in long-term care facilities, J. Am. Pharm. Assoc. **17:**739, 1977.

Comptroller General: Report to the Congress of the United States: problems remain in review of medi-

caid-financed drug therapy in nursing homes, (HRD-80-56) Washington, D.C., 1980, U.S. General Accounting Office.

Congress to cope with cutting health care costs: Today's Nursing Home **3**(2):11, 1982.

Cooper, J.W., and Bagwell, C.G.: Contribution of the consultant pharmacist to rational drug usage in the long-term care facility, J. Am. Geriatr. Soc. **26:**513, 1978.

Crooks, J., O'Malley, K., and Stevenson, I.H.: Pharmacokinetics in the elderly, Clin. Pharmacokinet. **1:**280, 1976.

Dementia and problems of aging: Clinical Pathological Conference, Am. J. Med. **67:**307, 1979.

Department of Health and Human Services: Conditions of participation for skilled nursing and intermediate care facilities, Fed. Register **47:**368, July 14, 1980.

Exton-Smith, A.N.: The use and abuse of hypnotics, Gerontol. Clin. **9:**264, 1967.

Freeman, H.: The therapeutic value of combinations of psychotropic drugs, a review, Psychopharm. Bull. **4:**1, 1967.

Greenblatt, D.J., and Miller, R.R.: Rationale use of psychotropic drugs: hypnotics, Am. J. Hosp. Pharm. **31:**990, 1974.

Hall, G.J.L., and Davis, A.E.: Inhibition of iron absorption by magnesium trisilicate, Med. J. Aust. **2:**95, 1969.

Hansten, P.D.: Drug interactions, ed. 4, Philadelphia, 1979, Lea & Febiger.

Hickox, R.F.: Expenditures will double by 1986, triple by 1990, Today's Nurs. Home **3**(2):9, 1982.

Hier, D.B., and Caplan, L.R.: Drugs for senile dementia, Drugs **20:**74, 1980.

Hoddinot, B.C.: Drug reactions and errors in administration on a medical ward, Can. Med. Assoc. J. **97:**1001, 1967.

Holland, O.B., Nixon, J.V., and Kuhnert, L.: Diuretic-induced ventricular ectopic activity, Am. J. Med. **70:**762, 1980.

Hollister, L.E.: Prescribing drugs for the elderly, Geriatrics **32**(8):71, 1977.

Hood, J.C., Lemberger, M., and Stewart, R.B.: Promoting appropriate therapy in a long-term care facility, J. Am. Pharm. Assoc. **15:**32, 1975.

Howard, J.B., Strong, K.E., Jr., Strong, K.E., Sr.: Medication procedures in a nursing home: abuse of p.r.n. orders, J. Am. Geriatr. Soc. **25:**83, 1977.

Howard, J.B., Strong, K.E., Sr., and Strong, K.E., Jr.: Nursing home medication costs, J. Am. Geriatr. Soc. **26:**228, 1978.

Hurwitz, N.: Predisposing factors in adverse reactions to drugs, Br. Med. J. **1:**536, 1969.

Hurwitz, N., and Wade, O.L.: Intensive hospital monitoring of adverse reactions surveillance program, Br. Med. J. **1:**531, 1969.

Ingbar, S.H., and Woeber, K.A.: Diseases of the thyroid. In Thorn, G.W., editor: Principles of internal medicine, ed. 8, New York, 1978, McGraw-Hill, Inc.

Ingelfinger, J.P., and Goldman, P.: The serum digitalis concentration—does it diagnose digitalis toxicity? N. Engl. J. Med. **295:**867, 1976.

Ingman, S.R., et al.: A survey of the prescribing and administration of drugs in a long term care institution for the elderly, J. Am. Geriatr. Soc. **23:**309, 1975.

Jarvick, M.E.: Drugs used in the treatment of psychiatric disorders. In Goodman, L.S., and Gilman, A.: The pharmacological basis of therapeutics, New York, 1970, Macmillan, Inc., pp. 151-203.

Kales, A., et al.: Comparative effectiveness of nonhypnotic drugs: sleep lab studies, J. Clin. Pharmacol. **17:**207, 1977.

Kitazawa, Y.: Primary angle-closure glaucoma, corticosteroid responsiveness, Arch. Ophthalmol. **84:**724, 1970.

Koda-Kimble, M.A.: Diabetes mellitus. In Koda-Kimble, M.A., Katcher, B., and Young, L., editors: Applied therapeutics for clinical pharmacists, San Francisco, 1979, Applied Therapeutics, Inc.

Krug, B.H.: Iron utilization in a skilled nursing facility, unpublished data, 1979.

Krug, B.H.: Digoxin level audit performed at metropolitan extended care facility, unpublished data, 1981.

Lamy, P.P.: Considerations in drug therapy of the elderly, J. Drug Issues **9**(3):27, 1979.

Lamy, P.P.: Drug interactions and the elderly—a new perspective, Drug Intell. Clin. Pharm. **14:**513, 1980a.

Lamy, P.P.: How your patient's diet can affect drug response, Drug Ther. **10**(8):82, 1980b.

Lamy, P.P., Misuse and abuse of drugs by the elderly—another view, Am. Pharm. **20:**14, 1980c.

Lamy, P.P.: Operation common sense: proposed new federal regulations for nursing homes, Contemp. Pharm. Practice. **3**(3):vi, 1980d.

Lamy, P.P.: Prescribing for the elderly, Littleton, Mass., 1980e, Publishing Sciences Group.

Lamy, P.P.: Drug prescribing for the elderly, Bull. NY Acad. Med. **57:**718, 1981a.

Lamy, P.P.: Special features of geriatric prescribing, Geriatrics **36**(12):42, 1981b.

Lamy, P.P., and Krug, B.H.: Review of laxative utilization in a skilled nursing facility, J. Am. Geriatr. Soc. **26:**544, 1978.

Lamy, P.P., and Vestal, R.E., Drug prescribing for the elderly, Hosp. Pract. **11**(10):111, 1976.

Lang, L.A., and Kabat, H.F.: Drug interactions in nursing home patient prescriptions, J. Am. Pharm. Assoc. **10:**674, 1970.

Laventurier, M.F., et al.: Drug utilization and potential drug-drug interactions, J. Am. Pharm. Assoc. **16:**77, 1976.

Letourneau, K.N.: Drug utilization review in an extended care facility, Drug Intell. Clin. Pharm. **8:**108, 1974.

Levine, P.J.: Quality drug care and cost containment in long-term care facilities, Perspectives, p. 17, Feb. 1980.

Liu, K., and Mossey, J.: The role of payment source in differentiating nursing home residents, services, and payments, Health Care Fin. Rev. **2**(1):51, 1980.

Martilla, J.K., and Green, B.A.: Auditing antiparkinson drugs: guidelines for appropriate medication use, Contemp. Pharm. Pract. **2**(1):11, 1979.

McGanity, W.J., and Cannon, R.O.: Iron deficiency in gynecologic patients, Am. J. Clin. Nutr. **7:**638, 1959.

McGhan, W.F., Wertheimer, A.I., and Martilla, J.K.: Assessing the need for pharmacist-conducted drug regimen reviews in skilled nursing and intermediate care facilities, Contemp. Pharm. Prac. **3:**203, 1980.

Michocki, R., Wiser, T., and Lamy, P.P.: Antibiotic audit, Washington, D.C., 1981, American Pharmaceutical Association.

Miller, D.A., et al.: Perceived clinical significance of consultant pharmacist recommendations in the skilled nursing facility, Drug Intell. Clin. Pharm. **14:**182, 1980.

Multicenter Diuretic Cooperative Study Group: Multiclinic comparison of amiloride, hydrochlorothiazide and hydrochlorothiazide plus amiloride in essential hypertension, Arch. Intern. Med. **141**:482, 1981.

Musher, D.M., and Griffith, D.P.: Generation of formaldehyde from methenamine: effect of pH and concentration and antibacterial effect, Antimicrob. Agents Chemother. **6**:708, 1974.

Naccarto, D.V., Bell, C.J., and Lamy, P.P.: Appraisal of ascorbic acid for acidifying the urine of methenamine-treated geriatric patients, J. Am. Geriatr. Soc. **27**:34, 1979.

Office of Long Term Care: Long-term care facility improvement campaign, Monograph No. 2, Physician's drug prescribing patterns in skilled nursing facilities, Rockville, Md., 1976, DHEW Pub. No. 75-50059.

Ogilvie, R.I., and Ruedy, J.: Adverse drug reactions during hospitalization, Can. Med. Assoc. J. **97**:1450, 1967.

Patry, R.A., and Kroeger, R.: Drug waste and prescribing patterns in two nursing homes, Contemp. Pharm. Pract. **1**(1):28, 1978.

Prein, R.F., Haber, P.A., Caffey, E.M.: The use of psychoactive drugs in elderly patients with psychiatric disorders: survey conducted in twelve Veterans Administration hospitals, J. Am. Geriatr. Soc. **23**:104, 1975.

Product Information: Macrodantin, Norwich, N.Y., Norwich-Eaton Pharmaceuticals.

Rawlings, J.L., and Frisk, P.A.: Pharmaceutical services for skilled nursing facilities in compliance with federal regulations, Am. J. Hosp. Pharm. **32**:905, 1975.

Rawlings, J., and Mathieson, D.: Unit dose packaging spurs optimum therapy in "Project ECG," Pharm. Times **36**:50, 1976.

Richey, D.P., and Bender, A.D.: Pharmacokinetic consequences of aging, Annu. Rev. Pharmacol. Toxicol. **17**:49, 1977.

Rosenwaike, I., Yaffe, N., and Sagi, O.C.: The recent decline in mortality of the extreme aged: an analysis of statistical data, Am. J. Public Health **70**:1074, 1980.

Ross, G.: Geriatric enteral hyperalimentation. II. Nutr. Supp. Serv. **1**(7):18, 1981.

Rowe, J.W., et al.: The effect of age on creatinine clearance in man: a cross-sectional and longitudinal study, J. Gerontol. **31**:155, 1976.

Segal, J.L., Thompson, J.F., and Floyd, R.A.: Drug

utilization and prescribing patterns in a skilled nursing facility: the need for a rational approach to therapeutics, J. Am. Geriatr. Soc. **27**:117, 1979.

Seidl, L.G., et al.: Studies on the epidemiology of adverse reactions. III. Reactions in patients on a general service, Bull. Johns Hopkins Hosp. **119**: 299, 1966.

Shepherd, M.D.: Medicaid and non-medicaid drug discards in long-term care facilities, Contemp. Pharm. Pract. **2**(1):14, 1979.

Souajian, J.: Iron supplements and the risks involved, Drug Ther. **5**(7):27, 1975.

Standards for certification and participation in medicare and medicaid programs, Fed. Register **39**:12, 1974.

Stewart, J.B., et al.: Monitoring drug therapy in skilled nursing facility patients, Drug Intell. Clin. Pharm. **12**:704, 1978.

Strandberg, L.R., et al.: Drug utilization and pharmacy services in the long-term care facility: an eight year study, Am. J. Hosp. Pharm. **37**:92, 1980a.

Strandberg, L.R., et al.: Effect of comprehensive pharmaceutical services on drug use in long-term care facilities, Am. J. Hosp. Pharm. **37**:92, 1980b.

Theodore, F.H.: External eye problems in the elderly, Geriatrics **30**(4):69, 1975.

Tomaiolo, P.P., Enman, S., and Kraus, V.: Preventing and treating malnutrition in the elderly, J. Parent Ent. Nutr. **5**(1):46, 1981.

Triggs, E.J., and Nation, R.L.: Pharmacokinetics in the aged: a review, J. Pharmacokinet. Biopharmaceut. **3**:387, 1975.

Triggs, E.J., Nation, R.L., and Long, A.: Pharmacokinetics in the elderly, Eur. J. Clin. Pharmacol. **8**:55, 1975.

Trunet, P., et al.: Iatrogenic disease and admissions to intensive care, J.A.M.A. **244**:2617, 1980.

U.S. National Center for Health Statistics: 1973-74 Nursing home survey—provisional data. (HRA 75-1120), Washington, D.C., 1974, U.S. Government Printing Office.

Vancura, E.J., and Martilla, J.K.: Monitoring drug therapy: an applied approach, Contemp. Pharm. Pract. **4**:238, 1981.

Vestal, R.E.: Drug use in the elderly: a review of problems and special considerations, Drugs **16**:358, 1978.

Vlasses, P.H., et al.: Drug therapy in a skilled nursing facility: an innovative approach, J. Am. Pharm. Assoc. **17:**93, 1976.

Williamson, J., and Chopin, J.M.: Adverse reactions to prescribed drugs in the elderly: a multicentre investigation, Age Ageing **9**(2):73, 1980.

Wintrobe, M.M.: Clinical hematology, ed. 7, Philadelphia, 1974, Lea & Febiger.

Wintrobe, M.M., and Bunn, H.F.: Iron deficiency anemia and the sideroblastic anemias. In Harrison, T.R., editor: Principles of internal medicine, ed. 8, New York, 1977, McGraw-Hill, Inc.

Young, L.Y., et al.: Decreased medication costs in a skilled nursing facility by clinical pharmacy services, Contemp. Pharm. Pract. **4:**233, 1981.

Zimmer, J.G.: Medical care evaluation studies in long-term care facilities, J. Am. Geriatr. Soc. **27:**62, 1979.

CHAPTER 6

Physiologic changes and clinical manifestations of aging

Duncan Robertson

The purpose of this chapter is to provide a brief overview of the physiologic changes that occur as a consequence of normal human aging. Some references will be made to common age-related disorders; however, only those changes that are universal, decremental, and irreversible will be considered as part of normal human aging.

It is not intended that all physiologic changes that occur with normal human aging be included, but changes, particularly those changes that affect drug handling or therapeutics, that are of relevance to the physician, pharmacist, nurse, and other health professionals are discussed. In this regard this chapter will serve as a basis for much of what will be discussed in following chapters. The physiologic changes and clinical manifestations of aging in various organs and body systems comprise the first sections of this chapter, followed by alterations in the homeostatic control and in the integrated function of several systems.

CARDIOVASCULAR SYSTEM

The high prevalence of atherosclerosis and its complications in North American and Western European populations leads to difficulty in separating changes caused by aging from those caused by atherosclerosis. In the absence of significant atherosclerosis there are a number of macroscopic and microscopic changes in the aged heart.

Autopsy studies have shown that the hearts of older subjects are generally smaller than those of younger subjects and that this difference persists even when heart weight is corrected for differences in body weight. Gross inspection shows increased density and sclerosis of the collagen of the cardiac skeleton and calcification, particularly of the aortic and mitral valve rings. Lipid deposits are found in the collagen layer of the aortic and mitral valve cusps, and there is a diffuse increase in the thickness of the endocardium, particularly in the atria. Within the myocardium, small fibrotic lesions, without the characteristics of healed infarcts, are present (Schwartz and Mitchell, 1962).

The myocardium itself, either externally or on its cut surface, may have a brown color that, when marked and associated with reduced heart size, is known as brown atrophy of the heart. The pigment responsible for this appearance, lipofuscin, forms yellow-brown granules at the poles of the myofiber nuclei. Lipofuscin probably derives from mitochondrial membranes and accumulates in these and other postmitotic cells with age. Lipofuscin, an intracellular deposit, is thought not to affect myofiber performance.

On the other hand, the intercellular deposition of cardiac amyloid may cause heart failure secondary to restrictive cardiomyopathy when severe. Between 12% and 15% of aged persons coming to autopsy have obvious cardiac amyloidosis (Cohen, 1965; Pomerance, 1976). Amyloid deposits are most commonly seen under the left atrial endocardium and between myocardial fibers. In one detailed study 42% of 300 autopsies performed on elderly persons showed some cardiac amyloid infiltration, with heavy ventricular involvement found in 5% (Pomerance, Slavin, and McWatt, 1976).

Of the age changes within the conducting system of the heart, the most marked change is seen in the sinoatrial (SA) node. Pacemaker cells (P cells) constitute about 50% of cells in the SA node region in young adults (James et al., 1966). There is a decline in P cells with age, and many persons aged 75 and over show fibrosis of the SA node region, with P cells accounting for less than 10% of all cells in the node (Davies and Pomerance, 1972). The atrial myocardium between the SA node and the atrioventricular (AV) node shows some increase in the content of elastin, collagen, and fat; however, the changes both in the internodal atrial myocardium and in the AV node are small in comparison with those in the SA node region. The bundle of His and the right and left bundle branches show loss of fascicles and an increase in fine fibrous tissue and elastin.

The anatomic changes in the SA node are reflected in a reduced intrinsic heart rate (Jose, 1966; Frick, Heikkila, and Kahanpaa, 1967). The intrinsic heart rate is a measure of the intrinsic rhythmicity of the SA node, which can be determined by simultaneous sympathetic and parasympathetic blockade. The presence of "lone fibrillation" or atrial fibrillation in the elderly, unaccompanied by significant cardiac disease or evidence of congestive heart failure (Evans and Swann, 1954), may be a result of the reduced number of P cells in the SA node.

The cardiac output in 67 healthy men aged 19 to 86 years was lower in the older men. The re-

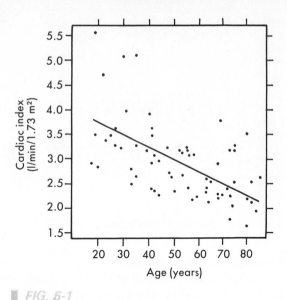

FIG. 6-1

Cardiac index versus age. (From Brandfonbrener, M., Landowne, M., and Shock, N.W.: Circulation **12**:557, 1955. By permission of the American Heart Association, Inc.)

duced cardiac output in older subjects would, if occurring longitudinally, correspond to a 1% drop in cardiac output each year (Brandfonbrener, Landowne, and Shock, 1955). When cardiac output was corrected for body size and the cardiac index calculated, approximately one half of this change was found to be caused by diminished body size of the older adult and one half resulted from changes in the stroke index and heart rate (Fig. 6-1).

The mean blood pressure rises with age; however, there is only a slight increase in diastolic pressure between early or middle adult life and old age (Fig. 6-2). The rise in systolic blood pressure with increasing age reflects diminished arterial compliance. Cross-sectional and longitudinal studies of blood pressure with age have been reviewed by Kohn (1977).

Postural hypotension, defined as a drop in systolic pressure of 20 mm Hg (or more) or diastolic

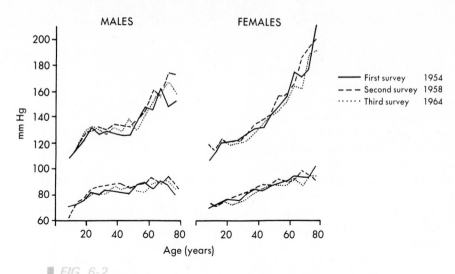

FIG. 6-2

Mean systolic and diastolic blood pressures in three
community surveys in South Wales. (From Miall, W.E., and
Lovell, H.G.: Br. Med. J. **2:**660, 1967.)

pressure of 10 mm Hg (or more) or both, when
a person moves from the supine to the standing
position, is a cause of light-headedness, falls, and
impaired mobility. It is perhaps of more clinical
significance than the absolute blood pressure
reading in the older person. Approximately 17%
of hospitalized elderly persons were found to
have postural hypotension (Johnson et al., 1964),
and 11% of reasonably healthy older persons living at home had postural hypotension by these
criteria (Caird, Andrews, and Kennedy, 1973).

The high prevalence of postural hypotension
in the older population must be kept in mind
when prescribing drugs that are intended to have
an effect on the blood pressure or that produce
postural hypotension as an adverse or side effect, such as tricyclic antidepressants, antiparkinsonian drugs, and phenothiazines.

NERVOUS SYSTEM

The structural and functional changes in the
central and peripheral nervous system that have

been ascribed to aging are complex, and some
are controversial.

That brains from older subjects weigh less
than those from younger subjects is well established (Pearl, 1922; Pakkenberg and Voigt, 1964).
Whether or not this represents a cohort effect,
in that brain weight correlates with body weight
and persons born in earlier generations are
lighter and smaller than those born more recently, is uncertain. Animal experiments comparing
brain weight of young and old animals of comparable size showed no change in brain weight
(Finch, 1973). Although there may be a slight
shrinkage of the gyri and enlargement of the
sulci, marked atrophy and ventricular dilatation,
when present, is not a feature of aging but of
dementia of the Alzheimer type.

Changes within neurons include the accumulation of lipofuscin, whose presence may or may
not affect neuronal function, and loss of horizontal dendrites of pyramidal cells of the cerebral
cortex (Schiebel and Schiebel, 1975). There have
been several studies that suggest loss of nerve

cells from the brain (Brody, 1955; Brody, 1970; Schefer, 1973; Tomlinson, 1976). The loss of cells is patchy, with up to 45% of cells being lost from the superior temporal gyrus by the ninth decade (Brody, 1955) but other areas, such as the inferior olive, showing no loss of cells with age (Monagle and Brody, 1974). There is a reduction in cerebellar cortical cells—about 25% during a lifetime—but the loss is barely appreciable until the sixth decade of life (Hall, Miller, and Corsellis, 1975). Shock (1960) reported some decline in nerve conduction velocity between ages 30 and 85, and Critchley (1931) reviewed the "normal" neurologic examination of the elderly, which includes depression or loss of ankle jerk and impaired vibration sense in the feet (Pearson, 1928).

There are certain changes in higher central nervous system function that are considered normal in old age. These include a decline in some intellectual functions that involve speed of response in nonverbal, perceptual-manipulative skills. This type of intelligence, sometimes called "fluid intelligence," is contrasted with "crystallized intelligence," which includes verbal skills and is well preserved in old age (Cattell, 1963; Horn and Cattell, 1967).

There are changes in memory, particularly in recall, which Kral (1962) called "benign senescent forgetfulness." These normal aging changes are distinct from dementia—a syndrome characterized by disorientation and impaired judgment, cognitive function, and memory. Senile dementia is estimated to occur in 10% of the population aged 65 and over.

The frequency with which adverse drug reactions affect the central nervous system in the elderly will be mentioned in Chapter 11, "Adverse Drug Reactions in the Geriatric Client." Most of the pharmacokinetic changes (see Chapter 10) that occur with advancing age tend to lead to an increased level of free drug in the plasma. Although this alone would increase the biologic effect and the chance of adverse drug reactions to any drugs, it appears that the central nervous system in the aged is particularly sensitive to the adverse effects of sedative and tranquilizing drugs. Demonstration of increased tissue sensitivity in the elderly, to the same plasma level of drugs, has been demonstrated in the case of nitrazepam (Castleden et al., 1975).

SPECIAL SENSES
Vision

The appearance of the eye and its surrounding tissues changes markedly with age. The shrunken appearance of the eye, laxity of the eyelids, and either entropion or ectropion are caused, in part, by the loss of periorbital fat. Arcus senilis (gerontoxon), a band of white lipid deposited at the periphery of the cornea, is frequently seen, and the pupil tends to be smaller than in middle adult life. Visual acuity is diminished, and the visual field is somewhat reduced (Weale, 1963).

Because of changes in the crystalline lens, the near point moves further from the eye and presbyopia develops. The lens becomes less elastic, more dense, and yellow. The yellowing of the lens has the effect of increasing the amount of illumination required to see clearly and to absorb wavelengths at the blue-green end of the spectrum, thus impairing color discrimination (Guth, 1957). The dividing point between normal age changes in the lens and senile cataract is not clear, but Nordmann (1965) has described a senile cataract as "an hereditary exaggeration of physiological aging."

One of the more common causes of visual impairment in elderly persons is macular degeneration. Macular degeneration is a progressive disorder affecting the macula of the retina where most of the cones are located. Estimates of the frequency of macular degeneration as a cause of visual problems in old age range as high as 45% (Gordon, 1965). Although glaucoma is more common in older individuals, it appears not to be intrinsically related to aging (Fozard et al., 1976).

The presence of visual impairment in the elderly should influence therapeutic decisions and plans for the older client on admission to the hospital. The management of an elderly person with diabetes and impaired vision may be changed from diet alone or with hypoglycemic agents to daily insulin injections without giving consideration to the problems that may arise when the client returns home. Even though the client may be taught to administer the injection, is vision adequate to ensure accurate dosage administration? If the client requires the daily assistance of another person to draw up the insulin, is the improved diabetic control of sufficient benefit to justify the increased dependency?

Medication instructions given with prescribed drugs may be typed in print too small for older clients (even with mild visual impairment) to read, and physicians, pharmacists, and nurses should be encouraged to provide drug dosage information printed in large type. Impaired color discrimination, particularly between colors at the blue-green end of the spectrum, may lead to confusion over tablets or capsules of similar size and shape, especially when they are stored in the same dispensing container.

Auditory perception

In the elderly the main morphologic changes observed in the ear include degeneration of the hair cells and supporting cells in the basal coil of the cochlea, loss of auditory neurons, atrophy of the stria vascularis in the scala media, and atrophic changes in the structures associated with vibration of the cochlear partition (Schuknecht and Igarashi, 1964). The clinical manifestations produced by these changes are generally known as presbycusis and involve some hearing loss at all frequencies, impaired sensitivity to sound, impaired high-frequency sensitivity, impaired loudness perception and sound localization, and a decline in discrimination of speech and time-related processing abilities. The impairment in the understanding of speech is more severe than would be predicted from audiometric tests. Reverberated, interrupted, or overlapping speech leads to a marked decrease in the intelligibility of speech in the elderly, particularly the very elderly (Bergman, 1971).

Surveys of the prevalence of hearing impairment in the elderly range from 12.2% (Wilkins, 1948) to 31.7% (Government Social Survey, 1962). One U.S. survey showed hearing loss in 48% of those aged 75 to 79 years (U.S. Department of Health, Education, and Welfare Reports, 1965). Clearly the criteria of significant hearing loss and the population's exposure to environmental noise will affect the reported prevalence of hearing impairment.

When giving instructions to clients concerning prescription and nonprescription drugs, the health professional should take into account these changes and conduct counseling in a quiet environment where distracting noises have been reduced or eliminated. Potentially remediable causes of impaired auditory reception, such as impacted cerumen or malfunctioning hearing aids, should first be identified and corrected.

Speech should be clearly and slowly articulated, and the speaker's mouth should be clearly visible to the client to permit lipreading. Lipreading of consonants can, to some extent, compensate for some of the high-frequency hearing loss. A simple, yet effective, method of testing reception of oral communication is for the clinician to request the client to repeat what was said. In this way misperceptions can be corrected, although when giving directions about the use of medications, the clinician should supplement verbal directions with simple written instructions.

Taste and smell

There is a reduction in the number of taste buds on the circumvallate papilla of older subjects, and taste buds present in the buccal mucosa and pharynx of the young are not found in older adults (Arey, Tremain, and Monzingo, 1936). Although a number of investigators report decreased taste sensitivity and impaired olfaction with advancing age, not all investigators have been able to verify this conclusion (Engen, 1976).

However, many older adults express a preference for highly seasoned or tart tastes, and medications in suspension and syrup form intended for the elderly may not need to contain as much sweetening to disguise a bitter taste.

Somesthesia

Somesthesia refers to awareness of the sensations arising from the skin, the locomotor system, and the viscera.

With advancing age there is a decline in touch sensitivity of the skin on the palm and sole but not on hairy skin. The vibratory threshold is increased in the elderly (Whanger and Wang, 1974), and absent vibratory sensation at the ankle of an octogenarian should not be considered pathologic. Loss of vibratory sense is by no means universal and may be preserved in many older persons. There appears to be no change in temperature perception in the healthy elderly, although thermoregulatory response to cold may be impaired (p. 123). It is a common observation that falls, fractures, and intra-abdominal events in older adults may occur without much apparent distress, and an increase in the threshold for pain in the elderly has been demonstrated (Procacci et al., 1970). An increased pain threshold may delay the diagnosis of a life-threatening illness. A disorder presenting with pain in the young may present in the elderly with confusion or with nonspecific findings such as malaise or weakness.

RESPIRATORY SYSTEM

Age changes in the respiratory system include anatomic changes within the lung and the chest wall. Rigidity of the chest wall contributes to the reduction in lung volume, and by the eighth decade about 30% of the total reduction in lung volume results from changes in the chest wall (Rizzato and Marazzini, 1970).

Degenerative changes in the intervertebral disks and thoracic vertebrae contribute to kyphosis and an increased anteroposterior diameter of the chest. There is a concomitant decrease in the transverse thoracic diameter, which on a chest roentgenogram appears as cardiac enlargement.

In the absence of lung disease there appears to be no loss in the total number of alveoli (Thurlbeck and Angus, 1975), although the thickness of the alveolar wall is reduced and fewer capillaries are present (Reid, 1967). The elastic tissue within the lungs increases with age, but the increase is localized to the pleural and septal tissues (Pierce and Ebert, 1965). Although there is some disruption or splitting of the elastic fibers, their ultramicroscopic appearance is unchanged (Adamson, 1968).

Nonsmoking subjects living in a pollution-free environment show a progressive fall in vital capacity of approximately 20 to 25 ml per year, and forced expiratory volume in 1 second has been shown to decline 32 ml per year for women (Morris, Koski, and Johnson, 1971). Carbon monoxide diffusing capacity decreases with age (Bates, Macklem, and Christie, 1971), although it is likely to be of little clinical significance.

In the absence of chronic obstructive pulmonary disease no elevation of arterial carbon dioxide tension is seen with advancing age; however, there is a decline in arterial oxygen saturation and a progressive increase in the alveolararterial oxygen difference (Bates, Macklem, and Christie, 1971). The decrease in arterial oxygen tension is thought to be caused by a decrease in the uniformity of distribution and ventilation in older men, which is possibly caused by lower zone airway closure and redistribution of blood preferentially to the upper zones of the lungs (Holland et al., 1968). This is supported by studies that show abolition of the alveolar-arterial gradient with deep breathing or when the inhaled gases are enriched with oxygen (Harris et al., 1974).

Some older individuals show an altered pattern of respiration. Cheyne-Stokes respiration, a form of periodic breathing consisting of cycles of crescendo-decrescendo respirations followed by apnea, is usually regarded as a poor prognostic sign in individuals with congestive heart failure or respiratory tract infections. Older clients without apparent illness may exhibit Cheyne-Stokes respiration while sleeping, or this may develop during the course of bronchopneumonia and disappear with its resolution. This form of periodic breathing is probably caused by impaired sensitivity of the respiratory center and a lowered arterial carbon dioxide tension.

The clinician working with the elderly will commonly encounter lower respiratory tract infections. The reasons for an increased incidence of bronchitis and bronchopneumonia in the elderly include impaired antibody production and impaired pulmonary defenses, such as the cough reflex, mucociliary escalators, and pulmonary macrophages. A diagnosis of pneumonia presents some difficulty because fine crepitations, presumably caused by microatelectasis, may be heard in the chests of healthy aged persons, and conversely, pneumonia may occur without fever or with few auscultatory findings.

BLOOD AND BLOOD-FORMING ORGANS

Throughout extrauterine life there is progressive involution of the red bone marrow. In fetal life and early childhood the long bones are filled with active bone marrow. In old age much is replaced with fatty bone marrow, and marrow aspirates adequate for diagnostic purposes may be obtained only from the sternum and the iliac spines. Where present, the red marrow shows no morphologic change in older subjects, and there appears to be no decline in marrow stem cell ability.

Each red cell undergoes a process of senescence from the time it enters the circulation. This process is practically the same in the old as in the young. There is a slight increase in mean cell diameter and mean corpuscular volume (Okuno, 1972), and there is a slight increase in osmotic fragility (Detraglisa et al., 1974).

There is a predisposition to lymphopenia and, therefore, total leukopenia in old age. The normal range for total leukocyte count in old age may well be 3000 to 8500/mm³ (Caird, Andrews, and Gallie, 1972). Although individual white cells show no significant morphologic change in the older person, their pentose phosphate metabolizing activity as assessed by transketolase activity is reduced (Markkanen, Peltola, and Heikinheimo, 1972), and there are other changes in enzyme activity, not all of which are decremental. Leukocyte alkaline phosphatase decreases with age (Ray and Pinkerton, 1969), but granulocyte pyruvate kinase and leukocyte peptidase increase with age (Stern et al., 1951; Rubinson et al., 1976).

With age there is a decline in cell-mediated functions that are T cell dependent. This occurs both with respect to the proliferative capacity of T cells in response to pokeweed mitogen (Mathies et al., 1973) and with respect to the regulatory function over B cells (Farrar, Loughman, and Nordin, 1974). It is tempting to speculate on the relationship between the development of autoimmunity and neoplasms and on the increased prevalence of infection at a time of life when T cell function is impaired. No change in morphology or function of platelets has been reported.

GASTROINTESTINAL SYSTEM

There are a number of aging changes in the teeth, their supporting structures, and the temporomandibular joint, but these do not directly affect drug therapy and will not be discussed.

Xerostomia, or dry mouth, may occur in severe form as a result of Sjogren's syndrome or in milder form as a normal consequence of aging. Parotid secretion has been found to be significantly reduced in individuals aged 70 to 88, compared with a younger control group (Kamocka, 1970).

Abnormal muscular function of the pharynx and esophagus is found in older persons without evidence of pharyngeal or esophageal disease. In one study 22% of subjects over 65 years of age showed evidence of pharyngeal muscle weakness or abnormal relaxation of the cricopharyngeus (Piaget and Fouillet, 1959). Presbyesophagus, a condition characterized by the absence of peristaltic waves, the presence of nonperistaltic or tertiary contractions, and the failure of the lower esophageal sphincter to relax, may be present in about one half of nonagenarians (Zboralske, Amberg, and Soergel, 1964).

There is an increasing tendency toward achlorhydria with advancing age (Baron, 1963). In 24 asymptomatic elderly individuals subjected to gastric biopsy all mucosal biopsies showed some degree of chronic atrophic gastritis and reduced acid secretion (Andrews et al., 1967). Reduced gastric acid production and reduced volume of gastric secretions may impair absorption of drugs best absorbed in an acid pH and conversely may improve the absorption of drugs, such as penicillin G, that are degraded by exposure to stomach acid.

Normal aging is associated with diminished absorption of substances that are actively transported across the small intestinal mucosa. The active transport of glucose, galactose, and 3-0-methyl-d-glucose declines with advancing age. The absorption of iron, calcium, and thiamine is diminished in older subjects. Most drugs are transported across the intestinal mucosa by simple diffusion, and there appears to be no specific age-related changes in the absorption of drugs such as phenylbutazone, acetaminophen, sulfamethizole, practolol, and aspirin (Triggs et al., 1975; Castleden, Volans, and Raymond, 1977).

Anatomic changes within the pancreas include hyperplasia of the ducts; however, there are few functional changes. Amylase and the bicarbonate content of pancreatic juice are unchanged in the

elderly, although a modest reduction in pancreatic lipase secretion has been reported (Necheles, Plotke, and Meyer, 1942).

There is a loss of weight of the liver, and cellular and mitochondrial changes have been described. The plasma half-life of a drug exclusively metabolized by the liver, such as antipyrine, is increased in the aged: 17.4 hours compared with 12 hours in young subjects (O'Malley et al., 1971). Sulfobromophthalein (BSP) clearance is diminished in the elderly; however, this reflects a lower storage capacity for BSP rather than a decline in the ability to extract and excrete the dye (Thompson and Williams, 1965). The physiologic changes outlined are minor, and because of the large functional reserve, changes in hepatic function are of little consequence in old age.

The decline in cardiac output with advancing age has been discussed already. The diminished cardiac output is not equally distributed because splanchnic circulation shows a greater decline in blood flow (Bender, 1965) than cerebral and coronary circulation. Hepatic and intestinal blood flow in a 65-year-old may be 40% less than that in a young adult. This may be of little significance in good health; however, when hepatic congestion from congestive heart failure occurs, or in the presence of hypoxia, then impairment in hepatic metabolism of drugs may occur.

Gastrointestinal transit time is markedly increased in the elderly, particularly those receiving anticholinergic or antidepressant drugs or major tranquilizers and those who are inactive or institutionalized. Constipation and impaired bowel function is an area of concern and sometimes of preoccupation with older adults. The prescribing clinician should be aware of the constipating effect of many drugs in common use and should be familiar with the different classes of drugs used in the management of constipation (e.g., stool softeners, bulk-forming agents, stimulants).

Fecal impaction, which may have signs as different as urinary incontinence or mental confusion, reflects inattention to diet and fluid intake and inadequate management of impaired bowel function.

KIDNEY AND EXCRETORY SYSTEM

Age-related changes in renal function are of great significance in clinical pharmacology and therapeutics because many of the drugs prescribed for the elderly are excreted either by glomerular filtration or tubular secretion. Glomerular filtration, which is measured by inulin, urea, and creatinine clearance (Rowe et al., 1976), declines with age even in the absence of renal disease (Fig. 6-3). The reduction in creatinine clearance starts around the mid-30s and accelerates after age 65. The serum creatinine level in the elderly gives an erroneously favorable impression of renal function because the impairment in creatinine clearance is compensated in part by reduced endogenous creatinine production. Endogenous creatinine production is closely related to lean body or muscle mass, which is reduced in the older person.

A reduced glomerular filtration rate in the elderly affects drugs that are excreted by the glomeruli, such as aminoglycosides, tetracyclines, and digoxin. Half-lives of such drugs are

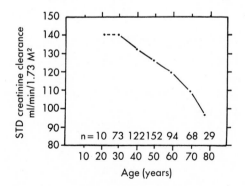

FIG. 6-3

Cross-sectional differences in standard creatinine clearance with age. (From Rowe, J.W., et al.: J. Gerontol. **31**:155, 1976.)

prolonged, and dosage intervals need to be changed when they are prescribed. The decline in clearance of digoxin has been extensively studied, and a close relationship exists between digoxin and creatinine clearance in elderly clients (Roberts and Caird, 1976).

Renal tubular secretion is the major route of excretion of organic acids, particularly penicillin and cephalosporin antibiotics. Tubular secretory capacity declines along with the decline in the glomerular filtration rate, and further inhibition of tubular secretion may occur when two or more drugs excreted by the tubules are used together.

Whether as a result of aging or of concomitant cerebrovascular or other neurologic disease, bladder function in the elderly is altered. The bladder capacity of normal older adults tends to decrease, and even in the absence of prostatic hypertrophy, residual urine volume (urine remaining in the bladder after voiding) increases. There are changes in the volume at which the desire to void is perceived, and uninhibited bladder contractions may occur (Brocklehurst and Dillane, 1966). These changes, which threaten the maintenance of urinary continence in old age, together with alterations in the diurnal rhythm of urine excretion (Lobban and Tredre, 1967), contribute to the high prevalence of nocturnal frequency (70% in men and 61% in women) (Brocklehurst et al., 1968).

Anatomic changes in the bladder include some trabeculation and diverticula formations that occur in women or in the absence of obvious bladder neck obstruction in men. In women the loss of hormone effect on the genital tract causes vulval atrophy, increased keratinization of vaginal and vulval mucosa, shortening and pallor of the vaginal wall, and recession of urethral meatus (Parsons and Sommers, 1962).

Age effects on bladder function are of significance to the prescriber of diuretic drugs. The use of rapid-acting diuretics, particularly in individuals whose mobility is impaired, may precipitate urinary incontinence; and drugs with an anticholinergic activity may benefit clients with uninhibited neurogenic bladders. The atonic neurogenic bladder is not a feature of aging but of autonomic neuropathy, usually secondary to diabetes. In this circumstance the administration of anticholinergic drugs may produce urinary retention.

MUSCULOSKELETAL SYSTEM

There is a loss of height with age, partly because of change in posture, dorsal kyphosis, and narrowing of intervertebral disks. With severe osteoporosis vertebral collapse may cause a more pronounced loss of height. Adult bone loss, osteoporosis or osteopenia, involves a decrease in bone mass, particularly cancellous bone; bone mass that is present is normal in appearance.

Bone loss has been estimated by measuring metacarpal cortical area/total area, and percentile ranking curves have been established for a normal population aged 2 to 85 years (Exton-Smith et al., 1971; Gryfe et al., 1971) (Fig. 6-4). There is a rapid increase in the amount of bone during the period of growth, but after puberty the increase continues at a slower rate; however, after age 45 loss of bone occurs in both sexes but more rapidly in women. The loss of bone in women is most rapid in the first 10 years after

menopause. The total bone mass is related to sex, racial factors, and body build, and for those with a large bone mass the loss of bone with age may not lead to clinical sequelae. For the individual starting with a smaller bone mass or where diseases such as Cushing's syndrome, rheumatoid arthritis, or immobilization are present and lead to accelerated bone loss, then clinically evident osteoporosis, perhaps with back pain, marked truncal shortening, and nerve root compression, will occur.

Muscle mass in relation to body weight declines in old age, and there is a decrease in the number and size of muscle fibers. There is a decline in physical strength with age (Ufland, 1933), and there are several studies of loss of hand grip strength (Anderson and Cowan, 1966; Walkley and Cowan, 1967). Gait is slowed and more cautious, and postural sway, after declining from high levels in childhood, increases again after age 60 so that the degree of sway in the very elderly is similar to that in young children. Marked postural sway is found particularly in persons with a history of falls caused by drop attacks, loss of balance, and giddiness (Overstall et al., 1975).

Age changes in skeletal profile, a changing center of gravity, and some impairment in sen-

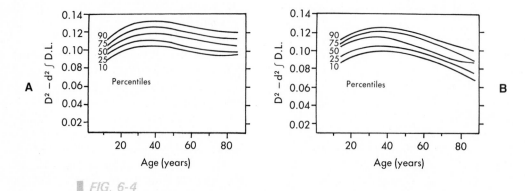

FIG. 6-4

Percentile curves for the ratio of bone density of the cortex of the metacarpal for men, **A,** and women, **B,** up to age 85 years. (From Exton-Smith, et al.: Lancet 1:523, 1971.)

sory input, nerve conduction, muscle strength, or vision make balance and gait more precarious, and the older individual is more likely to fall. Reduced bone mass increases the risk of fracture following relatively minor trauma.

Postural hypotension, caused or accentuated by diuretic therapy, and drugs with a central nervous system action are frequently responsible for precipitating falls in the elderly. Older persons are particularly sensitive to the effect of benzodiazepines on gait, and diazepam and flurazepam are common causes of iatrogenic locomotor instability and falls.

SKIN

Changes in the skin are among the earliest recognizable signs of aging. Graying of the scalp hair and wrinkling of the skin start to occur in middle adult life and increase progressively with age.

At a microscopic level age changes are present within the epidermis and dermis of the skin, and excessive exposure to actinic radiation produces an acceleration of the age changes. Although there is no change in the thickness of the epidermis with age, there are variations in the size and shape of cells of the epidermis and disorganization of the architecture of the cell layers. There is a slowing of the rate of cell replacement in the stratum corneum, which is more pronounced in men than in women (Baker and Blair, 1968), and wound healing is prolonged.

Microscopically, changes within the dermis are more prominent than those in the epidermis. There is an increased thickness of the dermis with age (Shuster, Black, and McVitie, 1975); however, there is a loss of collagen with aging and elastotic degeneration of the remaining collagen. This leads to friable and transparent skin and loss of strength and elasticity of the skin. The cellular elements of the dermis change with age; there is a reduced number of fibroblasts but no change in macrophages, lymphocytes, or mast cells. The ground substance of the dermis shows a reduction in the soluble pool of glycosaminoglycans (Fleischmajer, Perlish, and Bashley, 1973).

One effect of changes in the epidermis is an increased epidermal permeability to water and certain chemicals. This is important because topically applied drugs, such as steroid creams, may have a greater effect locally when applied to the elderly than to the young. When drugs, such as topical nitroglycerin, are applied topically and intended to produce a systemic effect, a corresponding increase in the serum level may not occur because diffusion in and absorption from the aged dermis appears to be reduced (Christophers and Kligman, 1965).

Skin color is a product of pigmentation and blood flow in the subepidermal venous circulation. There is a reduction in the number of capillary loops in the superficial dermis (Davis and Lawler, 1961) and a reduction in both the overall number of melanocytes and the number of dopareactive melanocytes. Eccrine sweat glands show minor morphologic changes; however, their numbers do not seem to be reduced in the aged. There is, however, a reduced maximum sweat output and an increased thermal threshold for sweating (Foster et al., 1976). Sebaceous glands show no morphologic change although decreased sebum production has been reported (Pochi and Strauss, 1965).

Although graying of the hair and temporal recession, which occur in both sexes, are recognized effects of aging, other changes in body hair distribution may be confused with endocrine disorders. In the absence of endocrine disorder or peripheral vascular disease there is a normal loss of lower leg hair in both sexes (Hamilton, 1958). After age 60 approximately 30% of women and 7% of men lose axillary hair, and this hair loss extends to the pubic area in approximately 5% of women in the absence of any endocrine disturbance other than menopause (Thomas and Ferriman, 1957). Coarse facial hair appears in about 40% of women over 55 years of age (Hamilton and Tereda, 1963).

ENDOCRINE SYSTEM

The anterior pituitary does not show any significant change in size or weight with advancing age, and microscopic studies show only minor changes in vascularity and the distribution of cell types. To date, no important changes in growth hormone or thyroid-stimulating hormone (TSH) secretion have been shown with advancing age, although a decline in the responsiveness of the anterior pituitary to thyroid-releasing hormone (TRH) stimulation has been shown (Snyder and Utiger, 1972).

However, age alone has no major effect on thyroid function. There is no change in the serum total or free thyroxine; however, a diminished rate of secretion of thyroid hormone is present.

The maintenance of a normal serum total and free thyroxine in the presence of a diminished rate of secretion suggests that thyroid hormone metabolism and excretion is reduced. A slight decline in the triiodothyronine level has been reported (Gregerman and Bierman, 1974). In the absence of thyroid dysfunction no change in plasma TSH is seen.

Normal levels of adrenocorticotrophic hormone (ACTH) were found in the morning blood sample of a number of elderly subjects, and the circadian rhythm of ACTH secretion was found to be normal in five elderly subjects (Jensen and Blichert-Toft, 1971). Despite the normal circadian rhythm in this small group, Romanoff et al. (1969) found a reduced 24-hour secretion

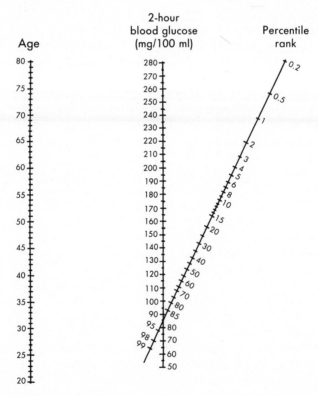

FIG. 6-5

Oral glucose tolerance test nomogram. (From Andres, R.: Med. Clin. North Am. **55:**835, 1971.)

rate of ACTH in elderly subjects, and this finding has subsequently been confirmed.

The adrenal gland shows no important change in weight with age, although histologic differences are apparent. The adrenal gland shows decreased sensitivity to circulating ACTH (West et al., 1961), and as with thyroxine there is a decreased rate of secretion of cortisol, decreased urinary excretion, and therefore maintenance of "normal" serum levels.

Impaired glucose tolerance is common in older persons. Given the criteria for the diagnosis of diabetes applicable to young subjects, about one half of persons in their eighth and ninth decade would be considered "diabetic." Fasting blood sugars of older subjects do not differ significantly from those in younger subjects, although it appears that pancreatic β-cells are less sensitive to the rise in serum glucose and that their response—secretion of insulin—is both attenuated and delayed, thus explaining the normal fasting levels and the elevated levels at 1 and 2 hours (Silverstone et al., 1957). There appears to be no change in the sensitivity to circulating insulin with increasing age (Martin, Pearson, and Stocks, 1968).

Andres (1971) has developed a nomogram showing the percentile rank of 2-hour blood glucose concentrations of subjects aged 20 to 80 years (Fig. 6-5). It is clear that the criteria for diagnosis of clinical diabetes, which can be applied to the young, cannot be applied to the very elderly. Impaired and delayed response to a glucose load is normal in old age, and inappropriate therapy and unnecessary anxiety may be avoided by considering the fasting and adjusted 2-hour serum glucose levels before making the diagnosis of diabetes mellitus.

INTEGRATIVE FUNCTION

Some of the anatomic and physiologic changes that occur in normal human aging have been discussed as if they occurred independent of each other and without overlying pathologic changes.

As illustrated, in many organ systems it is difficult to separate the effects of aging from those of accumulated, or age-related, pathologic conditions. The decremental changes within individual organs and body systems have complex interactive effects on other systems, and their final effect is on the "milieu intérieur," first described by Bernard (1859). In the resting state or in the absence of stress or the challenges produced by infection or disease, acid-base balance, serum chemistry, and tissue respiration are well maintained in the elderly. The impairment of integrative function and homeostatic control may be uncovered by stress.

Perhaps the best examples of failure in integrative function of several systems are the decline in maximum breathing capacity and maximum oxygen uptake. Maximum breathing capacity and maximum oxygen uptake require the integrated activity of the cardiovascular, nervous, musculoskeletal, and respiratory systems, and in cross-sectional studies maximum breathing capacity shows a decline of 60% to 70% between young adult life and the ninth decade (Shock, 1972).

Although normal acid-base balance can be maintained under normal conditions, the kidney's function, as an organ of acid-base balance, is impaired with advancing age. The depression of serum bicarbonate following an acid load persists longer in the elderly than in the young (Shock and Yiengst, 1950), and the response to base loads is similarly delayed and prolonged. Impairment in body temperature control predisposes older persons to hyperthermia (heat stroke) and hypothermia when they are challenged by extremes in environmental temperature.

The clinical condition of hypothermia (central body temperature less than 35° C) is seen more commonly in the United Kingdom where more elderly people live in inadequately heated homes than do their North American counterparts. The response to change in environmental temperature involves the integration of the central and peripheral nervous systems, the cardiovas-

cular, respiratory, musculoskeletal, and endocrine systems, and a behavioral response. With
many systems involved, heat or cold stress may
uncover deficient homeostatic control because
victims of hypothermia show deficient central
and peripheral response to low ambient temperatures. The possible presence of impaired thermo-
regulation must be considered when drugs such
as phenothiazines are prescribed for the elderly.

The relative proportions of various body compartments often differ between the young and the
old. In a cross-sectional study Fryer (1962)
showed the differences between body composition of men aged 25 and 70 years. Total body
water declined from 61% to 53%; total cell
solids, or lean body mass, declined from 19%
to 12% and fat increased from 14% to 30%. In a
longitudinal study of six subjects the decline of
lean body mass with age was confirmed (Forbes
and Reina, 1970).

These changes in body composition are of relevance to drug distribution. For drugs that distribute in the lean body mass or in body water
serum levels that are higher than anticipated
may be found. Drugs that are distributed in fatty
tissue, such as anesthetics and benzodiazepines,
may accumulate because of the greater volume
of distribution (Kotz et al., 1975).

SUMMARY

The appearance of robust health in the very
elderly may be deceptive because older persons
have accommodated to decrements in physiologic
function and impairments in regulatory mechanisms involved in integrating homeostatic control. It must be assumed that a reduction in the
reserve capacity of organs and systems has occurred and that this will affect pharmacokinetics,
tissue responsiveness, and the approach to therapeutics in old age. Against this background of impaired function, multiple pathology and polypharmacy further complicate the course of ill
health and the response to drug therapy in the
elderly.

REFERENCES

Adamson, J.R.: An electron microscopic comparison of the connective tissue from the lungs of young and elderly subjects, Am. Rev. Respir. Dis. **98**:399, 1968.

Anderson, W.F., and Cowan, N.R.: Hand grip pressure in older people, Br. J. Prevent. Soc. Med. **20**(3):141, 1966.

Andres, R.: Aging and diabetes, Med. Clin. North Am. **55**:835, 1971.

Andrews, G.R., et al.: Atrophic gastritis in the aged, Australas. Ann. Med. **16**:230, 1967.

Arey, L.B., Tremain, M.J., and Monzingo, F.L.: The numerical and topographical relations of taste buds to human circumvallate papillae throughout the life-span, Anat. Rec. **64**:9, 1936.

Baker, H., and Blair, C.P.: Cell replacement in the human stratum corneum in old age, Br. J. Dermatol. **80**:367, 1968.

Baron, J.H.: Studies of basal and peak acid output with an augmented histamine test, Gut **4**:136, 1963.

Bates, D.V., Macklem, P.T., and Christie, R.V.: Respiratory function in disease, ed. 2, Philadelphia, 1971, W.B. Saunders Co.

Bender, A.D.: Effect of increasing age on the distribution of peripheral blood flow in man, J. Am. Geriatr. Soc. **13**:192, 1965.

Bergman, M.: Hearing and aging, Audiology **10**:164, 1971.

Bernard, C.: Lecons sur les proprietes physiologiques et les alterations pathologiques des liquides de l'organisme, Paris, 1859, Baillière.

Brandfonbrener, M., Landowne, M., and Shock, N.W.: Changes in cardiac output with age, Circulation **12**:557, 1955.

Brocklehurst, J.C., editor: Textbook of geriatric medicine and gerontology, London, 1978, Churchill Livingstone.

Brocklehurst, J.C., and Dillane, J.B.: Studies of the female bladder in old age, Gerontol. Clin. **8**:285, 1966.

Brocklehurst, J.C., et al.: The prevalence and symptomatology of urinary infection in an aged population, Gerontol. Clin. **9**:242, 1968.

Brody, H.: Organization of cerebral cortex. III. A study of aging in the human cerebral cortex, J. Comp. Neurol. **102**:511, 1955.

Brody, H.: Structural changes in the aging nervous system, Interdisc. Topics Gerontol. **7**:9, 1970.

Caird, F.I., Andrews, G.R., and Gallie, T.B.: The leucocyte count in old age, Age Ageing **1**:239, 1972.

Caird, F.I., Andrews, G.R., and Kennedy, R.D.: Effect of posture on blood pressure in the elderly, Br. Heart J. **35**:527, 1973.

Castleden, C.M., Volans, C.N., and Raymond, K.: The effect of aging on drug absorption from the gut, Age Ageing **6**:138, 1977.

Castleden, C.M., et al.: The effect of aging on drug absorption from the gut, Eur. J. Clin. Pharmacol. **8**:55, 1975.

Cattell, R.B.: Theory of fluid and crystallized intelligence: a critical experiment, J. Educ. Psychol. **54**:127, 1963.

Christophers, E., and Kligman, A.M.: Percutaneous absorption in aged skin. In Montagna, W., editor: Advances in biology of skin, Oxford, 1965, Pergamon Press.

Cohen, A.S.: The constitution and genesis of amyloid, Int. Rev. Exp. Pathol. **4**:159, 1965.

Comfort, A.: The biology of senescence, ed. 3, New York, 1979, American Elsevier Publishers, Inc.

Critchley, M.: The neurology of old age. II. Clinical manifestations in old age, Lancet **1**:1221, 1931.

Davies, M.J., and Pomerance, A.: Quantitative study of aging changes in human sinoatrial nodes and internodal tracts, Br. Heart J. **34**:150, 1972.

Davis, M.J., and Lawler, J.C.: Capillary microscopy in normal and diseased human skin. In Montagna, W., and Ellis, R.E., editors: Advanced in biology of skin, Oxford, 1961, Pergamon Press.

Detraglisa, M., et al.: Erythrocyte fragility in aging, Biochem. Biophys. **345**:213, 1974.

Engen, T.: Taste and smell. In Birren, J.E., and Schaie, K.W., editors: Handbook of the psychology of aging, New York, 1976, Van Nostrand Reinhold Co.

Evans, W., and Swann, P.: Lone auricular fibrillation, Br. Heart J. **16**:189, 1954.

Exton-Smith, A.N., et al.: Pattern of development of bone in childhood and adolescence, Lancet **1**:523, 1971.

Farrar, J.J., Loughman, B.E., and Nordin, A.A.: Lymphopoietic potential of bone marrow cells from aged mice: comparison of the cellular constituents of bone marrow from young and aged mice, J. Immunol. **112**:1244, 1974.

Finch, C.E.: Catecholamine metabolism in the brains of aging mice, Brain Res. **52**:261, 1973.

Finch, C.E., and Hayflick, L., editors: Handbook of the biology of aging, New York, 1977, Van Nostrand Reinhold Co.

Fleischmajer, R., Perlish, J.S., and Bashley, R.I.: Aging of human dermis. In Robert, C.L., editor: Frontiers of matrix biology, Basel, Switz., 1973, S. Karger.

Forbes, G.B., and Reina, J.C.: Adult lean body mass declines with age: some longitudinal observations, Metabolism **19**:653, 1970.

Foster, K.G., et al.: Sweat responses in the aged, Age Ageing **5**:91, 1976.

Fozard, J.L., et al.: Visual perception and communication. In Birren, J.E., and Schaie, K.W., editors: Handbook of the psychology of aging, New York, 1976, Van Nostrand Reinhold Co.

Frick, M.H., Heikkila, J., and Kahanpaa, A.: Combined parasympathetic and beta-receptor blockade as a clinical test, Acta Med. Scand. **182**:621, 1967.

Fryer, J.H.: Studies of body composition in men aged 60 and over. In Shock, N.W., editor: Biological aspects of aging, New York, 1962, Columbia University Press.

Gordon, D.M.: Eye problems of the aged, J. Am. Geriatr. Soc. **13**:398, 1965.

Government Social Survey: Old people in Lewisham, London, 1962, King Edward VII Hospital Fund.

Gregerman, R.I., and Bierman, E.L.: Aging and hormones. In Williams, R.H., editor: Textbook of endocrinology, ed. 5, Philadelphia, 1974, W.B. Saunders Co.

Gryfe, C.I., et al.: Pattern of development of bone in childhood and adolescence, Lancet **1**:523, 1971.

Guth, S.K.: Effects of age on visibility, Am. J. Ophthalmol. **34**:463, 1957.

Hall, T.C., Miller, A.K.H., and Corsellis, J.A.N.: Variations in the human Purkinje cell population according to age and sex, Neuropathol. Applied Neurobiol. **1**:267, 1975.

Hamilton, J.B.: Age, sex and genetic factors in regulation of hair growth in man: a comparison of Caucasian and Japanese populations, In Montagna, W., and Ellis, R.H., editors: Biology of hair growth, New York, 1958, Academic Press, Inc.

Hamilton, J.B., and Tereda, H.: Interdependence of genetic aging and endocrine factors in hirsutism. In Greenblatt, R.B., editor: The hirsute female, Springfield, Ill., 1963, Charles C Thomas, Publisher.

Harris, E.A., et al.: The normal alveolar-arterial oxygen-tension gradient in man, Clin. Sci. Mol. Med. **46**:89, 1974.

Holland, J., et al.: Regional distribution of pulmonary ventilation and perfusion in elderly subjects, J. Clin. Invest. **47**:81, 1968.

Horn, J.L., and Cattell, R.B.: Age differences in fluid and crystallized intelligence, Acta Psychol. **6**:107, 1967.

James, T.N., et al.: Comparative structure of the sinus node in man and dog, Circulation **34**:139, 1966.

Jensen, H.K., and Blichert-Toft, M.: Serum corticotrophin, plasma cortisol and urinary excretion of 17-ketogenic steroids in the elderly age group (66-94 years), Acta Endocrinol. **74**:511, 1971.

Johnson, R.H., et al.: Effect of posture on blood pressure in elderly patients, Lancet **1**:731, 1964.

Jose, A.D.: Effect of combined sympathetic and parasympathetic blockade on heart rate and cardiac function in man, Am. J. Cardiol. **18**:476, 1966.

Kamocka, D.: Cytological studies of parotid glands secretion in people over 60 years of age, Roczn. Pom. Akad. Med. Swierczewskiego. **15**:247, 1969.

Kotz, U., et al.: The effects of age and liver disease on the disposition and elimination of diazepam in adult man, J. Clin. Invest. **55**:347, 1975.

Kohn, R.R.: Heart and cardiovascular system. In Finch, C.E., and Hayflick, L., editors: Handbook of the biology of aging, New York, 1977, Van Nostrand Reinhold Co.

Kral, V.A.: Senescent forgetfulness: benign and malignant, Can. Med. Assoc. J. **86**:257, 1962.

Lobban, M.C., and Tredre, B.E.: Diurnal rhythms of renal excretion and of body temperature in aged subjects, J. Physiol. **188**:48, 1967.

Markkanen, T., Peltola, O., and Heikinheimo, R.: Pentose phosphate metabolizing enzyme activity of leukocytes in patients of various age groups, Gerontol. Clin. **14**:149, 1972.

Martin, F.I.R., Pearson, M.J., and Stocks, A.E.: Glucose tolerance and insulin insensitivity, Lancet **1**:1285, 1968.

Mathies, M., et al.: Age-related decline in response to phytohemagglutinin and pokeweed mitogen by spleen cells from hamsters and a long-lived mouse strain, J. Gerontol. **28**:425, 1973.

Miall, W.E., and Lovell, H.G.: Relation between change of blood pressure and age, Br. Med. J. **2**:660, 1967.

Monagle, R.D., and Brody, H.: The effects of age upon the main nucleus of the inferior olive in the human, J. Comp. Neurol. **128**:109, 1974.

Morris, J.F., Koski, A., and Johnson, L.C.: Spirometric standards for healthy non smoking adults, Am. Rev. Respir. Dis. **103**:57, 1971.

Necheles, H., Plotke, F., and Meyer, J.: Studies in old age. V. Active pancreatic secretion in the aged, Am. J. Dig. Dis. **9**:157, 1942.

Nordmann, J.: Present state and perspectives in research of the lens, Invest. Ophthalmol. **4**:513, 1965.

Okuno, T.: Red cell size and age, Br. Med. J. **1**:569, 1972.

O'Malley, K., et al.: Effects of age and sex on human drug metabolism, Br. Med. J. **3**:607, 1971.

Overstall, P., et al.: Causes of falls and their relationship to postural imbalance, paper presented at the meeting of the British Geriatrics Society, London, 1975.

Pakkenberg, H., and Voigt, J.: Brain weight of the Danes, Acta Anat. **56**:297, 1964.

Parsons, L., and Sommers, S.C.: Gynecology, Philadelphia, 1962, W.B. Saunders Co.

Pearl., L.: The biology of death, Philadelphia, 1922, J.B. Lippincott Co.

Pearson, G.H.J.: Effect of age on vibratory sensibility, Arch. Neurol. Psychiatr. **20**:482, 1928.

Piaget, F., and Fouillet, J.: Le pharynx et l'esophage seniles: etude clinique, radiologique et radiocinematographique, J. Med. Lyon **40**:951, 1959.

Pierce, J.A., and Ebert, R.V.: Fibrous network of the lungs and its change with age, Thorax **20**:469, 1965.

Pochi, P.E., and Strauss, J.S.: The effect of aging on the activity of the sebaceous gland in man. In Montagna, W., editor: Advances in biology of skin, ed. 6, Oxford, 1965, Pergamon Press.

Pomerance, A.: Pathology of the myocardium and valves. In Caird, F.I., Dall, J.L.C., Kennedy, R.D., editors: Cardiology in old age, New York, 1976, Plenum Publishing Corp.

Pomerance, A., Slavin, G., and McWatt, J.: Experiences with the sodium sulphate alcian blue stain for amyloid in cardiac pathology, J. Clin. Pathol. **29**:22, 1976.

Procacci, P., et al.: The cutaneous pricking pain threshold in old age, Gerontol. Clin. **12**:213, 1970.

Ray, P.K., and Pinkerton, P.H.: Leukocyte alkaline phosphatase: the effect of age and sex, Acta Haematol. **42**:18, 1969.

Reid, L.: The aged lung. In Reid, L., editor: The

pathology of emphysema, London, 1967, Lloyd-Luke.

Rizzato, G., and Marazzini, L.: Thoraco-abdominal mechanics in elderly men, J. Appl. Physiol. **28**:457, 1970.

Roberts, M.A., and Caird, F.I.: Steady state kinetics of digoxin in the elderly, Age Ageing **5**:214, 1976.

Romanoff, L.P., et al.: Effect of ACTH on the metabolism of pregnenolone-7 alpha-3H and cortisol-4-14C in young and elderly men, J. Clin. Endocrinol. **29**:819, 1969.

Rowe, J.W., et al.: The effect of age on creatinine clearance in man: a cross sectional and longitudinal study, J. Gerontol. **31**:155, 1976.

Rubinson, H., et al.: Aging and accuracy of protein synthesis in man: search for inactive enzymatic cross-reacting material in granulocytes of aged people, Gerontology **22**:438, 1976.

Schefer, V.F.: Absolute number of neurons and thickness of cerebral cortex during aging, senile and vascular dementia and Pick's and Alzheimer's disease, Neurosci. Behav. Physiol. **6**:319, 1973.

Schiebel, M.D., and Schiebel, A.B.: In Brody, H., Harmon, D., and Mordy, J., editors: Clinical, morphological and neurochemical aspects of the aging central nervous system, New York, 1975, Raven Press.

Schuknecht, H.F., and Igarashi, M.: Pathology of slowly progressive sensori-neural deafness, Trans. Am. Acad. Ophthalmol. Otolaryngol. **68**:222, 1964.

Schwartz, C.J., and Mitchell, J.R.A.: The relation between myocardial lesions and coronary artery disease. I. An unselected necropsy study, Br. Heart J. **24**:761, 1962.

Shock, N.W.: Discussion on mortality and measurement. In Strehler, B.L., et al., editors: The biology of aging: a symposium, Washington, D.C., 1960, American Institute of Biological Science.

Shock, N.W.: Energy metabolism, caloric intake and physical activity of the aging. In Carlson, L.A., editor: Nutrition in old age (Tenth Symposium of the Swedish Nutrition Foundation), Stockholm, 1972, Almqvist & Wiksell International.

Shock, N.W., and Yiengst, M.J.: Age changes in the acid base equilibrium of the blood of males, J. Gerontol. **5**:1, 1950.

Shuster, S., Black, M.M., and McVitie, E.: Influence of age and sex on skin thickness, skin collagen and density, Br. J. Dermatol. **93**:639, 1975.

Silverstone, F.A., et al.: Age differences in the intravenous glucose tolerance tests and the response to insulin, J. Clin. Invest. **36**:504, 1957.

Snyder, P.J., and Utiger, R.D.: Response to thyrotropin releasing hormone (TRH) in normal man, J. Clin. Endocrinol. **34**:380, 1972.

Stern, K., et al.: Peptidase activity in leucocytes, erythrocytes and plasma of young, adult and senile subjects, J. Clin. Invest. **30**:84, 1951.

Thomas, P.K., and Ferriman, D.G.: Variation in facial and pubic hair growth in white women, Am. J. Phys. Anthropol. **15**:171, 1957.

Thompson, E.N., and Williams, R.: Effect of age on liver function with particular reference to bromsulphalein excretion, Gut **6**:266, 1965.

Thurlbeck, W.M., and Angus, G.E.: Growth and aging of the normal lung, Chest **67**(suppl.):38, 1975.

Tomlinson, B.E.: Some quantitative cerebral findings in normal and demented old people. In Terry, R.D., and Gershon, S., editors: Neurobiology of aging, New York, 1976, Raven Press.

Triggs, E.J., et al.: Pharmacokinetics in the elderly, Eur. J. Clin. Pharmacol. **8**:55, 1975.

Ufland, J.M.: Einfluss des Lebensalters, Geschlechts, der Konstitution und des Berufs auf die Kraft Verschiedener Muskelgruppen; über das dynamometrische Profil bei Vertretern verschiedener Berufe, Arbeitsphysiol **7**:238, 1933.

U.S. Department of Health, Education, and Welfare Reports: Hearing levels of adults by age and sex in U.S.A., 1960-62, Series 11, No. 11, Washington, D.C., 1965, National Center for Health Statistics.

Walkley, F.A., and Cowan, N.R.: Muscle strength, Gerontol. Clin. **9**:30, 1967.

Weale, R.A.: The aging eye, London, 1963, H.K. Lewis & Co., Ltd.

West, C.D., et al.: Adrenocortical function and cortisol metabolism in old age, J. Clin. Endocrinol. **29**:273, 1961.

Whanger, A.D., and Wang, H.S.: Clinical correlates of the vibratory sense in elderly psychiatric patients, J. Gerontol. **29**:39, 1974.

Wilkins, L.T.: The prevalence of deafness in the population of England, Scotland and Wales, London, 1948, Central Office of Information (revised December 1949).

Zboralske, F.F., Amberg, J.R., and Soergel, K.H.: Presbyesophagus: cineradiographic manifestations, Radiology **82**:463, 1964.

CHAPTER 7

Laboratory tests and the geriatric client

Keith Walker

Various conceptual ideas related to the development of physiologic and functional age have recently become of marked interest in an attempt to explain the individual differences in body organ and system performance noted in subjects of the same chronologic age. Two major studies, the Boston Veterans Administration Study of Normative Aging (Costa and McCrae, 1977) and the Baltimore Longitudinal Study of Aging (Borkan, 1978), have been used in an attempt to predict individual performance.

The Baltimore study included measurements of biochemical, physiologic, psychologic, anthropometric, and social variances. Numerous tests were eliminated when they were found to have changed very little over the adult age span of the average individual. The only definitive conclusion drawn from the Baltimore study was that the probability of surviving was less if the subjects' demonstrated abilities were less than the average scores achieved by subjects of the same average chronologic age.

The Boston Veterans Administration study included measurements of anthropometric, biomedical, psychologic, and psychosocial variables in normal men between 20 and 75 years of age. Repeat estimates on 18 anthropometric and physiologic tests were performed, and from the observations an attempt was made to test the use-

fulness of the results as a concept of "functional age." Costa and McCrae (1977) concluded from this study that "functional age" is of little value and that the effect of aging must be evaluated by the performance of specific tests.

Recently Strehler (1979), commenting on the theories of biologic aging, stated that "the solution of the puzzle of aging depends on the assignment of relative weights to the various potential processes involved." There appears to be selective repression of certain genes during later life, which may control the function of neurons, muscles, and endocrine cells. The exact site of these inhibitory functions is of course not yet fully identified. In addition to these inhibitory influences, perhaps the disturbances are controlled by malfunction of DNA and the genetic damage that accompanies disruption of this important biochemical material. Certainly with the declining function associated with aging, abnormalities in DNA could give rise to the accumulation of inactive enzymes, deceleration of protein synthesis, and inactivation of receptor sites on membranes. Shock (1977) has reported that progressive differences develop in physiologic function with age, and documentation of the changes in resting cardiac output (Fig. 7-1) and renal clearances in humans have been shown by Davies and Shock (1950), Brandfonbrener, Lan-

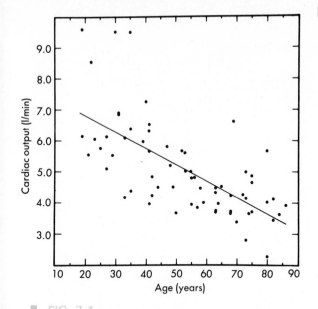

FIG. 7-1

Resting cardiac output (l/min) in normal men, aged 20 to 87 years. (Based on data from Brandfonbrener, M., Landowne, M., and Shock, N.W.: Circulation **12**:557, 1955.)

downe, and Shock (1955), and Rowe et al. (1976).

Over 100 years ago Bismark established 65 years as the normal retirement age, and in 1900 only 4% of the population exceeded this parameter. However, in 1970, 11% of the total population were over the age of 65, and it is anticipated that by the year 2000 this could well exceed 20% (New Encyclopaedia Britannica, 1975). Additionally, statistical information would indicate that with an increasing geriatric population, by the end of this century 50% of medical costs will be consumed by the elderly.

Consequently, because of the recent demonstration of changes in physiologic function with age and the greater emphasis on geriatric therapeutics, the requirement for the development of satisfactory reference ranges by which laboratory parameters can be accurately assessed has become a necessity.

REFERENCE VALUES IN THE GERIATRIC AGE GROUP

The normal reference value, as quoted in medical laboratory literature, is usually based on the 20- to 40-year-old age group. However, in the geriatric population, as in infancy and early childhood, variation in test results is well documented. Therefore to satisfactorily interpret laboratory values the determination of accurate reference ranges in the geriatric group is essential.

Gillibrand, Grewal, and Blattler (1979) conducted an analysis on chemistry reference values as a function of age and sex, including both pediatric and geriatric subjects. They demonstrated some interesting changes in the older age group, with findings similar to those established in my own series, which was conducted within a general population group admitted to a large reference teaching hospital. The resultant analyses, which are presented here, were performed using established automated instrumentation (e.g., Technicon SMA 12/60), and data were analyzed by means of a histogram select program, with subsequent calculation of means and standard deviations. The mean values for the analyses were then plotted against age groups, and the demonstrated variations were quite remarkable. Fig. 7-2 shows the values for calcium and phosphorus, and one can see the parallel relationship between these two minerals. Particularly, the fall in calcium within the female group occurs before that in the male group, although by the age of 50 they decrease in parallel. Undoubtedly, a contribution to this decrease in serum calcium is related to the commensurate fall in serum albumin, and Fig. 7-3 shows the mean distribution of total protein, the major constituent of which is serum albumin, because serum globulins tend to rise slightly with increasing age.

The age distribution for serum urea nitrogen and creatinine are shown in Fig. 7-4, and as can be seen, there is a gradual increase in the creatinine level, which occurs at a faster rate over the age of 50, becoming slightly greater in men

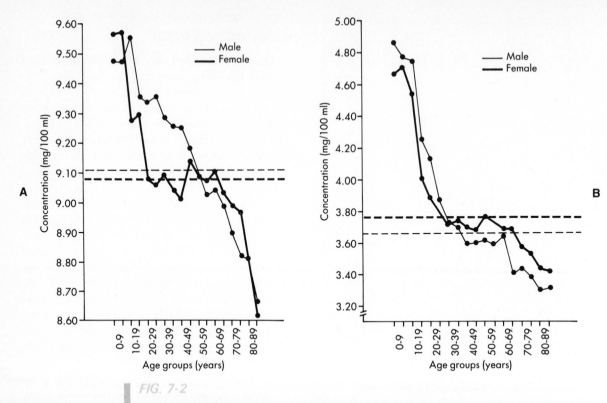

FIG. 7-2

A, Serum calcium reference range. **B,** Serum phosphorus reference range. Total number of subjects is greater than 10,000. Light dashes indicate mean normal range in males; heavy dashes indicate mean normal range in females.

than in women. This increase is also seen in urea nitrogen levels, although there is a tendency for a closer correlation between the male and female groups.

The increase in glucose intolerance shown with age is well demonstrated in Fig. 7-5, where the serum glucose can be seen to rise in men and women, although this becomes more marked in women over the age of 50. The interesting feature demonstrated by the glucose/age distribution is the decrease following onset of the menarche in women to levels significantly lower than in men, followed by a more marked intolerance in elderly women. It is interesting to postulate that these changes may be related to the hor-

monal changes accompanying the menarche and menopause in women, although presently this postulate has no direct experimental proof.

It becomes apparent that the importance of developing age-related reference ranges for the geriatric period is essential for appropriate interpretation of test results. Documentation of "normal ranges" has been done by Caird (1973) and Hodkinson (1977); however, many values do not differ greatly from the established values derived using the reference range of the general population. Nevertheless, under certain conditions the precise nature of the differences may be important as a discriminator, particularly in establishing an explanation for a metabolic disturbance

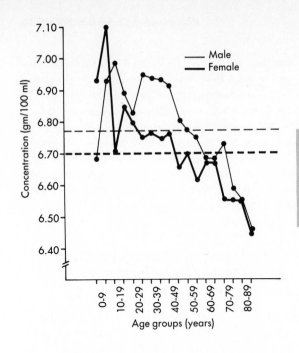

FIG. 7-3

Serum total protein reference range. Total number of subjects is greater than 10,000. Light dashes indicate mean normal range in males; heavy dashes indicate mean normal range in females.

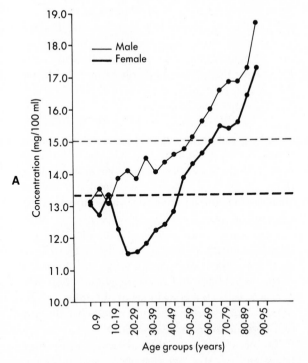

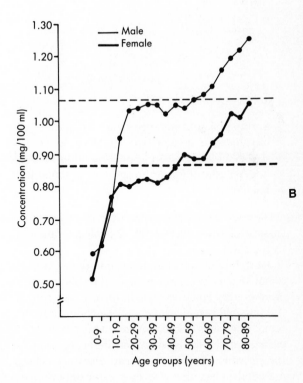

FIG. 7-4

A, Serum urea nitrogen reference range. **B,** Serum creatinine reference range. Total number of subjects is greater than 10,000. Light dashes indicate mean normal range in males; heavy dashes indicate mean normal range in females.

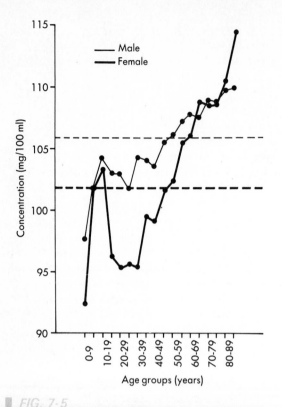

Serum glucose reference range. Total number of subjects is greater than 10,000. Light dashes indicate mean normal range in males; heavy dashes indicate mean normal range in females.

associated with decreasing physiologic function in the aged.

Certainly, if one is to determine the degree of organ dysfunction and degeneration as a result of laboratory analyses and, in turn, relate this to the possible responsiveness of the client to treatment, the necessity for accurate and precise reference values to assist in the determination of the possible effect of the organ disease on drug metabolism becomes of even greater importance. The well-recognized difference in the responsiveness of elderly persons to drugs, compared with younger adults, and the contrasting reactions

that are seen, may be related to metabolic processes that have changed or become deranged in dysfunctioning organs. Failure of excretion of the drug or its metabolites and differences in end organ responsiveness because of differences in cell receptor mediation may also be important.

Thus if any of the previously mentioned parameters can be assessed by appropriate biochemical function tests, the importance of an accurate reference range for the elderly is an absolute requirement.

PRINCIPLES OF DIAGNOSTIC LABORATORY INVESTIGATION IN GERIATRIC MEDICINE

Over the past 20 years screening for biochemical and hematologic disorders in laboratory medicine has become increasingly popular. This method involves the automated analysis of six or more tests, performed in a routine fashion on "sick," or in some instances "well," populations. Many papers (Screening in Medical Care, 1968) have been published concerning the abuse and misinterpretation of much of the data resulting from this type of program. The finding of abnormal results on a screening profile is obviously of value, but if one considers the 95% confidence limits of biologic and analytic variability in any single test procedure, it becomes obvious that a profile of 12 to 20 tests may carry a 60% chance of having an abnormal value unrelated to any clinical disorder.

Obviously, in an elderly population the previously mentioned finding will become increasingly apparent, and because of the advanced age of the individuals and the anticipated variability in test results, the possibility of obtaining an abnormal value in the absence of clinical disease will become even more prevalent.

In many instances this abnormal value may be related to the fact that the client is taking multiple medications, which appears to be a frequent problem in the elderly. Law and Chalmer (1976) have estimated in one British study that 87% of people over the age of 75 were found to be taking regular medication, and, more strikingly, 34% of the population were receiving a combination of more than three drugs. With this pattern of drug use in the elderly the possibility of interaction occurring between the analytic testing technique, or disordered organ function and the drug, gives rise to a greater likelihood of obtaining an abnormal false positive or false negative result in a screening profile. Consequently, as a result of these possible interferences, the performance of unrelated screening profiles would be nonbeneficial because they could quite easily lead to inappropriate investigations and false diagnoses.

The requirement for screening in the elderly should be limited to those tests related to the suspected clinical disease, and organ profiling is therefore the method of choice. Test profiles should be established aiming at the investigation of thyroid dysfunction, liver failure, myocardial and congestive cardiac failure, renal disease, bone disease, and nutritional disorders.

Similar screening should be established for hematologic disease, although in many instances the main requirement will be for the investigation of anemia in the elderly, which will require an estimate of the hemoglobin, hematocrit, red blood cell count, and an examination of a peripheral blood smear. Calculated red cell indices (i.e., mean corpuscular volume and mean corpuscular hemoglobin concentration) are also of assistance in subclassifying types of anemia. Any additional information required on mixed cell populations, observation for fragments or abnormal red and white cell forms, should be ascertained from a blood smear.

Many conditions in the elderly would be more efficiently diagnosed and monitored by the institution of a modified screening format. Diagnosis of the more occult disease presentations, such as hypothyroidism, may only be achieved by the use of a thyroid function study using serum thyroxine and T$_3$ resin uptake, with thyroid-stimulating hormone as a confirmatory procedure. Re-

stricted screening will prevent the considerable difficulty that can often arise in attempting to relate an abnormal test result to an otherwise normal clinical presentation.

SYSTEMATIC LABORATORY INVESTIGATION
Cardiovascular disease

Myocardial disease leading to congestive heart failure is not uncommon in the elderly, resulting from the gradual degeneration of myocardial muscle. Aggravation of this degeneration will be caused by any degree of anemia arising as a result of nutritional deficiencies or neoplastic disease, the latter giving rise to the normochromic, normocytic type of anemia quite often seen in the elderly. In addition, degeneration of myocardial muscle will be precipitated by the development of vascular occlusion, arising as a result of arteriosclerosis and hypertensive disease. Chronic obstructive pulmonary disease may also give rise to congestive heart failure as a result of inadequate transfer of oxygen to the myocardium. This could be aggravated by the reduced concentrations of hemoglobin found in chronic anemia.

Consequently, the laboratory investigation of congestive cardiac failure should include an evaluation of the hematologic profile, and corrective measures should be taken for any associated anemia. It is unlikely, unless the client has had recent chest pain, that an estimation of creatine kinase (CK) will be significant. However, if the client complains of chest pain, this estimation may be of assistance in determining the nature of the lesion, and if the symptom is followed during the period of hospitalization, it may indicate a progressive spread of acute damage to the myocardium.

Other enzymes of use in investigating congestive cardiac failure are lactate dehydrogenase (LDH) and its isoenzymes. The latter estimation will allow determination of whether the elevated lactate dehydrogenase results from congestive failure, leading to release of lactate dehydrogenase-5 from liver tissue or if it is elevated as a result of prolonged myocardial degeneration, in which case lactate dehydrogenase-1 will be dominant. Total lactate dehydrogenase, unless fractionated, is of little value.

Arteriosclerosis

The development of arteriosclerosis is certainly associated with aging; however, its underlying causes have been a topic of discussion for many years. It would appear that an elevated serum cholesterol and disorders of lipoprotein metabolism have a distinct role in the onset and progression of this disorder. Arteriosclerosis can be generalized or localized to various arterial groups; the clinical disorders commonly associated are intermittent claudication and angina pectoris, becoming a measure of the development and seriousness of this arterial problem.

Laboratory investigation of this disease in the elderly is of little assistance in terms of preventive medicine because the disease is usually fairly advanced and little can be done to prevent its progressive nature. However, should the diagnosis be made before the individual reaches 50 years of age, then the estimation of serum cholesterol and triglycerides should be performed along with fractionation of the lipoprotein entities. If it is found that the high density lipoprotein cholesterol is low, particularly in the presence of a high total serum cholesterol, then preventive measures should be taken to limit the cholesterol intake and redistribute the fractions to assist in promoting an elevation in the high density lipoprotein fraction.

Even in the elderly, maintenance of dietary restrictions to achieve these ends is not out of the question and could presumably have a beneficial effect on the life span of the individual. By the time a person reaches the age of 60 to 70 years the possibility of dietary measures having any success is doubtful; permanent damage has already been done to the arterial walls, and the progressive nature of arteriosclero-

sis is not altogether dependent on levels of cholesterol but is more associated with local damage, tissue reaction and regeneration, a process in which dietary manipulation of cholesterol restriction will probably not have any major effect.

The upper limits of the reference ranges for serum total cholesterol and triglycerides are quoted as 330 mg/100 ml and 190 mg/100 ml, respectively. In my opinion these values are too high, and the general aim in monitoring treatment of serum lipid levels in the elderly should be to achieve concentrations of less than 250 mg/100 ml for serum cholesterol and 150 mg/100 ml for serum triglycerides.

Renal disease

With increasing age, renal function, as measured by the usual standard function tests, shows a gradual deterioration. This can be demonstrated by the elevation of serum creatinine and urea, but it is shown more effectively by creatinine clearance, which in the normal adult lies between 110 and 120 ml/min; however, there is a gradual decrease with age, reaching levels of 60 to 70 ml/min in the 70- to 75-year age group.

The decrease in function results from a gradual reduction in effective renal filtration resulting from glomerular necrosis and tubular dysfunction. However, an important facet in the elderly is the associated dehydration, which quite often accompanies any constitutional upset in the individual.

Dehydration will cause a reduction in kidney perfusion and may lead to a false interpretation of laboratory predictors of disease, both hematologic and, more particularly, biochemical. Obviously, in the dehydrated elderly person, the volume depletion will lead to an apparent normalization of low biochemical parameters and an exaggeration of the biochemical serum analyses normally accepted as indicators of impaired renal function, such as urea and creatinine. Consequently, it is essential in the assessment of an elderly person's renal function to consider the possibility of dehydration because this can quite easily falsify the severity of renal perfusion and the subsequent degree of anticipated renal failure. Indeed, rehydration of an elderly person may easily improve creatinine clearance by as much as 200%.

Undoubtedly, control of osmoreception is far less efficient in the geriatric age group, and because of this, development of hyponatremia is not unusual, particularly in association with severe illness (Mukherjee, Coni, and Davison, 1973).

Geriatric clients, particularly those who are going to undertake a course of prolonged drug therapy with a pharmaceutical preparation mainly excreted through the kidney, require assessment of renal function as an important prerequisite. The most satisfactory test to assess functional impairment is creatinine clearance, performed on a 24-hour urinary collection. Reliance on serum creatinine or urea levels to assess renal function is less than satisfactory in the geriatric client because of the more static nature of these measures, leading quite often to a wrong evaluation of renal disease and the dangers associated with inappropriate drug therapy and response.

Hepatic disease

Little or no difference exists between the investigation of disorders of liver function in the elderly and other age groups. Anticipated hepatic disorders can be divided into the usual simple classification: hepatocellular or obstructive.

However, as mentioned in the discussion of cardiovascular disorders, perhaps the most commonly associated hepatocellular disorder in the geriatric age group results from congestive cardiac failure, leading to centrilobular necrosis and serum elevation of intracellular enzymes, alanine aminotransferase (ALT), aspartate aminotransferase (AST), and lactic dehydrogenase (LDH).

In a severe case of congestive cardiac failure the inability of the liver cells to excrete bilirubin may lead to a slight elevation in this excretory metabolite, and the level of unconjugated-to-con-

jugated bilirubin may be an estimate of the severity of the cellular necrosis. Eventually, should cardiac failure be sufficiently prolonged, fatty degeneration and, finally, fibrosis will occur with disruption in the liver pattern and the development of cirrhotic liver disease with the appropriate changes in liver cell enzymes. Cirrhosis can also develop from other disorders in the elderly, including alcoholism and postnecrotic fibrosis subsequent to acute hepatitis. Obviously, the latter two problems can be quite often excluded by client history and previous clinical presentation.

Obstructive liver disease in the elderly is quite another situation. Often this arises as a result of neoplasia, either from blockage of the porta hepatis from enlarged secondary neoplastic lymph glands or from primary involvement of the organ with metastases. Biochemical differentiation of this particular problem is often difficult, and on the basis of estimating bilirubin, along with alkaline phosphatase and 5'-nucleotidase, this may be insufficient to assist in differentiating blockage because of secondary carcinoma involving the lymphatic glands in the porta hepatis or early stages of carcinoma in the head of the pancreas. However, with metastases to the liver the marked differential increase between bilirubin and alkaline phosphatase, with a more marked elevation in the latter, quite often is a useful guide in predicting the presence of extensive hepatic secondaries.

Gallstone disease, although present in some geriatric clients, is usually not as prevalent as in the middle-aged group, and differentiation of biliary obstruction because of this disorder may easily be achieved by radiologic examination.

The importance of satisfactory hepatic function in the elderly age group undergoing drug therapy is obvious because the liver is the principal organ responsible for controlling the metabolism of pharmaceutical agents. Consequently, it becomes imperative in a client who is suspected of having liver disease that an appropriate biochemical assessment is made before the administration of pharmacologic preparations. Minimum liver function tests that should be performed are serum bilirubin, alkaline phosphatase, aspartate or alanine aminotransferase, and possibly γ-glutamyl transpeptidase in those clients suspected of having a history of alcohol indulgence. The major common metabolic function test of hepatic disease is probably the estimation of total serum protein, serum albumin, and protein electrophoresis. Serum albumin in the aged is usually 1 to 1.2 gm/100 ml lower than the quoted serum albumin for a younger adult population. Serum globulins are usually slightly elevated, and the total serum protein concentration may be normal. Fractionation is therefore essential, and a protein electrophoretic separation will often allow one to determine if the client has an inflammatory disorder or possible intrinsic liver disease leading to an increase in γ-globulin with β-γ bridging.

Gastroenterologic investigation

Overall function of the gastrointestinal tract generally decreases with age. The changes may be investigated biochemically in relation to the different segmental portions of this important organ. Many elderly people develop a hiatus hernia, and this can be very troublesome with regard to regurgitation of gastric contents into the distal portion of the esophagus, with the eventual production of an esophageal stricture leading to problems with deglutition. Frequently there is gastric atrophy with duodenal regurgitation, and the presence of bile in gastric contents is not unusual and may be associated with the development of gastric ulceration. The first stage in digestion may become severely disturbed, and in some cases gastric atrophy may be sufficient to prevent production of intrinsic factor with the subsequent development of megaloblastic anemia.

Small intestinal function tends to be satisfactorily retained, and development of frank malabsorption as a result of age is very rare. How-

ever, in the presence of primary disease of the biliary or pancreatic ducts, secondary malabsorption will occur. Muscular coordination of the intestinal tract appears to be a problem in the elderly, with subsequent development of delayed transit through the intestine, quite often leading to ileocecal regurgitation of colonic contents and bacteria. During an investigation of clients suffering from the malabsorption syndrome and suspected of having bacterial overgrowth, numerous elderly clients were found to have deconjugation of bile salts occurring in the small intestine, associated with a moderate degree of bile salt wastage. The deconjugation pattern shown in these clients improved dramatically when the bowel transit time was decreased by means of increasing the intestinal bulk through the administration of dietary fiber. This measure led to a physical as well as a biochemical improvement in their nutritional status. A further benefit also accrued, in that there was an increase in colonic function, inducing normal bowel action and overcoming the chronic constipative problems associated with increasing age.

Therefore, in investigating the intestinal tract of an elderly subject, it is recommended that if evidence of a nutritional or malabsorption problem exists, consideration should be given to the possibility of delayed transit with concomitant secondary bacterial contamination of the small intestine. Presence of bacteria in the small intestine may also have deleterious effects on drugs or pharmaceutical preparations that are being administered to the client because primary bacterial degradation of these products may occur before their absorption, with subsequent or apparent failure of therapeutic response.

Specific malabsorption defects may occur with aging, and a demonstration of a possible effect on fat-soluble vitamins has been reported by Hollander and Morgan (1979), who feel that the defect in absorption of vitamin A may have an effect on tissue aging.

Osteomalacia and osteoporosis, although distinctly different diseases of bone, are quite commonly associated with increasing age. Particularly, osteoporosis is common in postmenopausal women, and treatment with estrogens has been shown to be extremely beneficial. However, etiologically, osteoporosis is a loss of bony substance, whereas osteomalacia is a failure of mineralization of bony colloid because of the defective metabolism of calcium salts. The latter may arise as a result of intestinal malabsorption of calcium because of a lack of vitamin D in the diet or as a direct result of a failure of the primary absorptive mechanism. Diagnosis of osteomalacia may be made by estimating serum calcium and phosphorus; however, interpretation of the values should take into consideration any variations in serum albumin and also the normal reference range for these minerals. Unfortunately an estimation of serum alkaline phosphatase is of little value because so many other conditions in the elderly may contribute to an elevation in this enzyme.

Amelioration of geriatric osteomalacia may be achieved by vitamin D and calcium supplements, which tend to support a malabsorptive cause.

The establishment of investigational protocols to evaluate disease of the gastrointestinal tract in geriatric age groups should, therefore, be aimed mainly at determining the possible cause of any malabsorptive problems as a result of intrinsic intestinal disease or bacterial overgrowth. Consequently, the use of fecal fat measurement and serum carotene may be of initial value, followed by a possible trial of broad-spectrum antibiotics if a C^{14}-Glycocholic breath analysis is unavailable.

Endocrinologic investigation

During the course of aging there is a significant decline in hormone secretion by the thyroid, adrenal cortex, testes, and ovaries, and although the pituitary growth hormone level falls, gonadotropins continue to rise. The decline in excretion of testicular and ovarian steroids appears to be caused by an age change within the gonads, associated with necrosis of endocrine tissue. The thyroid similarly demonstrates a preponderance of nodular glands, showing tiny follicles with microscopic colloid nodules and associated fibrosis. Focal lymphocytic thyroiditis was also observed in 20% of thyroid glands examined by Denham and Wills (1980), but microscopic evidence of altered function, although common, could not always be correlated with the results of clinical thyroid function studies. Hypothyroidism in the elderly is not an uncommon disorder, but because of atypical presentations, its diagnosis may not occur until much later and may have serious consequences for the client. Thus, in this particular instance, thyroxine screening is of great assistance.

Adrenal function appears to be fairly well maintained, and it is only with the development of severely stressful situations that evidence of failure in the reserve capacity of the adrenal gland is recognized. However, this condition hardly ever requires investigation, and a plasma cortisol is rarely necessary.

Recognition of the development of decreased glucose tolerance is very important in the elderly, and often this is not related to any deficiency in the exocrine pancreas but probably more to peripheral end organ failure. Usually, hyperglycemia can be controlled by diet and oral hypoglycemic agents. An accepted interpretation of the glucose tolerance test in an elderly client without an elevated fasting serum glucose or positive family history of diabetes mellitus is to increase the normally accepted levels of 120 to 130 mg/100 ml at 1 hour and 60 to 80 mg/100 ml at 2 hours, by an increment of 10 mg/100 ml at 50 years, with an additional 10 mg/100 ml for each subsequent decade (Wallach, 1978).

Nevertheless, in the geriatric age group the determination of fasting and 2-hour postprandial blood glucose is important to ensure that early recognition of glucose intolerance can be recognized and, if necessary, treated to prevent the development of any complications associated with hyperglycemia.

Hematologic investigation

By far the most common hematologic disorder in the elderly client is anemia. Brunning (1974) states that after the age of 60, a person's normal hemoglobin level of 13.5 to 18 gm/100 ml decreases by about 1.5 gm/100 ml in men per decade; however, it remains remarkably stable in women at 12 to 16 gm/100 ml.

Howe (1979) believes that in an orderly approach to the correct diagnosis of anemia in the elderly one should classify anemia into three distinct types: (1) hypochromic microcytic, (2) normochromic, and (3) macrocytic. The diagnosis should be based on the hemoglobin, hematocrit, red blood cell count, and examination of a peripheral blood smear; in this manner it should therefore be possible to identify the cause of the anemia and establish the appropriate therapy. Additional biochemical analyses as a result of the initial hematologic screen can then be performed, thereby determining the presence of iron deficiency by performing serum iron and iron binding capacity in addition to measuring vitamin B_{12} and folic acid levels if macrocytic anemia is suspected.

LABORATORY INVESTIGATION IN RELATION TO DRUG THERAPY

Attention has been drawn to the problems associated with biochemical disturbances occurring in the elderly that may adversely affect the efficacy of drug treatment. It is not uncommon in clinical practice to observe in the geriatric age group an abnormal reaction to normal sedative administration, such as with barbiturates. Quite often the response of a geriatric client to the administration of a "sleeping pill" is exactly the converse, thus promoting hyperactivity. The biochemical disturbance underlying this reaction is not fully understood, although it may have some relationship to an imbalance between the normal serotonin-to-dopamine/epinephrine concentrations in the brain at the neuronal membrane level, as well as possible changes in hepatic metabolism.

However, the more important reactions are those that are known to have adverse effects as a result of treatment with a therapeutic agent, such as phenytoin, which decreases the level of serum thyroxine in clients and may easily be misinterpreted as evidence of underlying disease. Conversely, it is well known that many drugs bind to serum albumin and thus become inactive. Obviously, in geriatric clients who have low serum albumin levels, the degree of protein binding will consequently be less, thereby resulting in the presence of larger amounts of free drug that will have a possible greater effect at the target cell level.

Attention has already been given to the problems associated with renal and hepatic failure; therefore, if a client is suspected of having a disorder of these two important organs, the necessary functional tests must be performed before administration of the therapeutic agent. With the advent of further investigations into the pharmacokinetic relationships of drugs (see Chapter 10, "Pharmacokinetics in the Aged"), periodic therapeutic biochemical investigations (wich checks throughout the treatment period), using laboratory biochemical parameters associated with organ disease, have been shown to be increasingly important. In addition, the establishment of serum and urine assays for conveniently determining drug and metabolite levels is a reliable adjunct to satisfactory drug therapy.

CONCLUSION

Biochemical and hematologic reviews of the geriatric client from the diagnostic and pretreatment viewpoint are demonstrating increasing usefulness. These measures should be performed in such a manner as to assess the possibility of any detrimental reaction, particularly in relation to the administration of therapeutic agents, that may occur as a result of treatment. The investigational protocols do not need to be complex; simple procedures can convey the necessary information required to make a satisfactory assessment. Occasionally, more sophisticated biochemical analyses may be necessary. However, the preceding outline will hopefully serve as a guideline to the laboratory investigation of the geriatric client, particularly in relation to the establishment of normality before drug therapy.

REFERENCES

Borkan, G.A.: The assessment of biological age during adulthood, doctoral dissertation, Ann Arbor, Mich., 1978, University of Michigan.

Brandfonbrener, M., Landowne, M.M., and Shock, N.W.: Changes in cardiac output with age, Circulation **12:**557, 1955.

Brunning, R.D.: Differential diagnosis of anemia, Geriatrics **29:**52, 1974.

Caird, F.I.: Problems of interpretation of laboratory findings in the old, Br. Med. J. **4:**348, 1973.

Costa, P.T., Jr., and McCrae, R.R.: Functional age: a conceptual and empirical critique, paper presented at conference, Epidemiology of Aging, Bethesda, Md., Mar. 28-29, 1977, U.S. Government Printing Office.

Davies, D.F., and Shock, N.W.: Age changes in glomerular filtration rate, effective renal plasma flow and tubular excretory capacity in adult males, J. Clin. Invest. **29:**496, 1950.

Denham, M.J., and Wills, E.J.: A Clinico-pathological survey of thyroid glands in old age, Gerontology **26:** 160, 1980.

Gillibrand, D., Grewal, D., and Blattler, D.P.: Chemistry reference values as a function of age and sex, including pediatric and geriatric subjects. In Dietz, A.A., editor: Aging—its chemistry, proceedings of the Arnold O. Beckman conference in clinical chemistry. Washington, D.C., 1979, American Association for Clinical Chemistry.

Hodkinson, H.M.: Biochemical diagnosis of the elderly, London, 1977, Chapman & Hall.

Hollander, D., and Morgan, D.: Aging: its influence on vitamin A intestinal absorption in vivo by the rat, Exp. Gerontol. **14:**301, 1979.

Howe, R.B.: Tips on diagnosing and treating anemia in the aging, Geriatrics **34:**29, 1979.

Law, R., and Chalmer, C.: Medicines and elderly people: a general practice survey, Br. Med. J. **1:**565, 1976.

Mukherjee, A.P., Coni, N.K., and Davison, W.: Osmoreceptor functions among the elderly, Gerontol. Clin. **15:**227, 1973.

New Encyclopaedia Britannica: Macropaedia, vol 13, Chicago, 1975, Helen Hemingway Benton.

Rowe, J.W., et al.: The effect of age on creatinine clearance in men: a cross sectional and longitudinal study, J. Gerontol. **31:**155, 1976.

Screening in medical care: reviewing the evidence, Nuffield Provincial Trust, New York, 1968, Oxford University Press, Inc.

Shock, N.W.: The biological basis of aging. In Meade, G.M., editor: Frontiers of medicine, New York, 1977, Plenum Publishing Corp.

Strehler, B.L., A Critique of Theories of Biological Aging. In Dietz, A.A., editor: Aging—its chemistry, proceedings of the Arnold O. Beckman conference in clinical chemistry, Washington, D.C., 1979, American Association for Clinical Chemistry.

Wallach, J.: Interpretation of diagnostic tests, ed. 3, Boston, 1978, Little, Brown, & Co.

CHAPTER 8

Drug interactions in the geriatric client

Lawrence H. Block

The susceptibility of the elderly to drug-induced illness or adverse reactions is underscored by age-related differences in health and drug use patterns. Aging is associated with an increasing incidence of health problems requiring both medical intervention and the use of drugs with the subsequent potential of adverse reactions (see Chapter 11) and interactions (Seidl et al., 1966; Hurwitz, 1969a and 1969b; Wade, 1970; Lamy, 1974; Otten and Shelley, 1976; Freeman, 1979).

In one study (Hale, Marks, and Stewart, 1979) 77% of the ambulatory elderly screened used drugs regularly. There was a consistent increase in the average number of drug classes used with an increase in age. The greater frequency of multiple, chronic drug use in geriatric clients, coupled with a higher incidence of drug administration errors among the elderly (e.g., dose omission, incorrect time of administration), increases the risk of occurrence of adverse reactions and interactions (Holloway, 1974).

Age-related changes in pharmacokinetics (Chapter 10) and in receptor sensitivity to drugs predispose geriatric clients to adverse reactions and interactions. Altered drug disposition, such as altered renal or extrarenal clearance, changes in apparent volumes of distribution, and altered protein binding, are more likely to occur in the

elderly adult than in the younger adult because of progressive physiologic changes in body composition and organ function that occur with aging (Triggs and Nation, 1975; Schmucker, 1979; Vancura, 1979; Schumacher, 1980). (See Chapter 6, "Physiologic Changes and Clinical Manifestations of Aging.") In some instances the response of elderly individuals to drugs differs from that of younger individuals and appears to reflect an altered sensitivity of receptors to drugs rather than altered drug disposition (Bender, 1979; Fleisch, 1980). Vestal, Wood, and Shand (1979) noted the reduced responsiveness of the β-adrenoceptor to both agonist (isoproterenol) and antagonist (propranolol) with advancing years. The increased sensitivity of the elderly to warfarin may involve altered pharmacokinetics of warfarin enantiomers, altered vitamin K disposition, altered receptor sensitivity to vitamin K_1, or higher plasma concentrations of endogenous inhibitors of clotting factor activity in the aged (Shepherd, Wilson, and Stevenson, 1979).

Nutritional deficiencies in the aged can result from drug use (Roe, 1976) as well as from poor diet (Greene, 1979) and may well have serious consequences insofar as drug safety and efficacy in the elderly are concerned (Roe, 1976; Krishnaswamy, 1978).

Thus the clinician attempting to select appropriate drugs or individualize drug dosage for elderly clients may often be confronted with multiple pathologic conditions, existing drug use (sometimes surreptitious), poor compliance, altered pharmacokinetics, altered drug-receptor sensitivity, and altered nutritional status (Hyde et al., 1979; Knapp and Knapp, 1980). The predisposition, then, of geriatric clients to adverse drug reactions and interactions is hardly surprising.

A drug interaction occurs when the pharmacodynamics or pharmacokinetics of one drug is altered as a result of the administration of another drug. Rowland and Tozer (1980) distinguished between the two types of interactions on the basis of the relationship between response and the unbound concentration of the pharmacologically active species. A change in the response-unbound concentration curve implies a pharmacodynamic interaction; no change in the curve implies a pharmacokinetic interaction. Pharmacodynamic interactions probably account for most clinically important drug interactions (Ariens and Simonis, 1974; Prescott, 1980) because alterations of drug effects on receptors or physiologic systems are involved.

CLINICALLY IMPORTANT DRUG INTERACTIONS IN THE GERIATRIC CLIENT

The principal factors that affect the clinical importance or significance of interactions are (1) the frequency of occurrence of the interaction among those using the drugs and (2) the prognosis for the client as a result of the interaction (Block, 1977). One view is that drug interactions are only clinically important when the safety or efficacy of treatment is affected (Koch-Weser and Greenblatt, 1977). Furthermore, interactions involving frequently used drugs are generally of greater concern than those occurring with drugs that are infrequently used. Understandably, if all potential clinically important drug interactions could be detected by an appropriate monitoring

procedure, there would be no need to emphasize those interactions involving frequently used drugs. The frequency of use of drugs by geriatric clients (Moore, 1978; Christopher et al., 1979; Hale, Marks, and Stewart, 1979; Williamson, 1979) is listed in Table 8-1 by therapeutic category. Accordingly, the drugs most often employed are central nervous system (CNS) agents (other than analgesics), cardiovascular agents, anti-inflammatory agents and analgesics, and diuretics. The primary emphasis in this chapter is on interactions involving these widely used drugs. Interactions are described in terms of the effects of secondary agents on these primary drugs.

Interactions of drugs affecting the central nervous system

Elderly clients are prone to organic confusional psychoses with the onset of hypoxia, infection, or a cerebrovascular accident (e.g., hemorrhage, embolism, thrombotic infarction) (Grahame-Smith, 1977). The rate and extent of cerebral blood perfusion is reduced in the normal geriatric client and markedly reduced in the arteriosclerotic client. Marked structural and biochemical changes, coupled with neuronal loss in the aged brain (Cape, 1979), lead to a deterioration in brain function and unexpected or bizarre reactions to drug administration (Riley, 1977). The CNS is more prone to dysfunction with advancing age than any other organ system (Holloway, 1974). Thus combination drug therapy is associated with a high incidence of adverse effects (Grahame-Smith, 1977). Drug therapy involving two or more CNS depressants can result in oversedation (CNS underarousal), a loss of coordination, or confusion if the drug dosage is not properly adjusted. This may be particularly troublesome for elderly clients in the early evening and at night when orienting perceptual stimuli are decreased (Salzman, 1979). Clinicians should also be aware of the possible CNS depression or dysfunction induced by drugs not normally used

TABLE 8-1   **Ranking of frequency of use of drugs prescribed for and used by geriatric clients in various studies**

Therapeutic category	Moore (1978) N = 493*	Christopher et al. (1979) N = 873	Hale, Marks, and Stewart (1979) N = 1711	Williamson (1979) N = 1998
CNS agents (other than analgesics)	3	1	4	1
Cardiovascular agents	2	4	1	3
Anti-inflammatory agents and analgesics	1†	3	3	4
Diuretics	5	2	5	2
Vitamins	6	6	2	6
Endocrine agents	4	7	6-8‡	7-8‡
Antibiotics-antiinfectives	—	5	—	5

*N = number of geriatric clients in study.
†OTC analgesics were included with prescribed analgesics.
‡The ranges are a result of different classifications and pooling of therapeutic categories by the authors.

for their CNS activity. Examples of such drugs with secondary CNS effects include carbonic anhydrase inhibitors such as acetazolamide, cardiac glycosides, cimetidine, and cycloserine.

Anticonvulsants. Several anticonvulsants, such as phenobarbital, phenytoin, and carbamazepine, are enzyme inducers. The concurrent use of these anticonvulsants with other drugs in epileptic clients often leads to interactions manifested by changes in biophase concentrations of the induced drug following the addition or withdrawal of an inducer (Cereghino et al., 1975; Lai, Levy, and Cutler, 1978). Monitoring of concentrations at such times is necessary if toxicity or therapeutic failure is to be avoided.

Dravet et al. (1977) reported on the induction of carbamazepine toxicity in eight clients treated with the drug within 24 hours after the initiation of troleandomycin therapy for mild infections. All eight clients experienced nausea, vomiting,

disturbed balance, and pronounced drowsiness. The authors ascribed the toxicity to decreased hepatic biotransformation of carbamazepine in the presence of troleandomycin. Measurements of plasma carbamazepine concentrations supported this contention (Fig. 8-1). Thus troleandomycin should be avoided as should erythromycin (a structurally similar macrolide antibiotic), and other nonmacrolide antibiotics should be considered instead (Mesdjian et al., 1980). Dam and Christiansen (1977) also noted the prevalence of headache, dizziness, ataxia, nausea, and tiredness in clients receiving carbamazepine and propoxyphene concurrently. Plasma concentrations of carbamazepine and its 10,11-epoxide were determined in five clients before and after the addition of propoxyphene to the drug regimen. The results were indicative of an inhibition of carbamazepine oxidation with a consequent 32% to 44% decrease in carbamazepine clearance.

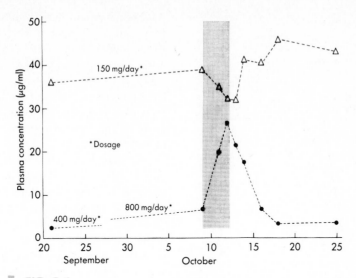

FIG. 8-1

Plasma concentrations of phenobarbital (△) and carbamazepine (●) as a function of time. The shaded area corresponds to the 4-day period during which troleandomycin (2 gm/day) was administered. (Modified from Dravet, C., et al.: Lancet **1**:810, 1977.)

The prudent clinician would be advised to avoid the use of propoxyphene or its combinations in clients treated with carbamazepine.

Phenytoin plasma concentrations may be increased to toxic levels (Fig. 8-2) as a result of the inhibition of biotransformation by concurrently administered drugs such as cimetidine or chloramphenicol (Christensen and Skovsted, 1969; Ballek, Reidenberg, and Orr, 1973; Rose et al., 1977; Greenlaw, 1979). This is of particular concern with phenytoin because of its nonlinear disposition kinetics. Accordingly, phenytoin concentrations should be monitored and the dose of phenytoin reduced if necessary. Antibiotics other than chloramphenicol should be considered for administration concurrently with phenytoin. Phenytoin biotransformation is significantly inhibited by dicumarol but not by warfarin or phenindione. Hansen, Kristensen, and Skovsted (1966) noted a fourfold increase in the half-life of phenytoin accompanying the addition of dicumarol to the regimen for 1 week. In some subjects elevated phenytoin concentrations persisted for 1 week after withdrawal of the dicumarol. Thus the use of dicumarol is not recommended for clients receiving phenytoin. If dicumarol must be used, phenytoin dose requirements will most likely be lower than they would be in the absence of dicumarol. Warfarin poses few problems for the client treated with phenytoin and would be the anticoagulant of choice. Plasma phenytoin concentrations are likely to be markedly increased in clients who begin to take disulfiram concurrently (Kiorboe, 1966; Olesen, 1966 and 1967), apparently as a result of noncompetitive inhibition of phenytoin biotransformation (Taylor, Alexander, and Lyon, 1981). The increase in phenytoin concentration can be rapid (within hours of the first dose of disulfiram) and prolonged (persisting for as long as 3 weeks after the

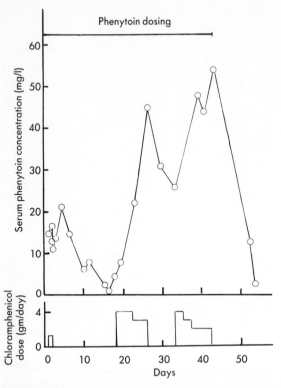

FIG. 8-2

Serum phenytoin concentrations as a function of time in a client receiving 300 mg/day phenytoin and intermittent doses of chloramphenicol. (From Rose, J.Q., et al.: J.A.M.A. **237:**2631, 1977. Copyright 1977, American Medical Association.)

discontinuation of disulfiram). A decrease in phenytoin dosage during concomitant therapy and a gradual increase in dosage after the discontinuation of disulfiram, in conjunction with the monitoring of plasma phenytoin concentrations, should be considered. Although plasma phenytoin concentrations are often higher than anticipated with concurrent disulfiram administration, phenytoin accumulation in clients taking isoniazid concurrently tends to be a problem only in those clients who demonstrate slow acetylation of isoniazid (Kutt et al., 1970).

Extensive monitoring of inpatients between 1966 and 1975 (Miller, Porter, and Greenblatt, 1979) revealed adverse CNS effects (e.g., disorientation, ataxia, nystagmus, dysarthria, psychotic behavior, convulsions, coma) in 2.7% taking phenytoin alone but in 27% of those taking both phenytoin and isoniazid. Age, weight, and mean daily doses of phenytoin were comparable in the two groups.

A clinically significant interaction between phenobarbital and valproic acid, resulting in an increase in phenobarbital concentrations, often necessitates a decrement in phenobarbital dosage (Loiseau, Brachet, and Henry, 1975; Mesdjian et al., 1978). Patel, Levy, and Cutler (1980), in a study of the interaction involving six normal subjects, demonstrated an increase in phenobarbital half-life, a decrease in phenobarbital clearance, and a decrease in the fraction of the phenobarbital dose metabolized consistent with decreased phenobarbital biotransformation. The specific metabolic pathways affected by valproic acid were not elucidated.

Antidepressants. Depression is a common psychiatric problem in the elderly, with the incidence and recurrence of depressive episodes increasing with age (Brathwaite, Montgomery, and Dawling, 1979).

Tricyclic antidepressants (TCAs) are the most widely used drugs for the treatment of depression (Norman et al., 1979; Fischer and Kroboth, 1980). Surveys of pharmacokinetic data reported for TCAs (Brathwaite, Montgomery, and Dawling, 1979; Norman et al., 1979) indicate that the variability in steady-state plasma TCA concentrations is substantially greater in geriatric clients than in young clients. Toxicity and therapeutic failure are consequently more often encountered in the elderly who are treated with these drugs.

The peripheral and central anticholinergic activity of TCAs leads to the most common unwanted effects of these drugs (Hollister, 1978). The coadministration of anticholinergic agents, such as antiparkinsonian agents and some antihistamines, with TCAs may result in excessive anticholinergic effects (e.g., paralytic ileus, acute glaucoma, or urinary retention) in geriatric clients (Ban, 1978; Gualtieri and Powell, 1978).

Notwithstanding their earlier introduction in the treatment of depression, monoamine oxidase inhibitors (MAOIs) are less often used than the TCAs. This reflects the association of MAOIs with adrenergic crises, particularly when used with sympathomimetic drugs and certain foods. Concomitant MAOI-TCA therapy may involve an interaction between the two drugs, resulting from the inhibition of deaminating enzymes by the MAOI and the inhibition of the presynaptic reuptake of biogenic amines in the CNS by the TCA. These actions ostensibly serve to increase the synaptic availability of the amines. Even though this "interacting" combination has been considered to be contraindicated in the past, experience has generally shown the combination to be safe as long as the client is closely monitored and low oral doses of the two drugs are used (Ponto et al., 1977; Goldberg and Thornton, 1978). Nonetheless, although the use of this combination may be warranted in the treatment of refractory depression, its use in elderly clients should be approached with caution in view of the greater frequency of toxic effects in geriatric clients and the decreased clearance of these drugs in the aged (Bender, 1979; Brathwaite, Montgomery, and Dawling, 1979; Norman et al., 1979; Robinson, 1979; Hirtz, 1980).

Also, it may be prudent to avoid tranylcypromine or phenelzine as the MAOI (because of their amphetamine-like–amine-releasing properties) and to employ amitriptyline rather than imipramine because the latter tends to evoke stimulation rather than sedation. The TCA can be added directly to the MAOI regimen if the MAOI has been used for less than 1 week. Otherwise, the TCA should not be used concomitantly until an MAOI-free period of several days to a week has elapsed (Goldberg and Thornton, 1978). A contrasting view has been proposed by other clinicians, such as Hollister (1980), who advocate the initiation of treatment with the TCA followed by the addition of the MAOI later on.

Antimanics. Lithium is eliminated by renal excretion; virtually all of an absorbed dose can ultimately be recovered in the urine. Renal excretion of lithium can be influenced by changes in electrolyte retention in the body. Sodium loading results in increased lithium excretion (and decreased effectiveness), whereas sodium depletion leads to increased lithium retention (and increased toxicity). The use of diuretics with lithium—occasionally in the treatment of lithium-induced edema—may pose special hazards for geriatric clients, particularly in view of reduced renal function and increased susceptibility to sodium depletion by diuretics with advancing age (Grahame-Smith, 1977). The concomitant administration of thiazide diuretics has been associated with a reduction of the renal clearance of lithium by 25% to 50% (Petersen et al., 1974; Himmelhoch et al., 1977a). Kerry, Ludlow, and Owen (1980) have pointed to the "dangers" of the uncontrolled use of diuretics in clients already receiving lithium. Nonetheless, sodium-depleting diuretics, such as the thiazides, can be used with lithium as long as lithium dosage is reduced and serum lithium concentrations are regularly assessed (Himmelhoch et al., 1977b). The effect of diuretics such as spironolactone or triamterene on lithium clearance has not been established with certainty as yet. The prudent clinician should monitor serum lithium concentrations and client response if potassium-sparing diuretics are used in conjunction with lithium.

Anxiolytics. Benzodiazepine clearance has been markedly decreased by coadministration of cimetidine (Klotz, Anttila, and Reimann, 1979; Klotz and Reimann, 1980; Desmond et al., 1980), apparently caused, in part at least, by decreased demethylation of the benzodiazepine (Fig. 8-3). The inhibitory effect of cimetidine on the clearance of intravenously administered chlordiazepoxide (Desmond et al., 1980) and diazepam (Klotz, Anttila, and Reimann, 1979; Klotz and Reimann, 1980) was not clinically evaluated but

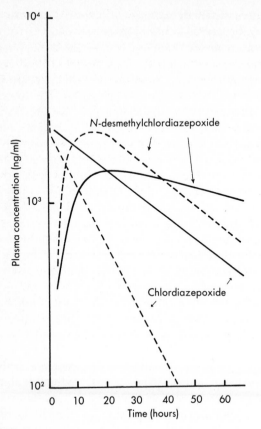

FIG. 8-3

Plasma chlordiazepoxide and N-desmethyl-chlordiazepoxide concentrations as a function of time, before (–––) and after (———) 7 days of treatment with cimetidine, 300 mg P.O. 4 times daily. (Modified from Desmond, P.V., et al.: Ann. Intern. Med. **93:**267, 1980.)

rather was studied in normal healthy subjects. Nonetheless, the frequency with which these benzodiazepines are prescribed concomitantly with cimetidine warrants some concern because more pronounced CNS depression or dysfunction may well be encountered than expected. In view of the substantial decrease in cimetidine clearance with age (Gugler and Somogyi, 1979; Rodolfi, Borgogelli, and Lodola, 1979) and in view of the association of mental confusion with high serum cimetidine concentrations (Schentag et al., 1979), this combination should be used cautiously in elderly clients. The client should be observed and the dose of the benzodiazepine reduced if necessary. Whether or not other less extensively metabolized benzodiazepines, such as oxazepam or lorazepam, would be more appropriate in conjunction with cimetidine remains to be seen, even though one study of cimetidine effects on the pharmacokinetics of lorazepam and oxazepam indicates no significant alteration in the pharmacokinetics of these two benzodiazepines in normal healthy young adults (Patwardhan et al., 1980). Ranitidine, a potent H_2-receptor antagonist similar to cimetidine but, apparently, without the microsomal enzyme-inhibiting activity of the latter, may offer an alternative to cimetidine that would not necessitate a change in the benzodiazepine (Henry et al., 1980).

Other interactions of drugs affecting the CNS are listed alphabetically in Table 8-2. These interactions tend to involve a less marked effect, a lower incidence, or minimal clinical documentation.

Interactions of cardiovascular drugs

The geriatric client's cardiovascular system presents a different picture from that of younger adults (Riley, 1977): cardiac output is decreased, and both the rate and extent of blood perfusion in tissues are diminished. The heart responds less readily to stress, and there is a predisposition to the development of cardiac dysrhythmias and failure. The vasculature is less resilient, leading to increased systolic pressure, whereas decreases in the luminal cross section of small vessels lead to increases in diastolic pressure. Furthermore, many of the drugs used to treat cardiovascular problems have a narrow therapeutic range, a steep dose-response relationship, and an effect that brings itself to the clinician's attention (Dollery, George, and Orme, 1975; Dollery, 1977).

TABLE 8-2 **Interactions of CNS agents other than analgesics**

CNS agent	Interacting drug	Result/mechanism of interaction	Circumvention or management of interaction	References
Haloperidol	Methyldopa	Dementia, increasing irritability, and aggressiveness; mechanism unknown	Avoid concomitant administration	Chouinard et al., 1973; Thornton, 1976; Nadel and Wallach, 1979
Levodopa	MAOIs	Hypertension, palpitations, increased possibility of akinesia, tremor; caused possibly by increased peripheral storage or release of dopamine and/or norepinephrine	Carbidopa (a peripheral decarboxylase inhibitor) may inhibit hypertensive effect of combination	Friend, Bell, and Kline, 1965; Kott, Bornstein and Eichhorn, 1971; Teychenne et al., 1975
	Papaverine	Antiparkinsonian effect antagonized by papaverine; mechanism unknown	Avoid concomitant use	Duvoisin, 1975; Posner, 1975
	Pyridoxine	As little as 10 mg pyridoxine daily can obliterate therapeutic response to levodopa by enhancing levodopa biotransformation	Avoid vitamin preparations containing pyridoxine or employ levodopa/carbidopa combination	Cohon, 1974
Lithium	Indomethacin	Increase in plasma lithium concentrations and risk of lithium toxicity; caused by decreased renal clearance of lithium resulting from inhibition of renal prostaglandin synthesis by indomethacin	Monitor plasma lithium concentrations in clients receiving combination; other nonsteroidal anti-inflammatory agents (NSAIAs) may also provoke increase in lithium concentrations	Frölich et al., 1979; Ragheb et al., 1980
	Methyldopa	Increase in plasma lithium concentrations and in toxicity; mechanism unknown	Monitor plasma lithium concentrations in clients receiving this combination	Byrd, 1975; O'Regan, 1976; Osanloo and Deglin, 1980
MAOIs	Sympathomimetic agents (e.g., amphetamines, dopamine, ephedrine, metaraminol, methylphenidate, phenylephrine, phenylpropanolamine)	Hypertensive crisis resulting from increased storage and/or release of norepinephrine	Avoid concomitant use	Elis et al., 1967; Marley and Blackwell, 1970

Continued.

TABLE 8-2 Interactions of CNS agents other than analgesics—cont'd

CNS agent	Interacting drug	Result/mechanism of interaction	Circumvention or management of interaction	References
Phenothiazines	Antacids	Aluminum- or magnesium-containing colloidal antacids may decrease bioavailability of simultaneously administered phenothiazines because of adsorption	Administer the phenothiazine at least 1 hour before or 2 hours after antacid	Forrest, Forrest, and Serra, 1970; Fann et al., 1973; Hurwitz, 1977
	Barbiturates and other known enzyme inducers (e.g., glutethimide, rifampin)	Increased biotransformation of the phenothiazine, leading to decreased plasma concentrations and diminished effectiveness	Avoid known enzyme inducers; modify dosage of phenothiazine appropriately when adding or discontinuing enzyme inducers	Forrest, Forrest, and Serra, 1970, Rawlins, 1978
	Lithium	Decreased peak chlorpromazine concentrations and areas-under-the-curve in normal subjects given single dose of chlorpromazine with lithium pretreatment (900 mg/day for 7 days); mechanism not established	Monitor clients for reduced effectiveness of phenothiazines	Rivera-Calimlin, Kerzner, and Karch, 1978
Phenytoin	Phenothiazines	Phenytoin concentrations altered when phenothiazines are started or stopped (thioridazine implicated more often than other phenothiazines); mechanism not established	Monitor plasma phenytoin concentrations as well as clinical response	Kutt and McDowell, 1968; Siris et al., 1974; Vincent, 1980
	Phenylbutazone (and oxyphenbutazone)	Increased plasma phenytoin concentrations and apparent half-life; mechanism not established	Monitor plasma phenytoin concentrations	Lunde, 1971; Andreasen, 1973
Tricyclic antidepressants (TCAs)	Barbiturates	Plasma TCA concentrations may be lowered substantially as a result of barbiturate-induced increase in TCA biotransformation; however, when plasma concentrations are relatively high, CNS toxicity may be potentiated by "antidotal" use of barbiturates	Avoid barbiturates	Alexanderson, Evans, and Sjoqvist, 1969; Burrows and Davies, 1971; Moody et al., 1977

Anticoagulants. Anticoagulants, such as heparin and warfarin, are used to suppress the synthesis or function of clotting factors. Heparin effectiveness is reportedly diminished in the elderly (Brodows and Campbell, 1972), although the incidence of bleeding complications and mortality appears to increase with age (Henry et al., 1981). The oral anticoagulants are more potent in geriatric clients than in younger clients (O'Malley et al., 1977). The increased sensitivity of elderly clients to oral anticoagulants has already been discussed. Drug interactions involving anticoagulants are among the most frequently described of any in the literature (Koch-Weser and Sellers, 1971). Their prominence is a reflection of the widespread use of anticoagulants, the concomitant use of other potent drugs, the risk of hemorrhagic complications with anticoagulants (particularly in the elderly), and the relative ease of detection of interactions arising from the necessity of monitoring the intensity of the effect of anticoagulants in the course of establishing or maintaining the appropriate dosage regimen.

Hemostatic mechanisms can be compromised to some extent by drugs (e.g., aspirin*) that prevent thrombus formation by inhibiting platelet function. Such drugs increase the risk of bleeding in clients receiving heparin or in those maintained on oral anticoagulants (O'Reilly, 1980a). The response to oral anticoagulants can also be markedly affected by the concurrent use of other drugs that alter either the plasma concentration of the anticoagulant or the rate of clotting factor synthesis or degradation. Table 8-3 lists oral anticoagulant interactions of importance. In general, adverse effects can be minimized if clients are monitored on a regular basis, particularly when dosage regimens are changed or when drugs are added to the regimen or discontinued. The development of a mathematically sound, predictive dose-response model for oral anticoagulants, as for heparin (McAvoy, 1979), would facili-

tate the dosage determination of these drugs and improve the ability of clinicians to detect significant drug interactions (and to distinguish them from individual variations per se in pharmacokinetics or pharmacodynamics).

Antihypertensives. Clinicians tend to avoid the use in the elderly of antihypertensive agents such as clonidine, methyldopa, and reserpine because of their potential for CNS depression, whereas guanethidine is often avoided because of the increased susceptibility of the elderly to postural hypotension (O'Malley and O'Brien, 1980). Instead, treatment is often begun with either an oral thiazide diuretic or a β-adrenergic blocking agent (O'Malley, Judge, and Crooks, 1980). Selected drug interactions involving antihypertensive drugs other than diuretics are listed in Table 8-4. Drug interactions affecting the efficacy of diuretics are discussed on p. 161.

Digitalis glycosides. Increased monitoring of plasma digitalis glycoside concentrations has led clinicians to a greater awareness of interactions involving these drugs. Thus a considerable number of studies attesting to the consistent rise in plasma or serum digoxin concentrations with the introduction and concomitant use of quinidine have been published in recent years (Fig. 8-4). Doering and König (1978), Ejvinsson (1978), and Leahey et al. (1978) were among the first to demonstrate a twofold (or larger) increase in plasma or serum digoxin concentrations within 24 hours of initiation of quinidine administration. Subsequent reports by others have confirmed the significance of the interaction between digoxin and quinidine (Hooymans and Merkus, 1978; Burkle and Matzke, 1979; Doering, 1979; Hager et al., 1979; Hooymans and Merkus, 1979; Reid and Meek, 1979; Mungall et al., 1980; Pedersen and Hvidt, 1980; Powell et al., 1980; Risler et al., 1980; Schenck-Gustafsson and Dahlqvist, 1981). The quinidine-induced rise in serum or plasma digoxin concentrations has been variously attributed to (1) reduced renal clearance of digoxin (Hooymans and Merkus, 1978; Doering, 1979; Hager et al., 1979; Hooymans and Merkus, 1979;

*Even low doses of aspirin (81 mg) appear to effectively inhibit platelet aggregation (Paccioretti and Block, 1980).

Text continued on p. 155.

TABLE 8-3 Oral anticoagulant drug interactions

INCREASED ANTICOAGULANT EFFECT*

Anticoagulant	Interacting drug	Effect/comment(s)	Mechanism	References
Dicumarol	Allopurinol	Plasma half-life of dicumarol in normal subjects (mean, 51 hr) markedly prolonged (mean, 152 hr) with concomitant allopurinol administration	Enzyme inhibition	Vesell, Passananti, and Greene, 1970
	Magnesium hydroxide†	Plasma dicumarol concentrations increased by 75%; area under-the-curve (AUC) increased 50%	Chelate formation leading to increased absorption	Ambre and Fischer, 1973
	Tricyclic antidepressants (TCAs)	Amitriptyline and nortriptyline	Apparent increase in dicumarol availability because of decreased intestinal transit rate or TCA-induced change in volume of distribution	Pond et al., 1975
Phenindione	Cimetidine	Prolongation of prothrombin time from 21 to 44 sec; 1 subject	Inhibition of hepatic microsomal enzyme oxidation	Serlin et al., 1979
Warfarin	Aspirin (see salicylates)			
	Cimetidine	Prolongation of prothrombin time from 29 to 40 sec (cimetidine, 1.0 gm/day); plasma warfarin concentrations increased from 0.96 µg/ml to 1.76 µg/ml with 1.0 gm/day cimetidine; warfarin clearance reduced from 3.4 ml/min to 2.5 ml/min following cimetidine at 1.6 gm/day	Inhibition of hepatic microsomal enzyme oxidation	Serlin et al., 1979
		Prothrombin time increased to 83 sec with 1.2 gm/day cimetidine		Silver and Bell, 1979
		Prothrombin time ratio increased to 3.8 with 1.2 gm/day cimetidine		Wallin, Jacknowitz, and Raich, 1979

Drug	Clinical description	Mechanism	Reference
	Prothrombin ratio increased by 40% to 50% with cimetidine doses of 0.8 to 1.0 gm/day; prothrombin ratio increased by 10% with only 0.4 gm/day cimetidine		Hetzel, Birkett, and Miners, 1979
Clofibrate	Marked hypoprothrombinemia, hemorrhaging; death	Displacement of warfarin from plasma protein binding sites; vitamin K turnover affected	Rogen and Campbell-Ferguson, 1963; Solomon and Rosner, 1973; Bjornsson et al., 1979
Co-trimoxazole	Prothrombin time ratio increased from approximately 1.5 to 5.1 with co-trimoxazole	Augmentation of plasma S-warfarin concentrations	Hassall et al., 1975; Errick and Keys, 1978; O'Reilly and Notley, 1979; O'Reilly, 1980b
Disulfiram	Prothrombin time and AUC increased by about 25% to 150% with 250 mg/day disulfiram	S-warfarin hypoprothrombinemia affected, but plasma concentrations of R and S enantiomorphs of warfarin were unaffected	O'Reilly, 1973; O'Reilly, 1981
Ethacrynic acid	Substantial increases in Sellers and Koch-Weser warfarin dose index after doses of ethacrynic acid suggested an interaction of the drugs in hypoalbuminemic client observed; prothrombin times were particularly elevated (29 to 39 sec) after 300 mg/day doses of ethacrynic acid	Displacement of warfarin from its protein binding sites	Petrick, Kronacher, and Alcena, 1975
Glucagon	Twenty-four clients with cardiac disease receiving warfarin therapy took glucagon, in daily doses of 2 to 96 mg, for its positive inotropic effect; in those clients receiving a total dose of glucagon >50 mg over at least 2 days, most exhibited markedly enhanced warfarin activity (prothrombin time more than two and a half times normal)	Unknown	Koch-Weser, 1970

Continued.

*These interactions can generally be managed by appropriately decreasing or increasing anticoagulant dosage in accordance with prothrombin times or other measures of anticoagulant efficacy. A lag of as much as 1 to 3 days may occur before the response to a given oral anticoagulant is fully developed. This should be kept in mind when dosage adjustment is being considered.

†Administration of the anticoagulant several hours or more before the adsorbent may avoid the interaction unless enterohepatic cycling is extensive. The prudent clinician should either avoid the combination or monitor anticoagulant efficacy if the interactants are coprescribed.

‡These factors increase the risk associated with concomitant use and warrant avoidance of the combination.

TABLE 8-3 Oral anticoagulant drug interactions—cont'd

INCREASED ANTICOAGULANT EFFECT*

Anticoagulant	Interacting drug	Effect(comment(s))	Mechanism	References
Warfarin—cont'd	Metronidazole	Plasma warfarin concentrations and hypoprothrombinemia increased	S-warfarin oxidation inhibited	O'Reilly, 1976b
	Phenylbutazone; oxyphenbutazone	Increased risk of gastrointestinal ulceration and bleeding.‡	Competitive displacement of warfarin from nonspecific binding sites in plasma and tissues; increased metabolism of R-warfarin and decreased metabolism of S-warfarin	O'Reilly and Levy, 1970; Lewis et al., 1974; Aarons, Schary, and Rowland, 1979
	Salicylates	Risk of bleeding because of gastrointestinal ulceration; aspirin inhibition of platelet adhesion among effects.‡	Displacement of warfarin from nonspecific binding sites; hypoprothrombinemia with large doses	Aarons, Schary, and Rowland, 1979; Rothschild, 1979
	Sulfamethoxazole (see co-trimoxazole)			
	Sulfinpyrazone	Prothrombin time ratio increased to as much as 10	Unknown	Weiss, 1979; Gallus and Birkett, 1980; Jamil, Reid, and Messer, 1981

DECREASED ANTICOAGULANT EFFECT*

Anticoagulant	Interacting drug	Effect(comment(s))	Mechanism	References
Dicumarol	Phenobarbital and other barbiturates	Daily maintenance dose requirements of dicumarol were significantly increased in 8 clients receiving chronic phenobarbital therapy (60 to 90 mg/day)	Enzyme induction by barbiturate	Goss and Dickhaus, 1965

Drug	Interacting agent	Effect	Mechanism	Reference
Phenprocoumon	Cholestyramine†	Phenprocoumon clearance increased one and a half to two times, whereas the anticoagulant effect was considerably reduced: area of prothrombin complex activity-time curves was reduced by 37% with concomitant administration of cholestyramine	Binding of phenprocoumon to resin	Meinertz et al., 1977
	Rifampin	Antagonistic effect of rifampin disappears slowly after discontinuation	Increased biotransformation because of enzyme induction by rifampin	Boekhout-Mussert et al., 1974
Warfarin	Carbamazepine	Prothrombin-proconvertin concentrations of plasma increased about fourfold	Warfarin biotransformation enhanced (carbamazepine induced)	Hansen, Siersbaek-Nielsen, and Skovsted, 1971
	Cholestyramine†	Plasma warfarin concentrations decreased by approximately 20% to 30%, even with 3-hr interval between ingestion of drugs; prothrombin time reduced from 17 to 14 sec with concomitant administration of cholestyramine	Binding of warfarin to resin	Robinson, Benjamin, and McCormack, 1971
	Glutethimide	Plasma warfarin concentrations and half-lives decreased	Glutethimide induces warfarin biotransformation	Corn, 1966; MacDonald et al., 1969
	Mercaptopurine	Increase in thrombotest to 30% to 40%	Enzyme induction by mercaptopurine	Spiers and Mibashan, 1974
	Phenobarbital and other barbiturates	Warfarin clearance increased	Enzyme induction by barbiturate of warfarin biotransformation; both R and S enantiomorphs are affected	Koch-Weser and Sellers, 1971; O'Reilly, 1976a; Orme, 1976
	Rifampin	Warfarin elimination increased	Rifampin-induced warfarin biotransformation	O'Reilly, 1974 and 1975

TABLE 8-4 **Selected antihypertensive drug interactions**

Antihypertensive agent	Interacting drug	Result/mechanism of interaction	Circumvention or management of interaction	References
β-adrenergic blockers	Cimetidine	Increased plasma β-blocker concentrations as a function of time resulting from decreased hepatic clearance of β-blocker when used with cimetidine; reduced clearance results mainly from inhibition of hepatic oxidative enzymes and reduction in liver blood flow rates by cimetidine	Avoid concomitant administration with β-blockers, particularly those that are predominantly eliminated by hepatic biotransformation; use β-blockers that are primarily renally excreted (e.g., atenolol, nadolol)	Feely, Wilkinson, and Wood, 1981
	Indomethacin and other NSAIAs	Indomethacin and, presumably, other prostaglandin synthesis inhibitors are capable of suppressing antihypertensive effect of β-blockers in some hypertensive clients	Avoid concomitant use	Durao, Prata, and Goncalves, 1977
Clonidine	β-adrenergic blockers	Hypertension induced on withdrawal of clonidine and maintenance or initiation of β-blocker therapy; possibly because of a withdrawal-induced increase in circulating catecholamines	Gradually withdraw the β-blocker before clonidine; if only clonidine is to be withdrawn and the β-blocker maintained or initiated, monitor blood pressure	Bailey and Neale, 1976; Cairns and Marshall, 1976; Harris, 1976; Lilja et al., 1980
	Tricyclic antidepressants	Loss of antihypertensive control; although TCAs may block peripheral synaptic clonidine uptake, the precise mechanism of this interaction is as yet unknown	Avoid concomitant use	Briant, Reid, and Pollery, 1973; VanZwieten, 1975; Risch, Groom, and Janowsky, 1981
Guanethidine	Chlorpromazine and other phenothiazines	The hypotensive effect of guanethidine may be reversed after several days when used with chlorpromazine; guanethidine uptake by nerve terminal and subsequent activity can be blocked by chlorpromazine	Avoid concomitant therapy or monitor client closely for hypertensive reversal if combined treatment is necessary; an increase in guanethidine dosage may be indicated	Fann et al., 1971; Ober and Wang, 1973; Poe, Edwards, and Taylor, 1979

Tricyclic antidepressants	The antihypertensive effect of guanethidine is antagonized; TCAs inhibit guanethidine uptake by adrenergic neurons	Avoid this combination	Leishman, Mathews, and Smith, 1963; Meyer, McAllister, and Goldberg, 1970; Poe, Edwards, and Taylor, 1979
Pargyline and other MAOIs	Severe reactions to concurrent therapy, including rigidity, hyperpyrexia, excitation, hypotension, dyspnea, and coma, as well as some deaths, have been attributed to acute use of meperidine in MAOI-treated clients; the interaction has been reported to occur within a short time after meperidine administration but is unpredictable; mechanism unknown	Avoid meperidine in clients receiving MAOIs; other narcotic analgesics may be used with somewhat less risk, perhaps, but as much caution	Shee, 1960; Taylor, 1962; Vigran, 1964

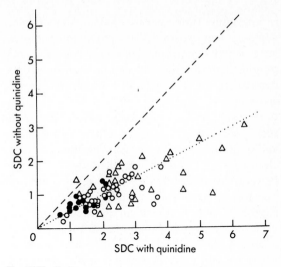

FIG. 8-4

Serum digoxin concentrations (SDC) in 80 clients with and without concomitant quinidine treatment. The dashed line (at 45-degree angle) and dotted line (at 30-degree angle) are provided to enhance visualization. (Based on data from Leahey, E.B., Jr., et al.: J.A.M.A. **240:**533, 1978, Δ; Doering, W.: N. Engl. J. Med. **301:**400, 1979, ○; and Mungall, D.R., et al.: Ann. Intern. Med. **93:**689, 1980, ●.)

Mungall et al., 1980; Risler et al., 1980; Schenck-Gustafsson and Dahlqvist, 1981); (2) decreased volume of distribution of digoxin resulting from its displacement from tissue binding sites (Hager et al., 1979; Hirsh, Weiner, and North, 1980; Schenck-Gustafsson and Dahlqvist, 1981), or (3) reduced nonrenal clearance of digoxin (Steiness et al., 1980; Schenck-Gustafsson and Dahlqvist, 1981). All three mechanisms may, in fact, be involved, depending on the client's renal function or the quinidine dosage employed. Although Doering (1979) noted that quinidine doses of less than 500 mg/day produced no appreciable changes in digoxin concentrations, Steiness et al. (1980) demonstrated, in healthy subjects, the abolition of the positive inotropic effect of digoxin by quinidine doses of only 400 mg/day. Hirsh, Weiner, and North (1980) provided evidence for a negative inotropic effect in normal subjects despite the quinidine-induced increase in serum digoxin concentration and the anticipated corresponding decrease in the left ventricular ejection time index and in the Q-S$_2$ index. It would seem, then, that the concurrent use of digoxin and quinidine is unwarranted even though many clients taking the drugs concurrently do not experience digoxin toxicity. The use of disopyramide or procainamide or other noninteracting antidysrhythmics rather than quinidine would be preferred. If digoxin and quinidine are to be used together, the clinician should consider employing a digoxin dose 50% lower than ordinarily used. The data of Steiness et al. (1980) and of Hirsh, Weiner, and North (1980) should give the clinician pause insofar as the advisability of digoxin dosage reduction is concerned, with the apparent attenuation of the inotropic effect of digoxin by quinidine. Subsequent monitoring of serum digoxin concentrations during the first 4 to 5 days of concomitant therapy (Mungall et al., 1980) can help to disclose any inordinate rise in serum digoxin concentrations and facilitate further dosage adjustment. Clients stabilized on digoxin should be observed closely for digoxin toxicity or loss of efficacy following the addition of quinidine. Digoxin dosage may need to be increased if quinidine is discontinued or decreased if quinidine dosage is increased. Chapron, Mumford, and Pitegoff (1979) reported the case of a 94-year-old woman who received daily doses of digoxin, quinidine, and pentobarbital. Discontinuation of the pentobarbital produced a sharp increase in serum digoxin concentrations from 1.3 to 4.5 ng/ml along with an apparent 3.8-fold increase in quinidine half-life.

Reports of the digoxin-quinidine interaction prompted studies of the effect of quinidine on serum or plasma digitoxin concentrations (Fenster et al., 1980; Keller and Kreutz, 1980; Ochs et al., 1980; Peters et al., 1980a and 1980b; Garty, Sood, and Rollins, 1981) because digitoxin might be considered as an alternative to

digoxin for clients receiving quinidine. In one study (Ochs et al., 1980) quinidine, at doses of 1000 mg/day, had no significant effect on the volume of distribution, elimination half-life, or total clearance of digitoxin in 10 healthy volunteers. Keller and Kreutz (1980) reported no marked change in plasma digitoxin concentrations with quinidine, whereas Peters et al. (1980a and 1980b) demonstrated a 32% increase in serum digitoxin concentrations. Pharmacokinetic evaluations of the interaction by Fenster et al. (1980) and Garty et al. (1981) in normal, healthy volunteers demonstrated a lengthening of the digitoxin half-life from 0.5- to 2.5-fold, respectively. Total body clearance of digitoxin was correspondingly reduced. There was no apparent change in the volume of distribution of digitoxin in any of the studies. The clinical significance of the digitoxin-quinidine interaction has yet to be fully resolved. Nonetheless, the clinician should not employ digitoxin as a digoxin alternative without considering the need for client monitoring when quinidine is used concurrently.

Most diuretics, with the exception of amiloride, spironolactone, and triamterene, increase the renal excretion of potassium. The risk of diuretic-induced hypokalemia (serum K$^+$ less than 3.5 mEq/l) does not appear to be significantly altered by either the duration of treatment with or dose of the diuretic employed. Furthermore, the risk of appreciable hypokalemia (serum K$^+$ less than 3.0 mEq/l) in the absence of severe heart failure or renal or hepatic disease is small in most clients (Morgan and Davidson, 1980). Nonetheless, hypokalemia in clients treated with digitalis glycosides has generally been considered a problem to be dealt with because of the increased risk of cardiac dysrhythmias and digitalis toxicity (Sloman and Manolas, 1980). Whether the increased risk is related to the increased binding of digitalis to and inhibition of the membrane-bound Na$^+$, K$^+$-activated adenosine triphosphatase (Hoffman and Bigger, 1980), or to the suppression of the renal excretion of digitalis (Steiness, 1978), the prognosis for the client is poorer if the hypokalemia is not corrected. Duke (1978), in a review of hospital records during a 10-year period, found that 59 of 1078 clients with an acute myocardial infarction experienced primary ventricular fibrillation. Of these 59 clients 10 (17%) were receiving a thiazide preparation at the time. Serum potassium concentrations were determined in 46 of the clients. Hypokalemia was noted in 7 of the 8 clients receiving a thiazide diuretic, whereas only 1 of the 38 clients not receiving a thiazide had a slightly reduced potassium level. Lehmann et al. (1978) observed digitalis toxicity in 13.1% of 4608 previously digitalized inpatients of a cardiopulmonary unit. Life-threatening toxicity was present in 286 of the clients. Clinical signs of severe intoxication were significantly ($p < 0.01$) more common among those simultaneously treated with diuretics than among those not taking diuretics. Hypokalemia was associated with a substantially greater incidence of ventricular extrasystoles, ventricular flutter and fibrillation, AV nodal rhythm, and SA and AV block. The death rate resulting from digitalis intoxication was three times greater among hypokalemic clients than normokalemic ones.

Whether hypokalemia occurs or not, Brater and Morelli (1977) consider digitalis toxicity to be enhanced by the depletion of intracellular potassium. Thus potassium supplementation is often beneficial for digitalis-induced dysrhythmias even in normokalemic clients. Potassium supplementation therapy or the use of potassium-sparing diuretics is generally preferable to dietary measures (Kosman, 1974). Morgan (1979) presented an overview of potassium replacement therapy.

Additional drug interactions with digitalis glycosides are listed in Table 8-5.

Interactions of anti-inflammatory agents and analgesics

Rheumatic diseases, affecting almost all people to a greater or lesser extent at some time in their lives, cause more continuous pain, more disability, and more loss of time from work than any other group of disorders (Hart, 1980). The erosion of health by rheumatic disorders is most evident in the elderly, 40% of whom require treatment (Lamy, 1980). Unfortunately, treatment of rheumatic disorders is palliative and centers primarily on the relief of pain and the control of inflammation. The drugs employed include corticosteroids and non-steroidal anti-inflammatory agents (NSAIAs): analgesics without anti-inflammatory action; miscellaneous compounds such as gold salts, antimalarials, and penicillamine; and immunosuppressive agents, which act more slowly on the rheumatoid disease process. Acute attacks of gout are generally treated with either colchicine or NSAIAs. Prophylactic treatment of gout with uricosuric agents or the xanthine oxidase inhibitor allopurinol is sometimes necessary.

Corticosteroids. Enhanced clearance of systemic corticosteroids by phenobarbital (Brooks et al., 1972; Jubiz and Meikle, 1979) and by phenytoin (Jubiz et al., 1970; Boylan, Owen, and Chin, 1976; Petereit and Meikle, 1977; Jubiz and Meikle, 1979) as a result of hepatic microsomal enzyme induction could result in diminished effectiveness of the corticosteroid, as reflected in a lack of response or an increase in corticosteroid dosage. In the latter instance, withdrawal of the barbiturate or hydantoin could lead to steroid toxicity if corticosteroid dosage were not then reduced. The substitution of an appropriate benzodiazepine, when feasible, would obviate the need to increase corticosteroid dosage.

Brooks et al. (1977) evaluated dexamethasone clearance in 21 clients with bronchial asthma. Sixteen of the clients later were treated over a 3-week period with either ephedrine (100 mg/day), oxtriphylline (800 mg/day), or placebo, followed by evaluation once again of dexamethasone clearance. Ephedrine treatment resulted in a 42% increase in dexamethasone clearance, compared with the pre-ephedrine or control period clearance ($p < 0.001$). Oxtriphylline or placebo treatment resulted in no significant change in dexamethasone clearance. The in-

TABLE 8-5 *Miscellaneous interactions of digitalis glycosides*

Digitalis glycoside(s)	Interacting drug	Result/mechanism of interaction	Circumvention or management of interaction	References
Digitoxin, digoxin	Cholestyramine	Decreased bioavailability because of adsorption or binding to the resin in gut; digitoxin may be affected to a greater extent than digoxin because of digitoxin's more extensive enterohepatic recycling and exposure to resin	Monitor clients for glycoside effectiveness; avoid simultaneous administration	Bazzano and Bazzano, 1972
	Rifampin	Hepatic enzyme induction by rifampin presumably was responsible for a four-fold increase in digitoxin clearance in normal healthy volunteers; the use of the less biotransformed digoxin, rather than digitoxin, has been recommended; a report of subtherapeutic serum digoxin concentrations in a rifampin-treated client has since appeared	Avoid rifampin; use ethambutol or other antitubercular agent instead; if rifampin is necessary, monitor the client for glycoside effectiveness	Zilly, Breimer, and Richter, 1977; Boman, Eliasson, and Odar-Cederlöf, 1980; Novi et al., 1980
	Spironolactone	Spironolactone has been variously reported to increase digitoxin biotransformation and to inhibit digoxin renal tubular secretion; a more recent study involving tritiated digoxin showed no significant changes in digoxin clearance; furthermore, evidence has been presented documenting radioimmunoassay interference by spironolactone and its metabolites; significance of interaction is uncertain at present	Monitor clients for glycoside effectiveness	Steiness, 1974; Wirth et al., 1976; Masson et al., 1978; Waldorff et al., 1978; Silber et al., 1979

| Digoxin | Antacids, colloidal | Decreased bioavailability, caused in part by adsorption to antacid, may lead to diminished digoxin effectiveness in clients receiving colloidal antacids on chronic basis | Monitor clients for glycoside effectiveness; digoxin should be administered at least 1 hour before or 2 hours after antacid dose if interaction is to be minimized | Brown and Juhl, 1976; Allen et al., 1981 |
| | Quinine | Serum digoxin concentrations elevated in subjects receiving quinine (600 mg/day); quinine treatment reduced total body clearance of digoxin by 26% but did not appear to affect digoxin's volume of distribution; nonrenal digoxin clearance was substantially altered | Monitor clients for glycoside toxicity | Wandell et al., 1980 |

creased clearance of dexamethasone was attributed to increased hepatic blood flow or to hepatic microsomal enzyme activity induced by ephedrine. Their recommendation, echoed by Jubiz and Meikle (1979), that theophylline is a more appropriate bronchodilator for use in clients receiving corticosteroids simultaneously should be considered in light of the experience of Buchanan, Hurwitz, and Butler (1979). The latter group reported the marked elevation of serum theophylline concentrations in three clients following the administration of hydrocortisone. Steady-state serum theophylline concentrations in the therapeutic range (10 to 20 μg/ml) rapidly increased to between 40 and 50 μg/ml following the intravenous administration of hydrocortisone. Buchanan, Hurwitz, and Butler observed similar effects of the interaction in three other clients but did not include their data in the published report.

Edwards et al. (1974) described a client with Addison's disease who required increased corticosteroid dosage while receiving rifampin. The apparent half-life of hydrocortisone was decreased during rifampin therapy, returning to normal when rifampin was stopped. In four other clients with normal pituitary-adrenal function, hydrocortisone biotransformation rates were increased as was the urinary excretion of glucaric acid, an index of hepatic microsomal enzyme activity. The conclusion drawn by Edwards et al. that rifampin increases the biotransformation of corticosteroids was corroborated by Yamada and Iwai (1976), who measured the urinary excretion of 6-hydroxycortisol in five clients with pulmonary tuberculosis treated with rifampin. The concomitant administration of hydrocortisone led to marked increases in metabolite formation relative to those observed in other tuberculous clients not treated with rifampin. The initiation of rifampin therapy appears to warrant increased doses of systemic corticosteroids: as a first approximation, the daily dose of the steroid at the outset would be doubled (Buffington et al., 1976; Jubiz and Meikle, 1979).

Nonsteroidal analgesic and anti-inflammatory agents. Of the nonsteroidal agents employed in the alleviation of symptoms of rheumatic disease, aspirin is the most widely used. Analgesia is often effected with doses of 1 to 2 gm/day, whereas substantial anti-inflammatory responses are not achieved unless substantially larger doses (e.g., 4 to 5 gm/day) are employed. The individualization of aspirin dosage regimens in the aged is complicated by (1) the dose-dependent kinetics of elimination exhibited by salicylate (Levy, 1979); (2) the relatively narrow therapeutic plasma concentration range (15 to 30 mg/100 ml) of salicylate for the treatment of inflammatory diseases; and (3) the reduction in salicylate clearance with increasing age (Cuny et al., 1979). Concomitant drug use affecting salicylate clearance can thus have profound effects on dosage requirements in the elderly.

The renal clearance of salicylate is markedly dependent on urinary pH (Smith et al., 1946). Levy and Leonards (1971) demonstrated that an average increase in urine pH of less than one unit—achieved by the administration of approximately 4 gm/day of sodium bicarbonate—reduced steady-state plasma salicylate concentrations by about one half in normal, healthy volunteers during the course of 1 week. Gibaldi, Grundhofer, and Levy (1974) found that the use of magnesium hydroxide, calcium carbonate-glycine, and aluminum-magnesium hydroxide suspensions increased average urine pH by 0.48, 0.41, and 0.86 unit, respectively. Aluminum hydroxide and dihydroxyaluminum aminoacetate suspensions had no effect on urine pH. Levy et al. (1975) pursued this further in their study of serum salicylate concentrations in three children with rheumatic fever receiving aspirin with or without aluminum-magnesium hydroxide suspension. Urinary pH increased appreciably and serum salicylate concentrations decreased by 30% to 70% with concurrent antacid administration. Limitations of this and other studies prompted Hansten and Hayton (1980) to attempt to delineate the interaction further. They found

a significant decrease in the serum salicylate concentration resulting from increased renal clearance of salicylate at higher urinary pH. When the steady-state salicylate concentration was below 10 mg/100 ml, antacid coadministration did not appear to significantly affect serum salicylate concentrations. The antacid effect on salicylate clearance appeared to be prominent only when the body load of salicylate was in the nonlinear, dose-dependent phase. Clients receiving less than 50 mg/kg/day of aspirin or its equivalent are not apt to experience marked changes in serum salicylate levels when antacids are administered concurrently (Hansten and Hayton, 1980). Antacid addition to or deletion from the drug regimen of a client maintained on high doses of salicylate could have a detrimental effect on salicylate efficacy because of decreased concentrations or increased toxicity. Haphazard use or unsupervised self-administration of antacids by such clients is to be avoided. The clinician may wish to recommend antacids with a minimal effect on urine pH, as previously noted. Clinicians employing an enteric-coated aspirin product may have an additional concern regarding the premature release of aspirin from such formulations when antacids are taken concurrently. Feldman and Carlstedt (1974) reported a decreased time of peak urinary excretion of salicylate when an enteric-coated aspirin formulation was administered along with aluminum-magnesium hydroxide suspension. More rapid excretion presumably reflected more rapid gastrointestinal availability of aspirin, but the mechanism of enhanced release was not elucidated. Moreover, the clinical significance of this apparent enhancement of release has not been evaluated. Nonetheless, the clinician should be aware of the potential effect of antacids on aspirin release, particularly for clients taking anti-inflammatory doses of aspirin.

Klinenberg and Miller (1965) concluded that corticosteroids appear to decrease steady-state salicylate concentrations during long-term aspirin therapy. They attributed the loss of salicylate to increased renal excretion. Graham et al. (1977) began a study of salicylate kinetics in two clients with rheumatoid arthritis receiving prednisone concomitantly, who responded poorly to high daily doses of aspirin. They later expanded the study to include 24 additional clients with rheumatoid arthritis. Using more specific assay procedures than Klinenberg and Miller, Graham et al. were able to show that little salicylic acid was excreted unconjugated when corticosteroids were employed concurrently. Most of the subjects given oral corticosteroids and aspirin (4.8 gm/day) did not attain plasma salicylate concentrations above 15 mg/100 ml, apparently as a result of corticosteroid-enhanced biotransformation of salicylate. It follows that a decrease in dosage of the corticosteroid without a corresponding alteration in salicylate dosage could lead to additional salicylate accumulation and toxicity.

Uricosuric agents. Selected interactions of uricosuric agents are noted in Table 8-6.

Interactions of diuretics

A survey of drug use among geriatric clients disclosed that diuretics were by far the most widely prescribed drugs (Williamson and Chopin, 1980). The most widely used diuretics are the thiazides (benzothiadiazines). All have parallel dose-response curves and comparable maximal chloruretic effects. Chlorthalidone, metolazone, and quinethazone differ structurally from the thiazides but are pharmacologically indistinguishable. Ethacrynic acid and furosemide are "high-ceiling" diuretics with a prompt onset of action and a peak diuresis far greater than that achieved with other diuretics (Mudge, 1980b). The use of the aldosterone antagonist spironolactone and the potassium-retaining (sparing) diuretics triamterene and amiloride offer alternatives to thiazide diuretics and high-ceiling diuretics in the treatment of refractory edema and potassium depletion.

Interactions that affect diuretic activity or increase the risk of adverse diuretic effects must be considered in the context of geriatric drug use. The decrease in the number of functioning nephrons with increasing age and the progressive decline in the rate and extent of renal blood flow compromise renal function to some extent in the elderly. The substantial functional reserve of the kidney is such, however, that the majority of aged clients are not at homeostatic risk unless other factors such as illness or inappropriate use of diuretics contravene (Riley, 1977). The risk of diuretic-induced hypokalemia and its consequences for clients treated with digitalis glycosides have already been discussed (pp. 156-157).

The concomitant use of potassium-losing diuretics with other drugs known to induce potassium loss (e.g., amphotericin B [Utz et al., 1964; McCurdy, Frederic, and Elkington, 1968], certain corticosteroids [Mudge, 1980a]) can be particularly hazardous and warrants the monitoring of serum electrolytes during the course of therapy. The aggressive or unwarranted use of potassium supplements in the elderly can rapidly lead to hyperkalemia and associated cardiotoxicity, which may prove fatal (Mudge, 1980a). Finally, drug-induced nephrotoxicity almost always results in reduced renal blood perfusion and glomerular filtration (Milne, 1975). The concurrent use of potentially nephrotoxic drugs should be viewed as another risk factor complicating diuretic therapy, particularly in the aged. Many anti-infective agents, such as the tetracyclines, aminoglycosides, and some cephalosporins (e.g., cephaloridine), are potentially nephrotoxic. The likelihood of renal damage increases when these agents are employed together with diuretics, particularly high-ceiling diuretics. In addition, ototoxicity—manifested by impaired hearing or vestibular dysfunction—has been reported following the use of diuretics, especially ethacrynic acid (Matz, 1976) and furosemide (Quick and Hoppe, 1975; Rifkin et al., 1978). Monitoring of cochlear and vestibular function is especially important in the elderly when these diuretics are used intravenously or in high dosages. Potentiation of diuretic-induced ototoxicity

TABLE 8-6   **Selected interactions of uricosuric agents**

Uricosuric agent	Interacting drug	Result/mechanism of interaction	Circumvention or management of interaction	References
Probenecid	Pyrazinamide	Probenecid uricosuria is suppressed substantially by the coadministration of pyrazinamide in spite of pyrazinamide's prolongation of probenecid's half-life from 5.5 to 8.4 hr; pyrazinamide apparently inhibits probenecid biotransformation and its uricosuric effects, the latter effect through inhibition of renal tubular secretion of urate	Avoid concurrent administration	Yü et al., 1977
	Salicylates	Probenecid uricosuria is decreased considerably or annulled with coadministration of salicylate, presumably as a result of competition for binding sites involved in tubular transfer of urate	Avoid chronic use of doses of salicylate sufficient to produce serum salicylate concentrations of 5 to 10 mg/100 ml	Pascale et al., 1955
Sulfinpyrazone	Salicylates	Sulfinpyrazone uricosuria may be inhibited considerably because of salicylate blockade of sulfinpyrazone's inhibition of tubular reabsorption of uric acid; salicylates and sulfinpyrazone also compete for plasma protein binding sites and for renal tubular secretion	Avoid chronic use of large doses of salicylates	Yü, Dayton, and Gutman, 1963

by aminoglycoside coadministration is well recognized (Johnson and Hamilton, 1970; Giusti, 1973; Brummett et al., 1975) and warrants avoidance of combined therapy.

A reduction in diuretic efficacy may be evident in clients receiving NSAIAs concurrently. The diuretic effect of furosemide has been ascribed, in part, to mediation by renal prostaglandins (Atallah, 1979). The effects of prostaglandin synthetase-inhibiting NSAIAs on renal hemodynamics and on glomerular and tubular function are complex and inadequately characterized at present (Mitnick et al., 1980). Nonetheless, indomethacin has been reported to diminish furosemide-induced natriuresis, plasma renin activity, and antihypertensive efficacy (Patak et al., 1975; Frölich et al., 1976), whereas Bartoli et al. (1980) provided evidence for the blunting of furosemide diuresis by aspirin. Pharmacokinetic evaluations of indomethacin's attenuation of furosemide's diuretic effect disclosed a relatively minimal effect of indomethacin on the disposition of furosemide, compared to the rather marked effect of indomethacin on natriuresis and diuresis (Frölich et al., 1976; Smith et al., 1979). This supports the contention that the mechanism of the furosemide-indomethacin interaction involves inhibition of prostaglandin synthesis. An alternative hypothesis involves the competition of furosemide and indomethacin for active renal tubular secretion (Smith et al., 1979). Bartoli et al. (1980) found that changes in furosemide clearance in clients pretreated with aspirin were significantly correlated ($p < 0.01$) with changes in urine flow rate and in osmolar clearance—additional evidence either for NSAIA competition with furosemide for the organic acid transport system of the proximal tubule or for NSAIA-compromised renal blood flow and diuretic access to the secretory site. An additional factor complicating the interpretation of these data involves the finding that the inhibitory effect of indomethacin is furosemide dose-dependent (Brater, 1979). In summary, clients receiving furosemide should be monitored for any indica-

tions of reduced diuretic efficacy when NSAIAs are added to the drug regimen. Diuretic dosage may well need to be increased. The continued use of NSAIAs with furosemide in clients with congestive heart failure (CHF) should be questioned, considering the reported shift in the natriuretic response–furosemide excretion curves in CHF clients (Brater, Chennavasin, and Seiwell, 1980).

Clients receiving thiazide diuretics occasionally experience hypercalcemia and hypocalciuria (Duarte et al., 1971). The reduction in renal excretion of calcium by thiazides has been employed in the management of hypercalciuria in clients with recurring calcium stones (Yendt and Cohanim, 1978). The concurrent ingestion of calcium-containing products with thiazides can lead to excessive serum calcium concentrations. Hakim et al. (1979) reported severe hypercalcemia (19.7 mg/100 ml) in a 67-year-old woman who had been taking both hydrochlorothiazide (50 mg/day) and an over-the-counter (OTC) calcium carbonate preparation (2.5 gm/day, for epigastric distress) for several years. Hypercalciuria developed when the client increased her calcium carbonate intake to 5 to 7 gm/day. Given the tendency of the elderly to self-medicate, the surreptitious and excessive use of OTC products can lead to serious complications as in this case report.

Miscellaneous interactions

Selected interactions affecting the use of antibiotics and anti-infective agents, bronchodilators, hypoglycemic agents, and thyroid hormone are briefly described in Table 8-7.

Drug-food interactions. Drug-food interactions have been the subject of numerous reviews in the literature (Block and Lamy, 1968; Place and Benson, 1971, Hethcox and Stanaszek, 1974; Cooper, 1976; Melander, 1978; Hathcock and Coon, 1978; Roe, 1976; Krishnaswamy, 1978; Levander and Cheng, 1980). Nonetheless, relatively few dietary interactions with drugs have,

Text continued on p. 168.

TABLE 8-7 *Miscellaneous drug interactions*

Primary drug	Interacting drug	Result/mechanism of interaction	Circumvention or management of interaction	References
Insulin	β-adrenergic blockers	As a result of β-blockade, warning symptoms of hypoglycemia in diabetics (e.g., palpitations, tremors) may be minimized or eliminated although sweating may be prolonged and excessive; in addition, β-blockers may enhance hypoglycemic response to insulin (or to insulin secretion stimulated by sulfonylureas); hypertension and bradycardia, during hypoglycemia, may also be encountered	Client should be monitored for alterations in hypoglycemic response to drug therapy; hypoglycemic drug dosage alterations are not necessary unless responsiveness has changed; use of relatively cardioselective β-blockers may reduce incidence of adverse cardiovascular effects (including impairment of peripheral circulation), but any advantage may be nullified if higher doses of cardioselective β-blocker were used	Barnett, Leslie, and Watkins, 1980; Hansten, 1980
	Corticosteroids	The intrinsic hyperglycemic activity of corticosteroids (gluconeogenesis) will increase blood glucose concentrations in some clients	Hypoglycemic drug dosage may require adjustment during and after corticosteroid therapy; monitor both blood and urine for evidence of loss of diabetic control	Miller and Neilson, 1964; Melby, 1974
	Diuretics, particularly thiazides	A double-blind, randomized, controlled trial of diuretic therapy in elderly hypertensives showed that after 2 years, active treatment group (which received 25 to 50 mg of hydrochlorothiazide and 50 to 100 mg of triamterene daily) had an average increase in fasting blood sugar of 9.6 mg/100 ml, compared with an average fall of 3.1 mg/100 ml in placebo group ($p < 0.001$); the hyperglycemic effect of diuretics appeared	Monitor hypoglycemic drug dosage requirements and increase dosage if necessary; some clients receiving both a thiazide diuretic and a sulfonylurea may require change from the latter to insulin if diuretic is not discontinued	Wolff and Lindeman, 1966; Breckenridge et al., 1967; Kohner et al., 1971; Amery et al., 1978; Cowley and Elkeles, 1978

to be related to potassium loss because glucose tolerance was most markedly impaired in those in whom serum potassium decreased over 2 years; about 30% of hypertensive clients receiving thiazide diuretics exhibit abnormal glucose tolerance, an incidence greater than that in the general population; high-ceiling diuretics have, on occasion, provoked hyperglycemia

Drug	Interactant	Mechanism	Recommendation	Reference
Methenamine	Acetazolamide	Methenamine may be rendered ineffectual; acetazolamide therapy can alkalinize the urine, thus preventing conversion in urine of methenamine to formaldehyde	Urine pH during methenamine therapy should be acidic (pH < 5.5); if acidity cannot be maintained to this degree, other urinary tract anti-infectives should be employed	Helmholz, 1932; Knight et al., 1952; Gandelman, 1967
	Antacids	Antacids may increase urine pH to >5.5, thus rendering methenamine compounds ineffective (see p. 160 for discussion of antacid effects on urine pH)	If urine acidity cannot be maintained, other urinary tract anti-infectives should be employed	Helmholz, 1932; Knight et al., 1952; Gandelman, 1967
	Sulfonamides	Some sulfonamides (sulfamethizole, sulfathiazole) can react with formaldehyde liberated from methenamine in acidic urine to form a precipitate; increased turbidity of the urine has been noted, but no instances of renal blockage or calculi have been reported	Avoid concomitant use of sulfonamides	Lipton, 1963
Sulfonylureas	β-adrenergic blockers	See Insulin (p. 164).		
	Corticosteroids	See Insulin (p. 164).		
	Diuretics	See Insulin (p. 164).		

Continued.

TABLE 8-7 Miscellaneous drug interactions—cont'd

Primary drug	Interacting drug	Result/mechanism of interaction	Circumvention or management of interaction	References
Sulfonylureas —cont'd	Phenylbutazone, oxyphenbutazone	Enhanced hypoglycemia may occur with combined therapy; renal clearance of acetohexamide's active metabolite hydroxyhexamide is ostensibly inhibited by phenylbutazone; inhibitory effect of phenylbutazone on tolbutamide biotransformation is time-dependent, taking 20 to 30 hr to become apparent; it has been suggested that this corresponds to induction of variant cytochrome P-450 with low activity for tolbutamide hydroxylation; sulfonylureas may also be subject to displacement from plasma protein binding sites by phenylbutazone, resulting in increased activity; one report described paradoxic decrease in hypoglycemic effect of tolbutamide in three previously well-controlled diabetic Africans given phenylbutazone	Adjust sulfonylurea dosage in accordance with client response when phenylbutazone or oxyphenbutazone is employed concomitantly	Christensen, Hansen, and Kristensen, 1963; Field et al., 1967; Owusu and Ocran, 1972; Tannenbaum, Anderson, and Soeldner, 1974; Dent and Jue, 1976; Pond, Birkett, and Wade, 1977
	Rifampin	Chlorpropamide dose requirements were increased in a client receiving 600 mg of rifampin daily because of rise in blood glucose; trough serum chlorpropamide concentration decreased markedly after rifampin therapy was started and rose dramatically on discontinuation of rifampin therapy; rifampin has also been reported to decrease half-life of tolbutamide. The effect of rifampin, presumably, is to induce hepatic biotransformation of sulfonylureas	Monitor client response to sulfonylurea and adjust dosage accordingly	Syvalahti, Pihlajamaki, and Iisalo, 1974; Self and Morris, 1980

			Clinical management	Reference
Sulfonamides		Hypoglycemia can be induced acutely with the addition of a sulfonamide to the drug regimen. Sulfaphenazole presumably inhibits carboxylation of tolbutamide; sulfisoxazole and sulfamethizole have both been reported to enhance effect of chlorpropamide; large doses of sulfonamides may also enhance hypoglycemia by displacing sulfonylureas from their protein binding sites	Monitor clients for sulfonylurea efficacy; hypoglycemia may occur after initiation of sulfonamide therapy, particularly if large doses of sulfonamides are used	Soeldner and Steinke, 1965; Tucker and Hirsch, 1972; Hansten, 1974
Theophylline	Allopurinol	Although 300 mg/day of allopurinol for 1 week was shown in one study to alter pattern of metabolite excretion without affecting plasma theophylline clearance, a longer term of allopurinol administration (2 to 4 weeks) at higher dose (600 mg/day) decreased theophylline clearance by 21%; neither absorption nor distribution was affected	Chronic allopurinol dosing may necessitate a decrease in theophylline dosage to avoid accumulation and toxicity	Grygiel et al., 1979; Manfredi and Vesell, 1981
	β-adrenergic blockers	Oral propranolol, 40 mg every 6 hr, induced a fall in theophylline clearance of about 50%; reduction was greatest in cigarette smokers, whose theophylline clearance is initially high; metoprolol, 50 mg every 6 hr, had no effect on theophylline clearance in normal subjects evaluated as a group; however, in smokers, effect of 200 mg/day of metoprolol seemed to parallel degree of β-blockade, with 30% to 50% reduction in theophylline clearance	Nonselective β-blockers should be avoided in asthmatics because of risk of bronchoconstriction; with cardioselective β-blockers, risk of exacerbation of asthma is reduced, but there is potential for theophylline toxicity, particularly in smokers; clients receiving concurrent therapy should be observed closely and theophylline dosage reduced if necessary	Conrad and Nyman, 1980
	Cimetidine	The half-life of theophylline may be considerably increased with the concurrent administration of cimetidine because of hepatic microsomal enzyme inhibition. A preliminary report notes a 60% increase in theophylline half-life with cimetidine dosages of 300 mg every 6 hr for 2 days	Avoid concomitant therapy; if cimetidine must be used, monitor client for theophylline accumulation and evidence of toxicity; theophylline dosage may need to be reduced	Jackson et al., 1980

Continued.

TABLE 8-7 **Miscellaneous drug interactions—cont'd**

Primary drug	Interacting drug	Result/mechanism of interaction	Circumvention or management of interaction	References
Theophylline—cont'd	Macrolide antibiotics (erythromycin, troleandomycin)	In one study of theophylline kinetics in nine normal subjects administration of erythromycin (500 mg initially, 250 mg every 6 hr thereafter for 24 hr) increased elimination half-life of theophylline from 7.9 to 10.3 hr and decreased clearance from 0.90 to 0.78 ml/min/kg; this interaction with erythromycin, when it does occur, usually increases theophylline concentration by less than two fold; troleandomycin has been reported to double serum theophylline concentration in all clients receiving concomitant therapy	If these drugs must be used concurrently, consider reducing theophylline dosage by 25% to 50%; monitor client for theophylline toxicity	Kozak, Cummins, and Gillman, 1977; Pfeifer, Greenblatt, and Friedman, 1979; Walker and Hendeles, 1979

in fact, been clearly established. Difficulties in characterizing drug-food interactions stem from the complexities inherent in defining diet and nutritional status, especially in the elderly.

Intrapersonal and interpersonal dietary variations arise because of palate *(de gustibus non disputandum)*, appetite, seasonal and regional availability of foods, religious reasons, cost, and therapeutic regimens. Aberrations may result from differences in food composition and sources. The influence of processing on nutrient composition, the effect of food additives (e.g., vitamins, minerals, preservatives, flavor enhancers, artificial sweeteners, colorants, suspending agents, emulsifiers) on nutritional status and drug therapy, and the effect of variations in the environment in which food is grown on food composition are all largely unknown.

The aging client is at risk, nutritionally, because of the interplay of many factors, including increasingly more limited financial resources, decreasing physical activity and food intake, changes in nutrient uptake and disposition, decreasing appetite (which may reflect diminutions or alterations in the frequency distributions of taste and smell receptors), mandibular atrophy or loss of teeth (about 50% of those over 65 years of age are edentulous) (Greene, 1979), diminished salivary flow (which may make mastication and swallowing more difficult), and increasing isolation (psychosocial as well as physical). Each of these factors may be affected by drug administration. Finally, the growing popularity of "health" foods and dietary supplements among the elderly should be viewed with some alarm because many such products (e.g., dolomite, potassium supplements), which are potentially hazardous, are promoted in a false, misleading, or deceptive manner ("Nutrition as Therapy," 1980).

The classic drug-food interaction is that of MAOIs (isocarboxazid, pargyline, phenelzine, procarbazine, tranylcypromine*) with foods such as aged cheese or chianti wine, which contain

*Furazolidone has been reported to function as an MAOI when administered for more than 5 days (Pettinger, Soyangco, and Oates, 1968).

pressor amines (e.g., tyramine, dopamine, serotonin, tryptamine). Inhibition of gut wall and hepatic monoamine oxidase prevents the presystemic oxidation of the pressor amine, permitting the amine to produce a systemic effect by stimulating the release of norepinephrine from its storage sites. That this combination can provoke severe hypertension, intracerebral hemorrhage, and heart failure was recognized as early as 1963 (Blackwell, 1963). Yet, in spite of the potentially fatal outcome of what should be a well-known interaction by now, reports of adrenergic crises arising from MAOI use persist (Wright, 1978). As Wright notes, there is a need for comprehensive instructions for the client about avoiding certain foods and self-medication. Table 8-8 summarizes current literature insofar as the pressor amine content of foods and beverages is concerned. Emphasis in Table 8-8 is placed on tyramine, the prototypical pressor amine (Barger and Walpole, 1901), which has been shown to provoke a substantial rise in systolic blood pressure (40 mm Hg) at a dose of 6 mg (Horwitz et al., 1964). Horwitz et al. were able to elicit a marked rise in systolic blood pressure (80 mm Hg) with the feeding of 20 gm of cheddar cheese containing about 25 mg of tyramine. Furthermore, only one tenth to one hundredth as much tyramine hydrochloride was required intravenously during monoamine oxidase inhibition to produce pressor effects equivalent to those when an MAOI was not employed. The pressor response to pressor amines other than tyramine has, for the most part, been ignored even though this interaction has been more extensively cited than any other drug-food interaction in the literature.

If, as Koch-Weser (1972) suggests, a low index of suspicion exists among clinicians and hampers the detection or avoidance of drug-drug interactions, then the multifactorial character of drug-food interactions further obscures their recognition. Nonetheless, the description of drug-food interactions as primarily pharmacokinetic or pharmacodynamic in nature can aid in their recognition and management.

Pharmacokinetic interactions. Drug-food interactions involving alterations either in gastrointestinal absorption or in disposition are numerous. Most reported interactions result from modifications in gastrointestinal absorption. The rate and extent of gastrointestinal absorption can be affected by (1) changes in the rate of gastric emptying, (2) changes in intestinal transit time, (3) increased viscosity of the contents of the gastrointestinal tract, (4) interaction between the drug and dietary components, (5) altered pH, especially in the gastric region, (6) stimulation of bile secretion, and (7) direct effect on membrane permeability at the absorbing surface. Altered disposition most frequently arises from (1) enzyme induction or inhibition or (2) changes in the extent of renal excretion because of changes in urinary pH. Table 8-9 lists some drug-food interactions that occur through a pharmacokinetic mechanism.

Pharmacodynamic interactions. Drug-food interactions that involve a pharmacodynamic perturbation include the enhanced toxicity of digitalis glycosides in clients rendered hypokalemic by the ingestion of licorice. Hypokalemia results from the systemic uptake of glycyrrhizic acid, a component of licorice with mineralocorticoid activity (Louis and Conn, 1956; Freycon et al., 1964; Wash and Bernard, 1975; Blachley and Knochel, 1980). The consumption of licorice or licorice-flavored products, including chewing tobacco (Blachley and Knochel, 1980), places the client maintained on potassium-losing diuretics at greater risk of developing hypokalemia. Gross, Dexter, and Roth (1966) reported the onset of severe hypokalemia in a client maintained on hydrochlorothiazide who consumed between 30 and 40 gm of licorice per day. Low diuretic dosage (50 mg 3 times weekly) and the regular consumption of citrus juice were apparently insufficient to offset the hypokalemic effect of licorice. A striking indication of the mineralocorticoid activity of licorice involves self-medication with licorice, as a palliative, by clients with Addison's disease (Baron, 1973; Cotterill and Cunliffe, 1973). This glycyrrhizophilia is a symptom of

Text continued on p. 175.

TABLE 8-8   *Pressor amine content* of foods and beverages (μg/gm or μg/ml)*

Food or beverage	Dopamine	2-phenyl-ethylamine	Serotonin	Tryptamine	Tyramine	Amount of food (gm) or beverage (ml) containing 25 mg tyramine†	References
FOODS							
Caviar, Russian	—	—	—	—	680	37	Isaac, Mitchell, and Grahame-Smith, 1977
Cheese‡							
American, processed	—	—	—	—	50	500	Horwitz et al., 1964
Blue (Gorgonzola type), Danish	—	—	—	—	31-256	98-806	Sen, 1969
Boursault, French	—	—	—	—	1116	22	Sen, 1969
Brick, natural, Canadian	—	—	—	—	524	48	Sen, 1969
Brie	—	—	—	—	180	139	Horwitz et al., 1964
Brie type, Danish	—	—	—	—	0	—	Sen, 1969
Camembert	—	—	—	—	86	291	Horwitz et al., 1964
Camembert type, Danish	—	—	—	—	23	1087	Sen, 1969
Camembert type, Mycella, Danish	—	—	—	—	1340	19	Sen, 1969
Camembert type, South African	—	—	—	—	13	1923	Kaplan, Sapeika, and Moodie, 1974
Cheddar, South African	—	—	—	—	175-775	32-143	Kaplan, Sapeika, and Moodie, 1974
Cheddar, Canadian	—	—	—	—	120-1530	16-208	Sen, 1969
Cheddar, New York State	—	—	—	—	1416	18	Horwitz et al., 1964
Cheddar, processed, pasteurized, Canadian	—	—	—	—	26	962	Sen, 1969
Cheshire, South African	—	—	—	—	297	84	Kaplan, Sapeika, and Moodie, 1974
Colby	—	—	—	—	100-560	45-250	Voigt et al., 1974
Cottage	—	—	—	—	<0.2	>12,500	Horwitz et al., 1964
Cream	—	—	—	—	<0.2	>12,500	Horwitz et al., 1964
Cream (cottage), South African	—	—	—	—	5-7	3571-5000	Kaplan, Sapeika, and Moodie, 1974
Edam	—	—	—	—	300-320	78-83	Voigt et al., 1974
Emmenthaler	—	—	—	—	225	111	Horwitz et al., 1964
Gouda type, Canadian	—	—	—	—	20	1250	Sen, 1969
Gruyère	—	—	—	—	516	48	Horwitz et al., 1964
Gruyère, South African	—	—	—	—	30	833	Kaplan, Sapeika, and Moodie, 1974
Mozzarella, Canadian	—	—	—	—	410	61	Sen, 1969

Food							Reference
Parmesan, Italian	—	—	—	—	65	385	Sen, 1969
Parmesan type, USA	—	—	—	—	4-290	86-6250	Sen, 1969
Provolone, Italian	—	—	—	—	38	658	Sen, 1969
Romano, Italian	—	—	—	—	238	105	Sen, 1969
Roquefort, French	—	—	—	—	27-520	48-926	Sen, 1969
Roquefort type, South African	—	—	—	—	656	38	Kaplan, Sapeika, and Moodie, 1974
Stilton	—	—	—	—	466; 2170	11.5-54	Horwitz et al., 1964; Sen, 1969
Swiss	—	—	—	—	0-1800	≥14	Voigt et al., 1974
Chocolate	—	≥107	—	—	—	—	Hanington, 1974
Condiments							
Soya sauce	—	—	—	—	1.76	14,204	Sen, 1969
Fruits							
Avocado	4-5	—	10	0	23	1087	Udenfriend, Lovenberg, and Sjoerdsma, 1959
Banana (skin or peel)	700	—	50-150	0	65	385	Udenfriend, Lovenberg, and Sjoerdsma, 1959
Banana (pulp)	8	—	28	0	7	3571	Udenfriend, Lovenberg, and Sjoerdsma, 1959
Grape	0	—	—	0	0	—	Udenfriend, Lovenberg, and Sjoerdsma, 1959
Orange (pulp)	0	—	0	0.1	10	2500	Udenfriend, Lovenberg, and Sjoerdsma, 1959
Plantain (pulp)	—	—	45	—	—	—	Udenfriend, Lovenberg, and Sjoerdsma, 1959
Plum, blue	—	—	0	5	—	—	Udenfriend, Lovenberg, and Sjoerdsma, 1959

Continued.

*Substantial variations in pressor amine content of foods and beverages are encountered in practice because of variations in processing, microbial contamination, extent of ripening or fermentation, type and concentration of preservative, and storage conditions.

†This corresponds to the amount of tyramine that can provoke a hypertensive crisis in a client receiving an MAOI (Horwitz et al., 1964).

‡Ripened or aged cheeses tend to have substantial concentrations of tyramine compared to unripened cheeses (e.g., cottage cheese, cream cheese).

§Other fermented sausages (e.g., bologna, pepperoni, salami) should be considered potential problems as well.

‖Broad beans have been shown to have little or no pressor amine content but do have a considerable amount of dopa that can be converted to dopamine.

¶Prolonged contact of the must with grape skins during processing may result in the introduction of extraneous fermenting organisms and the subsequent production of appreciable amounts of tyramine. This is true of red and, to a lesser extent, rosé wines.

TABLE 8-8 *Pressor amine content of foods and beverages ($\mu g/gm$ or $\mu g/ml$) — cont'd*

Food or beverage	Pressor amine					Amount of food (gm) or beverage (ml) containing 25 mg tyramine†	References
	Dopamine	2-phenyl-ethylamine	Serotonin	Tryptamine	Tyramine		
FOODS—cont'd							
Plum, blue-red	—	—	8	2	—	—	Udenfriend, Lovenberg, and Sjoerdsma, 1959
Plum, red	0	—	10	0-2	6	4167	Udenfriend, Lovenberg, and Sjoerdsma, 1959
Raspberry	—	—	—	—	13-93	269-1923	Coffin, 1971
Herring, pickled	—	—	—	—	3,030	8	Neussle, Norman, and Miller, 1965
Herring, salted, dry	—	—	—	—	470	53	Sen, 1969
Liver, beef	—	—	—	—	274	91	Boulton, Cockson, and Paulton, 1970
Liver, chicken	—	—	—	—	100	250	Hedberg, Gordon, and Glueck, 1966
Marmite (yeast extract)	—	—	—	—	2300	11	Blackwell et al., 1967
Marmite (yeast extract), English	—	—	—	—	1090-1640	15-23	Blackwell, Mabbitt, and Marley, 1969
Marmite (yeast extract), salt-free, English	—	—	—	—	190	132	Blackwell, Mabbitt, and Marley, 1969
Sausage,§ dry, fermented, Belgian	—	0-6	—	—	10-151	165-2500	Vandekerckhove, 1977
Vegetables							
Broad (fava) beans	=	—	—	—	—	—	Hodge, Nye, and Emerson, 1964

								Reference
Eggplant	0	—	0	2	0.5-3	3	8333	Udenfriend, Lovenberg, and Sjoerdsma, 1959
Potato	0	0	0	0	0	1	25,000	Udenfriend, Lovenberg, and Sjoerdsma, 1959
Sauerkraut	—	—	—	—	—	37	676	Mayer and Pause, 1980
Spinach	0	0	0	0	0	1	25,000	Udenfriend, Lovenberg, and Sjoerdsma, 1959
Tomato	0	—	0	12	4	4	6250	Udenfriend, Lovenberg, and Sjoerdsma, 1959
Yeast extracts, Brand A, English	—	—	—	—	—	2057-2256	11-12	Sen, 1969
Yeast extracts, Brand B, Canadian	—	—	—	—	—	0-84	≥298	Sen, 1969
Yogurt	—	—	—	—	—	<0.2	>12,500	Horwitz et al., 1964
BEVERAGES								
Milk, sweet, South African	—	—	—	—	—	22	1136	Kaplan, Sepeika, and Moodie, 1974
Ale and beer								
Unspecified brands	—	—	—	—	—	2-4	6250-12500	Horwitz et al., 1964
Unspecified brands, Canadian	—	—	—	—	—	6-11	2273-4167	Sen, 1969
Ale, Canadian	—	—	—	—	—	9	2778	Sen, 1969
Wines[‖] Chianti	—	—	—	—	—	2-12;25	1000-12,500	Horwitz et al., 1964; Sen, 1969
Sherry	—	—	—	—	—	4	6250	Horwitz et al., 1964

TABLE 8-9 Selected drug-food interactions

Drug	Interacting food or nutrient	Result/mechanism of interaction	Circumvention or management of interaction	References
Phenytoin	Calcium	In a chronic phenytoin dosing study of five healthy subjects with a high calcium intake (normal diet supplemented by 1 gm/day of calcium gluconate or lactate), plasma phenytoin concentrations were significantly lowered; a similar but less pronounced effect was observed when calcium-rich foods (e.g., dairy products) were excluded from diet, indicating need for balanced calcium intake during phenytoin treatment; a limited single dose study of effect of calcium gluconate on phenytoin availability in two subjects failed, not surprisingly, to demonstrate any appreciable influence of calcium intake (2 gm calcium gluconate) on phenytoin; hypothetical bases for this interaction include decreased solubility of phenytoin-calcium complex and calcium-induced alterations of membrane permeability	No special precautions need be taken unless calcium intake is marginal or excessive; it would then be prudent to monitor plasma phenytoin concentrations and adjust dosage if warranted	Herishanu, Eylath, and Ilan, 1976; Chapron et al., 1979
	Folic acid	Subnormal folate levels may be encountered in a high proportion of epileptic clients maintained on anticonvulsants; there are limited data that support the hypothesis that folates can enhance phenytoin biotransformation, resulting in decreased serum phenytoin concentrations; in addition, other data suggest that phenytoin's anticonvulsant activity, in part, is related to folate depletion; clinical relevance of this interaction has not been established	Folic acid supplementation may be necessary in some clients maintained on phenytoin; however, addition of folate to drug regimen should be done cautiously because seizure intensity and frequency may be increased	Baylis et al., 1971; Gerson et al., 1972; Reynolds, 1973; Furlanut et al., 1978

| Tetracyclines | Divalent or trivalent cations* | Divalent or trivalent cations (e.g., calcium, magnesium, iron, aluminum) impair gastrointestinal absorption of tetracyclines, presumably because of formation of poorly absorbed chelate with cation; increase in gastrointestinal pH because of food intake could also decrease tetracycline dissolution and consequent availability | Do not administer tetracyclines† within 2 to 3 hours of meals or nutritional supplements, particularly those with substantial calcium or iron content | DiGangi and Rogers, 1949; Neuvonen et al., 1970; Barr, Adir, and Garretson, 1971; Gothoni et al., 1972; Wood and Shannonhouse, 1977; Venho, Salonen, and Mattila, 1978; Martin, 1979 |

*In addition to food and nutritional supplements, other interactants include antacids and laxatives with these cations. They should be similarly avoided.
†Doxycycline is relatively insensitive to the effect of calcium and dairy foods.

some diagnostic significance. Licorice-induced sodium and water retention can complicate congestive heart failure, hypertension, edema, or other related problems. As noted earlier, lithium dosage requirements in the treatment of manic-depressive illness may increase with sodium retention. Thus concomitant licorice ingestion may increase manic symptoms in lithium-treated clients. The resurgence of natural foods and flavorings in recent years, coupled with the likelihood of impaired homeostasis in the elderly client, makes the possibility of a licorice-induced adverse reaction less remote than once thought.

Inordinate increases in dietary vitamin K intake because of consumption of substantial amounts of leafy, green vegetables or the use of nutritional supplements can antagonize anticoagulant effectiveness (Quick, 1964; O'Reilly and Ryland, 1980). The occurrence of warfarin tolerance could reflect dietary interaction and underlines the need for clinicians to discuss diet, as well as medication, with clients.

Drug-food interactions have not been studied as intensively or extensively as drug-drug interactions. This applies particularly to those interactions that occur through pharmacodynamic mechanisms. Given the subclinical malnutrition states of many elderly clients, the imposition of a drug regimen may exacerbate dietary problems and complicate treatment.

CONCLUSION

The vulnerability of geriatric clients to adverse drug reactions and interactions can be minimized if the clinician chooses drugs with the least risk and employs multiple drug therapy only when absolutely appropriate. The majority of drug interactions cited in this chapter are by no means definitively characterized. Few studies have delineated dosage limits or temporal constraints insofar as potential interactants are concerned or have interaction studies routinely considered the effect of other drugs on the interactants. The reader should be aware of the possibility of interacting drug combinations other than those described in this chapter. The American Pharmaceutical Association's *Evaluation of Drug Interactions* (1976) and its supplement (1978) list 211 interaction monographs, and Hansten's *Drug Interactions* (1979) contains 660 monographs.

Accordingly, monitoring client medication profiles and histories is increasingly more important. Given the low incidence of prescriber awareness and recognition of drug interactions (Koch-Weser, 1972; Hull et al., 1978) and the limited appreciation of the contents of preparations ordered for clients, computer aided screening and intervention can provide a distinct advantage to the concerned clinician. Computer monitoring of drug therapy should not be an end in itself. There is a need for the development of algorithms to facilitate the clinical decision-making process. Hansten (1979) has described a number of appropriate algorithms. Their integration with client education and with computer monitoring programs could ultimately result in safer, more efficacious drug use. Illich's description of the aged as "victims of treatments meted out for an incurable condition" (1976) warrants attention. A fuller understanding of the risks and benefits of drug therapy is necessary if the "symphony of life" is not to end "with the crash of a broken drum or cracked cymbals" (Yutang, 1939).

INDEX TO DRUG INTERACTIONS CITED IN CHAPTER 8

REFERENCES

Aarons, L.J., Schary, W.L., and Rowland, M.: An in vitro study of drug displacement interactions: warfarin-salicylate and warfarin-phenylbutazone, J. Pharm. Pharmacol. **31**:322, 1979.

Alexanderson, B., Evans, D.A.P., and Sjoqvist, F.: Steady state plasma levels of nortriptyline in twins: influence of genetic factors and drug therapy, Br. Med. J. **4**:764, 1969.

Allen, M.D., et al.: Effect of magnesium-aluminum hydroxide and kaolin-pectin on absorption of digoxin from tablets and capsules, J. Clin. Pharmacol. **21**: 26, 1981.

Ambre, J.J., and Fischer, L.J.: Effect of coadministration of aluminum and magnesium hydroxides on absorption of anticoagulants in man, Clin. Pharmacol. Ther. **14**:231, 1973.

American Pharmaceutical Association: Evaluations of drug interactions, ed. 2, Washington, D.C., 1976 (suppl., 1978), The Association.

Amery, A., et al.: Glucose intolerance during diuretic therapy, Lancet **1**:681, 1978.

Andreasen, P.B.: Diphenylhydantoin half-life in man and its inhibition by phenylbutazone: the role of genetic factors, Acta Med. Scand. **193**:561, 1973.

Ariens, E.J., and Simonis, A.M.: Drug interactions resulting in loss of action. In Cluff, L.E., and Petrie, J.C., editors: Clinical effects of interaction between drugs, New York, 1974, American Elsevier Publishers, Inc.

Atallah, A.A.: Interaction of prostaglandins with diuretics, Prostaglandins **18**:369, 1979.

Bailey, R.R., and Neale, T.J.: Rapid clonidine withdrawal with blood pressure overshoot exaggerated by beta-blockade, Br. Med. J. **1**:942, 1976.

Ballek, R.D., Reidenberg, M.M., and Orr, L.: Inhibition of diphenylhydantoin metabolism by chloramphenicol, Lancet **1**:150, 1973.

Ban, T.A.: Drug interactions in psychiatry, Int. Pharmacopsychiatry **13**:94, 1978.

Barger, G., and Walpole, G.S.: Isolation of the pressor principles of putrid meat, J. Physiol. **38**:343, 1901.

Barnett, A.H., Leslie, D., and Watkins, P.J.: Can insulin-treated diabetics be given beta-adrenergic blocking drugs? Br. Med. J. **2**:976, 1980.

Baron, J.H.: Glycyrrhizophilia, Lancet **1**:383, 1973.

Barr, W.H., Adir, J., and Garrettson, L.: Decrease of

tetracycline absorption in man by sodium bicarbonate, Clin. Pharmacol. Ther. 12:779, 1971.

Bartoli, E., et al.: Blunting of furosemide diuresis by aspirin in man, J. Clin. Pharmacol. 20:452, 1980.

Baylis, E.M., et al.: Influence of folic acid on blood-phenytoin levels, Lancet 1:62, 1971.

Bazzano, G., and Bazzano, G.S.: Digitalis intoxication: treatment with a new steroid-binding resin, J.A.M.A. 220:828, 1972.

Bender, A.D.: Drug sensitivity in the elderly. In Crooks, J., and Stevenson, I.H., editors: Drugs and the elderly, Baltimore, 1979, University Park Press.

Bjornsson, T.D., et al.: Clofibrate displaces warfarin from plasma proteins in man: an example of a pure displacement interaction, J. Pharmacol. Exp. Ther. 210:316, 1979.

Blachley, J.D., and Knochel, J.P.: Tobacco chewer's hypokalemia: licorice revisited, N. Engl. J. Med. 302:784, 1980.

Blackwell, B.: Hypertensive crisis due to monoamine-oxidase inhibitors, Lancet 2:849, 1963.

Blackwell, B., Mabbitt, L.A., and Marley, E.: Histamine and tyramine content of yeast products, J. Food Sci. 34:47, 1969.

Blackwell, B., et al.: Hypertensive interactions between monoamine oxidase inhibitors and foodstuffs, Br. J. Psychiatry 113:349, 1967.

Block, L.H.: Drug interactions and the elderly, U.S. Pharm. 2(10):46, 1977.

Block, L.H., and Lamy, P.P.: Legend drugs with OTC drugs . . . therapeutic incompatibilities, J. Am. Pharm. Assoc. NS8:66, 1968.

Boekhout-Mussert, R.J. et al.: Inhibition by rifampin of the anticoagulant effect of phenprocoumon, J.A.M.A. 229:1903, 1974.

Boman, G., Eliasson, K., and Odar-Cederlöf, I.: Acute cardiac failure during treatment with digitoxin—an interaction with rifampicin, Br. J. Clin. Pharmacol. 10:89, 1980.

Boulton, A.A., Cookson, B., and Paulton, R.: Hypertensive crisis in a patient on MAOI antidepressants following a meal of beef liver, Can. Med. Assoc. J. 102:1394, 1970.

Boylan, J.J., Owen, D.S., and Chin, J.B.: Phenytoin interference with dexamethasone, J.A.M.A. 235:803, 1976.

Brater, D.C.: Analysis of the effect of indomethacin on the response to furosemide in man: effect of dose of furosemide, J. Pharmacol. Exp. Ther. 210:386, 1979.

Brater, D.C., Chennavasin, P., and Seiwell, R.: Furosemide in patients with heart failure: shift in dose-response curves, Clin. Pharmacol. Ther. 28:182, 1980.

Brater, D.C., and Morelli, H.F.: Digoxin toxicity in patients with normokalemic potassium depletion, Clin. Pharmacol. Ther. 22:21, 1977.

Brathwaite, R., Montgomery, S., and Dawling, S.: Age, depression, and tricyclic antidepressant levels. In Crooks, J., and Stevenson, I.H., editors: Drugs and the elderly, Baltimore, 1979, University Park Press.

Breckenridge, A., et al.: Glucose tolerance in hypertensive patients on long-term diuretic therapy, Lancet 1:61, 1967.

Briant, R.H., Reid, J.L., and Pollery, C.T.: Interaction between clonidine and desipramine in man, Br. Med. J. 1:522, 1973.

Brodows, R.G., and Campbell, R.G.: Effect of age on post-heparin lipase, N. Engl. J. Med. 287:969, 1972.

Brooks, S.M., et al.: Adverse effects of phenobarbital on corticosteroid metabolism in patients with bronchial asthma, N. Engl. J. Med. 286:1125, 1972.

Brooks, S.M., et al.: The effects of ephedrine and theophylline on dexamethasone metabolism in bronchial asthma, J. Clin. Pharmacol. 17:308, 1977.

Brown, D.D., and Juhl, R.P.: Decreased bioavailability of digoxin due to antacids and kaolin-pectin, N. Engl. J. Med. 295:1034, 1976.

Brummett, R.E., et al.: Cochlear damage resulting from kanamycin and furosemide, Acta Otolaryngol. 80:86, 1975.

Buchanan, N., Hurwitz, S., and Butler, P.: Asthma—a possible interaction between hydrocortisone and theophylline, S. Afr. Med. J. 56:1147, 1979.

Buffington, G.A., et al.: Interaction of rifampin and glucocorticoids, J.A.M.A. 236:1958, 1976.

Burkle, W.S., and Matzke, G.R.: Effect of quinidine on serum digoxin concentrations, Am. J. Hosp. Pharm. 36:968, 1979.

Burrows, G.D., and Davies, B.: Antidepressants and barbiturates, Brit. Med. J. 4:113, 1971.

Byrd, G.J.: Methyldopa and lithium carbonate: suspected interaction, J.A.M.A. 233:320, 1975.

Cairns, S.A., and Marshall, A.J.: Clonidine withdrawal, Lancet 1:368, 1976.

Cape, R.D.T.: Drugs and confusional states. In Crooks, J., and Stevenson, I.H., editors: Drugs and the elderly, Baltimore, 1979, University Park Press.

Cereghino, J.J., et al.: The efficacy of carbamazepine combinations in epilepsy, Clin. Pharmacol. Ther. **18:**733, 1975.

Chapron, D.J., Mumford, D., and Pitegoff, G.I.: Apparent quinidine-induced digoxin toxicity after withdrawal of pentobarbital: a case of sequential drug interactions, Arch. Intern. Med. **139:**363, 1979.

Chapron, D.J., et al.: Effect of calcium and antacids on phenytoin bioavailability, Arch. Neurol. **36:**436, 1979.

Chouinard, G., et al.: Potentiation of haloperidol by alpha-methyl-dopa in the treatment of schizophrenic patients, Curr. Ther. Res. **7:**473, 1973.

Christensen, L.K., Hansen, J.M., and Kristensen, M.: Sulphaphenazole-induced hypoglycemic attacks in tolbutamide treated diabetics, Lancet **2:**1298, 1963.

Christensen, L.K., and Skovsted, L.: Inhibition of drug metabolism by chloramphenicol, Lancet **2:**1397, 1969.

Christopher, L.J., et al.: A survey of hospital prescribing for the elderly. In Crooks, J., and Stevenson, I.H., editors: Drugs and the elderly, Baltimore, 1979, University Park Press.

Coffin, D.E.: Tyramine content of raspberries and other fruit, J. Assoc. Off. Anal. Chem. **53:**1071, 1971. In Ough, C.S.: A comparison of tyramine in wine and other foods, U.S. Pharm. **5:**52, 1980.

Cohon, M.S.: Drug interactions involving levodopa, Rev. Drug Interact. **1:**45, 1974.

Conrad, K.A., and Nyman, D.W.: Effects of metoprolol and propranolol on theophylline elimination, Clin. Pharmacol. Ther. **28:**463, 1980.

Cooper, J.W.: Food-drug interactions, U.S. Pharm. **1**(10):16, 1976.

Corn, M.: Effect of phenobarbital and glutethimide on biological half-life of warfarin, Thromb. Diath. Haemorrh. **16:**606, 1966.

Cotterill, J.A., and Cunliffe, W.J.: Self-medication with liquorice in a patient with Addison's disease, Lancet **1:**294, 1973.

Cowley, A.J., and Elkeles, R.S.: Diabetes and therapy with potent diuretics, Lancet **1:**154, 1978.

Cuny, G., et al.: Pharmacokinetics of salicylates in elderly, Gerontology **25:**49, 1979.

Dam, M., and Christiansen, J.: Interaction of propoxyphene with carbamazepine, Lancet **2:**509, 1977.

Dent, L.A., and Jue, S.G.: Tolbutamide-phenylbutazone interaction, Drug Intell. Clin. Pharm. **10:** 711, 1976.

Desmond, P.V., et al.: Cimetidine impairs the elimination of chlordiazepoxide in man, Ann. Intern. Med. **93:**266, 1980.

Di Gangi, F.E., and Rogers, C.H.: Adsorption studies of Aureomycin Hydrochloride on aluminum hydroxide gel, J. Am. Pharm. Assoc., Sci. Ed. **38:**646, 1949.

Doering, W.: Quinidine-digoxin interaction: pharmacokinetics, underlying mechanism and clinical implications, N. Engl. J. Med. **301:**400, 1979.

Doering, W., and König, E.: Anstieg der digoxinkonzentration im serum unter chinidinmedikation, Med. Klin. **73:**1085, 1978.

Dollery, C.T.: Drug-drug and drug-disease interactions in cardiovascular therapy. In Grahame-Smith, D.G., editor: Drug interactions, Baltimore, 1977, University Park Press.

Dollery, C.T., George, C.F., and Orme, M.L.E.: Drug interactions affecting cardiovascular therapy. In Cluff, L.E., and Petrie, J.C., editors: Clinical effects of interaction between drugs, New York, 1974, American Elsevier Publishers, Inc.

Dravet, C., et al.: Interaction between carbamazepine and triacetyloleandomycin, Lancet **1:**810, 1977.

Duarte, C.G., et al.: Thiazide-induced hypercalcemia, N. Engl. J. Med. **284:**828, 1971.

Duke, M.: Thiazide-induced hypokalemia, J.A.M.A. **239:**43, 1978.

Durao, V., Prata, M.M., and Goncalves, L.M.P.: Modification of antihypertensive effect of β-adrenoceptor-blocking agents by inhibition of endogenous prostaglandin synthesis, Lancet **2:**1005, 1977.

Duvoisin, R.C.: Antagonism of levodopa by papaverine, J.A.M.A. **231:**845, 1975.

Edwards, O.M., et al.: Changes in cortisol metabolism following rifampicin therapy, Lancet **2:**549, 1974.

Ejvinsson, G.: Effect of quinidine on plasma concentrations of digoxin, Br. Med. J. **1:**279, 1978.

Elis, J., et al.: Modification by monoamine oxidase inhibitors of the effect of some sympathomimetics on blood pressure, Br. Med. J. **2:**75, 1967.

Errick, J.K., and Keys, P.W.: Co-trimoxazole and warfarin: case report of an interaction, Am. J. Hosp. Pharm. **35:**1399, 1978.

Fann, W.E., et al.: Chlorpromazine reversal of the antihypertensive action of guanethidine, Lancet **2:**436, 1971.

Fann, W.E., et al.: Chlorpromazine: effects of antacids on its gastrointestinal absorption, J. Clin. Pharmacol. **13:**388, 1973.

Feely, J., Wilkinson, G.R., and Wood, A.J.J.: Reduction of liver blood flow and propranolol metabolism by cimetidine, N. Engl. J. Med. **304:**692, 1981.

Feldman, S., and Carlstedt, B.C.: Effect of antacid on absorption of enteric-coated aspirin, J.A.M.A. **227:**660, 1974.

Fenster, P.E., et al.: Digitoxin-quinidine interaction: pharmacokinetic evaluation, Ann. Intern. Med. **93:**698, 1980.

Field, J.B., et al.: Potentiation of acetohexamide hypoglycemia by phenylbutazone, N. Engl. J. Med. **277:**889, 1967.

Fischer, J.M., and Kroboth, P.D.: Update: tricyclic antidepressant therapy, U.S. Pharm. **5**(4):33, 1980.

Fleisch, J.H.: Age-related changes in the sensitivity of blood vessels to drugs, Pharmacol. Ther. **8:**477, 1980.

Forrest, F.M., Forrest, I.S., and Serra, M.T.: Modification of chlorpromazine metabolism by some other drugs frequently administered to psychiatric patients, Biol. Psychiatry **2:**53, 1970.

Freeman, G.K.: Drug-prescribing patterns in the elderly—a general practice study. In Crooks, J., and Stevensen, I.H., editors: Drugs and the elderly, Baltimore, 1979, University Park Press.

Freycon, F., et al.: Licorice intoxication, Lyon Med. **12:**745, 1964.

Friend, D.G., Bell, W.R., and Kline, N.S.: The action of L-dihydroxyphenylalanine in patients receiving nialamide, Clin. Pharmacol. Ther. **6:**362, 1965.

Frölich, J.C., et al.: Suppression of plasma renin activity by indomethacin in man, Circ. Res. **39:**447, 1976.

Frölich, J.C., et al.: Indomethacin increases plasma lithium, Br. Med. J. **1:**1115, 1979.

Furlanut, M., et al.: Effects of folic acid on phenytoin kinetics in healthy subjects, Clin. Pharmacol. Ther. **24:**294, 1978.

Gallus, A., and Birkett, D.: Sulphinpyrazone and warfarin: a probable drug interaction, Lancet **1:**535, 1980.

Gandelman, A.L.: Methenamine mandelate: antimicrobial activity in urine and correlation with formaldehyde levels, J. Urol. **97:**533, 1967.

Garty, M., Sood, P., and Rollins, D.E.: Digitoxin elimination reduced during quinidine therapy, Ann. Intern. Med. **94:**35, 1981.

Gerson, C.D., et al.: Inhibition by diphenylhydantoin of folic acid absorption in man, Gastroenterol. **63:**246, 1972.

Gibaldi, M., Grundhofer, B., and Levy, G.: Effect of antacids on pH of urine, Clin. Pharmacol. Ther. **16:**520, 1974.

Giusti, D.L.: The clinical use of antimicrobial agents in patients with renal and hepatic insufficiency: the aminoglycosides, Drug Intell. Clin. Pharm. **7:**540, 1973.

Goldberg, R.S., and Thornton, W.E.: Combined tricyclic-MAOI therapy for refractory depression: a review, with guidelines for appropriate usage, J. Clin. Pharmacol. **18:**143, 1978.

Goss, J.E., and Dickhaus, D.W.: Increased bishydroxycoumarin requirements in patients receiving phenobarbital, N. Engl. J. Med. **273:**1094, 1965.

Gothoni, G., et al.: Iron-tetracycline interaction: effect of time interval between the drugs, Acta Med. Scand. **191:**409, 1972.

Graham, G.G., et al.: Patterns of plasma concentrations and urinary excretion of salicylate in rheumatoid arthritis, Clin. Pharmacol. Ther. **22:**410, 1977.

Grahame-Smith, D.G.: General aspects of drug interactions in psychopharmacology. In Grahame-Smith, D.G., editor: Drug interactions, Baltimore, 1977, University Park Press.

Greene, J.: Nutritional care considerations of older Americans, J. Natl. Med. Assoc. **71:**791, 1979.

Greenlaw, C.W.: Chloramphenicol-phenytoin drug interaction, Drug Intell. Clin. Pharm. **13:**609, 1979.

Gross, E.G., Dexter, J.D., and Roth, R.G.: Hypokalemic myopathy with myoglobinuria associated with licorice ingestion, N. Engl. J. Med. **274:**602, 1966.

Grygiel, J.J., et al.: Effects of allopurinol on theophylline metabolism and clearance, Clin. Pharmacol. Ther. **26:**660, 1979.

Gualtieri, C.T., and Powell, S.F.: Psychoactive drug interactions, J. Clin. Psychiatry **39:**720, 1978.

Gugler, R., and Somogyi, A.: Reduced cimetidine clearance with age, N. Engl. J. Med. **301:**435, 1979.

Hager, W.D., et al.: Digoxin-quinidine interaction: pharmacokinetic evaluation, N. Engl. J. Med. **300:** 1238, 1979.

Hakim, R., et al.: Severe hypercalcemia associated with hydrochlorothiazide and calcium carbonate therapy, Can. Med. Assoc. J. **121:**591, 1979.

Hale, W.E., Marks, R.G., and Stewart, R.B.: Drug use in a geriatric population, J. Am. Geriatr. Soc. **27:**374, 1979.

Hanington, E.: Monoamine oxidase and migraine, Lancet **2:**1148, 1974.

Hansen, J.M., Kristensen, M., and Skovsted, L.: Dicoumarol-induced diphenylhydantoin intoxication, Lancet **2:**265, 1966.

Hansen, J.M., Siersbaek-Nielsen, K., and Skovsted, L.: Carbamazepine-induced acceleration of diphenylhydantoin and warfarin metabolism in man, Clin. Pharmacol. Ther. **12:**539, 1971.

Hansten, P.D.: Concomitant use of antibacterial sulfonamides and sulfonylurea hypoglycemics, Northwest Med. J. **1:**25, 1974.

Hansten, P.D.: Drug interactions, ed. 4, Philadelphia, 1979, Lea & Febiger.

Hansten, P.D.: Beta-blocking agents and antidiabetic drugs, Drug Intell. Clin. Pharm. **14:**46, 1980.

Hansten, P.D., and Hayton, W.L.: Effect of antacid and ascorbic acid on serum salicylate concentration, J. Clin. Pharmacol. **20:**326, 1980.

Harris, A.L.: Clonidine withdrawal and blockade, Lancet **1:**596, 1976.

Hart, F.D.: Rheumatic disorders. In Avery, G.S., editor: Drug treatment, ed. 2, Sydney, 1980, ADIS Press.

Hassall, C., et al.: Potentiation of warfarin by cotrimoxazole, Lancet **2:**1155, 1975.

Hathcock, J.N., and Coon, J., editors: Nutrition and drug interrelations, New York, 1978, Academic Press, Inc.

Hedberg, D.L., Gordon, M.W., and Glueck, B.C.: Six cases of hypertensive crisis in patients on tranylcypromine after eating chicken livers, Am. J. Psychiatry **122:**933, 1966.

Helmholz, H.F.: The effectiveness of methenamine as a urinary antiseptic at various hydrogen-ion concentrations, J. Pediatr. **1:**73, 1932.

Henry, D.A., et al.: Cimetidine and ranitidine: comparison of effects on hepatic drug metabolism, Br. Med. J. **281:**775, 1980.

Henry, M.P., et al.: Bleeding complications of heparin treatment in geriatric patients, Methods Findings Exp. Clin. Pharmacol. **3:**95, 1981.

Herishanu, Y., Eylath, U., and Ilan, R.: Effect of calcium content of diet on absorption of diphenylhydantoin, Isr. J. Med. Sci. **12:**1453, 1976.

Hethcox, J.M., and Stanaszek, W.F.: Interactions of drugs and diet, Hosp. Pharm. **9:**373, 1974.

Hetzel, D., Birkett, D., and Miners, J.: Cimetidine interaction with warfarin, Lancet **2:**639, 1979.

Himmelhoch, J.M., et al.: Thiazide-lithium synergy in refractory mood swings, Am. J. Psychiatry **134:** 149, 1977a.

Himmelhoch, J.M., et al.: Adjustment of lithium dose during lithium-chlorothiazide therapy, Clin. Pharmacol. Ther. **22:**225, 1977b.

Hirsh, P.D., Weiner, H.J., and North, R.L.: Further insights into digoxin-quinidine interaction: lack of correlation between serum digoxin concentration and inotropic state of the heart, Am. J. Cardiol. **46:**863, 1980.

Hirtz, J.: La pharmacocinétique du sujet âgé, Pharm. Acta Helv. **55**(3):72, 1980.

Hodge, J.V., Nye, E.R., and Emerson, G.W.: Monoamine-oxidase inhibitors, broad beans and hypertension, Lancet **1:**1108, 1964.

Hoffman, B.F., and Bigger, J.T., Jr.: Digitalis and allied cardiac glycosides. In Goodman, A.G., Goodman, L.S., and Gilman, A., editors: The pharmacological basis of therapeutics, ed. 6, New York, 1980, Macmillan, Inc.

Hollister, L.E.: Drug therapy: tricyclic antidepressants, N. Engl. J. Med. **299:**1106, 1978.

Hollister, L.E.: Psychiatric disorders. In Avery, G.S., editor: Drug treatment, ed. 2, Sydney, 1980, ADIS Press.

Holloway, D.A.: Drug problems in the geriatric patient, Drug Intell. Clin. Pharm. **8:**632, 1974.

Hooymans, P.M., and Merkus, F.W.H.M.: Effect of quinidine on plasma concentration of digoxin, Br. Med. J. **2:**1022, 1978.

Hooymans, P.M., and Merkus, F.W.H.M.: The mechanism of the interaction between digoxin and quinidine, Pharm. Weekblad. Sci. Ed. **1:**36, 1979.

Horwitz, D., et al.: Monoamine oxidase inhibitors, tyramine and cheese, J.A.M.A. **188:**1108, 1964.

Hull, J.H., et al.: Potential anticoagulant drug interactions in ambulatory patients, Clin. Pharmacol. Ther. **24:**644, 1978.

Hurwitz, A.: Antacid therapy and drug kinetics, Clin. Pharmacokinet. **2:**269, 1977.

Hurwitz, N.: Admissions to hospitals due to drugs, Br. Med. J. **1:**539, 1969a.

Hurwitz, N.: Predisposing factors in adverse reactions to drugs, Br. Med. J. **1:**536, 1969b.

Hyde, N.A., et al.: Nonpharmacy outlets providing prescription medications to ambulatory patients, Contemp. Pharm. Pract. **2:**117, 1979.

Illich, I.: Medical nemesis: the expropriation of health, New York, 1976, Bantam Books, Inc.

Isaac, P., Mitchell, B., Grahame-Smith, D.G.: Mono-amine-oxidase inhibitors and caviar, Lancet **2:**816, 1977.

Jackson, J.E., et al.: Cimetidine-theophylline interaction, Pharmacologist **22:**231, 1980.

Jamil, A., Reid, J.M., and Messer, M.: Interaction between sulphinpyrazone and warfarin, Chest **79:**375, 1981.

Johnson, A.H., and Hamilton, C.H.: Kanamycin ototoxicity—possible potentiation by other drugs, South. Med. J. **63:**511, 1970.

Jubiz, W., and Meikle, A.W.: Alterations of glucorti-coid actions by other drugs and disease states, Drugs **18:**113, 1979.

Jubiz, W., et al.: Effect of diphenylhydantoin on the metabolism of dexamethasone, N. Engl. J. Med. **283:**11, 1970.

Kaplan, E.R., Sapeika, N., and Moodie, I.M.: Deter-mination of the tyramine content of South African cheeses by gas-liquid chromatography, Analyst **99:**565, 1974.

Keller, F., and Kreutz, G.: Keine chinidin-interak-tion mit digitoxin, Dtsch. Med. Wochenschr. **105:**701, 1980.

Kerry, R.J., Ludlow, J.M., and Owen, G.: Diuretics are dangerous with lithium, Br. Med. J. **281:**371, 1980.

Kiorboe, E.: Phenytoin intoxication during treatment with Antabuse (disulfiram), Epilepsia **7:**246, 1966.

Klinenberg, J.R., and Miller, F.: Effect of corticoste-roids on blood salicylate concentration, J.A.M.A. **194:**601, 1965.

Klotz, U., Anttila, V.J., and Reimann, I.: Cimetidine/diazepam interaction, Lancet **2:**699, 1979.

Klotz, U., and Reimann, I.: Delayed clearance of diazepam due to cimetidine, N. Engl. J. Med. **302:**1012, 1980.

Knapp, D.A., and Knapp, D.A.: The elderly and non-prescribed medications, Contemp. Pharm. Pract. **3:**85, 1980.

Knight, V., et al.: Methenamine mandelate: anti-microbial activity, absorption and excretion, Anti-biot. Chemother. **2:**615, 1952.

Koch-Weser, J.: Potentiation by glucagon of the hypo-prothrombinemic action of warfarin, Ann. Intern. Med. **72:**331, 1970.

Koch-Weser, J.: Clinical detection of drug interac-tions, Drug Info. J. **6**(1):42, 1972.

Koch-Weser, J., and Greenblatt, D.J.: Drug interac-tions in clinical perspective, Eur. J. Clin. Pharma-col. **11:**405, 1977.

Koch-Weser, J., and Sellers, E.M.: Drug interactions with coumarin anticoagulants, N. Engl. J. Med. **285:**487, 1971.

Kohner, E.M., et al.: Effect of diuretic therapy on glucose tolerance in hypertensive patients, Lancet **1:**986, 1971.

Kosman, M.E.: Management of potassium problems during long-term diuretic therapy, J.A.M.A. **230:**743, 1974.

Kott, E., Bornstein, B., and Eichhorn, F.: Excretion of dopa metabolites, N. Engl. J. Med. **284:**395, 1971.

Kozak, P.P., Cummins, L.H., and Gillman, S.H.: Administration of erythromycin to patients on the-ophylline, J. Allergy Clin. Immunol. **60:**149, 1977.

Krishnaswamy, K.: Drug metabolism and pharmaco-kinetics in malnutrition, Clin. Pharmacokinet. **3:**216, 1978.

Kutt, H., and McDowell, F.: Management of epilepsy with diphenylhydantoin sodium: dosage regulation for problem patients, J.A.M.A. **203:**969, 1968.

Kutt, H., et al.: Diphenylhydantoin intoxication: a complication of isoniazid therapy, Am. Rev. Respir. Dis. **101:**377, 1970.

Lai, A.A., Levy, R.H., and Cutler, R.E.: Time-course of interaction between carbamazepine and clonaze-pam in normal man, Clin. Pharmacol. Ther. **24:**316, 1978.

Lamy, P.P.: Geriatric drug therapy, Clin. Med. **81:**52, 1974.

Lamy, P.P.: Prescribing for the elderly, Littleton, Mass., 1980, PSG Publishing Co., Inc.

Leahey, E.B., Jr., et al.: Interaction between quini-dine and digoxin, J.A.M.A. **240:**533, 1978.

Lehmann, H.U., et al.: Lebensdrohliche digitalis intoxikationen mit und ohne saluretische zusatz-therapie, Dtsch. Med. Wochenschr. **103:**1566, 1978.

Leishman, A.W.D., Mathews, H.L., and Smith, A.J.: Antagonism of guanethidine by imipramine, Lancet **1:**112, 1963.

Levander, O.A., and Cheng, L., editors: Micronutrient interactions: vitamins, minerals and hazardous elements, Ann. N.Y. Acad. Sci. **355**:1, 1980.

Levy, G.: Pharmacokinetics of salicylate in man, Drug Metab. Rev. **9**:3, 1979.

Levy, G., and Leonards, J.R.: Urine pH and salicylate therapy, J.A.M.A. **217**:81, 1971.

Levy, G., et al.: Decreased serum salicylate concentration in children with rheumatic fever treated with antacid, N. Engl. J. Med. **293**:323, 1975.

Lewis, R.J., et al.: Warfarin—stereochemical aspects of its metabolism and the interaction with phenylbutazone, J. Clin. Invest. **53**:1607, 1974.

Lilja, M., et al.: Interaction of clonidine and β-blockers, Acta. Med. Scand. **207**:173, 1980.

Lipton, J.H.: Incompatibility between sulfamethizole and methenamine mandelate, N. Engl. J. Med. **268**:92, 1963.

Loiseau, P., Brachet, A., and Henry, P.: Etude du taux serique du phenobarbital chex des epiliptiques, Encephale **1**:341, 1975.

Louis, L.H., and Conn, J.W.: Preparation of glycyrrhizinic acid, the electrolyte-active principle of licorice: its effects upon metabolism and upon pituitary-adrenal function in man, J. Lab. Clin. Med. **47**:20, 1956.

Lunde, P.K.M.: Plasma protein binding of diphenylhydantoin in man, Acta. Pharmacol. Toxicol. **29**:152, 1971.

MacDonald, M.G., et al.: The effects of phenobarbital, chloral betaine and glutethimide administration on warfarin plasma levels and hypoprothrombinemic responses in man, Clin. Pharmacol. Ther. **10**:80, 1969.

Manfredi, R.L., and Vesell, E.S.: Inhibition of theophylline metabolism by long-term allopurinol administration, Clin. Pharmacol. Ther. **29**:224, 1981.

Marley, E., and Blackwell, B.: Interactions of monoamine oxidase inhibitors, amines and foodstuffs, Adv. Pharmacol. Chemother. **8**:185, 1970.

Martin, S.R.: Equilibrium and kinetic studies on the interaction of tetracyclines with calcium and magnesium, Biophys. Chem. **10**:319, 1979.

Masson, J.P., et al.: Zur eliminationskinetik des digoxin vor und während spironolactonbehandlung, Klin. Wochenschr. **56**:1071, 1978.

Matz, G.L.: The ototoxic effects of ethacrynic acid in man and animals, Laryngoscope **86**:1065, 1976.

Mayer, K., and Pause, G.: Biogenic amines in sauerkraut, Lebensm.-Wiss. Technol. **5**:108, 1972. Cited in Ough, C.S.: A comparison of tyramine in wine and other foods, U.S. Pharm. **5**:52, 1980.

McAvoy, T.J.: Pharmacokinetic modeling of heparin and its clinical implications, J. Pharmacokinet. Biopharm. **7**:331, 1979.

McCurdy, D.K., Frederic, M., and Elkington, J.R.: Renal tubular acidosis due to amphotericin B, N. Engl. J. Med. **278**:124, 1968.

Meinertz, T., et al.: Interruption of the enterohepatic circulation of phenprocoumon by cholestyramine, Clin. Pharmacol. Ther. **21**:731, 1977.

Melander, A.: Influence of food on the bioavailability of drugs, Clin. Pharmacokinet. **3**:337, 1978.

Melby, J.C.: Systemic corticosteroid therapy—pharmacology and endocrinologic considerations, Ann. Intern. Med. **81**:505, 1974.

Mesdjian, E., et al.: Effect of sodium valproate on phenobarbitone plasma levels in epileptic patients. In Meinardi, H., and Rowan, A.J., editors: Advances in epileptology, Amsterdam, 1978, Swets & Zeitlinger.

Mesdjian, E., et al.: Carbamazepine intoxication due to triacetyloleandomycin administration in epileptic patients, Epilepsia **21**:489, 1980.

Meyer, J.F., McAllister, C.K., and Goldberg, L.I.: Insidious and prolonged antagonism of guanethidine by amitriptyline, J.A.M.A. **213**:1487, 1970.

Miller, R.R., Porter, J., and Greenblatt, D.J.: Clinical importance of the interaction of phenytoin and isoniazid, Chest **75**:356, 1979.

Miller, S.E., and Neilson, J.M.: Clinical features of the diabetic syndrome appearing after steroid therapy, Postgrad. Med. J. **40**:660, 1964.

Milne, M.D.: Drug interactions and the kidney. In Cluff, L.E., and Petrie, J.C., editors: Clinical effects of interaction between drugs, Amsterdam, 1975, Excerpta Medica.

Mitnick, P.D., et al.: Effects of two nonsteroidal antiinflammatory drugs, indomethacin and oxaprozin, on the kidney, Clin. Pharmacol. Ther. **28**:680, 1980.

Moody, J.P., et al.: Pharmacokinetic aspects of protriptyline plasma levels, Eur. J. Clin. Pharmacol. **11**:51, 1977.

Moore, S.R.: Medication taking behavior of the elderly, Drug Intell. Clin. Pharm. **12**:739, 1978.

Morgan, T.O.: Potassium replacement: supplements or potassium-sparing diuretics? Drugs **18**:218, 1979.

Morgan, D.B., and Davidson, C.: Hypokalemia and diuretics: an analysis of publications, Br. Med. J. **1**:905, 1980.

Mudge, G.H.: Agents affecting volume and composition of body fluids. In Gilman, A.G., Goodman, L.S., and Gilman, A., editors: The pharmacological basis of therapeutics, ed. 6, New York, 1980a, Macmillan, Inc.

Mudge, G.H.: Diuretics and other agents employed in the mobilization of edema fluid. In Gilman, A.G., Goodman, L.S., and Gilman, A., editors: The pharmacological basis of therapeutics, ed. 6, New York, 1980b, Macmillan, Inc.

Mungall, D.R., et al.: Effects of quinidine on serum digoxin concentration, Ann. Intern. Med. 93:689, 1980.

Nadel, I., and Wallach, M.: Drug interaction between haloperidol and methyldopa, Br. J. Psychiatry 135:484, 1979.

Neussle, W.F., Norman, F.C., and Miller, H.E.: Pickled herring and tranylcypromine reaction, J.A.M.A. 192:726, 1965.

Neuvonen, P.J., et al.: Interference of iron with the absorption of tetracyclines in man, Br. Med. J. 4:532, 1970.

Norman, T.R., et al.: Pharmacokinetics and plasma levels of antidepressants in the elderly, Med. J. Aust. 1:273, 1979.

Novi, C., et al.: Rifampin and digoxin: possible drug interaction in a dialysis patient, J.A.M.A. 244:2521, 1980.

Nutrition as therapy: Consumer Rep. 45(1):21, 1980.

Ober, K.F., and Wang, R.I.: Drug interactions with guanethidine, Clin. Pharmacol. Ther. 14:190, 1973.

Ochs, H.R., et al.: Noninteraction of digitoxin and quinidine, N. Engl. J. Med. 303:672, 1980.

Olesen, O.V.: Disulfiram (Antabuse) as inhibitor of phenytoin metabolism, Arch. Pharmacol. Toxicol. 24:317, 1966.

Olesen, O.V.: The influence of disulfiram and calcium carbamide on the serum diphenylhydantoin. Excretion of HPPH in the urine, Arch. Neurol. 16:642, 1967.

O'Malley, K., and O'Brien, E.: Management of hypertension in the elderly, N. Engl. J. Med. 302:1397, 1980.

O'Malley, K., Judge, T.G., and Crooks, J.: Geriatric clinical pharmacology and therapeutics. In Avery, G.S., editor: Drug treatment, ed. 2, Sydney, 1980, ADIS Press.

O'Malley, K., et al.: Determinants of anticoagulant control in patients receiving warfarin, Br. J. Clin. Pharmacol. 4:309, 1977.

O'Regan, J.B.: Adverse interactions of lithium carbonate and methyldopa, Can. Med. Assoc. J. 115:385, 1976.

O'Reilly, R.A.: Interaction of sodium-warfarin and disulfiram (Antabuse) in man, Ann. Intern. Med. 78:73, 1973.

O'Reilly, R.A.: Interaction of sodium warfarin and rifampin. Studies in man, Ann. Intern. Med. 81:337, 1974.

O'Reilly, R.A.: Interaction of chronic daily warfarin therapy and rifampin, Ann. Intern. Med. 83:506, 1975.

O'Reilly, R.A.: Enantiomers of warfarin and phenobarbital (reply), N. Engl. J. Med. 295:1482, 1976a.

O'Reilly, R.A.: The stereoselective interaction of warfarin and metronidazole in man, N. Engl. J. Med. 295:354, 1976b.

O'Reilly, R.A.: Anticoagulant, antithrombotic, and thrombolytic drugs. In Gilman, A.G., Goodman, L.S., and Gilman, A., editors: The pharmacological basis of therapeutics, ed. 6, New York, 1980a, Macmillan Inc.

O'Reilly, R.A.: Stereoselective interaction of trimethoprim-sulfamethoxazole with the separated enantiomorphs of racemic warfarin in man, N. Engl. J. Med. 302:33, 1980b.

O'Reilly, R.A.: Dynamic interaction between disulfiram and separated enantiomorphs of racemic warfarin, Clin. Pharmacol. Ther. 29:332, 1981.

O'Reilly, R.A., and Levy, G.: Pharmacokinetic analysis of potentiating effect of phenylbutazone on anticoagulant action of warfarin in man, J. Pharm. Sci. 59:1258, 1970.

O'Reilly, R.A., and Notley, C.H.: Racemic warfarin and trimethoprim-sulfamethoxazole interaction in humans, Ann. Intern. Med. 91:34, 1979.

O'Reilly, R.A., and Ryland, D.A.: Resistance to warfarin due to unrecognized vitamin K supplementation, N. Engl. J. Med. 303:160, 1980.

Orme, M.: Enantiomers of warfarin and phenobarbital, N. Engl. J. Med. 295:1482, 1976.

Osanloo, E., and Deglin, J.H.: Interaction of lithium and methyldopa, Ann. Intern. Med. 92:433, 1980.

Otten, I., and Shelley, F.D.: When your parents grow old, New York, 1976, Funk & Wagnalls, Inc.

Owusu, S.K., and Ocran, K.: Paradoxical behaviour of phenylbutazone in African diabetics, Lancet 1:440, 1972.

Paccioretti, M.J., and Block, L.H.: Effects of aspirin

on platelet aggregation as a function of dosage and time, Clin. Pharmacol. Ther. **27**:803, 1980.

Pascale, L.R., et al.: Inhibition of the uricosuric action of Benemid by salicylate, J. Lab. Clin. Med. **45**:771, 1955.

Patak, R.V., et al.: Antagonism of the effects of furosemide by indomethacin in normal and hypertensive man, Prostaglandins **10**:649, 1975.

Patel, I.H., Levy, R.H., and Cutler, R.E.: Phenobarbital-valproic acid interaction, Clin. Pharmacol. Ther. **27**:515, 1980.

Patwardhan, R.V., et al.: Cimetidine spares the glucuronidation of lorazepam and oxazepam, Gastroenterology **79**:912, 1980.

Pedersen, K.E., and Hvidt, S.: Quinidine-digoxin interaction, N. Engl. J. Med. **302**:176, 1980.

Petereit, L.B., and Meikle, A.W.: Effectiveness of prednisolone during phenytoin therapy, Clin. Pharmacol. Ther. **22**:912, 1977.

Peters, U., et. al.: Interaktion von chinidin und digitoxin beim menschen, Dtsch. Med. Wochenschr. **105**:438, 1980a.

Peters, U., et al.: Keine chinidin-interaktion mit digitoxin, Dtsch. Med. Wochenschr. **105**:701, 1980b.

Petersen, V., et al.: Effect of prolonged thiazide treatment on renal lithium clearance, Br. Med. J. **2**:143, 1974.

Petrick, R.J., Kronacher, N., and Alcena, V.: Interaction between warfarin and ethacrynic acid, J.A.M.A. **231**:843, 1975.

Pettinger, W.A., Soyangco, F.G., and Oates, J.A.: Inhibition of monoamine oxidase in man by furazolidone, Clin. Pharmacol. Ther. **9**:442, 1968.

Pfeifer, H.J., Greenblatt, D.J., and Friedman, P.: Effects of three antibiotics on theophylline kinetics, Clin. Pharmacol. Ther. **26**:36, 1979.

Place, V.A., and Benson, H.: Dietary influences on therapy with drugs, J. Mond. Pharm. **4**:261, 1971.

Poe, T.E., Edwards, J.L., and Taylor, R.B.: Hypertensive crisis possibly due to drug interaction, Postgrad. Med. **66**:235, 1979.

Pond, S.M., Birkett, D.J., and Wade, D.N.: Mechanisms of inhibition of tolbutamide metabolism: phenylbutazone, oxyphenbutazone, sulfaphenazole, Clin. Pharmacol. Ther. **22**:573, 1977.

Pond, S.M., et al.: Effects of tricyclic antidepressants on drug metabolism, Clin. Pharmacol. Ther. **18**:191, 1975.

Ponto, L.B., et al.: Drug therapy reviews: tricyclic antidepressant and monoamine oxidase inhibitor combination therapy, Am. J. Hosp. Pharm. **34**:954, 1977.

Posner, D.M.: Antagonism of levodopa by papaverine, J.A.M.A. **233**:768, 1975.

Powell, J.R., et al.: Quinidine-digoxin interaction, N. Engl. J. Med. **302**:176, 1980.

Prescott, L.F.: Clinically important drug interactions. In Avery, G.S., editor: Drug treatment, Sydney, 1980, ADIS Press.

Quick, A.: Leafy vegetables in diet after prothrombin time in patients taking anticoagulant drugs, J.A.M.A. **187**:27, 1964.

Quick, C., and Hoppe, W.: Permanent deafness associated with furosemide, Ann. Otol. Rhinol. Laryngol. **84**:94, 1975.

Ragheb, M., et al.: Interaction of indomethacin and ibuprofen with lithium in manic patients under a steady-state lithium level, J. Clin. Psychiatry **41**: 397, 1980.

Rawlins, M.D.: Drug interactions and anaesthesia, Br. J. Anaesth. **50**:689, 1978.

Reid, P.R., and Meek, A.G.: Digoxin-quinidine interaction, Johns Hopkins Med. J. **145**:227, 1979.

Reynolds, E.H.: Anticonvulsants, folic acid, and epilepsy, Lancet **1**:1376, 1973.

Rifkin, S.I., et al.: Deafness associated with oral furosemide, South. Med. J. **71**:86, 1978.

Riley, G.: How aging influences drug therapy, U.S. Pharm. **2**(10):28, 1977.

Risch, S.C., Groom, G.P., and Janowsky, D.S.: Interfaces of psychopharmacology and cardiology—part one, J. Clin. Psychiatry **42**:23, 1981.

Risler, T., et al.: Quinidine-digoxin interaction, N. Engl. J. Med. **302**:175, 1980.

Rivera-Calimlin, L., Kerzner, B., and Karch, F.E.: Effect of lithium on plasma chlorpromazine levels, Clin. Pharmacol. Ther. **23**:451, 1978.

Robinson, D.S.: Age-related factors affecting antidepressant drug metabolism and clinical response. In Nandy, K., editor: Geriatric psychopharmacology, New York, 1979, Elsevier North-Holland, Inc.

Robinson, D.S., Benjamin, D.M., and McCormack, J.J.: Interaction of warfarin and nonsystemic gastrointestinal drugs, Clin. Pharmacol. Ther. **12**:491, 1971.

Rodolfi, A., Borgogelli, E., and Lodola, E.: Blood level of cimetidine in relation to age, Eur. J. Clin. Pharmacol. **15**:257, 1979.

Roe, D.A.: Drug-induced nutritional deficiencies, Westport, Conn., 1976, Avi Publishing Co., Inc.

Rogen, A.S., and Campbell-Ferguson, J.: Clinical observations on patients treated with Atromid and anticoagulant, J. Atheroscler. Res. **3**:671, 1963.

Rose, J.Q., et al.: Intoxication caused by interaction of chloramphenicol and phenytoin, J.A.M.A. **237**:2630, 1977.

Rothschild, B.M.: Hematologic perturbations associated with salicylates, Clin. Pharmacol. Ther. **26**:145, 1979.

Rowland, M., and Tozer, T.N.: Clinical pharmacokinetics: concepts and applications, Philadelphia, 1980, Lea & Febiger.

Salzman, C.: Polypharmacy and drug drug interactions in the elderly. In Nandy, K., editor: Geriatric psychopharmacology, New York, 1979, Elsevier North-Holland, Inc.

Schenck-Gustafsson, K., and Dahlqvist, R.: Pharmacokinetics of digoxin in patients subjected to the quinidine-digoxin interaction, Br. J. Clin. Pharmacol. **11**:181, 1981.

Schentag, J.J., et al.: Pharmacokinetic and clinical studies in patients with cimetidine-associated mental confusion, Lancet **1**:177, 1979.

Schmucker, D.L.: Age-related changes in drug disposition, Pharmacol. Rev. **30**:445, 1979.

Schumacher, G.E.: Using pharmacokinetics in drug therapy. VII. Pharmacokinetic factors influencing drug therapy in the aged, Am. J. Hosp. Pharm. **37**:559, 1980.

Seidl, L.G., et al.: Studies on the epidemiology of adverse drug reaction. III. Reactions in patients on a general medical service, Bull. Johns Hopkins Hosp. **119**:299, 1966.

Self, T.H., and Morris, T.: Interaction of rifampin and chlorpropamide, Chest **77**:800, 1980.

Sen, N.P.: Analysis and significance of tyramine in foods, J. Food Sci. **34**:22, 1969.

Serlin, M.J., et al.: Cimetidine: interaction with oral anticoagulants in man, Lancet **2**:317, 1979.

Shee, J.C.: Dangerous potentiation of pethidine by iproniazid and its treatment, Br. Med. J. **2**:507, 1960.

Shepherd, A.M.M., Wilson, N., and Stevenson, I.H.: Warfarin sensitivity in the elderly. In Crooks, J., and Stevenson, I.H., editors: Drugs and the elderly, Baltimore, 1979, University Park Press.

Silber, B., et al.: Spironolactone-associated digoxin radioimmunoassay interference, Clin. Chem. **25**:48, 1979.

Silver, B.A., and Bell, W.R.: Cimetidine potentiation of the hypoprothrombinemic effect of warfarin, Ann. Intern. Med. **90**:348, 1979.

Siris, J.H., et al.: Anticonvulsant drug serum levels in psychiatric patients with seizure disorders: effects of certain psychotropic drugs, N.Y. State J. Med. **74**:1554, 1974.

Sloman, J.G., and Manolas, E.: Cardiovascular diseases. In Avery, G.S., editor: Drug treatment, ed. 2, Sydney, 1980, ADIS Press.

Smith, D.E., et al.: Attenuation of furosemide's diuretic effect by indomethacin: pharmacokinetic evaluation, J. Pharmacokinet. Biopharm. **7**:265, 1979.

Smith, P.K., et al.: Studies on the pharmacology of salicylates, J. Pharmacol. Exp. Ther. **87**:237, 1946.

Soeldner, J.S., and Steinke, J.: Hypoglycemia in tolbutamide-treated diabetes: report of two cases with measurement of serum insulin, J.A.M.A. **193**:398, 1965.

Solomon, R.B., and Rosner, F.: Massive hemorrhage and death during treatment with clofibrate and warfarin, N.Y. State J. Med. **73**:2002, 1973.

Spiers, A.S.D., and Mibashan, R.S.: Increased warfarin requirement during mercaptopurine therapy: a new drug interaction, Lancet **2**:221, 1974.

Steiness, E.: Renal tubular secretion of digoxin, Circulation **50**:103, 1974.

Steiness, E.: Suppression of renal excretion of digoxin in hypokalemic patients, Clin. Pharmacol. Ther. **23**:511, 1978.

Steiness, E., et al.: Reduction of digoxin-induced inotropism during quinidine administration, Clin. Pharmacol. Ther. **27**:791, 1980.

Syvalahti, E.K.G., Pihlajamaki, K.K., and Iisalo, E.J.: Rifampicin and drug metabolism, Lancet **2**:232, 1974.

Tannenbaum, H., Anderson, L.G., and Soeldner, J.S.: Phenylbutazone-tolbutamide drug interaction, N. Engl. J. Med. **290**:344, 1974.

Taylor, D.C.: Alarming reaction to pethidine in patients on phenelzine, Lancet **2**:401, 1962.

Taylor, J.W., Alexander, B., and Lyon, L.W.: Mathematical analysis of a phenytoin-disulfiram interaction, Am. J. Hosp. Pharm. **38**:93, 1981.

Teychenne, P.F., et al.: Interactions of levodopa with inhibitors of monoamine oxidase and *L*-aromatic amino acid decarboxylase, Clin. Pharmacol. Ther. **18**:273, 1975.

Thornton, W.E.: Dementia induced by methyldopa with haloperidol, N. Engl. J. Med. **294:**1222, 1976.

Triggs, E.I., and Nation, R.I.: Pharmacokinetics in the aged: a review, J. Pharmacokinet. Biopharm. **6:**387, 1975.

Tucker, H.S.G., Jr., and Hirsch, J.I.: Sulfonamide-sulfonylurea interaction, N. Engl. J. Med. **286:**110, 1972.

Udenfriend, S., Lovenberg, W., and Sjoerdsma, A.: Physiologically active amines in common fruits and vegetables, Arch. Biochem. Biophys. **85:**487, 1959.

Utz, J.P., et al.: Amphotericin B toxicity, Ann. Intern. Med. **61:**334, 1964.

Vancura, E.J.: Guard against unpredictable drug responses in the aging, Geriatrics **34**(4):63, 1979.

Vandekerckhove, P.: Amines in dry fermented sausage, J. Food Sci. **42:**283, 1977.

VanZwieten, P.A.: Interaction between centrally acting hypotensive drugs and tricyclic antidepressants, Arch. Int. Pharmacodyn. Ther. **214:**12, 1975.

Venho, V.M.K., Salonen, R.O., and Mattila, M.J.: Modification of the pharmacokinetics of doxycycline in man by ferrous sulphate or charcoal, Eur. J. Clin. Pharmacol. **14:**277, 1978.

Vesell, E.S., Passananti, G.T., and Greene, F.E.: Impairment of drug metabolism in man by allopurinol and nortriptyline, N. Engl. J. Med. **283:**1484, 1970.

Vestal, R.E., Wood, A.J.J., and Shand, D.G.: Reduced β-adrenoceptor sensitivity in the elderly, Clin. Pharmacol. Ther. **26:**181, 1979.

Vigran, I.M.: Dangerous potentiation of meperidine hydrochloride by pargyline hydrochloride, J.A.M.A. **187:**953, 1964.

Vincent, F.M.: Phenothiazine-induced phenytoin intoxication, Ann. Internal Med. **93:**56, 1980.

Voigt, M.N., et al.: Tyramine, histamine and tryptamine content of cheese, J. Milk Food Technol. **37:**377, 1974.

Wade, O.L.: Adverse reactions to drugs, London, 1970, Heinemann Medical Books.

Waldorff, S., et al.: Spironolactone-induced changes in digoxin kinetics, Clin. Pharmacol. Ther. **24:**162, 1978.

Walker, J., and Hendeles, L.: The interaction of erythromycin and theophylline in the asthmatic dental patient, J. Am. Dent. Assoc. **99:**995, 1979.

Wallin, B.A., Jacknowitz, A., and Raich, P.C.: Cimetidine and effect of warfarin, Ann. Intern. Med. **90:**993, 1979.

Wandell, M., et al.: Effect of quinine on digoxin kinetics, Clin. Pharmacol. Ther. **28:**425, 1980.

Wash, L.K., and Bernard, J.D.: Licorice-induced pseudoaldosteronism, Am. J. Hosp. Pharm. **32:**73, 1975.

Weiss, M.: Potentiation of coumarin effect by sulphinpyrazone, Lancet **1:**609, 1979.

Williamson, J.: Adverse reactions to prescribed drugs in the elderly. In Crooks, J., and Stevenson, I.H., editors: Drugs and the elderly, Baltimore, 1979, University Park Press.

Williamson, J., and Chopin, J.M.: Adverse reactions to prescribed drugs in the elderly: a multicentre investigation, Age Ageing **9:**73, 1980.

Wirth, K.E., et al.: Metabolism of digitoxin in man and its modification by spironolactone, Eur. J. Clin. Pharmacol. **9:**345, 1976.

Wolff, F.W., and Lindeman, R.D.: Effects of treatment in hypertension: results of a controlled study, J. Chronic Dis. **19:**227, 1966.

Wood, J.H., and Shannonhouse, W.R.: Milk inactivation of tetracycline, Drug Intell. Clin. Pharm. **11:**495, 1977.

Wright, S.P.: Hazards with monoamine-oxidase inhibitors: a persistent problem, Lancet **1:**284, 1978.

Yamada, S., and Iwai, K.: Induction of hepatic cortisol-6-hydroxylase by rifampicin, Lancet **2:**366, 1976.

Yendt, E.R., and Cohanim, M.: Prevention of calcium stones with thiazides, Kidney Int. **13:**397, 1978.

Yü, T.F., Dayton, P.G., and Gutman, A.B.: Mutual suppression of the uricosuric effects of sulfinpyrazone and salicylate: a study in interactions between drugs, J. Clin. Invest. **42:**1330, 1963.

Yü, T.F., et al.: The effect of the interaction of pyrazinamide and probenecid on urinary uric acid excretion in man, Am. J. Med. **63:**723, 1977.

Yutang, L.: The Importance of Living, Devon, Eng., 1939, Readers Union Ltd. Reprinted in Cape, R.: Aging: its complex management, New York, 1978, Harper & Row, Publishers, Inc.

Zilly, W., Breimer, D.D., and Richter, E.: Pharmacokinetic interactions with rifampicin, Clin. Pharmacokinet. **2:**61, 1977.

CHAPTER 9

Geriatric poisoning

Ronald T. Coutts

The number of poisonings that occur in North America each year is difficult to estimate because many incidents, including those that result from drug abuse, are never reported. Based on reported data (Poison Control Program Statistics, 1974), approximately 1 in every 400 persons is poisoned each year. Most victims are children under the age of 5 years; elderly victims form the second largest group.

This chapter is primarily devoted to the treatment of acute overdoses of drugs and chemicals. The methods employed to treat both young and old victims are essentially identical. However, the geriatric client may also experience toxic reactions to drugs that are administered in therapeutic doses, and these reactions (i.e., chronic poisoning incidents) may require treatment.

ADVERSE EFFECTS OF DRUGS IN GERIATRIC CLIENTS

Studies have shown that the risk of developing an adverse drug reaction increases with age, and clients over 60 years of age are more likely to develop drug-induced illnesses (Hurwitz, 1969; Caranasos, Stewart, and Cluff, 1974; Wallace and Watanabe, 1977; Gotz and Gotz, 1978). Numerous factors contribute to these toxic effects in the elderly (Wallace and Watanabe, 1977). The elderly are particularly prone to accidental poi-

soning incidents. They generally receive more medication than other age groups, which may result in adverse drug interactions (see Chapter 8). They often have dietary deficiencies caused mainly by inadequate food intake. Vitamin and mineral deficiencies are common, and the self-administration of laxatives also contributes to these effects. (See Chapter 11, "Adverse Drug Reactions in the Geriatric Client," for more details on vitamin and mineral deficiencies in the elderly.)

The elderly often suffer from chronic illnesses that can result in an exaggerated drug response. In one investigation of client errors in the self-administration of drugs it was found that 59% of an elderly outpatient population with chronic illnesses made errors involving prescribed medications. More than 25% committed potentially serious errors (Copper, 1978). Many geriatric clients hoard drugs and use them inappropriately to self-treat illnesses that develop later and appear to be similar to the original illness for which the drug was prescribed. In these situations more than one drug is often administered. Some elderly clients are unaware of or have forgotten the appropriate dose of the medication and the frequency with which it has to be taken. This can result in poisoning incidents.

With increasing age there is a general decline in the physiologic state of the body (see Chapter 6). Various systems are adversely affected, including the central nervous system (CNS), the cardiovascular system, the respiratory system, the gastrointestinal (GI) system, the hepatic system, and the renal system (Crooks, O'Malley, and Stevenson, 1976). As a result, drug responses in the elderly differ appreciably from the responses observed in younger people. Because drug absorption is not appreciably altered in old age, poisoning incidents cannot generally be attributed to this factor. However, total body water and body mass decrease with age, whereas body fat increases significantly. This can result in an accumulation and prolongation of action of lipid-soluble drugs.

Plasma albumin levels decrease with advancing years, and protein binding of some drugs (e.g., meperidine, phenylbutazone) also decreases. Plasma levels of unbound drugs therefore increase sometimes to toxic levels. Binding of drugs to red blood cells also decreases in the elderly.

No significant changes with age have been observed in the apparent volume of distribution of some drugs (e.g., acetaminophen, phenylbutazone, warfarin). Diazepam is the exception. The plasma half-life of diazepam increases dramatically with an increase in age. In a 65- to 70-year-old person the half-life may be three to four times longer than that observed in a 20-year-old person. This effect is caused mainly by an increase in the volume of distribution of diazepam.

In the aged there is a reduction in liver microsomal drug metabolizing enzyme activity. Because most drugs are inactivated by metabolic oxidation in the liver, an increased plasma level of most drugs would be expected as a result of this reduction in metabolizing activity. However, an altered liver metabolism of only a few drugs has been unequivocally demonstrated; plasma half-lives of antipyrine, amobarbital, and propranolol are increased in the elderly as a result, at least in part, of decreased rates of metabolism.

Many drugs are eliminated by the kidneys.

Changes in renal function, therefore, will have important toxicologic implications for many therapeutic agents. The glomerular filtration rate, tubular reabsorptive capacity, and tubular excretory capacity are all reduced with advancing years. A combination of these effects can result in potentially dangerous increased levels of drugs (e.g., digoxin, sulfamethazole). (For detailed coverage of pharmacokinetics in the aged, see Chapter 10.)

SUICIDE

In most age groups poisonings are usually accidental occurrences. It is with the geriatric client that most deliberate poisonings occur. Suicide by the elderly is a serious social problem in the Western world and is one of the ten leading causes of death in the United States for persons aged 45 to 64 years (Bennett, 1967). As people age there is an increase in both physical and mental illnesses, and the incidence of insomnia increases. Serious physical disease is undoubtedly a factor in the decision to take one's own life. Elderly clients are often depressed and in poor health, and the combination of these two states contributes to the decision to attempt suicide. It has been claimed that at least 80% of suicidal people over the age of 60 suffer from depression (Batchelor, 1955). Serious mental disease (e.g., manic-depressive psychosis and chronic brain syndrome) and other psychiatric illnesses occur more frequently in older people and often lead to serious suicide attempts (O'Neal, Robins, and Schmidt, 1956).

Elderly clients generally have easy access to drugs, especially tranquilizers, antidepressants, barbiturates, and other drugs that are prescribed for a variety of geriatric illnesses. These are the drugs that are used most often in suicide attempts. Despite the fact that there has been a decrease in the prescribing of barbiturates in recent years, there are still many barbiturate suicides in the United States (Benson and Brodie, 1975).

CONTROL OF POISONING

All health professionals have a role to play in the control of accidental and deliberate poisoning. This is especially true when it is realized that 50% of the poisonous substances ingested are drugs. Ideally, health professionals must use their expertise to educate the public and thus prevent or reduce the occurrence of accidental poisoning. They must be able to judge whether a poisoning incident exists and, if so, offer sound advice on how and where to obtain prompt treatment. They should be capable of providing effective emergency treatment. Various aspects of poisoning are now presented.

Definition

A poison is any substance that can induce undesirable alterations in biologic systems. Most poisons are exogenous substances (foreign to the body), but some endogenous substances (e.g., insulin, iron) in excessive amounts can also be poisons.

Exposure routes

Poisoning results from (1) topical contact with, (2) inhalation of, (3) oral ingestion of, and (4) parenteral administration of poisonous substances. Local tissue damage and entry of the poison into the systemic circulation can occur through all exposure routes. The degree of local tissue damage and the quantity of poison absorbed can be reduced significantly if emergency first aid is applied as soon as possible after the person is exposed to the poison. After administration of emergency first aid, the client should be taken to a hospital's emergency department for further treatment.

Emergency outpatient treatment of poisoning can be applied if exposure is by topical contact, inhalation, or oral ingestion. If the poison is administered by injection, immediate hospitalization is usually required.

Topical contact. Most nonphysiologic chemicals are absorbed by passive transport across cell membranes. To be absorbed, they must be lipid soluble. Normally the dead cornified outer layer of the skin impedes the approach of chemicals to the living inner layers, but if the skin area is damaged (e.g., abraded or burned) to a considerable extent or if the chemical is dissolved in a solvent that can penetrate the skin (e.g., lead in gasoline), then the amount that is systemically absorbed can be appreciable. Corrosive materials are usually water soluble and are not systemically absorbed. These materials, however, can cause extensive epidermal damage and considerable irritation of the deeper layers of the skin. Various chemicals, especially corrosive acids and bases, are toxic to the eyes or exposed mucous membranes (mouth, nasal passages, anus, genital organs). A few compounds, including carbon tetrachloride, other halogenated hydrocarbons, and organophosphorus insecticides, are absorbed transcutaneously into the circulation and can cause damage to organs and tissues (e.g., liver).

Inhalation. Most deaths from this cause are the result of inhaling lethal quantities of gases or volatile liquids that are rapidly absorbed from the alveoli of the lungs. Mildly irritating substances can be deeply inhaled, but more severe irritants generally are not because they induce reflex holding of the breath. Typical examples of toxic gases or volatile liquids that are accidentally or deliberately inhaled are carbon monoxide, carbon tetrachloride, volatiles in glues, aerosols (Freons), and petroleum distillates. Gasoline sniffing is dangerous for two reasons: hydrocarbons cause lung damage, and the lead content of the gasoline easily enters the blood and can reach lethal levels.

If a person is exposed to a toxic gas, liquid, or dust, the obvious treatment is to remove the person from the toxic source into fresh air; occasionally the toxic material can be removed from the immediate surroundings of the affected person. Artificial respiration may be necessary if exposure to the gas or volatile liquid has been prolonged. In some instances, decontamination of clothing (by their removal) or skin (by washing) may be practical.

Oral ingestion. Most poisoning incidents in North America are the result of oral ingestion of a toxic material. This route can expose the mucous membranes of the entire GI tract to the poison. The results of this are rapid absorption of the poison into the systemic circulation or possible damage to mucous membranes if caustic or irritant poisons have been ingested.

There are five general goals in the treatment of the oral ingestion of a poison:

1. To minimize damage to mucous membranes if it is a corrosive substance
2. To prevent the absorption of the poison

If the poison has already been absorbed, then:

3. To accelerate its elimination
4. To counteract the systemic effects of the poison (with a specific antidote if available)
5. To provide supportive treatment to ensure that the body's vital systems (respiratory, cardiovascular, CNS, renal, hepatic) continue to function

CORROSIVE SUBSTANCES

Ingestion of corrosive alkalis or acids must be treated immediately to minimize the damage that will occur to the mucous membranes of the mouth, esophagus, and stomach. The corrosive substance most commonly encountered in emergency situations is sodium hydroxide, which is present in solid form in Clinitest tablets, in concentrated aqueous solution (up to 90%) in lye, and in drain and oven cleaners, such as Draino and Easy-Off. Additional common caustic alkalis are potassium hydroxide, cement, and solid detergents. Concentrated inorganic acids (e.g., sulfuric acid, nitric acid) and some organic acids (e.g., oxalic acid, found in metal cleaners or used as a bleach) are also corrosive. Many liquid bleaching solutions are 3% to 6% solutions of sodium hypochlorite in water (e.g., Clorox Bleach and Javex Bleach). When sodium hypo-

chlorite reaches the stomach, hypochlorous acid, which is irritant and corrosive to mucous membranes, is released.

Emergency treatment of the oral ingestion of a corrosive substance entails diluting the substance as rapidly as possible with copious quantities of water or milk. For example, at least 2 l of fluid must be given if 20 to 30 ml (i.e., one mouthful in an adult) of lye has been ingested. Vomiting must *not* be induced because emesis will increase the possibility of gastric perforation, and any aspiration of vomitus would result in pulmonary damage. Immediately after the administration of emergency first aid, the individual should be rushed to a hospital emergency department.

PREVENTION OF ABSORPTION OF AN INGESTED POISON

Two different emergency treatments are used for this purpose. An adsorbent may be administered, which complexes with a poison in the GI tract and thus prevents its absorption into the systemic circulation. Alternatively, an emetic may be given to promote evacuation of the stomach contents by inducing vomiting.

Both treatments are of value as long as the poison is in the stomach and must therefore be applied as soon as possible after ingestion of the poison.

Adsorbents

If a poisonous substance has been ingested, emergency treatments can be applied that will prevent or reduce the absorption of the poisonous material into the circulation. One important method of accomplishing this is to administer an adsorbent to the client. An adsorbent is a nontoxic substance that cannot be absorbed into the systemic circulation and that is capable of combining strongly with a poison to produce an inert product (e.g., a charcoal-poison complex), which also cannot be absorbed into the systemic circulation. The complex then passes through the GI tract and is excreted in the feces.

Numerous preparations (activated charcoal, charcoal tablets, burnt toast, "universal antidote," montmorillonite, attapulgite, evaporated milk, and various resins) have been claimed to be efficient adsorbents, but of these only one, activated charcoal, has proven to be an effective adsorbent of most poisons. The other preparations are either noneffective or are of doubtful efficacy. One, the "universal antidote," may actually aggravate a toxic situation if it is administered in a poisoning incident involving a hepatotoxin.

Activated charcoal. Activated charcoal (carbo activatus, medicinal charcoal) is the residue of the destructive distillation of various organic materials that has been chemically treated to increase its adsorptive properties. Numerous activation processes are used, including treatment with steam, air, oxygen, carbon dioxide, zinc chloride, sulfuric acid, and phosphoric acid at elevated temperatures (500° C to 900° C). These procedures remove substances that are adsorbed on the surface of the carbon residue and greatly reduce mineral content and particle size, thereby increasing effective surface area. It is important that the surface area of the charcoal preparation be as large as possible because the adsorption of the poison occurs on the surface of the activated charcoal. The greater the surface area presented, the greater the amount of poison complexed.

Organic materials commonly used in the production of activated charcoal are wood, sucrose, lactose, starch, bone, animal blood, and various organic industrial waste products. Activated charcoal is a fine, black, odorless, tasteless powder that is free from gritty matter. It must be stored in tightly closed containers because lengthy exposure to the atmosphere greatly reduces its adsorptive properties as a result of adsorption of gaseous and particulate materials present in the atmosphere.

Adsorptive properties. Activated charcoal can adsorb a wide range of organic compounds (e.g.,

most drugs, alkaloids, and petroleum products) and many inorganic compounds. It is an effective adsorbent of most substances involved in poisoning incidents. All the compounds in the following list are efficiently adsorbed by activated charcoal. This is not a complete list. Its inclusion illustrates the diversity in structure of the many compounds that are adsorbed. However, activated charcoal is *not* an effective adsorbent of cyanide, mineral acids, caustic alkalis, ferrous sulfate, boric acid, methanol, or ethanol (Decker, Combs, and Corby, 1968; Chin, Picchioni, and Duplisse, 1970):

Organic substances effectively adsorbed by activated charcoal

Acetaminophen	Chlorpromazine	Penicillin
Amphetamines	Cocaine	Phenobarbital
Antipyrine	Digitalis	Phenol
Aspirin	Digoxin	Phenolphthalein
Atropine	Glutethimide	Phenothiazines
Barbiturates	Ipecac	Phenytoin
Benzodiazepines	Malathion	Propoxyphene
Camphor	Meprobamate	Quinine
Chlorinated hydro-	Morphine	Salicylates
carbons (e.g.,	Nicotine	Strychnine
DDT)	Opium	Sulfonamides
Chloroquine	Oxalates	Tricyclic
Chlorpheniramine	Parathion	antidepressants

Inorganic substances effectively adsorbed by activated charcoal

Antimony salts	Lead	Potassium permanganate
Arsenic	Mercury	Selenium
Iodine	Phosphorus	Silver

Adsorptive capacity. This depends on the size of the carbon particles, the total surface area, the mineral content, and the degree of activation. Recently activated charcoal powder of very small particle size and minimum mineral content is best. Commercially available charcoal tablets and granules are less effective than powdered charcoal because of their reduced surface area. Burnt toast has a very low surface area, a high mineral content, and has not been subjected to an activation procedure; it has *no* adsorptive capacity.

Effect of pH. There is controversy in the literature about the effect of the pH of the medium on the adsorptive capacity of activated charcoal.

In vitro studies (Andersen, 1947; Smith et al., 1967) have shown that adsorptive capacity is increased at pH values that enhance the nonionization of a chemical. In vitro investigations (Smith et al., 1967; Tsuchiya and Levy, 1972) have also shown that activated charcoal–poison complexes dissociate to some extent and release the poison when the pH of the medium is significantly altered. In contrast, more informative in vivo studies (Decker and Corby, 1970) have revealed that activated charcoal–poison complexes that are formed in the acid medium of the stomach do not dissociate when they pass from the stomach into the alkaline medium of the small intestine.

Administration. The longer the time delay between the ingestion of a poison and the administration of the activated charcoal, the less effective is the treatment (Atkinson and Azarnoff, 1971). During this time interval, the poison can enter the small intestine and become inaccessible to the complexing action of the activated charcoal. Appreciable absorption of the poison into the bloodstream from the stomach and the small intestine can also occur when the administration of the activated charcoal is delayed.

Activated charcoal may also be effective in increasing the clearance rate of drugs (e.g., carbamazepine, phenobarbital) that have already been systemically absorbed (Berg, 1982; Levy, 1982).

Optimum antidotal dose. Doses of activated charcoal for the treatment of poisoning are often selected arbitrarily on the basis of data obtained from various in vitro studies (Andersen, 1947 and 1948). The application of in vitro data to the treatment of an in vivo poisoning situation is inappropriate and, in most instances, would lead to the use of inadequate amounts of the adsorbent. In vivo studies in rats (Chin et al., 1973) suggest that the optimum activated charcoal/poison ratio for the treatment of poisoning is at least 8:1. Given this ratio, the absorption of three drugs (pentobarbital, chloroquine, and isoniazid) by rats was reduced by 80% to 96%. Medical consultants ("Initial Management of Acute Poisoning," 1971) suggest that between 10 and 50 gm of activated charcoal, depending on the known or estimated amount of drug or poison ingested, should be administered. I recommend administration of a tenfold excess of activated charcoal, compared to the amount of poison ingested, with a minimum adult dose of 30 gm.

Dosage form and palatability. A major disadvantage of the use of activated charcoal is its unattractive physical appearance. A former Alberta Pharmaceutical Association Council ("Universal Antidote," 1964) adopted the concept of the black bottle (i.e., 10 gm of activated charcoal in a bottle, to which water can be added and the contents shaken to give a slurry that is swallowed directly from the bottle). This is probably still the best way of administering the adsorbent, but the appearance of the preparation, its strange taste and consistency, and the ready manner in which some of the charcoal sticks to the mucous membranes of the mouth and throat have dissuaded many from swallowing even one mouthful. Unfortunately, there is a limit to how its appearance can be improved.

Various attempts have been made to improve the palatability of activated charcoal. The use of ice cream and sherbet (Levy, Soda, and Lampman, 1975) or milk and cocoa powder (De Neve, 1976) to produce a palatable charcoal antidote is not recommended. The presence of these additives significantly decreases the adsorptive properties of the charcoal. The addition of jams, jellies, and marmalades to activated charcoal gives an acceptable, better tasting product that, however, still retains an unattractive appearance (De Neve, 1976). Various thickening agents (bentonite, sodium carboxymethylcellulose, carrageenan, and sodium alginate) have been added to aqueous suspensions of activated charcoal to overcome the problem of adhesion of charcoal to the mouth (Manes and Mann, 1974; Gwilt and Perrier, 1976). All of these thickening agents, especially bentonite, are effective for this purpose, without interfering with the adsorptive properties of the activated charcoal.

Activated charcoal has become available in Great Britain in an effervescent form (Medicoal), which should aid significantly in its administration ("Emergency Treatment of Poisoning," 1978). This preparation has been shown to be particularly useful in the adsorption of tricyclic antidepressants, salicylates, and barbiturates. These three drug classes accounted for 64% of deaths from poisoning in England and Wales in 1975. In Australia a palatable strawberry-flavored activated charcoal preparation has been developed and has been found suitable for home use (Boehm, Brown, and Oppenheim, 1978). It is supplied as a powder (20 gm) in a 200 ml bottle to which water is added before use.

"Universal antidote." This is a charcoal product that has been highly recommended in the past but that should *no* longer be used in the emergency treatment of poisoning. "Universal antidote" is composed of activated charcoal (2 parts), magnesium oxide (1 part), and tannic acid (1 part). It was believed that such a mixture would possess the adsorptive properties of activated charcoal, and, in addition, the magnesium oxide present would neutralize the stomach contents and precipitate acidic poisons. The tannic acid component would cause the precipitation as tannates of any basic poisons. Whether magnesium oxide and tannic acid are truly effective for these purposes is not known. Many studies (Picchioni et al., 1966) have shown that both activated charcoal and "universal antidote" are effective adsorbents of various drugs and poisons but that activated charcoal alone is more effective than "universal antidote" containing the same amount of activated charcoal. It was believed that the activated charcoal in "universal antidote" adsorbed some of the tannic acid and magnesium oxide, thus reducing its adsorptive efficiency. Medical consultants ("Charcoal as an Adsorbent," 1965) object to the use of "universal antidote" for a more serious reason—tannic acid is a hepatotoxin.

Emetics

Another important method of preventing or reducing the absorption of an ingested poison into the circulation is to empty the stomach as soon as possible after the ingestion of the poison. This can be accomplished by means of gastric aspiration and lavage or by the administration of an emetic.

An emetic is a chemical substance that induces vomiting. Various emetics are known. Some act directly by stimulating the chemoreceptor trigger zone (CTZ) in the medulla oblongata region of the brain (e.g., ipecac, apomorphine); others (e.g., copper sulfate, zinc sulfate, tartar emetic, saltwater, mustard powder, certain phosphates) act reflexly by means of their irritating action on the GI tract.

Although some authorities (Matthew, 1970) suggest that gastric aspiration and lavage is a safer and more efficient means of emptying the stomach when compared with emesis, most literature reports favor induced emesis with either syrup of ipecac or apomorphine (Oderda, 1974). Induced emesis can result in the emptying of not only the stomach but also the duodenum and can remove materials (e.g., tablets, capsules) that are too large for removal by a lavage tube.

Syrup of ipecac. Two ipecac preparations are described in the *U.S. Pharmacopeia.* Powdered ipecac is the dried and finely powdered rhizome and root of a small shrub *(Cephaelis acuminata)* native to Central and South America, which has been adjusted to a potency of between 1.9% and 2.1% of ether-soluble alkaloids. The major alkaloids of ipecac are emetine and cephaeline, but other minor alkaloids (e.g., psychotrine) are also present. Syrup of ipecac (Ipecac Syrup) is prepared from powdered ipecac. The alkaloid content (emetine and cephaeline) of the syrup is 7% (often described as one fourteenth) of that of powdered ipecac.

Emetic properties. Ipecac has long been known to possess emetic properties, but its routine use for this purpose began less than 20 years ago (Manno and Manno, 1977). The emetic properties of ipecac result from the presence of emetine and cephaeline. The latter alkaloid is twice as potent as emetine in producing vomiting, but it is present in lower quantities than emetine in ipecac.

Ipecac has two modes of action: local irritation of the gastric mucosa, which produces a reflex vomiting, and a centrally mediated emetic action—the emesis-producing alkaloids act directly on the CTZ of the brain's medulla oblongata region and induce vomiting. Early (within 30 minutes) and late (30 minutes or longer) phases of vomiting have been observed after administration of syrup of ipecac. If early vomiting occurs, it is caused by the direct irritant action of ipecac. Late vomiting is the result of stimulation of the CTZ, which is delayed until sufficient amounts of the alkaloids are absorbed and reach the brain. The average time interval between the administration of ipecac until induction of emesis is approximately 19 minutes. Slightly more than half (54%) of the treated clients vomit within 15 minutes; most (88%) vomit within 30 minutes; almost all (98%) vomit within 1 hour. The failure rate is less than 2% (Veltri and Temple, 1976; Manno and Manno, 1977).

Emetic properties in adults. Syrup of ipecac is widely accepted as being an efficient, reliable emetic for children who have ingested a poison (Hurst and Dozzi, 1975), but as recently as 1977 it was claimed ("Emetics for Acute Poisoning," 1977) that although syrup of ipecac may be the treatment of choice for acute poisoning of children, there was no convincing evidence of the effectiveness of the syrup in adults for whom gastric lavage remained the treatment of choice. This claim was quickly refuted (Gibb, Unsworth, and Ilett, 1977), and data were provided to show that syrup of ipecac was an efficient emetic in adults. Sixty-seven acutely poisoned adults were given one or two 15 ml doses of the syrup, and virtually all vomited successfully (96% success rate). Another study (Veltri and Temple, 1976) confirmed the effectiveness of syrup of ipecac in both adults and children.

Toxicity. Ingestion of excessive amounts of emetine or cephaeline results in undesirable toxic effects. Most toxic incidents are associated with the ingestion of fluid extract of ipecac, which, like powdered ipecac, is approximately fourteen times more concentrated than the syrup (Manno and Manno, 1977). The fluid extract is not readily obtainable, but occasional reports still appear in the literature of accidental poisoning caused by administration of the fluid extract. When excessive amounts of ipecac are administered, various toxic effects are observed, including GI tract disturbances (stenosis of the esophageal lumen, bloody diarrhea, protracted vomiting), cardiac toxicity (tachycardia, ECG irregularities) and neuromuscular toxicity (transient or prolonged muscle weakness). Most toxic effects are associated with the emetine content of ipecac preparations. Deaths have certainly resulted from the ingestion of fluid extract of ipecac (Manno and Manno, 1977), but syrup of ipecac, when taken in the recommended dosage, has not been associated with fatalities (Hurst and Dozzi, 1975).

Dosage. For adults the most commonly recommended dosage of syrup of ipecac is 15 ml, followed by approximately 250 ml (8 fl oz) of water or a noncarbonated flavored drink. This dosage may be repeated once in about 20 minutes if emesis has not occurred (Oderda, 1974; Hurst and Dozzi, 1975; Gibb, Unsworth, and Ilett, 1977).

To minimize the possibility of administering excessive amounts of syrup of ipecac, the emetic is commercially available in 15 ml capacity containers, which can be purchased without prescription in pharmacies.

Contraindications. Emesis should not ordinarily be induced if *petroleum distillates*, such as kerosene, burning paraffin, lamp oil, gasoline, fuel oil, coal oil, paint thinners, cleaning fluids, charcoal igniting fluids, camp stove fluids; *corrosives*, such as alkalis (lyes) and strong acids; or *strychnine* have been ingested. Induced emesis is also contraindicated if the person is *unconscious* or *comatose* or if a *health condition* exists (e.g., cardiac disease, pregnancy) that may be adversely affected by vomiting. In summary, emesis can be employed in all situations except those in which the violent physical activity of vomiting may be dangerous.

The reasons behind these contraindications are fairly obvious. Induced emesis of an unconscious or comatose person may result in aspiration of vomitus into the lungs and, subsequently, lung damage or blockage of the air passages. A person who is unconscious, comatose, in shock, deeply cyanotic, in convulsions, or who has a health condition that could be aggravated or adversely affected by the physical act of vomiting should be rushed to a hospital for gastric lavage.

Ingestion of petroleum distillates is potentially dangerous because there is always the chance that some of the ingested product may enter the lungs and cause pulmonary pneumonitis, hemorrhage, and edema, which may be fatal. Experiments with rabbits (Richardson and Pratt-Thomas, 1951) have shown that only 0.25 ml of kerosene per kg of body weight caused fatal pneumonitis when injected directly into the trachea, whereas 35 ml/kg was necessary when the kerosene was instilled directly into the stomach. This observation provides an explanation of why some persons have died as a result of swallowing as little as 10 ml (0.3 fl oz) of a petroleum distillate, whereas others have recovered following ingestion of approximately 250 ml (8 fl oz) (Dreisbach, 1977). Despite the potential dangers of inducing emesis in persons who have ingested petroleum distillates, some sources claim increasing evidence that, in a hospital setting, syrup of ipecac is safe for evacuating the stomach after hydrocarbon ingestion. However, virtually all other authorities on the subject emphasize that induction of emesis is contraindicated when petroleum distillates are swallowed. The only exception to this rule would be if the petroleum distillates contain additional toxic additives (e.g., insecticides, nitrobenzene).

If a corrosive substance (alkali or strong acid) has been swallowed, it will cause damage mainly to the mouth and esophagus. If emesis is induced, it may result in aspiration of vomitus and subsequent pulmonary damage, as well as dangerous esophageal perforation. Most people who ingest caustic alkalis and survive have permanent esophageal damage.

In addition to the contraindication just listed, some authorities ("Emetics for Acute Poisoning," 1977) claim that syrup of ipecac should not be administered if the ingested poison is an antiemetic drug. On theoretical grounds this appears to be a reasonable suggestion. An examination of Poison Control Center data (Thoman and Verhulst, 1966), however, showed that syrup of ipecac was successful in inducing emesis in 94.5% of the 291 cases reviewed in which antiemetics (phenothiazines, antihistamines, and others) had been ingested. The conclusion from these data would seem to be that ingestion of toxic quantities of antiemetics can be treated successfully with syrup of ipecac.

Strychnine is a potent CNS stimulant. Strychnine causes involuntary muscular spasm and generalized tetanic convulsions, which would be exacerbated, perhaps fatally, if vomiting were induced.

Home administration. Provided that syrup of ipecac is not administered in situations where its use is contraindicated, authorities in the United States (Veltri and Temple, 1976), Australia (Hurst and Dozzi, 1975), and England ("Emetics for Acute Poisoning," 1977) believe that it can be kept at home in first aid kits and administered to the person who has ingested a poison as soon as possible after the ingestion. It is recommended that when such an action is taken, the approval of a medically qualified person should be obtained. In the United States (Veltri and Temple, 1976) a program to manage poisoning exposures at home by inducing emesis with syrup of ipecac has been successfully initiated. The study included telephone supervision and evaluation of the program by qualified personnel at a regional poison control center. In this program 776 cases were studied during a 6-month period, and it was concluded that induction of emesis in both adults and children could be successfully managed at home by telephone supervision. The innovators of the program describe it as an overwhelming success that resulted in substantial financial savings in emergency room costs.

Apomorphine. Apomorphine is a compound that is structurally related to morphine. It is administered subcutaneously (dose 0.09 mg/kg body weight) (Decker et al., 1969) and produces emesis rapidly (within 5 minutes) by direct stimulation of the CTZ in the medulla oblongata. Emesis is usually violent and efficient.

There are disadvantages to the use of apomorphine. It is a respiratory depressant and is therefore contraindicated in clients whose respiration is shallow and labored or in cases when the ingested poison is itself a respiratory depressant. It is not effective in deep narcosis or shock, and sometimes it produces protracted vomiting. Many clinicians who use apomorphine administer an antagonist (i.e., naloxone) after the client has completed productive vomiting. Administration of the antagonist counteracts vomiting and any CNS depression. A comparison of the effectiveness of activated charcoal with apomorphine in inhibiting aspirin absorption showed both to be similar; each separately caused a 50% reduction. The use of both activated charcoal and apomorphine simultaneously caused a greater reduction in serum salicylate concentration than did either single treatment (Decker et al., 1969).

Saltwater. Saltwater (15 to 60 ml [1 to 4 tbsp] of sodium chloride, or table salt, in a glass of warm water) used to be recommended as an efficient, easily prepared, and readily available emetic by many authorities. The current medical view is that salt may be an occasionally successful but dangerous emetic with an efficacy about one fourth that of syrup of ipecac. Numerous examples of death occurring from hypernatremia, caused by ingestion of excessive doses of sodium chloride and its subsequent absorption into the systemic circulation, have been reported ("Emetics for Acute Poisoning," 1977). In most of these fatalities victims would probably not have died from the toxic effects of the originally ingested poison if supportive treatment in a hospital setting had been given instead of a saltwater emetic.

It has been suggested (Oderda, 1974) that a saltwater emetic may possibly be useful in emergencies, especially if the client has a tendency to vomit and if other emetic procedures are not available. Generally, however, its use should be *avoided* ("Emetics for Acute Poisoning," 1977).

Mustard water. Some first aid charts include mustard water (generally 10 ml [2 tsp] of powdered mustard in a glass of warm water) in the list of preparations that can be used to induce emesis. In fact, it is an unreliable, unpalatable preparation, which, like saltwater, is difficult to swallow. It should *not* be used as an emetic.

Mechanically induced vomiting ("gagging"). This is achieved by gentle stroking of the pharynx with a blunt instrument or a finger. It is a very unreliable method; the percentage of individuals who vomit is low and so is the average volume of vomitus (Oderda, 1974; Veltri and Temple, 1976). In a study of the effectiveness of mechanically induced vomiting it was found that of 30 children who were gagged at a hospital by a physician, only two vomited (vomitus 60 and 120 ml), whereas all vomited (mean vomitus 380 ml) when subsequently given syrup of ipecac. No comparable studies on adults have been reported.

CATHARSIS

A cathartic is a drug that is used for the purpose of promoting defecation. Numerous cathartics are known, and some have been used for centuries. Often they are self-administered by lay persons, sometimes resulting in overdoses and possible toxic reactions.

Cathartics have different modes of action. They may irritate the colon or small intestine, lubricate the GI tract, stimulate peristalsis, or promote oil-water emulsion formation to keep stools soft. Because catharsis speeds the passage of substances through the intestinal tract, it decreases the time available for absorption of these substances into the systemic circulation. This is of no significance if the substance is normally rapidly absorbed, but it is of value if the substance is absorbed slowly. Administration of a cathartic would hasten the excretion of a poison-activated charcoal complex or a poison conjugate that was excreted into the bile and hence into the intestinal tract.

In practice, cathartics are rarely used in the emergency treatment of poisoning. On those occasions when they are administered, only saline cathartics should be used. The common saline cathartics (magnesium sulfate, magnesium citrate, potassium acid tartrate, potassium tartrate, potassium sodium tartrate, potassium sulfate, and sodium sulfate) are not readily absorbed from the intestine and therefore reduce the normal absorption of water from the intestine. The resulting bulky fluid content distends the bowel and induces peristalsis, which empties the bowel 1 to 2 hours afterward. Of the common saline cathartics, sodium sulfate (Glauber's salt) is probably the one most suitable for the elimination of unabsorbed poisons because it is nontoxic even if it is absorbed to any extent (ex-

cept for the consequences of excess sodium absorption). The normal dose for adults is 30 gm in water. In contrast, when magnesium sulfate (Epsom salt) is administered, it may be absorbed and produce magnesium intoxication (CNS depression).

ANTIDOTES

Antidotes are substances that are administered to neutralize a poison. Local antidotes are used to neutralize a poison within the GI tract, whereas systemic antidotes are capable of counteracting the systemic effects of an absorbed poison. Few locally acting antidotes are ever used. Some are identified in Table 9-1.

Systemic antidotes are administered only when the identity of the poison is known and an antidote for it exists. Relatively few poisons have systemic antidotes. Such antidotes are classified as specific or nonspecific, depending on whether they act on the poison or its receptors (specific antidote) or whether they simply oppose the toxic symptoms produced (nonspecific antidote). Deferoxamine, for example, is a specific systemic antidote for iron poisoning, whereas atropine is a nonspecific systemic antidote for poisons that inactivate cholinesterase. Systemic antidotes that are in current use are listed in Table 9-2.

TABLE 9-1   *Locally acting antidotes*

Toxic agent	Antidote	Mechanism of action
Barium salts	Sodium sulfate, 0.3 gm/kg	Precipitation
Fluoride	Calcium lactate or gluconate, lime water, milk (for calcium salts, administer 10 gm in 250 ml of water)	Precipitation
Iodine	5% starch solution	Complexation
Phenol	Vegetable oil (e.g., olive oil)	Dissolution, absorption retarded
Numerous poisons	Activated charcoal slurry (30 to 50 gm in water)	Adsorption

TABLE 9-2 Systemic antidotes*

Toxic agent	Antidote	Mechanism of action
Amphetamines and related CNS stimulants	Chlorpromazine, 1 mg/kg IV or IM every 0.5 hr as indicated	Blockage of CNS excitation
Anticholinesterases (e.g., organophosphates, carbamates, neostigmine, physostigmine)	Atropine, 1 to 4 mg/kg IV or IM; repeated every 0.5 hr until atropinization is observed	Blockage of muscarinic effect
	Pralidoxime, 25 to 50 mg/kg IV; repeat in 12 hr p.r.n.	Regenerates cholinesterase
Cholinergic compounds (e.g., pilocarpine, arecoline)	Atropine (dosage as above)	Blockage of muscarinic effect
Cyanide	Amyl nitrite inhalation; then sodium nitrite and sodium thiosulfate IV (dosage instructions are supplied with kit)	Methemoglobin formed, the iron component of which competes with cytochromes for cyanide; also cyanide converted to thiocyanate
Ethylene glycol	Ethanol (50%), 1.0 ml/kg IV; then 0.5 ml/kg IV q.2hr for 4 days	Enzyme competition; formation of toxic metabolite (oxalate) retarded
	Calcium gluconate (10%), administer 10 ml IV	Precipitation of oxalic acid
Metals		
Iron	Deferoxamine (Desferal) initially, 1 gm at rate *not* to exceed 15 mg/kg/hr IV, followed by two doses of 500 mg each at 4-hr intervals or 90 mg/kg IM up to 1 gm q.8hr; *note:* do *not* exceed 6 gm per 24 hr; monitor renal function; use IV route only for clients in cardiovascular collapse	Chelation
Lead	Dimercaprol (BAL) 4 mg/kg IM q.4hr; calcium disodium edetate (EDTA) 12.5 mg/kg IV, IM, SC q.4hr P.O. D-penicillamine (Cuprimine) 500 mg q.8hr for 1 wk then 250 mg q.8hr as indicated	Chelation
Copper	D-penicillamine (dosage as above)	Chelation
Antimony, arsenic, bismuth, gold, mercury, and nickel	Dimercaprol (dosage as above)	Chelation
Cadmium, manganese, and other heavy metals	EDTA (dosage as above)	Chelation
Methanol	Ethanol (dosage as above); sodium bicarbonate, 4 mEq/kg IV q.4hr p.r.n.	Enzyme competition; formation of toxic metabolites (formaldehyde and formic acid) retarded; prevention or correction of acidosis

Continued.

*Doses may vary depending on individual client parameters (e.g., renal and hepatic function) and on clinical response.

TABLE 9-2   **Systemic antidotes—cont'd**

Toxic agent	Antidote	Mechanism of action
Methemoglobinemic agents (e.g., aromatic amines, phenacetin, nitrites)	Methylene blue (1%), 1 ml/kg IV in solution over 5 to 10 min	Reduces methemoglobin to hemoglobin
Narcotics (e.g., codeine, heroin, morphine, meperidine)	Naloxone (Narcan), 0.4 mg IV; repeat at 2 to 3 min intervals as indicated	Specific antagonism at receptor site
Venoms	Various antivenoms are available commercially	Specific antagonism
Warfarin and other oral anticoagulants	Phytonadione (AquaMEPHYTON), 2.5 to 25 mg IM or SC; *note:* monitor prothrombin time	Reversal of hypoprothrombinemia

GASTRIC LAVAGE

If emesis cannot be induced or if it is contraindicated, gastric lavage should be instituted. This involves the removal by suction of the stomach contents and the subsequent washing of the stomach with a suitable lavage fluid. The procedure is generally worthwhile during the first 3 hours after ingestion of a poison, but its benefits decrease with the passage of time as a result of stomach emptying. If the stomach is full or if there is reason to suspect delayed stomach emptying, then lavage may be of value well after 3 hours have elapsed since ingestion of the poison. Irritation delays emptying of the stomach, and, therefore, irritant poisons remain in the stomach for relatively long times. Fats, milk or cream, protein solutions, and some drugs, including the tricyclic antidepressants and methyl salicylate, also leave the stomach slowly (Matthew, 1970; Arena, 1975). In these instances repeated gastric lavage is warranted even several hours after ingestion.

Compared with emesis, gastric lavage is less easily performed because it requires special equipment and expertise. There is much conflict of opinion as to whether gastric lavage is as effective as emesis for the removal of stomach contents. Matthew (1970) believes that the two methods are probably equally effective, provided that the proper gastric tube (e.g., Jacques tube of 30 French gauge) is used, and sufficient volumes of lavage fluid (up to 10 l) are employed. Unfortunately, a Levine gastroduodenal tube is sometimes used, but it is not appropriate for the purpose.

Lavage has fewer contraindications than emesis because there is less chance of aspiration of stomach contents into the lungs, provided the client has a cough reflex, and less physical activity is involved. There are situations, however, in which gastric lavage is contraindicated: (1) ingestion of corrosive acids or alkalis because perforation could result; and (2) ingestion of CNS stimulants, especially strychnine, because manipulation of the tube and the resulting excitation of the client may induce convulsions. Some authorities include ingestion of petroleum products as a contraindication because of the danger of aspiration, but it is generally accepted that lavage can be performed to treat ingestion of petroleum products and the unconscious and anesthetized client in a hospital setting, provided an

TABLE 9-3   **Lavage fluids**

Lavage fluid	Toxic agent
Activated charcoal slurry	Numerous organic and inorganic compounds
Ammonium acetate or ammonium hydroxide (1%)	Formaldehyde
Lime water; calcium lactate solution (3%)	Fluoride; oxalate
Milk or evaporated milk	Copper sulfate; chlorates; thioglycolic acid
Mineral oil	Yellow phosphorus
Potassium ferrocyanide (0.1%)	Iron and copper salts
Potassium permanganate (1:5000)	Oxidizable substances: strychnine, physostigmine, nicotine, quinine
Sodium bicarbonate (5%)	Ferrous sulfate
Sodium chloride (0.9%)	Silver nitrate
Sodium sulfate or magnesium sulfate (5%)	Lead and barium salts
Sodium thiosulfate (5%)	Cyanides; hypochlorites
Starch solution (7.5%)	Iodine
Tannic acid (4% aqueous solution)	Alkaloids and organic bases (e.g., strychnine, morphine); salts of silver and lead
Vegetable oil	Phenol

endotracheal tube with an inflatable cuff is employed (Matthew, 1970; Arena, 1975).

In the normal procedure the client is placed on his left side with his head hanging over the edge of the bed and with his face down. This position minimizes the chance of aspiration. The lavage tube is inserted, and the stomach contents are aspirated. The lavage fluid (water or another solution) is then introduced into the stomach. The client is turned to allow mixing, and the fluid is withdrawn. This procedure is repeated until the washings are clear; 10 l or more of the lavage fluid may be necessary. The washings are reserved for analysis, the first separate from the others, which may be combined.

Because lavage washings are completely removed from the stomach, lavage fluids may contain chemicals in nonphysiologic quantities that have antidotal properties and that are capable of neutralizing the poison within the stomach. Substances that have proven useful as gastric lavage fluids are listed in Table 9-3.

ACCELERATED ELIMINATION

If a specific systemic antidote is not available, other methods of eliminating an absorbed toxic substance may be required. Hydrophilic poisons are readily excreted by the kidneys because they are poorly reabsorbed in the renal tubules. Lipophilic poisons, however, are well reabsorbed in the kidneys into the systemic circulation. Passive reabsorption of lipophilic poisons can be reduced so that the excretion of these poisons is accelerated. This can be achieved in two ways. First, the pH of the urine can be altered. The rate of excretion of basic toxic agents can be accelerated by acidifying the urine either by administering ammonium chloride or ascorbic acid (vitamin C). In an acid urine, basic poisons are in ionized form and therefore are poorly reabsorbed. Similarly, the rate of excretion of acidic toxic agents can be accelerated by alkalinization of the urine. This is usually achieved by administration of sodium bicarbonate. Examples of toxic compounds that may be excreted more rapidly as a result of urine pH manipulations are the weak acids, such as glutethimide, phenobarbital, and other barbiturates; salicylic acid and other organic acids; many basic drugs, including amphetamines and phenothiazines; and alkaloids, such as strychnine. Second, the volume of urine excreted can be increased. This procedure reduces the poison's concentration gradient between the urine and the blood, and it is usually achieved by the administration of an osmotic diuretic. Mannitol and urea are particularly suitable because they are active throughout the length of the renal tubule. Probably the most useful treatment combines the use of an osmotic agent and manipulation of urinary pH. This combination has proven useful in the treatment of poisonings with salicylates, phenobarbital, amphetamines, quinine, and strychnine (Oderda, 1974).

DIALYSIS

Absorbed poisons can also be removed from the blood by means of dialysis. In this procedure unwanted solutes in the plasma are allowed to diffuse across a dialysis membrane into a solution (the dialysate), which is replaced regularly with fresh solution.

Extracorporeal hemodialysis ("the artificial kidney") is an elaborate procedure in which blood is removed continuously from a peripheral artery and pumped through the dialysis tubing back into a peripheral vein. In *peritoneal dialysis* the dialysate is introduced into the peritoneal cavity and is exchanged every 1 or 2 hours. The membranes of the abdominal cavity and of the organs within it serve as the dialysis membrane. In general, solutes that circulate in the blood unbound or reversibly bound to plasma protein can be efficiently removed by dialysis, whereas irreversibly bound compounds cannot. The list of currently known dialyzable poisons is large (Oderda, 1974) and is continually growing. The list includes barbiturates; glutethimide; depressants, sedatives, and tranquilizers; antidepressants; ethanol, methanol, and other alcohols; analgesics, such as salicylates and acetaminophen; antibiotics; various metals; halides; toxins; and other miscellaneous substances.

Solutes pass from the blood into the dialysate solution, provided a concentration gradient exists. The dialysate must therefore contain nor-

mal plasma solutes so that these do not leave the body. It is also common to add 5% albumin to the dialysate. Many dialyzed poisons bind to the albumin, thus maintaining a favorable concentration gradient.

With peritoneal dialysis, the pH of the dialysate must be physiologic, but this is not a requirement of solutions used in extracorporeal hemodialysis. By suitably altering dialysate pH, the dialysis of acidic and basic poisons can be enhanced.

Lipid dialysis is a technique that can be used to remove lipid-soluble toxic materials from the blood. Because many such materials cannot be effectively removed by extracorporeal hemodialysis with an aqueous dialysate, it is beneficial to replace the aqueous dialysate with a nonpyrogenic oil, such as soybean oil. Lipid-soluble toxic materials, such as gluthethimide, pentobarbital, secobarbital, and phenothiazines, are removable from the blood by lipid dialysis.

The technique of *charcoal hemoperfusion* is expected to play a more significant role in the management of the severely poisoned client. In this procedure the client's blood is passed through a column of activated charcoal that has been suitably coated to prevent charcoal embolism and reduce the possibility of thrombocytopenia. Blood levels of salicylate, barbiturates, glutethimide, and digoxin are lowered appreciably after charcoal hemoperfusion (Vale et al., 1975; Temple, Walker, and Done, 1977).

SOME COMMON HOUSEHOLD POISONS
Petroleum products

These products are obtained by the fractionation of crude petroleum oil. The most volatile fraction is termed petroleum ether (or benzin). In order of decreasing volatility are the following fractions: petroleum ether, gasoline, mineral spirits, kerosene, fuel oil, mineral oils (paraffin oils), lubricating oils, paraffin wax, and asphalt (or tar). The first five fractions in this list (petroleum ether through fuel oil) are toxic if ingested; most of the remainder (mineral oils through paraffin wax) are essentially nontoxic because they are not absorbed from the alimentary tract. Indeed, purified mineral oil (medicinal-grade liquid petrolatum) is used medicinally as a demulcent and mild cathartic (although its use is not recommended). The toxicity of asphalt is not well documented, but it should be considered as a toxic petroleum product because it is a mixture of many compounds, including long-chain hydrocarbons, unsaturated hydrocarbons, aromatic compounds, heterocyclic compounds, and particulate material.

Volatile petroleum products (petroleum ether through fuel oil) are toxic for two reasons. They can be aspirated and can cause "aspiration pneumonia". There is also some evidence that when they are absorbed from the alimentary tract and carried in the bloodstream to the lungs, they cause pulmonary lesions (Schneider, 1949).

It is difficult to determine the lethal dose of volatile petroleum products. In adults death has resulted from the ingestion of less than 15 ml (0.5 fl oz) of kerosene, whereas recovery has occurred after the ingestion of more than 250 ml (8 fl oz) (Dreisbach, 1977). In the latter instance aspiration of the kerosene did not occur; however, in the former case it did. Gosselin et al. (1976) suggest that 90 to 120 ml (3 to 4 fl oz) of kerosene is probably the oral mean lethal dose of kerosene in adults, provided aspiration does not occur.

Volatile petroleum products are used for many purposes. They are commonly used as paint thinners and dry cleaning solvents and as motor, heating, and illuminating fuels. Common petroleum products are kerosene (kerosine, range oil, home heating oil), fuel oil (gas oil, home heating oil), gasoline, diesel oil (diesel fuel), mineral seal oil (signal oil, common constituent of furniture polish), petroleum ether (petroleum benzin, benzin, light ligroin), lighter fluid, charcoal igniting fluid, camp stove fluid, white spirit (high flash naphtha), mineral spirits (ligroin, printer's naphtha), burning paraffin, rubber solvent, and others.

Emergency treatment. Administration of emetics is definitely contraindicated because of the danger of aspiration and consequent severe and perhaps fatal lung damage. There are differences of opinion about what constitutes an acceptable emergency treatment of the ingestion of toxic petroleum products. In the United Kingdom some authorities (Gosselin et al., 1976) recommend the administration of several ounces of mineral oil (medicinal-grade liquid petrolatum) for the following reasons. Mineral oil possesses demulcent properties; it may reduce gastric irritation and, in so doing, reduce the possibility of vomiting. In addition, the mineral oil would mix completely with the volatile petroleum product and produce a mixture with a viscosity higher than that of the volatile petroleum product alone, thus reducing the possibility of aspiration if vomiting did occur (Gerarde, 1963). Also, mineral oil is a mild cathartic and would be expected to accelerate the fecal excretion of the ingested volatile petroleum product and thus reduce the amount absorbed into the systemic circulation.

The administration of activated charcoal may also reduce the toxicity of ingested volatile petroleum products. Studies in rats (Chin, Picchioni, and Duplisse, 1969) have shown that blood levels of kerosene in animals treated promptly with activated charcoal were significantly lower than those in control animals over a 12-hour period.

Gosselin et al. (1976) suggest that the best course of treatment of kerosene ingestion is probably symptomatic and supportive but state that activated charcoal or mineral oil (medicinal grade) may be given. Neither of the latter methods has been the subject of a detailed clinical study.

Turpentine

Turpentine (oil of turpentine, spirits of turpentine, gum turpentine) is a common solvent found in most homes and is used as a thinner of oil-base paints and to clean paintbrushes and remove paint stains. Ingestion of turpentine can cause death, but exposure to turpentine vapors while painting with oil-base paint containing turpentine has no toxicologic implications.

Turpentine is a mixture of oil and resin obtained by tapping certain pine trees. It consists mainly of compounds classified chemically as terpenes, especially α-pinene, β-pinene, and Δ^3-carene (Mirov, Zavarin, and Bicho, 1962; Williams and Bannister, 1962). Turpentine is readily absorbed through the skin and from the GI tract and the respiratory tract. When ingested, it is less toxic than methyl salicylate or kerosene. However, several fatalities have been reported. The mean lethal dose in adults is believed to be between 120 and 180 ml (4 and 6 fl oz). Turpentine is a local irritant and CNS depressant. Prolonged exposure can cause renal damage, but this is rarely observed. Some reports have described the results of aspiration of turpentine. This can lead to pulmonary edema, pneumonitis, fever, tachycardia, and other manifestations (Gosselin et al., 1976).

Emergency treatment. There are no detailed reports on the usefulness of activated charcoal in the prevention of absorption of ingested turpentine. It can be predicted that if used for this purpose, it would be beneficial. Induction of emesis is contraindicated. The best emergency treatments are to (1) administer a demulcent, such as milk or beaten egg whites mixed with water, or (2) administer a saline cathartic, such as sodium sulfate or magnesium sulfate (15 to 30 gm in water).

Methanol

Methanol (methyl alcohol, wood alcohol) is a common laboratory solvent and is also widely used as a solvent in paints, varnishes, shellacs, and paint removers. It is sometimes used as a fuel and as an antifreeze liquid. It is readily absorbed from the GI tract. The fatal dose in adults is

variable but is accepted as being between 50 and 250 ml (2 and 8 fl oz), although ingestion of as little as 10 ml may produce toxic symptoms. The mortality rate after ingestion of methanol is high; death may be quite rapid or may be delayed for several days.

Ingestion of methanol causes CNS depression, metabolic acidosis, and visual disturbances. Treatment must be started promptly or death will ensue. If treatment is delayed, the poisoned person may still recover but be permanently blind or, at best, may have permanent ocular damage. Formaldehyde, formed metabolically in the retina of the eye, is believed to be the cause of the ocular damage (Potts and Johnson, 1952; Praglin, Spurney, and Potts, 1955; Kini, Wing, and Cooper, 1962).

In humans, ethanol and methanol are metabolized by the same enzyme (alcohol dehydrogenase); hence if both are administered concomitantly, the one will inhibit the metabolism of the other (Kini and Cooper, 1961). Ethanol is therefore an antidote for methanol poisoning (Zatman, 1946).

Emergency treatment. The best emergency treatment is to administer 30 ml (1 fl oz) of whiskey, or its equivalent, or 50% ethanol in water, every 3 or 4 hours for 24 hours or so, until the person can receive hemodialysis and supportive medical treatment. Minimum treatment would be to administer 4 gm of sodium bicarbonate every 15 minutes for 1 or 2 hours (to treat the acidosis that results from methanol ingestion) while transporting the client for treatment. Activated charcoal is not considered to be an effective absorbent of methanol (Decker, Combs, and Corby, 1968). Emesis is probably contraindicated in methanol poisoning because the victim may not be fully conscious and may aspirate vomitus.

Ethanol

Ethanol (alcohol, ethyl alcohol, grain alcohol, neutral spirits) is the major constituent of intoxicating spirits in concentrations up to 50%.

It is also a constituent of medicinal tinctures and rubbing alcohol and is present in some cosmetic preparations. "Denatured alcohol" is used as a solvent and as a cleaning agent. It contains small amounts of various additives (e.g., brucine, pyridine, methyl alcohol) to discourage the consumption of "denatured alcohol" as a beverage.

Ethanol is rapidly absorbed after ingestion and is distributed throughout the body water. It is a potent CNS depressant. Rapid ingestion of 960 ml (1.5 to 2 pt) of an alcoholic beverage containing 40% or more ethyl alcohol will probably be fatal (Webster, 1930). The rate of metabolic degradation of ethanol is remarkably similar in all individuals and is virtually independent of the amount consumed. Excretion of ethanol is not significantly increased by administration of diuretics, and its rate of metabolism cannot be significantly increased by drinking coffee or by the administration of hormones, vitamins, or glucose (Loomis, 1950; Jacobsen, 1952). Administration of fructose, however, can increase the rate of metabolism of ethanol up to 50% (Lowenstein et al., 1970; Brown, Forrest, and Roscoe, 1972).

Emergency treatment. Artificial respiration may be required. If vomiting occurs, steps should be taken to avoid aspiration of vomitus by the client. Activated charcoal is not an effective adsorbent of ethanol (Decker, Combs, and Corby, 1968). A comatose person should be transported to a hospital's emergency department for supportive therapy.

Strychnine

Strychnine is an alkaloid obtained from the seeds of *Strychnos nux-vomica*. Preparations containing strychnine are used as vermicides, especially to control populations of mice, rats, gophers, prairie dogs, moles, and predatory animals. Strychnine is a potent convulsant. Symptoms normally begin 10 to 30 minutes after ingestion; violent and characteristic convulsions occur, which are repeated every 10 to 15 minutes. Death often occurs after two or more convulsions

as a result of tetanic contractions of the diaphragmatic, abdominal, and thoracic muscles, which terminate respiration. The mean lethal dose of strychnine is thought to be in the 100 to 120 mg range for adults.

Emergency treatment. Treatment must be initiated as soon as possible after ingestion and before signs of hyperexcitability (which precede convulsions) are apparent. The safest method is to administer activated charcoal. Emesis is normally contraindicated in strychnine poisoning, but it can be induced before the development of hyperexcitability. Syrup of ipecac must therefore be administered *immediately* after the ingestion of the strychnine. If the administration of syrup of ipecac is delayed, its action may coincide with the initial stages of tetanic convulsions induced by the strychnine, with distressing and sometimes fatal results. If activated charcoal is not available, clients should be protected from harming themselves during convulsions and protected from any stimuli that could exacerbate convulsions, such as noise, bright light, and the unnecessary presence of people. If clients are kept warm and in a quiet, dark room, the severity and number of convulsions may be reduced. Intravenous injection of diazepam or a short-acting barbiturate (amobarbital, pentobarbital) will also reduce or prevent further convulsions.

Cyanide

Hydrocyanic acid (HCN, hydrogen cyanide, prussic acid), potassium cyanide (KCN), and sodium cyanide (NaCN) are the most common substances involved in cyanide poisoning, although other much less frequently encountered sources of cyanide are known. For example, amygdalin and the controversial laetrile are glucosides that release benzaldehyde and HCN on hydrolysis and have occasionally been implicated in cyanide poisoning. These glucosides are found in the seeds and other parts of various plants, such as apricots and cherries.

Hydrocyanic acid and sodium and potassium

cyanide are components of some insecticides, rodenticides, vermicidal fumigants, metal polishes, and electroplating and photographic solutions. The average lethal dose of potassium cyanide is approximately 200 mg (Gettler and Baine, 1938), although some people have survived larger doses (up to 6 gm), especially if prompt treatment was given (Miller and Toops, 1951; DeBusk and Seidl, 1969). Based on this figure for KCN, the average lethal dose of sodium cyanide would be 150 mg and that of hydrocyanic acid 80 to 85 mg. This last amount corresponds to about 4 ml of a 2% solution of HCN.

Cyanide is a potent inhibitor of cytochrome oxidase enzymes. It prevents all body cells from using the oxygen carried in the blood, with the result that all body functions rapidly cease. The brain is the organ that is the most sensitive to oxygen lack. Convulsions precede death, which is caused by respiratory arrest.

Emergency treatment. Emergency treatment must be applied immediately after ingestion of the cyanide when the client is still free of symptoms of cyanide poisoning. The best emergency treatment (Gosselin et al., 1976) is to induce vomiting with syrup of ipecac. Activated charcoal should *not* be given. It is *not* an effective absorbent of cyanide (Andersen, 1946; Caranasos, Stewart, and Cluff, 1974). The contents of one ampule of sodium nitrite (cyanide antidote kit) are administered to adults as a specific antidote for cyanide poisoning. This is followed with appropriate supportive care.

Corrosive acids

Concentrated inorganic (mineral) acids (hydrochloric [muriatic], sulfuric, nitric, and phosphoric acids) are the most commonly encountered corrosive acids, but other inorganic acids (e.g., hypochlorous acid [present in some bleaches as sodium hypochlorite], boric acid), organic acids (e.g., formic, acetic, trichloroacetic, lactic, oxalic acids), and other compounds

(e.g., phenol, iodine and bromine solutions, ammonia, and lye) are also corrosive. Many household products contain corrosive mineral acids. Automobile batteries contain about 28% aqueous sulfuric acid, and some cleansing products contain sodium bisulfite or hydrochloric or phosphoric acids. Some industrial cleaning agents and other products may contain corrosive acids. Some rust removers contain oxalic acid.

It is difficult to predict the lethal doses of concentrated hydrochloric acid (36% HCl), concentrated nitric acid (69% HNO_3), concentrated sulfuric acid (95% H_2SO_4), dilutions of these acids, or other corrosive acids. It has been suggested (Polson and Tatersall, 1959) that 30 ml (1 fl oz) of the three concentrated mineral acids just mentioned would constitute a lethal dose in adults, but another authority (Arena, 1974) suggests that much lower volumes (5 ml) are lethal. Ingestion of caustic acids can cause damage to the esophagus, stomach, and pyloric sphincter. Pyloric stenosis is frequently observed in clients who survive the ingestion of concentrated mineral acid, but evidence of pyloric obstruction may be delayed for years. Other corrosive-induced lesions, including esophageal stricture, are less frequently observed when mineral and organic acids are ingested.

Emergency treatment. If corrosive acids have been ingested, *vomiting should not be induced.* This could result in perforation of the esophagus or stomach or could result in aspiration of the acid.

The initial emergency treatment should be to have the client drink large amounts of water and a noneffervescent neutralizer (e.g., 60 ml [2 fl oz] of milk of magnesia or aluminum hydroxide gel). The use of carbonates and bicarbonates should be avoided because during the neutralization reaction they release carbon dioxide, which will distend the stomach and may rupture it if it is damaged. Demulcents (milk, egg whites, mineral oil, olive oil, melted butter, starch water) may also be given (Gosselin et al., 1976). Activated charcoal is *not* an effective adsorbent of mineral acids (Decker, Combs, and Corby, 1968).

Corrosive alkalis

Corrosive alkalis are commonly referred to as "lyes" and include sodium hydroxide, potassium hydroxide, caustic soda, and caustic potash. Some peroxides, carbonates, oxides, and alkaline phosphates (e.g., trisodium phosphate), and other substances (e.g., powdered cement, solid detergents) are also caustic. As mentioned earlier in this chapter, drain and oven cleaners (e.g., Draino, Easy-Off) are common domestic corrosive alkalis. Some paint removers and denture cleaners are also caustic. Urine glucose reagent tablets (e.g., Clinitest) can also be dangerous.

It is difficult to predict lethal doses of caustic alkalis because the toxic effect is dependent on the concentration of the lye solution. Many studies have been conducted with animals, and data from these studies and from human poisonings with lye indicate that the lethal dose of sodium hydroxide in adults is less than 10 gm. In experiments with cats, liquid lye preparations, containing about 30% sodium or potassium hydroxide, when introduced into the mouth caused severe damage (esophageal necrosis) even when only 1 ml was introduced and exposure time was 1 second (Leape et al., 1971). Aqueous products that contained less than 10% lye produced severe damage after 30 seconds' exposure (Ashcraft and Padula, 1974). Ingestion of concentrated sodium hydroxide solutions is particularly dangerous ("The Management of Lye Burns of the Esophagus," 1972). Approximately 25% of those who ingest these substances die from the immediate effects. Damage to the esophagus and stomach after ingestion may progress for 2 to 3 weeks. Death from peritonitis may occur 1 month or more after ingestion. Approximately 95% of those who ingest strong alkali and recover from immediate effects suffer from persistent esophageal stricture and have difficulty swallowing.

There are two stages of lye toxicity: (1) liquefaction necrosis followed by stricture and (2) an intense, progressive inflammatory reaction ("The Management of Lye Burns of the Esophagus," 1972; Gosselin et al., 1976). Lye has a dehydrating action on tissue cells; it solubilizes protein and collagen and saponifies lipid material.

Emergency treatment. If corrosive alkalis have been ingested, *vomiting should not be induced* because, as in the case of corrosive acids, this could result in perforation of the esophagus or stomach or could result in aspiration of the alkali. *Immediately*, the client should drink large volumes of water or milk to dilute the ingested alkali. Demulcent drinks, such as egg whites, may also be given. Analgesics are administered to relieve pain, and steroid and antibiotic therapy is used to decrease granulation and scar tissue contracture and to control possible infection (Cardona and Daly, 1971). In instances where esophageal stricture cannot be prevented, bougienage or reconstructive surgery may be necessary. Intravenous administration of fluids (electrolyte solutions, plasma, whole blood) may be necessary to control shock.

Liquid bleaches (containing hypochlorite)

Numerous liquid household bleaches are 3% to 10% solutions of sodium hypochlorite (NaOCl) in water, containing small amounts of sodium chloride (3% to 8%) and sodium hydroxide (0.01% to 0.5%). Javex bleach is a 6% solution of NaOCl; Clorox bleach contains 5.25% NaOCl. Attempted suicides have involved liquid household bleaches. In a reported instance a man survived the ingestion of 0.95 l (1 qt) (Strange et al., 1951). Ingestion of liquid household bleach promptly induces emesis. Although not commonly observed, permanent esophageal stricture can result from the ingestion of liquid household bleach. From the figures quoted by Gosselin et al. (1976), the incidence of esophageal stricture is about 4%. Hypochlorite solutions are corrosive to mucous membranes, but damage is rarely permanent.

Emergency treatment. It is best to administer milk of magnesia, an antacid with adsorbent and demulcent properties. Alternatively, aluminum hydroxide gel or magnesium trisilicate gel can be given, but sodium bicarbonate should be *avoided* because it releases carbon dioxide. If an antacid is not available, milk or egg whites in water should be administered. Analgesics are given for the control of pain. It may be necessary to treat shock with intravenous fluids.

Carbon monoxide

Carbon monoxide (CO) is a colorless, odorless, tasteless gas that has a density similar to that of air. The main sources of CO are exhaust from internal combustion engines and flue gas from furnaces, but there are other sources (e.g., the burning of vinyl plastics and poorly aerated restaurant kitchens). Carbon monoxide combines with hemoglobin in the blood, forming carboxyhemoglobin, thus rendering the hemoglobin unable to combine with and transport oxygen. The cells of the body are therefore deprived of necessary oxygen. The affinity of hemoglobin for carbon monoxide is 200 times that for oxygen (Lilienthal et al., 1946); the result of this high affinity is that small concentrations of CO in air (e.g., 1%) can, within a few hours, inactivate most of the blood's hemoglobin. High concentrations of carboxyhemoglobin in the blood impart a cherry-red color to the skin of most, but not all, victims. This is the most obvious symptom of acute CO intoxication. Other symptoms are mild-to-throbbing headache, irritability, impaired judgment and memory, weakness, nausea, and defective vision because the organ most sensitive to oxygen lack is the brain.

Emergency treatment. The victim should be removed from the CO source and artificial respiration should be applied until pure oxygen can be administered. Antibiotics may be necessary if pulmonary infection occurs. A whole blood transfusion may also be necessary.

COMMON DRUGS INVOLVED IN POISONING

It is impossible to list all the drugs that are involved in poisoning episodes. Six important examples have been selected because of their involvement in many instances of geriatric poisoning.

Barbiturates

Most barbiturate poisonings are the result of attempted suicides. It is estimated (Berman et al., 1956; Gosselin et al., 1976) that an oral dose of 1 gm of most barbiturates will produce serious poisoning in an adult, and death is probable after the ingestion of from 2 to 10 gm, depending on which barbiturate has been swallowed. In the adult the lethal doses of pentobarbital, amobarbital, and secobarbital are similar (around 3 gm); the lethal dose of phenobarbital is approximately 5 gm; barbital is much less toxic. In some instances death from barbiturate ingestion occurs within a few hours of ingestion of a fatal dose, but in most instances death is delayed for many hours and even for 4 to 5 days.

Emergency treatment. There are no effective antidotes that can be used in barbiturate poisoning. The best emergency treatments are the use of syrup of ipecac or activated charcoal if the client is awake and is not in imminent danger of losing consciousness. If the client is not fully conscious, gastric lavage should be performed. Precautions against aspiration are essential. Alkaline diuresis may increase the renal clearance of these compounds; in severe poisonings hemodialysis may be used. Throughout treatment, appropriate cardiovascular and respiratory support should be applied.

Benzodiazepines

The most commonly prescribed drugs of this class are diazepam (e.g., Valium, Vivol), chlordiazepoxide (e.g., Librium), and oxazepam (e.g., Serax). These drugs are widely used, and it is inevitable that both accidental and deliberate overdosing occurs with them. Diazepam is currently one of the most commonly involved drugs in poisoning episodes in North America. However, few deaths have been associated with these three drugs. In adults, doses of chlordiazepoxide of 600 mg and greater have produced no serious effects. In one case, when 400 mg of diazepam was ingested, the client was drowsy but recovered without treatment. Oxazepam is significantly less toxic than either diazepam or chlordiazepoxide. All are less toxic than the tricyclic antidepressants. It would appear from the limited data available that ingestion by adults of 10 mg/kg or more of any of these three antianxiety drugs will produce toxic symptoms requiring treatment (Gosselin et al., 1976).

Emergency treatment. Activated charcoal or syrup of ipecac can be administered. In a hospital setting gastric lavage is performed, followed by symptomatic and supportive treatment. Diuresis or hemodialysis may be required for the severely intoxicated client.

Digoxin

Digoxin is a digitalis glycoside, which has a specific and powerful effect on the myocardium and is used as a cardiotonic. The usual daily dose is 0.125 to 0.25 mg, and the single oral lethal dose lies between 20 and 50 times the daily maintenance dose, although adults have survived single doses in excess of 20 mg (Smith and Willerson, 1971; Dobson and Zettner, 1973). Digoxin is rated as a "supertoxic" substance (Gosselin et al., 1976) and is involved in numerous accidental poisonings and suicide attempts. This is of particular significance in the geriatric client who is being treated with digoxin for atrial fibrillation

or flutter, paroxysmal atrial tachycardia, cardiogenic shock, congestive heart failure, or other heart ailments.

Emergency treatment. If overdosage is recognized promptly, activated charcoal or syrup of ipecac can be administered. Gastric lavage is also effective. None of these three procedures is of any value if toxic signs and symptoms are evident. Further treatment is symptomatic and depends on the results of continuous ECG monitoring. Potassium chloride is often administered if the client is hypokalemic, and phenytoin is often used to treat associated dysrhythmias.

Phenothiazines

Phenothiazines are used as antipsychotic tranquilizers, antiemetics, and antihistaminics. Many drugs that possess the phenothiazine ring system are therefore available commercially; their toxicities, however, vary widely. One of the most widely used phenothiazines is chlorpromazine (Largactil, Thorazine), which is an effective CNS depressant and is used in the treatment of a wide range of psychiatric disturbances, as well as for its antiemetic properties. Because of its widespread use, its toxicity has been established. Poisoning as a result of overdose occurs frequently, but human fatalities are only rarely encountered. The lethal dose is difficult to estimate. One woman died after ingesting only 2 gm of chlorpromazine (Algeri, Katsas, and McBay, 1959), whereas some adults have recovered after the ingestion of ten times that amount (Brophy, 1967).

Emergency treatment. Because cardiotoxicity is an infrequent result of phenothiazine poisoning and because emetic drugs tend to be ineffective when phenothiazines are ingested, the use of emetic drugs generally should be avoided. The safest emergency treatment is to administer activated charcoal. Gastric lavage is also indicated. Fluid and electrolyte therapy and exchange transfusion may be necessary in severely poisoned individuals.

Salicylates

Poisoning by salicylates is termed salicylism. Its signs and symptoms include headache, tinnitus, dimness of vision, confusion, hyperpnea, bizarre behavior, emesis, convulsions, and coma. Hyperthermia may also be observed. Death is often the result of respiratory failure or cardiovascular collapse while the client is in a coma (Riley and Worley, 1956). The commonly encountered salicylates include salicylic acid, sodium salicylate, potassium salicylate, and other salts; methyl salicylate, phenyl salicylate, and other esters; and aspirin. The most commonly encountered salicylates in poisoning incidents are aspirin and methyl salicylate (oil of wintergreen).

The toxicity of salicylates is underestimated by many. Recently in the United States, of 536 deaths from salicylism, 61% were caused by methyl salicylate ingestion (and the number who ingested it was very low); 31% were caused by ingested aspirin; and 8% were caused by other salicylates. From these data it would appear that methyl salicylate is much more toxic than other salicylates, but, on a molar basis, this is not true. The fact that methyl salicylate is a liquid means that it can be ingested more easily in large doses than aspirin or salicylic acid, which are solids.

The mean lethal oral dose of aspirin or sodium salicylate is estimated to be between 0.4 and 0.5 gm/kg of body weight, which is equivalent to about ninety 325 mg aspirin tablets or 20 ml of methyl salicylate for a 150-pound adult. Toxic effects usually appear whenever an adult has ingested more than 10 gm of aspirin (equivalent to about thirty 325 mg aspirin tablets) in a single dose. However, there are reports that less than 1 gm of aspirin (i.e., two to three 325 mg tablets) has caused death (a hypersensitivity reaction), and ingestion of more than 130 gm of aspirin has been survived (with treatment) (Gosselin et al.,

1976). The overall incidence of all types of hypersensitivity to aspirin is probably about 0.2% of the population.

Emergency treatment. This should be applied to adults who have ingested more than 10 gm of aspirin. It should also be applied if methyl salicylate (any volume) is accidentally swallowed.

Either activated charcoal or syrup of ipecac should be administered as soon as possible after ingestion of aspirin or methyl salicylate. In a hospital environment various other treatments are applied, depending on the severity of the poisoning. Gastric lavage may be instigated. Most cases of salicylism are effectively treated with intravenous fluids. This treatment corrects dehydration and shock by expanding the volume of the extracellular fluid. If acidosis has been established, alkali therapy is used. Intravenous sodium bicarbonate is usually administered. Forced alkaline diuresis, hemodialysis, peritoneal dialysis, and exchange transfusion are other procedures used to treat acute salicylism.

Tricyclic antidepressants

Tricyclic antidepressants (e.g., amitriptyline, imipramine, desipramine, nortriptyline) are widely used in the treatment of psychiatric depression. Because of this wide use, accidental and intentional overdosing with these drugs has become common. Ingestion by adults of 500 mg of imipramine or 1000 mg of desipramine, amitriptyline, or nortriptyline can be expected to result in severe intoxication or death. From the limited data available it would appear that ingestion by adults of 5 mg/kg or more of any of these four drugs will produce toxic symptoms requiring treatment (Gosselin et al., 1976).

Emergency treatment. Because ingestion of excessive doses of tricyclic antidepressants can result in cardiac disturbances and CNS stimulation resulting in convulsions, the administration of an emetic is contraindicated. A safe emergency treatment is to administer activated charcoal. Gastric lavage is indicated only in the absence of convulsions. In the hospital, treatment is generally symptomatic and supportive. Convulsions may need to be controlled and the ECG continuously monitored. Physostigmine, 0.03 mg/kg, is administered IV slowly over 2 to 3 minutes to treat the anticholinergic effects of tricyclic antidepressant overdose.

EMERGENCY TREATMENT SUMMARY

Inhaled poisons. If a gas or irritant powder has been inhaled, remove the person from the source into *fresh air;* be prepared to administer *artificial respiration.* Provide necessary supportive care.

Ingested poisons. Determine if possible what was swallowed, when it was swallowed, and how much was swallowed. If a toxic amount of the poison appears to have been ingested and less than 1 or 2 hours have elapsed, steps should be taken to prevent the absorption of the poison still in the stomach. For this purpose, always have the following readily available:

1. Activated charcoal—Either a commercial preparation ready for use or a 200 ml bottle containing 20 gm of activated charcoal to which water is added and the mixture thoroughly shaken just before use
2. Syrup of ipecac—Commercially available in 15 ml capacity containers; normal treatment is to administer 15 ml followed by about 200 ml of water or a flavored drink, and if vomiting does not occur within 20 minutes, another 15 ml of syrup of ipecac should be administered.
3. Mineral oil (medicinal grade)
4. Milk of magnesia or aluminum hydroxide gel
5. Milk
6. Eggs

A summary of the appropriate emergency treatment is given in Table 9-4.

TABLE 9-4   Summary of emergency treatment of poisoning

State of client or nature of poison	Emergency treatment
Syrup of ipecac *can be used to induce vomiting in all poisonings* except in the following instances, *which should be treated as indicated.*	
Corrosive acids or alkalis	Administer copious quantities of water or milk (up to 2 l may be required)
Ethanol	Be prepared to administer artificial respiration
Household detergents	Administer liberal quantities of milk or water
Liquid bleaches	Give milk of magnesia or aluminum hydroxide gel
Methanol	Give 30 ml (1 fl oz) of an ethanol-containing beverage (e.g., gin, vodka, whiskey) every 3 or 4 hours
Petroleum products	Give several ounces of mineral oil (medicinal grade) or give activated charcoal
Pregnancy or cardiac disease	Administer activated charcoal if appropriate
Strychnine	Give activated charcoal; keep client warm, quiet, and in subdued lighting. (Emesis may be induced [syrup of ipecac] provided the emetic is administered *immediately* after the ingestion of the strychnine.)
Tricyclic antidepressants Phenothiazines	Induction of emesis is probably contraindicated; the safest emergency treatment is to administer activated charcoal

Continued.

TABLE 9-4 **Summary of emergency treatment of poisoning—cont'd**

State of client or nature of poison	Emergency treatment
Turpentine	Administer a demulcent, milk, or several egg whites mixed with water
Unconscious, very drowsy, very agitated, or convulsing client	Keep the client warm and provide supportive care

Activated charcoal *can be given in all poisonings* except in the following instances, *which should be treated as indicated.*

Boric acid	Give syrup of ipecac
Corrosive acids and alkalis	Administer copious quantities of water or milk (up to 2 l may be required)
Cyanide	Give syrup of ipecac
Ethanol	Administer artificial respiration if necessary
Iron preparations	Give syrup of ipecac
Methanol	Administer 30 ml (1 fl oz) of an ethanol-containing beverage (e.g., gin, vodka, whiskey) every 3 or 4 hours
Turpentine	Give milk or several egg whites beaten with water
Unconscious, very drowsy, very agitated, or convulsing client	Keep the client warm and provide supportive care

REFERENCES

Algeri, E.J., Katsas, G.G., and McBay, A.J.: Toxicology of some new drugs: glutethimide, meprobamate and chlorpromazine, J. Forensic Sci. 4:111, 1959.

Andersen, A.H.: Experimental studies on the pharmacology of activated charcoal. I. Adsorption power of charcoal in aqueous solution, Acta Pharmacol. Toxicol. 2:69, 1946.

Andersen, A.H.: Experimental studies on the pharmacology of activated charcoal. II. The effect of pH on the adsorption by charcoal from aqueous solutions, Acta Pharmacol. Toxicol. 3:199, 1947.

Andersen, A.H.: Experimental studies on the pharmacology of activated charcoal. III. Adsorption from gastro-intestinal contents, Acta Pharmacol. Toxicol. 4:275, 1948.

Arena, J.M.: Poisoning—toxicology, symptoms, treatments, ed. 3, Springfield, Ill., 1974, Charles C Thomas, Publisher.

Arena, J.M.: Poisoning—treatment and prevention. I. J.A.M.A. 232:1272, 1975.

Arena, J.M.: Poisoning—treatment and prevention. II. J.A.M.A. 233:358, 1975.

Ashcraft, K.W., and Padula, R.T.: The effect of dilute corrosives on the esophagus, Pediatrics 53:226, 1974.

Atkinson, J.P., and Azarnoff, D.L.: Comparison of charcoal and attapulgite as gastrointestinal sequestrants in acute drug ingestions, Clin. Toxicol. 4:31, 1971.

Batchelor, I.R.C.: Management and prognosis of suicidal attempts in old age, Geriatrics 10:291, 1955.

Bennett, A.E.: Recognizing the potential suicide, Geriatrics 22:175, 1967.

Benson, R.A., and Brodie, D.C.: Suicide by overdoses of medicines among the aged, J. Am. Geriatr. Soc. 23:304, 1975.

Berg, M.J., et al.: Acceleration of the body clearance of phenobarbital by oral activated charcoal, N. Engl. J. Med. 307:642, 1982.

Berman, L.B., et al.: Hemodialysis, an effective therapy for acute barbiturate poisoning, J.A.M.A. 161:820, 1956.

Boehm, J.J., Brown, T.C.K., and Oppenheim, R.C.: Flavored activated charcoal as an antidote, Aust. J. Pharm. Sci. 7:119, 1978.

Brophy, J.J.: Suicide attempts with psychotherapeutic drugs, Arch. Gen. Psychiatry 17:652, 1967.

Brown, S.S., Forrest, J.A.H., and Roscoe, P.: A controlled trial of fructose in the treatment of acute alcoholic intoxication, Lancet 2:898, 1972.

Caranasos, G.J., Stewart, R.B., and Cluff, L.I.: Drug-induced illness leading to hospitalization, J.A.M.A. 228:713, 1974.

Cardona, J.C., and Daly, J.F.: Current management

of corrosive esophagitis; an evaluation of results in 239 cases, Ann. Otol. Rhinol. Laryngol. **80**:521, 1971.

Carter, R.O., and Griffith, J.F.: Factors relating to accidental ingestion hazard, Soap Chem. Specialties **37**:49, 1961.

Charcoal as an adsorbent: Med. Letter **7**:52, 1965.

Chin, L., Picchioni, A.L., and Duplisse, B.R.: Comparative antidotal effectiveness of activated charcoal, Arizona montmorillonite and evaporated milk, J. Pharm. Sci. **58**:1353, 1969.

Chin, L., Picchioni, A.L., and Duplisse, B.R.: The action of activated charcoal on poisons in the digestive tract, Toxicol. Appl. Pharmacol. **16**:786, 1970.

Chin, L., et al.: Optimal antidotal dose of activated charcoal, Toxicol. Appl. Pharmacol. **26**:103, 1973.

Cooper, J.W.: Drug therapy in the elderly: is it all it could be? Am. Pharm. **18**:353, 1978.

Crooks, J., O'Malley, K., and Stevenson, I.H.: Pharmacokinetics in the elderly, Clin. Pharmacokinet. **1**:280, 1976.

DeBusk, R.F., and Seidl, L.G.: Attempted suicide by cyanide, Calif. Med. **110**:394, 1969.

Decker, J.D., et al.: Inhibition of aspirin absorption by activated charcoal and apomorphine, Clin. Pharmacol. Ther. **10**:710, 1969.

Decker, W.J., Combs, H.F., and Corby, D.G.: Adsorption of drugs and poisons by activated charcoal, Toxicol. Appl. Pharmacol. **13**:454, 1968.

Decker, W.J., and Corby, D.C.: Activated charcoal as a gastrointestinal decontaminant: experiences with experimental animals and human subjects, Clin. Toxicol. **3**:1, 1970.

De Neve, R.: Antidotal efficacy of activated charcoal in presence of jam, starch and milk, Am. J. Hosp. Pharm. **33**:965, 1976.

Dobson, J.D., and Zettner, A.: Digoxin serum half-life following suicidal digoxin poisoning, J.A.M.A. **233**:147, 1973.

Dreisbach, R.H.: Handbook of Poisoning, Los Altos, Calif., 1977, Lange Medical Publications.

Emergency treatment of poisoning: Pharm. J. **220**:452, 1978.

Emetics for acute poisoning—treatment or hazard?: Br. Med. J. **2**:977, 1977.

Gerarde, H.W.: Toxicological studies on hydrocarbons. IX. The aspiration hazard and toxicity of hydrocarbons and hydrocarbon mixtures, Arch. Environ. Health **6**:329, 1963.

Gettler, A.O., and Baine, J.O.: The toxicology of cyanide, Am. J. Med. Sci. **195**:182, 1938.

Gibb, S.M., Unsworth, R.W., and Ilett, K.F.: Ipecacuanha as an emetic for adults, Br. Med. J. **2**:1474, 1977.

Gosselin, R.E., et al.: Clinical toxicology of commercial products, ed. 4, Baltimore, 1976, The Williams & Wilkins Co.

Gotz, B.E., and Gotz, V.P.: Drugs and the elderly, Am. J. Nurs. **78**:1347, 1978.

Gwilt, P.R., and Perrier, D.: Influence of thickening agents on the antidotal efficiency of activated charcoal, Clin. Toxicol. **9**:89, 1976.

Hurst, J.A., and Dozzi, A.M.: The emergency treatment of poisoning in children, Med. J. Aust. **2**:432, 1975.

Hurwitz, N.: Predisposing factors in adverse reactions to drugs, Br. Med. J. **1**:536, 1969.

Initial management of acute poisoning: Med. Letter **13**:35, 1971.

Jacobsen, E.: The metabolism of ethyl alcohol, Pharmacol. Rev. **4**:107, 1952.

Kini, M.M., and Cooper, J.R.: The biochemistry of methanol poisoning. III. The enzymic pathway for the conversion of methanol to formaldehyde, Biochem. Pharmacol. **8**:207, 1961.

Kini, M.M., Wing, D.W., and Cooper, J.R.: Biochemistry of methanol poisoning. V. Histological and biochemical correlates of effects of methanol and its metabolites on the rabbit, J. Neurochem. **9**:119, 1962.

Leape, L.L., et al.: Hazard to health—liquid lye, N. Engl. J. Med. **284**:578, 1971.

Levy, G.: Gastrointestinal clearance of drugs with activated charcoal, N. Engl. J. Med. **307**:676, 1982.

Levy, G., Soda, D.M., and Lampman, T.: Inhibition by ice cream of the antidotal efficacy of activated charcoal, Am. J. Hosp. Pharm. **32**:289, 1975.

Lilienthal, J.L., et al.: The relationships between carbon monoxide, oxygen and hemoglobin in the blood of man at altitude, Am. J. Physiol. **145**:351, 1946.

Loomis, T.A.: A study of the rate of metabolism of ethyl alcohol with special reference to certain factors reported as influencing this rate, Q.J. Stud. Alcohol **11**:527, 1950.

Lowenstein, L.M., et al.: Effect of fructose on alcohol concentrations in the blood in man, J.A.M.A. **213**:1899, 1970.

The management of lye burns of the esophagus: Med. Letter **14**:18, March 1972.

Manes, M., and Mann, J.P.: Easily swallowed formulations of antidote charcoals, Clin. Toxicol. 7:355, 1974.

Manno, B.R., and Manno, J.E.: Toxicology of ipecac: a review, Clin. Toxicol. 10:221, 1977.

Matthew, H.: Gastric aspiration and lavage, Clin. Toxicol. 3:179, 1970.

Miller, M.H., and Toops, T.C.: Acute cyanide poisoning: recovery with sodium thiosulfate therapy, J. Indiana State Med. Assoc. 44:1164, 1951.

Mirov, N.T., and Zavarin, E., and Bicho, J.G.: Composition of gum turpentine of pines, *Pinus nelsonii* and *Pinus occidentalis,* J. Pharm. Sci. 51:1131, 1962.

Oderda, G.M.: Clinical toxicology, J. Am. Pharm. Assoc. 14:626, 1974.

O'Neal, P., Robins, E., and Schmidt, E.H.: Psychiatric study of attempted suicide in persons over 60 years of age, Arch. Neurol. Psychiat. 75:275, 1956.

Picchioni, A.L., et al.: Activated charcoal vs "universal antidote" as an antidote for poisons, Toxicol. Appl. Pharmacol. 8:447, 1966.

Poison Control Program Statistics 1974: Ottawa, 1977, Health and Welfare Canada.

Polson, C.J., and Tatersall, R.N.: Clinical toxicology, Philadelphia, 1959, J.B. Lippincott Co.

Potts, A.M., and Johnson, L.V.: Studies on the visual toxicology of methanol. I. The effects of methanol and its degradation products on retinal metabolism, Am. J. Ophthalmol. 35:107, 1952.

Praglin, J., Spurney, R., and Potts, A.M.: An experimental study of electroretinography. I. The electroretinogram in experimental animals under the influence of methanol and its oxidation products, Am. J. Ophthalmol. 39:52, 1955.

Richardson, J.A., and Pratt-Thomas, H.R.: Toxic effects of varying doses of kerosene administered by different routes, Am. J. Med. Sci. 221:531, 1951.

Riley, H.D., and Worley, L.: Salicylate intoxication, Pediatrics 18:578, 1956.

Schneider, L.: Pulmonary hazard of the ingestion of mineral oil in the apparently healthy adult, N. Engl. J. Med. 240:284, 1949.

Smith, R.P., et al.: Comparison of the adsorptive properties of activated charcoal and Alaskan montmorillonite for some common poisons, Toxicol. Appl. Pharmacol. 10:95, 1967.

Smith, T.W., and Willerson, J.T.: Suicidal and accidental digoxin ingestion: report of five cases with serum digoxin level correlations, Circulation 44:29, 1971.

Strange, D.C., et al.: Corrosive injury of the stomach; report of a case caused by ingestion of Clorox and experimental study of injurious effects, Arch. Surg. 62:350, 1951.

Temple, A.R., Walker, J., and Done, G.A.: A comparative evaluation of activated charcoal hemoperfusion devices, Clin. Toxicol. 10:481, 1977.

Thoman, M.E., and Verhulst, H.L.: Ipecac syrup in antiemetic ingestion, J.A.M.A. 196:433, 1966.

Tsuchiya, T., and Levy, G.: Relationship between effect of activated charcoal on drug absorption in man and its drug adsorption characteristics *in vitro,* J. Pharm. Sci. 61:586, 1972.

Universal antidote for accidental poisoning: "Black bottle" adopted: Can. Pharm. J. 97:258, 1964.

Vale, J.A., et al.: Use of charcoal haemoperfusion in the management of severely poisoned patients, Br. Med. J. 1:5, 1975.

Veltri J.C., and Temple, A.R.: Telephone management of poisonings using syrup of ipecac, Clin. Toxicol. 9:407, 1976.

Wallace, D.E., and Watanabe, A.S.: Drug effects in geriatric patients, Drug Intell. Clin. Pharm. 11:597, 1977.

Webster, R.W.: Legal medicine and toxicology, Philadelphia, 1930, W.B. Saunders Co.

Williams, A.L., and Bannister, M.H.: Composition of gum turpentines from twenty-two species of pines grown in New Zealand, J. Pharm. Sci. 51:970, 1962.

Zatman, L.J.: The effect of ethanol on the metabolism of methanol in man, Biochem. J. 40:lxvii, 1946.

CHAPTER 10

Pharmacokinetics in the aged

W.A. Ritschel

Physiologic changes that occur with increasing age and the increased side effects or toxicity of many drugs in the geriatric client require special attention for drug therapy in the aged. Observed differences in drug response seem to be primarily caused not by increased sensitivity of drug receptors in the aged but by altered pharmacokinetic parameters.

The response to some drugs, however, seems to be unrelated to changes in blood and tissue levels. Differences in the physiologic and pathologic status of tissues may be responsible for altered mechanisms of drug action (see Chapter 6). Most likely such differences may be caused by a change in the number of viable receptors, by a change in receptor sensitivity, or by a change in homeostatic capacity.

For a pharmacologic response to occur, a drug must reach a certain minimum concentration at the site of action. The entire process of reaching and, if necessary, maintaining a therapeutic concentration in the body is pharmacokinetically described by the LADME System: liberation, absorption, distribution, metabolism, elimination (Ritschel, 1973) (Fig. 10-1).

Most of the studies done so far are based on single dose administration. There is a definite need for further investigations to study the pharmacokinetics of drugs in the elderly at steady state and on chronic dosing.

Of all the pharmacokinetic processes studied in the elderly, there are two processes particularly that show some consistent pattern: renal elimination and volume of distribution (Vd). The higher the extent of renal elimination of the unchanged drug from the body, the more pronounced is the prolongation of biologic half-life associated with the reduction of renal function with increasing age. The volume of distribution may change, depending on the lipophilic character of the drug and the extent of protein binding.

Even if correction of any changed parameter is made and a therapeutic range is obtained as found desirable for the young adult, there is no proof that such a therapeutic window is also applicable to the aged. Combined pharmacokinetic and pharmacodynamic studies are needed in this area.

LIBERATION

A prerequisite for a drug to be absorbed is its presence in aqueous solution at the absorption site, except in the rare cases of absorption by pinocytosis. In all cases, except when the drug is administered in solution form (IV solution, IM solution, oral elixir, oral syrup, rectal enema), it has to be released from the dosage form.

Because the amount of gastric secretion is re-

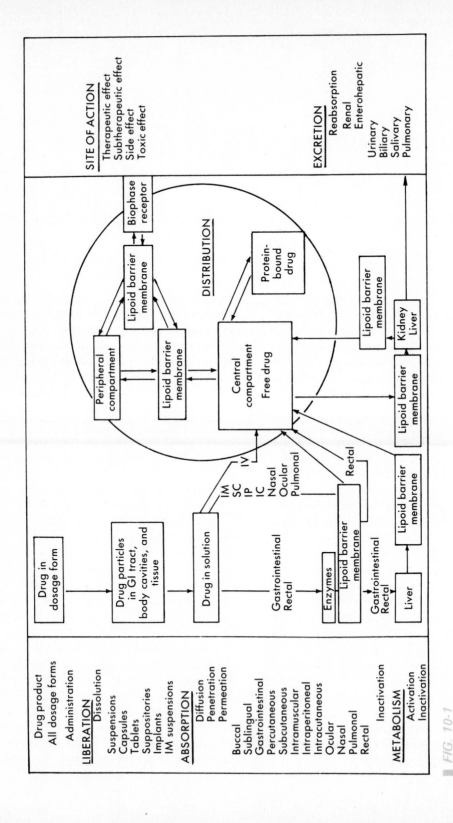

FIG. 10-1   LADME system in biopharmaceutics. (Reprinted with permission from Ritschel, W.A.: Handbook of basic pharmacokinetics, ed. 2., Hamilton, Ill., 1980, Drug Intelligence Publications, Inc., pp. 315-316.)

duced in the elderly, it can be assumed that the disintegration and dissolution of oral dosage forms will be prolonged. The higher gastric pH will affect the degree of ionization of some drugs. Acidic drugs, particularly, which might be absorbed from the acidic stomach, can be in the ionized, nonabsorbable moiety. However, at the present time there is not enough information available to draw definite conclusions.

ABSORPTION

Absorption from the gastrointestinal (GI) tract may be impaired in the geriatric client because of atrophy of the absorbing intestinal epithelium, a delay in gastric emptying, or a decrease in GI tract motility (Bender, 1965).

The reduction in the number of absorbing cells resulting from mucosal atrophy reduces the surface area available for absorption. A decreased gastric emptying rate may result in an increased lag time before the drug is absorbed from the small intestine.

Other factors that may affect GI tract absorption are a decreased splanchnic blood flow and an increased occurrence of duodenal diverticula. The decreased splanchnic blood flow may minimize the concentration gradient between the drug concentration in the luminal content and in mesenteric blood; hence it will delay absorption. The occurrence of duodenal diverticula caused by a change in bacterial flora of the upper GI tract may result in malabsorption not only of food but also of drugs. For some agents absorbed by active transport, impaired absorption was found in the aged. Examples are xylose, galactose, 3-methylglucose, calcium, thiamine, and iron (Bender, 1968; Dietze et al., 1971; Webster and Leeming, 1974). However, most drugs are absorbed from the GI tract by passive diffusion. So far no evidence has been found that passive transport is impaired in the aged (Fikry and Aboul-Wafa, 1965; Bender, 1968).

Intramuscular (IM) and subcutaneous (SC) absorption seems to be delayed in the elderly for some drugs. Absorption of an injection wheal from the skin requires 80 minutes at age 10 years, whereas 140 minutes are required in clients above 60 years of age (Schultz, 1965). This has been explained by reduced blood flow and altered permeability of the capillary walls.

Also, percutaneous absorption seems to be impaired. The extent of absorption of radioactive labeled testosterone from the skin of the back was 37.9% in a group aged 20 to 40 years versus 12.5% in a group aged 70 to 82 years (Christophers and Kligman, 1964).

DISTRIBUTION

Distribution is the process by which the absorbed drug is transported in the organism, reaches organs and peripheral tissues, and is localized in the tissues. Although there is no significant change with age (Schröder and Börner, 1958; Smith, 1958; Cohen, Gitman, and Lipschutz, 1960) in blood or plasma volume per unit of body weight, there are several changes in the aged that may influence Vd: body composition, regional blood flow rates associated with decreased cardiac output, and binding to plasma albumin and red blood cells.

Body composition

Even if body weight remains constant throughout adulthood, body composition changes with increasing age, resulting in less lean body mass and more fat tissue (Goldman, 1970; Novak, 1972). The change in body composition is shown in the schematic diagram in Fig. 10-2. With increasing age, body fat increases from 18% to 36% of total body weight in males and from 33% to 48% in females.

Total body fluid (TBF) decreases significantly with age (Shock, Yiengst, and Watkin, 1953; Olbrich, Woodford-Williams, and Attwood, 1957; Parker et al., 1958; Fryer, 1962; Novak, 1972). Extracellular fluid (ECF) remains unchanged but constitutes a larger proportion of TBF in the aged

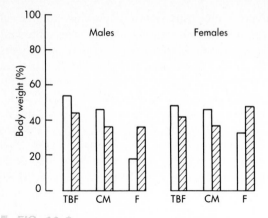

FIG. 10-2

Body composition for males and females in percent of body weight. *TBF*, total body fluid; *CM*, cell mass; *F*, fat; open rectangle, age 25 years; slashed rectangle, age 75 years.

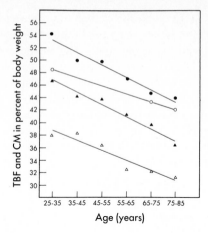

FIG. 10-3

Age versus mean total body fluid (TBF) and mean cell mass (CM) in percent of body weight in males and females. ●, TBF in males; ○, TBF in females; ▲, CM in males; △, CM in females. (From Ritschel, W.A.: J. Am. Geriatr. Soc. **24:**344, 1976b.)

(Cohn and Shock, 1949; Kohn, 1971). Because the intracellular water concentration does not change with age, it is interpreted that the reduction in TBF reflects loss of viable tissue with increasing age (Shock, 1961), and hence the intracellular fluid (ICF) is also reduced (Nöcker, 1965; Goldman, 1970). On replotting of the data of Shock, Yiengst, and Watkin (1953) and of Novak (1972) for TBF and cell mass (CM), respectively (Fig. 10-3), an apparent zero-order decrease was found for both. The reduction in TBF per year in males is 0.37% and in females 0.27%. CM decreases at approximately parallel slopes (Ritschel, 1976b).

Since drug receptors are usually found in the cell and because CM and TBF apparently decrease at a constant rate, it might be reasonable to assume that the Vd for drugs of low lipid solubility or low apparent lipid/water partition coefficient (i.e., for drugs that are distributed in the lean body mass) decreases proportionally with increasing age. I derived correction factors for the

Vd of drugs that are distributed in lean body mass (Ritschel, 1976b)

$$Vd[l/kg] \text{ GerM} = \frac{Vdnorm \times [54.25 - 0.199 \times (Age - 25)]}{54.25} \quad (1)$$

$$Vd[l/kg] \text{ GerF} = \frac{Vdnorm \times [49.25 - 0.130 \times (Age - 25)]}{49.25} \quad (2)$$

where Vd GerM and Vd GerF are the volumes of distribution in l/kg in geriatric males and females, respectively, and Vdnorm is the drug's volume of distribution in "normal" adults in l/kg ("normal" = 70 kg body weight, 25 years of age).

Since fat content increases with age, it can be assumed that the Vd might increase for drugs of high lipid solubility or high apparent lipid/water partition coefficient (i.e., for drugs that particularly accumulate in fat tissue).

TABLE 10-1 *Change of blood flow with age*

Organ	Approximate average rate of change (decrease) per year above 25 years of age (%)
Cardiac output	−0.75 to −1.01
Brain	−0.35 to −0.5
Heart	−0.5
Liver	−0.3 to −1.5
Kidney	−1.1 to −1.9
Tissue	−1.3

Based on data from Goldman, R.: Decline in organ function with aging. In Rossman, I., editor: Clinical geriatrics, Philadelphia, 1971, J.B. Lippincott Co.

Regional blood flow

Cardiac output decreases with age approximately 1% per year (Bender, 1965).

Regional blood flow decreases at different rates and is the most prominent for renal blood flow. Regional blood flow rate decreases are summarized in Table 10-1 (Goldman, 1971).

Reduced metabolism and delayed renal elimination may therefore be well explained by reduction in hepatic and renal blood flow, respectively.

On the other hand, degenerative changes in tissue may be responsible for altered response. The decrease with age in the amount of local anesthetic required for epidural block has been attributed to greater penetration into nerve fibers because of degeneration of the surrounding connective tissue and to delayed removal of the drug from the area because of thickening of the walls of the blood vessels (Bromage, 1962).

Binding to plasma albumin and red blood cells

Although there does not seem to be a large change with age in total plasma proteins (Morgan, Murai, and Gillum, 1955; Zerman and Franca, 1956; Eckerstrom, 1958), there is a significant reduction in plasma albumin (Chresrow et al., 1958). However, the γ-globulin concentration is increased (Woodford-Williams et al., 1964).

The effect of reduced plasma albumin depends on the extent to which the drug is normally bound. If the drug is not extensively bound, a reduction in plasma albumin will not be of clinical significance. If the drug is bound extensively, more than 80% or 90%, a decrease in the amount of albumin will make more free drug available for tissue distribution. Whether this may result in a significant change in the pharmacokinetics depends on the magnitude of the Vd. If the Vd is large, the tissue concentration will rise and the Vd will increase, but the plasma clearance will remain unchanged. If the Vd is small, the rate of drug clearance will increase. This means that the plasma clearance is unchanged but the amount of drug per milliliter of plasma available for clearance is increased.

A decrease in plasma albumin might cause an increase in the free, unbound concentration drugs highly bound to protein. Since only the nonbound moiety is available for drug-receptor interaction, the intensity of the effect of such drugs would increase in the aged, or it might result in toxic levels. If more free drug is available, the Vd might change. The data available on the extent of protein binding are inconclusive. For some drugs, such as meperidine, phenylbutazone, phenytoin, and warfarin, reduction in binding has been reported.

The question of protein binding becomes important in polypharmacy because highly bound acidic drugs might be displaced from their binding sites by other drugs, resulting in higher free drug levels, as has been observed for phenylbutazone, salicylate, and sulfadiazine in multiple-drug therapy in the elderly (Wallace, Whiting, and Runcie, 1976).

Also, the possibility of binding to structures other than plasma proteins should be considered.

At least in the case of meperidine, higher serum levels in the aged were explained by reduced binding to red blood cells (Chan et al., 1975).

The total clearance (Cl tot) from the body of a drug that is practically completely metabolized is proportional to the product of the ratio of free to total drug in plasma (F free) and the intrinsic metabolic clearance (Cl met intr) (Levy, 1976 and 1977):

$$\text{Cl tot} = \text{F free} \times \text{Cl met intr} \qquad (3)$$

Since liver blood flow (LBF) decreases with age, a reduction in Cl tot can be expected for drugs whose clearance is limited by LBF, as shown in Equation 4:

$$\text{Cl tot} = \frac{\text{LBF} \times \text{F free} \times \text{Cl met intr}}{\text{LBF} + \text{F free} \times \text{Cl met intr}} \qquad (4)$$

If LBF is significantly greater than F free × Cl met intr, a decrease in metabolic function or Cl met intr may not cause a decrease in Cl tot if F free compensates for the decreased Cl met intr because of reduced albumin concentration (i.e., increased F free). If F free changes more than Cl met intr, the Cl tot will increase with age. However, if F free × Cl met intr is significantly greater than LBF, the Cl tot will decrease because of a decreased liver perfusion rate (Levy, 1977).

METABOLISM

Metabolism is the sum of all chemical reactions in biotransformation of foreign compounds to more polar, water-soluble, ionized structures that can be eliminated more easily. Although there are definite structural changes in the liver—its size and liver blood flow decrease with age—there seems to be no significant change in liver function (Cohen, Gitman, and Lipschutz, 1960; Kattwinkel et al., 1973). No age-related difference in the rate of clearing of sulfobromophthalein and bilirubin was found (Calloway and Merrill, 1965).

Most of the drugs studied regarding me-tabolism in the elderly are oxidized by the hepatic metabolizing system. For some drugs an increase in half-life has been observed, but not for all drugs. Even if metabolism is decreased, it does not necessarily mean that the Cl tot is changed because the Vd may also change.

In general, no conclusive pattern can be established at this time. Each drug has to be studied for a possible change in the rate of metabolism.

In evaluating blood level and urinary excretion data for the influence of age on metabolism, it is essential to consider the clearance, Cl tot, which is the product of the Vd during the β-phase (Vdβ) and the terminal disposition rate constant (β):

$$\text{Cl tot} = \text{Vd}\beta \times \beta \qquad (5)$$

The Cl tot can be obtained from IV data according to Equation 6

$$\text{Cl tot} = \frac{\text{D IV}}{\text{AUC}(\text{o} \to \infty)} \qquad (6)$$

where AUC(o → ∞) is the total area under the blood level–time curve.

Most drugs are cleared from the body by more than one pathway. If besides renal clearance (Cl r), metabolic clearance (Cl m) is also involved, the Cl tot is a composite of the different clearances:

$$\text{Cl tot} = \text{Cl r} + \text{Cl m} \qquad (7)$$

Each metabolite has its own clearance; hence Equation 5 can be modified with as many Cl m terms as there are metabolites. The fraction of unchanged drug eliminated through the kidneys (Fe) is given in Equation 8

$$\text{Fe} = \frac{\text{Cl r}}{\text{Cl tot}} \qquad (8)$$

and the fraction of drug metabolized (Fm) is thus:

$$\text{Fm} = \frac{\text{Cl m}}{\text{Cl tot}} \qquad (9)$$

Since renal function is decreased in the elderly, the fraction of unchanged drug excreted in the urine will decrease, and the fraction of drug metabolized will increase. One might erroneously conclude that the activity of the drug biotransformation pathways is higher in the aged (Levy, 1977). It is therefore necessary to determine all the clearances involved.

ELIMINATION

Elimination is described as the loss of unchanged drug from the body by excretion through the kidneys, bile, lungs, saliva, sweat, or skin and by metabolism. The elimination of drugs through bile, the lungs, saliva, and skin is of minor importance. The main route is the excretion of drugs through the kidneys.

The overall elimination rate constant (ke) of a drug is composed of the rate constants for the loss of unchanged drug into urine (ku), for the loss of drug by extrarenal excretion through bile, saliva, the lungs, and sweat (ker), and for the loss of drug because of metabolism (km)

$$ke = ku + ker + km \qquad (10)$$

whereby ku comprises the rate constant for excretion by glomerular filtration and active tubular secretion.

The fraction of unchanged drug eliminated into urine (Fe) is given in Equation 11

$$Fe = \frac{Ae\,^{(\infty)}}{F \times D} \qquad (11)$$

where Ae $^{(\infty)}$ is the total amount of unchanged drug excreted into urine, F is the fraction of drug absorbed, and D is the size of the dose administered.

The elimination rate constant for unchanged drug excreted into urine follows:

$$ku = Fe \times ke \qquad (12)$$

Substituting Equation 12 for Equation 10 and solving for ker + km, one obtains Equation 15:

$$ke = Fe \times ke + ker + km \qquad (13)$$

$$ker + km = ke - Fe \times ke \qquad (14)$$

$$ker + km = ke \times (1 - Fe) \qquad (15)$$

Since the extrarenal nonmetabolic route of elimination is negligible for most drugs, the ku will depend, for those drugs that are primarily excreted through the kidneys (drugs with relatively large Fe), on the glomerular filtration rate (GFR) and the capacity for active tubular secretion or transport maximum (Tm). It is evident that elderly clients have a reduced renal function even without kidney disease (Shock, 1958; Heider and Brest, 1963; Friedman et al., 1972).

The linear regression equations for inulin clearance, creatinine clearance (Cl cr), and transport maximum in different groups of subjects in relation to age are listed in Table 10-2.

The average decrease in GFR and Tm is 0.66% and 0.62% per year, respectively (Ritschel, 1976b). These data, and the fact that the average inulin clearance per unit of Tm remains constant between the ages of 20 and 90 years, support the hypothesis that a nephron loses its function as a unit (Shock, 1958; Bricker, Morrin, and Kine, 1960). This means that GFR and Tm decrease parallel with increasing age. Hence the ku, as measured by Cl cr, is valid for both functions. Correction for the change in Cl cr with increasing age should therefore be applicable for all drugs excreted through the kidneys.

The rate of elimination of unchanged drug into the urine in the aged (ku Ger) can therefore be expressed by Equation 16

$$ku\ Ger = ku \times \frac{Cl\ cr\ Ger}{Cl\ cr\ norm} \qquad (16)$$

where Cl cr Ger is the creatinine clearance in the aged in ml/min/1.73 m², and Cl cr norm is the creatinine clearance in normal young adults aged 25 years in ml/min/1.73 m². The overall elimination rate constant of unchanged drug into urine in the aged (ke Ger) can be expressed by Equation 17:

$$ke\ Ger = ku\ Ger + ker + km \qquad (17)$$

By substituting Equation 16 for Equation 17, substituting the expression ker + km in Equation 17 for Equation 15, and substituting ku in

Equation 16 by Equation 12, Equation 18 is obtained, which can be rewritten as Equation 19:

$$ke\ Ger = \tag{18}$$

$$Fe \times ke \times \frac{Cl\ cr\ Ger}{Cl\ cr\ norm} + ke \times (1 - Fe)$$

$$ke\ Ger = ke \times \left\{ \left[\left(\frac{Cl\ cr\ Ger}{Cl\ cr\ norm} - 1 \right) \times Fe \right] + 1 \right\} \tag{19}$$

Correction factors have been derived for the overall elimination rate constant in elderly males (ke GerM) and elderly females (ke GerF) (Ritschel, 1976b), as given in Equations 20 and 21:

$$ke\ GerM = \tag{20}$$

$$ke \times \left\{ \left[\left(\frac{120.7 - 0.988 \times (Age - 25)}{120.7} - 1 \right) \times Fe \right] + 1 \right\}$$

$$ke\ GerF = \tag{21}$$

$$ke \times \left\{ \left[\left(\frac{105.9 - 0.988 \times (Age - 25)}{105.9} - 1 \right) \times Fe \right] + 1 \right\}$$

As seen in Equations 20 and 21, the overall elimination rate constant will decrease or the biologic half-life will increase with increasing age and greater Fe.

In medical practice the Cl cr is often obtained by conversion from serum creatinine values,

since there is a log-log linear relationship between the two. In the elderly, however, the decrease in Cl cr is not necessarily accompanied by an increase in serum creatinine because of a decrease in muscle mass, the primary source of serum creatinine. The GFR in the elderly must fall much more before the serum creatinine concentration will change. Siersbaek-Nielsen et al. (1971) constructed a nomogram for determination of Cl cr from serum creatinine values, corrected for age and sex, as shown in Fig. 10-4.

However, it must be pointed out that this nomogram can be used only in stabilized kidney function and not in changing kidney function because an altered GFR will be reflected in corresponding serum creatinine values only after some time (1 to 4 days).

It can be assumed that the elimination process is the most important one within the LADME system in relation to age, since (1) many drugs are eliminated through the kidneys, (2) a significant fraction (large Fe) of many drugs is renally eliminated, and (3) there is well-documented evidence of a decrease in renal function with increasing age.

Table 10-3 summarizes the physiologic and

TABLE 10-2 **Regression equations for inulin and creatinine clearance and transport maximum**

Linear regression equation	Decrease in renal function by GFR or Tm (% per year)		References
Cl inulin = 153.2 − 0.96 × age	0.63		Shock, 1958
Cl inulin = 157.0 − 1.16 × age	0.74		Watkin and Shock, 1955
Cl inulin = 150.9 − 0.904 × age	0.60	$\bar{x} = 0.66$ ± 0.08 SD	Miller, McDonald, and Shock, 1952
Cl inulin = 150.3 − 0.892 × age	0.59		Dost, 1968
Cl cr = 135.8 − 1.027 × age	0.75		Siersbaek-Nielsen et al., 1971
Tm PAH = 120.6 − 0.865 × age	0.72		Watkin and Shock, 1955
Tm Diodrast = 66.7 − 0.40 × age	0.60	$\bar{x} = 0.62$ ± 0.09 SD	Shock, 1958
Tm Diodrast = 64.78 − 0.359 × age	0.55		Dost, 1968

TABLE 10-3 **Physiologic and pathologic changes and their pharmacokinetic and therapeutic consequences in the geriatric client**

Parameter	Physiologic or pathologic change	Organ consequences	Pharmacokinetic consequences	Therapeutic consequences
Body weight	Generally reduced, including vital organs	Loss of fluid; reduction in heart, kidney, muscle tissue; atrophic tissue	Normal adult dose results in higher blood levels and higher drug concentration/receptor ratio	Overdosing; increased side effects and toxic effects
GI tract	Reduced secretion; reduced GI motility	Higher gastric pH; longer stomach emptying rate; less mixing of GI tract contents	Altered dissolution rate of tablets and capsules; delayed transition to small intestine; prolonged absorption rate	Longer time for onset of effect; lower intensity of effect; prolonged duration of effect
Body fluid	TBF and ICF reduced	Hypokalemia and hypernatremia	Reduced Vd; increased blood levels	Overdosing; increased side effects and toxic effects; dehydration
Heart and blood flow	Reduced cardiac output; reduced vascular elasticity and permeability; reduced blood flow	Possible venous congestion and arterial hypovolemia	Slower absorption rate from GI tract, muscle, skin, and rectum; delayed distribution; reduced Vd; increased blood levels	Longer time for onset; overdosing; increased side effects and toxic effects; hypoxia
Body composition	Reduced lean body mass; increased adipose tissue	Organ function changed	Decrease in Vd in general storage of drugs with high lipid solubility in fat depots and slower elimination	Overdosing; increased side effects; reduced response for drugs of high lipid solubility; hangover phenomenon; delayed onset followed by accumulation and overdosing in multiple dosing
Kidneys	Reduced renal blood flow; reduced glomerular filtration and active secretion	Lower Cl cr; reduced renal function	Increase in biologic half-life of drugs eliminated through kidneys	Overdosing; longer duration of effect; increased side effects and toxic effects
Plasma proteins	Reduction in albumin	Hypoalbuminemia	Saturation of protein binding and increased concentration of free drug; shorter half-life if highly bound	Increased intensity of effect; increased side effects and toxic effects; overdosing
Homeostasis	Abnormal lability	Restricted range of regulatory functions	Possible change in Vd	Paradoxic drug reactions

From Ritschel, W.A.: Sci. Pharm. **45**:304, 1977.

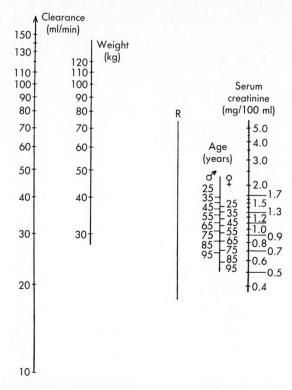

FIG. 10-4

Nomogram for rapid determination of creatinine clearance from serum creatinine data dependent on age, sex, and weight. Using a ruler, join weight to age (based on appropriate sex). Keeping the ruler at crossing point of line marked *R*, move right-hand side of ruler to the appropriate serum creatinine value. Read the client's clearance from the left-hand side of the nomogram. (From Siersbaek-Nielsen, K., et al.: Lancet **1**:1113, 1971.)

pathologic changes in the aged and the resulting pharmacokinetic and therapeutic consequences (Ritschel, 1977).

DOSAGE REGIMEN IN THE AGED

With the exception of renally excreted drugs, there is at the present time not enough information available to make generalized recommendations for determination of dose and dosage regimens applicable to all drugs for the elderly. Even the observed changes in the Vd for some drugs on single dosing do not permit conclusions to be made for clinical significance on multiple dosing. Apparent changes in metabolism caused by some drugs do not permit drawing overall conclusions until such changes are evaluated in the context of clearance and Vd. The pharmacokinetic approach presented in this section may therefore serve as a guideline only for the initial design of dosage regimens. Monitoring of blood levels and clinical response is necessary, and corrections or adjustments will have to be made accordingly.

Steady state concentration

The steady state concentration in blood, plasma, or serum (Css) is obtained when the drug input and output to and from the body are equal. The steady state or plateau concentration can be achieved by IV infusion or by intermittent IV or extravascular administration of constant doses (D) at constant dosing intervals (τ). The Css is a function of Cl tot.

In IV infusion the average steady state concentration (Css av) can be expressed by Equation 22

$$Css\ av = \frac{RO}{Cl\ tot} \qquad (22)$$

where RO is the constant infusion rate.

On extravascular administration the Css av can be expressed by Equation 23

$$Css\ av = \frac{D \times F/\tau}{Cl\ tot} \qquad (23)$$

where F is the fraction of drug absorbed. Because

$$\frac{D \times F}{Cl\ tot} = AUC(o \to \infty) \qquad (24)$$

Equation 23 can be rewritten:

$$Css\ av = \frac{AUC\ (\tau n \to \tau n + 1)}{\tau} \qquad (25)$$

On extravascular administration, the Css is a hypothetical average concentration (Css av) with fluctuations between a maximum and minimum concentration, Css max and Css min, respectively. Using identical dose sizes, AUC($o \to \infty$) on a single dose is equal to the AUC during any dosing interval at steady state AUC($\tau n \to \tau n + 1$) in the absence of dose-dependent kinetics.

To calculate the dosing rate, that is, RO for IV infusion, or D/τ for extravascular administration, the Cl tot must be known. Unfortunately,

in most studies on the elderly only $T_{\frac{1}{2}}$ has been determined. To assume an unchanged Vd might be erroneous. For example, the $T_{\frac{1}{2}}$ of diazepam increases from 20 to 90 hours from age 20 to age 80 years (Klotz et al., 1975). But the Vd increases also, and, consequently, the Cl tot seems to be independent of age. Hence the dosing rate remains unchanged with increasing age. Yet there is an important clinical aspect associated with it: the time to reach Css is a function of $T_{\frac{1}{2}}$ and is approximately 4.5 $\times$ $T_{\frac{1}{2}}$. Therefore it takes about 405 hours for 80-year-old clients to reach steady state versus 90 hours for 20-year-old clients. Additionally, $T_{\frac{1}{2}}$ also affects the fluctuations between Css max and Css min. The longer the $T_{\frac{1}{2}}$, the smaller the fluctuations during the dosing interval.

Dose size determination

For the selection of the appropriate dosage regimen calculation according to pharmacokinetic principles, drugs can be classified into two groups (Ritschel, 1972):

1. Minimum inhibitory concentration (MIC) pattern
2. Log dose-response pattern

The MIC pattern is indicated for bacteriostatic antibiotics, sulfonamides, and other antimicrobial agents for which it is essential to reach and maintain a definite drug concentration in blood, serum, or plasma above an MIC throughout the entire dosing interval. The log dose-response pattern is applicable for all other drugs (e.g., analgesics, antidysrhythmics, anticoagulants, antidiabetics, tranquilizers) for which it is essential to reach a definite Css with fluctuations of the maximum and minimum concentration, Css max and Css min, respectively, throughout the dosing interval that are below the toxic concentration and above the minimum effective concentration. For Css, a drug concentration is selected that is approximately the mean or less of the therapeutic range. The pattern is shown in Fig. 10-5 (Ritschel, 1976b).

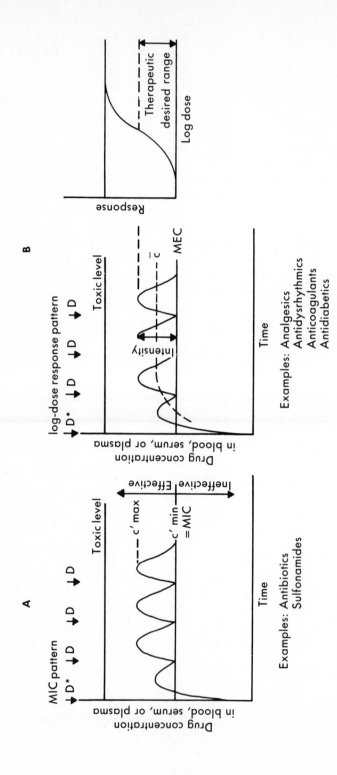

Schematic diagram for pharmacokinetic classification with respect to dosage regimen calculation for drugs following the MIC pattern, **A**, or the log dose-response pattern, **B**. D^*, loading dose; D, maintenance dose; *MIC*, minimum inhibitory concentration; *MEC*, minimum effective concentration; c'_{max}, maximum blood level concentration at steady state; c'_{min}, minimum blood level concentration at steady state; $\bar{c}$, average steady state blood level concentration. (From Ritschel, W.A.: J. Am. Geriatr. Soc. **24**:344, 1976b.)

I derived equations for the determination of the loading dose size in geriatric males (DL GerM) and geriatric females (DL GerF) and the corresponding maintenance doses for males (DM GerM) and females (DM GerF) according to the MIC pattern and log dose-response pattern, as given in Equations 26 through 31 (Ritschel, 1976b).

$$DL\ GerM = \tag{26}$$

$$\frac{D\ GerM}{1 - \exp\left(-ke \times \left\{\left\{\left[\dfrac{120.7 - 0.988 \times (Age - 25)}{120.7} - 1\right] \times Fe\right\} + 1\right\} \times \tau\right)}$$

$$DL\ GerF = \tag{27}$$

$$\frac{D\ GerF}{1 - \exp\left(-ke \times \left\{\left\{\left[\dfrac{105.9 - 0.988 \times (Age - 25)}{105.9} - 1\right] \times Fe\right\} + 1\right\} \times \tau\right)}$$

These equations are based on the Css min (Ritschel, 1974, 1975, and 1976a) and Css av (Wagner, 1967) equations using the correction factors for Vd (Equations 1 and 2) and for elimination (Equations 20 and 21). Equations 26 through 31 should be applicable for drugs of relatively low lipid solubility or low partition coefficient that are exclusively or predominantly cleared in unchanged form through the kidneys, having an Fe value of greater than 0.5 (Ritschel and Eldon, 1979).

PHARMACOKINETIC PARAMETERS OF DRUGS ALTERED IN THE AGED

For a respectable number of drugs, changes in pharmacokinetic parameters have been found. The changes are related to altered renal function, loss in liver weight per body weight, change in body composition, and reduced protein synthesis.

In general, an increase in the biologic half-life is observed, as seen in Fig. 10-6, *A* to *D* (Ritschel, 1978b). However, an increase in T$_{\frac{1}{2}}$

does not necessarily warrant change in dosage regimen. In some cases the Vd increases too, resulting in unchanged clearance.

In the past few years many drugs have been studied in the aged. Most of the investigations were performed with single dose administration. Sometimes literature values have been used for young adults to compare the pharmacokinetic data between the two age groups. This is problematic because different analytic methodologies may have been used; thus the results must be viewed with caution.

There is definitely no arbitrary age at which a person automatically joins the elderly age group. It is not the calendar age but the biologic age that counts. And there is no abrupt change from the young adult to the old age group. Rather there is a gradient from age 20 or 25 years with increasing age. It is only between the fifth and seventh decade of life that body functions are sufficiently reduced to make changes in drug disposition apparent.

The drugs that are discussed in the remainder of the chapter have been studied regarding possible differences in disposition between young and elderly subjects.

Acenocoumarol

In a study of the anticoagulant acenocoumarol higher plasma concentrations of the drug were found in clients older than 70 years for any given prothrombin level than in clients younger than 51 years (Hirtz et al., 1979). It is interesting to note that higher acenocoumarol levels are required in the elderly to produce prothrombin levels comparable to those in younger subjects.

Acetaminophen

The time to reach peak plasma levels did not differ between a group of young subjects aged 22 to 27 and a group aged 51 to 68 years (Triggs et al., 1975). However, the T$_{\frac{1}{2}}$ was statistically different between the two groups, with values of

Dose for males (maintenance dose): DM GerM:

$$DM\ GerM = \frac{\left\{Vd \times \left[\dfrac{54.25 - 0.199 \times (Age - 25)}{54.25}\right] \times BW\right\} \times MIC \times \left(1 - \exp\left(-ke \times \left\{\left[\left[\dfrac{120.7 - 0.988 \times (Age - 25)}{120.7}\right] - 1\right] \times Fe\right\} + 1\right\} \times \tau\right)\right)}{\left(\exp\left(-ke \times \left\{\left[\left[\dfrac{120.7 - 0.988 \times (Age - 25)}{120.7}\right] - 1\right] \times Fe\right\} + 1\right\} \times \tau\right) \times F \times 1000}$$
(28)

Dose for females (maintenance dose); DM GerF:

$$DM\ GerF = \frac{\left\{Vd \times \left[\dfrac{49.25 - 0.130 \times (Age - 25)}{49.25}\right] \times BW\right\} \times MIC \times \left(1 - \exp\left(-ke \times \left\{\left[\left[\dfrac{105.9 - 0.988 \times (Age - 25)}{105.9}\right] - 1\right] \times Fe\right\} + 1\right\} \times \tau\right)\right)}{\left(\exp\left(-ke \times \left\{\left[\left[\dfrac{105.9 - 0.988 \times (Age - 25)}{105.9}\right] - 1\right] \times Fe\right\} + 1\right\} \times \tau\right) \times F \times 1000}$$
(29)

Dose for males (maintenance dose); DM GerM:

$$DM\ GerM = \frac{Css\ av \times \left\{Vd \times \left[\dfrac{54.25 - 0.199 \times (Age - 25)}{54.25}\right] \times BW \times \tau\right\}}{1.44 \times T_{1/2} \times Fe \times \left[\dfrac{120.7 - 0.988 \times (Age - 25)}{120.7} - 1\right] + 1 \times F \times 1000}$$
(30)

Dose for females (maintenance dose); DM GerF:

$$DM\ GerF = \frac{Css\ av \times \left\{Vd \times \left[\dfrac{49.25 - 0.130 \times (Age - 25)}{49.25}\right] \times BW \times \tau\right\}}{1.44 \times T_{1/2} \times Fe \times \left[\dfrac{105.9 - 0.988 \times (Age - 25)}{105.9} - 1\right] + 1 \times F \times 1000}$$
(31)

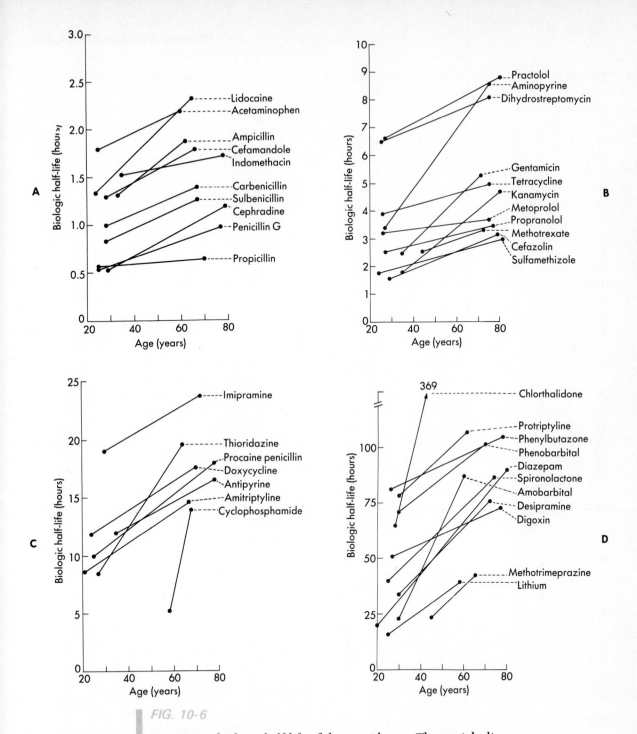

FIG. 10-6

Increase in biologic half-life of drugs with age. The straight lines between the half-lives of drugs in the young and elderly do not necessarily imply linear increase with age or is extrapolation permitted beyond the age range given. **A,** Half-life for drugs ranges from 0.5 to 3 hours. **B,** Half-life for drugs ranges from 1 to 10 hours. **C,** Half-life for drugs ranges from 5 to 25 hours. **D,** Half-life for drugs ranges from 20 to 370 hours.

1.8 and 2.17 hours, respectively. Acetaminophen is nearly completely metabolized. A reduced metabolic capacity may be responsible. No difference in Vd was found (1.03 versus 1.05 l/kg). The Cl tot was reduced from 477 to 379 ml/min.

Other studies showed a rise in acetaminophen $T_{\frac{1}{2}}$ from 1.75 hours, measured in 28 persons between the ages of 20 and 40 years, to 2.17 hours in a group of 28 persons over 65 years of age. The Cl tot of the drug also changed, dropping from 0.340 l/kg/hr to 0.254 l/kg/hr in the same groups, respectively, but no change was found in the drug's Vd. The sex of the aged person was not found to be a factor (Briant et al., 1976).

Acetaminophen plasma levels were found to be elevated by 36% 6 hours after dosing, and the $T_{\frac{1}{2}}$ increased by 19% (Creasey, 1979).

In a study of young subjects aged 24 years and elderly subjects aged 76 years acetaminophen was administered intravenously and orally according to a crossover design. The Vd of the central compartment was significantly reduced as a function of age from 0.62 l/kg to 0.48 l/kg. Also, the Cl tot decreased significantly from 363.5 ml/min to 240.8 ml/min. The extent of bioavailability was the same for both groups: 0.98% in the young and 0.95% in the elderly (Fulton, Rawlins, and James, 1979). The reduced Cl tot indicates impairment of conjugation with age.

Acetanilid

Although a decline in microsomal oxidation of acetanilid has been seen with age (Smithard and Langman, 1977), which would tend to lengthen the drug's half-life, other studies have shown no statistical differences between the half-lives of the drug in young and old persons (Playfer et al., 1978).

Alprenolol

In 1975 the prescribed daily dose for this drug ranged from 462 mg/day in the 15- to 59-year age group to 393 mg/day in the 80-year-old

and older age group (Boethius and Sjoquist, 1978).

Aminopyrine

Aminopyrine is approximately 90% metabolized (Brodie and Axelrod, 1950). The $T_{\frac{1}{2}}$ increases with age from 3.4 hours at age 25 to 30 years to 8.5 hours at age 65 to 85 years (Jori, DiSalle, and Quadri, 1972). Practically the same change in $T_{\frac{1}{2}}$ was found in a later study (Carulli et al., 1977).

Amitriptyline

In young clients older than 21 years the mean steady state plasma level of amitriptyline was 81.7 ng/ml and increased in clients aged 65 to 68 to 138.7 ng/ml, whereas the steady state plasma levels of the metabolite nortriptyline remained unchanged with 122.8 ng/ml (Nies et al., 1977). Assuming an F of 0.65 and an unchanged Vd during the β-phase, Vdβ, of 8.84 ml/gm, I calculated an increase in $T_{\frac{1}{2}}$ from 8.6 hours to 14.6 hours according to the steady state concentrations, applying the Css av equation. Doses given in 1975 ranged from a mean of 70 mg/day for 15- to 59-year-old subjects to a mean dose of 45 mg/day in persons over the age of 70 (Boethius and Sjoquist, 1978).

Amobarbital

After single dosing amobarbital blood levels were considerably higher in elderly subjects than in younger subjects (Irvine et al., 1974). The amount of the metabolite 3-hydroxyamylobarbitone excreted in the urine in 24 hours decreased from 14.2% for the group aged 20 to 40 years to 4.3% in clients above 65 years, with an average increase in the plasma drug level of 30%. The authors assume an age-related decrease in metabolism because more of the subjects had significantly reduced Cl cr values. Under the assumption that the Vd does not change for amobarbital, hence the distribution rate constants remain unchanged and loss of drug occurs from the central compartment only, data were analyzed with the analog computer and an increase in $T_{\frac{1}{2}}$ was found from 22.8 hours in subjects aged 20 to 40 years to 86.6 hours in elderly subjects older than 65 years (Ritschel, 1978a).

Ampicillin

In one study the $T_{\frac{1}{2}}$ of ampicillin in young healthy subjects aged 33 years was 1.31 hours, with a Vd coefficient of 0.55 ml/gm (Jusco and Lewis, 1973), and increased to $T_{\frac{1}{2}}$ of 1.88 hours in geriatric cirrhotic clients aged 62 years, with a Vd of 0.43 ml/gm. The fraction of drug eliminated through the kidneys decreased from 0.92 to 0.65 (Jusco and Lewis, 1973). In another study the $T_{\frac{1}{2}}$ increased from 1 hour in young subjects (21 to 30 years) to 1.2 hours in older clients (60 to 76 years) (Richey and Bender, 1977). In geriatric clients with cirrhosis the $T_{\frac{1}{2}}$ increased from 1.31 to 1.9 hours. A dramatic increase was found in the volume of distribution at steady state (Vdss) and the volume of distribution of the central compartment (Vdc) from 19.5 to 59.1 l and 13.4 to 20.4 l, respectively. The Cl tot decreased from 342 to 280 ml/min (Lewis and Jusko, 1976).

Antipyrine

Antipyrine is not bound to plasma proteins but is evenly distributed in the TBF and is more or less completely metabolized.

The age-related effect on $T_{\frac{1}{2}}$ of antipyrine was studied by different investigators. An increase in $T_{\frac{1}{2}}$ from 12 hours to 17.4 hours was reported for two groups of subjects aged 20 to 50 years and 70 to 100 years, respectively. The Vd decreased from 40.6 l to 31.2 l and the clearance from 2.4 l/hr to 1.5 l/hr for these groups (O'Malley et al., 1971). Similar changes in $T_{\frac{1}{2}}$ were found in other studies from 12.7 to 14.8 hours, respectively, for

the groups from 18 to 39 and 60 to 92 years of age (Vestal et al., 1975) and from 12.5 to 16.8 hr for the groups aged 20 to 40 years and over 65 years (Liddell, Williams, and Briant, 1975). A significant increase in $T_{\frac{1}{2}}$ and decrease in Cl tot was found between young (20 to 29 years) and old (75 to 86 years) clients from 11.8 to 16.7 hours and 41.8 to 24.1 ml/min, respectively (Swift et al., 1978). It was found that the antipyrine clearance per unit of liver volume was reduced in the elderly. The decreased liver mass and decreased hepatic enzyme activity contribute to the impairment of drug oxidation (Swift et al., 1977).

In elderly clients with vitamin C (ascorbic acid) deficiency the antipyrine $T_{\frac{1}{2}}$ decreased, and the Cl tot increased after treatment with vitamin C (Smithard and Langman, 1978). In clients without deficiency vitamin C supplementation did not change $T_{\frac{1}{2}}$ and Cl tot. Longer biologic half-lives of antipyrine of 18.6 hours were observed in elderly clients with vitamin deficiencies of ascorbic acid, folic acid, vitamin A, and vitamin B, either singly or in combination (Smithard and Langman, 1977). Poor nutrition in the elderly may, at least in part, be responsible for the decline in microsomal enzyme function with age.

Aspirin

For aspirin, changes from young (20 to 40 years) to old (over 65 years) persons were an increase in peak plasma concentration (from 35 ± 3 $\mu g/ml$ to 40.5 ± 11.7 $\mu g/ml$), increases in time to peak plasma levels (from 48 ± 32 minutes to 69 ± 29.9 minutes), an increased AUC (from 136 ± 36.1 [$\mu g/ml$] × hr to 287 ± 141.67 [$\mu g/ml$] × hr, statistically significant), and a decrease in the absorption rate constant (from 13.8 ± 2.5 l/hr to 12.5 ± 6.2 l/hr). (All values are $\pm$ SD.) The Vd was practically unchanged, with 0.08 l/kg in the young and 0.11 l/kg in the elderly. The Cl tot decreased with age from 0.024 l/kg/hr to 0.017 l/kg/hr (Salem and Stevenson, 1977).

Carbenicillin

The $T_{\frac{1}{2}}$ of carbenicillin in young subjects aged 28 years was 1 hour, with a Vd of 0.215 ml/gm at a Cl cr of 95 ml/min and increased in normal geriatric subjects aged 67 to a $T_{\frac{1}{2}}$ of 1.4 hours, with a Vd of 0.272 ml/gm at a Cl cr of 73 ml/min (Hansen, Jacobsen, and Weis, 1975).

Carbenoxolone

With carbenoxolone the change for aldosterone displacement by the drug from plasma proteins was from 2.5% in persons under 40 (9% total free aldosterone), to 3.2% in persons over 65 years of age (13% total free aldosterone). In the same age groups, respectively, there was a change in Cl tot from 4.72 ml/kg/hr to 3.28 ml/kg/hr, a change in half-life from 16.3 hours to 22.9 hours, and no change in the Vd from 0.105 l/kg to 0.098 l/kg (Hayes, Sprackling, and Langman, 1977). Similar results were reported by the same authors in another publication (1975).

Cefamandole

The $T_{\frac{1}{2}}$ of cefamandole in young adults aged 28 years was found to be 1.3 hours (Meyers et al., 1976) and increased to 1.8 hours at age 66 (Mellin, Welling, and Madsen, 1977). The Vd for the two groups was 18.5 and 29.4 l, respectively. Hence, the Cl tot is practically unchanged with age with 10.49 and 11.09 l/hr, respectively. In spite of the increased $T_{\frac{1}{2}}$, dosage regimens should be unchanged with increasing age. Yet it will take longer (4.5 × $T_{\frac{1}{2}}$) to reach steady state.

Cefazolin

The $T_{\frac{1}{2}}$ of cefazolin increased from 1.56 hours in young subjects aged 24 to 33 years to 3.15 hours in those aged 70 to 88 years (Simon et al., 1976). The Cl tot decreased from 83 ml/min to 43 ml/min. I calculated the Vd, which is 11.7 l and 11.3 l respectively, for the two groups. The authors found no differences in the protein concentration of skin blisters; hence the differences in cefazolin concentration in the skin blisters between the two groups are explained by decreased elimination rate and decreased distribution rate constants. Dosage regimens for cefazolin should therefore be adjusted in the aged.

Cephradine

The $T_{\frac{1}{2}}$ of cephradine increases from 0.53 hours in young subjects aged 24 to 33 years to 1.2 hours in the elderly aged 70 to 88 years (Simon et al., 1976). The Cl tot decreases from 378 ml/min to 152 ml/min with age. The Vd calculated from these data seems not to differ significantly with 15.7 and 17 l respectively. Based on the difference in Cl tot, the dosage regimen should be adjusted in the elderly.

Chlorazepate

Chlorazepate undergoes acid-dependent hydrolysis and decarboxylation in the stomach, yielding desmethyldiazepam, which reaches the systemic circulation and exerts its antianxiety activity. Peak plasma concentrations of desmethyldiazepam of 371 ng/ml were reached within 1.1 hours in young (20 to 26 years) subjects, whereas peak concentrations of 185 ng/ml were reached within 2.3 hours in the elderly (50 to 75 years) (Ochs et al., 1979).

Chlordiazepoxide

On IV administration of chlordiazepoxide an increase in $T_{\frac{1}{2}}$ was observed from about 6 hours at age 20 years to about 36 hours at age 80 years. This increase in $T_{\frac{1}{2}}$ was associated with a significant decrease in Cl tot from about 30 to 8 ml/min. The Vdss increased from about 0.25 to 0.42 l/kg, whereas the Vdc was practically unchanged (Roberts, Wilkinson, and Schenker, 1978). Therefore the increase in $T_{\frac{1}{2}}$ with aging can be attributed to both an altered distribution, similar to that observed with diazepam, and a reduced hepatic metabolism capacity.

In a study of oral administration of chlordiazepoxide an increase in absorption half-life from 5.5 minutes in young (21 to 30 years) subjects to 19.6 minutes in elderly (63 to 74 years) subjects was found. The $T_{\frac{1}{2}}$ increased from 10.1 to 18.2 hours in these groups, and the Cl tot decreased from 43.3 to 26.6 ml/min (Shader et al., 1977). The findings were not influenced by smoking habits or by concurrent use of other drugs. The reduced Cl tot indicates that dosing in the aged should be adjusted accordingly to prevent increased accumulation.

Chlormethiazole

The $T_{\frac{1}{2}}$ of chlormethiazole increased from 4.1 hours in young subjects (25 to 28 years) to 8.5 hours in older subjects (70 to 91 years) and showed both a significant increase in Vd from 7.9 to 11.2 l/kg and a decrease in Cl tot from 23 to 16.1 ml/min/kg (Moore et al., 1975; Triggs, 1979). On oral administration an increase in F was observed from 8.6% in the young to 89.7% in the elderly.

Chlorthalidone

In a study by Collste et al. (1976) on chlorthalidone in six healthy volunteers aged 25 to 31 a $T_{\frac{1}{2}}$ of 64.8 hours was found with a Vd of 7.6 ml/gm ranging from 3.2 to 12.9 ml/gm, with a much larger variation of Vd than $T_{\frac{1}{2}}$. They also studied the pharmacokinetics in clients, including two elderly subjects aged 72 and 75 years, respectively. The elderly clients had much higher Css av of 1138 and 799 ng/ml, respectively, versus Css av varying from 211 to 700 ng/ml for the group aged 21 to 62 years of age. All clients had serum creatinine concentrations between 0.7 and 1.4 mg/100 ml. Since

$$\text{Css av} = \frac{\text{AUC } (\tau n \rightarrow \tau n + 1)}{\tau} \qquad (32)$$

AUC $(\tau n \rightarrow \tau n + 1)$ can be calculated from the Css av given. From the fraction of drug absorbed (F = 0.5), and because

$$\text{Cl tot} = \frac{D \times F}{\text{AUC } (\tau n \rightarrow \tau n + 1)} \qquad (33)$$

and under the assumption that $Vd\beta$ remains unchanged, I calculated β according to Equation 34:

$$\beta = \frac{\text{Cl tot}}{Vd\beta} \qquad (34)$$

$T_{\frac{1}{2}}$ in the two elderly subjects were 471.6 and 267.7 hours, averaging 369.7 hours. However, the $Vd\beta$ fluctuated considerably, even in the younger group. This might be explained by the binding to plasma proteins and erythrocytes. The drug is completely eliminated through the kidneys in unchanged form. The higher Css av levels are probably influenced by both a change in $T_{\frac{1}{2}}$ and $Vd\beta$. A more reliable interpretation is therefore in terms of Cl tot, which decreased from 92.8 ± 40.5 ml/min at age 25 to 31 years to 18.5 ± 4.6 ml/min at age 72 to 75 years.

Cimetidine

In a study of blood level–time profiles on oral administration of cimetidine a significant relationship was found between the area under the curve and age. The age-related increased bioavailability was probably a result of decreased Cl tot, which resulted from a decreased Vd and increased $T_{\frac{1}{2}}$ with age. The $T_{\frac{1}{2}}$ was prolonged from 2.1 hours in young (22 to 57 years) subjects to 2.6 hours in older (66 to 84 years) subjects, whereas the Vd decreased for these groups from 1.6 to 1.37 l/kg (Redolfi, Borgogelli, and Lodola, 1979). The Cmax in the elderly was 1374 ng/ml versus 945 ng/ml in the younger volunteers. These authors suggest a reduction of the oral cimetidine dose by one third to one half.

In another study with orally administered cimetidine an increase was found in $T_{\frac{1}{2}}$ from 1.8 hours at age 30 years to 2.3 hours at age 65 years. At the same time the Vd at steady state decreased from about 80 l to 35 l, and the Cl tot decreased from about 600 ml/min to 100 ml/min (Somogyi, Rohner, and Gugler, 1980).

Cyclophosphamide

Cyclophosphamide is biotransformed in the liver to active alkylating metabolites that are predominately excreted through the kidneys (Graul et al., 1967). Although no conclusive studies are available, the decrease in renal function with increasing age probably affects cyclophosphamide kinetics. A $T_{\frac{1}{2}}$ of approximately 5.3 hours was found in clients aged 44 to 72 years, with a Vd of approximately 36 l (Mouridsen, Faber, and Skovsted, 1976). In middle-aged and elderly (57 to 79 years) clients with renal failure a $T_{\frac{1}{2}}$ of 14 hours and a Vd of 41 l for cyclophosphamide were found (Mouridsen and Jacobsen, 1975).

Desipramine

After chronic administration of imipramine (150 mg/day in younger clients and 50 to 150 mg/day in older clients) for 21 days, steady state blood levels of the metabolite desipramine were determined. The mean steady state desipramine levels were 21.2 ng/ml in the younger and 57.2 ng/ml in the older clients. The biologic half-life was determined from blood samples taken between 48 and 72 hours after discontinuation of dosing. The mean half-lives ($\pm$ SEM) were 34.2 $\pm$ 2.7 hours for young subjects and 75.8 $\pm$ 18.2 hours for elderly subjects (Nies et al., 1977).

Desmethyldiazepam

Desmethyldiazepam is the major metabolite of diazepam, which also possesses pharmacologic activity like the parent compound. During multiple-dose therapy with diazepam, steady state concentrations of diazepam and desmethyldiazepam are nearly equal. Two other benzodiazepines, chlorazepate and prazepam, are prodrugs and are biotransformed to the phar-

macologically active desmethyldiazepam. This compound, desmethyldiazepam, is a minor metabolite of several other benzodiazepines, such as chlordiazepoxide and medazepam.

On oral administration of 20 mg desmethyldiazepam to four young (29 to 34 years) and four elderly (65 to 85 years) volunteers the biologic half-lives were 51 $\pm$ 6.2 and 151 $\pm$ 60 hours, the Vdβ 0.64 $\pm$ 0.17 and 0.85 $\pm$ 0.14 l/kg, and the Cl tot 11.3 $\pm$ 3.1 and 4.3 $\pm$ 1.5 ml/min, respectively. The largely reduced clearance indicates that dosing should be reduced in treatment of elderly clients (Klotz and Müller-Seydlitz, 1979).

Diazepam

Diazepam is the most widely used benzodiazepine for treatment of anxiety and insomnia. Reports on the drug disposition of diazepam in the elderly are somewhat conflicting, which might be caused by different analytic methodology and the possibility of influencing factors other than age. Indeed, recent studies indicate that the Vd is more extensive in the elderly than in the young and in females regardless of age. The $T_{\frac{1}{2}}$ is significantly prolonged in the elderly but is not influenced by sex, whereas the Cl tot depends on sex. Age has less effect in females than in males (Greenblatt et al., 1979b). In this study with two age groups, 26 to 37 years and 61 to 84 years, the $T_{\frac{1}{2}}$ for males increased from 38.7 to 93.8 hours, the Vd increased from 1.16 to 1.7 l/kg, and the Cl tot decreased from 0.37 to 0.24 ml/min/kg. For the females the $T_{\frac{1}{2}}$ increased from 44 to 86.3 hours and the Vd from 1.69 to 2.97 l/kg, whereas the Cl tot decreased only slightly from 0.47 to 0.43 ml/min/kg.

The first report on the influence of age on the disposition of diazepam was published by Klotz et al. (1975). In this study the $T_{\frac{1}{2}}$ of diazepam increased linearly from 20 hours at age 20 years to 90 hours at age 80 years after both intravenous and oral administration. However, no significant change in Cl tot was found, being approximately

26 ml/min for both groups. This is explained by a significant age-dependent change in the Vd of the central compartment, Vdc (0.2 l/kg in the young subjects and 0.55 l/kg in the elderly subjects), and the Vd at steady state, Vdss (0.7 l/kg versus 1.7 l/kg), both corrected for body weight, whereby the change in Vdss seems to be a result of the change in Vdc. No significant change was found in the extent of protein binding (97.4%). In multiple dosing the Css av will therefore be unaffected with increasing age. However, it will take about 4.5 times longer in the elderly to achieve Css av.

Although pharmacokinetic data do not suggest the necessity of changing the diazepam dosage regimen, there seems to be a significant increase in CNS side effects from age 40 to 70 years (Boston Collaborative Surveillance Program, 1973). This might be explained by either (1) an increased drug concentration at the receptor site, which cannot be evaluated at present by the compartmental analysis of the data, (2) the increasing sensitivity of receptors with age, or (3) the decreasing number of receptors.

In another study on age- and gender-related differences in diazepam pharmacokinetics the $T_{\frac{1}{2}}$ increased from 24 hours in young (21 to 29 years) subjects to 35.8 hours in elderly (73 to 88 years) subjects. The Vd increased in these groups from 1.0 to 1.6 l/kg, whereas the Cl tot remained practically constant with 34.5 and 32.8 ml/min (Macleod et al., 1979). In females the values for $T_{\frac{1}{2}}$, Vd, and Cl tot in the young (21 to 30 years) subjects were 43.9 hours, 1.28 l/kg, and 20.7 ml/min, and those in the elderly (70 to 85 years) group were 56.6 hours, 1.9 l/kg, and 25.5 ml/min (Macleod et al., 1979). According to this study, age had no significant effects on Cl tot of diazepam, although in males diazepam showed a shorter half-life and higher Cl tot than in females. The extent of protein binding and plasma protein concentrations were not determined in this study. Because the elderly usually have lower serum albumin concentrations and because diazepam is highly protein bound

(97.5%), differences may be a result of binding changes.

In a study by Greenblatt et al. (1980) previous findings (Greenblatt et al., 1979b) were verified. Additionally, a decreased extent of protein binding was found in the elderly. Clearance of unbound diazepam was reduced in elderly as opposed to young individuals of the same sex but was generally greater in females than in males in both age groups. Smoking resulted in higher diazepam clearance, particularly in younger subjects.

It is important to note that age-related changes in diazepam clearance may not be recognizable if only total (free plus bound drug) diazepam blood levels are measured because reduction of protein binding with increasing age may mask differences in intrinsic clearance. The observed increased sensitivity to diazepam in the elderly may well be explained by a higher fraction of free diazepam.

Digoxin

Digoxin intoxication is higher in geriatric clients than in young adults (Feibush, 1959; Dall, 1965; Beller et al., 1971; Evered and Chapman, 1971; Ogilvie and Ruedy, 1972). However, it has been shown that the elderly have in fact essentially the same sensitivity to digoxin as younger clients but need a lower dose to obtain the desired serum concentration (Chamberlain et al., 1970). A considerable increase in the digoxin plasma concentration was noted when the GFR was reduced by at least 50%, and Falch (1973) concluded that age-related increased blood levels are a result of reduction in kidney function. An increased $T_{\frac{1}{2}}$ from 51 hours to 73 hours was found with increasing age from 27 to 77 years, and a significant reduction in renal clearance from 83 to 53 ml/min/1.73 m^2 was found for the same groups (Ewy et al., 1969). However, a decreased Vd may be responsible for cerebral side effects in the aged (Rietbrock and Abshagen, 1973).

Regarding absorption, there is no evidence so far that the absorption of orally administered digoxin is impaired in the elderly. Any influence of protein binding is unlikely to have any effect on digoxin disposition in the aged because the extent of protein binding is low (23%) and the Vd is large (6.8 1/kg). Also, reduced liver function should be of no clinical significance because the drug is primarily cleared through the kidneys (76%) (Ritschel, 1980).

The renal clearance of digoxin is assumed to be similar to that of creatinine (Bloom and Nelp, 1966). However, there is evidence that renal elimination of digoxin not only involves glomerular filtration but also active secretion (Marcus, 1972; Steiness, 1974) and tubular reabsorption (Doherty, Ferrell, and Towbin, 1969). Because renal function is reduced with increasing age, despite apparently normal serum creatinine values, extrarenal clearance (Cl er) also becomes important in the elderly. In young healthy individuals the Cl er accounts for approximately 30% of Cl tot (Sumner, Russell, and Whiting, 1976). If, for instance, Cl cr falls in the aged to 30 ml/min and Cl er is maintained at normal values, the Cl er will account for about 60% of Cl tot. The Cl er can be calculated from the F, D, Css av, and Cl cr (Whiting et al., 1978) as follows:

$$Cl\ er = (F \times D/Css\ av) - Cl\ cr \qquad (35)$$

A wide variation of Cl cr was found in 18 elderly clients (64 to 80 years), ranging from 5 to 67 ml/min. A significant relationship was found between Cl er and age. The influence of Cl er will have more influence on dosage the lower Cl cr becomes. This concept was recently used for development of a dosing nomogram for digoxin based on both Cl er and Cl cr (Whiting, Lawrence, and Sumner, 1979). This new approach may be advantageous, since it was reported that although serum digoxin levels obtained by routine pharmacokinetic calculations based on Cl cr provided statistically significant correlations with measured digoxin levels, the individual data were clinically not acceptable be-

cause of wide scatter (Dimant and Merrit, 1978; Simonson and Stennett, 1978).

In a recent study with IV and oral administration of digoxin to young (34 to 61 years) and elderly (72 to 91 years) subjects a faster rate of absorption was found in the younger subjects, but there was no statistically significant difference in the extent of absorption after oral administration (84.3% versus 76%) (Cusack et al., 1979). The $T_{\frac{1}{2}}$ for these groups showed an increase from 38.2 to 68.8 hours, and a trend in decrease of Vd from 5.3 to 4.1 l/kg (not significant). However, the decrease in Cl tot from 1.7 to 0.8 ml/min/kg was statistically significant (Cusack et al., 1979).

Dihydrostreptomycin

The $T_{\frac{1}{2}}$ of dihydrostreptomycin increases from 6.55 hours in young adults aged 18 to 33 years to 8.1 hours in elderly clients aged 63 to 87 years (Vartia and Leikola, 1960). Similar values of 5.2 and 8.4 hours were found for two age groups with mean ages of 27 and 75 years (Richey and Bender, 1977). The increase in $T_{\frac{1}{2}}$ is probably caused by a decrease in glomerular filtration in the elderly.

Doxycycline

The $T_{\frac{1}{2}}$ of doxycycline increased from 11.9 hours in young clients aged 20 to 28 years to 17.7 hours in a geriatric group aged 60 to 80 years. However, the differences were not statistically significant. The Vd was practically unchanged, with 0.73 and 0.70 ml/gm, respectively (Simon et al., 1975). The authors conclude that both distribution and disposition of doxycycline in geriatric clients are similar to those in younger adults.

Ethambutol

After oral administration of 25 ml/kg ethambutol to subjects with a mean age of 40 years, peak plasma concentrations of 7.9 ± 4.5 μg/ml were obtained (Braun, 1976), whereas in elderly subjects (60 to 78 years) the peak levels were significantly lower with 2.55 ± 1.9 $\mu g/ml$ (Omer, 1978). Unfortunately, Braun and Omer did not analyze the blood level–time profiles for pharmacokinetic parameters.

Ethotoin

For ethotoin nonlinear kinetics exist within the therapeutic range, probably because of saturation of hepatic metabolism. The $T_{\frac{1}{2}}$ below dose-dependent kinetics of 8 $\mu g/ml$ varies between 5 and 9 hours (Sjö et al., 1975). Since the therapeutic concentrations of 5 to 20 $\mu g/ml$ are in the range where saturation kinetics apply, monitoring seems to be necessary, particularly in the elderly.

Flurazepam

In a study of 2542 hospitalized patients receiving flurazepam, with a mean age of 54.5 years (40% were over 60 years of age), only 3.4% died while in the hospital, although unwanted side effects did increase with age: under 60 years old, 1.9%; over 80 years, 7.9%. This was speculated to be a result of an increased sensitivity of the CNS in older clients (Greenblatt, Allen, and Shader, 1977).

Gentamicin

The $T_{\frac{1}{2}}$ in a group of healthy young adults aged 35 years was found to be 2.5 hours, with a Cl tot of 82 ml/min (Dobbs and Mawer, 1976). In a group of elderly clients aged 71 years a $T_{\frac{1}{2}}$ of 5.3 hours was observed, with a Cl tot of 27.3 ml/min (Mosegard, Welling, and Madsen, 1975). Because the Vd for the central compartment was practically identical, 0.106 versus 0.090 ml/gm, respectively, the change in Cl tot is apparently associated with a decrease of the elimination rate constant (k13) from the central compartment, 0.68 versus 0.26 hr^{-1} for the two groups.

Heparin

For heparin, which has a $T_{\frac{1}{2}}$ for the anticoagulant activity of 1.5 hours in the adult (Estes, 1970), an increased incidence of bleeding was reported in clients above age 60 years, particularly in females (Jick et al., 1968; Vieweg et al., 1970).

Imipramine

Mean steady state plasma levels increased from 32.3 ng/ml in young clients above 27 years of age to 83.8 ng/ml in clients aged 65 to 78 years. At the same time the mean steady state plasma levels of the metabolite desipramine increased from 21.2 ng/ml to 52.2 ng/ml. The $T_{\frac{1}{2}}$ of imipramine increased for the same age groups from 19 hours to 23.8 hours, and the $T_{\frac{1}{2}}$ of the metabolite desipramine increased from 34.2 hours to 75.8 hours (Nies et al., 1977).

Indomethacin

The $T_{\frac{1}{2}}$ of indomethacin increases from 1.53 hours in the group aged 20 to 50 years to 1.73 hours in the group aged 71 to 83 years (Triggs and Nation, 1975; Crooks, O'Malley, and Stevenson, 1976). The rate and extent of absorption do not differ between young and elderly subjects (Traeger et al., 1973). Also, the rate and extent of absorption are not influenced by age (Crooks, O'Malley, and Stevenson, 1976). However, less free drug is eliminated in urine in the aged (30% versus 13% of the administered dose) (Triggs and Nation, 1975).

Iron

In a study on iron absorption in young (19 to 49 years) and elderly (65 to 83 years) subjects no significant differences in mucosal iron uptake (40.2% versus 47.4%) or iron retention (23% versus 31.5%) were found. Age apparently has no influence on iron absorption from the gastrointestinal tract. However, the red cell uptake decreased from 91.2% to 66.0% (Marx, 1979).

Kanamycin

In three age groups, 20 to 50 years, 50 to 70 years, and 70 to 90 years, an increase in $T_{\frac{1}{2}}$ from 1.8 hours to 2.48 hours to 4.7 hours, respectively, was found. The serum creatinine concentrations were normal—between 0.95 and 0.98 mg/100 ml; however, Cl cr decreased from 94 to 75 to 43 ml/min, respectively, for the three groups (Kristensen et al., 1974).

Levodopa

For levodopa only preliminary studies on two young subjects (22 and 26 years) and two elderly subjects (74 and 84 years) are available. The peak plasma concentrations after a 300 mg dose administered orally were 238 and 1007 ng/ml in the young subjects and 2030 and 7128 ng/ml in the elderly subjects after oral doses of 300 and 600 mg, respectively (Triggs, 1979). The AUC(o → ∞) was substantially greater for both doses in the elderly subjects.

Lidocaine

In a study on the pharmacokinetics of lidocaine in young and aged subjects aged 24 and 65 years a statistically significant increase in $T_{\frac{1}{2}}$ from 1.34 hours to 2.33 hours was found (Nation, Triggs, and Selig, 1977). Whereas the volume of the central compartment remained practically unchanged (0.33 versus 0.35 ml/gm), the $Vd\beta$ increased significantly from 0.895 ml/gm to 1.586 ml/gm with age. However, the Cl tot remained unchanged (543 ml/min versus 556 ml/min). Since Cl tot does not change with age, no adjustment of the dosage regimen seems to be necessary. However, it will take longer to achieve steady state because $T_{\frac{1}{2}}$ is prolonged.

Lithium

Symptoms of lithium toxicity at therapeutic serum levels have been reported in elderly clients, and a reduction of daily doses has been suggested (Van der Velder, 1971; Hewick et al.,

1977). The dose reduction to achieve therapeutic plasma levels is approximately 30% from age 20 to age 80 years (Hewick et al., 1977). The Cl tot decreases from 41.5 ml/min at age 25 years to 16.8 ml/min at age 58 years to 7.7 ml/min at age 63 years (Lehmann and Merten, 1974). Under the assumption of unchanged Vd, I calculated an increase in $T_{\frac{1}{2}}$ from 16 hours to 39.5 hours to 86 hours for the age increase from 25 to 58 to 63 years, respectively. However, since the drug is exclusively eliminated through the kidneys, the Vd is somewhat larger than TBF, and TBF decreases with increasing age, a decrease in Vd should thus also be expected.

A conflicting report stated that the concentration in the circulatory system needed for therapeutic effect was the same in younger adults and geriatric clients, but the incidence of toxic effects increased with age (Foster, Gershell, and Goldfarb, 1977). This increase in toxic effects was seen in four cases of toxicity out of 31 clients 60 to 79 years old but was found in only 2 out of 164 persons under 60 years of age (Roose et al., 1979).

Lorazepam

In a study on IV administration of lorazepam to a small number of subjects between 15 and 73 years no age-related changes in lorazepam disposition were found (Kraus et al., 1978). In a later study with 30 volunteers aged 19 to 84 years again no significant difference in $T_{\frac{1}{2}}$ was found between the young and the older groups (14.1 hours versus 15.9 hours). The Cl tot decreased from about 1 ml/min/kg to 0.8 ml/min/kg (Greenblatt et al., 1979a) and just reached statistical significance. There was no influence by gender on the disposition of lorazepam in either group.

Meperidine

Plasma levels of meperidine are more than twice as great in clients over 70 years of age than in younger ones (Chan et al., 1975). This is believed, at least in part, to be a result of a decrease in binding to erythrocytes, which is reduced from 50% in the young to 20% in the elderly (Mather et al., 1975). The plasma protein binding decreases from 75% in the young to 35% in the elderly. Elderly persons excrete more normeperidine than younger ones, which might be explained by the larger amount of free drug available at any time for metabolism (Chan et al., 1975).

Methotrexate

The information on pharmacokinetic parameters of methotrexate is still conflicting. However, since up to 90% of the drug is eliminated through the kidneys, age-dependent pharmacokinetics can be expected (Kristensen, Weismann, and Hutters, 1975). It was observed that the Vd of methotrexate decreased from 0.63 ml/gm in subjects aged 20 to 69 years at a creatinine clearance greater than 70 ml/min to 0.52 ml/gm in subjects older than 70 years at a creatinine clearance less than 65 ml/min. The $T_{\frac{1}{2}}$ of methotrexate increased from 2.55 hours in the group aged 20 to 69 to 3.33 hours in the group over 70 years of age. The Cl tot decreased in these groups from 182 to 99.7 ml/min. Hence the Cl tot is influenced by both $T_{\frac{1}{2}}$ and Vd.

Based on pharmacokinetic studies the following dosage regimens were recommended for treatment of recalcitrant psoriasis in the elderly, based on their creatinine clearance: doses of 50 μg/kg should be given at 12-hour intervals to clients having a Cl cr greater than 60 ml/min; at 16-hour intervals to those with a Cl cr between 40 and 60 ml/min; and clients with a Cl cr of 20 to 40 ml/min should receive the dose just mentioned at 24-hour intervals (Weismann, 1977). The age-dependent decrease in renal function that significantly alters methotrexate elimination has also led other authors to modified dosage regimen recommendations for this drug. Serum creatinine is inferior for monitoring the decrease of renal function in the elderly, compared with endogenous Cl cr. Whenever possible, en-

dogenous Cl cr should be determined. Dosage modification for methotrexate, which is eliminated by glomerular filtration and tubular secretion, has been proposed by Shinn et al. (1977) by reduction in dose size between 50% and 90%, dependent on Cl cr. Straus (1976) proposed a modification of methotrexate dosage according to renal function:

SERUM CREATININE (mg/100 ml)	METHOTREXATE DOSE (%)
<1.6	100
1.6 to 2.5	67
2.6 to 3.5	33
>3.5	0

Methotrimeprazine

From a study by Dahl, Strandjord, and Sigfusson (1977) a $T_{\frac{1}{2}}$ of 23.2 hours was calculated for a group aged 45 years and a $T_{\frac{1}{2}}$ of 42.5 hours for a group aged 65 years. Although the differences were not significant for the two groups of four subjects each, an age-dependent disposition was suggested. The Cl tot relative to the fraction of unchanged drug absorbed (Cl tot/F) decreased insignificantly from 3.3 to 3.2 l/min for the two groups. The Vd relative to the fraction absorbed (Vd/F) was not significantly different (102.5 versus 109.1 l) (Dahl, Strandjord, and Sigfusson, 1977). The difference was not statistically significant because of the large individual variations caused by differences in $T_{\frac{1}{2}}$, Vd, and F. Methotrimeprazine shows a first-pass effect (Dahl, Strandjord, and Sigfusson, 1977).

Metoprolol

For young adults aged 23 to 28 years a $T_{\frac{1}{2}}$ of 3.2 hours was reported (Regardh et al., 1974), and for elderly clients aged 61 to 88 years a $T_{\frac{1}{2}}$ of 3.7 hours was found (Lundberg and Steen, 1976). Like propranolol, metoprolol also undergoes extensive first-pass effect. In older subjects higher peak levels were observed, the peaks occurred later, and 24-hour blood levels were higher than the 12-hour levels of young subjects. From data presented the increase in $T_{\frac{1}{2}}$ can be roughly estimated to be from 3 hours at age 23 to 5.7 hours at age 67 (Kendall, Brown, and Yates, 1977). The mean Cmax after a single dose of 100 mg metoprolol was 110 ng/ml in the young subjects, compared to 150 ng/ml in the elderly. The time to peak concentration (tmax) increased from 2 hours in the young subjects to 4 hours in the elderly subjects.

Minocycline

In a study of IV minocycline in subjects between 34 and 78 years, with a varying decrease in renal function, no statistically significant differences were found for any of the pharmacokinetic parameters, $T_\frac{1}{2}$, Vd, and Cl tot. The average age was 58 years. In the group with normal renal function and that with mild uremia (Cl cr less than 30 ml/min) the values for $T_\frac{1}{2}$ were 17.9 and 13.9 hours; for Vdc, 0.15 and 0.15 l/kg; and for Cl r, 1.52 and 1.39 ml/min, respectively (Welling et al., 1975).

Morphine

A relationship was found between serum morphine concentration and age. Two minutes after IV administration morphine serum concentration averaged 0.29 µg/ml in the group aged 23 to 50 years and 0.49 µg/ml in the group 51 to 75 years of age (Berkowitz et al., 1975). However, no change in $T_\frac{1}{2}$ was observed with increasing age. Administration of morphine in cor pulmonale may cause severe suppression of the responsiveness of the respiratory center, thus adding to the existing hypoxemia in the elderly (Hun, 1971).

Netilmicin

In three groups of clients with mean ages of 54, 74, and 73 years and Cl cr of 124, 73, and 32 ml/min, the following pharmacokinetic parameters were found after 1 mg/kg IV injection: $T_\frac{1}{2}$ was 2.3, 5, and 10.3 hours; Vdβ was 24.8%,

27.0%, and 23.8% of body weight; and Cl tot was 64, 54, and 21 ml/min. The Vd did not change with either age or renal function. Drug elimination, expressed by $T_\frac{1}{2}$ and Cl tot, was significantly correlated with renal function but not with age per se (Welling et al., 1977).

Nitrazepam

In a study involving 25 healthy young subjects aged 21 to 38 years and 12 elderly clients aged 66 to 89 years, the latter suffering from various diseases (e.g., heart failure, coronary heart disease, leukemia, diabetes), significant differences were found: for $T_\frac{1}{2}$, 28.9 hours versus 40.4 hours; for Vd, 2.4 versus 4.8 l/kg. No significant differences were observed for Cl tot: 4.1 versus 4.7 l/hr (Iisalo, Kangas, and Ruikka, 1977).

In persons over 69 years of age, at 12, 36, and 60 hours after administration of a single oral dose, the concentration of nitrazepam in plasma went from 168 to 105 to 59 nmole/l. Likewise, in persons under 40 years of age the concentrations at the same time points were 149, 94, and 53 nmole/l. The mean half-life of nitrazepam in the elderly was 32.5 hours, and that in the younger subjects was 33 hours. The Vd in the elderly was 2.7 l/kg and in the younger adults 2.9 l/kg (Castleden et al., 1977). Despite the small changes in pharmacokinetic parameters, there was an increased sensitivity to nitrazepam with increased age.

In the first study cited the two groups were not comparable, and it seems that disease rather than age might have been the responsible factor in altered pharmacokinetic parameters. It seems from the second study mentioned that increased sensitivity to nitrazepam is found in the elderly and is not necessarily related to altered kinetics. Unfortunately, the extent of protein binding was not investigated in either study. Nevertheless, the increased sensitivity warrants a reduction of dose in the elderly.

Nitrofurantoin

The mean dose prescribed in 1974 fell from 169 mg/day for 15- to 59-year-olds to 153 mg/day for persons over 80 years of age (Boethius and Sjoquist, 1978).

Nortriptyline

There are a number of studies on nortriptyline after single oral doses in both volunteers and clients. The following pharmacokinetic parameters were reported: $T_{\frac{1}{2}}$ in young volunteers aged 20 to 35 years was 26.9 (Alexanderson, 1972), 25.5 (Gram and Fredricson-Overø, 1975), and 24.9 (Braithwaite, Dawling, and Montgomery, 1979) hours; and Cl tot in the same groups was 50.0 (Alexanderson, 1972), 63.1 (Gram and Fredricson-Overø, 1975), and 44.0 l/hr (Braithwaite, Dawling, and Montgomery, 1979). This would result in a Vd of 1941 (Alexanderson, 1972), 2322 (Gram and Fredricson-Overø, 1975), and 1746 l (Braithwaite, Dawling, and Montgomery, 1979). In elderly volunteers aged 47 to 53 the values for $T_{\frac{1}{2}}$, Cl tot, and Vd were 37.6 hours, 52.6 l/hr, and 2854 l, respectively (Alexanderson, 1973). In clients aged 22 to 74 years the mean $T_{\frac{1}{2}}$ was 43.1 hours, the Cl tot was 27.1 l/hr, and the Vd was 1685 l (Braithwaite, Montgomery, and Dawling, 1978).

By combining all data from reported studies, one can see a significant positive correlation between age and $T_{\frac{1}{2}}$ of about 26 hours in the young and 55 hours in the elderly and between age and Cl tot of about 50 l/hr in the young and 37 l/hr in the elderly subjects (Braithwaite, Montgomery, and Dawling, 1979). Apparently, the Vd remains unchanged. Further studies are needed for final evaluation and dosage recommendation because wide fluctuations were observed in all studies.

Oxazepam

In persons of mean age 53.6 ± 4.5 years a mean half-life of 6.4 ± 0.4 hours was found, and a Vdβ of 61.2 ± 4.6 l/kg was found. The percentage of unchanged drug excreted in the urine was 0.09% ± 0.024%. In persons of mean age of 25 ± 2.3 years the same parameters were 7.1 ± 1.2 hours, 47.7 ± 6.3 l/kg, and 0.23% ± 0.05%, respectively (Wilkinson, 1978). In another study with single oral doses of oxazepam no significantly different values were found for $T_{\frac{1}{2}}$, Vd, and Cl tot (Shull et al., 1976). In a series of 38 healthy volunteers aged 22 to 85 years the $T_{\frac{1}{2}}$ ranged from 5 to 12 hours in 35 of the 38 volunteers. In three elderly females half-lives between 15 and 20 hours were observed. However, there were no age-related changes in oxazepam clearance in either male or female groups (Greenblatt and Shader, 1980).

Penicillin G

For penicillin G an increase in $T_{\frac{1}{2}}$ from 0.54 hours in a group aged 15 to 33 years to 0.98 hours in a group aged 71 to 86 was observed (Leikola and Vartia, 1957). In another study the $T_{\frac{1}{2}}$ of penicillin G in women younger than 50 years was 0.4 hour, and in women older than 70 years it was 0.93 hour; in men younger than 30 years it was 0.35 hour, and in men older than 65 years it was 0.65 hour (Molholm Hansen, Kampmann, and Laursen, 1970). Since approximately 80% of the drug is eliminated by active tubular transport, the increase in $T_{\frac{1}{2}}$ is apparently associated with a general decrease in tubular secretion in the aged. No change in the rate of IM absorption was observed.

It has been found that age did not affect the binding of penicillin G to plasma proteins, which was 42% in subjects younger than 50 years and 45% in the elderly (Bender et al., 1975).

Phenobarbital

Phenobarbital is approximately 35% eliminated in unchanged form through the kidneys and approximately 65% metabolized with a $T_{\frac{1}{2}}$ of 50 to 120 hours (Hvidberg and Dam, 1976). A $T_{\frac{1}{2}}$

of 71 hours in a group aged 20 to 40 years, of 77 hours in a group aged 50 to 60 years, and of 107 hours for elderly above 70 years was reported (Traeger, Kiesewetter, and Kunze, 1974). The extent of protein binding was found to be equal in subjects below and above 50 years (Bender et al., 1975). Barbiturates, which depress cardiac or respiratory function, should be used in the elderly with great care (Stieglitz, 1952; Bare, 1961; Keyes, 1965).

Phenylbutazone

The $T_{\frac{1}{2}}$ of phenylbutazone increases slightly, although not significantly, with age. An increase in $T_{\frac{1}{2}}$ from 81 hours to 105 hours from age 26 to age 78 years was found (O'Malley et al., 1971). No significant differences in $T_{\frac{1}{2}}$ were found in another study (young subjects 110 hours, elderly 87 hours), but a decrease, although not significant, was reported in Vd with age from 0.172 ml/gm to 0.165 ml/gm (Triggs et al., 1975). The $T_{\frac{1}{2}}$ correlated inversely with plasma albumin concentration. The extent of protein binding decreased with age from 96% to 94% from age 19 to 40 to age 69 to 85 (Wallace, Whiting, and Runcie, 1976). Higher free phenylbutazone levels were found in elderly as well as in drug-free and in multiple-drug therapy clients. The clearance decreased from 0.086 l/hr to 0.065 l/hr (O'Malley, 1973).

Definitely, more studies are required with phenylbutazone. Even if there are no significant changes in $T_{\frac{1}{2}}$ and Vd, the decrease in protein binding, resulting in more free drug in circulation, may influence the pharmacologic response.

Phenytoin

A positive correlation was found between phenytoin serum concentrations and age in epileptic clients (Houghton, Richens, and Leighton, 1975). The low multiple correlation coefficient indicated that variables other than age seem to be more important for serum concentration. A decrease in protein binding was observed from 90.1% at age 17 to 87.3% at age 53 years (Hooper et al., 1974). On oral dosing a significant increase in Cl tot was obtained from 26 ml/kg/hr for two groups aged 20 to 43 years to 42 ml/kg/hr for the group aged 67 to 95 years, and on IV administration an increase in Cl tot from 44 ml/kg/hr for the group aged 20 to 38 years to 67 ml/kg/hr for the group aged 65 to 86 years was found (Hayes, Langman, and Short, 1975). At the same time a decrease of plasma protein binding of 18% was found. The increased clearance can thus be explained by the higher amount of drug in the free form. The clearance was found not to be affected by hepatic enzyme induction. The Vd is increased in the aged because of the greater amount of free drug.

A positive correlation was found between age and steady state serum concentrations with administration of 300 mg phenytoin daily (Houghton and Richens, 1975). This finding is supported by the fact that the average dose sizes prescribed are 0.33 gm/day in clients aged 15 to 59 years and 0.27 gm/day for clients above 70 years of age (Boethius and Sjoquist, 1978).

Practolol

Practolol is almost completely eliminated through the kidneys (Bodem and Chidsey, 1973). In a comparison of a group of young subjects, 27 years of age, with older subjects, 80 years of age, no significant differences were found between the two groups during the first 2 hours. However, subsequent blood levels were higher in the elderly. Peak concentrations in the elderly were less than twice those of the young group. The differences seem to be related to decreasing kidney function with age. From the data published the $T_{\frac{1}{2}}$ and Vd were calculated. The $T_{\frac{1}{2}}$ increased from 6.6 hours to 8.83 hours from age 27 years to age 80 years (Castleden, Kaye, and Parsons, 1975). The ka decreased for these groups from 1.13 hr^{-1} to 0.71 hr^{-1} and the Vd from 1.5 to 0.88 l/kg.

Procaine penicillin

The $T_\frac{1}{2}$ of procaine penicillin increased from 10 hours in a group aged 15 to 33 years to 18 hours in a group of aged volunteers of 71 to 86 years (Leikola and Vartia, 1957). Again, the increase in $T_\frac{1}{2}$ is apparently associated with a decrease in active renal tubular function. The increase in $T_\frac{1}{2}$ was higher in females (134%) than in males (88.9%). The rate or extent of absorption on IM administration is not influenced by age.

An increase in plasma levels of procaine penicillin of threefold to fifteenfold in the elderly was reported (Creasey, 1979).

Propicillin

The $T_\frac{1}{2}$ of propicillin in young healthy subjects aged 20 to 30 years of 0.57 hour increases slightly in geriatric clients aged 60 to 80 years to 0.65 hour, whereas the Vd decreases significantly from 0.43 l/kg to 0.26 l/kg for these groups (Simon et al., 1972). The absorption rate constants were identical for both groups, 1.54 l/hr versus 1.46 l/hr, as was the percent of urinary recovery, 53.4% versus 51.4%. The increase in blood levels and the doubling in AUC are therefore primarily caused by a decrease in Vd with increasing age.

Propranolol

Propranolol is almost entirely metabolized (Paterson et al., 1970). In 77-year-old clients substantially higher blood levels were found at all times than in 27-year-old subjects (Castleden, Kaye, and Parsons, 1975). The authors assume a substantially reduced first-pass effect in the elderly. From the data presented the $T_\frac{1}{2}$ and Vd were calculated. The $T_\frac{1}{2}$ increased from 2.54 hours to 3.47 hours from age 27 to 77. The Vd decreased from 263 l to 69 l in the same groups. The rate constant of absorption (ka) decreased for these groups from 2.1 hr^{-1} to 1.66 hr^{-1}. There is also an increase in bioavailability with oral administration, which suggests a diminished

amount of inactivation by metabolism (Castleden and George, 1979).

The average prescribed dose in 1975 decreased from 160 mg/day for 15- to 59-year-olds to 70 mg/day for persons over 80 years of age (Boethius and Sjoquist, 1978).

In one study involving young and elderly subjects aged 27 and 80 years (mean age) no statistically significant difference was found for $T_\frac{1}{2}$ (Carulli et al., 1977).

Protriptyline

In a study comparing the pharmacokinetics of protriptyline on single-dose administration in a group of young subjects with that on multiple dosing in elderly clients aged 61 years, an increase of $T_\frac{1}{2}$ from 78.4 hours to 107 hours was observed, although the difference was not statistically significant because of the wide range of individual half-life (Moody et al., 1977). There was practically no difference in Vd; hence the decrease in Cl tot from 0.213 l/kg/hr in the young subjects to 0.123 l/kg/hr in the elderly seems to be caused by a change in $T_\frac{1}{2}$ only.

Quinidine

Cl tot of quinidine decreased with age, indicating a need for, on the average, higher doses of quinidine in young adults, compared to elderly individuals. The changes in pharmacokinetic parameters from young to old persons were as follows: peak plasma concentration changed from 1.1 ± 0.4 $\mu g/ml$ to 2.3 ± 0.74 $\mu g/ml$; time to peak changed from 77.2 ± 28.8 minutes to 110 ± 75.0 minutes; AUC changed from 10 ± 3.2 to 25.7 ± 13.5; and absorption rate constant changed from 2.1 ± 1.6 hr^{-1} to 6 ± 4.6 hr^{-1} (Salem and Stevenson, 1977). Others report a change in half-life from 7.3 hours in the young (23 to 34 years) to 9.7 hours in the elderly (60 to 69 years). The Vd values were 2.39 l/kg versus 2.18 l/kg; those for Cl tot were 4.04 ml/min/kg versus 2.64 ml/min/kg (Ochs et al.,

1978). Reduced Cl tot of quinidine and prolongation of $T_{\frac{1}{2}}$ may predispose to toxicity in the elderly unless an adjustment in the dosage regimen is made.

A significant decrease was also found in Cl tot in clients with cardiac disease from 11 ml/min/kg at age 20 years to 2 ml/min/kg at age 80 (Drayer et al., 1980).

Salicylate

No change in the extent of protein binding has been found with age for salicylates. However, in multiple-drug therapy, significantly higher free levels of salicylate were found in the elderly, suggesting that either reduced concentration of albumin for binding is available and/or the strength of binding to plasma albumin is decreased in the elderly (Wallace, Whiting, and Runcie, 1976).

Spironolactone

In a study including five young volunteers aged 19 to 31 years the $T_{\frac{1}{2}}$ from 36 to 96 hours was 65.8 hours, and from 96 to 144 hours it was 39.8 hours. In a geriatric client aged 74 years the corresponding $T_{\frac{1}{2}}$ was 182.6 hours and 86.9 hours, respectively. The division into two half-lives is probably an artifact, since total radioactivity was measured. It might have been more appropriate to use a linear regression for all data points past 36 hours. No differences were found in tmax, which was approximately 0.5 hour, and urinary recovery, which ranged for all subjects from 46.7% to 57.8%. The Cmax was higher for the aged subject than for the younger individuals (Abshagen, Rennekamp, and Luszpinski, 1976).

Sulbenicillin

In young normal adults aged 28 years a $T_{\frac{1}{2}}$ of 0.97 hour and a Vd of 0.18 ml/gm were found at normal Cl cr of 106 ml/min. In normal geri-

atric clients aged 67 years the $T_{\frac{1}{2}}$ was 1.27 hours, with a Vd of 0.22 ml/gm at a Cl cr of 65 ml/min. In geriatric clients with renal impairment the $T_{\frac{1}{2}}$ of sulbenicillin was found to be 2.5 hours, with a Vd of 0.235 ml/gm at a Cl cr of 27 ml/min. An inverse correlation exists between renal function and sulbenicillin half-life (Hansen, Jacobsen, and Weis, 1975).

Sulfadiazine

Significantly increased free sulfadiazine levels were reported in the aged receiving multiple-drug therapy. Wallace, Whiting, and Runcie (1976) suggested that the elevated drug levels might be caused by displacement from protein binding sites because of a decrease in the strength of binding of drugs to plasma albumin in the aged.

Sulfamethizole

The $T_{\frac{1}{2}}$ of sulfamethizole increased from 1.75 hours in young subjects aged 24 years to 3.0 hours in elderly subjects aged 81 years (Triggs et al., 1975). The Vd was practically unchanged for the two groups, with 0.36 and 0.34 ml/gm, respectively, and the Cl tot decreased from 167 ml/min/1.73 m^2 to 90 ml/min/1.73 m^2.

The average number of tablets prescribed (containing 80 mg trimethoprim and 400 mg sulfamethizole) decreases from 3.5 in clients aged 15 to 59 years to 2.8 tablets in clients over 80 years (Boethius and Sjoquist, 1978). No statistically significant difference was found with respect to rate and extent of absorption. The elevated blood levels are therefore caused by reduction in the elimination rate constant. Sulfamethizole is primarily excreted in unchanged form.

Sulfisomidine

On IV administration of sulfisomidine to young subjects aged 24 to 33 years and older individuals aged 70 to 87 years for total sulfonamide (free plus acetylated) a significant difference was found 8 and 15 minutes after administration (Simon et al., 1976). From the data presented in the paper I calculated for the young and elderly subjects $T_{\frac{1}{2}}$, Vd, and Cl tot, which were 6.6 hours versus 16.2 hours, 11.6 l versus 13.9 l, and 20.2 ml/min versus 9.9 ml/min, respectively. The study indicates that the dose might have to be adjusted for the elderly.

Tetracycline

After IM injection of tetracycline, significantly higher 6-hour and 12-hour blood levels were found in the group of older subjects (63 to 87 years) than in the younger group (18 to 33 years). The $T_{\frac{1}{2}}$ increased from 3.9 hours in the young subjects to 4.9 hours in the elderly. These changes are probably a result of decreased renal function with age (Vartia and Leikola, 1960).

Even with these elevated levels the average dose of tetracycline in 1974 went from 0.89 gm/day in 15- to 59-year-olds to 0.98 gm/day in persons over 70 years of age (Boethius and Sjoquist, 1978).

Theophylline

Theophylline is a drug for which the biologic half-life varies over a fivefold range in normal subjects from about 3 to 15 hours. The mean $T_{\frac{1}{2}}$, Vd, and Cl tot in young adults are 4.4 hours, 0.45 l/kg, and 72 ml/kg/hr (Koysooko, Ellis, and Levy, 1974; Chrzanowski et al., 1977). In a study involving ten elderly subjects aged 60 to 72 years the following pharmacokinetic parameters were found after IV injection of 5.6 mg/kg; $T_{\frac{1}{2}}$ of 7.68 hours, Vdβ of 0.39 l/kg, and Cl tot of 35.7 ml/kg/hr (Nielsen-Kudsk, Magnussen, and Jakobsen, 1978).

Thioridazine

The $T_{\frac{1}{2}}$ of thioridazine increases from 8.5 hours at age 27 years (Martensson and Roos, 1973) to

19.6 hours at age 64 (Muusze and Vanderheeren, 1977). The prolonged $T_{\frac{1}{2}}$ might explain the poor tolerance to phenothiazines by the elderly (Ayd, 1960; Hamilton, 1966; O'Malley et al., 1971).

Tobramycin

In a study of IV administration of tobramycin a $T_{\frac{1}{2}}$ of 1.4 to 1.7 hours in a group of 30 subjects aged 25 to 87 years was observed, and an increase in $T_{\frac{1}{2}}$ was observed in subjects older than 60 years, with a $T_{\frac{1}{2}}$ of 1.9 hours. The Vdβ in the aged (mean 55 years) was 0.066 l/kg and the Cl tot was 71.1 ml/min (Gillette et al., 1976). In comparison, in younger subjects (mean 34.5 years) the Vdβ was 0.08 l/kg, and the Cl tot was 89.1 ml/min (Dobbs and Mawer, 1976).

Tolbutamide

Tolbutamide pharmacokinetics were studied in two age groups, one composed of subjects between 15 and 45 years and one with volunteers aged 70 to 96 years. The parameters found in the two groups were $T_{\frac{1}{2}}$ of 6.4 hours versus 10.4 hours, Vd of 10.2 l versus 8.2 l, and Cl tot of 18.9 ml/min versus 9.3 ml/min (Carulli et al., 1977). The increase in $T_{\frac{1}{2}}$ and decrease in Cl tot were statistically significant. One may conclude that tolbutamide dosage in the elderly should be adjusted accordingly.

Warfarin

The $T_{\frac{1}{2}}$ of prothrombin complex activity after warfarin administration in normal subjects was 13.8 hours (O'Reilly, Aggeler, and Leony, 1963). The maximum binding of warfarin to protein decreased from 561 μmole/l in the group aged 20 to 45 years to 451 μmole/l in the group aged 65 to 90 years (Hayes, Langman, and Short, 1975). The association constant, however, was not influenced by age. The decrease in protein binding was suggested to be caused by a decrease in plasma albumin concentration from 3.9% to 3%

in these groups. The increase in anticoagulant effect with potential toxicity in the aged on warfarin can be explained by a reduction in protein binding; hence more free drug is available (Hewick et al., 1975). The warfarin $T_{\frac{1}{2}}$ increased from 37 hours in the young subjects (27 to 37 years) to 44 hours in the elderly subjects (62 to 89 years). The Vd was practically unchanged, with 193 ml/kg versus 200 ml/kg. The plasma clearance was slightly, however not significantly, reduced from 3.8 ml/kg/hr to 3.26 ml/kg/hr (Shepherd et al., 1977). For warfarin apparently no dosage regimen adjustment is required for the aged based on pharmacokinetic parameters. However, the anticoagulant response to warfarin is greater in the elderly, resulting in greater inhibition of vitamin K–dependent clotting factor synthesis. The increased intrinsic sensitivity of the elderly to warfarin warrants a reduction in dose (Shepherd et al., 1977).

CONCLUSION AND OUTLOOK

It is evident that for many drugs pharmacokinetic parameters change with age. The determination or evaluation of one parameter alone, such as the biologic half-life, is not sufficient. The volume of distribution and binding to biologic material, particularly the total clearance, also have to be considered. Much more research is necessary in this area to develop guidelines for practical application. The problem is complicated by three aspects: there are large interindividual variations; any attempted correction cannot be based on actual age but on physiologic or biologic age; and any correction would apply only to elderly persons without certain concomitant diseases, such as renal and hepatic impairment, acute myocardial or coronary infarction, severe edemas, obesity, and hypoproteinemia. In these cases larger than expected changes for a given age would apply. For some drugs it is possible now to calculate and adjust appropriate dosage regimens for a given age. However, it is indispensable to monitor drug concentrations in blood and make adjustments as necessary.

In many instances a change in intrinsic activity or sensitivity must also be considered and may require altering the dosage regimen even if the pharmacokinetic parameters do not alter with age.

REFERENCES

Abshagen, U., Rennekamp, H., and Luszpinski, G.: Pharmacokinetics of spironolactone in man, Naunyn-Schmiedeberg's Arch. Pharmacol. **296**:37, 1976.

Alexanderson, B.: Pharmacokinetics of nortriptyline in man after single and multiple oral doses: the predictability of steady-state plasma concentrations from single dose plasma level data, Eur. J. Clin. Pharmacol. **5**:82, 1972.

Alexanderson, B.: Prediction of steady-state plasma levels of nortriptyline from single oral dose kinetics: a study in twins, Eur. J. Clin. Pharmacol. **6**:44, 1973.

Ayd, F.J.: Tranquilizers and the ambulatory geriatric patient, J. Am. Geriatr. Soc. **8**:909, 1960.

Bare, W.W.: Correction of erratic response to hypnotics in elderly people, Am. J. Med. Sci. **241**:766, 1961.

Beller, G.A., et al.: Digitalis intoxication: a prospective clinical study with serum level correlation, N. Engl. J. Med. **284**:989, 1971.

Bender, A.D.: The effect of increasing age on the distribution of peripheral blood flow in man, J. Am. Geriatr. Soc. **13**:192, 1965.

Bender, A.D.: Effect of age on intestinal absorption: implications for drug absorption in the elderly, J. Am. Geriatr. Soc. **16**:1331, 1968.

Bender, A.D., et al.: Plasma protein binding of drugs as a function of age in adult human subjects, J. Pharm. Sci. **64**:1771, 1975.

Berkowitz, B.A., et al.: The disposition of morphine in surgical patients, Clin. Pharmacol. Ther. **17**:629, 1975.

Bloom, P.M., and Nelp, W.B.: Relationship of the excretion of tritiated digoxin to renal function, Am. J. Med. Sci. **251**:133, 1966.

Bodem, G., and Chidsey, C.A.: Pharmacokinetic studies of practolol, a beta adrenergic antagonist in man, Clin. Pharmacol. Ther. **14**:26, 1973.

Boethius, G., and Sjoquist, F.: Dosage and dosage intervals of drugs—clinical practice and pharmacokinetic principles, Clin. Pharmacol. Ther. **24**:255, 1978.

Boston Collaborative Surveillance Program: Clinical depression of the central nervous system due to diazepam and chlordiazepoxide in relation to cigarette smoking and age, N. Engl. J. Med. **288**:277, 1973.

Braithwaite, R.A., Dawling, S., and Montgomery, S.: Difference in nortriptyline pharmacokinetics between healthy volunteers and depressed patients. In Crooks, J., and Stevenson, I.H., editors: Drugs and the elderly, Baltimore, 1979, University Park Press.

Braithwaite, R.A., Montgomery, S., and Dawling, S.: The pharmacokinetics of nortriptyline in depressed patients with high plasma levels, Clin. Pharmacol. Ther. **23**:303, 1978.

Braithwaite, R.A., Montgomery, S., and Dawling, S.: Age, depression and tricyclic antidepressant levels. In Crooks, J., and Stevenson, I.H., editors: Drugs and the elderly, Baltimore, 1979, University Park Press.

Braun, M.: Zur Pharmakokinetik von Ethambutol bei Magenresezierten, Diss. Fachbereich Medizin., München, 1976, Techn. Univ.

Briant, R.H., et al.: The rate of acetaminophen metabolism in the elderly and the young, J. Am. Geriatr. Soc. **24**:359, 1976.

Bricker, N.S., Morrin, P.A.F., and Kine, S.W.: The pathologic physiology of chronic Bright's disease, Am. J. Med. **28**:77, 1960.

Brodie, B.B., and Axelrod, J.: The fate of aminopyrine (pyramidone) in man and methods for estimation of aminopyrine and its metabolites in biological material, J. Pharmacol. Exp. Ther. **99**:171, 1950.

Bromage, P.R.: Exaggerated spread of epidural analgesia in arteriosclerotic patients, Br. Med. J. **2**:303, 1962.

Calloway, N.O., and Merrill, R.S.: The aging adult liver. I. Bromsulphalein and bilirubin clearances, J. Am. Geriatr. Soc. **13**:594, 1965.

Carulli, N., et al.: Il metabolismo epatico dei farmaci nella persona arziani, G. Geront. **25**:901, 1977.

Castleden, C.M., and George, C.F.: The effect of aging on the hepatic clearance of propranolol, Br. J. Clin. Pharmacol. **7**:49, 1979.

Castleden, C.M., Kaye, C.M., and Parsons, R.L.: The effect of age on plasma levels of propranolol and practolol in man, Br. J. Clin. Pharmacol. **2**: 303, 1975.

Castleden, C.M., et al.: Increased sensitivity to nitrazepam in old age, Br. Med. J. **1**:10, 1977.

Chamberlain, D.A., et al.: Plasma digoxin concentrations in patients with atrial fibrillation, Br. Med. J. **3**:429, 1970.

Chan, K., et al.: The effect of aging on plasma pethidine concentration, Br. J. Clin. Pharmacol. **2**:297, 1975.

Chresrow, E.F., et al.: Serum proteins in the aged: means and stability of mucoprotein levels and electrophoretic partitions, Geriatrics **13**:20, 1958.

Christophers, E., and Kligman, A.M.: Visualization of the cell layers of the stratum corneum, J. Invest. Dermatol. **42**:407, 1964.

Chrzanowski, F.A., et al.: Kinetics of intravenous theophylline, Clin. Pharmacol. Ther. **22**:188, 1977.

Cohen, T., Gitman, L., and Lipschutz, E.: Liver function studies in the aged, Geriatrics **15**:828, 1960.

Cohn, J.E., and Shock, N.W.: Blood volume studies in middle aged and elderly males, Am. J. Med. Sci. **217**:388, 1949.

Collste, P., et al.: Interindividual differences in chlorthalidone concentration in plasma and red cells of man after single and multiple doses, Eur. J. Clin. Pharmacol. **9**:319, 1976.

Creasey, W.A.: Drug disposition in humans, New York, 1979, Oxford University Press.

Crooks, J., O'Malley, K., and Stevenson, I.H.: Pharmacokinetics in the elderly, Clin. Pharmacokinet. **1**:280, 1976.

Cusack, B., et al.: Digoxin in the elderly: pharmacokinetic consequences of old age, Clin. Pharmacol. Ther. **25**:772, 1979.

Dahl, S.G., Strandjord, R.E., and Sigfusson, S.: Pharmacokinetics and relative bioavailability of levomepromazine after repeated administration of tablets and syrup, Eur. J. Clin. Pharmacol. **11**:305, 1977.

Dall, J.L.C.: Digitalis intoxication in elderly patients, Lancet **1**:194, 1965.

Dietze, V.F., et al.: Geriatrische Aspekte der Eisenresorption, Z. Alternsforsch. **24**:229, 1971.

Dimant, J., and Merrit, W.: Serum digoxin levels in elderly nursing home patients: appraisal of routine periodic measurements, J. Am. Geriatr. Soc. **26**: 378, 1978.

Dobbs, S.M., and Mawer, G.E.: Intravenous injection of gentamicin and tobramycin without impairment of hearing, J. Infect. Dis. **134**:S114, 1976.

Doherty, J.E., Ferrell, C.B., and Towbin, E.J.: Localization of the renal excretion of tritiated digoxin, Am. J. Med. Sci. **258**:181, 1969.

Dost, F.H.: Grundlagen der Pharmakokinetik, Stuttgart, 1968, Georg Thieme Verlag.

Drayer, D.E., et al.: Prevalence of high (3S)-3-hydroxyquinidine/quinidine ratios in serum, and clearance of quinidine in cardiac patients with age, Clin. Pharmacol. Ther. **27**:72, 1980.

Eckerstrom, S.: Serum proteins in aged people: electrophoretic separation of protein, Geriatrics **13**:744, 1958.

Estes, J.W.: Kinetics of the anticoagulant effect of heparin, J.A.M.A. **212**:1492, 1970.

Evered, D.C., and Chapman, C.: Plasma digoxin concentrations and digoxin toxicity in hospital patients, Br. Heart J. **33**:540, 1971.

Ewy, G.A., et al.: Digoxin metabolism in the elderly, Circulation **39**:449, 1969.

Falch, D.: The influence of kidney function, body size and age on plasma concentration and urinary excretion of digoxin, Acta Med. Scand. **194**:251, 1973.

Feibush, J.S.: Unusual sensitivity to digitalis, Am. J. Cardiol. **3**:121, 1959.

Fikry, M.E., and Aboul-Wafa, M.H.: Intestinal absorption in the old, Gerontol. Clin. **7**:171, 1965.

Foster, J.R., Gershell, W.J., and Goldfarb, A.I.: Lithium treatment in the elderly. I. Clinical usage, J. Gerontol. **32**:299, 1977.

Friedman, S.A., et al.: Functional defects in the aging kidney, Ann. Intern. Med. **76**:41, 1972.

Fryer, J.H.: Studies of body composition in men aged 60. In Shock, N.N., editor: Biological aspects of aging, New York, 1962, Columbia University Press.

Fulton, B., Rawlins, M.D., and James, O.: Influence of age on bioavailability and metabolism of paracetamol, Gut **20**:448, 1979.

Gillette, A.P., et al.: Rapid intravenous injection of tobramycin: suggested dosage schedule and concentration in serum, J. Infect. Dis. **134**:S110, 1976.

Goldman, R.: Speculations on vascular changes with age, J. Am. Geriatr. Soc. **18**:765, 1970.

Goldman, R.: Decline in organ function with aging. In Rossman, I., editor: Clinical geriatrics, Philadelphia, 1971, J.B. Lippincott Co.

Gram, L.F., and Fredricson-Overø, K.: First-pass metabolism of nortriptyline in man, Clin. Pharmacol. Ther. **18**:305, 1975.

Graul, E.H., et al.: Metabolism of radioactive cyclophosphamide, Cancer **20**:896, 1967.

Greenblatt, D.J., Allen, M.D., and Shader, R.I.: Toxicity of high-dose flurazepam in the elderly, Clin Pharmacol. Ther. **21**:355, 1977.

Greenblatt, D.J., and Shader, R.I.: Effect of age and other drugs on benzodiazepine kinetics, Arzneim.-Forsch. **30**:886, 1980.

Greenblatt, D.J., et al.: Lorazepam kinetics in the elderly, Clin. Pharmacol. Ther. **26**:103, 1979a.

Greenblatt, D.J., et al.: Age, sex, and diazepam kinetics, Clin. Pharmacol. Ther. **25**:227, 1979b.

Greenblatt, D.J., et al.: Diazepam disposition determinants, Clin. Pharmacol. Ther. **27**:301, 1980.

Hamilton, L.D.: The aged brain and the phenothiazines, Geriatrics **21**:131, 1966.

Hansen, I.B., Jacobsen, E., and Weis, J.: Pharmacokinetics of sulbenicillin: a new broad-spectrum semisynthetic penicillin, Clin. Pharm. Ther. **17**:339, 1975.

Hayes, M.J., and Langman, M.J.S.: An analysis of carbenoxolone plasma binding and clearance in young and elderly people. In Avey Jones, F., and Parke, D.V., editors: Fourth symposium on carbenoxolone, London, 1975, Butterworth.

Hayes, M.J., Langman, M.J.S., and Short, A.H.: Changes in drug metabolism with increasing age. I. Warfarin binding and plasma proteins, Br. J. Clin. Pharmacol. **2**:69, 1975.

Hayes, M.J., Sprackling, M., and Langman, M.J.S.: Changes in the plasma clearance and protein binding of carbenoxolone with age, and their possible relationship with adverse drug effects, Gut **18**:1054, 1977.

Heider, C.H., and Brest, A.N.: Renal insufficiency in the aged, Geriatrics **18**:489, 1963.

Hewick, D.S., et al.: The effect of age on the sensitivity to warfarin sodium, Br. J. Clin. Pharmacol. **2**:189, 1975.

Hewick, D.S., et al.: Age as a factor affecting lithium therapy, Br. J. Clin. Pharmacol. **4**:201, 1977.

Hirtz, J., et al.: Clinical pharmacology studies with acenocoumarol, Int. J. Clin. Pharmacol. Biopharm. **17**:361, 1979.

Hooper, W.D., et al.: Plasma protein binding in diphenylhydantoin: effects of sex hormones, renal and hepatic disease, Clin. Pharmacol. Ther. **15**:267, 1974.

Houghton, G.W., Richens, A., and Leighton, M.: Effect of age, height, weight and sex on serum phenytoin concentration in epileptic patients, Br. J. Clin. Pharm. **2**:251, 1975.

Hun, F.: Some fundamental therapeutic problems of geriatrics, Ther. Hung. **19**:81, 1971.

Hvidberg, E.F., and Dam, M.: Clinical pharmacokinetics of anticonvulsants, Clin. Pharmacokinet. **1**:161, 1976.

Iisalo, E., Kangas, L., and Ruikka, I.: Pharmacokinetics of nitrazepam in young volunteers and aged patients, Br. J. Clin. Pharmacol. **4**:646P, 1977.

Irvine, R.E., et al.: The effect of age on the hydroxylation of amylobarbitone sodium in man, Br. J. Clin. Pharmacol. **1**:41, 1974.

Jick, H., et al.: Efficacy and toxicity of heparin in relation to age and sex, N. Engl. J. Med. **279**:284, 1968.

Jori, A., DiSalle, E., and Quadri, A.: Rate of aminopyrine disappearance from plasma in young and aged humans, Pharmacol. **8**:273, 1972.

Jusco, W.J., and Lewis, G.P.: Comparison of ampicillin and hetacillin pharmacokinetics in man, J. Pharm. Sci. **62**:69, 1973.

Kattwinkel, J., et al.: The effect of age on alkaline phosphatase and other serological liver function tests in normal subjects and patients with cystic fibrosis, J. Pediatr. **82**:234, 1973.

Kendall, M.J., Brown, D., and Yates, R.A.: Plasma metoprolol concentrations in young, old and hypertensive subjects, Br. J. Clin. Pharmacol. **4**:497, 1977.

Keyes, J.W.: Problems in drug management in cerebrovascular disorders, J. Am. Geriatr. Soc. **13**:118, 1965.

Klotz, U., and Müller-Seydlitz, P.: Altered elimination of desmethyldiazepam in the elderly, Br. J. Clin. Pharmacol. **7**:119, 1979.

Klotz, U., et al.: The effects of age and liver disease on the disposition and elimination of diazepam in adult man, J. Clin. Invest. **55**:347, 1975.

Kohn, R.R.: Principles of mammalian aging, Englewood Cliffs, N.J., 1971, Prentice-Hall, Inc.

Koysooko, R., Ellis, E.F., and Levy, G.: Relationship between theophylline concentration in plasma and saliva of man, Clin. Pharmacol. Ther. **15**:454, 1974.

Kraus, J.W., et al.: Effects of aging and liver disease on disposition of lorazepam, Clin. Pharmacol. Ther. **24**:411, 1978.

Kristensen, L.Ø., Weismann, K., and Hutters, L.: Renal function and rate of disappearance of methotrexate from serum, Eur. J. Clin. Pharmacol. **8**:439, 1975.

Kristensen, M., et al.: Drug elimination and renal function, J. Clin. Pharmacol. **14**:307, 1974.

Lehmann, K., and Merten, K.: Die Elimination von Lithium in Abhängigkeit vom Lebensalter bei Gesunden und Niereninsuffizienten, Int. J. Clin. Pharmacol. **10**:292, 1974.

Leikola, E., and Vartia, K.O.: On penicillin levels in young and geriatric subjects, J. Gerontol. **12**:48, 1957.

Levy, G.: Clinical implications of interindividual differences in plasma protein binding of drugs and endogenous substances. In The effect of disease state on drug pharmacokinetics, Washington, D.C., 1976, American Pharmaceutical Association, Academy of Pharmaceutical Sciences.

Levy, G.: Pharmacokinetic assessment of the effect of age on the disposition and pharmacologic activity of drugs. Presented at the Second Philadelphia Symposium on Aging, Valley Forge, Penn., May 26-28, 1977.

Lewis, G.P., and Jusko, W.J.: Pharmacokinetics of ampicillin in cirrhosis, Clin. Pharmacol. Ther. **18**: 475, 1976.

Liddell, D.E., Williams, F.M., and Briant, R.H.: Phenazone (antipyrine) metabolism and distribution in young and elderly adults, Clin. Exp. Pharmacol. Physiol. **2**:481, 1975.

Lundberg, P., and Steen, B.: Plasma levels and effect on heart rate and blood pressure of metoprolol after acute oral administration in 12 geriatric patients, Acta Med. Scand. **200**:397, 1976.

Macleod, S., et al.: Age and gender related differences in diazepam pharmacokinetics, J. Clin. Pharmacol. **19**:15, 1979.

Marcus, F.I.: Metabolic factors determining digitalis dosage in man. In Marks, B.H., and Weissler, A.M., editors: Basic and clinical pharmacology of digitalis, Springfield, Ill. 1972, Charles C Thomas, Publisher.

Martensson, E., and Roos, B.E.: Serum levels of thioridazine in psychiatric patients and volunteers, Eur. J. Clin. Pharmacol. **6**:181, 1973.

Marx, J.J.M.: Normal iron absorption and decreased red cell iron uptake in the aged, Blood **53**:204, 1979.

Mather, L.E., et al.: Meperidine kinetics in man: intravenous injection in surgical patients and volunteers, Clin. Pharmacol. Ther. **17**:21, 1975.

Mellin, H.E., Welling, P.G., and Madsen, P.O.: Pharmacokinetics of cefamandole in patients with normal and impaired renal function, Antimicrob. Agents Chemother. **10**:262, 1977.

Meyers, B.R., et al.: Pharmacological studies with cefamandole in human volunteers, Antimicrob. Agents Chemother. **9**:140, 1976.

Miller, J.H., McDonald, R.K., and Shock, N.W.: Age changes in the maximal rate of renal tubular reabsorption of glucose, J. Gerontol. **7**:196, 1952.

Molholm Hansen, J., Kampmann, J., and Laursen, H.: Renal excretion of drugs in the elderly, Lancet **1**:1170, 1970.

Moody, P.O., et al.: Pharmacokinetic aspects of protriptyline plasma levels; Eur. J. Clin. Pharmacol. **11**:51, 1977.

Moore, R.G., et al.: Pharmacokinetics of chlormethiazole in humans, Eur. J. Clin. Pharmacol. **8**:353, 1975.

Morgan, A.F., Murai, M., and Gillum, H.L.: Nutritional status of aging. VI. Serum protein, blood nonprotein nitrogen uric acid and creatinine, J. Nutr. **55**:671, 1955.

Mosegard, A., Welling, P.G., and Madsen, P.O.: Gentamicin and gentamicin C, in the treatment of complicated urinary tract infections: comparative study of efficacy, tolerance, and pharmacokinetics, Antimicrob. Agents Chemother. **7**:328, 1975.

Mouridsen, H.T., Faber, O., and Skovsted, L.: The metabolism of cyclophosphamide, Cancer **37**:665, 1976.

Mouridsen, H.T., and Jacobsen, E.: Pharmacokinetics of cyclophosphamide in renal failure, Acta Pharmacol. Toxicol. **36**:409, 1975.

Muusze, R.G., and Vanderheeren, F.A.J.: Plasma levels and half lives of thioridazine and some of its metabolites, Eur. J. Clin. Pharmacol. **11**:141, 1977.

Nation, R.L., Triggs, E.J., and Selig, N.: Lignocaine kinetics in cardiac patients and aged subjects, Br. J. Clin. Pharmacol. **4**:439, 1977.

Nielsen-Kudsk, F., Magnussen, K., and Jakobsen, P.: Pharmacokinetics of theophylline in ten elderly patients, Acta Pharmacol. Toxicol. **42**:226, 1978.

Nies, A., et al.: Relationship between age and tricyclic antidepressant plasma levels, Am. J. Psychiatry **134**::790, 1977.

Nöcker, J.: In Doberauer, W., editor: Handbuch der praktischen Geriatrie, Stuttgart, 1965, Enke.

Novak, L.P.: Aging, total body potassium, fat free mass and cell mass in males and females between the ages 18 and 85 years, J. Gerontol. **27**:438, 1972.

Ochs, H.R., et al.: Effect of age and Billroth gastrectomy on absorption of desmethyldiazepam from chlorazepate, Clin. Pharmacol. Ther. **26**:449, 1979.

Ochs, H.R., et al.: Reduced quinidine clearance in elderly persons, Am. J. Cardiol. **42**:481, 1978.

Ogilvie, R.J., and Ruedy, J.: An educational program in digitalis therapy, J.A.M.A. **222**:50, 1972.

Olbrich, O., Woodford-Williams, E., and Attwood, E.C.: Proceedings of Congress International Association of Gerontologists, Merano, Italy **2**:387, 1957.

O'Malley, K.: Ph.D. Dissertation, University of Dundee, 1973.

O'Malley, K., et al.: Effect of age and sex on human drug metabolism, Br. Med. J. **3**:607, 1971.

Omer, L.M.O.: Tagesprofile und Profilverlaufskontrollen von Ethambutol bei älteren Tuberkulosekranken, Prax. Klin. Pneumol. **32**:252, 1978.

O'Reilly, R.A., Aggeler, P.M., and Leony, L.S.: Studies on the coumarin anticoagulant drugs: the pharmacodynamics of warfarin in man, J. Clin. Invest. **42**:1542, 1963.

Parker, H.W., et al.: Body water compartments throughout the life span. In Wolstenholme, G., and O'Conner, C., editors: Water and electrolytic metabolism in relation to age and sex, vol. 4 (Ciba Foundation Colloquium on Aging), Boston, 1958, Little, Brown & Co.

Paterson, J.W., et al.: The pharmacodynamics and metabolism of propranolol in man, Pharmacol. Clin. **2**:127, 1970.

Playfer, J.R., et al.: Age related differences in the disposition of acetanilide, Br. J. Clin. Pharmacol. **6**:529, 1978.

Redolfi, A., Borgogelli, E., and Lodola, E.: Blood level of cimetidine in relation to age, Eur. J. Clin. Pharmacol. **15**:257, 1979.

Regardh, C.G., et al.: Pharmacokinetic studies on the selective β-receptor antagonist metoprolol in man, J. Pharmacokinet. Biopharm. **2**:347, 1974.

Richey, D.P., and Bender, A.D.: Pharmacokinetic consequences of aging, Annu. Rev. Pharmacol. Toxicol. **17**:49, 1977.

Rietbrock, N., and Abshagen, U.: Stoffwechsel und Pharmakokinetik der Lanataglykoside beim Menschen, Dtsch. Med. Wochenschr. **98**:117, 1973.

Ritschel, W.A.: Bioavailability in the clinical evaluation of drugs, Drug Intell. Clin. Pharm. **6:**246, 1972.

Ritschel, W.A.: Angewandte Biopharmazie, Stuttgart, 1973, Wissenschaftliche Verlagsgesellschaft.

Ritschel, W.A.: Limitations in dosage regimen adjustment, Sci. Pharm. **42:**228, 1974.

Ritschel, W.A.: Dose size and dosing interval determination, Arzneim.-Forsch. **25:**1442, 1975.

Ritschel, W.A.: Handbook of basic pharmacokinetics. Drug Intelligence Publications, Hamilton, Ill., 1976a.

Ritschel, W.A.: Pharmacokinetic approach to drug dosing in the aged, J. Am. Geriatrics Soc. **24:**344, 1976b.

Ritschel, W.A.: Drug action and interaction in the geriatric patient, Sci. Pharm. **45:**304, 1977.

Ritschel, W.A.: Age-dependent disposition of amobarbital: analog computer evaluation, Am. J. Geriatr. Soc. **26:**540, 1978a.

Ritschel, W.A.: Pharmacokinetics of drugs in the elderly patient, Sixth Annual Midyear Clinical Meeting, New York State Council of Hospital Pharmacists with the Section on Geriatric Medicine, The New York Academy of Medicine, New York, April 14-15, 1978b.

Ritschel, W.A.: Handbook of Basic Pharmacokinetics, ed. 2, Hamilton, Ill., 1980, Drug Intelligence Publications.

Ritschel, W.A., and Eldon, M.: Prediction of biological half-life and volume of distribution in geriatric patients: limitations of a recently developed pharmacokinetic dosing method, Sci. Pharm. **47:**142, 1979.

Roberts, R.K., Wilkinson, G.R., and Schenker, S.: Effect of age and parenchymal liver disease on the disposition and elimination of chlordiazepoxide (Librium), Gastroenterology **75:**479, 1978.

Roose, S.P., et al.: Lithium treatment in older patients, Am. J. Psychiatry **136:**843, 1979.

Salem, S.A.M., and Stevenson, I.H.: Absorption kinetics of aspirin and quinine in elderly subjects, Br. J. Clin. Pharmacol. **4:**397P, 1977.

Schröder, J., and Börner, W.: Zur Frage der Altersabhängigkeit der zirkulierenden Blutmenge und der Blutströmungsgeschwindigkeit, Ärztl. Wochschr. **13:**578, 1958.

Schultz, F.: In Doberauer, W., editor: Handbuch der Praktischen Geriatrie, Stuttgart, 1965, Enke.

Shader, R.I., et al.: Absorption and disposition of chlordiazepoxide in young and elderly male volunteers, J. Clin. Pharmacol. **17:**709, 1977.

Shepherd, A.M.M., et al.: Age as a determinant of sensitivity to warfarin, Br. J. Clin. Pharmacol. **4:** 315, 1977.

Shinn, A.F., et al.: Dosage modifications of cancer chemotherapeutic agents in renal failure, Drug Intell. Clin. Pharm. **11:**140, 1977.

Shock, N.W.: The role of the kidney in electrolyte and water regulation in the aged. In Wolstenholme, G., and O'Conner, C., editors: Water and electrolyte metabolism in relation to age and sex, vol. 4, (Ciba Foundation Colloquium on Aging) Boston, 1958, Little, Brown & Co.

Shock, N.W.: Physiological aspects of aging in man, Annu. Rev. Physiol. **23:**97, 1961.

Shock, N.W., Yiengst, M.J., and Watkin, D.M.: Age changes in body water and relationship to basal oxygen consumption in males, J. Gerontol. **8:**388, 1953.

Shull, H., et al.: Normal disposition of oxazepam in acute viral hepatitis and cirrhosis, Ann. Intern. Med. **84:**420, 1976.

Siersbaek-Nielsen, K., et al.: Rapid evaluation of creatinine clearance, Lancet **1:**1113, 1971.

Simon, C., et al.: Zur Pharmacokinetik von Propicillin bei geriatrischen Patienten im Vergleich zu jüngeren Erwachsenen, Dtsch. Med. Wochenschr. **97:**1999, 1972.

Simon, C., et al.: Die Pharmacokinetik von Doxycyclin bei Niereninsuffizienz und geriatrischen Patienten im Vergleich zu jüngeren Erwachsenen, Schweiz. Med. Wochenschr. **105:**1615, 1975.

Simon, C., et al.: Die geriatrische Pharmakologie von Cefazolin, Cefradin und Sulfisomidin, Arzneim.-Forsch. **26:**1377, 1976.

Simonson, W., and Stennett, D.J.: Estimation of serum digoxin levels in geriatric patients, Am. J. Hosp. Pharm. **35:**943, 1978.

Sjö, O., et al.: Dose-dependent kinetics of ethotoin in man, Clin. Exp. Pharmacol. Physiol. **2:**185, 1975.

Smith, R.H.: Normal blood volumes in men and women over sixty years of age as determined by a modified C^{51} method, Anesthesiology **19:**752, 1958.

Smithard, D.J., and Langman, M.J.S.: Drug metabolism in the elderly, Br. Med. J. **2:**520, 1977.

Smithard, D.J., and Langman, M.J.S.: The effect of vitamin supplementation upon antipyrine metabolism in the elderly, Br. J. Clin. Pharmacol. **5:**181, 1978.

Somogyi, A., Rohner, H.G., and Gugler, R.: Pharmacokinetics and bioavailability of cimetidine in gastric and duodenal ulcer patients, Clin. Pharmacokinet. **5**:84, 1980.

Steiness, E.: Renal tubular secretion of digoxin, Circulation **50**:103, 1974.

Stieglitz, E.J.: Geriatric medicine: therapeutic aspects, J. Gerontol. **7**:100, 1952.

Straus, M.J.: Combination chemotherapy in advanced lung cancer with increased survival, Cancer **38**:2232, 1976.

Sumner, D.J., Russell, A.J., and Whiting, B.: Digoxin pharmacokinetics: multicompartmental analysis and its clinical implications, Br. J. Clin. Pharmacol. **3**: 221, 1976.

Swift, C.G., et al.: A study of antipyrine kinetics in relation to liver size in the elderly, Br. J. Clin. Pharmacol. **4**:730P, 1977.

Swift, C.G., et al.: Antipyrine disposition and liver size in the elderly, Eur. J. Clin. Pharmacol. **14**:149, 1978.

Traeger, A., Kiesewetter, R., and Kunze, M.: Zur Pharmakokinetik von Phenobarbital bei Erwachsenen und Greisen, Dtsch. Ges. Wesen **29**:1040, 1974.

Traeger, A., et al.: Zur Pharmakokinetik von Indomethazin bei alten Menschen, Z. Alternsforsch. **27**: 151, 1973.

Triggs, E.J.: Pharmacokinetics of lignocaine and chlormethiazole in the elderly: with some preliminary observations on other drugs. In Crooks, J., and Stevenson, I.H., editors: Drugs and the elderly, Baltimore, 1979, University Park Press.

Triggs, E.J., and Nation, R.L.: Pharmacokinetics in the aged: a review. J. Pharmacokinet. Biopharm. **3**:387, 1975.

Triggs, E.J., et al.: Pharmacokinetics in the elderly, Eur. J. Clin. Pharmacol. **8**:55, 1975.

Van der Velder, C.D.: Toxicity of lithium carbonate in elderly patients, Am. J. Psychiatry **127**:115, 1971.

Vartia, K.O., and Leikola, E.: Serum levels of antibiotics in young and old subjects following administration of dihydrostreptomycin and tetracycline, J. Gerontol. **15**:392, 1960.

Vestal, R.E., et al.: Antipyrine metabolism in man: influence of age, alcohol, caffeine, and smoking, Clin. Pharmacol. Ther. **18**:425, 1975.

Vieweg, W.V.R., et al.: Complication of intravenous administration of heparin in elderly women, J.A.M.A. **213**:1303, 1970.

Wagner, J.G.: Drug accumulation, J. Clin. Pharmacol. **7**:84, 1967.

Wallace, S., Whiting, B., and Runcie, J.: Factors affecting drug binding in plasma of elderly patients, Br. J. Clin. Pharmacol. **3**:327, 1976.

Watkin, D.M., and Shock, N.W.: Agewise standard value for C_{IN}, C_{PAH}, and $T_{m\ PAH}$ in adult males, J. Clin. Invest. **34**:969, 1955.

Webster, S.G.P., and Leeming, J.T.: Assessment of small bowel function in the elderly using a modified xylose tolerance test, Gut **16**:109, 1974.

Weismann, K.: Methotrexate therapy for psoriasis in elderly patients with impaired renal function, Acta Dermatovener. **57**:185, 1977.

Welling, P.G., et al.: Pharmacokinetics of minocycline in renal failure, Antimicrob. Agents Chemother. **8**:532, 1975.

Welling, P.G., et al.: Netilmicin pharmacokinetics after single intravenous doses to elderly male patients, Antimicrob. Agents Chemother. **12**:328, 1977.

Whiting, B., Lawrence, J.R., and Sumner, D.J.: Digoxin pharmacokinetics in the elderly. In Crooks, J., and Stevenson, I.H., editors: Drugs and the elderly, Baltimore, 1979, University Park Press.

Whiting, B., et al.: A computer assisted review of digoxin therapy in the elderly, Br. Heart J. **40**:8, 1978.

Wilkinson, G.R.: The effects of liver disease and aging on the disposition of diazepam, chlordiazepoxide, oxazepam, and lorazepam in man, Acta Psychiatr. Scand. **274**(Suppl.):56, 1978.

Woodford-Williams, E., et al.: Serum protein patterns in "normal" and pathological aging, Gerontologia **10**:86, 1964.

Zerman, A.M., and Franca, F.: Serum eucolloid in healthy aged individuals, G. Geront. **4**:519, 1956.

CHAPTER 11

Adverse drug reactions in the geriatric client

Abram J.D. Friesen

For a variety of reasons, such as reduced organ function, presence of disease, noncompliance, and greater drug consumption, geriatric clients are more vulnerable to adverse drug reactions than other clients (Williamson and Chopin, 1980). However, if proper precautions are taken, the incidence of side effects or therapeutic failures can be substantially reduced. In this regard it is important to emphasize that health professionals will have to work as a team, each using his or her own expertise in a cooperative manner, if safer and more effective drug therapy for the elderly person is to become a reality. In addition, more research in the general area of geriatric therapeutics is required because there are still many gaps in the understanding of the aging process and how this in turn affects the health, presentation of disease symptoms, and the safety or efficacy of different treatment methods in the elderly.

DEFINITION OF AN ADVERSE DRUG REACTION

A broad definition of an adverse drug reaction can be stated as any undesirable or unwanted consequence that occurs when drugs are used to diagnose or treat disease states (Melmon and Morrelli, 1978). Adverse drug reactions there-fore include not only the undesirable noxious effects of drugs but also the concept of diagnostic or therapeutic failures in a setting where success could reasonably be expected. This latter aspect of the definition is often ignored by investigators. For this reason the magnitude of the adverse drug reaction problem may be substantially underestimated in the literature.

Diagnostic or therapeutic failures can arise from many causes. For example, they may result from a drug interaction in which one agent nullifies or inhibits the pharmacologic effect of another drug (e.g., propranolol versus the bronchodilation caused by epinephrine, or tricyclic antidepressants versus the antihypertensive effects of guanethidine); they can also result from choosing an inappropriate drug (e.g., using penicillin G to treat a penicillinase-producing staphylococcal infection) or selecting a drug dosage that is too low (e.g., narcotic analgesics are frequently used in too low a dosage to relieve postoperative or cancer pain).

Experience over many years has taught that no clinically useful drug is completely safe under all circumstances or in all clients. In most cases it generally takes at least 5 years of fairly widespread use of a new drug before its full potential for producing side effects is reasonably well established. The common undesirable effects are readily detected during the initial clinical trials, but less common toxic reactions or those that only occur after prolonged treatment may not be detected or elicited for many years following the introduction of a new therapeutic agent. Although it must be acknowledged that many safe and highly efficacious new drugs have been discovered over the past 30 years, the clinician should not automatically assume that a new drug is superior to older established agents.

Adverse effects of commonly prescribed drugs for geriatric clients are presented in Table 11-3.

REASONS FOR THE FAILURE TO DIAGNOSE DRUG-INDUCED ILLNESS

A low level of suspicion on the part of the clinician has been cited as one reason why drug-induced illness is so seldom diagnosed in clinical

practice (Melmon and Morrelli, 1978). This may stem from the fact that many clinicians do not generally consider major side effects to be common events. In turn, this latter attitude may be a result of inadequate knowledge about drugs and their potential for producing adverse effects (see Tables 11-1, 11-2, and 11-3 for adverse effects of drugs). In reality, toxic effects are so common that, on the average, clinicians should be detecting a drug-induced illness at least once a day in one of their clients (Savett, 1980).

Especially in the elderly it is tempting to ascribe new symptoms to a newly emerging disease state, to an exacerbation of an existing illness, or to the aging process. As a consequence another drug may be prescribed to treat these drug-induced symptoms, thereby compounding the problem, whereas the best solution would be

TABLE 11-1   *Diseases and clinical conditions caused by drugs commonly used by the elderly*

Disease or clinical condition	Drug
Adrenal insufficiency	Anti-inflammatory steroids
Bleeding or hemorrhage	Aspirin and related anti-inflammatory drugs, heparin, indomethacin, phenylbutazone, vitamin E (megadoses), and warfarin
Blood dyscrasias	
Agranulocytosis	Antihistamines (H_1-blockers), benzodiazepines, clindamycin, phenothiazines, phenytoin, procainamide, sulfonamides, sulfonylureas, and tricyclic antidepressants
Aplastic anemia	Chloramphenicol, hydralazine, phenylbutazone, phenytoin, sulfonylureas, and thiazide diuretics
Eosinophilia	Chloral hydrate, erythromycin, and phenothiazines
Hemolytic anemia	Methyldopa, sulfonamides, sulfonylureas, and vitamin C (megadoses)
Leukocytosis	Haloperidol, lithium, phenothiazines, and tetracyclines
Leukopenia	Antihistamines (H_1-blockers), chloral hydrate, chloramphenicol, haloperidol, phenytoin, and primidone

TABLE 11-1 **Diseases and clinical conditions caused by drugs commonly used by the elderly —cont'd**

Disease or clinical condition	Drug
Megaloblastic anemia	Phenobarbital, phenytoin, primidone, and triamterene
Neutropenia	Indomethacin and phenytoin
Reticulocytopenia	Chloramphenicol
Thrombocytopenia	Clindamycin, chloramphenicol, heparin, indomethacin, phenytoin, primidone, quinidine, sulfonamides, and tetracyclines
Bronchospasms	Iron (parenteral), propranolol, and may result from allergic reaction to many drugs (e.g., aspirin and penicillins)
Candida infections	Aminoglycosides, beclomethasone (inhalation), chloramphenicol, and tetracyclines
Cardiac failure	Disopyramide, guanethidine, lidocaine, and propranolol
Cataracts	Anti-inflammatory steroids
Colitis, pseudomembranous	Clindamycin, chloramphenicol, and tetracyclines
Confusional states	Alcohol, antidepressants, antidiabetic drugs, antiparkinsonian agents, antipsychotics, atropine-like drugs, cimetidine, clonidine, digitalis glycosides, ephedrine, indomethacin, lidocaine, methyldopa, narcotic analgesics, phenytoin, quinidine, reserpine, and sedative-hypnotics
Conjunctivitis	Hydralazine and drugs topically applied to the eye(s)
Constipation	Aluminum hydroxide, atropine-like drugs, calcium carbonate, cimetidine, diuretics, iron (oral), MAOIs, narcotic analgesics, and verapamil
Convulsions or seizures	Haloperidol, iron (parenteral), lidocaine, lithium, MAOIs, penicillin (megadoses), and theophylline
Cushing's disease	Anti-inflammatory steroids
Deafness	Aminoglycosides, aspirin, erythromycin, furosemide, and quinidine
Depression, psychic	Clonidine, levodopa, methyldopa, and reserpine
Diarrhea	Ampicillin, benzodiazepines, clindamycin, chloramphenicol, digitalis glycosides, disopyramide, guanethidine, iron (oral), KCl, laxatives, lithium, magnesium carbonate, magnesium hydroxide, phenylbutazone, quinidine, reserpine, spironolactone, tetracyclines, thyroid hormones, and vitamin C (megadoses)
Dysrhythmias, cardiac	β-adrenergic agonists, digitalis glycosides, levodopa, lithium, procainamide, quinidine, theophylline, thyroid hormones, and tricyclic antidepressants

Continued.

TABLE 11-1 *Diseases and clinical conditions caused by drugs commonly used by the elderly —cont'd*

Disease or clinical condition	Drug
Edema	Antihypertensive agents, anti-inflammatory steroids, carbenoxolone, estrogens, lithium, nifedipine, phenylbutazone, sodium salts, and tricyclic antidepressants
Enterocolitis, staphylococcal	Chloramphenicol and tetracyclines
Exfoliative dermatitis	Chlorpropamide, phenobarbital, phenytoin, and sulfonamides
Extrapyramidal syndromes	Haloperidol, methyldopa, metoclopramide, phenothiazines, and reserpine
Galactorrhea	Cimetidine, haloperidol, methyldopa, and phenothiazines
Gingival hyperplasia	Phenytoin
Gingivitis	Vitamin A (megadoses)
Glaucoma	Anti-inflammatory steroids (ophthalmic) and drugs possessing atropine-like activity
Goiter/hypothyroidism	Lithium, saturated solution of potassium iodide, and sulfonamides
Gout (hyperuricemia)	Furosemide, thiazide diuretics, and vitamin C (megadoses)
Gynecomastia	Cimetidine, diazepam, digitalis glycosides, haloperidol, phenothiazines, and spironolactone
Hallucinations	Alcohol, amantadine, digitalis glycosides, ephedrine, haloperidol, levodopa, MAOIs, pentazocine, phenytoin, procainamide, and propranolol
Hemochromatosis	Iron
Hirsutism	Anti-inflammatory steroids, minoxidil, phenytoin, and spironolactone
Hyperglycemia	Anti-inflammatory steroids, carbenoxolone, estrogens, furosemide, sympathomimetic amines, and thiazide diuretics
Hypoglycemia	Alcohol, insulin, propranolol, and sulfonylureas
Hypotension	Antihypertensive drugs, iron (parenteral), lithium, MAOIs, meprobamate, procainamide, quinidine, and theophylline
Hypotension, postural	Clonidine, guanethidine, haloperidol, levodopa, MAOIs, methyldopa, narcotic analgesics, nitroglycerin, phenothiazines, prazosin, reserpine, and tricyclic antidepressants
Involuntary movement disorders	Levodopa and phenothiazines
Liver dysfunction	Acetaminophen, alcohol, erythromycin estolate, haloperidol, methyldopa, phenothiazines, phenylbutazone, phenytoin, sulfonamides, sulfonylureas, tetracyclines, thiazide diuretics, and vitamin A (megadoses)

TABLE 11-1   **Diseases and clinical conditions caused by drugs commonly used by the elderly—cont'd**

Disease or clinical condition	Drug
Lymphadenopathy	Iron (parenteral) and primidone
Neuropathy, peripheral	Hydralazine, isocarboxazid, isoniazid, phenelzine, and phenytoin
Nystagmus	Phenobarbital, phenytoin, and primidone
Osteomalacia	Aluminum hydroxide, phenobarbital, phenytoin, and primidone
Osteoporosis	Anti-inflammatory steroids, heparin, thyroid hormones, and vitamin D (megadoses)
Peptic ulcers	Alcohol, anti-inflammatory steroids, aspirin, caffeine, chloral hydrate, non-steroidal anti-inflammatory agents, reserpine, and tobacco smoke
Photosensitivity	Haloperidol, sulfonamides, tetracyclines, and thiazide diuretics
Pneumonitis	Mineral oil
Porphyria	Barbiturates
Psychosis	Amphetamines, anti-inflammatory steroids, levodopa, primidone, procainamide, quinidine, and tricyclic antidepressants
Renal dysfunction	Aminoglycosides, cephalosporins, furosemide, phenylbutazone, sulfonamides, tetracyclines, thiazide diuretics, and vitamin C (megadoses)
Renal stones	Aluminum hydroxide, calcium carbonate, magnesium trisilicate, vitamin C (megadoses), and vitamin D (megadoses)
Skin rashes	Are caused by numerous drugs and are often caused by a hypersensitivity reaction
Stevens-Johnson syndrome	Phenolphthalein, phenylbutazone, phenytoin, and sulfonamides
Systemic lupus erythematosus	Hydralazine, phenolphthalein, phenylbutazone, phenytoin, procainamide, and sulfonamides
Thrombophlebitis	IV administration of cephalosporins, clindamycin, erythromycin, phenytoin, and tetracyclines
Tremor	Antihistamines (H_1-blockers), hydralazine, lithium, MAOIs, and tricyclic antidepressants
Vertigo/vestibular dysfunction	Aminoglycosides, benzodiazepines, haloperidol, indomethacin, MAOIs, methyldopa, minocycline, phenytoin, and primidone
Visual dysfunctions	Anti-inflammatory steroids, drugs possessing atropine-like activity, digitalis glycosides, phenothiazines, phenylbutazone, phenytoin, quinidine, and vitamin E (megadoses)

to reduce the dosage of the offending drug or to substitute an alternate agent.

Another reason for failure to detect adverse drug reactions is that the clinician may be unaware of all drugs that the client is taking. About 30% of elderly clients may receive drugs from more than one prescriber (Ascione et al., 1980), so unless there is good communication between the various prescribers they will not know all drugs that have been issued for a particular client.

In addition, the older person may be taking several over-the-counter (OTC) or nonprescription drugs on a fairly regular basis (e.g., antihistamines, analgesics, antacids, laxatives, nasal decongestants, cough suppressants, and vitamins). Although OTCs are, on the whole, safer than products requiring a prescription, they can and do cause problems for certain individuals, depending on the status of their health and on the other types of drugs being consumed. For example, antacids decrease the absorption of tetracyclines and iron, MAOIs can potentiate the pressor effects of nasal decongestants and cause excessive hypertension, and antihistamines cause additive sedative effects when used concomitantly with other CNS depressants.

MAGNITUDE OF THE PROBLEM IN THE ELDERLY

Although more studies are still required, available data indicate that clients over 65 years of age experience more adverse reactions to drugs than do younger clients (see p. 263). On the average, the geriatric client is at least twice as likely to suffer a potentially serious side effect from a particular drug than a younger adult. Because elderly clients also consume more drugs—about twice as many as 30- to 50-year-old clients (Skoll, August, and Johnson, 1979; Vener, Krupka, and Climo, 1979)—the overall incidence of adverse effects must be at least four times higher in the geriatric population. Some of the probable reasons for the vulnerability of the elderly to drug-induced illness are discussed in the next section.

Commonly used drugs that cause CNS depression

Effects produced include sedation, drowsiness, decreased mental acuity, confusion, ataxia, and respiratory depression. Coma and death can occur if excessive doses are used. When used concomitantly, CNS depressants usually produce additive effects.

Antiepileptics	Phenobarbital Phenytoin Primidone
Antihistamines (H₁-receptor blockers)	Diphenhydramine Tripelennamine Promethazine
Antihypertensives	Clonidine Methyldopa Reserpine
Antipsychotics	Haloperidol Phenothiazines (e.g., chlorpromazine and thioridazine)
Narcotic analgesics	Codeine Meperidine Methadone Morphine Pentazocine Propoxyphene
Sedative-hypnotics	Alcohol (ethanol) Barbiturates (e.g., amobarbital, phenobarbital, pentobarbital, and secobarbital) Benzodiazepines (e.g., chlordiazepoxide, diazepam, flurazepam, and oxazepam) Chloral hydrate Meprobamate
Tricyclic antidepressants	Amitriptyline Desipramine Imipramine

Commonly used drugs that cause atropine-like effects

Effects produced include dry mouth, tachycardia, blurred vision, constipation, urinary retention, hyperthermia in a hot environment, delirium, and confusion. They may also precipitate an acute attack of glaucoma in clients with a narrow drainage angle. When used concomitantly, these drugs usually produce additive atropine-like effects.

Antidysrhythmics	Disopyramide
Anticholinergics (antiparkinsonian)	Benztropine Cycrimine Trihexyphenidyl
Antidepressants	MAOIs (e.g., isocarboxazide, phenelzine, and tranylcypromine) Tricyclic antidepressants (e.g., amitriptyline, doxepin, and imipramine)
Antihistamines (H_1-receptor blockers)	Chlorpheniramine Cyclizine Diphenhydramine Promethazine
Antipsychotics	Haloperidol Phenothiazines (e.g., chlorpromazine and thioridazine)
Muscarinic blockers	Atropine Belladonna tincture Glycopyrrolate Isopropamide Mepenzolate Propantheline

Statistics on the incidence of adverse drug reactions in geriatric clients

A. Drug-induced illness as the sole or major contributing cause for admission to hospital

	Drug-induced illness as a percentage of those admitted
General population[*]	2% to 8%
Elderly over 65 yr[†]	5% to 30%

B. Incidence of adverse drug effects in hospitalized clients as a function of age[‡]

Age (years)	Experiencing adverse effects during hospitalization (%)
20 to 29	3.0
30 to 39	5.7
40 to 49	7.5
50 to 59	8.1
60 to 69	10.7
70 to 79	21.3

C. About 25% of elderly persons living at home complain of side effects to drugs[§]

[*]Smith et al., 1966; Hurwitz, 1969a; Boston Collaborative Drug Surveillance Program, 1974; Caranasos, Stewart, and Cluff, 1974; McKenney and Harrison, 1976.
[†]Caranasos et al., 1974; Frisk, Cooper, and Campbell, 1977; Williamson, 1979; Williamson and Chopin, 1980.
[‡]Hurwitz, 1969b.
[§]Eberhardt and Robinson, 1979.

COMMON CAUSES AND PREDISPOSING FACTORS
Excessive dosage

The most common cause of adverse drug effects is the administration of a dosage schedule that is excessive for a particular client (Melmon and Morrelli, 1978). The average suggested dose merely represents the starting point from which the appropriate dosage for a given client is arrived at by monitoring for therapeutic and toxic effects and, if necessary, by measuring serum concentrations of the drug. Wide differences can exist from client to client in the way each responds to drugs. Common factors that may vary in different persons include rate and extent of drug absorption, volume of drug distribution, rate of drug metabolism, rate of drug excretion, responsiveness of the target tissues to the drug, and the influence of concurrently administered drugs on these processes (Fig. 11-1).

In most cases geriatric clients require lower doses than those suggested for younger adults. The pharmacokinetic reasons for this have been discussed in Chapter 10. Decreased ability to excrete drugs and perhaps a decreased rate of drug metabolism in some cases are the major factors

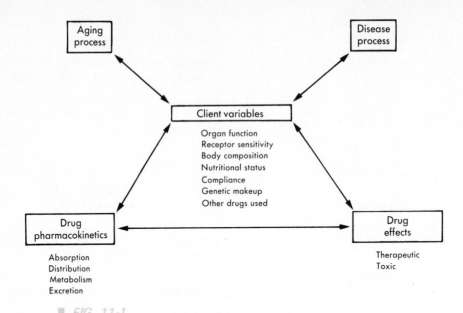

FIG. 11-1

Interacting variables that influence the safety and efficacy of drug therapy in the elderly client.

responsible. For these reasons therapeutic blood levels can often be achieved by administering drugs in lower doses or by administering the dose less frequently. If these dosage adjustments are not made, the accumulation of toxic levels of the drug in the body may occur.

Reduced functional reserve capacity of vital organs

It has been suggested that under ideal conditions humans could live for about 120 years, but disease, stress, and genetic and environmental factors shorten a human's life span (Cape, 1978). Organs reach their peak performance by age 3 to 25 years, depending on the organ studied; for example, the skin develops early, but sex organs and the brain reach maturity more slowly. After this maturation period, a gradual decline in organ performance begins, even in the absence of disabling disease states (Cape, 1978; Ritschel, 1980). Fortunately the vital organs (e.g., heart, kid-

neys, liver, lungs, and brain) have fairly large functional reserve capacities such that significant impairment may not occur in some elderly persons until they reach age 80 or 90 years. However, many elderly persons' organ functions may border on the critical level; these individuals may be more vulnerable to any insult, be it a disease state or a drug effect, which further suppresses organ function below this critical level (Fig. 11-1).

Predisposing diseases

Elderly adults, on the average, suffer from more acute or chronic diseases than younger adults. Such diseases may further reduce the functional reserve capacity of vital organs or make the client more susceptible to the side effects of drugs. For example, a client with latent heart failure may experience frank congestive heart failure when given propranolol; CNS depressants (e.g., sedatives and hypnotics, tranquilizers, and narcotic analgesics) may readily induce confusional states in the elderly; antihypertensive agents are likely to cause orthostatic hypotension, and if the client has advanced osteoporosis, a fall could result in a broken hip, arm, or leg (see Table 11-1 for drug-induced illnesses). Following is a list of common diseases of geriatric clients:

Allergies
Arthritic conditions
Cardiovascular disorders
    Anemias
    Congestive heart failure
    Dysrhythmias
    Hypertension
    Ischemic heart disease
    Peripheral vascular diseases
Central nervous system disorders
    Confusional states
    Epilepsy
    Parkinsonism
    Reactive depression
    Senile dementia
Diabetes and other endocrine disorders
Gastrointestinal tract disorders
    Biliary tract diseases
    Colonic cancer
    Colonic polyps
    Constipation
    Diverticular disease
    Peptic ulcers
Hearing disorders
Infections, especially of the respiratory and urinary tracts
Osteoporosis
Renal diseases
Respiratory tract diseases
    Asthma
    Bronchitis
    Cancer
    Emphysema
Skin conditions
Vision disorders

About 15% of those over 65 years of age may suffer from mild to severe senile dementia (Katzman, 1976). About one half of these may be of the Alzheimer type (Tomlinson, Blessed, and Roth, 1970), but the rest are caused by underlying disease states, nutritional deficiencies, and drugs. It has been estimated that drugs may account for 16% of these cases (Learoyd, 1972). Clearly, an effort should be made to seek an underlying cause of the particular senile dementia because some of them (e.g., anemia, diabetes, nutritional deficiencies, and hypothyroidism) are amenable to therapy. A careful drug history should also be taken, and, if possible, certain drugs should be withdrawn (see Table 11-1 for drugs causing confusional states) or their dosage reduced in order to verify that they are not the cause of the problem.

Polypharmacy and excessive drug prescribing

Geriatric clients commonly consume more than twice the amount of drugs taken by younger adults (Skoll, August, and Johnson, 1979; Vener, Krupka, and Climo, 1979; Lamy, 1980). Some of this increased drug use is justified because the elderly also contract more diseases, and one cannot deny the fact that drugs frequently improve the quality and length of their lives. However, there is substantial evidence that clinicians overprescribe drugs, especially the psychoactive agents.

Clinicians often find it easier and less time consuming to prescribe one of these drugs than to provide a counseling service or to seek a nonpharmaceutical solution for psychosocial problems. If clinicians feel they cannot provide such a service because of lack of training, time, or interest, they should refer the client to a trained psychologist or to a social agency for help rather than merely treat the symptoms of such disorders with a drug. The greater the number of drugs prescribed, the greater will be the risk of inducing side effects (Cluff, Thornton, and Seidl, 1964; Smith et al., 1966) or an adverse drug-drug reaction (Armstrong, Driever, and Hays, 1980). For these reasons drugs should only be prescribed when necessary and only when the potential benefits outweigh the possible risks. The drugs most commonly prescribed for the elderly follow:

Analgesics and anti-inflammatory drugs
Antidiabetic drugs
Antihistamines (H_1-receptor blockers)
Antimicrobial drugs
Antiulcer drugs
Bronchodilators
Cardiovascular drugs
  Antianginals
  Anticoagulants
  Antidysrhythmics
  Antihypertensives
  Digitalis glycosides
  Peripheral vasodilators
Central nervous system drugs
  Analgesics
  Antidepressants
  Antiepileptics
  Antiparkinsonian drugs
  Antipsychotics
  Sedative-hypnotics
Diuretics
Hormones
  Estrogens
  Insulin
  Thyroid hormones
Laxatives
Minerals
  Calcium
  Iron
  Potassium
Vitamins

In various surveys that have deen done, CNS drugs usually head the list of the most frequently prescribed agents, followed by cardiovascular drugs (Skoll, August, and Johnson, 1979; Vener, Krupka, and Climo, 1979; Williamson and Chopin, 1980; Steinberg, 1981).

Wrong diagnosis

A false diagnosis may lead to prescribing of an inappropriate drug and the needless exposure of clients to potential adverse effects. Accurate diagnosis of disease conditions may be difficult in the elderly client for a number of reasons. In one study (Miller and Elliot, 1976) newly admitted clients to a nursing home were reassessed, and it was estimated that about 60% of previous diagnoses were incorrect. Geriatric clients frequently exhibit atypical disease symptoms that are at variance with those described in standard textbooks (Caird and Judge, 1974; Hodkinson, 1980). There are at least four factors that can modify or alter the types of symptoms experienced by the elderly client: (1) the inflammatory response is often blunted; (2) there is often more referred pain, making it difficult to precisely locate the organ responsible; (3) the pain threshold is often higher; therefore a greater injurious stimulus may be required to elicit pain; and (4) loss of functional reserve capacity of organs can cause symptoms seldom experienced by a younger adult.

In some cases it may be difficult to communicate with the client because of hearing and visual loss or dementia and confusional states. As a result it may be difficult to obtain an accurate history. A spouse, close friend, or relative may be able to assist the clinician in obtaining a clearer picture of the client's history and current symptoms.

Noncompliance

Up to 60% of clients who self-medicate do not comply with instructions (Schwartz, 1965; Neely and Patrick, 1968; Sackett, 1976). Those clients taking more than three drugs usually are the least compliant. Too high a dosage can lead to toxic effects, whereas too low a dosage or suddenly stopping therapy can lead to exacerbation of the disease state and in some cases severe rebound toxic effects (e.g., propranolol—increased number of anginal attacks and possibly myocardial infarction; clonidine—rebound hypertension; and antibiotics—infections with drug-resistant bacteria). More detailed aspects of drug compliance are discussed in Chapter 1.

Subclinical and overt vitamin or mineral deficiencies

Marginal or obvious vitamin and mineral deficiencies may make the client more susceptible to side effects of drugs. On the other hand, the *chronic* use of some drugs that interfere with the absorption, storage, or use of one of these nutrients may convert a subclinical deficiency condition into a serious deficiency state (Table 11-2).

The most common deficiencies seen in the elderly are those involving vitamins A, C, D, B_1, B_2, folic acid, and the minerals calcium and iron (Todhunter, 1980).

A number of factors have been identified to explain the poor nutritional status of some elderly individuals: poverty; lack of interest in food because of depression, anorexia, or loss of taste and smell; poorly fitting dentures

TABLE 11-2 *Examples of vitamin and mineral deficiencies that may be caused by chronic drug use*

Drug used	Vitamin and mineral deficiency
Alcohol (ethanol)	Deficiencies of *vitamins B_1, B_2, B_6, C, folic acid and vitamins A, D, and K* if bile acid secretion is inadequate because of liver cirrhosis
Antacids	Deficiency in *iron* is possible because of decreased absorption; aluminum hydroxide decreases *phosphate* absorption and causes hypophosphatemia
Anticonvulsants (e.g., phenobarbital, phenytoin, and primidone)	Deficiencies of *vitamin D and folic acid*
Anti-inflammatory steroids (e.g., prednisolone, prednisone, and triamcinolone)	Deficiencies of *calcium and vitamin D*
Cholestyramine	Deficiencies of *vitamins A, D, and K*
Folic acid antagonists (e.g., methotrexate, pyrimethamine, and trimethoprim)	Deficiency of *folic acid*
Hydralazine	Deficiency of *pyridoxine*
Isoniazid	Deficiency of *pyridoxine*
Laxatives	Excessive chronic use can cause *sodium* and *potassium* depletion
MAOIs (e.g., hydrazine derivatives such as isocarboxazid and phenelzine)	Deficiency of *pyridoxine*
Mineral oil	Deficiencies of *vitamins A, D, and K*
Oral anticoagulants (e.g., warfarin)	Deficiency of *vitamin K*
Penicillamine	Deficiency of *pyridoxine*
Triamterene	Deficiency of *pyridoxine*

and resultant avoidance of hard-to-chew foods; and physical disabilities that may make it difficult to prepare nutritious meals. In addition to the factors just mentioned, there is some evidence that older clients may require a higher dietary intake of nutrients (Todhunter, 1980) perhaps because of less efficient absorption, storage, or use.

However, more research in this area is required in order to establish the *optimum* vitamin and mineral requirements of geriatric clients. Because multiple vitamin preparations that contain the recommended daily allowances are relatively inexpensive, it would probably be prudent to advise all elderly individuals to take vitamin supplements. However, they should be cautioned against taking megadoses of vitamins A and D because excessive doses of these vitamins are toxic. Megadoses of vitamins C and E, although comparatively safer, do occasionally represent a possible risk of inducing adverse reactions (see Table 11-3 for adverse effects of megadoses of vitamins A, C, D, and E).

SUGGESTIONS ON HOW TO REDUCE THE INCIDENCE OF ADVERSE DRUG REACTIONS IN THE ELDERLY

It has been claimed that at least 50% of the adverse effects experienced by geriatric clients can be prevented by certain precautionary measures (Melmon, 1971; Frisk, Cooper, and Campbell, 1977). Following is a discussion of the most relevant suggestions, but this by no means should be considered an exhaustive list of methods that can be used. Each case is unique, and clinicians must use their professional judgment and decide what is best for the client under the prevailing circumstances. Questions that may be used to reduce the incidence of adverse drug reactions in the elderly follow, and an outline of preventive suggestions is presented in Fig. 11-2.

1. Is the diagnosis correct?
2. Has a careful and detailed drug history been taken?
3. Is drug treatment really necessary?
4. Is the dosage correct?
5. Can compliance be improved?
6. Are the follow-up procedures adequate?
7. Are the new symptoms drug-induced?

Is the diagnosis correct?

As previously mentioned, the elderly often have atypical presentations of disease symptoms. This factor, coupled with communication problems, may make it difficult to arrive at an accurate diagnosis. There is a need for more accurate information on disease states in the geriatric client with respect to symptoms experienced and methods of diagnosis. General practitioners require more training in this area, and, especially in North America, more geriatric specialists are needed to deal with some of the more complex cases. England and some of the other European countries are more advanced in this regard than are Canada or the United States, and clinicians elsewhere could learn a great deal from their experiences.

Disease symptoms can also be caused by drugs (Table 11-1); therefore a careful, detailed drug history should be taken so that this possibility can be ruled out. The client should be questioned about the use of OTC products and any drugs prescribed by other clinicians. Ideally, the other clinician should be contacted to verify the accuracy of such information. If the client is obtaining all drugs from one pharmacy, the pharmacist should be able to provide an accurate history of all prescription drugs issued for that particular client.

Is drug treatment really necessary?

Wherever possible, other modes of treatment should be tried first. Perhaps rest, physiotherapy, changes in diet, or counseling sessions may be effective alternatives to drug therapy; one of the easiest ways of avoiding an adverse drug reaction is not to take the drug in the first place. Even if drug treatment may appear to be the best

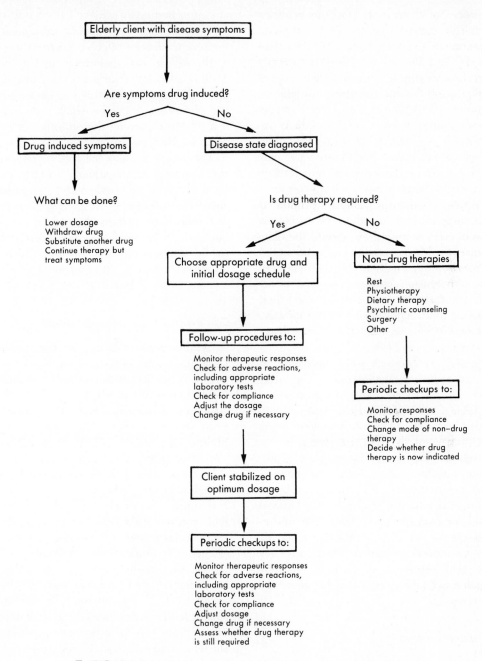

FIG. 11-2

Summary of suggestions for decreasing adverse drug effects and improving therapeutic efficacy in the geriatric client.

solution, one should seriously consider whether the benefits are greater than the potential risks.

The treatment of mild hypertension (less than 105 mm Hg diastolic and 180 mm Hg systolic) with powerful antihypertensive drugs is an example of the possible misuse of drugs in the elderly (Moore-Smith, 1980). The risk of adverse effects from these agents is often greater than the possible long-term benefits of lowering mildly elevated blood pressure. The elderly are particularly sensitive to the postural hypotensive effects caused by these drugs. If drugs are used for this condition, therapy should be initiated with low doses. Doses can then be increased as required over a period of weeks to allow ample time for cardiovascular adjustment to occur, which will eventually lessen the degree of orthostatic hypotension. However, weight reduction and salt restriction should be tried first when treating mild hypertension in the elderly. Other adverse effects of antihypertensive drugs are presented in Table 11-3.

Occasionally, drugs that were necessary at one time are no longer needed and can be safely withdrawn. In this regard, several studies (Gibson and O'Hare, 1968; Dall, 1970; Lamy, 1980) suggest that up to 60% of clients who were being treated with one of the digitalis glycosides no longer required the drug. These clients presumably only suffered from temporary congestive heart failure provoked by another disease (e.g., anemia, respiratory tract infection, hyperthyroidism, or hypertension). Once the underlying condition is corrected, the extra strain on the heart is removed and cardiac function is back in balance with the needs of the body, thereby obviating the need for agents that improve cardiac efficiency.

Is the dosage correct?

Geriatric clients usually require lower doses than younger clients. Therefore, in most cases, it is wiser to start therapy with low doses and then gradually increase them until an optimum

dosage schedule is achieved (i.e., one that provides satisfactory therapeutic responses with a minimum of side effects). Current therapeutic textbooks are now beginning to list some suggested doses for elderly clients; however, more research is required in this area because there are still numerous drugs for which little information is available regarding the optimum dosage schedules for this age group.

The major reasons for the decreased dosage requirements in the elderly include decreased renal function, altered body composition, increased sensitivity to drugs, and decreased liver metabolism of certain drugs (e.g., acetaminophen, barbiturates, and propranolol). (See Chapter 6, "Physiologic Changes and Clinical Manifestations of Aging," and Chapter 10, "Pharmacokinetics in the Aged.")

Can compliance be improved?

Well-educated clients, or ones who understand the nature of their disease and the reasons why compliance is important for their future health, are more likely to comply with the instructions for proper drug use (Schwartz, 1965; Cole and Emmanuel, 1971; Boyd et al., 1974; Sharpe and Mikeal, 1974). Verbal instructions should be reinforced by giving written instructions, especially if these are rather complicated to follow. Prescribing as few drugs as possible and simplifying drug-taking intervals to suit the daily routine of the client (e.g., on arising, mealtime, and bedtime) will also help to improve compliance. The clinician should always ask the older person to verbally repeat or physically demonstrate instructions to ensure that they have been understood. If it is obvious that the individual cannot follow instructions because of dementia or other disabilities, a responsible adult living with the client should assume the responsibility for administering the drug, or suitable arrangements should be made with a social service agency to perform this task. A detailed discussion of compliance is presented in Chapter 1, "Medication-taking Behavior and Compliance in the Elderly."

Are the follow-up procedures adequate?

Once a new prescription has been issued, the clinician should schedule appointments at appropriate intervals to monitor drug responses, make dosage adjustments if necessary, and change drugs if a satisfactory response cannot be achieved with the original agent. After the client has been stabilized on an optimum dosage schedule, periodic checkups are still required to verify compliance and to change treatment modalities when changes occur in the health status of the client. In this regard, prescriptions for chronic conditions should require a renewal order about every 6 months (or some other appropriate interval based on clinical experience). This maneuver would ensure that the client visited a clinician on a regular basis, at which time the client's condition and medication requirements can be thoroughly reevaluated.

Health care professionals trained in geriatric medicine can assist the primary care clinician with some of these follow-up procedures. More than 85% of senior citizens live in their own homes and are otherwise independent. These specially trained professionals who can make periodic home visits to check for compliance, adverse drug effects, and to investigate other aspects related to the health of the client may provide a valuable service and relieve some of the burden placed on the primary care clinician.

Are the new symptoms drug-induced?

During drug therapy new symptoms may emerge. If this occurs, one should not automatically assume that these result from exacerbation of an existing disease, the start of a new disease process, or just a result of the aging process. Drug-induced illness should always be considered as a definite possibility. For example,

propranolol may provoke bronchospasms or heart failure, reserpine may cause peptic ulcers or psychic depression, lithium and theophylline can cause seizures in excessive doses, and antipsychotic drugs may cause extrapyramidal reactions. (See Table 11-1 for more examples of drug-induced illness.) Lowering the dosage, withdrawing the drug, or substituting it with another agent may provide the least harmful solution to these problems. In other cases (e.g., parkinsonism caused by phenothiazines) it may be necessary and appropriate to treat these new symptoms with another drug.

SUMMARY

Drug consumption by persons over 65 years of age is at least two times greater than drug consumption by younger adults. The elderly person is also twice as likely to suffer an adverse reaction to a given drug than a person 30 to 50 years of age. Therefore the overall incidence of adverse drug effects is about four times greater in senior citizens than the incidence experienced by younger adults.

The causes or predisposing factors that make the geriatric client more vulnerable are numerous and include excessive dosage, reduced organ function, predisposing disease states, polypharmacy, faulty diagnosis, noncompliance, and poor nutritional status.

A realistic estimate is that 50% or more of these adverse reactions can be prevented by (1) making an accurate diagnosis of the cause of the symptoms, (2) making maximum use of nonpharmaceutical methods of treatment where feasible, (3) individualizing drug dosage, (4) monitoring and ensuring compliance, (5) using appropriate procedures after treatment has begun to monitor drug responses, (6) being aware that drug-induced illness is fairly common, and (7) using the expertise of all health professionals to assist in the delivery of health care to the geriatric client.

TABLE 11-3 **Adverse effects of drugs commonly used by the elderly**

Medication	Adverse effects	Cautions and comments
ANALGESICS AND ANTI-INFLAMMATORY AGENTS		
Acetaminophen	Hypersensitivity reactions characterized by skin rashes; drug fever or mucosal lesions occur occasionally. Potentially fatal hepatic necrosis occurs in overdosages (more than 10 gm/day).	Cross-allergic reactions may occur with aspirin. It is a well-tolerated analgesic for mild-to-moderate pain and also possesses antipyretic properties but lacks anti-inflammatory activity.
Aspirin	Epigastric distress, nausea, vomiting, and exacerbation of peptic ulcers are fairly common adverse effects. Chronic use may induce gastric ulcers in some clients. GI tract bleeding is usually minor but occasionally is excessive and leads to development of anemia. Hypersensitivity reactions may cause rhinitis, urticaria, hypotension, bronchospasms, and, rarely, anaphylactic shock. Tinnitus and impaired hearing may occur with higher anti-inflammatory doses.	Concurrent use with other ulcerogenic drugs should be avoided if possible (e.g., alcohol, anti-inflammatory steroids, and reserpine). Aspirin causes small erosions of GI tract; this effect, coupled with its ability to inhibit platelet aggregation, causes bleeding. Because of its antiplatelet effects, aspirin tends to potentiate effects of anticoagulants. Allergic reactions are most likely to occur in asthmatic clients, especially those with nasal polyps (about 20%). They are relatively uncommon in nonasthmatics (about 0.2%). Aspirin inhibits uricosuric effects of probenecid and sulfinpyrazone, even in lower analgesic doses.
Indomethacin	GI tract symptoms are common and are similar to those caused by aspirin. CNS symptoms occur frequently and include severe frontal headache, dizziness, vertigo, and mental confusion. Pancreatitis, neutropenia, and thrombocytopenia occur occasionally.	This drug is poorly tolerated by up to 50% of clients. Cross-allergic reactions may occur with aspirin.

Narcotic analgesics
  Codeine
  Meperidine
  Methadone
  Morphine
  Pentazocine
  Propoxyphene
	Nausea, vomiting, dizziness, sedation, mental clouding, constipation, miosis, and respiratory depression occur fairly frequently. Psychologic dependence may occur with chronic use. In doses greater than 60 mg pentazocine is likely to cause anxiety, psychosis, hallucinations, and nightmares. Orthostatic hypotension may occur after parenteral administration.	Tolerance and physical dependence develop in chronic users, and abstinence symptoms will develop with abrupt withdrawal of these agents. Pentazocine probably has lower abuse potential than morphine. Propoxyphene in doses less than 60 mg has lower analgesic efficacy than codeine but probably also has lower abuse potential.

TABLE 11-3 **Adverse effects of drugs commonly used by the elderly—cont'd**

Medication	Adverse effects	Cautions and comments
ANALGESICS AND ANTI-INFLAMMATORY AGENTS—cont'd		
Phenylbutazone	GI tract symptoms are common and are similar to those caused by aspirin. Skin rashes, diarrhea, vertigo, nervousness, insomnia, blurred vision, edema, and hematuria occur fairly frequently. Serious, but less frequent, adverse effects include a hypersensitivity reaction of the serum sickness type, ulcerative stomatitis, hepatitis, and nephritis. Aplastic anemia is a rare but potentially fatal reaction to this drug.	This drug is poorly tolerated by up to 50% of clients. Because of its propensity to produce serious adverse effects, its use is not advised for elderly clients. If it is prescribed, duration of therapy should be limited to maximum of 1 week.

Steroids
  Cortisol
  Prednisolone
  Prednisone
  Triamcinolone
	After chronic use for more than 1 month, acute adrenal insufficiency can be caused by too rapid a withdrawal of these agents. Numerous adverse effects are likely to occur with chronic therapy. They include hyperglycemia, increased susceptibility to infections, impaired wound healing, Cushing's habitus, myopathy of arms and legs, hypokalemic alkalosis, edema, osteoporosis and vertebral compression fractures, aggravation of peptic ulcers, striae, ecchymoses, acne, and hirsutism. Behavioral disturbances may also occur and are characterized by nervousness, insomnia, changes in mood, or psychosis. Topical application to the eye for more than 2 weeks may induce irreversible glaucoma. Cataracts have been reported to occur in clients who have used steroids continuously for 4 years.	Whenever possible, these drugs should not be used for more than 7 days. The incidence and severity of adverse effects is directly related to duration of treatment and dosage used. Hyperglycemia can be controlled by dietary measures or by insulin therapy. Fluid and electrolyte imbalances are rarely caused by 16 substituted steroids (e.g., triamcinolone). Spine should be checked periodically for signs of osteoporosis when steroids are used for more than 2 months. Therapy should be discontinued if osteoporosis has occurred. Peptic ulcer disease may worsen insidiously until ulcer perforates or causes major hemorrhage. Prior absence of psychiatric illness is no guarantee against the induction of psychosis during steroid therapy.

ANTICOAGULANTS		
Heparin	Bleeding and hemorrhage are the major problems encountered. Transient alopecia or thrombocytopenia may occasionally occur. Osteoporosis has been reported after long-term therapy (more than 4 months). Hypersensitivity reactions, probably caused by preservatives used in certain preparations, have been reported. They include chills, fever, urticaria, and, rarely, anaphylactic shock.	It is important to individualize the dosage by monitoring partial thromboplastin time. Protamine sulfate, 1 mg IV for every 100 units of heparin *remaining* in the client, is used as an antidote for treating excessive bleeding. Aspirin and other antiplatelet drugs may potentiate anticoagulant activity of heparin. Risk of adverse effects with full heparinization is greatest in women over 60 years of age.

Continued.

TABLE 11-3 *Adverse effects of drugs commonly used by the elderly—cont'd*

Medication	Adverse effects	Cautions and comments
ANTICOAGULANTS—cont'd		
Warfarin	Bleeding and hemorrhage are major problems encountered. Numerous drugs may potentiate (e.g., aspirin-like drugs, phenylbutazone, and clofibrate) or reduce (e.g., barbiturates, glutethimide, and rifampin) anticoagulant activity of warfarin.	It is important to individualize dosage by monitoring prothrombin time. Doses may have to be adjusted as new drugs are added to or withdrawn from therapeutic regimen of a particular client. Vitamin K_1 (phytonadione) is a specific antidote and can be given orally (10 to 20 mg) for minor bleeding or IV (50 to 100 mg) for major hemorrhage.
ANTIDEPRESSANTS		
Lithium carbonate	Goiter may be induced, but most clients remain euthyroid. Leukocytosis may occur with long-term therapy. Sodium retention and edema are usually transient but occasionally are persistent. Moderately elevated doses can produce the following adverse effects: nausea, vomiting, abdominal pain, diarrhea, dysarthria, mental confusion, fine or gross tremor, seizures, cardiac dysrhythmias, hypotension, and albuminuria.	Lithium has low margin of safety, and, therefore, doses must be individualized, ideally by monitoring plasma levels of the drug. Clients must maintain adequate fluid and salt intake during therapy. Drug is eliminated by renal excretion. Clients with impaired renal function will therefore require lower doses. Diuretics have been reported to inhibit excretion of lithium and may therefore potentiate its toxicity. Dialysis is considered to be most effective method of removing drug from body after severe intoxication.
Monoamine oxidase inhibitors (MAOIs) Isocarboxazid Phenelzine Tranylcypromine	Orthostatic hypotension and constipation are the most common adverse effects observed. Less common side effects include atropine-like effects, vertigo, headache, fatigue, excessive sweating, skin rashes, tremor, agitation, and insomnia. Hallucinations, confusion, or convulsions may occur occasionally. Hepatotoxicity, with currently used drugs of this class, is a comparatively rare complication. Peripheral neuropathy, responsive to pyridoxine therapy, may occur after chronic use of hydrazine derivatives, such as isocarboxazid and phenelzine.	Hypertensive crises may occur if clients consume tyramine-containing foods or beverages while receiving MAO inhibitors. MAOIs may also potentiate the pressor effects of other sympathomimetic agents (e.g., epinephrine, metaraminol, norepinephrine, phenylephrine, phenylpropanolamine, and pseudoephedrine). MAOIs have been reported to potentiate the central effects of levodopa unpredictably; therefore concurrent use of these agents is best avoided.

TABLE 11-3   **Adverse effects of drugs commonly used by the elderly—cont'd**

Medication	Adverse effects	Cautions and comments
ANTIDEPRESSANTS—cont'd		

Tricyclic antidepressants
  Amitriptyline
  Desipramine
  Doxepin
  Imipramine
  Protriptyline
	Atropine-like effects are fairly common as are tachycardia, postural hypotension, dizziness, sedation, delirium, fatigue, fine tremor, edema, and excessive sweating. Manic excitement, cardiac dysrhythmias, and impotence may occur occasionally. Jaundice, agranulocytosis, and skin rashes are relatively rare side effects.	Desipramine and protriptyline are less likely to produce severe atropine-like effects than other drugs in this class. The antihypertensive effects of guanethidine (and related drugs) and clonidine can be nullified by these agents. These drugs may markedly potentiate the pressor effects of epinephrine and norepinephrine.

ANTIDIABETIC AGENTS		
Insulin	Hypoglycemia caused by overdosage is the most serious adverse effect. Allergies, usually characterized by skin rashes, may occur occasionally. Urticaria, angioedema, or anaphylactic shock are rare reactions. Lipodystrophy in the injected area can occur.	Doses must be individualized by monitoring blood or urine glucose levels. Highly purified preparations are available, which have a lower potential for producing allergic reactions and lipodystrophy.

Sulfonylureas
  Acetohexamide
  Chlorpropamide
  Tolazamide
  Tolbutamide
	Hypoglycemia as a result of overdosage is the most serious adverse effect. Nausea, vomiting, epigastric distress, and photosensitivity are fairly common reactions. Less common effects include cholestatic jaundice, leukopenia, agranulocytosis, hemolytic anemia, pancytopenia, and hyponatremia. A disulfiram-like reaction with concurrent use of alcohol occurs occasionally.	Doses must be individualized by monitoring blood or urine glucose levels. Prolonged periods of hypoglycemia and cholestatic jaundice are more likely to occur with chlorpropamide. The University Group Diabetic Program study suggested that long-term use of these agents may increase risk of death resulting from cardiovascular causes. Appropriate dietary restrictions and correction of obesity will often eliminate need for using these drugs.

ANTIEPILEPTIC AGENTS		
Phenobarbital	Sedation is the most common adverse effect, but paradoxic CNS excitement may occur in some clients. Skin rashes occur in 1% to 2% of clients treated. Megaloblastic anemia, responsive to folic acid therapy, and osteomalacia, responsive to vitamin D supplements, may occur with chronic usage. Porphyria may be induced in susceptible persons. Potentially fatal exfoliative dermatitis is a rare complication. Respiratory depression, nystagmus, and ataxia occur when excessive doses are used.	Doses should be individualized, if necessary by monitoring blood levels of the drug, to lessen the incidence of side effects and to optimize the therapeutic effects. If withdrawal of therapy is necessary, it should be done gradually to minimize risk of precipitating status epilepticus. As with other barbiturates, physical dependence and perhaps psychologic dependence can develop with chronic therapy. Its sedative effects can be potentiated by alcohol, and other CNS depressants can be expected to produce additive effects if used concurrently.

Continued.

TABLE 11-3   **Adverse effects of drugs commonly used by the elderly—cont'd**

Medication	Adverse effects	Cautions and comments
ANTIEPILEPTIC AGENTS—cont'd		
Phenytoin	Skin rashes, gingival hyperplasia, GI tract disturbances, and hirsutism are the most common adverse effects observed. Peripheral neuropathy may occur when high doses are used on a chronic basis. Megaloblastic anemia and osteomalacia, similar to that seen with phenobarbital, may occur with long-term therapy. Hematologic disorders may occasionally occur and include neutropenia, leukopenia, thrombocytopenia, agranulocytosis, and aplastic anemia. Stevens-Johnson syndrome, systemic lupus erythematosus, and potentially fatal hepatic necrosis are rare complications of therapy.	Doses should be individualized, if necessary by monitoring blood levels of the drug, to reduce the risk of adverse effects and to optimize therapeutic effects. Moderate overdoses produce a variety of CNS effects. These include nystagmus, ataxia, blurred vision, vertigo, mydriasis, hyperactive tendon reflexes, hyperactivity, sedation, confusion, and hallucinations. If withdrawal of therapy is necessary, it should be done gradually to minimize risk of precipitating status epilepticus.
Primidone	Common side effects include sedation, ataxia, dizziness, vertigo, nausea, vomiting, nystagmus, and diplopia. Megaloblastic anemia and osteomalacia, similar to that seen with phenobarbital, may occur with long-term therapy. Skin rashes, leukopenia, thrombocytopenia, systemic lupus erythematosus, and lymph adenopathy are relatively uncommon side effects. Acute psychotic reactions have been reported in clients with temporal lobe epilepsy.	Primidone is converted to two active metabolites, phenobarbital and phenylethylmalonamide. Doses should be individualized, if necessary by measuring blood levels of phenobarbital, to reduce risk of adverse reactions and to optimize therapeutic effects. Combination therapy with phenobarbital is illogical because the drug is in part converted to this barbiturate and no additional beneficial effects can be expected by such a maneuver. Its sedative effects can be potentiated by alcohol, and other CNS depressants can be expected to produce additive effects if used concurrently.
ANTIHISTAMINES		
(H$_1$-receptor blocking agents) Chlorpheniramine Cyclizine Diphenhydramine Pyrilamine Tripelenamine	Sedation and atropine-like effects are the most common side effects observed. Side effects that occur less frequently include dizziness, tinnitus, lassitude, fatigue, nervousness, insomnia, tremor, and GI tract symptoms. Allergic dermatitis occurs more commonly with topical use. Leukopenia and agranulocytosis are rare complications of therapy.	Adverse effects are rarely serious. Sedation is more pronounced with ethanolamine derivatives such as diphenhydramine. Additive effects can be expected with concurrent use of alcohol and other CNS depressants. CNS excitement, nervousness, and insomnia are more likely to occur with alkylamine derivatives such as chlorpheniramine. Pyrilamine is least likely to produce atropine-like effects.

TABLE 11-3   **Adverse effects of drugs commonly used by the elderly—cont'd**

Medication	Adverse effects	Cautions and comments
ANTIHYPERTENSIVE AGENTS		
Note:	*Diuretics are discussed under a separate heading. With the exception of diuretics, all antihypertensive agents tend to produce edema.*	*Thiazide diuretics and related agents are used to control edema caused by these drugs. They are also used alone for treatment of milder forms of hypertension.*
Clonidine	Sedation and dry mouth are common adverse effects and may be severe. Psychic depression, impotence, and orthostatic hypotension may occur occasionally.	Sucking a hard sugarless candy can help relieve dry mouth. Rebound hypertension may occur on withdrawal of this drug. This effect can be controlled with a combination of propranolol and phentolamine. Tricyclic antidepressants may nullify clonidine's antihypertensive action.
Guanethidine	Orthostatic hypotension occurs frequently. Diarrhea is also a fairly common side effect. Impotence may occur. Guanethidine decreases cardiac contractility and can aggravate congestive heart failure. Severe hypertension can occur in clients with pheochromocytoma. This effect is related to guanethidine's ability to potentiate the pressor effects of direct-acting sympathomimetic agents such as epinephrine, norepinephrine, phenylephrine, and methoxamine.	It is poorly tolerated by most clients. Orthostatic hypotension is worsened by hot weather, alcohol, and exercise. Diarrhea associated with use of this drug is usually responsive to low doses of atropine or opioids. Tricyclic antidepressants nullify its antihypertensive action. Phenothiazines have been reported to have similar inhibitory effect.
Hydralazine	Common side effects include anorexia, nausea, dizziness, headache, reflex tachycardia, and sweating. A lupuslike syndrome may occur in 15% of clients treated with doses greater than 400 mg/day. Nasal congestion, flushing, lacrimation, conjunctivitis, tremor, and muscle cramps also occur fairly frequently. Rarer adverse effects include skin rashes, urticaria, drug fever, GI tract hemorrhage, anemia, and pancytopenia.	Concurrent therapy with a β-adrenergic blocker, such as propranolol, will prevent tachycardia and reduce dose required to control hypertension. Incidence of side effects is generally dose related; therefore dose of this agent should be kept as low as possible. Peripheral neuropathy may occur, but this effect can be prevented (or treated) with dietary supplements of pyridoxine.
Methyldopa	This drug regularly produces sedation and a decrease in mental acuity. Orthostatic hypotension, vertigo, extrapyramidal syndromes, nightmares, psychic depression, dry mouth, nasal stuffiness, galactorrhea, and impotence occur less frequently. Relatively rare adverse effects include severe drug fever, jaundice, and hemolytic anemia.	Up to 25% of clients receiving chronic therapy develop a positive Coombs' test, and hemolytic anemia occurs in about 5% of those showing a positive reaction. Rebound hypertension may occur on abrupt withdrawal of this drug. Incidence of this effect is apparently lower than that occurring after clonidine withdrawal. *Continued.*

TABLE 11-3   **Adverse effects of drugs commonly used by the elderly—cont'd**

Medication	Adverse effects	Cautions and comments
ANTIHYPERTENSIVE AGENTS—cont'd		
Minoxidil	Reflex tachycardia, hirsutism, and severe edema are common adverse effects. Pericardial effusion occurs less frequently and is probably caused by edema.	Reflex tachycardia can be controlled by coadministration of propranolol or other β-adrenergic blocking agents. Edema may be difficult to control, even with use of furosemide. This agent is usually reserved for clients with severe hypertension who are unresponsive to other drugs.
Prazosin	Orthostatic hypotension, tachycardia, and perhaps syncope may occur when therapy is initiated. Tolerance to these effects usually occurs with continued therapy. Drowsiness, dizziness, headache, and fatigability are fairly common side effects.	Therapy should be initiated with low doses. Doses can then be increased gradually to avoid excessive postural hypotension and syncope.
Propranolol	This drug reduces cardiac contractility and AV conduction. It increases airway resistance in lungs and tends to cause hypoglycemia. Less common adverse effects include nausea, vomiting, diarrhea or constipation, hallucinations, nightmares, insomnia, lassitude, dizziness, and depression. Hypersensitivity reactions characterized by skin rashes, fever, and purpura are rare but require withdrawal of therapy.	This drug is contraindicated in clients with frank heart failure, asthma, partial heart block, and in those clients who are prone to hypoglycemic episodes. It should be used with caution in diabetic clients being treated with antidiabetic drugs. Abrupt withdrawal of this agent should be avoided because this may cause anginal attacks, some rebound increase in blood pressure, and possibly myocardial infarction.
Reserpine	Common side effects include sedation, nasal congestion, abdominal cramps, diarrhea, aggravation of peptic ulcers, and nightmares. Psychic depression can occur and may lead to suicide attempts. Orthostatic hypotension occurs less frequently than with guanethidine. Extrapyramidal reactions are relatively rare when doses do not exceed 1 mg/day.	Drug is best avoided in clients with a history of peptic ulcer disease. Drug is contraindicated in clients who are depressed or in those who have had a history of depression. Earlier reports of an increased risk of carcinoma of the breast have *not* been confirmed by more recent studies.
ANTIMICROBIAL AGENTS		

Aminoglycosides
  Amikacin
  Gentamicin
  Tobramycin
	Ototoxicity (vestibular/auditory) and nephrotoxicity occur fairly frequently and are the most feared adverse effects of these drugs. Nausea, vomiting, headache, a variety of allergic reactions, and overgrowth of *Candida* organisms may occur.	These drugs have narrow margins of safety; therefore doses should be individualized by monitoring blood levels of drug given. They are largely eliminated unchanged by the kidneys. Those clients with renal impairment will require lower and less frequent doses. Additive nephrotoxic effects have been reported with concurrent cephalosporin therapy.

TABLE 11-3   *Adverse effects of drugs commonly used by the elderly—cont'd*

Medication	Adverse effects	Cautions and comments
ANTIMICROBIAL AGENTS—cont'd		

Cephalosporins
  Cefaclor
  Cefamandole
  Cefazolin
  Cefoxitin
  Cephalexin
  Cephaloridine
  Cephalothin
  Cephradine
	Hypersensitivity reactions of same type and incidence as those produced by penicillins can be expected. Renal tubular necrosis has occasionally been reported during cephaloridine therapy, but incidence appears to be lower for other cephalosporins. Hypernatremia may occur when high doses of sodium salts are injected parenterally in clients with impaired renal function. IV administration can cause thrombophlebitis.	Cross-allergic reactions may occur in up to 20% of clients who are allergic to penicillin. These drugs are best avoided in clients who have previously experienced severe hypersensitivity response to one of the penicillins.

Clindamycin	Diarrhea and skin rashes occur fairly frequently. Pseudomembranous colitis occurs occasionally and can cause death unless promptly treated with oral vancomycin. Granulocytopenia, thrombocytopenia, and anaphylactic reactions are rare complications. IV administration may cause thrombophlebitis.	Any diarrhea that occurs during therapy should be promptly investigated to ensure that it is not pseudomembranous colitis. The latter condition is caused by a suprainfection with *Clostridium difficile* and is responsive to oral vancomycin therapy.
Chloramphenicol	Nausea, vomiting, diarrhea, and perineal irritation may occur after oral administration. Hypersensitivity reactions are relatively uncommon and are characterized by skin rashes, fever, or angioedema. Suprainfections similar in type and incidence to those produced by tetracyclines may occur with chronic therapy. Blood disorders can occur and include reticulocytopenia, anemia, leukopenia, thrombocytopenia, and, rarely, irreversible pancytopenia.	Most blood dyscrasias occur when large doses are used for prolonged periods. In contrast, fatal pancytopenia appears to be an idiosyncratic reaction (perhaps allergic) that is unrelated to dosage used. Pancytopenia occurs in about 1 in 30,000 clients treated with chloramphenicol. Drug should not be used unless safer agents have proven ineffective and unless microorganisms have been demonstrated to be sensitive to chloramphenicol.
Erythromycin	Epigastric distress is frequently observed, especially after large oral doses. Hypersensitivity reactions occur occasionally and are characterized by skin rashes, fever, and eosinophilia. Cholestatic jaundice may occur, especially with estolate form of the drug. IV administration regularly produces thrombophlebitis.	Incidence of serious adverse effects is probably lowest of all currently used antibiotic agents. Transient auditory impairment may occur after large doses but is otherwise a rare reaction.

Continued.

TABLE 11-3 *Adverse effects of drugs commonly used by the elderly—cont'd*

Medication	Adverse effects	Cautions and comments
ANTIMICROBIAL AGENTS—cont'd		
Penicillins	Hypersensitivity reactions occur in up to 10% of clients treated. They include skin rashes, angioedema, serum sickness, fever, and, rarely, anaphylactic shock. Arachnoiditis or severe and potentially fatal encephalopathy may occur with intrathecal injection of penicillin G. This route of administration should therefore be avoided. In the presence of renal impairment, 10 to 20 million U of penicillin G may cause lethargy, confusion, or seizures. High doses of sodium or potassium salts should also be avoided in such clients because these may cause hypernatremia or hyperkalemia. Accidental injection of the penicillins into the sciatic nerve causes severe pain and dysfunction of the nerve, which may last for weeks.	Cross-allergic reactions are likely to occur in 80% of individuals receiving different penicillins and in 20% of those receiving cephalosporins. Lack of a skin reaction to benzylpenicilloylpolylysine (Pre-Pen) makes it unlikely that a person will have a serious hypersensitivity reaction to the penicillins. Epinephrine is drug of choice for treating anaphylactic shock. Because penicillins rely on renal excretion for their elimination from the body, toxic reactions may occur when very large doses are administered to clients with renal impairment.
Sulfonamides	Fairly common side effects include anorexia, nausea, vomiting, and allergic reactions. Allergic reactions are characterized by skin and mucous membrane lesions, drug fever, and less commonly by vascular lesions. Renal damage from crystalluria may occur in about 0.2% of clients treated. Hemolytic anemia may occur in clients with erythrocyte deficiency of glucose 6-phosphate dehydrogenase. Agranulocytosis occurs in about 0.1% of clients treated. Goiter, hypothyroidism, and thrombocytopenia are relatively rare complications.	Cross-allergic reactions with different sulfonamides occur in about 20% of cases. Although crystalluria is now less common with newer sulfonamides, this adverse effect still occurs to a significant extent. It can be largely prevented by ensuring an adequate fluid intake such that urine output is at least 1200 ml/day.
Tetracyclines	Fairly common side effects include epigastric distress, nausea, vomiting, diarrhea, and photosensitivity. Hepatotoxicity may occur when doses exceeding 2 gm/day are given parenterally. Leukocytosis, atypical lymphocytes, toxic granulation of granulocytes, and thrombocytopenia may occur occasionally with long-term therapy. Weight loss caused by catabolic effects of drug is likely to occur in debilitated clients. Suprainfections involving *Candida* organisms, staphylo-	Any diarrhea occurring during tetracycline therapy should be immediately investigated to rule out potentially fatal staphylococcal enterocolitis or pseudomembranous colitis. In both of these conditions tetracycline therapy should be withdrawn and clients should be given oral vancomycin. Calcium in milk products or antacids and other antacids containing aluminum or magnesium can inhibit absorption of tetracyclines. Oral iron preparations have also been re-

TABLE 11-3   Adverse effects of drugs commonly used by the elderly—cont'd

Medication	Adverse effects	Cautions and comments
ANTIMICROBIAL AGENTS—cont'd		
Tetracyclines—cont'd	cocci, or *Clostridium difficile* may occur. Vestibular toxicity has been reported in clients receiving minocycline. It is reversible on withdrawal of the drug. Renal toxicity may occur if renal function is already impaired. IV administration may cause thrombophlebitis.	ported to impair absorption of these drugs. Tetracyclines form water-insoluble chelates with these divalent and trivalent cations, thereby becoming unavailable for absorption.
ANTIPARKINSONIAN AGENTS		
Amantadine	Insomnia, dizziness, lethargy, drowsiness, and slurred speech may occasionally occur. Hallucinations, confusion, and nightmares can occur, especially with combined anticholinergic therapy or if client has an underlying psychiatric disorder. Nausea, vomiting, anorexia, and constipation are observed relatively infrequently. Livedo reticularis in lower extremities may occur with long-term treatment and represents a cosmetic problem.	Amantadine is less likely to produce serious adverse effects than levodopa but is also less efficacious in treatment of Parkinson's disease. However, doses exceeding 200 mg/day can markedly increase incidence of side effects.
Anticholinergics Benztropine Cycrimine Procyclidine Trihexyphenidyl	Atropine-like side effects may be prominent. Mental confusion, delirium, somnolence, and hallucinations may also occur.	These agents are therapeutically less efficacious than levodopa, but concurrent therapy with levodopa or amantadine often provides additional amelioration of symptoms.
Levodopa	Adverse effects are frequently encountered and can be expected in majority of clients. GI tract symptoms and orthostatic hypotension are worse during initiation of therapy, and then tolerance to them usually develops. Abnormal involuntary movements develop eventually in majority of clients receiving long-term therapy. Behavioral disturbances develop in about 15% of clients treated and include confusion, delirium, depression, paranoid delusions, hallucinations, and psychotic episodes. Cardiac dysrhythmias may occur, but their incidence is fairly low.	Concurrent administration of a peripheral dopa decarboxylase inhibitor (carbidopa dosage and reduces incidence of dosage to about 25% of the pre–carbidopa dosage and reduces indicence of adverse GI tract and cardiac effects. However, abnormal involuntary movements may occur earlier and become more severe with combination therapy. Supplements of pyridoxine increase activity of dopa decarboxylase, but this effect can be prevented by carbidopa. Phenothiazines and haloperidol are contraindicated because they nullify effects of levodopa. MAO inhibitors are also best avoided because they may potentiate central effects of levodopa in an unpredictable manner. Dosages should be individualized and gradually increased at weekly intervals as required.

Continued.

TABLE 11-3 **Adverse effects of drugs commonly used by the elderly—cont'd**

Medication	Adverse effects	Cautions and comments
ANTIPSYCHOTIC AGENTS		
Haloperidol	Sedation, orthostatic hypotension, tachycardia, and atropine-like side effects are less frequently observed than during phenothiazine therapy; however, extrapyramidal syndromes are of the same type and occur at about the same frequency as that seen with phenothiazines. Anorexia, nausea, vomiting, vertigo, agitation, headache, confusion, and hallucinations may occur. Rarer adverse effects include cholestatic jaundice, photosensitivity, convulsions, gynecomastia, galactorrhea, leukopenia, and leukocytosis.	Extrapyramidal syndromes usually respond to therapy with amantadine or anticholinergic agents. For reasons discussed later (see Phenothiazines) levodopa should be avoided.

Phenothiazines
  Chlorpromazine
  Fluphenazine
  Mesoridazine
  Perphenazine
  Prochlorperazine
  Thioridazine
  Trifluoperazine
	Common adverse effects include sedation, skin rashes, extrapyramidal syndromes, orthostatic hypotension, and tachycardia. Atropine-like side effects, gynecomastia, galactorrhea, interference with ejaculation, and disturbances in temperature regulation may also occur. Obstructive jaundice, leukocytosis, and eosinophilia occur less frequently. Agranulocytosis and pigmentary degeneration of retina are rare complications.	Extrapyramidal syndromes observed include parkinsonism, akathisia, acute dystonic reactions, tardive dyskinesia, and perioral tremor. Severe symptoms can be treated with anticholinergics or amantadine; levodopa should be avoided because it usually aggravates psychotic state being treated. Thioridazine is usually better tolerated by elderly clients because it is less likely to cause sedation, orthostatic hypotension, and extrapyramidal reactions.

ANTIULCER AGENTS		
Antacids	These agents tend to decrease absorption of iron. Those containing aluminum, calcium, or magnesium will decrease absorption of tetracyclines.	
Aluminum hydroxide	Constipation is the most common side effect. Hypophosphatemia and its sequelae (osteomalacia and calcium nephroliths) may occur with long-term usage in clients receiving low-phosphate diet. Intestinal obstruction or concretions in stools are fairly rare complications.	Concurrent therapy with magnesium hydroxide usually prevents constipation. The aluminum ion binds phosphate and prevents phosphate absorption. Use with caution in presence of gastric outlet obstruction because aluminum ions inhibit smooth muscle contraction.

TABLE 11-3   Adverse effects of drugs commonly used by the elderly—cont'd

Medication	Adverse effects	Cautions and comments
ANTIULCER AGENTS—cont'd		
Antacids—cont'd		
Calcium carbonate	Hypercalcemia may occur in clients with impaired renal function, and this in turn can cause nephrolithiasis. Milk-alkali syndrome may occur with chronic usage. Belching occurs because of the release of CO_2 in the stomach.	Hypercalcemia can potentiate cardiac toxicity of digitalis glycosides. Calcium carbonate is now seldom used for chronic therapy of peptic ulcers because of its greater toxicity and because it usually causes a rebound increase in stomach acid secretion.
Magnesium hydroxide	Diarrhea is most common side effect. Hypermagnesemia may occur in clients with limited kidney function. Fecal stones are a rare complication.	Concurrent therapy with aluminum hydroxide usually prevents diarrhea. A related drug, magnesium trisilicate, possesses same adverse effects and, in addition, may cause siliceous nephroliths.
Sodium bicarbonate	Chronic use leads to systemic alkalosis and when combined with milk can cause milk-alkali syndrome. The excess sodium absorbed may be detrimental to clients with congestive heart failure, hypertension, or edema. Belching occurs because of release of CO_2 in the stomach.	Chronic use is not advised because of potential toxicity and because sodium bicarbonate tends to cause a rebound increase in stomach acid secretion.
Atropine-like agents Atropine Belladonna tincture Glycopyrrolate Isopropamide Mepenzolate Propantheline	Common adverse effects include dry mouth, tachycardia, blurred vision, urinary retention, constipation, nausea, and vomiting. CNS excitement and mental confusion may occur but are unlikely to occur with quaternary ammonium derivatives (e.g., propantheline). They can precipitate acute attacks of glaucoma in clients with narrow drainage angle. Mucous plugs may form in clients with asthma or chronic obstructive lung disease. Hyperthermia can occur in a hot environment. Impotence and some decrease in neuromuscular transmission may occur with quaternary ammonium derivatives.	Dry mouth can be relieved by sucking on hard sugarless candy. Urinary retention is likely to occur in clients with prostate hypertrophy. These drugs are contraindicated in clients with narrow-angle glaucoma. These drugs inhibit perspiration and therefore reduce one of the mechanisms for heat loss from the body. Quaternary ammonium derivatives are contraindicated in clients with myasthenia gravis.
Carbenoxolone	This drug regularly produces mineralocorticoid-like effects with chronic usage (e.g., sodium and fluid retention and potassium loss). Hyperglycemia may occur in diabetics. Diabetics should therefore monitor their blood or urine glucose levels more frequently when therapy with this agent is initiated or withdrawn.	Drug is best avoided in clients with congestive heart failure, hypertension, or edema. Fluid and electrolyte imbalance are best treated with thiazide diuretics and potassium supplements. Spironolactone interferes with its ulcer-healing effects and therefore should not be used to treat edema caused by this drug. *Continued.*

TABLE 11-3 **Adverse effects of drugs commonly used by the elderly—cont'd**

Medication	Adverse effects	Cautions and comments
ANTIULCER AGENTS—cont'd		
Cimetidine	Headache, dizziness, fatigue, constipation or diarrhea, and skin rashes are the most commonly reported side effects. Slurred speech, confusion, delirium, or coma may occur when high doses are used in clients with impaired renal function. Gynecomastia and galactorrhea may occur when high doses are used for more than 8 weeks.	About 60% of the drug is excreted in unchanged form by the kidneys. Dosage interval should therefore be increased in those clients with impaired renal function (i.e., 300 mg every 8 to 12 hours, depending on degree of renal impairment).
BRONCHODILATORS		

Adrenergic agonists
  Albuterol
  Epinephrine
  Ephedrine
  Isoproterenol
  Metaproterenol
  Terbutaline
	Cardiac symptoms include tachycardia, angina pain, and dysrhythmias. CNS excitement characterized by anxiety, confusion, hallucinations, and insomnia is more likely to occur with ephedrine. Hyperglycemia may develop in diabetic clients. Paradoxic airway resistance may develop with repeated excessive inhalations.	Cardiac dysrhythmias are more likely to occur on concurrent therapy with volatile anesthetics and digitalis glycosides and in those clients with coronary artery disease or hyperthyroidism. β_2-agonists, such as metaproterenol, albuterol, and terbutaline, are less likely to produce adverse cardiac effects.

Theophylline	This drug has narrow margin of safety, and toxic effects can occur at twice the therapeutic blood levels. Toxic symptoms include nausea, vomiting, headache, hypotension, tachycardia, angina pain, cardiac dysrhythmias, CNS excitement, and seizures.	Dosage must be individualized by monitoring blood levels of drug to arrive at safe and effective maintenance dosage. Seizures may be severe but usually respond to diazepam therapy.
CARDIAC AGENTS		
Digitalis glycosides	These drugs have narrow margin of safety and readily produce toxic effects. Anorexia, nausea, vomiting, diarrhea, and abdominal discomfort are usually the earliest signs of toxicity. Headache, fatigue, drowsiness, neurologic pain resembling trigeminal neuralgia, and paresthesias may also occur with slight overdoses. Visual disturbances, which include blurred vision and chromatopsia for yellow and green, occur in toxic doses. Toxic mental symptoms are characterized by disorientation, confusion, aphasia, delirium, nightmares, and hallucinations. Toxic cardiac symptoms in-	Doses must be individualized by monitoring cardiac effects and, if necessary, by measuring blood concentrations of these drugs. Hypokalemia and hypercalcemia potentiate cardiac toxicity of these drugs. Common causes of hypokalemia include chronic use of potassium-losing diuretics, prolonged diarrhea or excessive chronic use of laxatives, and inadequate dietary intake of potassium. Severe cardiac dysrhythmias can be treated by administration of potassium, phenytoin, or lidocaine. Potassium should *not* be used if serum potassium levels are higher than normal because

TABLE 11-3   *Adverse effects of drugs commonly used by the elderly—cont'd*

Medication	Adverse effects	Cautions and comments
CARDIAC AGENTS—cont'd		
Digitalis glycosides—cont'd	clude severe sinus bradycardia, various degrees of heart block, and variety of atrial and ventricular dysrhythmias.	this can lead to complete AV conduction block and cardiac arrest. Atropine can be used to control excessive sinus bradycardia and second- or third-degree AV block. (See Chapter 12, "Drug Selection and Dosage in the Elderly," for further discussion.)
Disopyramide	Atropine-like effects, nausea, abdominal pain, and diarrhea occur fairly frequently. Depression of ventricular function may be noted in clients with latent or overt heart failure.	About 50% of disopyramide is excreted in unchanged form by the kidneys. Maintenance doses should be carefully adjusted for those with renal impairment, according to rate of creatinine clearance.
Lidocaine	Depression of ventricular function may be noted in clients with latent or overt heart failure. Moderate overdoses may produce feelings of dissociation, paresthesias, mild drowsiness, or mild agitation. Higher concentrations cause disorientation, muscle twitching, convulsions, and respiratory arrest.	Rate of lidocaine metabolism is related to rate of hepatic blood flow. Heart failure reduces hepatic blood flow and therefore slows rate of its inactivation. For this reason smaller doses should be given to clients whose cardiac output is depressed.
Nitroglycerin	Headache is common and can be severe. Postural hypotension and possibly syncope may occur if client remains in standing position after sublingual administration. Skin rashes may occasionally occur.	Longer duration of action than that achieved by sublingual administration can be obtained by applying ointment form of drug to the skin. However, tolerance may develop with chronic use of the agent in this manner.
Phenytoin	When used IV to treat dysrhythmias the drug may produce drowsiness, nystagmus, vertigo, ataxia, or nausea. Side effects to orally administered phenytoin are described under the heading *Antiepileptic Agents.*	IV administration is preferred because drug's absorption after IM administration is unreliable. Intermittent IV injections should be given because constant IV infusion of drug causes severe phlebitis. If necessary, blood levels of this drug can be monitored.
Procainamide	Incidence of adverse effects is relatively high. Hypersensitivity reactions are the most common and troublesome. Allergic reactions include fever, agranulocytosis, myalgias, angioedema, skin rashes, and a systemic lupus erythematosus-like syndrome. Anorexia, nausea,	Dosage should be individualized by monitoring ECG and, if necessary, by measuring blood levels of drug. Initiation of therapy by IV route should be done cautiously to avoid excessive hypotension. *Continued.*

TABLE 11-3   **Adverse effects of drugs commonly used by the elderly—cont'd**

Medication	Adverse effects	Cautions and comments
CARDIAC AGENTS—cont'd		
Procainamide—cont'd	and vomiting may occur. IV administration tends to cause hypotension. CNS symptoms occur occasionally and include giddiness, psychoses, hallucinations, and mental depression. Cardiac toxicities resemble those caused by quinidine and require same precautionary measures.	
Propranolol	Adverse effects of propranolol are discussed under the heading *Antihypertensive Agents.*	
Quinidine	About one third of clients cannot tolerate GI tract symptoms, which are characterized by nausea, vomiting, and diarrhea. Excessive ventricular tachycardia may occur during course of treating atrial fibrillation. Pretreatment of such clients with digitalis glycosides is generally advised to avoid the problem. Hypotension tends to occur when drug is given by IV route. Hypersensitivity reactions rarely occur but may be serious (e.g., fever, thrombocytopenia, or anaphylactic shock). Excessive doses cause cinchonism and cardiac dysrhythmias, which are characterized by SA block or arrest, high-grade AV block, and ventricular asystole or ventricular dysrhythmias.	Dose should be individualized by monitoring ECG and, if necessary, by measuring blood levels of drug. IV infusion should be slow to prevent nypotension. Blood pressure and ECG should be monitored continuously. Cinchonism is characterized by tinnitus, loss of hearing, blurred vision, altered color perception, confusion, delirium, and psychosis.
DIURETICS		
Furosemide	This drug has high diuretic efficacy and can readily produce dehydration, hyponatremia, hypokalemia, and alkalosis. Hyperuricemia occurs fairly frequently and may precipitate gouty arthritis in susceptible clients. Painful distention of bladder may occur in clients with prostatic hypertrophy. Rarer complications include hyperglycemia, interstitial nephritis, transient deafness, and GI tract disturbances with or without bleeding.	Doses should be individualized and serum electrolytes checked periodically to ensure that imbalances do not occur. Potassium supplements may be required to prevent hypokalemia. Hypokalemia potentiates toxicity of digitalis glycosides. This drug tends to inhibit renal excretion of lithium and therefore may enhance its toxicity.

TABLE 11-3   *Adverse effects of drugs commonly used by the elderly—cont'd*

Medication	Adverse effects	Cautions and comments
DIURETICS—cont'd		
Spironolactone	Hyperkalemia is the most serious adverse effect observed. Nausea, vomiting, cramping, and diarrhea occur but are usually mild. Gynecomastia and androgen-like effects in women are fairly common with chronic usage.	Hyperkalemia occurs more readily in clients on diet rich in potassium or in those with renal impairment. This drug inhibits the ulcer healing effects of carbenoxolone and may enhance toxicity of lithium because it tends to inhibit renal excretion of this drug.
Triamterene	Hyperkalemia is most serious adverse effect observed. Most common side effects include nausea, vomiting, leg cramps, dizziness, and mild azotemia. Megaloblastic anemia, responsive to folic acid therapy, may occur, especially in clients with alcoholic liver cirrhosis.	Hyperkalemia occurs more readily in clients on diet rich in potassium or in those with renal impairment. The drug tends to inhibit renal excretion of lithium and may enhance its toxicity by this mechanism.

Thiazides and related diuretics
  Chlorthalidone
  Hydrochlorothiazide
  Metolazone
  Quinethazone
	Hypokalemia may occur unless clients are on potassium-rich diet. Hyperglycemia may occur in diabetics. Hyperuricemia also tends to occur, and this can precipitate gouty arthritis in susceptible clients. Borderline renal or hepatic insufficiency may be unpredictably aggravated by these drugs. Rarer complications include hypersensitivity reactions, cholestatic jaundice, photosensitivity, bone marrow depression, necrotizing vasculitis, and interstitial nephritis.	Potassium supplements are not routinely required if client's diet contains foods rich in potassium (e.g., orange, pineapple, and tomato juices; dried apricots and peaches; bananas; potatoes; broccoli; brussels sprouts; yams; and winter squash). Hypokalemia potentiates toxicity of digitalis glycosides. These drugs tend to inhibit renal excretion of lithium and therefore may potentiate its toxicity.

HORMONES		

Estrogens
  Conjugated estrogens
  Diethylstilbestrol
  Estradiol
  Ethinyl estradiol
	Morning nausea, especially when therapy is initiated, is the most common complaint. Anorexia, vomiting, and mild diarrhea are less common side effects. Edema, conversion of latent to overt diabetes, and periodic uterine bleeding may occur with chronic use. Long-term therapy has been reported to increase the risk of endometrial and, possibly, breast cancer.	Risk of developing endometrial carcinoma is directly related to duration of therapy. This risk has been reported to be 2 to 15 times greater than incidence of this cancer in clients who have not used estrogens. Periodic examination should be performed to ensure that this complication does not occur. Data on breast cancer are still controversial.

Thyroid hormones	Excessive doses cause hyperthyroidism, which is characterized by tachycardia, heat intolerance, hyperactivity, anxiety insomnia, and diarrhea. Angina pectoris, cardiac dysrhythmias, heart failure, muscle wasting, and osteoporosis may ensue if hyperthyroidism is allowed to continue.	Doses should be individualized by monitoring responses, especially cardiac effects. These hormones should be taken on an empty stomach to minimize irregular absorption caused by foods.

Continued.

TABLE 11-3   **Adverse effects of drugs commonly used by the elderly—cont'd**

Medication	Adverse effects	Cautions and comments
SEDATIVE-HYPNOTICS		
Barbiturates Amobarbital Barbital Butabarbital Pentobarbital Phenobarbital Secobarbital	Oversedation and "hangover" are the most common side effects. Physical dependence, tolerance, and psychologic dependence can develop with chronic use. Paradoxic excitement may occur in some clients. Porphyria may be induced in susceptible individuals. Nightmares frequently occur when hypnotic therapy is withdrawn.	Barbiturates are poorly tolerated by most elderly clients and have been largely replaced in therapy by benzodiazepines. Alcohol potentiates CNS-depressant effects, and additive effects can be expected with concurrent use of other CNS-depressant drugs. Respiratory depression occurs with excessive doses.
Benzodiazepines Chlordiazepoxide Diazepam Flurazepam Oxazepam	Oversedation, light-headedness, ataxia, confusion, slurred speech, retrograde amnesia, dry mouth, headache, vertigo, nausea, vomiting, epigastric distress, skin rashes, and diarrhea may occur during therapy. Cognition is generally less affected than motor performance. Physical dependence may occur when high doses are used for prolonged periods of time. Psychologic dependence may develop with chronic use. Paradoxic excitement, anxiety, and hostility have been reported in some clients. Agranulocytosis is a rare complication.	Drugs with a shorter half-life (e.g., oxazepam) are less likely to accumulate in body and therefore may be safer for elderly clients. Alcohol potentiates CNS-depressant effects, and additive effects can be expected with concurrent use of other CNS depressants. Overdoses are less likely than other sedative-hypnotics to depress respiration.
Chloral hydrate	Unpleasant taste, epigastric distress, aggravation of peptic ulcers, light-headedness, malaise, ataxia, and nightmares are the most frequently observed side effects. Allergic skin rashes, eosinophilia, and leukopenia may occur in some clients. Physical dependence, tolerance, and possibly psychologic dependence can develop with chronic use.	Epigastric distress can be reduced by diluting drug in water or milk before ingestion. Additive CNS depressant effects can be expected with concurrent use of alcohol and other CNS depressants. Excessive doses cause respiratory depression.
Meprobamate	Drowsiness and ataxia are major adverse effects observed. Hypotension and allergic skin rashes may occur in some clients. Physical dependence, tolerance, and psychologic dependence can occur with chronic use.	Respiratory depression occurs when excessive doses are used. Alcohol potentiates the CNS-depressant effects, and additive effects can be expected with concurrent use of other CNS depressants.
LAXATIVES *Note:*	*Habituation may occur with chronic laxative use. Colon may become dilated and defecation reflex blunted. These ef-*	*In most cases constipation can be relieved by increasing fluid intake, increasing amount of nondigestable fiber in*

TABLE 11-3   Adverse effects of drugs commonly used by the elderly—cont'd

Medication	Adverse effects	Cautions and comments
LAXATIVES—cont'd		
Note:—cont'd	fects in turn tend to reinforce need for laxatives. Laxatives should not be used when signs and symptoms of inflamed appendix exist because they may induce perforation.	diet, and by regular moderate exercise. Fruits, vegetables, nuts, and cereals are rich sources of dietary fiber.
Bulk-forming agents Bran Psyllium Celluloses	Flatulence, especially during first few days, is the most common complaint. Intestinal obstruction and impaction have been reported in clients with gross intestinal pathologic conditions.	Psyllium and celluloses should be mixed with 240 ml of fluid before ingestion and followed with additional 240 ml. Adequate fluid intake should be ensured.
Docusates	These agents may enhance absorption of coadministered drugs.	These are stool softeners; they possess limited laxative activity but do allow easier passage of stools without straining. Adequate fluid intake should be ensured. They should not be coadministered with mineral oil.
Magnesium citrate, hydroxide, and sulfate	Adverse effects of these agents are discussed under the heading *Antiulcer Agents.*	Chronic use of these agents should be avoided. Adequate fluid intake should be ensured.
Mineral oil	Chronic usage may lead to deficiencies of vitamins A, D, E, and K. Leakage of oil past anal sphincter is an annoying side effect and is occasionally the cause of pruritus ani. Accidental aspiration can cause lipid pneumonitis.	Habitual use of this agent should be avoided. This agent inhibits absorption of fat-soluble vitamins and perhaps other lipoid substances or drugs. Docusates may enhance mineral oil absorption; therefore concurrent use of these agents is not recommended.
Sodium phosphate Sodium sulfate	Some sodium does get absorbed, and this can be harmful to clients with edema, congestive heart failure, and hypertension. Sodium sulfate has an unpleasant taste.	Chronic use of these agents should be discouraged. Adequate fluid intake should be ensured.
Stimulant laxatives Bisacodyl Cascara sagrada Danthron Phenolphthalein Senna	Excessive usage can cause dehydration, hyponatremia, and hypokalemia. Phenolphthalein may occasionally cause hypersensitivity reactions characterized by skin rashes, lupus erythematosus-like syndrome, or Stevens-Johnson syndrome.	Chronic use of these agents should be discouraged. Adequate fluid intake should be ensured. Pink to red-brown discoloration of urine may occur with cascara sagrada, danthron, phenolphthalein, or senna. The client should be informed of this possibility to avoid unnecessary anxiety. Concurrent ingestion of milk or antacids with oral bisacodyl tablets may cause enteric coating to dissolve in the stomach; if this occurs, severe gastric irritation may result.

Continued.

TABLE 11-3   **Adverse effects of drugs commonly used by the elderly—cont'd**

Medication	Adverse effects	Cautions and comments
VITAMINS AND MINERALS		
Note:	With the exception of vitamins A and D, megadoses of vitamins cause few adverse effects. Water-soluble vitamins (B-complex and ascorbic acid) are readily excreted by the kidneys if excessive amounts are used. Fat-soluble vitamins (A, D, E, and K), however, may accumulate in body.	There are few established therapeutic reasons for using megadoses of vitamins. Therefore use of vitamins in excess of daily requirements should be discouraged.
Iron (oral) Ferrous salts	GI tract symptoms are the most common effects and include heartburn, epigastric distress, nausea, and constipation or diarrhea. Hemochromatosis may occur with long-term excessive use.	Lowering dosage or taking iron with meals will lessen GI tract symptoms but will also decrease amount available for absorption. Antacids tend to decrease absorption of iron. Iron will darken stools, and client should be informed of this effect to avoid unnecessary anxiety.
Iron (parenteral) Iron dextran	IM administration causes persistent pain and discoloration at site of injection. Headache, malaise, muscle and joint pains, hypotension, tachycardia, nausea, vomiting, and bronchospasms may occur and are more commonly observed after IV administration. Allergic-like reactions occur occasionally and include skin rashes, fever, urticaria, bronchospasms, and, rarely, anaphylactic shock. Generalized or local lymphadenopathy and seizures have also been reported.	Because of their greater toxicity, parenteral iron preparations should only be used in clients who cannot tolerate or do not respond to oral preparations. It is advisable to administer a small test dose to check for idiosyncratic or allergic-like reactions before administering larger amounts. IV doses should be injected slowly (20 to 50 mg/min) to lessen severity of adverse effects.
Potassium supplements Potassium chloride	Hyperkalemia may occur in clients with impaired renal function. Nausea, vomiting, and diarrhea can occur because of the irritative properties of potassium chloride. Solutions of potassium chloride have an unpleasant taste, and this may decrease compliance. Enteric-coated tablets may cause small bowel ulcerations; wax matrix tablets, such as Slow-K, are probably less likely to produce such ulcerations.	Potassium-sparing diuretics (e.g., spironolactone and triamterene) and salt substitutes containing potassium are contraindicated because they can contribute to development of hyperkalemia. Serum potassium levels should be checked periodically to ensure that this complication does not occur.
Vitamin A (retinol)	Chronic ingestion of 10,000 μg or more of retinol per day can cause toxic symptoms. Toxic signs include irritability, headache, drowsiness, anorexia, vomiting, gingivitis, mouth fissures,	Megadoses of vitamin A are seldom justified. They may, however, be helpful in treatment of certain skin diseases such as psoriasis and ichthyosis.

TABLE 11-3 *Adverse effects of drugs commonly used by the elderly—cont'd*

Medication	Adverse effects	Cautions and comments
VITAMINS AND MINERALS—cont'd		
Vitamin A (retinol)—cont'd	skin desquamation, liver damage, enlarged spleen, loss of body hair, and elevation of cerebrospinal fluid. Latter effect may mimic symptoms of brain tumor.	
Vitamin C (ascorbic acid)	Although it is a relatively nontoxic substance, some adverse effects have been reported to occur when megadoses (0.5 to 10 gm/day) are used chronically. GI tract symptoms of nausea, vomiting, and diarrhea are most common. Oxalate kidney stones have been reported. Hyperuricemia tends to occur, and this may precipitate gouty arthritis in susceptible persons. Hemolytic anemia may occur in clients with erythrocyte deficiency of glucose 6-phosphate dehydrogenase. Scurvy may occasionally occur in clients who have been taking large doses for long periods and then abruptly stop taking the vitamin.	As the amount of this vitamin ingested is increased, efficiency of absorption decreases (e.g., 50 mg of which 100% is absorbed versus 10 gm of which 20% is absorbed). The excess not absorbed acts as osmotic agent and induces diarrhea. Some ascorbic acid is normally metabolized to oxalate. When doses are increased, more oxalate is produced, and this can in turn lead to formation of oxalate kidney stones. Plasma concentrations greater than 1.4 mg/100 ml are readily excreted, thereby acidifying urine. Claims for effectiveness of megadoses of vitamin C in prevention or treatment of common cold or other conditions have not been substantiated by most investigators and remain controversial.
Vitamin D (cholecalciferol)	Chronic use of more than 50,000 IU per day in person with normal sensitivity to this vitamin can cause toxic reactions. Initial signs and symptoms of toxicity include weakness, fatigue, headache, nausea, and vomiting. These symptoms are the result of hypercalcemia. Osteoporosis also occurs. Prolonged hypercalcemia causes deposition of calcium in soft tissues (e.g., kidney, heart, blood vessels, lungs, and skin). Death can occur because of renal or heart damage.	Hypercalcemia results from excessive absorption of calcium, increased resorption of bone mineral, and decreased renal excretion of calcium. Hypercalcemia increases cardiac toxicity of digitalis glycosides. Use of megadoses of vitamin D is seldom justified. Some clients may inherit or develop an inability to convert vitamin D to its active form, calcitriol. Such individuals can be treated with *physiologic doses* of calcitriol.
Vitamin E	Doses as high as 1000 IU per day have been used with relative safety. Adverse effects that have been reported include nausea, muscle weakness, fatigue, blurred vision, mouth fissures, and an increased bleeding tendency.	With possible exception of intermittent claudication, all other claims for therapeutic effectiveness of megadoses of this vitamin remain unsubstantiated. Megadoses of vitamin E may potentiate effects of anticoagulants.

REFERENCES

Armstrong, W.A., Driever, C.W., and Hays, R.L.: Analysis of drug-drug interactions in a geriatric population, Am. J. Hosp. Pharm. **37**:385, 1980.

Ascione, F.J., et al.: Seniors and pharmacists: improving the dialogue, Am. Pharm. **20**:30, 1980.

Boston Collaborative Drug Surveillance Program: Hospital admissions due to adverse drug reactions, Arch. Intern. Med. **134**:219, 1974.

Boyd, J.R., et al.: Drug defaulting. II. Analysis of noncompliance patterns, Am. J. Hosp. Pharm. **31**:455, 1974.

Caird, F.I., and Judge, T.G.: The assessment of the geriatric patient, London, 1974, Pitman Medical.

Cape, R.: Aging: its complex management, New York, 1978, Harper & Row, Publishers, Inc.

Caranasos, G.J., Stewart, R.B., and Cluff, L.E.: Drug-induced illness leading to hospitalization, J.A.M.A. **228**:713, 1974.

Cluff, L.E., Thornton, C.F., and Seidl, L.G.: Studies on the epidemiology of adverse drug reactions, J.A.M.A. **188**:979, 1964.

Cole, P., and Emmanuel, S.: Drug consultation: its significance to the discharged hospital patient and relevance as a role for the pharmacist, Am. J. Hosp. Pharm. **28**:954, 1971.

Dall, J.L.C.: Maintenance digoxin in elderly patients, Br. Med. J. **2**:705, 1970.

Eberhardt, R.C., and Robinson, L.A.: Clinical pharmacy involvement in a geriatric health clinic at a high-rise apartment center, J. Am. Geriatr. Soc. **27**:514, 1979.

Frisk, P.A., Cooper, J.W., and Campbell, N.A.: Community-hospital pharmacist detection of drug-related problems upon patient admission to small hospitals, Am. J. Hosp. Pharm. **33**:738, 1977.

Gibson, I.I., and O'Hare, M.O.: Prescription drugs for old people at home, Gerontol. Clin. **10**:271, 1968.

Hodkinson, H.M.: Common symptoms of disease in the elderly, ed. 2, Oxford, 1980, Blackwell Scientific Publications.

Hurwitz, N.: Admissions to hospital due to drugs, Br. Med. J. **1**:539, 1969a.

Hurwitz, N.: Predisposing factors in adverse reactions to drugs, Br. Med. J. **1**:536, 1969b.

Katzman, R.: The prevalence and malignancy of alzheimer disease: a major killer, Arch. Neurol. **33**:217, 1976.

Lamy, P.P.: Misuse and abuse of drugs by the elderly, Am. Pharm. **20**:254, 1980.

Learoyd, B.M.: Psychotropic drugs and the elderly patient, Med. J. Aust. **1**:1131, 1972.

McKenney, J.M., and Harrison, W.L.: Drug-related hospital admissions, Am. J. Hosp. Pharm. **33**:792, 1976.

Melmon, K.L.: Preventable drug reactions—causes and cures, N. Engl. J. Med. **284**:1361, 1971.

Melmon, K.L., and Morrelli, H.F.: Drug reactions. In Melmon, K.L., and Morrelli, H.F., editors: Clinical pharmacology: basic principles of therapeutics, ed. 2, New York, 1978, Macmillan, Inc.

Miller, M.B., and Elliot, D.F.: Errors and omissions in diagnostic records on admission of patients to a nursing home, J. Am. Geriatr. Soc. **24**:108, 1976.

Moore-Smith, B.: The management of hypertension in the elderly. In Denham, M.J., editor: The treatment of medical problems in the elderly, Baltimore, 1980, University Park Press.

Neely, E., and Patrick, M.L.: Problems of aged persons taking medications at home, Nursing Res. **17**:52, 1968.

Ritschel, W.A.: Disposition of drugs in geriatric patients, Pharm. Int. **1**:226, 1980.

Sackett, D.L.: The magnitude of compliance and noncompliance. In Sackett, D.L., and Haynes, R.B., editors: Compliance with therapeutic regimens, Baltimore, 1976, Johns Hopkins University Press.

Savett, L.A.: Drug-induced illness: causes for delayed diagnosis and a strategy for early recognition, Postgrad. Med. **67**:155, 1980.

Schwartz, D.: The elderly patient and his medications, Geriatrics **20**:517, 1965.

Sharpe, T.R., and Mikeal, R.L.: Patient compliance with antibiotic regimens, Am. J. Hosp. Pharm. **31**:479, 1974.

Skoll, S.L., August, R.J., and Johnson, G.E.: Drug prescribing for the elderly in Saskatchewan during 1976, Can. Med. Assoc. J. **121**:1074, 1979.

Smith, J.W., et al.: Studies on the epidemiology of adverse drug reactions. V. Clinical factors influencing susceptibility, Ann. Intern. Med. **65**:629, 1966.

Steinberg, S.: Drug therapy in the elderly: problems and recommendations, On Continuing Practice **8**:15, 1981.

Todhunter, E.N.: Nutrition of the elderly. In Alfin-Slater, R.B., and Kritchevsk, D., editors: Human nutrition a comprehensive treatise: Nutrition and adult micronutrients, vol. 3B, New York, 1980, Plenum Press Corp.

Tomlinson, B.E., Blessed, G., and Roth, M.: Observations on brains of demented people, J. Neurol. Sci. 11:205, 1970.

Vener, A.M., Krupka, L.R., and Climo, J.J.: Drug usage and health characteristics in noninstitutional-ized retired persons, J. Am. Geriatr. Soc. 27:83, 1979.

Williamson, J.: Adverse reactions to prescribed drugs in the elderly. In Crooks, J., and Stevenson, I.H., editors: Drugs and the elderly: perspectives in geriatric clinical pharmacology, Baltimore, 1979, University Park Press.

Williamson, J., and Chopin, J.M.: Adverse reactions to prescribed drugs in the elderly: a multicentre investigation, Age Ageing 9:73, 1980.

CHAPTER 12

Drug selection and dosage in the elderly

John J. Peto

David Skelton

Behold the drug advertisement:
the bold print giveth,
the fine print taketh away.
The Epistle to the Geriatricians

Geriatric care is first and foremost good medical care. This implies that diagnosis is of paramount importance, since easily remediable conditions or symptomatically relievable states may go unrecognized or be labeled as "old age" or senility. Symptomatic management is unacceptable if it merely replaces well-reasoned diagnostic efforts. Once the diagnoses are established, the art and science of clinical therapeutics come to the fore. Many disease conditions, although not curable, can be successfully controlled, their distressing features alleviated, and their progress slowed or even halted. In this area "symptomatic management" is no mean feat and can often tax the skills of even the most proficient therapist.

All therapeutic decisions must be tempered with the humane judgment of the clinician, which takes into consideration the client as an individual. The concept of nontreatment as the "lesser evil" enters into geriatric decision making frequently. However, such an approach must not

be permitted to become the means of dealing with a complex situation, thus bypassing the steps of assessment, investigation, diagnosis, and logical treatment strategies.

The goal of this chapter is to provide a readily accessible source of reference for the clinician treating elderly clients. The vast field of geriatric medicine is divided in this chapter according to organ systems. Under each of these rubrics, diagnostic or pathophysiologic headings are given so that readers can turn to the appropriate section to locate the disease or condition their clients suffer from.

We emphasize that if treatment is given for any condition that has not been correctly or adequately diagnosed, subsequent success is unlikely, yet the side effects of medications will crop up with distressing regularity. We do not advocate, for example, the use of vitamin B_{12} unless appropriate studies confirm the diagnosis of B_{12} deficiency. Naturally, however, to make this diagnosis is a matter of utmost urgency, since subacute, combined degeneration of the spinal cord, if missed, may cripple the client for life.

Under the individual disease headings, readers will find the drugs recommended, with the doses and dosages appropriate for the geriatric population. Where indicated, initial investigations, follow-up studies, and common side effects are listed. Additional information will be discussed under *Cautions and comments.*

Some conditions may overlap two organ systems. In these instances we have arbitrarily assigned the topic to one of these systems (e.g., dementias are classified under *Psychiatry*, not *Central nervous system*). An outline of the disease or condition classification schema used in this chapter follows:

Central nervous system
 Stroke
 Epilepsy
 Parkinson's disease
 Pain
Cardiovascular system
 Peripheral vascular disease
  Arterial disease
  Deep venous thrombosis
 Hypertension
 Hypotension and syncope
 Pulmonary embolic disease
 Cardiac dysrhythmias
 Cardiac failure
Respiratory system
 Chronic obstructive pulmonary disease
Endocrine system
 Diabetes mellitus
 Thyroid disease
  Hyperthyroidism
  Hypothyroidism
Gastrointestinal system
 Peptic ulcer disease
 Constipation
 Diverticular disease
 Irritable bowel syndrome
 Intestinal obstruction
Genitourinary system
 Urinary tract infections
 Urinary incontinence
Musculoskeletal system
 Rheumatoid arthritis
 Osteoarthritis
 Pseudogout
 Paget's disease of the bone
 Giant cell arteritis
Psychiatry
 Affective disorders
 Insomnia
 Dementia

Readers are therefore encouraged to scan several systems, if the diagnosis is not found in their first choice of heading, or to consult the general index of this text. Several conditions, for which treatment is surgical or for which no known pharmacologic approach exists, have been purposely omitted. This chapter is not intended to take the place of textbooks of geriatric medicine but rather to serve as a useful aid and guide in dealing with some of the more frequently encountered geriatric conditions.

Drug therapy in the elderly must be established on an individual basis. The effects of aging on the interpretation of laboratory test results in relation to diagnosis and monitoring of therapy are presented in Chapter 7. Pharmacokinetics of these agents and the effects of renal or hepatic dysfunction on dosage are discussed more fully in Chapter 10. For more specific information on the adverse effects of a particular agent readers are referred to Chapter 11.

CENTRAL NERVOUS SYSTEM (CNS)

Disorders of the CNS account for a large amount of disease and disability in the elderly. We have elected to discuss only four topics: stroke, epilepsy, Parkinson's disease, and pain.

We have endeavored to avoid areas where little effective pharmacologic help can be offered, as well as others that are important but clinically less common in the elderly.

Stroke

A discussion of stroke syndromes must include (1) transient ischemic attacks (TIAs), (2) stroke-in-evolution, (3) acute completed stroke, and (4) prevention of stroke or its recurrence.

DRUG	USUAL GERIATRIC DOSAGE	SIDE EFFECTS/ CONTRAINDICA- TIONS/COMMENTS
TIAs		
Aspirin	325 mg P.O. q.i.d. (enteric-coated form preferred)	Sex difference (Canadian Cooperative Study Group, 1978); observe for gastrointestinal (GI) tract irritation; rule out correctable cause
Stroke-in-evolution		
Warfarin	5 to 10 mg P.O. q.d.	Maintain prothrombin time at 2 to 3 times control value; *note:* do not use if anticoagulation is contraindicated
Acute completed stroke		
Hydrochloro-thiazide	25 to 50 mg P.O. q.AM (to control blood pressure)	Hypokalemia; dehydration; hepatic failure; gout; diabetes
Dexametha-sone	2 to 4 mg P.O./IM/ IV (for cerebral edema only)	Sodium retention; cardiac failure
Prevention of stroke or its recurrence		
Aspirin	325 mg P.O. b.i.d.	See above
Warfarin	5 to 10 mg P.O. q.d.	For embolic strokes; also see above
Hydrochloro-thiazide	25 to 50 mg P.O. q.AM	See above
Other antihy-pertensive agents (e.g., methyldopa, propranolol)		Also see *Hypertension*

Cautions and comments

1. Arterial thromboembolization from the extracranial circulation is the leading cause of TIAs. Antiplatelet agents (e.g., aspirin, dipyridamole) may be effective against platelet-fibrin emboli, but cholesterol debris is not removed. Accordingly, aspirin is least effective in extensive multiple vessel atheromatosis.

2. Surgical therapy (carotid endarterectomy and extra-cerebral/intracerebral bypass surgery) may prove beneficial for clients who have cortical lesions *appropriate* to the symptoms. Since benefits are marginal, investigation and treatment should be carried out in centers with experience performing these procedures. The value of operating on asymptomatic clients with physical signs suggestive of significant arterial lesions—or following a completed stroke—has not yet been conclusively established.

3. Cardiac lesions, hypertensive arteriolar crises, and other vasculopathies should be diagnosed and treated appropriately. Invasive angiographic studies, tissue biopsy, or extensive biochemical workup may be required. If a correctable lesion is discovered, surgery may be indicated to prevent a major stroke or a recurrence.

4. Because of the risk of intracerebral hemorrhage, anticoagulation is not advised in thrombotic strokes, except for stroke-in-evolution, where it continues to advance over many hours or even days ("stuttering stroke").

5. CAT scanning is useful in ruling out a potentially correctable intracranial lesion.

6. Unless there are clinical signs of cerebral herniation, urea, dexamethasone, or mannitol therapy is not indicated in the management of the acute stroke. If therapy for cerebral edema is necessary, dexamethasone (2 to 4 mg P.O./IM/IV q.6hr) is recommended, although neurosurgical dosages are often much higher.

Epilepsy

Seizure disorders may be present for decades, with clients surviving into old age, or they may first occur in later life. After appropriate investigations, treatment will often be effective.

DRUG	USUAL GERIATRIC DOSAGE	SIDE EFFECTS/ CONTRAINDICA- TIONS/COMMENTS
Generalized (tonic-clonic)		
Phenytoin	100 mg P.O. t.i.d. or 300 mg P.O. q.h.s.	See *Cautions and comments*
Carbam-azepine	50 to 100 mg P.O. b.i.d.	Even at these dosages hypotension, hypotonicity, and somnolence are common in the elderly
Partial (focal)		
Phenytoin	100 mg P.O. t.i.d. or 300 mg P.O. q.h.s.	See *Cautions and comments*
Carbam-azepine	50 to 100 mg P.O. b.i.d.	See above

DRUG	USUAL GERIATRIC DOSAGE	SIDE EFFECTS/ CONTRAINDICA- TIONS/COMMENTS
Status epilepticus		
Diazepam	5 to 10 mg slow IV or IM	Look for respiratory depression
Phenytoin	15 mg/kg slow IV (minimum 15 to 20 minutes)	Monitor for cardiac dysrhythmias
Amobarbital	1 mg/min IV; then titrate q.30min (maximum dose 1 gm/24 hr)	Look for respiratory depression; *note:* high risk of cardiac arrest

Cautions and comments

1. Elderly clients who experience a seizure for the first time deserve detailed investigation. This is expected to reveal a cause in 50% of cases, focal seizures being more likely to yield a structural abnormality than seizures generalized from the onset. Vascular disease, subdural hematomas, and tumors will be found most frequently (Schold, Yarnell, and Earnest, 1977).

2. Elderly epileptics receiving chronic therapy deserve a review using sophisticated methods of investigation, including radionuclide imaging and, if available, CAT scanning. Such a workup may reveal unexpected findings of space-occupying lesions not giving rise to focal neurologic signs or symptoms.

3. The current trend in drug management is to achieve seizure control with a single agent. It has been repeatedly demonstrated that optimum blood levels of a single agent will lead to better control (Penry and Newmark, 1979).

4. The correct interpretation of drug blood levels requires appreciation of the following facts:
   a. If seizure control is achieved at lower than recommended drug levels, there is nothing to be gained from increasing the dosage (Reynolds, 1978).
   b. Even within the "therapeutic range" there is increasing likelihood of side effects at higher levels.
   c. Indications for blood level determinations include baseline steady-state determination, sudden recurrence of seizures after good control, detection of toxicity, persistence of seizures despite adequate dosage, and realignment of a multiple-drug regimen (Penry and Porter, 1979).

5. Because phenytoin demonstrates saturation kinetics and hepatic reserves are diminished in the elderly, increases in dosage should be performed slowly, with small increments, especially in the upper ranges of therapeutic drug levels. Since phenytoin is eliminated slowly from the body and because compliance with a t.i.d. regimen is poor, a single daily dose regimen is recommended.

6. Elderly epileptics, in our opinion, should not be started on barbiturates because of the frequent occurrence of sedation. If clients have previously been given phenobarbital, there may be an argument for continuing with the previous regimen, but subtle mental impairment is one of the side effects to be monitored.

7. Polypharmacy, combination therapy using multiple drugs, is reserved for the most brittle epileptics and, in general, the use of more than two drugs is not recommended. Discontinuing medications can be very difficult and should always be attempted through tapering of dosages rather than by sudden cessation of therapy because of the risk of precipitating status epilepticus.

8. The elderly are a highly *heterogeneous* population; therefore predicting how the individual client will handle medications is fraught with uncertainty. Reliance on continuing close clinical scrutiny and measurement of drug blood levels is essential.

Parkinson's disease

Parkinson's disease is a disorder of the basal ganglia (in particular the substantia nigra and nigrostriatal dopaminergic pathways). The more common form of presentation in the elderly is one-sided *tremor*. *Akinesia* may be the initial symptom in a smaller group. The former group usually progresses quite slowly, making a reasonable life-style an attainable goal for most elderly persons. Although medications are of paramount importance, they only represent the foundations of treatment; physical and occupational therapy can enhance the quality of life of these individuals immensely.

DRUG	USUAL GERIATRIC DOSAGE	SIDE EFFECTS/ CONTRAINDICA- TIONS/COMMENTS
Diphenhydramine	12.5 mg P.O. t.i.d.	Sedation
Benztropine	0.5 mg P.O. t.i.d. (start with single q.h.s. dose)	Glaucoma
Trihexyphenidyl	1 mg P.O. t.i.d. (start with single q.h.s. dose)	Glaucoma: monitor intraocular pressure; confusion; agitation; parotitis; urinary retention
Amantadine	100 mg P.O. b.i.d. (start 100 mg P.O. q.d.)	Mental symptoms; congestive heart failure; tolerance may develop rapidly
Levodopa/ carbidopa	100 mg/10 mg P.O. b.i.d.	Nausea; dyskinesias; narrow-angle glaucoma; GI tract bleeding
Levodopa/ benserazide	100 mg/25 mg P.O. q.d. to b.i.d.	Postural hypotension; psychoses

Cautions and comments

1. Before initiating antiparkinsonian therapy, the diagnosis of Parkinson's disease must be established. Other tremors should be considered and ruled out.

    a. Physiologic tremor is a fine tremor that is caused by activation of peripheral β-adrenergic receptors. Isoproterenol enhances it, whereas intraarterial propranolol averts its occurrence.

    b. Essential tremor, a motor disturbance, is a central tremor; consequently, intraarterial propranolol does not block it. However, chronic oral therapy with the same agent is beneficial. The characteristic nodding head tremor of essential tremor is not found in Parkinson's disease. Alcohol is known to diminish the amplitude of this tremor.

    c. Cerebellar tremor has both postural and intention components. It is slower than parkinsonian tremors. Ataxia may coexist with it (Jankovic and Fahn, 1980).

2. Anticholinergic medications are more likely to produce confusion in the elderly than in younger clients. A drug-induced pseudodementia state can result from accumulating drug doses. However, in low doses these drugs may be sufficient to control tremor.

3. Amantadine may be beneficial for akinesia, which is the most disabling symptom of Parkinson's disease. With increasing use, side effects of this drug have been recognized. These include vivid auditory and visual hallucinations, anorexia, nausea and vomiting, congestive heart failure, orthostatic hypotension, and cardiac dysrhythmias. Since many of these toxic effects have been described in clients with renal failure, the relevance of these findings is obvious in the geriatric age group (Ing et al., 1979).

4. If levodopa therapy becomes necessary, it is wise to keep in mind that there seems to be a time-related diminution of the drug's effectiveness, as well as an increased frequency of side effects. It appears that the period of benefit can be extended if the goal is set at less-than-perfect control of akinesia, rigidity, and tremor. Despite individual variations, the elderly as a group seem to absorb levodopa more efficiently. It has also been discovered that in 45% of clients more than one peak of levodopa concentration can be demonstrated following oral administration (Evans et al., 1980).

Today levodopa is most commonly used in combination with a dopa-decarboxylase inhibitor (e.g., carbidopa or benserazide). The advantage of the combination is a drop in the levodopa dosage required and the resultant reduction in nausea, vomiting, hypotension, and cardiac effects induced by the peripheral action of dopamine. The combination should be started at a low dose (Sinemet 100/10 or Prolopa 100/25 q.AM). Further dose increases may be introduced at 4- to 5-day intervals. GI tract upset can be minimized by administering the medication with meals.

5. Movement disorders are the major CNS side effects. The on-off phenomenon is defined as sudden onset of akinesia, followed by an abrupt return of mobility, which may be accompanied by dyskinesia (Goldstein, 1980). This may develop at any time during treatment, but younger clients, who achieved dramatic results initially but who were also plagued by dyskinesias, are more likely to be afflicted. Some types (early morning, start-dose, peak- and end-dose akinesias) depend on timing of the doses of levodopa, whereas others do not. Theories accounting for these symptoms include degeneration of nerve terminal granules resulting in cytoplasmic leakage (Granerus, 1978), receptor site desensitization, and short levodopa plasma half-life (Lesser et al., 1979).

Research suggests the existence of two types of dopaminergic receptors, and some authors propose that the on-off phenomenon may be caused by both fluctuations of the relative sensitivities of the two sets of dopaminergic receptors and changes in brain dopamine levels (Lee et al., 1978; Goldstein, 1980).

6. None of the drugs described here will halt or reverse the destruction of dopaminergic neurons and their connections. Their use is only justified if they produce symptomatic benefit for the client ("Levodopa," 1981). Parkinsonian clients should be reviewed clinically every 3 months when stable to detect side effects early. Occupational therapy and physiotherapy are crucial to maintain the drug-produced gains.

Retropulsion, "the backward leaning syndrome," is often noted in akinetic parkinsonian clients, confining them to wheelchairs (Braverman, 1980). We found that Sinemet proved effective for treatment of the syndrome. Its benefit may be augmented by periods of the client lying *prone* during the day, if this position is tolerated.

Pain

The management of acute and chronic pain in the elderly must be based on accurate diagnosis of the underlying disorder. The best treatment is, of course, the elimination of the condition producing pain.

Chronic or recurrent pain can lead to a state of mind that reflects the dehumanizing cycle of pain—inadequate relief—anticipation—recurrence of pain.

Pain often has complex causes. Its severity is seldom directly related to objective physical changes, and individual clients do not have fixed thresholds of pain. In addition to somatic factors, depression, denial, frustration over unfulfilled expectations, and benefits derived from the sick role contribute to the perception of pain. We have found the concept of "total pain syndrome" useful to describe this mental and physical state.

If the underlying causes of the "total pain syndrome" cannot be eliminated, management has to be guided by the goal of complete pain relief without clouding the sensorium. Two observations are relevant to the elderly. Their pain threshold is commonly higher than that of younger adults. They are also more sensitive to analgesics, usually requiring lower dosages. Neither of these findings can, however, justify the inadequate treatment of pain in elderly clients.

Addiction to analgesics is a process that usually has its roots in *too little* medication *too late* rather than the opposite (Marks and Sachar, 1973; Twycross, 1978). Chronic, severe pain must therefore be treated *before* it recurs. The p.r.n. approach is inexcusable under these circumstances.

Development of new knowledge in the field of pain perception has come about largely as a result of the birth of hospice programs and palliative care units both in the United Kingdom and North America. In these settings many long-standing myths about narcotics have been dispelled, and the outcome has been great improvement in the quality of life for clients in the terminal phase of illness.

DRUG	USUAL GERIATRIC DOSAGE	SIDE EFFECTS/ CONTRAINDICA- TIONS/COMMENTS
Mild-to-moderate pain		
Aspirin	650 mg P.O. q.3 to 4hr	Aspirin may cause deafness without tinnitus; confusion; acid-base disturbance; bleeding tendency may develop
Acetamin- ophen	650 mg P.O. q.4hr	High dose may cause liver damage; *note:* avoid concurrent phenobarbital use
Codeine	30 to 60 mg P.O. q.4hr	Cough suppression; constipation; may combine with either of the above drugs
Severe pain		
Morphine	10 mg P.O. or 5 mg IM q.4hr	At high doses respiratory depression may occur with all narcotics; nausea; vomiting; drowsiness; constipation
Pentazocine	50 mg P.O. q.3hr 30 mg IM q.3hr	As above
Meperidine	100 mg P.O. q.3hr 75 mg IM q.3hr	Elevated cerebrospinal fluid pressure; hypotension; increased airway resistance

DRUG	USUAL GERIATRIC DOSAGE	SIDE EFFECTS/ CONTRAINDICA- TIONS/COMMENTS
Levorphanol	2 mg P.O./IM 3 mg PR q.4hr	Pruritus; sweating
Methadone	5 mg P.O. q.8hr	
Hydromor- phone	2 to 3 mg P.O./ IM q.4hr	

All narcotics are potentiated by the following drugs when administered concurrently:

Prochlor- perazine	5 mg P.O. q.4hr	
Chlorprom- azine	15 mg P.O. q.4hr	
Hydroxyzine	10 to 25 mg P.O. t.i.d.	

Special pain syndromes

Trigeminal neuralgia Carbam- aze- pine	50 to 100 mg P.O. t.i.d.	See *Epilepsy*

Cautions and comments

1. In the unique setting of terminal care, the goal of comfort without narcotization can frequently be achieved with oral preparations. In our experience narcotic addiction is not a problem. Dosage escalation is the exception once the initial stabilization has taken place. An increase in requirements usually signals progression of the underlying condition, not the development of tolerance.

2. Experience both at the terminal care service of the Department of Geriatric Medicine, St. Boniface Hospital, Winnipeg, and the Royal Victoria Hospital, Montreal, indicates that a simplified morphine mixture is as effective as the original Brompton cocktail and is distinctly preferred in the clinical setting (Melzack, Mount, and Gordon, 1979). Our experience suggests that the following mixtures meet most requirements:

Analgesic Liquid No. 1

Morphine sulfate 1 mg/ml
Alcohol 12.5%
Sorbitol* q.s.

Analgesic Liquid No. 2

Morphine sulfate 2 mg/ml
Alcohol 12.5%
Chocolate syrup q.s.

3. Successful pain management demands skill in techniques other than safe and efficacious use of medications. The patient care team must offer support, direction, and counseling to both the patient and the family. Behavior modification, reality orientation, and the normalizing atmosphere of milieu therapy may also be used. In this way patients can regain control of many aspects of their lives while dealing with questions related to their own mortality.

---

*Sorbitol in high doses causes diarrhea.

░ CARDIOVASCULAR SYSTEM

Cardiovascular disease afflicts a large proportion of the elderly in North America. The following conditions are discussed:

1. Peripheral vascular disease
2. Hypertension
3. Hypotension and syncope
4. Pulmonary embolic disease
5. Cardiac dysrhythmias
6. Cardiac failure

░ *Peripheral vascular disease*

Arterial disease. Arteriosclerosis obliterans is common in the elderly population. Treatment must be aimed at reduction of risk factors, since there is no known pharmacologic agent that will reverse the atheromatous changes in blood vessels. A partial list of risk factors follows:

1. *Smoking:* Like thromboangiitis obliterans, arteriosclerosis obliterans is also accelerated by smoking. Nicotine is only one of the factors deleterious to limb perfusion (e.g., the inhaled carbon monoxide also contributes to the metabolic impairment of the affected extremities).
2. *Obesity:* This places an increased load on the lower extremities. Tissue responsiveness to insulin is diminished as well.

The consensus of experts in the field is that cessation of smoking and weight loss are more beneficial in salvaging limbs with impaired circulation than is pharmacologic intervention (Juergens and Bernatz, 1980).

The argument for using vasodilator therapy in peripheral vascular disease is that an increase in luminal diameter affords more flow to areas of ischemia. However, the hypoxic tissues themselves generate local metabolites that induce maximum vasodilation. Exogenous stimuli are more likely, therefore, to affect the vasculature in less impaired regions. Skin temperature may rise but at the cost of reducing flow to already ischemic muscles. More potent vasodilators (e.g., nitroglycerin) may redistribute blood flow so ef-

fectively that severe systemic hypotension may result (Coffman, 1979).

Certain drugs may cause peripheral vasoconstriction. Propranolol blocks β-adrenergic receptors, whereas clonidine stimulates α-adrenergic receptors. Both should be avoided in elderly persons suffering from severe peripheral vascular disease.

The chronically progressive symptoms of arterial impairment are most commonly caused by atheromatous degeneration. However, artery-to-artery embolization may also occur. In these cases impairment develops acutely and frequently requires surgical intervention. If the operative procedure is successful, further recurrences may be reduced in incidence by maintenance anticoagulation. Recent myocardial infarction and the presence of atrial fibrillation predispose to arterial embolization. Unfortunately, when chronic atrial fibrillation is successfully converted to normal sinus rhythm, a shower of emboli may be expelled from the atrium, which has again been rendered capable of synchronized contraction.

Deep venous thrombosis (DVT). This is a common occurrence in the elderly. Recommendations have been made both for prophylaxis of the population at risk and for the treatment of the acute thrombotic episode (Thomas, 1978).

DRUG	USUAL GERIATRIC DOSAGE	SIDE EFFECTS/ CONTRAINDICA- TIONS/COMMENTS
Prophylaxis		
Surgical:		
Heparin	5000 U SC q.12hr	One preoperative dose
After myocardial infarction:		
Heparin	5000 U SC q.8hr	Until client mobilized
Acute DVT		
Heparin	5000 to 10,000 U IV load 1000 U continuous IV	Monitor partial thromboplastin time (PTT); maintain at 2 to 3 times control value
Prevention of recurrence		
Warfarin	5 to 10 mg P.O. q.d. for 3 months	Monitor prothrombin time (PT); maintain at 2 times control value

Cautions and comments

1. Complications of anticoagulation are more frequent in the elderly. Therefore appropriate diagnostic measures are essential to confirm the presence of DVT and to rule out superficial phlebitis, cellulitis, and contusion of calf muscles. The objectives of therapy are: (a) to prevent progression of the thrombus and the development of pulmonary emboli and (b) to avert chronic venous insufficiency.

2. The prophylactic use of heparin in the postoperative setting is undoubtedly effective. In hip surgery, however, the risk of hematoma formation, resulting in failure of the operative procedure, is a major deterrent to its use. Unfortunately, this is the setting in which DVT is the most common and the protective effect of heparin is the least impressive (Sagar et al., 1976). We personally recommend its use provided the client is hemostatically competent and the operating surgeon has no objections. The dosage used is based on American Heart Association guidelines (heparin 5000 U SC q.12hr) (Council on Thrombosis, 1977).

In nonsurgical conditions, which characteristically result in prolonged bedrest (e.g., myocardial infarction, bronchopneumonia, and stroke), heparin prophylaxis using a higher dosage regimen of 5000 U SC q.8hr is safe and recommended.

Hemorrhagic episodes are reported to be more common with intermittent IV heparin administration than with continuous IV infusion (Salzman et al., 1975). It is assumed that the portion of the time when the client is in the absolutely incoagulable state represents the vulnerable period. However, other studies (Mant et al., 1977) raise the suspicion that the total heparin dose, rather than the mode of administration, is the crucial determinant.

3. The hazards of long-term anticoagulation must be carefully balanced against the risk of recurrent thrombotic episodes. After the client has had several bouts with DVT, chronic oral anticoagulation may become necessary. Elderly women as a group are at especially high risk for hemorrhagic complications (Vieweg et al., 1970).

Hypertension

DRUG	USUAL GERIATRIC DOSAGE	SIDE EFFECTS/ CONTRAINDICA- TIONS/COMMENTS
Hydrochloro- thiazide	25 to 50 mg P.O. q.AM	Hypokalemia; hypovole- mia; diabetes mellitus; gout; above this dosage risk of hyperkalemia high (Hollifield, 1978)
Hydrochloro- thiazide +	25 mg P.O. q.AM	See *Cautions and comments*
Triamterene	50 mg P.O. q.AM	Hyperkalemia
Amiloride	5 to 10 mg q.d.	Hyperkalemia

DRUG	USUAL GERIATRIC DOSAGE	SIDE EFFECTS/ CONTRAINDICA- TIONS/COMMENTS
Propranolol	20 mg P.O. t.i.d.	*Note:* cardiac failure; chronic obstructive pulmonary disease (COPD); diabetes mellitus
Methyldopa	250 mg P.O. q.d.	*Note:* depression; syncope
Hydralazine	10 mg P.O. b.i.d.	Systemic lupus erythematosus-like syndrome; myocardial ischemia; tachycardia; postural hypotension

Cautions and comments

1. Both systolic and diastolic hypertension are more common in the elderly. Large population studies (Kannel and Gordon, 1974) demonstrated that hypertension is an important risk factor for cardiovascular mortality. This is true of all age groups, both for systolic and diastolic blood pressure elevation. In fact, the deleterious effects of hypertension increase with age. In the 65- to 74-year age group the annual mortality rate of those whose systolic pressure was above 160 mm Hg was double the rate found in the group with the systolic pressure below 130 mm Hg (Koch-Weser, 1978).

2. It has been demonstrated by the European Working Party on High Blood Pressure in the Elderly (EWPHE) that the use of thiazide diuretics was effective in achieving normal blood pressure in 88% of clients (Amery et al., 1977). Another 12% required the addition of methyldopa.

3. The Hypertension Detection and Follow-up Program (HDFP) Cooperative Group (1979 a and b) study used stepped care. Step 1 was chlorthalidone ± triamterene or spironolactone. In Step 2, if Step 1 failed to normalize blood pressure, reserpine or methyldopa was added. Step 3 combined hydralazine with the previous regimen. Guanethidine was chosen in Step 4. Step 5 represented the addition of any other drugs. The study demonstrated that normalization of blood pressure was achieved in a larger number of older subjects (age 60 to 69) than in either of the younger groups (age 30 to 49 and 50 to 59).

4. The EWPHE study reported significant elevation of creatinine, uric acid, and blood glucose in the thiazide-treated group when compared with the control population (Amery, 1978).* Although statistically significant, the clinical relevance of these changes is not yet certain, except as far as clients with diabetes and gout are concerned. Even here one may argue that the use of thiazide diuretics is not absolutely contraindicated in diabetes, and the increases reported are not very substantial. Grimm et al. (1981) discovered that thiazides may induce hyperlipoproteinemia, potentially can-

---

*EWPHE study was announced in Amery et al., 1977; pilot study results were reported in Amery et al., 1978.

celing the risk factor benefit attained by treatment. The relevance of this finding in geriatric populations is not yet clear.

Although the EWPHE has not yet published mortality and morbidity data, the HDFP has. They found that 5-year all-cause death rates were lowered by 25.3% in the 50- to 59-year age group and by 16.4% in the 60- to 69-year age group when stepped care was used. The comparison was made against matched controls, who were treated by their own physicians. This setup logically minimizes the benefit of step care because the control group also received some antihypertensive therapy.

The other remarkable finding of the HDFP study was that mortality from all causes was reduced *most* in the *mild* hypertensive group (diastolic pressure 90 to 104). The report does not stratify the 60- to 69-year age group according to diastolic pressure at entry and does not state whether the reduction in mortality holds true for the elderly as well.

5. We concur with Dyer et al. (1977) that elderly clients demonstrating target organ damage should be adequately treated. Asymptomatic hypertensive clients with systolic pressures above 160 mm Hg on two occasions or with a diastolic pressure persistently above 100 mm Hg should be treated. All clients should be screened for postural and postexertional hypotension before treatment is initiated. In our opinion α-adrenergic blockers (e.g., guanethidine) and agents with depressant actions (e.g., reserpine, clonidine) should *not* be used in geriatric practice. We recommend stepped therapy, starting with a thiazide diuretic, combined with a potassium-sparing diuretic (e.g., triamterene), if dietary potassium deficiency is suspected. β-blockers are added in the second step, whereas methyldopa and hydralazine are reserved for the more resistant cases.

Hypotension and syncope

Blood pressure is maintained in a narrow range by neural, vascular, cardiac, and endocrine mechanisms that resist changes induced by gravity. If they fail, episodes of orthostatic hypotension result, which in turn may cause presyncope or syncope (defined as loss of consciousness caused by impairment of cerebral perfusion). When the elderly client experiences dizziness, syncope, or falls, hypotension as a cause must always be carefully ruled out. The workup of such a client can be complex, but the client's life may be threatened if the syncopal episode recurs; therefore detailed investigation is justified (Sobel and Roberts, 1980).

The first step in investigation is a review of all medications because *drug effect* is a common cause. Diuretics, tranquilizers, sedative-hypnotics, antihypertensives, antidepressants, anti-

histamines, digitalis preparations, quinidine, and alcohol, either alone or in complex combinations, have all been implicated (see Chapter 11, "Adverse Drug Reactions in the Geriatric Client").

Neurologic disorders frequently interfere with the normal functioning of other systems. Such conditions may involve the afferent or the efferent arm of the nervous system, or both.

Carotid sinus hypersensitivity is an example of an afferent disturbance. Atheromatous changes need not necessarily be present in the arterial wall.

The CNS is affected in the Bradbury-Eggleston syndrome and in Parkinson's disease. Degeneration of the peripheral sympathetic nervous system is common in diabetes mellitus and tabes dorsalis, whereas effector fibers are damaged in the numerous peripheral neuropathies. The not uncommon Shy-Drager syndrome presents a mixed central and peripheral abnormality. Primary *vascular* pathologic conditions that may result in symptoms of hypotension and syncope include atherosclerosis and systemic amyloidosis. In the latter condition blood vessel infiltration has been implicated, resulting in the inability of the arterial system to generate effective systemic vasoconstriction. *Cardiac* causes of a sudden drop in blood pressure can be divided into three main groups:

1. Various dysrhythmias
2. Conditions resulting in outflow tract obstruction
3. Impaired ventricular performance

Endocrine disturbances rarely give rise to syncope. However, hypoaldosteronism, pheochromocytoma, hyporeninemia in diabetics, and serotonin- and kinin-secreting tumors should be considered in the differential diagnosis of such events.

Baroreceptor deconditioning is an important cause of hypotension in elderly clients confined to bed for any length of time. This condition represents a complex disturbance of neural, cardiovascular, and endocrine mechanisms. If one rules out such specific causes, many clients remain who do not fit into any of the previous categories. For them, skillful symptomatic management must be offered. This should include physical and pharmacologic treatment. Some individuals respond well to elevation of the head of the bed at night, whereas others need foot binders or g suits to maintain adequate cardiac return. Drug regimens follow:

DRUG	USUAL GERIATRIC DOSAGE	SIDE EFFECTS/ CONTRAINDICA- TIONS/COMMENTS
Single agents		
Fludrocorti-sone	0.1 mg P.O. q.d.	Sodium retention; cardiac failure
Dihydroergot-amine		Bevegard, Castenfors, and Lindblad, 1974
Combinations		
MAOI + tyra-mine		Frewin, Robinson, and Willing, 1973
MAOI + levo-dopa		Sharpe, Marquez-Julio, and Ashby, 1972
		Note: the last three treatment modalities are *not* generally recommended but in our experience may be required in the elderly who are resistant to therapy

Pulmonary embolic disease

Deep venous thrombophlebitis is the most common source of pulmonary emboli. Certain conditions predispose both to deep venous thrombophlebitis and pulmonary emboli. Immobilization, congestive heart failure, myocardial infarction, stroke, trauma, and postoperative states are prominent among them (see also "Deep Venous Thrombosis").

DRUG	USUAL GERIATRIC DOSAGE	SIDE EFFECTS/ CONTRAINDICA- TIONS/COMMENTS
Prevention		
Heparin	5000 U SC q.12hr	For surgical procedures
Heparin	5000 U SC q.8hr	For medical indications

DRUG	USUAL GERIATRIC DOSAGE	SIDE EFFECTS/ CONTRAINDICA- TIONS/COMMENTS
Treatment		
Heparin	5000 to 10,000 U IV loading dose, 1000 to 1200 U/hr	Monitor PTT; maintain at 2 to 3 times control value

Cautions and comments

1. Although the efficacy of the higher dosage regimen has been amply demonstrated in preventing pulmonary emboli, postoperative bleeding complications have occurred frequently enough to convince the American Heart Association to opt for the lower q.12hr regimen (Council on Thrombosis, 1977). One preoperative dose of 5000 U is given.

2. Research suggests that in certain operative procedures (e.g., total hip replacement) enough heparin-neutralizing activity is released from platelets to inactivate the heparin prophylactically delivered (Sagar et al., 1976). We feel that in hemostatically competent elderly clients the potential benefits outweigh the risks, and we recommend the preventive regimen as outlined previously.

3. A small group of clients suffer from recurrent pulmonary embolization, which may lead to pulmonary insufficiency. Even when extensive investigations, including pelvic venography, fail to disclose a source of emboli, venous thrombi are usually implicated in these episodes. Surgical treatment options may include inferior vena cava plication and the placement of various antiembolic devices. Before embarking on these procedures, however, a trial of chronic oral anticoagulation with warfarin should be given (McNamara, Takaki, and Yao, 1977; Sharma and Sasahara, 1979).

Cardiac dysrhythmias

Routine electrocardiograms (ECGs) undertaken in the community have shown abnormalities in up to half of the healthy elderly.

Although ECG changes may imply cardiac disease, the use of ECGs as a screening procedure may misidentify 30% to 50% of these individuals. The presence of ECG abnormalities may not have prognostic implications and is frequently unassociated with clinical or historic evidence of heart disease.

Dosage of antidysrhythmics must be individualized for the elderly, based on response and tolerance. ECG and blood pressure should be continuously monitored during the parenteral administration of these agents.

DYSRHYTHMIA	DRUG	USUAL GERIATRIC DOSAGE	SIDE EFFECTS/CONTRA-INDICATIONS/COMMENTS
Atrial			
Sinus bradycardia	Atropine	0.3 mg IV	Prostatic hypertrophy; glaucoma
	Isoproterenol	5 to 10 mg sublingual (SL)	*Note:* treat only if symptomatic
Atrial fibrillation	Digoxin	0.5 to 0.75 mg (loading dose slow IV or, if feasible, in divided doses over 24 hr)	See *Cautions and comments*
	Verapamil	0.08 mg/kg IV push over 3 min (if fibrillation continues or recurs, an additional 5 mg can be administered after 5 min and repeated twice at 6 hr intervals; oral dosage form for maintenance should be started with 80 mg b.i.d. and then titrated to patient response)	Monitor ECG and blood pressure continuously; contraindicated in AV block, acute myocardial infarction, sick sinus syndrome, and severe hypotension
Ventricular			
Ventricular tachycardia	Lidocaine	75 to 100 mg IV load administered at a rate of 25 mg/min and followed by an IV infusion of 1 mg/min (then titrate)	Monitor ECG and blood pressure continuously
	Quinidine	200 mg P.O. t.i.d.	*Note:* digoxin-quinidine effect; syncope; idiosyncrasy
	Disopyramide	100 mg P.O. t.i.d. (IV load: 2 mg/kg over 15 min; add 1 mg/kg if required; maintenance dose 0.4 mg/kg/hr IV for 24 hr)	Prostatic hypertrophy; dry mouth; heart failure may worsen; reduce dose in renal insufficiency

Cautions and comments

1. Complete treatment of this topic is not attempted here. In general, dysrhythmias should be considered in the differential diagnosis of falls and syncope, as well as seizures. Long-term ambulatory (Holter) monitoring may be advisable, preferably under circumstances similar to those that prevailed at the time of the event being investigated.

2. Sinus bradycardia as an isolated finding is not uncommon, especially in elderly men. The diagnosis depends on demonstrating that the heart rate *can* be raised by exercise. If the client is asymptomatic, treatment is not indicated. If no other rhythm disturbance can be held responsible for the bradycardia, a trial of therapy from the drugs listed previously is recommended.

3. Chronic atrial fibrillation may have several causes (e.g., ischemic heart disease, thyrotoxicosis, pulmonary or other infection). If the ventricular rate is not too high, and the atrial kick is not essential to keep the client out of congestive heart failure, conversion need not be attempted.

4. Cardioversion, either by electric or pharmacologic means, can lead to thromboembolic complications. Therefore prophylactic anticoagulation may be necessary. Treatment must be individualized to take into consideration clients' histories and their current condition.

5. The widespread use of the ambulatory monitoring technique has led to the recognition that unexpected episodes of ventricular tachycardia are not uncommon. Loss of the filling contribution provided by atrial contraction and the inadequate diastolic filling time produce a rapid fall in cardiac output. Low-energy electric conversion may be required to achieve conversion of acute episodes. Lidocaine can only be delivered intravenously. For individuals sustaining recurrent attacks, initial investigation should carefully search for evidence of myocardial ischemia, hypoxia, bradycardia, electrolyte imbalance, and cardiac failure. If the attacks persist after treatment of such precipitating conditions, the specific antidysrhythmic agents should be used. In coronary artery disease and the syndrome of mitral valve prolapse, propranolol can be useful. Other agents, such as quinidine and disopyramide, should be carefully monitored clinically; serum levels of both of these drugs can be obtained to rule out toxicity or to determine that an adequate dose is being used. Procainamide is no longer recommended as the drug of first choice.

6. The sick sinus syndrome is a well-recognized clinical condition that usually presents as episodes of cerebral ischemia, sometimes compounded by cardiac symptoms. The mechanism may be a sinus nodal or atrial dysrhythmia or AV junctional disease. The tachycardia-bradycardia syndrome may result from sinus arrest, SA block, impaired automaticity of the AV junction while conduction is preserved, or from atrial tachycardias. Tachycardia induces a low cardiac output by hindering adequate diastolic filling, whereas bradycardia may reduce foreward output by overdistending the left ventricle beyond its optimum size (Kaplan, 1976).

Treatment of the sick sinus syndrome is aimed at protecting the client from clinically significant bradycardia through the use of demand pacing, whereas digoxin or propranolol prevents the episodes of tachycardia. If it is suspected that atrial fibrillation is the sole mechanism maintaining an adequate cardiac function (e.g., AV automaticity impaired, conduction impaired), a pacemaker should be implanted before digitalization. Unfortunately, this is frequently uncovered only when asystole develops with digitalis use. Careful preliminary assessment of these clients is therefore essential.

Cardiac failure

Heart disease caused by valvular abnormalities, coronary artery disease, hypertension, cardiomyopathy, pericardial disorders, and disorders of other systems will often result in signs and symptoms of heart failure in the elderly. The clinical presentation can be classified as predominantly left- or right-sided heart failure or pulmonary venous or systemic venous hypertension.

The absolute prerequisite of successful therapy is again an accurate etiologic diagnosis. Although propranolol can be lifesaving in asymmetrical septal hypertrophy, it may further reduce already diminished cardiac output in failure caused by hypertension. It is also essential that precipitating or exacerbating causes of heart failure be identified. Examples include infection, fever, apathetic thyrotoxicosis, hypothyroidism, Paget's disease of the bone, and other high output states. Treatment of these conditions lessens the demand on the impaired myocardium and may obviate the use of a cardiac glycoside.

DRUG	USUAL GERIATRIC DOSAGE	SIDE EFFECTS/ CONTRAINDICA- TIONS/COMMENTS
Diuretics		
Hydrochloro- thiazide	50 to 100 mg q.d.	May produce hypokale- mia, hypovolemia; also see *Hyperten- sion*
Furosemide	40 mg P.O. q.AM	As above; may titrate as needed
Ethacrynic acid	50 mg P.O. q.AM	As above; may succeed when furosemide is no longer effective
Triamterene	50 mg P.O. q.AM	May produce hyperka- lemia
Spironolac- tone	25 mg P.O. q.AM	See *Triamterene*; gyne- comastia
Amiloride	5 to 10 mg P.O. q.d.	Hyperkalemia; drug available in United Kingdom and Canada
Cardiac glycosides		
Digoxin	0.125 mg P.O. q.d.	See *Cautions and com- ments*
Deslanoside	0.2 to 0.4 mg IV	If rapid digitalization is needed

DRUG	USUAL GERIATRIC DOSAGE	SIDE EFFECTS/ CONTRAINDICA- TIONS/COMMENTS
Vasodilator agents		
Nitrites		
Nitroglycer- in	0.2 mg q.3 to 4hr SL	Monitor BP; headache; use *fresh* medication
Isosorbide dinitrate	5 mg P.O. t.i.d. to q.i.d.	Monitor BP; headache
Nitroglycer- in oint- ment	1.25 cm/chest q.4hr	As above
Pentaeryth- ritol tetra- nitrate	10 to 20 mg P.O. q.8hr	As above; alcohol en- hances hypotensive effect
Hydralazine	10 mg P.O. t.i.d.	Lupus-like syndrome; postural hypotension
Prazosin	0.5 mg P.O. t.i.d.	First dose and all in- creased doses at night; *note:* syncope

Cautions and comments

1. Sodium retention is a characteristic finding in cardiac failure. Diuretic therapy is indicated to reduce ventricular preload. Because secondary hyperaldosteronism is not uncommon, thiazide diuretics can be combined with spironolactone. Potassium wasting can also be reduced by adding triamterene. One of us had highly favorable results with amiloride in this setting.

2. If renal failure reduces free water clearance, fluid restriction may become necessary. Usually, with mild renal impairment, only sodium intake needs to be curtailed.

3. Digitalis preparations may become necessary for the management of heart failure. We favor the use of digoxin as the standard medication.

Under nonemergent conditions, an oral maintenance dosage can be used to achieve adequate digitalization. If more rapid methods are needed, an oral loading dose of digoxin or IV deslanoside should be used.

4. In circumstances requiring the long-term use of digoxin, symptoms of digitalis toxicity should be repeatedly monitored for. These include GI tract disturbances such as anorexia, nausea, and vomiting, as well as CNS symptoms. Headache, fatigue, general malaise, confusion, disorientation, and seizures are typical nonspecific findings; visual disturbances may present as scotomata, flickering halos, and altered color vision. Since the therapeutic ratio is low, it is not unreasonable to attribute any new cardiac event or one of the symptoms described previously to toxicity until proven otherwise. The commonly accepted therapeutic range for serum digoxin levels is 0.8 to 1.2 ng/ml, measured 6 hours after the last administered dose.

5. Digitalis-induced dysrhythmias are dangerous and potentially lethal. Attention to serum potassium levels and especially to the general state of hydration can reduce the risk of these complications. Hypomagnesemia may interfere with the correction of hypokalemia.

Hypokalemia, hypercalcemia, elevated or depressed magnesium levels, acute hypoxemia, acidosis and alkalosis, hypothyroidism, increased sympathetic tone, and ischemic heart disease all predispose clients to digitalis toxicity. These conditions need to be corrected as completely as possible.

6. Digitalis toxicity may present as frequent ectopic beats, first-degree AV block, or atrial fibrillation, with a slow ventricular response. Withholding the medication may be sufficient to correct these rhythm and conduction abnormalities.

More advanced dysrhythmias are hazardous. Ventricular tachycardia caused by digitalis toxicity has been associated with a 66% mortality rate in one reported study (Dreifus et al., 1963).

Bradydysrhythmias may respond to atropine, but high-grade AV block usually does not. This condition necessitates temporary ventricular pacing.

Tachydysrhythmias require drug therapy with IV phenytoin or lidocaine. Potassium infusion can be useful if hypokalemia is demonstrated but is contraindicated in paroxysmal atrial tachycardia with AV block, since hyperkalemia can increase the grade of the block, resulting in either complete heart block or asystole.

Propranolol can be useful because it slows automaticity and depolarization, but, unfortunately, AV conduction and subsidiary pacemakers are also depressed; asystole may ensue.

Quinidine and procainamide are currently not recommended for treatment of digitalis toxicity because they can cause additional cardiotoxicity.

As the ultimate recourse, direct current countershock using low energy levels may become necessary if all else fails.

7. If cardiac failure is refractory to diuretics and digitalis therapy, the next step is to carefully reassess the cause of the disorder. After all correctable problems have received appropriate and adequate treatment, vasodilator therapy may be used. If management is individualized, good results can be expected, although an ideal drug has not yet been discovered.

8. Long-acting nitrates are useful when the main problem is dyspnea resulting from elevated left ventricular end-diastolic pressure. Venous dilatation produced by these agents reduces preload, thereby returning the ventricle to a smaller, more efficient configuration.

9. Hydralazine is useful in low cardiac output states in which the chief complaint is fatigue. This drug reduces both preload and afterload, although the effect is most prominent on afterload (i.e., relaxation of arterioles). Cautious administration may improve the client's condition without inducing clinically appreciable hypotension or reflex tachycardia.

10. When excessive preload and dyspnea are combined with reduced cardiac output and fatigue, prazosin can benefit the client. The first dose should always be given at night to avoid initial hypotension. Subsequent dosage escalation should also be accomplished at night.

11. Other useful combinations include hydralazine with nitrates, as well as prazosin with hydralazine. Since myocardial oxygen demand is reduced, angina may improve noticeably.

12. Mitral insufficiency caused by papillary muscle dysfunction can occur both in ischemic and nonischemic cardiomyopathies. Hydralazine and prazosin may correct this by reducing aortic impedance. In severe cases nitrates can perhaps also help because reduction of the left ventricular size improves the anatomic position of the papillary muscles.

13. It is worth emphasizing that arterial vasodilators (e.g., hydralazine) are also valuable in the therapy of primary valvular disorders. Care of mitral and aortic insufficiency as well as of aortic stenosis has changed with this insight, and these agents should also be considered in such clinical settings.

RESPIRATORY SYSTEM

Pulmonary disease is common in the elderly. Dyspnea causes a great deal of physical disability. It reduces mobility and frequently threatens the client's independence.

Our discussion is limited to chronic obstructive pulmonary disease. For information regarding pulmonary infections readers are referred to standard textbooks of pharmacology and infectious diseases.

Chronic obstructive pulmonary disease (COPD)

This term covers a broad spectrum, including asthma, chronic bronchitis, and emphysema.

Although there are clients who have one of these conditions in its pure form, the majority have overlapping findings of each. Thus most clients with chronic bronchitis have a measurable bronchospastic component, and many asthmatic clients produce bronchial secretions to excess.

From long-term follow-up of asthmatic clients it appears that bronchospasm, which was initially fully reversible, will gradually give way to a fixed airway resistance. This is especially true if bronchodilator therapy has been inadequate or episodic. Secondary emphysema may then develop. Clients may fail to recognize the objectively demonstrable improvement in airway resistance (Eaton, et al., 1980).

Finally, clients whose condition is predominantly caused by emphysema may nevertheless have enough reversible airway obstruction to materially interfere with gas exchange because of ventilation/perfusion mismatch. They may then benefit from bronchodilators, although these drugs do not of course affect the primary underlying pathologic condition.

DRUG	USUAL GERIATRIC DOSAGE	SIDE EFFECTS/ CONTRAINDICA-TIONS/COMMENTS
Sympathomimetics		
Albuterol	1 to 2 puffs q.i.d. (by inhaler)	Headache; dizziness; tremor; tachycardia; also see *Cautions and comments*
Albuterol	2 mg P.O. t.i.d.	As above; side effects more common with oral administration
Terbutaline	2.5 mg P.O. t.i.d.	Nervousness; tremor; tachycardia less common than with albuterol
Theophylline derivatives		
Aminophylline	200 mg P.O. t.i.d. (then titrate)	Nausea; vomiting; headache; tachydysrhythmias; seizures; coma; see *Cautions and comments*
Oxtriphylline	200 mg P.O. t.i.d. (then titrate)	As above
Aminophylline	5.6 mg/kg IV (over 20 to 30 minutes; for maintenance see *Cautions and comments*)	As above
Steroids		
Beclomethasone	2 puffs q.i.d. (by inhaler)	See *Cautions and comments*
Prednisone	5 to 10 mg P.O. q.d. (then titrate)	In severe asthma only

Cautions and comments

1. The treatment of COPD is aimed at improving gas exchange, reducing the work of breathing, and combatting infectious exacerbations. Since most clients have some degree of bronchospasm, bronchodilator therapy is the cornerstone of management.

2. Three groups of agents are used: sympathomimetics, theophylline derivatives, and steroids.

a. Sympathomimetics were developed to retain the β-agonist effect of epinephrine while eliminating the α-adrenergic cardiac side effects.

The nonselective β-stimulants (e.g., isoproterenol) frequently cause excessive CNS stimulation and tachycardia. The new generation of selective β_2-agonists have been demonstrated to produce fewer cardiac complications (Light, Taylor, and George, 1979). In current practice albuterol is used frequently because it is available in both oral and inhaled forms. Terbutaline is more β_2-selective, and if oral medication is acceptable, tachycardia is a less frequent event. The mode of drug delivery is a contentious issue. The agent may be administered orally, parenterally, or directly into the tracheobronchial tree.

Oral sympathomimetics have the disadvantage of common systemic effects and prolonged half-lives. Their onset of action is slower than that of aerosols. They should only be used in situations where the latter do not provide relief without excessively frequent administration.

Aerosol preparations may be driven by an inert propellant, a positive pressure breathing apparatus, or a nebulizer generating hot or cold vapors. These modalities vary in the concentration delivered and droplet size, as well as user convenience.

Cannister-type inhalers require a fair degree of manual coordination. If the discharge is not timed correctly, only the oropharynx and larynx will be sprayed. The following "patient drill" is useful:

(1) Take a deep breath.
(2) Exhale fully.
(3) Discharge cannister in the *middle* of the second deep breath.
(4) Complete second deep breath.
(5) Hold breath as long as possible.
(6) Return to normal breathing.

This "patient drill" requires frequent reinforcement from the treatment team and the family.

The use of intermittent positive pressure breathing may be difficult in confused clients, who tend to blow against the jet of air rather than continue to inhale.

Nebulizers are simple to administer, although some dyspneic elderly clients resist the use of a mask.

b. Theophylline derivatives inhibit phosphodiesterases with a consequent increase in cyclic AMP in bronchial smooth muscle. These agents are available in various oral forms (e.g., aminophylline, oxtriphylline). Dosage conversion tables are available (100 mg theophylline anhydrous = 127 mg aminophylline dihydrate = 156 mg oxtriphylline = 110 mg theophylline monohydrate = 116 mg aminophylline anhydrous = 133 mg theophylline monethanolamine = 208 mg theophylline calcium salicylate = 196 mg theophylline sodium glyconate) (Piafsky and Ogilvie, 1975).

We do not favor the use of combined preparations with antihistamines, barbiturates, and expectorants added. Side effects may be complex, and benefits are not obvious.

Clients commonly have significant airway obstruction in the absence of overt symptoms. Chronic administration of bronchodilators is recommended in such cases to reduce the frequency of exacerbations and to enhance exercise tolerance.

Intravenously administered aminophylline is an essential agent in acute attacks of asthma and asthmatic bronchitis. Over the past decade several significant changes in dosage have occurred. The early method of pushing the dosage until side effects occurred has been abandoned, since it became evident that seizure may be the first sign of toxicity (Weinberger et al., 1976). Through the use of pharmacokinetic studies a nomogram has been developed that recommends both loading and maintenance dosages (Jusko et al., 1977).

Renal impairment reduces the rate of elimination of theophylline; the recommended maintenance dosage for otherwise healthy elderly clients is 0.68 mg/kg/hr. This represents a 25% reduction from the dosage used in young adults. Theophylline is enzymatically inactivated in the liver. Therefore clients who have congestive heart failure or hepatic failure should only receive 0.45 mg/kg/hr of IV aminophylline. If the client has had no previous theophylline therapy, the loading dose is 5.6 mg/kg IV over 20 to 30 minutes. If the client has taken oral theophylline within 12 hours of the attack, the loading dose should be halved, or even omitted, depending on the dose taken and on clinical circumstances (Jusko et al., 1977).

The next step in development is expected to be similar to gentamicin dosage calculations, using programmable calculators to further individualize therapy (de Repentigny et al., 1981).

Frequent serum theophylline determinations in acutely ill COPD clients should be undertaken in order to keep the level in the 10 to 20 mg/l range. Close observation of all clients for signs of theophylline toxicity also markedly improves the quality of care.

c. Management of severe asthma or asthmatic bronchitis may necessitate the use of glucocorticoids. The treatment of these individuals has changed in recent years with the introduction of new steroidal molecular forms that are virtually void of systemic corticosteroid action when applied directly into the tracheobronchial tree. Harvey, Nair, and Kass (1976) demonstrated that for 59% of their steroid-dependent clients it was possible to replace oral prednisone therapy completely with beclomethasone aerosol. In this group the pituitary-adrenal axis recovered fully from steroid suppression. In the rest of their clients the maintenance dosage of prednisone could be significantly reduced when beclomethasone was concurrently used.

In our experience some clients may have a bronchospastic response to the propellant. It is therefore advisable to use a sympathomimetic aerosol before the administration of beclomethasone.

3. Although expectorants and cough suppressants are freely and frequently used, their justifiable applications are few (Zanjanian, 1980). Since the cough reflex is a defense mechanism, its elimination may enhance the risk of lower respiratory tract infection. Only in cases where cough no longer serves a useful purpose should codeine or dextromethorphan be used (e.g., malignancy).

Expectorants may not be beneficial when the underlying cause of difficulty is inspissation of secretions secondary to inadequate bronchodilator therapy. When needed, a saturated solution of potassium iodide is recommended.

4. Discussion of this topic is not complete without briefly outlining some of the other components of the treatment program for COPD clients.

Physical modalities include postural drainage and chest percussion. These are only beneficial if bronchial secretions are increased in amount or in viscosity. Therapy sessions should be timed to coincide with the peak of bronchodilator effect.

General physical conditioning and breathing exercises, as well as training in energy-saving techniques and breath-preserving methods, are all parts of a well-balanced program. With respiratory rehabilitation teams providing follow-up in the community, many clients may return to their home environment.

5. Long-term management of COPD clients often includes oxygen therapy. It appears that low-flow oxygen administration is safer in clients who are prone to retain carbon dioxide (Warren et al., 1980).

Respiratory failure is the lethal complication of such therapy. The current impression is that the mortality rate in the group of clients whose pH falls below 7.26 ([H$^+$] above 55 nmole/l) is greatly increased, when compared with less severely acidotic clients. Repeated arterial blood gas monitoring is justified in this highly compromised population, especially because this dangerous nadir of pH can occur at any time during the clinical course of the acute episode, not just before initiation of intensive therapy.

ENDOCRINE SYSTEM

Only two major topics, diabetes mellitus and thyroid disease, are discussed here.

Diabetes mellitus

Glucose tolerance diminishes with age; this trend was clearly demonstrated by Silverstone and Shock (Silverstone et al., 1957). This fact adds considerably to the difficulty of making the diagnosis in elderly clients, especially those who do not initially have the classic catabolic findings of diabetes. Controversies abound because uncertainty exists about the primary lesion. If one believes that insulin deficiency initiates the process (vascular changes being secondary), then vigorous maintenance of euglycemia is of paramount concern (Cahill, Etzwiler, and Freinkel, 1976). If, on the other hand, vascular degeneration is primary, with insulin deficiency a consequence of this, then tight blood sugar control will not avoid the complications of diabetes, and only duration of illness will determine the outcome (Siperstein et al., 1977). Ingelfinger (1977), in an outstanding editorial, indicated that a balance has to be achieved between these two views.

Dietary management is the cornerstone of treatment. Recent challenge to traditional diets comes from studies showing that carbohydrates can provide up to 70% of caloric intake, as long as 75% of the carbohydrate ingested is in the complex form and high fiber content is guaranteed (25 gm of plant fiber/1000 cal) (Anderson, 1980). This regimen results in a reduction of plasma glucose levels and insulin or oral hypoglycemic agent requirements. The goal of dietary management is to tailor the glucose peaks to available endogenous insulin. When this is insufficient to control hyperglycemia, then an oral agent or insulin has to be added. These supplement but do not supplant good dietary care.

DRUG	USUAL GERIATRIC DOSAGE	SIDE EFFECTS/ CONTRAINDICA- TIONS/COMMENTS
Oral hypoglycemic agents		
Chlorpropamide	100 mg to 500 mg P.O. q.d.	*Note:* prolonged hypoglycemia
Tolbutamide	500 mg P.O. t.i.d.	
Insulins		
Lente } NPH }	Intermediate action	Adjust dose to individual need and response	See *Cautions and comments*
CZI regular } Semi-lente }	Short action	Adjust dose to individual need and response	
Ultra-lente }	Long action	Adjust dose to individual need and response	

Cautions and comments

1. In all instances of asymptomatic diabetes, proper diet alone should first be instituted. Education of the "cook" may be as important and more effective than education of the client.

2. Non–insulin-dependent or type II diabetics (maturity-onset diabetics) with less than a 10-year history of illness, who fail to respond to diet alone, should be started on oral hypoglycemic agents. The lowest possible dosage should always be used. Blood levels may not equilibrate until after 7 to 10 days of therapy, and dosage escalation should be slow.

3. Elderly clients are at higher risk of severe and prolonged hypoglycemia induced by oral agents. If this develops, admission to the hospital is mandatory.

4. It is felt by clinicians who specialize in treatment of diabetes (Cahill, Etzweiler, and Freinkel, 1976) that normoglycemia may reduce the risk of infection, cataract formation, retinopathy, neuropathy, and perhaps thromboemboli. However, hypoglycemia is an ever-present hazard.

5. If oral agents become ineffective, insulin therapy will be necessary. Most clients can be satisfactorily managed on intermediate acting insulins (NPH or lente). Although there is no hard-and-fast rule, the initial dose can be estimated in units of insulin by dividing the fasting blood sugar (in mg/100 ml) by 10.

6. In our experience hyperosmolar hyperglycemic nonketotic coma is one of the more common geriatric emergencies. It complicates mild and moderate diabetes in the elderly. It is usually initiated by several days of reduced fluid intake, resulting in marked dehydration, and is worsened by glycosuria and osmotic diuresis. Management of this condition is a geriatric medical emergency. Rapid rehydration with hypotonic saline (0.45%) and low-dose insulin therapy are necessary (e.g., 25 U regular crystalline insulin IV initially, followed by 5 to 9 U/hr by infusion as dictated by blood glucose levels). Special attention must be given to serum K^+ levels, since total body K^+ loss is very large. Ketosis, as well as lactic acidosis, can coexist in some of these clients.

7. Clients can now survive to old age with brittle diabetes; therefore diabetic ketoacidosis is not unheard of in geriatric clients. Added attention must be given to the cardiovascular status, and hemodynamic monitoring may be needed in the rapid rehydration phase.

Thyroid disease

Hyperthyroidism may be caused by diffuse toxic goiter (in Graves' disease), toxic multinodular goiter (in the setting of a preexisting multinodular nontoxic goiter), or, rarely, toxic adenoma.

Signs and symptoms of hyperthyroidism may be difficult to recognize in the elderly (apathetic hyperthyroidism). However, if atrial fibrillation or congestive heart failure develops de novo in a geriatric client, investigations should include thyroid indices.

DRUG	USUAL GERIATRIC DOSAGE	SIDE EFFECTS/ CONTRAINDICA- TIONS/COMMENTS
Radioiodine 131	7 to 10 mCi (140 to 160 μCi/ gm of tissue) P.O.	Long-term monitoring for hypothyroidism
Propylthiouracil	50 mg P.O. q.6hr	Monitor white cell count Discontinue (D/C) immediately if sore throat, fever, and headache noted
Propranolol	40 mg P.O. q.i.d.	Observe for cardiac failure and broncho- spasm; may need to digitalize client first

Hypothyroidism may be caused by iatrogenic destruction of thyroid tissue (postthyroidectomy, postradiation thyroiditis), involution following inflammation (burnt-out Graves' disease, Hashimoto's thyroiditis), or primary thyroprival hypothyroidism.

It may be difficult to make the diagnosis clinically, and a high index of suspicion is required. Thyroid studies should be obtained as a baseline investigation of dementias, as well as unexplained heart failure.

DRUG	USUAL GERIATRIC DOSAGE	SIDE EFFECTS/ CONTRAINDICA- TIONS/COMMENTS
Levothyroxine	0.10 to 0.15 mg P.O. q.d.	Initial dose is *much lower*; dosage escalation must be slow; see *Cautions and comments*

Cautions and comments

1. Because of the limited life expectancy of geriatric clients, the concern regarding development of late hypothyroidism is outweighed by the reliability of conventional dose ^{131}I therapy. Follow-up of thyrotoxic clients is necessary both for detection of recurrence of hyperthyroidism and the development of hypothyroidism caused by radioactive iodine.

2. Some authorities recommend much *higher* dosages than indicated above, especially if thyrotoxicosis is suspected to *cause* congestive heart failure. This approach would reliably produce hypothyroidism.

3. Propylthiouracil may be used after ^{131}I therapy to reduce the period of thyrotoxicosis. Agranulocytosis can rapidly develop but usually occurs early in the course of therapy. Clients must be warned to discontinue propylthiouracil at the first sign of sore throat or fever. Fortunately these are rare complications of the drug.

4. Propranolol is beneficial in alleviating the peripheral manifestation of thyrotoxicosis, but it does not block the hypermetabolic effect of thyroxine. Thus it is only a stopgap measure until definitive therapy takes hold.

5. The dosage of levothyroxine listed is the maintenance dosage. Under no circumstances should this be the initial dosage in the newly diagnosed myxedematous client. Extreme caution needs to be used, and in view of the prolonged half-life dosages as low as 0.025 mg q.d. may be necessary, with only weekly dosage increases.

6. We caution against the use of liothyronine (T_3) in the management of hypothyroidism, having witnessed acute myocardial infarction associated with its use in the elderly.

Although a pseudodementia can be produced by myxedema, the amount of improvement with treatment is limited by two factors.

First, cardiovascular symptoms may emerge, preventing attainment of the euthyroid state. Second, certain aspects of mental functioning may be affected irreversibly. Therefore cognitive recovery may not be complete. Early diagnosis is a sine qua non of geriatric endocrinologic practice.

7. Myxedema coma is a medical emergency that should be managed in an intensive care setting with careful consideration of fluid and electrolyte abnormalities, effects of hypothermia, and relative adrenal insufficiency. It is the only indication for intravenous thyroid therapy. We prefer the use of levothyroxine (T_4) over liothyronine (T_3) in this situation.

GASTROINTESTINAL SYSTEM

Peptic ulcer disease, constipation, diverticular disease, irritable bowel syndrome, and intestinal obstruction will be discussed in this section.

Peptic ulcer disease

Duodenal and gastric ulcers are common in elderly clients; the ulcer diathesis tends to be chronic and recurrent, although the natural history is variable. Currently three major issues are being debated:

1. Does treatment influence ulcer healing?
2. Does treatment provide pain relief?
3. Is the treatment beneficial in preventing recurrence?

Spontaneous healing of ulcers can be demonstrated in 30% to 50% of cases studied. There seems to be a correlation between ulcer size and likelihood of healing. Pharmacologic intervention improves healing rates by 20% to 30% (Winship, 1978).

Clinical experience suggests that treatment

definitely relieves ulcer pain. However, several studies attempting to confirm this impression produced equivocal findings (Littman et al., 1977). Placebo effect may play a significant role; in addition, a dilutional component may also apply when antacids are matched by volume with inert liquids.

There is now convincing evidence in the literature showing that long-term treatment with H_2-antagonists does reduce rates of recurrence (Bodemar and Walan, 1978).

In general, medications may either act to *reduce aggressive factors* (they affect acid and/or pepsin secretion) or to *promote protective factors* (they make the mucosa more impervious to noxious influence). Anticholinergics, antacids, and H_2-blockers diminish the impact of agents injurious to the mucosa.

Anticholinergic agents. These were traditionally used to delay gastric emptying and reduce acid secretion. The major objection to their use is the dose-related development of side effects: CNS stimulation, confusion, exacerbation of glaucoma, drying of respiratory tract secretions, precipitation of bladder neck obstruction, and interference with sweat production.

Recent research suggests that the old approach of pushing anticholinergic dosage to the point of toxicity, then cutting back slightly, is not warranted. Feldman et al. (1977) showed that propantheline at 15 mg produced the same meal-stimulated acid output reduction as the near-toxic 45 mg dose. It was also demonstrated that combining cimetidine with propantheline at the lower dose resulted in additive reduction of acid secretion. In this dose range their use may be acceptable in the elderly.

Antacids. In the British literature antacids used to be considered useful for symptomatic relief only (Morris and Rhodes, 1979). However, in the United States, Peterson et al. (1977) demonstrated that a regimen involving seven doses of antacids with neutralizing capacity sufficient to counteract 1000 mEq of hydrochloride definitely encourages healing.

Antacids work by raising the gastric and duodenal pH. Antacids containing calcium are the most potent alkalinizers; however, they may cause acid rebound. The use of these compounds in the presence of impaired renal function may result in hypercalcemia.

Aluminum hydroxide is an effective antacid; however, it frequently causes constipation. There is also some question whether aluminum is absorbed to a significant extent. Since aluminum hydroxide is converted to aluminum phosphate in the gut, hypophosphatemia may develop (Spencer and Lender, 1979). Clients initially have anorexia, muscle weakness, and osteomalacia, symptoms beginning as early as after 2 weeks of use (Shields, 1978).

Magnesium hydroxide is another commonly used antacid. It may produce diarrhea. In renally impaired clients, magnesium can accumulate, resulting in somnolence and possibly confusion.

All these cations are capable of chelating many other drugs and interfering with their absorption. Antibiotics, anticonvulsants, anticoagulants, and digoxin may be malabsorbed when administered concurrently with an antacid (Hurwitz, 1977).

Most antacids on the market today combine aluminum and magnesium hydroxide, but depending on the particular formulation, individual products can range in acid neutralizing capacity from 0.3 to 4.2 mEq/ml (Drake and Hollander, 1981). This finding accounts for widely varying dose requirements. Whereas only 33 ml of Maalox TC are required to neutralize 140 mEq of hydrochloride, 100 ml of Amphojel would be necessary to achieve the same result.

In the elderly another consideration is sodium content. Newer, high potency antacids have been formulated to avoid Na^+ overload (Maalox TC, Riopan Plus, Mylanta-II).

It has been demonstrated in numerous studies that the elderly, as a group, secrete less gastric acid than the younger population. Consequently, lower doses of antacids may be required to neutralize the aggressive factors. However, no systematic study has succeeded yet in correlating acid secretion with antacid requirements, or is it reasonable to perform gastric intubation and pentagastrin stimulation on every elderly individual who develops peptic ulcer disease.

H$_2$-receptor antagonists. The theory currently favored regarding the mechanism of action of these agents is that the parietal cell has specific histamine, gastrin, and acetylcholine receptors. When histamine occupies its own receptor site, affinity for the other two molecules is heightened. Thus H$_2$-blockade acts to inhibit acid secretion through all of these pathways. The most commonly used agent is cimetidine. In studies cimetidine was shown to reduce meal-stimulated acid secretion by 70%, being twice as effective as the anticholinergic agents (Henn et al., 1975; Finkelstein and Isselbacher, 1978).

Treatment with cimetidine resulted in healing of duodenal ulcers in 70% of the cases studied; the placebo group showed a 37% healing rate. The initial concerns about side effects were directed at bone marrow depression caused by metiamide, an earlier H$_2$-antagonist.

However, since cimetidine was introduced, this side effect has not been reported. The usual recommended dosage (300 mg P.O. q.6hr) must be reduced in clients with renal impairment.

The side effects most commonly encountered in the elderly are mental confusion (McMillen, Ambis, and Siegel, 1978), toxic psychosis (Barnhart and Bowden, 1979), and paranoia with hallucinations (Adler, Sadja, and Wilets, 1980). The common factors identified are old age, serious underlying medical conditions, renal impairment, and doses in the high dose range.

Although confusion can be a prominent feature of cimetidine toxicity, this may clear while an underlying paranoid psychosis may remain. Early, complete cessation of therapy is necessary to reverse the psychosis (Adler, Sadja, and Wilets, 1980).

Studies on *gastric* ulcers and cimetidine are less conclusive (Freston, 1978). However, the consensus is that in this condition the agent is also effective. Since ulcers do occur under conditions of normal and low acid secretion, other factors must also be operative (e.g., bile reflux and mucosal barrier dysfunction).

Protective agents promote healing by either encouraging better mucosal resistance against aggressive factors or by forming a physical barrier over the ulcer surface.

Carbenoxolone promotes production of gastric mucus and improves its quality; gastric mucosal epithelial cells have prolonged half-lives under its influence; it also interferes with pepsin activity. This agent has been effective in promoting healing of gastric ulcers in 75% of clients. A special formulation was developed to cause duodenal rather than gastric release. Archambault et al. (1977) found the drug to be significantly better than a placebo in treating duodenal ulcers.

In the geriatric population, however, carbenoxolone cannot be recommended as a drug of first choice because it has potent aldosterone-like effects, resulting in hypokalemia, weight gain, and hypertension.

Colloidal bismuth has been shown in some studies (Salmon et al., 1974) to be effective in the treatment of duodenal ulcers. Since it is not an antacid or effective antipepsin agent, it is assumed to form a physical barrier against gastric secretion reaching the duodenum.

Related issues. Prevention of recurrence has been shown to improve with long-term low-dosage cimetidine therapy (e.g., 300 mg b.i.d. or q.h.s.), although this protection is not universal (Gray et al., 1978). Twenty percent of chronic ulcer clients will have a recurrence within 1 year, even with cimetidine therapy. Since long-term studies with this agent have not yet been reported, a risk-benefit equation cannot be reliably arrived at. However, in selected clients, this approach may prove preferable to surgery as long as toxicity is diligently avoided.

In critically ill clients, gastric ulceration and hemorrhage often complicate the clinical course. Studies demonstrated that continuous nasogastric antacid infusion with periodic pH measurements to maintain pH was beneficial (Hastings et al.,

1978). Cimetidine proved less effective than antacid therapy.

Recommended therapy. Presently we tend to start ulcer clients on antacids, selecting a high-potency, low-sodium preparation. If a p.r.n. regimen fails to achieve healing, we progress to the higher dosage range (15 to 30 ml 1 to 3 hr p.c. and h.s.). If diarrhea complicates therapy, we may switch to cimetidine.

DRUG	USUAL GERIATRIC DOSAGE	SIDE EFFECTS/ CONTRAINDICA- TIONS/COMMENTS
Antacids		
Maalox TC	15 to 30 ml 1 to 3 hr p.c. and h.s.	Observe for diarrhea or constipation
Mylanta II	15 to 30 ml 1 to 3 hr p.c. and h.s.	As above
Cimetidine	300 mg P.O. t.i.d. (normal renal function) 150 mg P.O. t.i.d. (reduced renal function)	See text
Propantheline	7.5 to 15 mg P.O. q.8hr (therapeutic dosage) 15 mg P.O. q.h.s. (prophylactic dos- age)	See text
Sucralfate	1 gm P.O. q.i.d., 1 hr a.c. and h.s.	Do *not* take antacids for 30 min before or following sucralfate; the elderly may have difficulty with swallowing tablet or with chalky taste if chewed

Constipation

The generation of persons currently in the geriatric age group have lived through the medical profession's great myth about autointoxication from bacteria in the colon and the supposed resulting evils of infrequent bowel actions.

Constipation may be defined either by infrequency of bowel movements or by passage of hard stools. Spurious diarrhea frequently occurs in the presence of an impacting fecal mass. Older individuals may be more prone to constipation, as shown in studies measuring intestinal transit time; such differences are confounded, however, by differences in physical activity levels. When institutionalized geriatric clients were compared with their peers living in the community, the active individuals showed normal or only minimally prolonged transit times, whereas the bed-bound group showed marked holdup in the descending colon, with clearly abnormal transit times.

Constipation may be caused by an abnormality of the lumen, causing the gut to be narrowed or immobile. Tumors encroach on and reduce the luminal cross section. Strictures, either caused by inflammation or ischemia, can also increase resistance to the passage of stools. Inflammatory and infiltrative disorders result in segments of fixed diameter as well. Prolonged laxative abuse can also be included under this heading, especially with those substances that damage the myenteric plexus. Certain systemic conditions interfere with intestinal motility. Hypothyroidism, hyperthyroidism, and hyperparathyroidism are such states. Treatment of these disorders invariably improves constipation. The irritable bowel syndrome will be discussed separately.

Drugs are notorious for slowing transit time. Narcotic analgesics, anticholinergic agents, antipsychotic tranquilizers, and antacids containing calcium and aluminum may produce constipation. Although diuretics do not influence intestinal motility directly, excessive dehydration can result in constipation, even to the point of the development of obstruction.

Certain other conditions are also associated with constipation, such as spinal cord lesions and disorders of the brain (e.g., multiple sclerosis). Immobility is naturally a contributing factor. The three most important factors in bowel habits of otherwise healthy elderly persons are diet, hydration, and activity. Both reduced fluid intake and a shift to a low-fiber, refined diet will promote constipation. Exercise is beneficial in stimulating intestinal motility.

Several different systems have been designed to classify all laxatives. Recent research has disproved several previously held beliefs about mechanisms of action, resulting in the emergence of new descriptive groupings.

Contact cathartics. These agents inhibit water and electrolyte absorption; some also stimulate peristalsis.

The anthraquinones (cascara, senna) produce soft or liquid stools through their absorption-blocking action. Although small bowel motility is not affected, the colon expels its contents more rapidly. The most common side effect is excessive purgation with dehydration and resultant electrolyte disturbances. Chronic abuse is a serious disorder that may result in a cathartic colon.

Diphenylmethanes include phenolphthalein and bisacodyl. Because of the mechanism of action, fluid and electrolyte losses and malabsorption can result from chronic abuse. Phenolphthalein can be detected by alkalinizing stool or urine, the appearance of pink or red color proving surreptitious laxative use. Bisacodyl suppositories may produce proctitis.

Hydroxy fatty acids are the active ingredients in castor oil. The peristaltic stimulation is most prominent in the small bowel, differentiating this agent from those listed previously. Therefore the onset of evacuation is much more rapid. Side effects are as noted previously.

Surfactants previously were not classified with the stimulant group; recent studies, however, reveal that one of their mechanisms of action is blocking intestinal absorption. This probably accounts for the increase in the water content of stools. Docusate calcium and docusate sodium are the best known members of the group.

When surfactants are administered with mineral oil, absorption of the latter is enhanced. We therefore caution against the use of this combination in less severe cases or for prolonged periods of time.

Saline cathartics. The traditional view that inorganic salts containing magnesium, sulfate, or phosphate simply act as intraluminal osmotic agents is no longer tenable. The volume of fluid that would render the usual dose isosmotic is only 100 to 200 ml; this amount is insufficient to cause diarrhea.

Magnesium sulfate is now known to have actions on bowel motility and secretion similar to cholecystokinin. The exact mechanism is not clear, but saline cathartics definitely act through nonosmotic pathways as well.

These agents may cause electrolyte disturbance; in addition, hypermagnesemia may occur in clients with diminished renal function.

Bulk-forming agents. When polysaccharides (e.g., cellulose derivatives), psyllium, or bran is taken orally, they absorb water to form a gelatin-like mass. Although there is an increase in stool bulk, other effects can be related to changes in the bile salt pool and its composition.

In excessive amounts, these agents can markedly harden stools and even lead to intestinal obstruction.

Lubricants. Mineral oil is the best known example. It softens stools and reduces surface tension. The risk of aspiration of mineral oil is increased in all debilitated clients, especially those who have CNS or neuromuscular disorders, resulting in a deficient gag reflex. Unfortunately, chronic aspiration results in lipoid pneumonia, and it may go unnoticed until pulmonary function declines dramatically. Mineral oil may also absorb fat-soluble vitamins and cause annoying anal leakage. Its routine or regular use is therefore discouraged.

Lactulose. This agent is a synthetic sugar. It is not broken down until it reaches the colon. Bacteria there break it down to produce lactic and pyruvic acids, which stimulate both colonic secretions and motility.

Sanders (1978) found that in dosages of 15 to 30 ml P.O. q.h.s., institutionalized clients had significant reduction in cramping, griping, flatulence, tenesmus, and bloating. Sanders also noted marked reduction in the incidence of fecal impaction.

It should be noted here that Martelli et al.

(1978) compare chronic, severe constipation to Hirschsprung's disease and recommend surgical management with anorectal myectomy.

Our current approach to constipation in elderly clients follows: after screening for the list of conditions mentioned previously, a comprehensive dietary history is taken with special attention to adequate fluid and dietary fiber intake. The client is then encouraged to alter incorrect eating and exercise habits. Since a high-fiber diet may result in undue flatulence and bloating, its benefit in the elderly must be weighed against its side effects. Fiber content must be gradually and cautiously built up, and the clinician should assess the extent of these side effects and weigh them against the benefit derived.

If laxatives are required, we prefer to administer bulk-forming agents, followed by contact cathartics, such as bisacodyl and docusate sodium.

We are reluctant to administer lubricants because of the risk of aspiration and usually discourage the use of saline cathartics. However, their judicious use in initial therapy of severe constipation has its place. Our experience with lactulose syrup is limited but encouraging.

Finally, in institutionalized clients good nursing care plays an enormous role in avoiding impaction by encouraging activity, encouraging adequate fluid and dietary fiber intake, minimizing bedrest, and diligently seeking out those most likely to develop fecal buildup.

DRUG	USUAL GERIATRIC DOSAGE	SIDE EFFECTS/ CONTRAINDICA- TIONS/COMMENTS
Plantago seed	1 packet P.O. q.d. to t.i.d.	Mix in cool fruit juice
Bisacodyl	10 to 15 mg P.O./ PR q.h.s.	
Docusate calcium	240 mg P.O. q.h.s.	
Docusate sodium	100 to 200 mg P.O. q.h.s.	
Magnesium sulfate	10 to 30 mg P.O. (in solution)	

Note: Administer adequate fluid with all laxatives.

Diverticular disease

Over the past 60 to 70 years there has been a dramatic increase in the number of clients with diverticular disease.

Pathologically defined as *pseudodiverticula*, these mucosal outpouchings through the muscularis mucosae occur predominantly in the sigmoid colon. The condition may be asymptomatic, accidentally discovered on administration of a barium enema; clients may initially have episodes of diverticulitis and its complications. Alternatively, intermittent constipation and diarrhea with diffuse abdominal pain may be reported. Finally, and unfortunately not rare in the elderly, previously asymptomatic diverticula may cause major colonic hemorrhage.

The current theory of the pathogenesis of diverticular disease states that refined, low-fiber diets cause excessive colonic segmentation with resulting muscular hypertrophy. Higher than normal intracolonic pressure is generated; this causes mucosal herniation at the site of the vascular pedicles. This theory does not account for recent findings that show that intraluminal pressures expressed as the motility index are not elevated in individuals who had x-ray evidence of diverticulosis but no symptoms. Undoubtedly, pressures are elevated in individuals who have acute or chronic symptoms. On the other hand, in the group suffering from the "colicky sigmoid syndrome," pressures are very high, yet no diverticula are evident on barium examination (Weinreich and Anderson, 1976). Therefore the mechanics of diverticulum development are probably separate from the disturbance of visceral sensations.

The current approach to treatment is to increase dietary fiber content (Gear et al., 1979). Some skeptics find the benefit nonspecific: "Dietary treatment of diverticular disease with bran has blown fresh air into dark passages as it reminds the low-residue fans of the importance of keeping their bowels open" (Spiro, 1977).

There is some evidence that bran is more effective for uncomplicated diverticular disease than other types of fiber. The excessive use of bran can, however, lead to flatulence and abdominal distention (Brodribb and Humphreys, 1976). Other agents such as antispasmodics (e.g., dicyclomine) and anticholinergics (e.g., propantheline and methscopolamine) are occasionally helpful but are not recommended in the uncomplicated case (Ivey, 1975).

Since diverticulitis is a relatively uncommon complication, the prophylactic use of antibiotic therapy in the usual case is contraindicated.

Irritable bowel syndrome

By clarifying the difference between hysterical conversion reactions, manifesting as diffuse abdominal pain, and psychophysiologic disturbance, which is capable of disrupting smooth muscle physiology, recent research has shed more light on this chronic bowel disturbance. It is characterized by prolonged constipation, intermittent diarrhea confined to the daytime, and diffuse abdominal pain (Spiro, 1977).

It is evident that pentagastrin or cholecystokinin stimulation results in exaggerated segmenting response in the sigmoid colon of these clients. In addition, visceral sensations are heightened so that intraluminal pressures within the normal range cause excruciating pain.

Myoelectric activity, measured in the rectosigmoid area, reveals an abnormal preponderance of slow waves in these clients (Snape et al., 1977). Meal-stimulated motor activity is prolonged as well (Sullivan, Cohen, and Snape, 1978).

These observations may demonstrate the electric equivalent of failure of relaxation before contraction, which normally results in propagation of stool.

Irritability has now been reliably demonstrated. The mechanism by which certain foods (coffee, alcohol, or high-fiber diet), as well as emotions, can stimulate the gut is unclear. Therefore treatment can only be pragmatic.

In clients with irritable bowel syndrome whose primary complaint is constipation, in-creased fluid intake (hot water preferred) and a high-fiber diet are beneficial. The treatment apparently works by enhancing stool bulk. Both fruit and vegetable fiber are used; the servings can be raw or cooked. Laxatives should be avoided as much as possible, since over time they tend to exacerbate the condition.

Clients whose primary complaint is diarrhea initially require a low-fiber diet. If this is not sufficient, then diphenoxylate (2.5 to 5 mg P.O. q.i.d.) or codeine (15 mg P.O. t.i.d.) is added. Once the diarrhea is under control, fiber is cautiously reintroduced. Although theoretic considerations would seem to justify the use of anticholinergics for pain in the predominantly constipated group, there is insufficient evidence that they are better than placebo in doses tolerated by elderly clients (Ivey, 1975).

Obviously, emotional crises can precipitate further attacks. By the same token, careful experimentation with various foods may reveal sensitivity to a particular item.

The essence of treatment is to support clients without encouraging them to assume the sick role. Therefore investigation should be thorough but not excessive. The purpose of each test must be clearly explained to the client. Negative studies do not "prove" that the client is hysterical; they only serve to rule out processes other than a motility disturbance.

In elderly clients who have suffered from the irritable bowel syndrome for decades diverticular disease is not an uncommon complication. The coexistence of these conditions provides a special challenge to the clinician.

Intestinal obstruction

Many terminally ill elderly clients develop intestinal obstruction. This is characteristically slow in onset. Abdominal distention, pain, borborygmi, nausea, vomiting, and early diarrhea with later constipation are the classic symptoms associated with this condition.

Such an occurrence does not have to result in

surgical intervention—a course of action that may in fact add to the misery of the client. Medical management has made this final stage of illness much more bearable and allows the sufferer to exercise some control over the condition.

The treatment goal is simply to gain control over pain and nausea. Although the client may continue to vomit—even twice daily—this is usually not too distressing a feature of the last days, weeks, or even months of life.

In the early phases of obstruction a stool softener is prescribed, but any direct chemical stimulation of peristalsis is carefully avoided. Docusate sodium may be given once or twice daily. Narcotic medications are used orally whenever possible to control pain, and an antiemetic, such as prochlorperazine syrup, is routinely advocated. If abdominal cramping becomes especially problematic, diphenoxylate, 2.5 to 5 mg, with atropine, 0.025 mg, is given every 4 hours.

With increasing constipation, laxatives should be discontinued. In the later stages of obstruction, medications may have to be administered by parenteral or rectal route. Saunders (1978) has recommended the rectal route and advocates the use of oxycodone, 20 to 60 mg, and prochlorperazine maleate suppositories, 25 mg, every 8 hours.

The careful therapeutic management of this condition often enables clients to continue with a fluid diet, and even favorite solids may be taken if the almost inevitable vomiting induced some hours later is considered an acceptable price to pay for such self-determination. Although dehydration is common in the later stages of treatment, it must be clearly appreciated by the clinician that the only distress experienced in this condition is that of a dry mouth. This can be adequately relieved by the use of small drinks or crushed ice frequently administered. The highest standards of nursing care are required, although treatment may be given by attentive and supportive relatives at home, provided the clinician is willing to offer unstinting

services and time to the family and community support agencies.

GENITOURINARY SYSTEM

Disturbances of this system cause almost as much disability in the geriatric population as those of the CNS. Discussion here will deal with infections and incontinence.

Urinary tract infections

Infection involves colonization of a previously sterile space or organ, accompanied by an inflammatory response at a systemic and/or local level. Symptoms may arise from irritation, secondary to edema, as well as from toxic products released by the invading organisms and/or defending host mechanisms.

Acute cystitis is a symptomatic bladder infection, usually caused by a single organism that arises from fecal-perineal flora. Pyuria is present; the bacterial count is usually 10^5/ml or more. There are two qualifying conditions often imposed on this figure: Enterobacteria are required to reach this count before giving rise to symptoms, whereas other organisms may be held responsible for cystitis at lower concentrations. In addition, the 10^5 bacteria per ml figure was arrived at from studies on pyelonephritis, not cystitis (Kass, 1957).

Acute pyelonephritis is a symptomatic infection of the upper urinary tract. Clients are usually more toxic when this occurs than with cystitis, with toxicity partly caused by gram-negative endotoxins. However, with repeated exposure, tolerance may develop. Taking into account the fact that the elderly may be less able to mount a toxic response, a common mistake is to underestimate the frequency of upper urinary tract infections in that age group (Riff, 1978).

A technique to improve differentiation between lower and upper urinary tract infection uses the detection of antibody-coated bacteria. Since these antibodies are presumed to be synthesized only in response to tissue invasion, the method can distinguish the two types of involvement (Jones, Smith, and Sanford, 1974). Prostatitis is characterized by tissue involvement, thus making the technique less useful in elderly men.

Asymptomatic bacteriuria is a condition that is usually detected on routine urinalysis. In the current literature the central issue is the natural history of this condition (Freeman et al., 1975; Dontas et al., 1981). It is common in elderly women who do not demonstrate any radiologic abnormality on urography.

The *urethral syndrome* is a recently described entity. Clients have dysuria with or without frequency, but according to classic criteria, they do not have cystitis, since bacteria are not identified in sufficient numbers. On further study, some clients in this group only have bacteriuria; a larger group of clients, however, also show pyuria. Usually *Escherichia coli, Staphylococcus saprophyticus,* and *Klebsiella* species are identified.

Another subset within the group with urethral and bladder irritation have no bacteriuria, but *Chlamydia* infection can be demonstrated.

Finally, some symptomatic clients have neither bacteriuria nor pyuria. No bacteriologic or other obvious cause can be found for their complaints (Stamm et al., 1980).

The relevance of these findings in elderly women has yet to be determined, but the broader implications are that bacterial isolation at lower than previously accepted counts may be indicative of infection requiring antibiotic therapy.

Relapse is defined as recurrence of infection caused by a previously identified organism.

Reinfection is a new infection produced by a different microorganism.

Persistence of infection may occur in two settings:

1. If there is no significant reduction in bacterial count, the wrong antibiotic was probably selected.
2. If the count is reduced but treatment failed to sterilize the urine, a structural abnormality (e.g., tumor, stone) or development of bacterial resistance should be suspected.

Prophylaxis for urinary tract infection is usually accomplished with antimicrobial therapy in dosages lower than full therapeutic regimens. The risk-benefit equation is affected by the natural history of recurrent infections in the urinary tract. Recent trials have demonstrated that in the absence of severe urologic disease or concomitant noninfectious renal disease (e.g., incomplete obstruction), persistent bacteriuria does not result in renal failure. Therefore such prophylaxis would have to be both effective and free of side effects to justify large-scale treatment of clients at risk (Freeman et al., 1975). Other studies seem to contradict these findings, at least as far as institutionalized elderly persons are concerned (Dontas et al., 1981).

Both low-dose nitrofurantoin (Bailey et al., 1971) and co-trimoxazole (Stamey, Condy, and Mihara, 1977) have been shown to be effective in reducing recurrence of urinary tract infections. The literature has not yet dealt with geriatric populations; therefore only inferences can be drawn.

Our policy with regard to treating urinary tract infections is as follows: after cultures are obtained, any symptomatic infection is treated with appropriate antibiotics. Because of the origin of the organisms, elderly clients in the community are initially treated with sulfonamides or ampicillin. Treatment is continued for 10 days, although this approach may change in the near future (Fang, Tolkoff-Rubin, and Rubin, 1978).

Institutionalized clients may carry different bacterial flora, thus necessitating broad-spectrum antibiotics (Sherman et al., 1980).

Clients who suffer from recurrent infections are intensively investigated to rule out structural abnormality. In the group with no underlying pathologic cause, low-dose prophylactic therapy with co-trimoxazole is tried (Santoro and Kaye, 1978).

Those with abnormalities not amenable to correction are given sequential, full-dose antibiotic therapy.

Asymptomatic bacteriuria is not treated in the absence of renal impairment. If, however, serial determinations suggest a *decline* in the glomerular filtration rate, treatment is instituted.

If aminoglycoside therapy is required, the Siersbaek-Nielsen dosing chart is used to avoid nephrotoxicity. In all severely ill clients, serum aminoglycoside levels should be determined as well (Siersbaek-Nielsen et al., 1971; Hull and Sarubbi, 1976). The incidence of toxic side effects is further reduced when individual pharmacokinetic calculations are carried out. This is now feasible based on as few as two serum levels through the use of computer technology (de Repentigny et al., 1981).

Finally, there is good evidence that clients suffering from chronic bacterial prostatitis may benefit from prolonged treatment with co-trimoxazole at full dosage (Meares, 1975).

Urinary incontinence

Incontinence may occur in two different settings in geriatrics. *Transient* incontinence is often the result of acute confusional states. It can also be caused by urinary tract infection, impending prostatic obstruction ("overflow incontinence"), fecal impaction, and relative or absolute immobility, thus preventing ready access to bathroom facilities. This group of clients will respond to removal of the underlying disorder, with a high probability that continence will return to normal.

Established incontinence warrants a five-stage investigation process:

1. History relating to timing and circumstances of incontinence
2. Physical examination, including pelvic examination
3. Biochemical workup with urinalysis and culture to rule out infection
4. Invasive studies—complete urodynamic study, cytoscopy, and voiding cystogram
5. Incontinence charting to assess and document timing, volume, and circumstances of incontinence

The pathologic substrate may either be a urologic abnormality (e.g., cystocele, tumor, stone, or prostatic hypertrophy) or a disturbance of neural control of bladder function (Bissada, Finkbeiner, and Welch, 1977a). Pharmacologic intervention may be required in the latter.

Neural control depends on the integrity of sensory (afferent) nerves delivering information about the degree of bladder filling and distention (Bissada, Finkbeiner, and Welch, 1977b); it uses the sacral parasympathetic micturition centers for efficient emptying; the spinal cord provides access for higher inhibitory stimuli; the brain adds the component of conscious inhibition, making social continence possible (Bissada, Finkbeiner, and Welch, 1977c). Although no classification is perfect, the following headings are practical and useful:

1. *Autonomous bladder.* Sensory and motor fibers disrupted. Only local control from within the bladder can cause emptying.
2. *Atonic bladder.* Sensory fibers damaged. The bladder is large and overdistended. Incontinence is of the overflow type.
3. *Reflex bladder.* Spinocerebral connections severed. The bladder is small and spastic. Small volumes are voided at irregular intervals.
4. *Uninhibited bladder.* Higher centers of the brain are disrupted. Sensation is intact, but inhibition is ineffective. This disturbance is common following multiple cerebral infarcts and diffuse degenerative brain diseases.

Management of incontinence. Following are the goals of treatment (Vallarino, 1978):

1. Reduce or eliminate incontinence
2. Maintain residual bladder volume at a minimum to avoid urinary tract infections

Successful treatment requires a closely coordinated team approach.

Pharmacologic modalities are aimed at heightening bladder tone in an atonic bladder, relaxing the small spastic bladder, and reducing the frequency of spontaneous bladder contractions by blocking smooth muscle irritability (Bissada, Finkbeiner, and Welch, 1977a, b, and c and 1979; Finkbeiner, Bissada, and Welch, 1977a, b, and c and 1979; Mahony, Laferte, and Blais, 1977; Bissada and Finkbeiner, 1980).*

It is important to emphasize that within limits the bladder can be "reconditioned." Skill in handling the atonic bladder may restore some function with resulting improvement in emptying. Combination of frequent, scheduled toileting and muscle-relaxing agents can increase the capacity of a small spastic bladder. The advantages of restoring a degree of continence include protection of skin from maceration, reduction in the frequency of urinary tract infections, lessening of nursing requirements, and last but foremost, vast improvement in the quality of life for the client suffering from incontinence. Morale and self-respect can be expected to return with dramatic consequences in up to 80% to 90% of incontinent clients admitted to active treatment geriatric medical services.

Parasympathomimetic agents. These agents affect the muscarinic receptors without significantly influencing ganglionic transmission (Finkbeiner, Bissada, and Welch, 1977a). Their place in therapy is in the management of the atonic bladder.

Bethanechol is a commonly used agent (Finkbeiner, Bissada, and Welch, 1977b). Administered subcutaneously, within 7 to 15 minutes after intravesical pressure rises, the desire to urinate becomes intense, and voiding is accomplished. Oral administration results in voiding within 1 hour. Because of a differential effect on detrusor and bladder neck, bethanechol produces muscarinic stimulation of bladder muscle, promoting voiding, while through its weak nicotinic action, it heightens urethral pressure, which may block micturition. This is not of major im-

portance in most cases of atonic bladder without urethral disturbance, but in cases of associated functional outflow obstruction bethanechol alone may not be useful. Combination with phenoxybenzamine results in a reduction of outlet pressure, and thus voiding may be accomplished.

Finally, in the vesical-sphincteric dyssynergia group, bethanechol causes heightened pressures throughout, with obstruction more likely than successful voiding. Even if micturition is accomplished, it is at a cost of excessive pressure (Diokno and Koppenhoefer, 1976).

Therapy is usually started subcutaneously, followed by oral administration, once success is demonstrated. Side effects are caused by excessive cholinergic stimulation (e.g., flushing, lacrimation). Headaches and blurred vision may also occur.

Parasympathetic antagonists. These agents are antimuscarinic in action, making tissues insensitive to acetylcholine. Their therapeutic role is in managing spastic, irritable bladders by depressing the uninhibited contractions of smooth muscle. In appropriate doses detrusor tonicity is well maintained, resulting in enhanced bladder capacity yet complete emptying (Finkbeiner, Bissada, and Welch, 1977c).

Propantheline is useful in treating symptoms produced by contractions of the uninhibited bladder. It relieves frequency and urgency while sensation is preserved. Since it is a quarternary amine, it is less likely to cause CNS symptoms because it penetrates the blood-brain barrier poorly.

In the elderly, symptoms of reduced salivation, mydriasis and blurred vision, glaucomatous attacks, tachycardia, and other dysrhythmias are of concern. In higher doses excitation, delirium, and psychotic episodes may occur. Since the antimuscarinic effect is nonspecific, some of these side effects may in fact need to be anticipated and dealt with as a trade-off for urinary incontinence.

Central nervous system depressants. As a

---

*Bissada and Finkbeiner published a series of 12 excellent articles in *Urology* over a period of several years; the authorship sequence varied.

peripheral side effect, these agents may interfere with bladder function. However, they can be useful in certain settings (Bissada, Finkbeiner, and Welch, 1979).

Imipramine has been found effective in treating uninhibited bladder contractions, provided sufficient time is allowed for its action (2 to 3 weeks may be needed) (Cole and Fried, 1972). As expected, insomnia, restlessness, irritability, and confusion may develop, limiting its usefulness in the elderly. Cautious dosage management with careful observation, including incontinence charting, is necessary, but beneficial results have been obtained.

Adrenergic-blocking agents. Because α-receptors are present at the bladder outlet, their stimulation results in resistance to flow. β-receptors are most prevalent in the dome of the bladder. They relax smooth muscle, enhancing bladder capacity (Finkbeiner, Welch, and Bissada, 1979).

Phenoxybenzamine is an α-blocker. A relatively recent discovery is its effectiveness in clients who have functional obstruction caused by heightened outlet tone. In clients with neurogenic disturbances, the use of this drug can reduce or eliminate residual volumes, as well as improve flow (McQuire, Wagner, and Weiss, 1976).

Side effects of phenoxybenzamine are caused by its nonselective α-blockade. Postural hypotension and reflex tachycardia have been reported, an effect exacerbated by hypovolemia.

Propranolol has been successfully used in the management of stress and postprostatectomy incontinence by promoting α-adrenergic tone at the bladder outlet (Gleason et al., 1974; Khanna, 1976). Because it can be effective for clients who would not be able to tolerate α-adrenergic stimulants, this drug can be beneficial in elderly clients with cardiac disease. A comprehensive review is found in Mahony, Laferte, and Blais (1977) and Bissada and Finkbeiner (1980).

DRUG	USUAL GERIATRIC DOSAGE	SIDE EFFECTS/ CONTRAINDICA-TIONS/COMMENTS
Bethanechol	10 to 50 mg P.O. q.6hr 2.5 mg to 5 mg SC q.6hr	Escalate dosage with caution
Propantheline	7.5 to 15 mg P.O. q.6hr	
Imipramine	10 to 25 mg P.O. b.i.d.	Escalate cautiously over 2 to 3 weeks
Phenoxy-benzamine	5 to 10 mg P.O. b.i.d.	Observe for hypotension
Propranolol	10 mg P.O. b.i.d. to q.i.d.	*Note:* relatively contra-indicated in heart failure; diabetes mellitus; asthma

MUSCULOSKELETAL SYSTEM

In addition to a brief discussion of common forms of arthritis, we will cover Paget's disease and giant cell arteritis. Only rheumatoid arthritis, osteoarthritis, and chondrocalcinosis will be mentioned because they are the arthritic conditions most commonly seen in the elderly.

Rheumatoid arthritis

This syndrome of systemic inflammation gives rise to two types of presentations in the elderly. Chronic rheumatoid clients survive to old age, their articular disabilities often compounded by persistent inflammation. The other group of clients develop rheumatoid arthritis for the first time in later life. It is important to consider this diagnosis in all elderly clients who initially have articular complaints.

The diagnosis depends on a constellation of signs and symptoms, with laboratory evidence confirming the clinical impression. Seronegative forms are not uncommon in the elderly, making the condition more challenging to identify. Treatment combines rest, physical therapy, and medications. The cornerstone of therapeutic management is salicylate therapy.

Aspirin is a potent anti-inflammatory agent

when given in sufficiently large doses. However, its use is often difficult in the elderly for the following reasons:

1. Salicylates are protein bound, but with increasing blood levels the percentage bound declines, making more free drug available.
2. Both hepatic-metabolic processes and renal excretion tend to deteriorate with age, prolonging the half-life of aspirin. Since some metabolites obey first-order kinetics, whereas others depend on Michaelis-Menten kinetics, the actual outcome of these changes is difficult to predict.
3. The elderly may not be able to protect their systemic pH as accurately as younger subjects, causing fluctuations in the amount of nonionized salicylates available (the molecular form capable of cellular penetration).
4. The classic CNS side effect heralding toxicity is tinnitus. In elderly clients this may not occur; instead, deafness may set in insidiously. Reduction in blood levels reverses the hearing loss, although reports are lacking about chronic toxicity (Mongan et al., 1973).
5. GI tract irritation is a common complaint. There is debate about whether achlorhydria protects the gastric mucosa from ulceration, but since salicylates are mucosal barrier toxins, they may injure the atrophic gastric wall independent of acid secretion.

If care is taken to consider these facts, management with frequent salicylate level determinations may elicit the response necessary.

Other nonsteroidal anti-inflammatory agents

Indomethacin. This drug is beneficial for many arthritic conditions. Although its side effects are potentially troublesome, it may be a reasonable alternative to salicylates.

In some centers CNS complaints of dissociation from reality have been reported. In our ex-perience this is a rare complication. Na^+ retention is of potential concern in the elderly population with cardiac disease. Cautious monitoring of weight early in the clinical course is recommended. GI tract complaints may occur, and some cases of GI tract bleeding, initially asymptomatic, have been reported. The suppository form of indomethacin can bring dramatic results with control of morning symptoms. The drug is contraindicated in clients who are allergic to aspirin.

Ibuprofen, fenoprofen, ketoprofen, and naproxen. These agents all appear to be similar in effectiveness. Their side effects are fairly unpredictable, and perhaps one or two of these drugs should be given adequate trial, since lack of response to one does not necessarily preclude benefit with another. Individual clients may respond favorably to one of them, having failed to benefit from another member of the group. Similarly, a side effect that precludes the use of one medication (e.g., gastric irritation) may not occur with another one. Therefore we recommend adequate trial of at least two of the agents listed.

Sulindac. Fasching and Eberl (1976) have found this indene derivative to be useful in managing inflammatory joint disease. We tend to give it a trial before turning to the agents discussed on the following pages (Fasching and Eberl, 1976). Because sulindac is a prodrug that is only converted to its active form after absorption, gastric irritation is less common than with other agents (Duggan et al., 1977; Kwan et al., 1978). As with the other medications, a low dosage regimen is recommended.

Gold therapy. When it is determined that the elderly client with rheumatoid arthritis needs additional therapy, gold is one of the treatment options to be considered.

It must be stressed that response to treatment may take 2 to 3 months. Because of potential toxicity, clients should be observed closely. Measurement of gold blood or urine levels has not proven helpful in predicting which clients will develop complications (Billings et al., 1975).

The important side effects follow:

1. Dermatitis, ranging from rashes to exfoliation
2. Renal toxicity with the nephrotic syndrome
3. Hematologic abnormalities (thrombocytopenia is the most common, followed by leukopenia; aplastic anemia is rare but highly lethal once developed)

Therefore clients should be monitored with complete blood count determinations and urinalyses, as well as be reviewed for other undesirable effects. If any of the major complications develop, therapy should be discontinued immediately.

Exfoliative dermatitis, severe bone marrow depression, and nephritis are life-threatening conditions; following treatment of these toxic manifestations, the client should *not* be rechallenged with gold salts.

Antimalarials. Chloroquine and hydroxychloroquine have an antirheumatoid effect that takes as long or longer than gold therapy to manifest. Retinopathy and ototoxicity, as well as skin rash, may complicate their use. Because the retinal damage may progress to blindness despite cessation of therapy, we recommend the use of these agents only for clients who cannot tolerate gold therapy. The dosage in elderly clients should be low. The ocular fundus should be reviewed every 2 to 3 months by an ophthalmologist familiar with the drugs.

Penicillamine. Like the previous two groups of agents, this drug is indicated only in aggressive, erosive forms of rheumatoid arthritis (Crawhall, 1980).

The side effects of penicillamine include rashes, GI tract and taste disturbances, proteinuria, thrombocytopenia, and leukopenia (Stein et al., 1980). If the medication is well tolerated, there is a 70% chance of clinical improvement. There seems to be an increased risk of side effects with higher dosages.

DRUG	USUAL GERIATRIC DOSAGE	SIDE EFFECTS/ CONTRAINDICATIONS/COMMENTS
Aspirin	650 mg P.O. t.i.d.	GI tract irritation; measure blood salicylate levels; also see text
Gold sodium thiomalate	10 mg IM q. wk × 2 (then titrate; maintenance dosage 25 mg IM q. mo)	Dermatitis; nephritis; hematologic disorders; monitor CBC; urinalysis; see text
Chloroquine	125 mg P.O. q.d.	Observe fundi; see text
Hydroxy-chloroquine	200 mg P.O. q.d.	Observe fundi; see text
Penicillamine	125 to 250 mg P.O. q.d. (increase after 3 months)	See text

Osteoarthritis

Osteoarthritis is a primary degenerative condition that causes a great deal of disability among the elderly. Involvement of weight-bearing joints interferes with mobility, whereas if the small joints of the hands are affected, prehensile and manipulative difficulties result. The long-continued debate about whether cartilage destruction is primary or secondary to abnormalities of the underlying bone is of more than theoretic interest. Important, too, is the research to determine if osteoarthritic cartilage is excessively vulnerable to damage or is less capable of self-repair. Until these questions are answered satisfactorily, treatment can only be palliative.

Physical therapy has the following goals:

1. Maintenance of range of movement of joints
2. Bolstering of muscle strength
3. Correction of abnormal loading factors that place excessive strain on the involved joints

Rest is an integral part of treatment. Medical therapy relies on the use of analgesics to control pain. Aspirin is the mainstay of treatment because it combines analgesic and anti-inflammatory properties. Acetaminophen is helpful for clients unable to take salicylates. This medication relieves pain but *not* inflammation.

Codeine in low doses can be combined with salicylates or acetaminophen, although chronic use is not recommended.

Although the dominant process is a degenerative arthropathy, low-grade synovitis can be demonstrated as well. In addition, episodes of acute or chronic relapse are clearly inflammatory, with effusion and more florid synovitis. The use of nonsteroidal anti-inflammatory agents described under *Rheumatoid Arthritis* can be beneficial. Indomethacin can afford impressive relief. In elderly clients, low dosages (25 mg P.O. b.i.d.) should be used initially, and dosage escalation requires caution.

In the treatment of osteoarthritis sulindac compares favorably with aspirin (Gengos, 1978).

Although systemic steroids have not been shown to be very effective, intraarticular use can be recommended. Since this approach is not without hazard, its application should be restricted to one injection per year for each large joint involved. Both infectious complications and tendon damage resulting from local catabolic effects have been seen when steroids are used more frequently.

Current research carries the promise of solutions that will prevent excessive cartilage degradation and even stimulate effective healing of damaged joints.

Pseudogout

Pseudogout is an arthritic condition that is now known by the tongue-twisting designation *calcium pyrophosphate crystal deposition (CPCD) disease*. The disease may have multiple patterns.

Pseudogout (McCarty type A). The knee is the most frequently involved joint. Attacks may be as acute as in gout. Abortive attacks with less painful manifestations outnumber full-blown episodes. Surgery, trauma, stroke, and myocardial infarction can incite an attack. Clustering of joint involvement has been observed.

Pseudo–rheumatoid arthritis (McCarty type B). Subacute attacks with systemic manifestations (e.g., fatigue, elevated erythrocyte sedimentation rate [ESR], fever) are seen. The disease may even assume an acute form, with multiple inflamed joints, high fever, and leukocytosis. Because it occurs in elderly clients, confusion can compound matters.

Pseudoosteoarthritis (McCarty types C and D). A chronic arthritis with symmetrical involvement is seen, which appears to be classically osteoarthritic. The pattern of joints affected is different from osteoarthritis: wrist, metacarpophalangeal joints, elbow, and shoulder are afflicted, whereas proximal interphalangeal and distal interphalangeal joints are spared. However, the two conditions may coexist.

Asymptomatic (McCarty type E) pseudogout. This appears to be the most common form. In fact, symptoms in joints without CPCD deposits are noted, whereas radiologically chondrocalcinotic joints are pain free.

Pseudoneuropathic (McCarty type F) pseudogout. Charcot's joints have been reported in some clients with CPCD. Treatment is presently symptomatic. In the acute episode colchicine is occasionally helpful, whereas indomethacin is more reliably effective. Phenylbutazone may be necessary, although we would first try intraarticular steroids. Interval treatment has not been shown effective in reducing the frequency of attacks but is necessary in the chronic forms (Fam et al., 1981).

Since CPCD disease afflicts the elderly, it must always be entertained in the differential diagnosis of arthritis.

DRUG	USUAL GERIATRIC DOSAGE	SIDE EFFECTS/ CONTRAINDICA- TIONS/COMMENTS
Indometha- cin	25 mg P.O. t.i.d.	GI tract irritation; GI bleeding; do not use if aspirin allergy is documented

DRUG	USUAL GERIATRIC DOSAGE	SIDE EFFECTS/ CONTRAINDICA- TIONS/COMMENTS
Methylpred- nisolone	10 to 40 mg (intra- articular)	Do not inject when infec- tion is present
Sulindac	150 mg P.O. b.i.d. with food	GI tract irritation

Paget's disease of the bone

This condition affects bone synthesis and re- sorption in a focal fashion. Although involvement is commonly multiple, it is not a diffuse disor- der.

The radiologic changes are often not associated with symptoms, and treatment is not warranted under such circumstances. Five complications of Paget's disease justify therapy (Evans, 1979):

1. Bone pain (not simply osteoarthritic dis- comfort)
2. Immobilization hypercalcemia
3. Recurrent fractures
4. Neurologic complications (nerve and root entrapment)
5. Preoperative and postoperative manage- ment (orthopedic procedures)

The occasionally encountered decompensated heart failure reported in Europe is rarely seen in North America.

Apart from agents used for articular manifes- tations, which are discussed under *Osteoarthritis*, three groups of medications are beneficial.

Calcitonins. Porcine extract, synthetic salmon, and synthetic human calcitonins have all been used. Biochemical evidence attests to improve- ment with this treatment (Sturtridge, Harrison, and Wilson, 1977). The hormone is injected sub- cutaneously on a daily basis. The usual dose is 100 U/day.

Calcitonin preparations currently available are antigenic (porcine and salmon). Antibodies de- velop in up to 50% of clients, but relapse only occurs in 10% of clients receiving treatment. Re- lapse is caused by excessively high antibody titers. Synthetic human calcitonin appears to be much less antigenic, and its use promises better control for longer periods.

Paget's disease may cause both radiographical- ly sclerotic and lytic lesions. Lytic lesions, espe- cially with resorptive fronts, make clients more prone to fracture and deformity. For sclerotic lesions that are painful but do not threaten to produce anatomic deformity, regimens with lower daily dosages or less frequent administra- tion of full dosages (e.g., three doses per week) may be sufficient. This approach could perhaps reduce the rate of antibody production. For lytic lesions pain relief alone is not an acceptable end point for treatment; only radiologic proof of heal- ing should be accepted.

Deafness is a common, progressive, neuro- logic complication of Paget's disease. Unfortu- nately, treatment with calcitonin does not appear to be beneficial in preventing this complication (Walker et al., 1979).

Diphosphonates. Diphosphonates have been investigated in Paget's disease. Ethane hydroxy- diphosphonate (EHDP) is currently available for use. Clinical evidence shows improvement in up to 61% of symptomatic clients (Khairi et al., 1977).

Findings indicate that intermittent therapy with EHDP is preferable. The dosage currently recommended is 5 mg/kg/day because larger amounts do not accrue benefits commensurate with the risk of toxicity (e.g., diarrhea, increased bone pain). The main obstacle to widespread use is the now confirmed mineralization delay that predisposes clients to fractures and is more pro- nounced in the higher dose range (de Deux- chaisnes et al., 1980). Dichloromethylene diphos- phonate holds promise of being both more effec- tive and less toxic than EHDP (Douglas et al., 1980).

Mithramycin is an antibiotic with strong anti- osteoclastic activity. It has hematologic toxicity resulting in thrombocytopenia, which limits its usefulness. However, it is effective for treatment of bone pain associated with Paget's disease. A new, low-dose regimen, using 10 μg/kg of mi-thramycin daily, administered intravenously for 10 days, has resulted in complete pain relief in 4 to 5 days (Russell, 1980). Careful hematologic monitoring is necessary for safe use.

Giant cell arteritis

The spectrum of this disease encompasses rheumatic manifestations (polymyalgia rheumatica) and temporal arteritis, as well as other disabling and diverse forms.

Although much has been written about this condition, it is still often not suspected in the elderly. Many of the reviews emphasize the nonspecific nature of the clinical presentation.

It is often debated whether the diagnosis can be entertained in the absence of an elevated ESR. It may be that the ESR fluctuates with the clinical course, and some authors note that in the "burnt-out" phase of the condition the ESR may not be abnormal. The other difficulty lies in defining the normal ESR which tends to rise with age.

Strachan, How, and Bewsher (1980) introduced a new classification, with masked giant cell arteritis as a major subdivision:

1. Malignant (cachectic)
2. Anemic
3. Febrile
4. Aneurysmal (aortic regurgitation, aneurysm)
5. Occlusive (stroke, amaurosis, intermittent claudication, myocardial ischemia)

Diagnosis requires an elevated ESR, as well as a biopsy of the temporal artery. The biopsy may be positive even when the artery is not tender and is normally pulsatile. Because of segmental involvement, the surgeon and pathologist should cooperate to excise a sufficiently long portion of the artery, which is then examined microscopically at multiple points on the specimen.

The use of steroids is an effective treatment. Initially high doses must be used. Symptomatic improvement, coupled with normalization of the ESR and reversal of anemia, is rapidly achieved. Actual dosage recommendations vary, depending on the investigator's experience. Fernandez-Herlihy (1980) uses 40 to 80 mg of prednisone initially, then tapers this to 15 to 20 mg after 3 weeks. The average maintenance dosage in his series is 8 mg/day.

The European experience is summarized by Mumenthaler (1978). The recommended dosage is 1 mg/kg of prednisone for 3 weeks. If the ESR is 10 by the end of this period, the dosage is reduced by 5 mg every 2 days. The maintenance dosage is set at 10 to 15 mg/day. Mumenthaler cautions against sudden interruption of therapy because blindness, secondary to occlusive arteritis, may develop overnight. Unfortunately, once this happens, treatment will almost uniformly fail to restore vision.

PSYCHIATRY

Mental illness is common in old age. Clients with chronic psychiatric disorders survive to late life, but new mental disorders also develop in the elderly.

Affective disorders

Depression is often a disease of later life. It can take on psychotic proportions; suicide is a common outcome unless effective treatment intervenes.

The diagnosis of depression may be obvious in the lethargic, apathetic, melancholic client who manifests the expected biologic symptoms and signs (e.g., anorexia, weight loss, insomnia with early awakening, psychomotor retardation).

If thoughts of worthlessness and guilt and morbid preoccupation with death and suicide are demonstrated, treatment is of the *utmost urgency*. Depression may occur in other forms as well; guilt and self-reproach can produce agitation, which may also be caused by coexistent mania or paranoid thought content. Although pure paranoia is rare in the elderly, clients may initially have depression with paranoid features. Another guise depression may assume is phobia with obsessions. This atypical form is less responsive to usual management approaches than the others. Chronic hypochondriasis and pseudo-dementia are often rooted in an underlying depression.

Finally, in our experience, whenever a somatic complaint, most commonly unexplained pain, does not appear to have a pathologic substrate, depression must be excluded.

Depression may occur in cycles or may occur only once in a lifetime. The classic bipolar manic-depressive illness is much less common in the elderly than recurrent, unipolar depressive episodes. The regular return of symptoms is important to identify, since lithium carbonate has been found effective in cyclic depression even if no manic episodes intervene.

Tricyclic antidepressants. Neurotransmitter research has defined some abnormalities of brain function, although both the specificity and predictive potential of these studies is limited at present (Hall, 1974). In general, the tricyclic antidepressants can be classified as stimulant or sedative antidepressants. They seem to affect norepinephrine and serotonin fluxes, respectively (Maas, 1975). The sedative group includes amitriptyline and doxepin. They are most likely to benefit agitated clients, but this is far from being an absolute rule, since paradoxic responses to therapy are commonly encountered.

Imipramine, desipramine, and protriptyline are stimulant antidepressants. Lethargic clients improve after receiving these agents, and they begin to feel better under their influence. Because of the large area of overlap, tricyclic antidepressants should not be deemed to have failed until one agent from each group is given an adequate trial.

As a rule, the geriatric antidepressant dosage is *one third* of the customary adult dose. It is now possible to measure tricyclic antidepressant blood levels. Although debate abounds as to whether "therapeutic" levels guarantee a benefi-

cial effect, it has been demonstrated that different clients may have subtherapeutic or toxic blood levels despite receiving the same dose. Toxic levels of tricyclic antidepressants may produce depressive symptoms indistinguishable from the untreated condition (Appelbaum et al., 1979).

The "start low–go slow" slogan should apply to tricyclic antidepressant therapy in the elderly. The disadvantage of this approach is that the hazardous period when the side effects of these medications are obvious to the client, while affective reversal has not yet taken place, is prolonged.

The major common side effects include anticholinergic complications, extrapyramidal symptoms, and quinidine-like cardiac manifestations (e.g., ventricular dysrhythmias, syncope).

The strongly anticholinergic agents, such as amitriptyline, are safer when given in a single, bedtime dose; imipramine, on the other hand, can be administered in divided doses. Prostatic obstruction, glaucoma, xerostomia, and tachycardia can limit the usefulness of these agents, but preventive monitoring can reduce the hazards of administration. Although it has not been conclusively proven for all tricyclic antidepressants, it is likely that a therapeutic "window" exists, above and below which serum concentration the agent is not effective in the treatment of depression. This range may be narrower in the elderly than in younger adults (Comfort, 1980).

MAO inhibitors. These agents are effective antidepressants, but because they have to be accompanied by a special diet low in tyramine and other biologically active amines, they may be hazardous to the elderly population. Although the classically described response to foods high in tyramine (e.g., blue cheese, Chianti wine) is a hypertensive crisis, protracted hypotension might occur in the elderly. (See Chapter 8, "Drug Interactions in the Geriatric Client," for further information on this interaction.)

In atypical depression, associated with phobias and obsessional thought content, tricyclic antidepressants may not be effective. Under these conditions, MAO inhibitors can be tried. It is preferable to institutionalize the client for the initial phase of treatment.

Phenelzine may be useful for depressed clients who display increased anxiety, as long as precautions with regard to diet are accompanied by careful blood pressure monitoring, with the client in both the supine and erect positions. An adequate trial is at least 3 weeks of therapy. The usual adult dosage is 15 mg P.O. t.i.d.; however, in the elderly, lower dosage (e.g., 7.5 mg P.O. t.i.d. or 15 mg P.O. b.i.d.) is advisable.

Tranylcypromine is a potent MAO inhibitor, with side effects similar to phenelzine. Hypertensive crises have been reported with both drugs. Deaths have occurred in clients with underlying intracerebral vascular abnormalities. The usual adult dosage is 10 mg P.O. b.i.d., followed by a boost of the morning dose. In geriatric clients all dosages should be reduced by one half. Although the literature is not uniform in this regard, we strongly recommend this approach.

Lithium carbonate. This agent has been successful in the prevention of recurrence of the manic phase of bipolar affective illness. More recently it has also been demonstrated to benefit those clients whose depressive episodes are clearly cyclic in occurrence. This drug may be helpful for depressed clients who cannot tolerate tricyclic antidepressants.

Since toxic blood levels are close to the therapeutic range, frequent monitoring is essential. Because lithium and sodium share a common reabsorptive mechanism, a dangerous accumulation of lithium may occur when intake of sodium is restricted or when diuretics are used concurrently. Lithium carbonate is excreted through the kidneys; therefore significant renal impairment is a contraindication to its use.

Blood levels should be drawn 9 to 12 hours after the last dose. The therapeutic range is 1.0 to 1.5 mEq/l. Elderly clients may become toxic even at levels below 1.0 mEq/l (Foster, Gershell, and Goldfarb, 1977). Symptoms include fatigue, weakness, drowsiness, tremor, and GI tract symptoms.

It has been documented that as the manic episode subsides a significant decline in lithium dosage requirement can be anticipated. The lowest recommended dosage is 300 mg P.O. b.i.d., and while levels are closely monitored, it can be cautiously increased.

Electroconvulsive therapy (ECT). This topic is included in the discussion to emphasize its occasional usefulness and considerable safety in older clients. Bilateral or full-thickness ECT is more effective than unilateral, nondominant hemisphere discharges, but it is also associated with more amnesia. In situations where the client is at risk of either suicide or death because of inanition or general debilitation caused by severe depression, ECT can be a lifesaving measure.

The fact that recovery after ECT takes five to seven times longer in the elderly must be considered when treatment is planned. It is now becoming evident from recent studies that a coexisting dementia may just be unmasked rather than caused by ECT.

Comments on dosages. All of the dosages listed are meant for initiation of therapy. Except for extraordinary cases, tricyclic antidepressants and MAO inhibitors should *not* be combined by the general clinician. When used sequentially, at least a 10- to 14-day drug-free interval is recommended. Monitoring tricyclic antidepressant blood levels may be useful; if unavailable, failure to respond to a previously effective dose should be approached through dose *reduction* before escalation is embarked on.

DRUG	USUAL GERIATRIC DOSAGE	SIDE EFFECTS/ CONTRAINDICA- TIONS/COMMENTS
Amitriptyline	25 mg P.O. q.h.s.	*Note:* anticholinergic effects: prostate, glaucoma, colon
Amoxapine	12.5 to 25 mg P.O. t.i.d.	Our limited experience with this agent indicates that rapid onset of action may not be beneficial in the elderly (i.e., CNS excitation has been observed); reportedly minimal cardiac toxicity must be further evaluated

DRUG	USUAL GERIATRIC DOSAGE	SIDE EFFECTS/ CONTRAINDICA- TIONS/COMMENTS
Desipramine	25 mg P.O. q.h.s.	Least anticholinergic; first choice in stimulant group
Doxepin	25 mg P.O. q.h.s.	Sedative; least cardiotoxic; one of our first choice drugs
Imipramine	25 mg P.O. q.h.s.	
Lithium car- bonate	300 mg. P.O. b.i.d.	*Note:* monitor blood levels; avoid salt restriction and diuretics
Nomifensine	25 mg P.O. t.i.d.	Minimal anticholinergic ef- fects; reduced dosage in renal impairment
Phenelzine	5 mg P.O. t.i.d.	*Note:* dietary restrictions; monitor blood pressure in supine and standing posi- tions
Protriptyline	10 to 25 mg P.O. q.d.	
Tranylcy- promine	5 mg P.O. b.i.d.	*Note:* dietary restrictions; monitor blood pressure in supine and standing posi- tions

Insomnia

This is a common complaint in the elderly. Sleep studies are now beginning to report about disturbances in this age group. The quality of sleep may be more important than its quantity. Aging is accompanied by a reduction in Stage IV (deep) sleep in the sleep cycle.

Early awakening may signify depression. The overall duration of sleep is shorter in the elderly than in the young.

Large segments of the population use seda- tive-hypnotics and minor tranquilizers routinely. The elderly purchase over-the-counter sleeping aids, as well as prescription medications, in large quantities.

Barbiturates. Although these agents have been immensely popular in the past, in our opinion they are strongly contraindicated in the elderly. They are addictive and cause overseda- tion and drowsiness. In addition, they may in- duce hepatic microsomal enzymes. The degree of induction is a confounding, age-related variable, making predictions before treatment regarding the actual outcome of drug interaction nearly

impossible. We thus recommend discontinuation of barbiturates through tapering whenever fea- sible.

Benzodiazepines. Diazepam and flurazepam are frequently prescribed. Unfortunately, both of these agents have prolonged half-lives in the elderly, resulting in daytime drowsiness, confu- sion, and ataxia.

Hepatic glucuronidation does not seem to be impaired by the aging process. Oxazepam and lorazepam do not require any other steps before becoming inactive; therefore their half-lives are unchanged in the geriatric age group.

Triazolam is a newer agent with a specific geri- atric dosage form (0.25 mg tablet). Our personal experience is generally unfavorable, since we have seen many elderly clients who became con- fused and developed feelings of depersonaliza- tion. These symptoms responded to cessation of therapy. Lower dosage may perhaps prevent these side effects.

Chloral hydrate is an age-old sedative that does not accumulate. Combination with alcohol is of "Mickey Finn" fame; clients therefore need to be cautioned against a "nightcap."

In our clinical practice we prefer to avoid pre- scribing nighttime sedation. Daytime activity, early evening walks, and intellectual stimulation in the later hours, together with careful attention to physical comfort and relief of anxiety, can obvi- ate the need of such drugs in most of the elderly who live in the community.

If the client with insomnia fails to respond to conservative measures, our first choice is still chloral hydrate.

Among the benzodiazepines, oxazepam is rec- ommended. It is important to inform the client that it will take up to 1 hour for drowsiness and sleep to occur; therefore it should be taken earli- er. We have not yet seen problematic morning drowsiness or confusion with this agent.

Antidepressants of the sedative type are useful in depressive illness. In fact, clients may com- ment favorably that they finally had a good night's rest after receiving treatment. For insti- tutionalized clients it may be useful to chart and document actual sleep duration. Rather than sedation at night, vigorous activity in the evening may be the long-term solution to insomnia. We deplore the occasionally observed routine use of sedation for the sole purpose of "crowd control."

DRUG	USUAL GERIATRIC DOSAGE	SIDE EFFECTS/ CONTRAINDICA- TIONS/COMMENTS
Chloral hydrate	500 mg P.O./PR q.h.s.	Do not use concurrently with alcohol
Oxazepam	15 mg P.O. q.h.s.	Take 1 hour before desired sleep

Dementia

It is appropriate to discuss this topic for two reasons: to emphasize the treatable nature of some dementias and to aid in interpreting some claims in the literature.

Senile dementia has an extensive differential diagnosis. The leading dementias are senile dementia of the Alzheimer type, multiinfarct dementia, alcohol-related dementia, and pseudo-dementia of depression.

Recent research dictates abandonment of the term *organic brain syndrome* with its nihilistic connotations of a uniform cause and irreversible course (Seltzer and Sherwin, 1978; Besdine et al., 1980).

Dementia has to be carefully defined to avoid mislabeling of nondemented clients. Dementia is a global decline in intellectual function from some clearly defined, previously attained level. This decline encompasses the realms of memory, orientation, judgment, and problem-solving ability. Associated behavioral disturbances often occur. These include diminished performance of customary functions in the home and in the community and withdrawal from leisure activities, social activities, or business and financial dealings. An inflexible daily routine is often adopted, with emotional outbursts occurring if the schedule deviates from this.

All of these changes take place in the absence of disturbance of consciousness or delirium. Although motor, special sensory, or other disability may be present, each is insufficient to account for the mental changes.

The onset is subacute, or chronic and gradual, and progression must be demonstrated for at least 6 months. We found in a review of over 300 elderly persons that 27% of the cases were secondary dementias with a potentially curable cause. Of those studied, 7% represented end-stage manifestations of other neurologic diseases. The remaining 64% could be classified as primary dementias (heredodegenerative disease, multiinfarct, Alzheimer's disease, Jakob-Creutzfeldt disease, or dementias associated with long-standing alcohol abuse, schizophrenia, or head trauma).

Alzheimer's disease. Recent research emphasizes the pathologic similarities between young and old clients. Plaques, neurofibrillary tangles, and granulovacuolar degeneration are prevalent in both groups.

Biochemical studies have shed new light on underlying neurotransmitter abnormalities. Acetylcholine deficiency, cholinergic neuronal fallout in the cortical and hippocampal regions, and abnormally low levels of choline acetyltransferase, acetylcholinesterase, and other enzyme transmitters have now been documented.

There is striking similarity between Alzheimer's disease, Huntington's chorea, and Parkinson's disease, each manifesting as a neurotransmitter deficiency state. Just as levodopa therapy benefits clients with Parkinson's disease and GABA aids clients with Huntington's chorea, it may be reasonable to speculate that if brain acetylcholine levels can be replenished, similar results may be evidenced in Alzheimer's disease. Administration of choline is limited by dosage difficulties. Lecithin, a precursor of choline, may be more effective (Perry, Perry, and Tomlinson, 1977; Wurtman, Hirsch, and Growdon, 1977). The obvious problem in testing such agents is to identify clients with early changes, since they would be expected to benefit most.

Multiinfarct dementia. Atherosclerosis of intracerebral arteries has been found to be unrelated to dementia. The downhill, saw-toothed progression of multiinfarct dementia is punctuated by clearly defined episodes of neurologic deficit, caused by occlusive arterial disease.

Some of these clients suffer embolic strokes, and this group may dramatically benefit from early anticoagulant therapy. Late in the course of the disease, areas of infarction may become hemorrhagic; anticoagulation is then hazardous. When reduced blood flow to areas of the brain was postulated as the cause of dementia, cerebral vasodilators became popular. However, metabolites in hypoxic regions would already produce maximum vasodilation, and, in fact, through the intracerebral steal mechanism, hypoxia may become more pronounced with such treatment.

It now appears that some of the agents tested, such as cyclandelate and ergoloid mesylates, may work because they influence cyclic-AMP metabolism, platelet or granulocyte aggregation, or neurotransmitter flux.

Alcohol-induced dementia. Although Korsakoff's psychosis is well known, it is far less common in its pure form than the gradual onset of a less flamboyant mental deterioration. Thiamine does not produce spectacular results in the latter condition, but cessation of alcohol intake may improve the course.

It is mandatory to consider alcohol abuse as an underlying or at least a contributing factor in dementia. The already damaged brain is particularly susceptible, and a last "binge" may result in irreversible loss of cognitive function. This is one of the reasons why alcohol must *not* be used as a "geriatric wonder-drug."

We purposely have not concluded this section with a list of drugs, since we do not believe that there are agents in current use that improve primary dementias. Data on choline, lecithin, and dihydroergotamine are not sufficient to justify their inclusion in a table of recommended medications.

Behavioral disturbances in demented clients may be the final development that results in institutionalization. Skillful management of these situations with low-dose antipsychotic tranquilizers, as well as provision of community backup in the form of homemaker and day hospital services, respite care, and lay self-help and support groups (e.g., Alzheimer's Society), can either delay or avert admission to institutions (Eisdorfer and Cohen, 1981).

REFERENCES

Adler, L.E., Sadja, L., and Wilets, G.: Cimetidine toxicity manifested as paranoia and hallucinations, Am. J. Psychiatry **137**(9):1112, 1980.

Amery, A., and de Schaepdrijver, A.: Should elderly hypertensives be treated? Lancet **1**:272, 1975.

Amery, A., et al.: Antihypertensive therapy in elderly patients: pilot trial of the European Working Party on High Blood Pressure in the Elderly, Gerontology **23**:426, 1977.

Amery, A., et al.: Aging and the cardiovascular system, Acta. Cardiol. **33**:443, 1978.

Anderson, J.W.: High-fibre diets for diabetics and hypertriglyceridemic patients, Can. Med. Assoc. J. **123**:975, 1980.

Andres, R.: Relation of physiological changes in aging to medical changes of disease in the aged, Mayo Clin. Proc. **42**:674, 1967.

Appelbaum, P.S., et al.: Clinical utility of tricyclic antidepressant blood levels: a case report, Am. J. Psychiatry **136**:339, 1979.

Archambault, N., et al.: Evaluation of Duogastrone (carbenoxolone sodium) for the treatment of duodenal ulcer: a multicentre study, Can. Med. Assoc. J. **117**:1155, 1977.

Bailey, R.R., et al.: Prevention of urinary tract infection with low-dose nitrofurantoin, Lancet **2**:1112, 1971.

Barnhart, C., and Bowden, C.L.: Toxic psychosis with cimetidine, Am. J. Psychiatry **136**(5):725, 1979.

Beattie, A., and Caird, F.I.: The occupational therapist and the patient with Parkinson's disease, Br. Med. J. **1**:1354, 1980.

Besdine, R.W., et al.: Senility reconsidered: treatment possibilities for mental impairment in the elderly; task force sponsored by the National Institute on Aging, J.A.M.A. **244**:259, 1980.

Bevegard, S., Castenfors, J., and Lindblad, L.-E.: Haemodynamic effects of dihydroergotamine in patients with postural hypotension, Acta Med. Scand. **196**:473, 1974.

Billings, R., et al.: Blood and urine gold levels during chrysotherapy for rheumatoid arthritis, Rheumatol. Rehabil. **14**:13, 1975.

Bissada, N.K., and Finkbeiner, A.E.: Concept of pharmacodynamics of urinary storage and micturition, Urology **16**:118, 1980.

Bissada, N.K., Finkbeiner, A.E., and Welch, L.T.: Lower urinary tract pharmacology. I. Anatomic considerations, Urology **9**:107, 1977a.

Bissada, N.K., Finkbeiner, A.E., and Welch, L.T.: Lower urinary tract pharmacology. II. Review of neurology, Urology **9**:113, 1977b.

Bissada, N.K., Finkbeiner, A.E., and Welch, L.T.: Lower urinary tract pharmacology. III. Neuropharmacologic basis for lower urinary tract dynamics, Urology **9**:357, 1977c.

Bissada, N.K., Finkbeiner, A.E., and Welch, L.T.: Uropharmacology. X. Central nervous system stimulants and depressants, Urology **13**:464, 1979.

Blazer, D.: The diagnosis of depression in the elderly, J. Am. Geriatr. Soc. **28**:52, 1980.

Bodemar, G., and Walan, A.: Maintenance treatment of recurrent peptic ulcer by cimetidine, Lancet **1**: 403, 1978.

Braverman, A.M.: The backward leaning syndrome, J. Clin. Exp. Geront. **2**:99, 1980.

Brodribb, A.J., and Humphreys, D.M.: Diverticular disease: three studies. II. Treatment with bran, Br. Med. J. **1**:425, 1976.

Cahill, G.F., Jr., Etzwiler, D.D., and Freinkel, N.: "Control" and diabetes, N. Engl. J. Med. **294**:1004, 1976.

The Canadian Cooperative Study Group: A randomized trial of aspirin and sulfinpyrazone in threatened stroke, N. Engl. J. Med. **299**:53, 1978.

Coffman, J.D.: Vasodilator drugs in peripheral vascular disease, N. Engl. J. Med. **300**:713, 1979.

Cole, A.T., and Fried, F.A.: Favorable experiences with imipramine in the treatment of neurogenic bladder, J. Urol. **107**:44, 1972.

Comfort, A.: Practice of geriatric psychiatry, New York, 1980, American Elsevier Publishing, Inc.

Coppen, A., et al.: Mianserin and lithium in the prophylaxis of depression, Br. J. Psychiatry **133**:206, 1978.

Council On Thrombosis of the American Heart Association: Special report: prevention of venous thromboembolism in surgical patients by low-dose heparin, Circulation **55**:423A, 1977.

Crawhall, J.C.: Penicillamine: twenty-five years later, Ann. Intern. Med. **93**:367, 1980.

de Deuxchaisnes, C.N., et al.: Calcitonin or diphosphonates for osteolytic Paget's disease? Lancet **1**: 374, 1980.

Diokno, A.C., and Koppenhoefer, R.: Bethanechol chloride in neurogenic bladder dysfunction, Urology **7**:455, 1976.

Dontas, A.S., et al.: Bacteriuria and survival in old age, N. Engl. J. Med. **304**:939, 1981.

Douglas, D.L., et al.: Effect of dichloromethylene diphosphonate in Paget's disease of bone and in hypercalcaemia due to primary hyperparathyroidism or malignant disease, Lancet **1**:1043, 1980.

Drake, D., and Hollander, D.: Neutralizing capacity and cost effectiveness of antacids, Ann. Intern. Med. **94**:215, 1981.

Dreifus, L.S., et al.: Digitalis intolerance, Geriatrics **18**:494, 1963.

Duggan, D.E., et al.: Identification of the biologically active form of sulindac, J. Pharmacol. Exp. Ther. **201**:8, 1977.

Dyer, A.R., et al.: Hypertension in the elderly, Med. Clin. North. Am. **61**:513, 1977.

Eaton, M.L., et al.: Efficacy of theophylline in "irreversible" airflow obstruction, Ann. Intern. Med. **92**: 758, 1980.

Eisdorfer, C., and Cohen, D.: Management of the patient and family coping with dementing illness, J. Fam. Pract. **12**:831, 1981.

Evans, I.M.A.: Calcitonin treatment of Paget's disease, Lancet **2**:1232, 1979.

Evans, M.A., et al.: Systemic availability of orally administered L-dopa in the elderly Parkinsonian patient, Eur. J. Clin. Pharmacol. **17**:215, 1980.

Fam, A.G., et al.: Clinical and roentgenographic aspects of pseudogout: a study of 50 cases and a review, Can. Med. Assoc. J. **124**:545, 1981.

Fang, L.S.T., Tolkoff-Rubin, N.E., and Rubin, R.H.: Efficacy of single-dose and conventional amoxicillin therapy in urinary-tract infection localized by the antibody-coated bacteria technic, N. Engl. J. Med. **298**:413, 1978.

Fasching, V., and Eberl, R.: Sulindac: Klinische Prufung eines neuen Antiphlogisticums bei der chronischen Polyarthritis, Wien, Klin. Wochenschr. **59** (suppl.):1, 1976.

Feldman, M., et al.: Effect of low-dose propantheline on food-stimulated gastric acid secretion, N. Engl. J. Med. **297**:1427, 1977.

Fernandez-Herlihy, L.: Duration of corticosteroid therapy in giant cell arteritis, J. Rheumatol. **7**:361, 1980.

Finkbeiner, A.E., Bissada, N.K., and Welch, L.T.: Uropharmacology. IV. Parasympathomimetic agents, Urology **9**:474, 1977a.

Finkbeiner, A.E., Bissada, N.K., and Welch, L.T.: Uropharmacology. V. Choline esters and other parasympathomimetic drugs, Urology **10**:83, 1977b.

Finkbeiner, A.E., Bissada, N.K., and Welch, L.T.: Uropharmacology. VI. Parasympathetic depressants, Urology **10**:503, 1977c.

Finkbeiner, A.E., Welch, L.T., and Bissada, N.K.: Uropharmacology. XI. Adrenergic-blocking agents and drugs affecting catecholamines binding and release, Urology **13**:693, 1979.

Finkelstein, W., and Isselbacher, K.J.: Cimetidine, N. Engl. J. Med. **299**:992, 1978.

Foster, J.R., Gershell, W.J., and Goldfarb, A.I.: Lithium treatment in the elderly. I. Clinical usage, J. Gerontol. **32**:299, 1977.

Freeman, R.B., et al.: Long-term therapy for chronic bacteriuria in men. U.S. Public Health Service Cooperative Study, Ann. Intern. Med. **83**:133, 1975.

Freston, J.W.: Cimetidine in the treatment of gastric ulcer, Gastroenterology **74**:426, 1978.

Frewin, D.B., Robinson, S.M., and Willing, R.L.: The use of a new mode of therapy in the management of orthostatic hypotension, Aust. NZ J. Med. **3**:180, 1973.

Gear, J.S.S., et al.: Symptomless diverticular disease and intake of dietary fibre, Lancet **1**:511, 1979.

Gengos, D.: Long term experience with sulindac in the treatment of osteoarthritis, Eur. J. Rheumatol. Inflam. **1**(1):51, 1978.

Gleason, B.M., et al.: The urethral continence zone and its relation to stress incontinence, J. Urol. **112**:81, 1974.

Goldstein, L.: The "on-off" phenomena in Parkinson's disease—treatment and theoretical considerations, Mt. Sinai J. Med. **47**:80, 1980.

Granerus, A.-K.: Factors influencing the occurrence of "on-off" symptoms during long-term treatment with L-dopa, Acta Med. Scand. **203**:75, 1978.

Gray, G.R., et al.: Long term cimetidine in the management of severe duodenal ulcer dyspepsia, Gastroenterology **74**:397, 1978.

Grimm, R.H., Jr., et al.: Effects of thiazide diuretics on plasma lipids and lipoproteins in mildly hypertensive patients: a double-blind controlled trial, Ann. Intern. Med. **94**:7, 1981.

Hall, P.: Differential diagnosis and treatment of depression in the elderly, Gerontol. Clin. **16**:126, 1974.

Harvey, L.L., Nair, S.V., and Kass, I.: Beclomethasone diproprionate aerosol in the treatment of steroid-dependent asthma, Chest **70**:345, 1976.

Hastings, P.R., et al.: Antacid titration in the prevention of acute gastrointestinal bleeding: a controlled, randomized trial in 100 critically ill patients, N. Engl. J. Med. **298**:1041, 1978.

Henn, R.M., et al.: Inhibition of gastric acid secretion by cimetidine in patients with duodenal ulcer, N. Engl. J. Med. **293**:371, 1975.

Hollifield, J.W.: Biochemical consequences of diuretic therapy in hypertension, Tenn. State Med. Assoc. J. **71**(1):757, 1978.

Hull, J.H., and Sarubbi, F.A., Jr.: Gentamicin serum concentrations: pharmacokinetic predictions, Ann. Intern. Med. **85**:183, 1976.

Hurwitz, A.: Antacid therapy and drug kinetics, Clin. Pharmacokinet. **2**:269, 1977.

Hypertension Detection and Follow-up Program Cooperative Group: Five-year findings of the Hypertension Detection and Follow-up Program. I. Reduction in mortality of persons with high blood pressure, including mild hypertension, J.A.M.A. **242**: 2562, 1979a.

Hypertension Detection and Follow-up Program Cooperative Group: Five-year findings of the Hypertension Detection and Follow-up Program. II. Mortality by race, sex and age, J.A.M.A. **242**:2572, 1979b.

Ing, T.S., et al.: Toxic effects of amantadine in patients with renal failure, Can. Med. Assoc. J. **120**: 695, 1979.

Ing, T.S., Daugirdas, J.T., and Soung, L.S.: The posology of amantadine: a note of caution, J.A.M.A. **243**:1844, 1980.

Ingelfinger, F.J.: Debates on diabetes, N. Engl. J. Med. **296**:1228, 1977.

Ivey, K.J.: Are anticholinergics of use in the irritable colon syndrome? Gastroenterology **68**:1300, 1975.

Jankovic, J., and Fahn, S.: Physiologic and pathologic tremors: diagnosis, mechanism and management, Ann. Intern. Med. **93**:460, 1980.

Jones, S.R., Smith, J.A., and Sanford, J.P.: Localization of urinary tract infections by detection of antibody-coated bacteria in urine sediment, N. Engl. J. Med. **290**:591, 1974.

Juergens, J.L. and Bernatz, P.E.: Atherosclerosis of the extremities. In Juergens, J.L., Spittell, J.A., Jr., and Fairbairn, J.A., II, editors: Allen-Barker-Hines peripheral vascular diseases, Philadelphia, 1980, W.B. Saunders Co.

Jusko, W.J., et al.: Intravenous theophylline therapy: nomogram guidelines, Ann. Intern. Med. **86**:400, 1977.

Kannel, W.B., and Gordon, T., editors: The Framingham Study: an epidemiologic investigation of cardiovascular disease, Washington, D.C., 1974, U.S. Government Printing Office.

Kaplan, B.M.: The tachycardia-bradycardia syndrome, Med. Clin. North. Am. **60**:81, 1976.

Kass, E.H.: Bacteriuria and the diagnosis of infections of the urinary tract: with observations on the use of methionine as a urinary antiseptic, Arch. Intern. Med. **100**:709, 1957.

Khairi, M.R.A., et al.: Sodium etidronate in the treatment of Paget's disease of bone: a study of long-term results, Ann. Intern. Med. **87**:656, 1977.

Khanna, O.P.: Disorders of micturition: neuropharmacologic basis and results of drug therapy, Urology **8**:316, 1976.

Koch-Weser, J.: Treatment of hypertension in the elderly. In Crooks, J., and Stevenson, I.H., editors: Drugs and the elderly: perspectives in geriatric clinical pharmacology, Baltimore, 1978, University Park Press.

Kwan, K.C., et al.: Sulindac: chemistry, pharmacology and pharmacokinetics, Eur. J. Rheumatol. Inflam. **1**(1):9, 1978.

Lee, T., et al.: Receptor basis for dopaminergic supersensitivity in Parkinson's disease, Nature **273**:59, 1978.

Lesser, R.P., et al.: Analysis of the clinical problems in parkinsonism and the complications of long-term levodopa therapy, Neurology **29**:1253, 1979.

Levodopa: long-term impact on Parkinson's disease: Br. Med. J. **282**:417, 1981.

Light, R.W., Taylor, R.W., and George, R.B.: Albuterol and isoproterenol in bronchial asthma, Arch. Intern. Med. **139**:639, 1979.

Littman, A., et al.: Controlled trials of aluminum hydroxide gels for peptic ulcer, Gastroenterology **73**:6, 1977.

Maas, J.W.: Biogenic amines and depression: biochemical and pharmacologic separation of two types of depression, Arch. Gen. Psychiatry **32**:1357, 1975.

Mahony, D.T., Laferte, R.D., and Blais, D.J.: Integral storage and voiding reflexes: neurophysiologic concept of continence and micturition, Urology **9**:95, 1977.

Mant, M.J., et al.: Haemorrhagic complications of heparin therapy, Lancet **1**:1133, 1977.

Marks, R.M., and Sachar, E.J.: Undertreatment of medical inpatients with narcotic analgesics, Ann. Intern. Med. **78**:173, 1973.

Martelli, H., et al.: Mechanisms of idiopathic constipation: outlet obstruction, Gastroenterology **75**:623, 1978.

McMillen, M.A., Ambis, D., and Siegel, J.H.: Cimetidine and mental confusion, N. Engl. J. Med. **298**:284, 1978.

McNamara, M.F., Takaki, H.S., and Yao, J.S.T.: Venous disease. Surg. Clin. North. Am. **57**:1201, 1977.

McQuire, E.J., Wagner, F.M., and Weiss, R.M.: Treatment of autonomic dysreflexia with phenoxybenzamine, J. Urol. **115**:53, 1976.

Meares, E.M., Jr.: Long-term therapy of chronic bacterial prostatitis with trimethoprim-sulfamethoxazole, Can. Med. Assoc. J. **112**:22S, 1975.

Melzack, R., Mount, B.M., and Gordon, J.M.: The Brompton mixture versus morphine solution given orally: effects on pain, Can. Med. Assoc. J. **120**:435, 1979.

Mongan, E., et al.: Tinnitus as an indication of therapeutic serum salicylate levels, J.A.M.A. **226**:142, 1973.

Morris, T., and Rhodes, J.: Progress report: antacids and peptic ulcer—a reappraisal, Gut **20**:538, 1979.

Mumenthaler, M.: Giant cell arteritis (cranial arteritis, polymyalgia rheumatica), J. Neurol. **218**:219, 1978.

Penry, J.K., and Newmark, M.E.: The use of antiepileptic drugs, Ann. Intern. Med. **90**:207, 1979.

Penry, J.K., and Porter, R.J.: Epilepsy: mechanisms and therapy, Med. Clin. North Am. **63**:801, 1979.

Perry, E.K., Perry, R.H., and Tomlinson, B.E.: Dietary lecithin supplements in dementia of Alzheimer's type? Lancet **2**:242, 1977.

Petersen, W.L., et al.: Healing of duodenal ulcer with an antacid regimen, N. Engl. J. Med. **297**:341, 1977.

Piafsky, K.M., and Ogilvie, R.I.: Dosage of theophylline in bronchial asthma, N. Engl. J. Med. **292**:1218, 1975.

de Repentigny, L., et al.: Gentamicin: use of a programmable calculator to determine dosages from pharmacokinetic data for individual patients, Can. Med. Assoc. J. **124**:1459, 1981.

Reuler, J.B., Girard, D.E., and Nardone, D.A.: The chronic pain syndrome: misconceptions and management, Ann. Intern. Med. **93**:588, 1980.

Reynolds, E.H.: Drug treatment of epilepsy, Lancet **2**:721, 1978.

Riff, L.J.M.: Evaluation and treatment of urinary infection, Med. Clin. North Am. **62**:1183, 1978.

Russell, A.S.: Calcitonin or mithramycin for Paget's disease, Lancet **1**:884, 1980.

Sagar, S., et al.: Efficacy of low-dose heparin in prevention of extensive deep-vein thrombosis in patients undergoing total-hip replacement, Lancet **1**:1151, 1976.

Salmon, P.R., et al.: Evaluation of colloidal bismuth (De-Nol) in the treatment of duodenal ulcer employing endoscopic selection and follow up, Gut **15**:189, 1974.

Salzman, E.W., et al.: Management of heparin therapy: controlled prospective trial, N. Engl. J. Med. **292**:1046, 1975.

Sanders, J.F.: Lactulose syrup assessed in a double-blind study of elderly constipated patients, J. Am. Geriatr. Soc. **26**:236, 1978.

Santoro, J., and Kaye, D.: Recurrent urinary tract infections: pathogenesis and management, Med. Clin. North. Am. **62**:1005, 1978.

Saunders, C.M., editor: The management of terminal disease, London, 1978, Edward Arnold, Publishers.

Schold, C., Yarnell, P.R., and Earnest, M.P.: Origin of seizures in elderly patients, J.A.M.A. **238**:1177, 1977.

Seltzer, B., and Sherwin, I.: "Organic brain syndromes": an empirical study and critical review, Am. J. Psychiatry. **135**:1, 1978.

Sharma, G.V.R.K., and Sasahara, A.A.: Diagnosis and treatment of pulmonary embolism, Med. Clin. North. Am. **63**:239, 1979.

Sharpe, J., Marquez-Julio, A., and Ashby, P.: Idiopathic orthostatic hypotension treated with levodopa and MAO inhibitor: a preliminary report, Can. Med. Assoc. J. **107**:296, 1972.

Sherman, F.T., et al.: Nosocomial urinary-tract infections in a skilled nursing facility, J. Am. Geriatr. Soc. **28**:456, 1980.

Shields, H.M.: Rapid fall of serum phosphorus secondary to antacid therapy, Gastroenterology **75**:1137, 1978.

Siersbaek-Nielsen, K., et al.: Rapid evaluation of creatinine clearance, Lancet **1**:1133, 1971.

Silverstone, F.A., et al.: Age differences in the intravenous glucose tolerance tests and the response to insulin, J. Clin. Invest. **36**(3):504, 1957.

Siperstein, M.D., et al.: Control of blood glucose and diabetic vascular disease, N. Engl. J. Med. **296**:1060, 1977.

Snape, W.J., Jr., et al.: Evidence that abnormal myoelectrical activity produces colonic motor dysfunction in the irritable bowel syndrome, Gastroenterology **72**:383, 1977.

Sobel, B.E., and Roberts, R.: Hypotension and syncope. In Braunwald, E., editor: Heart disease: a textbook of cardiovascular medicine, Philadelphia, 1980, W.B. Saunders Co.

Spencer, H., and Lender, M.: Adverse effects of aluminum-containing antacids on mineral metabolism, Gastroenterology **76**:603, 1979.

Spiro, H.M.: Motor abnormalities. In Spiro, H.M.: Clinical gastroenterology, ed. 2, New York, 1977, MacMillan, Inc.

Stamey, T.A., Condy, M., and Mihara, G.: Prophylactic efficacy of nitrofurantoin macrocrystals and trimethoprim-sulfamethoxazole in urinary infections: biologic effects on the vaginal and rectal flora, N. Engl. J. Med. **296**:780, 1977.

Stamm, W.E., et al.: Causes of the acute urethral syndrome in women, N. Engl. J. Med. **303**:409, 1980.

Stein, H.B., et al.: Adverse effects of D-penicillamine in rheumatoid arthritis, Ann. Intern. Med. **92**:24, 1980.

Strachan, R.W., How, J., and Bewsher, P.D: Masked giant-cell arteritis, Lancet **1**:194, 1980.

Sturtridge, W.C., Harrison, J.E., and Wilson, D.R.: Long-term treatment of Paget's disease of bone with salmon calcitonin, Can. Med. Assoc. J. **117**:1031, 1977.

Sullivan, M.A., Cohen, S., and Snape, W.J., Jr.: Colonic myoelectric activity in the irritable bowel syndrome: effect of eating and anticholinergics, N. Engl. J. Med. **298**:878, 1978.

Thomas, D.P.: Heparin in the prophylaxis and treatment of venous thromboembolism, Semin. Hematol. **15**:1, 1978.

Twycross, R.: The relief of pain. In Saunders, C., editor: The management of terminal disease, London, 1978, Edward Arnold, Publishers.

Vallarino, R.: Basic protocol for the treatment of urinary incontinence, New Hyde Park, N.Y., 1978, Jewish Institute For Geriatric Care, Unpublished manuscript.

Vieweg, W.V.R., et al.: Complications of intravenous administration of heparin in elderly women, J.A.M.A. 213:1303, 1970.

Walker, G.S., et al.: Effects of calcitonin on deafness due to Paget's disease of skull, Br. Med. J. 2:364, 1979.

Warren, P.M., et al.: Respiratory failure revisited: acute exacerbations of chronic bronchitis between 1961-68 and 1970-76, Lancet 1:467, 1980.

Weinberger, M.W., et al.: Intravenous aminophylline dosage: use of serum theophylline measurement for guidance, J.A.M.A. 235:2110, 1976.

Weinreich, J., and Anderson, O.: Intraluminal pressure in the sigmoid colon. II. Patients with sigmoid diverticula and related conditions, Scand. J. Gastroenterol. 11:581, 1976.

Winship, D.H.: Cimetidine in the treatment of duodenal ulcer, Gastroenterology 74:402, 1978.

Wurtman, R.J., Hirsch, M.J., and Growdon, J.H.: Lecithin consumption raises serum free-choline levels, Lancet 2:68, 1977.

Zanjanian, M.H.: Expectorants and antitussive agents: are they helpful? Ann. Allergy 44:290, 1980.

ACKNOWLEDGMENT

We wish to express our thanks to Mr. J. Vande Brink, MALS, Health Sciences Librarian of the Edmonton General Hospital, for his assistance in compiling the list of references for this chapter.

Appendix A

ABBREVIATIONS USED IN THE TEXT

AbNLab	abnormal laboratory (tests)
ACTH	adrenocorticotropic hormone
ADA	American Diabetic Association
Adm	admission
ADR	adverse drug reaction
Ae (∞)	total amount of unchanged drug excreted into urine
ALT	alanine aminotransferase
AMP	adenosine monophosphate
ASA	aspirin
AST	aspartate aminotransferase
AUC(o → ∞)	total area under the blood level-time curve
AV	atrioventricular
BAL	dimercaprol
b.i.d.	twice a day
BP	blood pressure
BSP	Bromsulphalein (Sulfobromophthalein)
BUN	blood urea nitrogen
BW	body weight
C	centigrade
Ca^{++}	calcium
cal	calorie
CAT	computerized axial tomography
CBC	complete blood count
CHF	congestive heart failure
CK	creatine kinase
Cl cr	creatinine clearance
Cl er	extrarenal clearance
Cl m	metabolic clearance
Cl met intr	intrinsic metabolic clearance
Cl r	renal clearance
Cl tot	total clearance
cm	centimeter
CM	cell mass
Cmax	maximum concentration
CNS	central nervous system

CO	carbon dioxide
C/O	complaint of
COPD	chronic obstructive pulmonary disease
CPCD	calcium pyrophosphate crystal deposition disease
Css	steady state drug concentration in blood, plasma, or serum
Css av	mean steady state concentration
Css max	maximum steady state concentration
Css min	minimum steady state concentration
CTZ	chemoreceptor trigger zone
CZI	crystalline zinc insulin
D	dose administered
D/C	discontinue
DIMES	drug intake and management system
DL	loading dose
DM	maintenance dose
DNA	deoxyribonucleic acid
DPT	diphtheria, pertussis, tetanus
DRR	drug regimen review
DVT	deep venous thrombosis
ECF	extracellular fluid
ECG	electrocardiogram
ECT	electroconvulsive therapy
EDTA	edetate calcium disodium
EHDP	ethane hydroxydiphosphonate
ESR	erythrocyte sedimentation rate
EWPHE	European Working Party on High Blood Pressure in the Elderly
F	fraction of drug absorbed
FBS	fasting blood sugar
Fe	fraction of unchanged drug eliminated through the kidneys
F free	ratio of free to total drug in plasma
fl oz	fluid ounce
Fm	fraction of drug metabolized

337

GABA	gamma-aminobutyric acid	**LBF**	liver blood flow
Ger	geriatric	**LDH**	lactate dehydrogenase
GerF	geriatric female(s)	**LTCF**	long-term care facility
GerM	geriatric male(s)		
GFR	glomerular filtration rate	**MAOI**	monoamine oxidase inhibitor
GI	gastrointestinal	**MAR**	medication administration record
gm	gram	**MBE**	management by exceptions
GU	genitourinary	**MCHC**	mean corpuscular hemoglobin concentration
		mCi	millicurie(s)
Hb	hemoglobin	**MCV**	mean corpuscular volume
H₂-blockers	histamine-receptor blockers	**MEC**	minimum effective concentration
HCl	hydrochloric acid	**mEq**	milliequivalent
HCN	hydrogen cyanide	**μg**	microgram
Hct	hematocrit	**mg**	milligram
HDFP	Hypertension Detection and Follow-up Program	**MIC**	minimum inhibitory concentration
Hg	mercury	**min**	minute
HHS	Health and Human Services	**ml**	milliliter
HNO₃	nitric acid	**mm Hg**	millimeters of mercury
hr	hour	**mo**	month
h.s.	bedtime		
H₂SO₄	sulfuric acid	**Na⁺**	sodium
		NaCN	sodium cyanide
¹³¹I	radioactive iodine	**NaOCl**	sodium hypochlorite
IC	intracardiac	**ng**	nanogram
ICF	intracellular fluid	**nmole**	nanomole
IM	intramuscular	**NPH**	neutral protamine Hagedorn
IU	international unit(s)	**NSAIA**	nonsteroidal anti-inflammatory agent
IV	intravenous		
		OTC	over-the-counter (nonprescription)
K⁺	potassium		
k13	rate constant of elimination from the central compartment	**p.c.**	after meals
		P cell	pacemaker cell
ka	rate constant of absorption	**PE**	physical examination
KCN	potassium cyanide	**pH**	hydrogen ion concentration
ke	overall elimination rate constant of a drug	**P.O.**	by mouth (orally)
		POMR	problem-oriented medical record
ker	rate constant for loss of drug by extra-renal excretion	**PR**	by rectum (rectally)
		p.r.n.	as needed
kg	kilogram	**PSRO**	professional standards review organization
km	rate constant for loss of drug caused by metabolism		
		PT	prothrombin time
ku	rate constant for loss of unchanged drug into urine	**PTT**	partial thromboplastin time
		PTU	propylthiouracil
l	liter	**q.**	every
LADME	liberation, absorption, distribution,	**q.AM**	every morning
system	metabolism, elimination	**q.d.**	every day
lb	pound	**q.h.s.**	every bedtime

q.i.d.	four times daily
qt	quart
RO	constant infusion rate
ROS	review of symptoms
Rx	prescription
SA	sinoatrial
SC	subcutaneous
SD	standard deviation
SEM	standard error of measurement
SGOT	serum glutamic oxaloacetic transaminase
SL	sublingual
SLE	systemic lupus erythematosus
SOAP	subject, objective, assessment plan
S/P	status post
SSKI	saturated solution of potassium iodide
stat	immediately
τ	constant dosing interval
$T_{\frac{1}{2}}$	half-life of elimination
T_3	liothyronine
T_4	levothyroxine
TBF	total body fluid
tbsp	tablespoonful
TCA	tricyclic antidepressant

TIA	transient ischemic attack
t.i.d.	three times daily
Tm	capacity for active tubular secretion (transport maximum)
tmax	time of maximum plasma concentration
TRH	thyroid-releasing hormone
TSH	thyroid-stimulating hormone
Tx	treatment
U	unit(s)
USP	United States Pharmacopeia
UTI	urinary tract infection
Vd	volume of distribution
Vdβ	volume of distribution beta
Vdc	volume of distribution of the central compartment
Vdnorm	volume of distribution in 70 kg, 25-year-old, "normal" adults
Vdss	volume of distribution at steady state
VS	vital signs
wk	week
wt	weight
yr	year

Appendix B

DRUG NAMES THAT LOOK OR SOUND ALIKE

Generally, as people age, their senses gradually deteriorate. This can often lead to much confusion in the elderly in relation to drug therapy. Following is a list of drug names that may be confused by sight or sound with other drug names.

DRUG NAME	MAY BE CONFUSED WITH

A

Acetaminophen	Acetophen
Acetazolamide	Acetohexamide
Acetohexamide	Acetazolamide
Acetophen	Acetominophen
Achromycin	Aureomycin
Adroyd	Android
Aerolone	Aralen, Arlidin
Afrin	Aspirin
Agoral	Argyrol
Aldactazide	Aldactone
Aldactone	Aldactazide
Aldomet	Aldoril
Aldoril	Aldomet, Elavil, Mellaril
Ambenyl	Ambodryl, Aventyl
Ambodryl	Ambenyl, Aventyl
Amcill	Amoxil
Amoxil	Amcill

Android	Adroyd
Antuitrin	Anturane, Artane
Anturane	Antuitrin, Artane
Anusol	Aquasol
Aquasol	Anusol
Aralen	Aerolone, Arlidin
Argyrol	Agoral
Arlidin	Aerolone, Aralen
Artane	Antuitrin, Anturane
Arthralgen	Auralgan, Ophthalgan
Aspirin	Afrin
Atarax	Enarax, Marax
Auralgan	Arthralgen, Ophthalgan
Aureomycin	Achromycin
Avazyme	Orenzyme
Aventyl	Ambenyl, Ambodryl, Bentylol
Azathioprine	Azulfidine
Azulfidine	Azathioprine

B

Bacitracin	Bactrim
Bactrim	Bacitracin, Zactirin
Banthine	Brethine
Belladenal	Belladonna, Benadryl
Belladonna	Belladenal

Beminal	Benemid
Benadryl	Belladenal, Bentyl, Benylin
Benemid	Beminal
Benoxyl	PanOxyl
Bentyl	Benadryl, Benylin
Bentylol	Aventyl
Benylin	Benadryl, Bentyl, Betalin
Betalin	Benylin
Bicillin	V-Cillin, Wycillin
Brethine	Banthine
Butabarbital	Butalbital
Butabell	Butibel
Butalbital	Butabarbital
Butazolidin	Butisol, Sterazolidin
Butibel	Butabell
Butisol	Butazolidin

C

Calamine	Calomel, Coramine
Calomel	Calamine
Catapres	Combipres, Diupres, Hydropres, Ser-Ap-Es
Cefazolin	Cephalothin
Cepacol	Sebisol
Cephalothin	Cefazolin
Cheracol	Geritol
Chloromycetin	Chlor-Trimeton
Chlor-Trimeton	Chloromycetin
Clinistix	Clinitest
Clinitest	Clinistix
Clofibrate	Clorazepate

Clonidine	Clonopin, Quinidine
Clonopin	Clonidine
Clorazepate	Clofibrate
Codeine	Coldene
Coldene	Codeine
Combex	Combid
Combid	Combex
Combipres	Catapres, Diupres, Hydropres
Coramine	Calamine
Cort-Dome	Cortone
Cortone	Cort-Dome
Coumadin	Kemadrin
Cuprex	Cuprimine
Cuprimine	Cuprex
Cytarabine	Vidarabine
Cytosar	Cytoxan
Cytoxan	Cytosar

D

Danthron	Dantrium
Dantrium	Danthron
Daricon	Darvon
Darvocet-N	Darvon-N
Darvon	Daricon
Darvon-N	Darvocet-N
Decadron	Percodan
Delalutin	Dilantin
Deltalin	Dilantin
Demerol	Demulen, Deprol, Dicumarol
Demulen	Demerol

Deprol	Demerol	Equanil	Elavil
Desoxyn	Digoxin	Esidrix	Lasix
Dianabol	Donnatal	Ethamide	Ethionamide
Diazepam	Diazoxide	Ethinamate	Ethionamide
Diazoxide	Diazepam	Ethionamide	Ethamide, Ethinamate
Dicumarol	Demerol	Eurax	Serax, Urex
Digitoxin	Digoxin	Euthroid	Thyroid
Digoxin	Desoxyn, Digitoxin		

F

Feosol	Fer-in-Sol, Festal
Fer-in-Sol	Feosol
Festal	Feosol
Flagyl	Flexical
Flexical	Flagyl
Fostex	pHisoHex
Fulvicin	Furacin
*Furacin	Fulvicin

Dilantin	Delalutin, Deltalin, Dilaudid, Phe-lantin
Dilaudid	Dilantin
Diupres	Catapres, Combipres, Hydropres
Diuril	Doriden
Diutensin	Salutensin, Unitensin
Donnagel	Donnatal
Donnatal	Dianabol, Donnagel
Donnazyme	Entozyme
Dopar	Dopram
Dopram	Dopar
Doriden	Diuril, Doxidan, Loridine
Doxidan	Doriden
Dyrenium	Pyridium, Serenium

G

Ganatrex	Kantrex
Gantanol	Gantrisin
Gantrisin	Gantanol
Garamycin	Terramycin
Gelfoam	Ger-O-Foam
Geritol	Cheracol
Ger-O-Foam	Gelfoam
Glutethimide	Guanethidine
Guanethidine	Glutethimide

E

Ecotrin	Edecrin
Edecrin	Ecotrin
Elavil	Aldoril, Equanil, Mellaril
Emetine	Emetrol
Emetrol	Emetine
Enarax	Atarax
Entozyme	Donnazyme

H

Haldol	Halog, Winstrol
Halog	Haldol

Haloperidol	Haloprogin
Haloprogin	Haloperidol
Halotestin	Halotex, Halothane
Halotex	Halotestin, Halothane, Herplex
Halothane	Halotex, Halotestin
Herplex	Halotext, Hiprex
Hiprex	Herplex
Hycodan	Hycomine
Hycomine	Hycodan
Hydropres	Catapres, Combipres, Diupres
Hygroton	Regroton
Hyperstat	Nitrostat
Hytone	Vytone

I

Ilosone	Ionosol
Imferon	Imipramine, Imuran, Inderal
Imipramine	Imferon
Imuran	Imferon, Inderal
Inderal	Imferon, Imuran, Isordil
Indocin	Lincocin, Minocin
Ionosol	Ilosone
Ismelin	Isuprel, Ritalin
Isordil	Inderal, Isuprel
Isuprel	Ismelin, Isordil

K

Kafocin	Keflin
Kantrex	Ganatrex
Kaolin	Kaon
Kaon	Kaolin

Keflex	Keflin
Keflin	Kafocin, Keflex
Kemadrin	Coumadin

L

Lasix	Esidrix, Lidex
Leritine	Loridine
Levallorphan	Levorphanol
Levodopa	Methyldopa
Levorphanol	Levallorphan
Lidex	Lasix
Lincocin	Indocin
Loridine	Doriden, Leritine
Lotrimin	Otrivin
Luminal	Tuinal, Tylenol

M

Marax	Atarax
Mebaral	Medrol, Mellaril, Tegretol
Mebendazole	Metronidazole
Medrol	Mebaral, Mellaril
Mellaril	Aldoril, Elavil, Mebaral, Medrol, Moderil
Meperidine	Meprobamate
Mephenytoin	Mesantoin
Mephyton	Methadone
Meprobamate	Meperidine
Mesantoin	Mephenytoin
Methadone	Mephyton
Methiodal	Methionine
Methionine	Methiodal

Methyldopa	Levodopa	Otobione	Otobiotic
Metrazol	Mintezol	Otobiotic	Otobione, Urobiotic
Metronidazole	Mebendazole	Otrivin	Lotrimin
Milontin	Miltown, Minocin, Mylanta	Ovral	Ovulen
Miltown	Milontin, Minocin	Ovulen	Ovral
Minocin	Indocin, Lincocin, Milontin		
Mintezol	Metrazol	**P**	
Moderil	Mellaril		
Modicon	Mylicon	Pabalate	Pabanol, Robalate
Myambutol	Nembutal	Pabanol	Pabalate
Mylanta	Milontin	PanOxyl	Benoxyl
Mylicon	Modicon	Penicillin	Polycillin
		Pentazine	Pentazocine
N		Pentazocine	Pentazine
		Pentobarbital	Phenobarbital
Nembutal	Myambutol	Pentothal	Pentritol
Nilstat	Nitrostat, Nystatin	Pentritol	Pentothal
Nitrostat	Hyperstat, Nilstat, Nystatin	Percobarb	Percodan, Periactin
Norlestrin	Nystatin	Percodan	Decadron, Percobarb, Percogesic, Periactin
Norlutate	Norlutin	Percogesic	Percodan
Norlutin	Norlutate	Periactin	Percobarb, Percodan, Peritrate, Persantine
Nystatin	Nilstat, Nitrostat, Norlestrin	Peritrate	Periactin
		Persantine	Periactin, Pertofrane, Trasentine
O		Pertofrane	Persantine
		Phelantin	Dilantin
Omnipen	Unipen	Phenaphen	Phenergan, Theragran
Ophthalgan	Arthralgen, Auralgan	Phenergan	Phenaphen, Theragran
Orenzyme	Avazyme, Orinase	Phenobarbital	Pentobarbital
Orinase	Orenzyme, Ornade, Ornex	Phentermine	Phentolamine
Ornacol	Orthoxicol	Phentolamine	Phentermine
Ornade	Orinase, Ornex		
Ornex	Orinase, Ornade		
Orthoxicol	Ornacol		

pHisoHex	Fostex
Piperacetazine	Piperazine
Piperazine	Piperacetazine
Pitocin	Pitressin
Pitressin	Pitocin
Polycillin	Penicillin
Ponstel	Pronestyl
Pralidoxime	Pyridoxine
Prednisolone	Prednisone
Prednisone	Prednisolone
Pronestyl	Ponstel
Propadrine	Propoxyphene
Propoxyphene	Propadrine
Pyridium	Dyrenium, Pyridoxine
Pyridoxine	Pralidoxime, Pyridium

Q

Quaalude	Quinidine
Quarzan	Questran
Questran	Quarzan
Quinidine	Clonidine, Quaalude, Quinine
Quinine	Quinidine

R

Regonal	Regroton
Regroton	Hygroton, Regonal
Rifadin	Ritalin
Ritalin	Ismelin, Rifadin
Robalate	Pabalate

S

Salutensin	Diutensin, Unitensen
Sebisol	Cepacol, Sebulex
Sebulex	Sebisol, Sebutone
Sebutone	Sebulex
Ser-Ap-Es	Catapres
Serax	Eurax, Xerac
Serenium	Dyrenium
Sparine	Sterane
Sporicidin	Sporostacin
Sporostacin	Sporicidin
Stelazine	Sterazolidin
Sterane	Sparine
Sterazolidin	Butazolidin, Stelazine
Sudafed	Sudodrin
Sudodrin	Sudafed
Sulfamethazine	Sulfamethizole
Sulfamethizole	Sulfamethazine
Surbex	Surfak
Surfak	Surbex
Synalar	Syntar
Syntar	Synalar

T

Taractan	Tinactin
Tegopen	Tegretol, Tegrin
Tegretol	Mebaral, Tegopen, Tegrin
Tegrin	Tegopen, Tegretol
Terramycin	Garamycin
Theragran	Phenaphen, Phenergan
Thiamine	Thiomerin, Thorazine

Thiomerin	Thiamine
Thorazine	Thiamine
Thyrar	Thyrolar
Thyroid	Euthroid
Thyrolar	Thyrar
Timoptic	Viroptic
Tinactin	Taractan
Tobramycin	Trobicin
Tolectin	Toleron, Tolinase
Toleron	Tolectin, Tolinase
Tolinase	Tolectin, Toleron
Trasentine	Persantine
Triamcinolone	Triaminic, Triaminicin
Triaminic	Triamcinolone, Triaminicin, Tri-Hemic
Triaminicin	Triamcinolone, Triaminic
TriHemic	Triaminic
Trobicin	Tobramycin
Troph-Iron	Trophite
Trophite	Troph-Iron
Tuinal	Luminal, Tylenol
Tylenol	Luminal, Tuinal
Tyzine	Visine

U

Unicap	Unipen
Unipen	Omnipen, Unicap
Unitensen	Diutensin, Salutensin
Uracel	Uracid
Uracid	Uracel
Urex	Eurax, Serax
Uristat	Uristix

Uristix	Uristat
Urobiotic	Otobiotic

V

Valium	Valmid, Valpin
Valmid	Valium, Valpin, Velban
Valpin	Valium, Valmid, Velban
Vasocidin	Vasodilan
Vasodilan	Vasocidin
V-Cillin	Bicillin, Wycillin
Velban	Valmid, Valpin
Vibramycin	Viomycin
Vidarabine	Cytarabine
Vigran	Wigraine
Viomycin	Vibramycin
Viroptic	Timoptic
Visine	Tyzine
Vontrol	VoSol
VoSol	Vontrol
Vytone	Hytone

W

Wigraine	Vigran
Winstrol	Haldol
Wycillin	Bicillin, V-Cillin

X

Xerac	Serax

Z

Zactirin	Bactrim, Zarontin, Zaroxolyn
Zarontin	Zactirin, Zaroxolyn
Zaroxolyn	Zactirin, Zarontin

Appendix C

TRADE NAMES AND GENERIC EQUIVALENTS

The medications discussed in this text are generally referred to by their nonproprietary (generic) names. However, because it is recognized that the clinician is often aware of the trade (brand) name of a particular medication but does not have ready access to the corresponding nonproprietary name, an appendix listing trade names has been compiled.

This appendix lists in alphabetic order the major American and Canadian trade names for the medications discussed in this text and provides their corresponding nonproprietary names. Information about the medication may then be located by consulting the general index, which lists the medications by nonproprietary names only.

If one is aware of the nonproprietary name of the medication in question, then this appendix should be bypassed and the general index should be consulted.

TRADE NAME	NONPROPRIETARY NAME
Acetal	Aspirin
Acetazolam	Acetazolamide
Acetophen	Aspirin
Achromycin	Tetracycline
Adrenalin	Epinephrine
Aldactone	Spironolactone
Aldomet	Methyldopa
Algoverine	Phenylbutazone
Alka-Seltzer	Aspirin, sodium bicarbonate, citric acid
Afko-Lube	Docusate sodium

TRADE NAME	NONPROPRIETARY NAME
Alpen	Ampicillin
Aludrox	Magnesium hydroxide, aluminum hydroxide
Amcill	Ampicillin
Amikin	Amikacin
Amiline	Amitriptyline
Aminodur	Aminophylline
Aminophyl	Aminophylline
AmoxiCAN	Amoxicillin
Amoxil	Amoxicillin
Ampen	Ampicillin
Ampicin	Ampicillin
Ampilean	Ampicillin
Amytal	Amobarital
Anavac	Danthron
Ancef	Cefazolin
Anevral	Phenylbutazone
Anspor	Cephradine
Anturane	Sulfinpyrazone
Anuphen	Acetaminophen
APAP	Acetaminophen
Apresoline	Hydralazine
Aptine	Alprenolol

TRADE NAME	NONPROPRIETARY NAME	TRADE NAME	NONPROPRIETARY NAME
Aquamephyton	Vitamin K_1	Biquin	Quinidine
Aquasol A	Vitamin A	Biscolax	Bisacodyl
Aquasol E	Vitamin E	Brethine	Terbutaline
Aralen	Chloroquine	Bricanyl	Terbutaline
Artane	Trihexyphenidyl	Bristamycin	Erythromycin
A.S.A.	Aspirin	Bronkaid	Epinephrine
Ascoril	Vitamin C	Butagesic	Phenylbutazone
Ascriptin	Aspirin, magnesium hydroxide, aluminum hydroxide	Butazolidin	Phenylbutazone
Ascriptin A/D	Aspirin, magnesium hydroxide, aluminum hydroxide	Calcet	Calcium, vitamin D
		Carbolith	Lithium carbonate
Aspergum	Aspirin	Cardioquin	Quinidine
Asthmophylline	Theophylline	Catapres	Clonidine
Atarax	Hydroxyzine	Cedilanid-D	Deslanoside
Atasol	Acetaminophen	Ceporex	Cephalexin
Athrombin	Warfarin	Chloralex	Chloral hydrate
Ativan	Lorazepam	Chloralvan	Chloral hydrate
Aventyl	Nortriptyline	Chloromycetin	Chloramphenicol
Azolid	Phenylbutazone	Chloroptic	Chloramphenicol
Bactrim	Co-Trimoxazole	Chlorprom	Chlorpromazine
BAL	Dimercaprol	Chlor-Promanyl	Chlorpromazine
Bancaps	Acetaminophen	Chlor-Trimeton	Chlorpheniramine
Banlin	Propantheline	Chlor-Tripolon	Chlorpheniramine
Benadryl	Diphenhydramine	Chlortrone	Chlorpheniramine
Bendopa	Levodopa	Choledyl	Oxtriphylline
Benemid	Probenecid	Cleocin	Clindamycin
Betaloc	Metoprolol	Clinoril	Sulindac
Bicillin	Penicillin G	Cogentin	Benztropine
Bio-Tetra	Tetracycline	Colace	Docusate sodium
		Colisone	Prednisone

TRADE NAME	NONPROPRIETARY NAME	TRADE NAME	NONPROPRIETARY NAME
Coloctyl	Docusate sodium	Dibenzyline	Phenoxybenzamine
Comfolax	Docusate sodium	Dilantin	Phenytoin
Compazine	Prochlorperazine	Dimelor	Acetohexamide
Corax	Chlordiazepoxide	Dolene	Propoxyphene
Corophyllin	Aminophylline	Dopamet	Methyldopa
Coumadin	Warfarin	Dopar	Levodopa
Crystapen	Penicillin G	Dorbane	Danthron
C-Tran	Chlordiazepoxide	Dorbantyl	Danthron, docusate sodium
Cuprimine	Penicillamine	Doriden	Glutethimide
Cytoxan	Cyclophosphamide	Doxan	Danthron, docusate sodium
Dalmane	Flurazepam	Doxidan	Danthron, docusate calcium
Danilone	Phenindione	Doxinate	Docusate sodium
Dantoin	Phenytoin	Doxy-II	Doxycycline
Darvon	Propoxyphene	Drisdol	Vitamin D
Decaderm	Dexamethasone	Dulcolax	Bisacodyl
Decadron	Dexamethasone	Dyazide	Hydrochlorothiazide, triamterene
Delta-Cortef	Prednisolone	Dymelor	Acetohexamide
Deltasone	Prednisone	Ecotrin	Aspirin
Demerol	Meperidine	Edecrin	Ethacrynic acid
Dentogel	Quinine	E.E.S.	Erythromycin
Depen	Penicillamine	Elavil	Amitriptyline
Depo-Medrol	Methylprednisolone	Elixophyllin	Theophylline
Deprex	Amitriptyline	Elksosin	Sulfisomidine
Depronal-SA	Propoxyphene	Eltroxin	Levothyroxine
Dexameth	Dexamethasone	Empirin Compound	Aspirin, caffeine
Dexasone	Dexamethasone	E-mycin	Erythromycin
Dexone	Dexamethasone	Endep	Amitriptyline
Diabinese	Chlorpropamide	Entrophen	Aspirin
Diamox	Acetazolamide		

TRADE NAME	NONPROPRIETARY NAME	TRADE NAME	NONPROPRIETARY NAME
E-Pam	Diazepam	Geopen	Carbenicillin
Equanil	Meprobamate	Glysennid	Senna
Erthrocin	Erythromycin	Haldol	Haloperidol
Erythromid	Erythromycin	Hepalean	Heparin
Esidrix	Hydrochlorothiazide	Hexadrol	Dexamethasone
Eskabarb	Phenobarbital	Hiprex	Methenamine
Eskalith	Lithium carbonate	Histalon	Chlorpheniramine
Estinyl	Ethinyl Estradiol	Histantil	Promethazine
Estrace	Estradiol	Honvol	Diethylstilbestrol
Ethril	Erythromycin	Hydergine	Dihydroergotamine
Eutonyl	Pargyline	Hydro-Aquil	Hydrochlorothiazide
Excedrin	Aspirin, acetaminophen, salicyl-amide, caffeine	Hydrocil	Plantago seed
		Hydrodiuril	Hydrochlorothiazide
Exdol	Acetaminophen	Hydromox	Quinethazone
Ex-Lax	Phenolphthalein	Hydrozide	Hydrochlorothiazide
Falapen	Penicillin G	Hygroton	Chlorthalidone
Feen-A-Mint	Phenolphthalein	Iletin	Insulin
Fenicol	Chloramphenicol	Ilosone	Erythromycin
Fer-In-Sol	Ferrous sulfate	Ilotycin	Erythromycin
Fero-Grad	Ferrous sulfate	Imavate	Imipramine
Fesofor	Ferrous sulfate	Imferon	Iron-Dextran
Furadantin	Nitrofurantoin	Impril	Imipramine
Furanex	Nitrofurantoin	Inderal	Propranolol
Furatine	Nitrofurantoin	Inderide	Propranolol, hydrochlorothiazide
Furoside	Furosemide		
Gammacorten	Dexamethasone	Indocid	Indomethacin
Gantrisin	Sulfisoxazole	Indocin	Indomethacin
Garamycin	Gentamicin	Inflamase	Prednisolone
Gardenal	Phenobarbital	INH	Isoniazid
Geocillin	Carbenicillin	Intrabutazone	Phenylbutazone

TRADE NAME	NONPROPRIETARY NAME	TRADE NAME	NONPROPRIETARY NAME
Ismelin	Guanethidine	Librium	Chlordiazepoxide
Isobec	Amobarbital	Lipo-Hepin	Heparin
Isopto Fenicol	Chloramphenicol	Liquiprin	Acetaminophen
Isordil	Isosorbide dinitrate	Lithane	Lithium carbonate
Isotamine	Isoniazid	Lithizine	Lithium carbonate
Isuprel	Isoproterenol	Lithonate	Lithium carbonate
Janimine	Imipramine	Lithotabs	Lithium carbonate
K-10	Potassium chloride	Loniten	Minoxidil
Kantrex	Kanamycin	Lopressor	Metoprolol
Kaochlor	Potassium chloride	Loridine	Cephaloridine
Kaon	Potassium chloride	Luf-Iso	Isoproterenol
Ka-Pen	Penicillin G	Luminal	Phenobarbital
Kato	Potassium chloride	Maalox	Magnesium hydroxide, aluminum hydroxide
Kay Ciel	Potassium chloride	Macrodantin	Nitrofurantoin
Keflex	Cephalexin	Malgesic	Phenylbutazone
Keflin	Cephalothin	Mandelamine	Methenamine mandelate
Kefzol	Cefazolin	Mandol	Cefamandole
Klorvess	Potassium chloride	Marezine	Cyclizine
Konakion	Phytonadione	Maxidex	Dexamethasone
Laco	Bisacodyl	Measurin	Aspirin
Lan-Dol	Meprobamate	Medicycline	Tetracycline
Lanoxin	Digoxin	Medihaler-Iso	Isoproterenol
Largactil	Chlorpromazine	Medimet-250	Methyldopa
Larodopa	Levodopa	Mediphen	Phenobarbital
Lasix	Furosemide	Medi-Tran	Meprobamate
Levate	Amitriptyline	Medrol	Methylprednisolone
Levo-Dromoran	Levorphanol	Mefoxin	Cefoxitin
Levopa	Levodopa	Megacillin	Penicillin G
Levoprome	Methotrimeprazine		

TRADE NAME	NONPROPRIETARY NAME	TRADE NAME	NONPROPRIETARY NAME
Megapen	Penicillin G	Nebcin	Tobramycin
Mellaril	Thioridazine	Nembutal	Pentobarbital
Mellitol	Tolbutamide	Neo-Calme	Diazepam
Mep-E	Meprobamate	Neo-Codema	Hydrochlorothiazide
Mephyton	Phytonadione	Neo-Dibetic	Tolbutamide
Meprospan-400	Meprobamate	Neo-Serp	Reserpine
Meravil	Amitriptyline	Neo-Tretrine	Tetracycline
Metamucil	Plantago seed	Neo-Tran	Meprobamate
Methandine	Methenamine mandelate	Neo-Zoline	Phenylbutazone
Meticortelone	Prednisolone	Nephronex	Nitrofurantoin
Meval	Diazepam	Netromycin	Netilmicin
Mexate	Methotrexate	Nifuran	Nitrofurantoin
Midamor	Amiloride	Nitro-Bid	Nitroglycerin
Miltown	Meprobamate	Noctec	Chloral hydrate
Minipress	Prazosin	Norpace	Disopyramide
Minocin	Minocycline	Norpramin	Desipramine
Mobenol	Tolbutamide	Norsena	Senna
Modane	Danthron	Novadex	Dexamethasone
Mogadon	Nitrazepam	Nova-Phase	Aspirin
Motrin	Ibuprofen	Nova-Phenicol	Chloramphenicol
M.V.I.	Multiple vitamins	Nova-Pheno	Phenobarbital
Myambutol	Ethambutol	Nova-Pred	Prednisolone
Myochrysine	Aurothiomalate	Nova-Rectal	Pentobarbital
Myotonachol	Bethanechol	Novasen	Aspirin
Mysoline	Primidone	Novobutamide	Tolbutamide
Nadozone	Phenylbutazone	Novobutazone	Phenylbutazone
Nalfon	Fenoprofen	Novochlorhydrate	Chloral hydrate
Naprosyn	Naproxen	Novochlorocap	Chloramphenicol
Nardil	Phenelzine	Novodipam	Diazepam

TRADE NAME	NONPROPRIETARY NAME	TRADE NAME	NONPROPRIETARY NAME
Novoferrosulfa	Ferrous sulfate	Panmycin	Tetracycline
Novofuran	Nitrofurantoin	Panwarfin	Warfarin
Novohydrazide	Hydrochlorothiazide	Paracort	Prednisone
Novomedopa	Methyldopa	Paralgin	Acetaminophen
Novo-Mepro	Meprobamate	Parnate	Tranylcypromine
Novopen G	Penicillin G	Paveral	Codeine
Novopheniram	Chlorpheniramine	Paxel	Diazepam
Novopoxide	Chlordiazepoxide	Peganone	Ethotoin
Novopramine	Imipramine	Pen-A	Ampicillin
Novopropanthil	Propantheline	Penbritin	Ampicillin
Novopropoxyn	Propoxyphene	Penioral	Penicillin G
Novoridazine	Thioridazine	Pensyn	Ampicillin
Novorythro	Erythromycin	Pentamycetin	Chloramphenicol
Novosemide	Furosemide	Pentids	Penicillin G
Novosoxazole	Sulfisoxazole	Pentogen	Pentobarbital
Novotetra	Tetracycline	Peritrate	Pentaerythritol tetranitrate
Novotriptyn	Amitriptyline	Pertofrane	Desipramine
Nydrazid	Isoniazid	Pethidine	Meperidine
Omnipen	Ampicillin	Pfizer-E	Erythromycin
Ophthochlor	Chloramphenicol	Pfizerpen G	Penicillin G
Optomethasone	Dexamethasone	Phenbutazone	Phenylbutazone
Oramide	Tolbutamide	Phenergan	Promethazine
Orinase	Tolbutamide	Plaquenil	Hydroxychloroquine
Orudis	Ketoprofen	Polycillin	Ampicillin
Ostoforte	Vitamin D	Praminil	Imipramine
Oxalid	Oxyphenbutazone	Pred-5	Prednisolone
Pagitane	Cycrimine	Premarin	Conjugated estrogens
Panheprin	Heparin	Principen	Ampicillin

TRADE NAME	NONPROPRIETARY NAME	TRADE NAME	NONPROPRIETARY NAME
Pro-65	Propoxyphene	Robigesic	Acetaminophen
Probal	Meprobamate	Robimycin	Erythromycin
Pro-Banthine	Propantheline	Robinul	Glycopyrrolate
Progesic	Propoxyphene	Robitet	Tetracycline
Pronapen	Penicillin G	Rofact	Rifampin
Pronestyl	Procainamide	Rounox	Acetaminophen
Propanthel	Propantheline	Rum-K	Potassium chloride
Propyl-Thyracil	Propylthiouracil	Sal-Adult	Aspirin
Proternol	Isoproterenol	Secogen	Secobarbital
Purodigin	Digitoxin	Seconal	Secobarbital
Pyopen	Carbenicillin	Senokot	Senna
Pyribenzamine	Tripelennamine	Septra	Co-Trimoxazole
Quietal	Meprobamate	Septra DS	Co-Trimoxazole
Quinaglute	Quinidine	Ser-Ap-Es	Reserpine, hydralazine, hydro-chlorothiazide
Quinamm	Aminophylline, quinine	Serax	Oxazepam
Quinidex	Quinidine	Serpasil	Reserpine
Radiostol	Vitamin D	Sertan	Primidone
Rau-Sed	Reserpine	Sinemet	Levodopa, carbidopa
Redoxon	Vitamin C	Sinequan	Doxepin
Regulex	Docusate sodium	Sintrom	Acenocoumarol
Relaxil	Chlordiazepoxide	SK-65	Propoxyphene
Resercrine	Reserpine	SK-Lygen	Chlordiazepoxide
Reserpanca	Reserpine	SK-Soxazole	Sulfisoxazole
Retet-S	Tetracycline	Slow-Fe	Ferrous Sulfate
Rhonal	Aspirin	Slow-K	Potassium chloride
Rifadin	Rifampin	Slow-Phyllin	Theophylline
Rifamate	Rifampin, isoniazid	Solu-Medrol	Methylprednisolone
Rimactane	Rifampin	Somophylin	Aminophylline, theophylline
Rimifon	Isoniazid		

TRADE NAME	NONPROPRIETARY NAME	TRADE NAME	NONPROPRIETARY NAME
Sterine	Methenamine mandelate	Tolinase	Tolazamide
Stibilium	Diethylstilbestrol	Totacillin	Ampicillin
Stress-Pam	Diazepam	Tranxene	Clorazepate
Sumycin	Tetracycline	Tremin	Trihexyphenidyl
Supasa	Aspirin	Triaphen-10	Aspirin
Symmetrel	Amantadine	Tridil	Nitroglycerin
Synthroid	Levothyroxine	Trilium	Chlordiazepoxide
Tagamet	Cimetidine	Tums	Calcium carbonate
Talwin	Pentazocine	Turbinaire	Dexamethasone
Tandearil	Oxyphenbutazone	Tylenol	Acetaminophen
Tazone	Phenylbutazone	Ultramycin	Minocycline
T-caps	Tetracycline	Unigesic-A	Propoxyphene, aspirin
Tedral	Theophylline, ephedrine, phenobarbital	Urecholine	Bethanechol
		Uritol	Furosemide
Tegretol	Carbamazepine	Urozide	Hydrochlorothiazide
Tempra	Acetaminophen	Valadol	Acetaminophen
Tetracrine	Tetracycline	Valium	Diazepam
Tetracyn	Tetracycline	Vancenase	Beclomethasone
Tetralean	Tetracycline	Vanceril	Beclomethasone
Tetrex	Tetracycline	Vectrin	Minocycline
Theolair	Theophylline	Velosef	Cephradine
Theolixir	Theophylline	Ventolin	Albuterol
Theophyl-225	Theophylline	Vesicholine	Bethanechol
Thioril	Thioridazine	Vibramycin	Doxycycline
Thorazine	Chlorpromazine	Vimicon	Cyproheptadine
Tocopherex	Vitamin E	Vistaril	Hydroxyzine
Tofaxin	Vitamin E	Vivactil	Protriptyline
Tofranil	Imipramine	Vivol	Diazepam
Tolbutone	Tolbutamide	Warfilone	Warfarin

TRADE NAME	NONPROPRIETARY NAME
Warnerin	Warfarin
WinGel	Magnesium hydroxide, aluminum hydroxide
Winpred	Prednisone
Wycillin	Penicillin G
Wygesic	Propoxyphene, acetaminophen

TRADE NAME	NONPROPRIETARY NAME
X-Prep	Senna
Xylocaine	Lidocaine
Zaroxolyn	Metolazone
Zyloprim	Allopurinol

Index

Sulfonamides—cont'd
  interaction of
    with methenamine, 165
    with sulfonylureas, 167
Sulfonylureas
  adverse effects of, 275
  interaction of
    with β-adrenergic blocks, 165
    with corticosteroids, 165
    with diuretics, 165
    with oxyphenbutazone, 166
    with phenylbutazone, 166
    with rifampin, 166
    with sulfonamides, 167
Sulfuric acid, poisoning by, 195, 210
Sulindac in treatment
  of osteoarthritis, 324
  of pseudogout, 324-325
  of rheumatoid arthritis, 322
Surfactants in treatment of constipation, 314
Sympathomimetic agents, interaction of, with MAOIs, 147
Symptoms, drug-induced, determination of, in reducing incidence of adverse drug reactions, 271
Syncope and hypotension, drug selection and dosage for, 302-303
Syrup of ipecac
  contraindications to, 199-200, 215
  dosage of, 199
  emetic properties of, 198-199
  home administration of, 200-201
  toxicity of, 199
Systematic laboratory investigation in elderly, 133-138
Systemic antidotes, 202, 203-204
Systemic lupus erythematosus, drug-induced, 261
Systems model in quality assurance, 68-69

T

Taste in elderly, 115-116
TCA; *see* Tricyclic antidepressants
Team approach to care for the elderly
  to decrease drug misuse, 44
  to improve compliance, 25
  to maintain quality assurance, 66, 87-88
  to provide optimal care, 94
Terbutaline
  adverse effects of, 284
  in treatment of COPD, 307

Terpenes, 208
Tetracyclines
  adverse effects of, 280-281
  differences in, between young and elderly, 249
  interaction of, with divalent or trivalent cations, 175
Theophylline
  adverse effects of, 271, 284
  differences in, between young and elderly, 249
  interaction of
    with β-adrenergic blockers, 167
    with allopurinol, 167
    with cimetidine, 167
    with erythromycin, 168
    with hydrocortisone, 159
    with macrolide antibiotics, 168
    with troleandomycin, 168
Therapeutic end point of drug therapy, 3
Therapeutic goal for elderly, 61, 92
Thiazide(s), 4, 161
  adverse effects of, 287
  and diuretic-induced hypokalemia, 161
  interaction of, with insulin, 164
Thioridazine
  adverse effects of, 282
  differences in, between young and elderly, 249
Thrombocytopenia, drug-induced, 259
Thrombophlebitis
  deep venous, 303
  drug-induced, 261
Thrombosis, deep venous (DVT), drug selection and dosage for, 300-301
Thyroid disease
  drug selection and dosage for, 309-310
  indication for treatment of, 59
Thyroid function in elderly, 122
Thyroid hormones, adverse effects of, 287
Thyroid-releasing hormone (TRH), 122
Thyroid-stimulating hormone (TSH), 122
TIAs; *see* Transient ischemic attacks
Tobramycin
  adverse effects of, 278
  differences in, between young and elderly, 249
Tolazamide, adverse effects of, 275
Tolbutamide
  adverse effects of, 275
  differences in, between young and elderly, 249
  in treatment of diabetes mellitus, 309
Topical contact with poison, 194